# Dream-Child

Lear and Fool, Charles and Mary Lamb's *Tales from Shakespear*,
illustrated by William Mulready. (Courtesy of HathiTrust.)

# Dream-Child

## A LIFE OF
## CHARLES LAMB

Eric G. Wilson

Yale UNIVERSITY PRESS

New Haven & London

Published with assistance from the Annie Burr Lewis Fund.

Published with assistance from the foundation established in memory
of Henry Weldon Barnes of the Class of 1882, Yale College.

Yale University Press books may be purchased in quantity for educational,
business, or promotional use. For information, please e-mail sales.press@yale.
edu (U.S. office) or sales@yaleup.co.uk (U.K. office).

Set in Adobe Garamond type by Newgen North America, Austin, Texas.
Printed in the United States of America.

Library of Congress Control Number: 2021931501
ISBN 978-0-300-23080-2 (hardcover : alk. paper)

A catalogue record for this book is available from the British Library.

This paper meets the requirements of ANSI/NISO Z39.48-1992
(Permanence of Paper).

10 9 8 7 6 5 4 3 2 1

For Fielding

# Contents

# *Preface*

Charles Lamb has contributed substantially to English literature. He was one of the first writers to celebrate the transience, variety, and crowdedness of metropolitan life, thus challenging his friend Wordsworth's nature worship. He was also among the first to compose children's books more for imagination than morality. Perhaps influenced by his sister Mary, who enjoyed her own literary career, he proved one of the earliest male feminists. Along with De Quincey, he invented the addiction memoir. His satires about his life as an accountant anticipate the office-focused fiction of Melville (not to mention Kafka). Walter Pater, the theoretician of fin-de-siècle aestheticism, thrilled to Lamb's multifarious style, an assortment of "glimpses, suggestions, delightful half-apprehensions, profound thoughts of old philosophers, hints of the inner-most reason in things."[1] Virginia Woolf, experimental essayist as much as avant-garde novelist, delighted in the "wild flash[es]" of Lamb's imagination that left his essays "flawed and imperfect, but starred with poetry."[2] These groundbreaking writers most valued the essays Lamb wrote in the persona of Elia. Vertiginously self-referential and hilariously ironic, these excursions turn everything topsy-turvy, resembling David Foster Wallace more than Samuel Taylor Coleridge.[3] Lamb's witty pairings of himself and his literary persona feel contemporary, too; they prefigure the "autofiction" of Ben Lerner, Teju Cole, and Sheila Heti.

Just as an interlocutor in some of the most famous literary conversations of his day, Lamb is worth close attention. Fueled by egghot and tobacco, he helped the young Coleridge develop his groundbreaking conversational style. He joined (rather shyly) Coleridge and Wordsworth's talk at Nether Stowey, as the poets planned *Lyrical Ballads*. He was present at the "Immortal Evening" when Wordsworth, Keats, and other members of London's literati convened at artist Benjamin Robert Haydon's home to celebrate his *Christ's Entry into Jerusalem*. Lamb proved a stable, albeit absurd, companion for other Romantic luminaries, including Wordsworth's sister Dorothy, Leigh Hunt, William Hazlitt, Robert Southey, and William Godwin. One of his closest friends, Thomas Manning, the Cambridge mathematician who became the first Englishman to enter Lhasa, is emerging as a major travel writer and pioneer in East Asian studies. Lamb didn't meet Blake but knew his work well and was one of the first to recognize his genius.

Lamb's companions attended the weekly dinners he and Mary hosted, hodgepodges of punning, pot roast, ale, gin, tobacco, whist, literary talk, eccentricity. The scene was uproariously democratic. In addition to poets, dramatists, and essayists, the Lambs opened their door to seamen, card aficionados, and barristers. The only rule: do your thing.

But there was horror beneath the frolic. In a fit of madness, Mary murdered her and Charles's mother with a kitchen knife. With courage and compassion, a twenty-one-year-old Lamb saved Mary from life in a nightmarish asylum by volunteering to care for her for the rest of his days—mostly to his delight, since his sister, whose seasons of sanity exceeded her spells of madness, was astute, patient, maternal, brilliant, lovely. Their relationship is one of the most fascinating in all of literature, on par with the interactions of the Brontë sisters.

Given Lamb's compelling life, his significant literary contributions, his vital presence in the work of major authors, and his unique humor, why has no full-scale biography of him appeared since 1905, when E. V. Lucas published his elegant volumes?[4]

When Lucas completed his work, Lamb's reputation was ascendant. To the sentimental Victorian Age, he was a hero, a man who sacrificed his own happiness to care for his ill sister and who, despite his daily grind, turned out charming essays on life's simple pleasures. The epitome of this Victorian worship was Thackeray holding a letter by Lamb to his forehead and exclaiming, "St. Charles!" Lamb became his admirers: a tender-hearted fellow who championed children, gardens, bachelorhood, domesticity, his country, tender English meat, tobacco, and his glass of port. This Lamb is apolitical, asexual, complacent.

Hard-edged critics between the world wars excoriated Lamb. Especially Denys Thompson. In league with F. R. Leavis and his magazine *Scrutiny,* Thompson cringed at "appreciationist" literary criticism and espoused rigorous textual analysis, which revealed Lamb as "proudly ignorant and hostile to serious art and intelligence."[5] Thompson injected his vituperation into his textbook *Reading and Discrimination,* published in 1934. For decades, students were encouraged to view Lamb as an example of how *not* to write. Eventually Lamb was expunged from this text, no longer deemed worthy of the canon.

This popular textbook seriously damaged Lamb's reputation.[6] He is now rarely taught in high school or college classrooms, and scholarly attention to him for the last eighty-odd years has been middling, at least compared to work on Coleridge and Wordsworth. Fortunately, there is a Lamb renaissance in the academy.

Since Lucas's magisterial work of 1905, there have been fine brief or partial biographies of Charles, as well as excellent accounts of his life with Mary.[7] But no book has described the sweep of his life within the appropriate contexts of his times—literary, social, political, religious, gender, and so on. Significant new information on Lamb has come to light since Lucas wrote: on Lamb's participation in the British Empire, his position in the East India House, his Unitarian political radicalism, his interest in the philosophy of Joseph Priestley, his walking and psychogeography, his connection to Cockney literature, his work as a magazine writer, his children's books, his bending of gender roles, and his late poems for women's albums and highly particular occasions.[8] Incorporating this fresh material—which also includes novel perspectives on Lamb's drinking, melancholy, and sexuality—we are in a position to produce a more accurate, nuanced, and robust portrait of Lamb.[9] Fused into the "gentle and frolic" essayist Wordsworth cherished is a man bitter and desperate, addicted to outlandish invective as much as fanciful affection.

Scholarship aside, the time feels right for Charles Lamb. More than any other Romantic, he speaks to our age. Whereas Wordsworth idealizes a natural world inaccessible to most and quickly (and sadly) dwindling, Lamb celebrates the grit and speed and diversity of the urban. Likewise, in place of Wordsworth's "egotistical sublime" is Lamb's more fluid, collaborative vision of identity, much closer to our own postmodern ideas of selfhood. Most of all, Lamb's gentle irony, his ability to doubt without denouncing, to undercut while still holding aloft, addresses our epistemological moment, when social media, conspiracy theories, and paranoid invocations of fake news have fomented such extreme cynicism that the very notion of the real seems at risk.

But this biography did not begin in scholarship or timeliness. It started in humdrum coincidence. While living in an old house in the Hampstead area of London—I was directing a study abroad program for my university—I came across, in a miscellany of books in the parlor's corner, a green duodecimo. It was Lamb's Elia essays, which I knew, though a specialist in British Romanticism, only faintly. Like many in my field, I had devoted my critical energies to the Big Six Poets and neglected the prose of Lamb, Hazlitt, and Hunt. More out of distraction than interest, I flipped through the pages, dipped into "New Year's Eve," and enjoyed Lamb's witty exploration of Wordsworthian nostalgia.

I read little more of Lamb during that time in London, which is unfortunate, since the city would have animated the words of one of its most ardent lovers. But I did bring the volume home to the United States. (I promise to return it to Hampstead one day.) For several years, it lay neglected in my office, in another stack of random books. Then, while planning a literary nonfiction workshop, I picked it up again. This time I opened to "A Chapter on Ears." Two sentences in, I was enthralled—not by Lamb's Romantic vision but by his freaky prose.

I soon learned that Lamb the stylist is also Lamb the sage, however outlandish and skeptical. Life is terrible, he teaches, but here's how to love it anyway.

I wanted to be near Lamb, for a long time. I committed, seven years ago, to writing his life. I am the better for it.

# *Introduction*

## BETWEEN EDEN AND FLEET

You are walking westward from the lead-clad dome of St. Paul's, golden in the evening sun, and you find yourself on Ludgate Street, which soon rises into Ludgate Hill, whose apex bestows exquisite views of the cathedral. You reach the top. It is February 10, 1775, the day of Charles Lamb's birth.

In one minute you have descended the other side, and you hit New Bridge Street. It leads south to Blackfriars Bridge, the newest in London. The street covers the river Fleet, which once teemed with barges, sewage, and suicides, but now merely trickles in the rank ditches cutting north through Fleet Market. You cross, and you appear on Fleet Street.[1]

Look out! Coach-and-four! And another, another . . . another—segments of an immense vertiginous worm. Stay alert. Keep pushing west. Meat hawkers, costermongers, swindlers with viper oils, dogs barking, cocks crowing, blackened coalmen bearing seven stone of their stock, fiddles and hurdy-gurdies, beggars, pickpockets, church bells, shit, piss, boys hustling headlines, mumbling drunks, ginned-up prostitutes. "Your pleasure?" Begrimed taverns crowd hopped-up coffeehouses. Street fires burn high, warming seamen just unshipped and sundry ne'er-do-wells.[2]

Divert through a doorway to catch your breath. Rackstrow's Museum. In waxwork or floating in solution are deformed babies and fetuses contorted. A seventy-two-foot sperm whale skeleton spans the dim chamber. Here's a

Detail after John Horwood, *Plan of the Cities of London and Westminster,
the Borough of Southwark and Parts Adjoining Shewing Every House.*
(Royal Collection Trust / © Her Majesty Queen Elizabeth II 2020.)

coffin. It cradles a mummy; its flesh looks like black earwax. And over there
a plaster mold of the Giant of Staffordshire, seven foot two, looms; below, at
three foot three, the Norfolk Dwarf.

Crammed within Fleet's half mile is London journalism, some 250 papers and periodicals. The publishing trade thrives here as well, and writers
stay close to the action. Oliver Goldsmith wrote the *Vicar of Wakefield* just
off Fleet, at No. 6 Wine Office Court. Also right off Fleet, at No. 17 Gough
Square, Samuel Johnson completed his *Dictionary of the English Language.*
Johnson found green fields, when compared to Fleet, dull.

Fleet is a powder keg for riot. Mobs erupted in 1763 and 1769, incited by
followers of the radical John Wilkes, and again in 1794, because of the treason
trial of Thomas Hardy, founder of the London Corresponding Society.

Ready to go on, you press from the oddities back into the throng. You
are James Boswell, who wrote of Fleet, "The noise, the crowd, the glare of
the shops agreeably confused me."[3] You are Dickens: "Who could sit upon
anything in Fleet-street during the busy hours of the day, and not be dazed

and deafened by two immense processions, one ever tending westward with the sun, the other ever tending eastward from the sun, both ever tending to the plains beyond the range of red and purple where the sun goes down!"[4]

You are also you, and though you have hiked down Fleet only a quarter mile, you are *addlepated*.

But here is your turn, and your relief. Across from Chancery Lane, to your left, is No. 17 Fleet, the Inner Temple Gateway, extant since the twelfth century. You pass through the arched threshold, admiring the carved Pegasus on each spandrel.

Relax into Inner Temple Lane, Eden after Fleet's pandemonium. Stroll one hundred yards south, and to your left is the Temple Church, whose rare round nave, fifty-five feet in diameter, was constructed in 1185. Stone knights repose around the base. To the right is Farrar's Building. Its rust bricks and creamy trim exude understated dignity, in contrast to the colorful elegance of the surrounding rose bushes and apple trees.

Proceed Thames-ward. In two minutes, you spy a line of buildings to your right, positioned perpendicularly to your southerly drift. Crown Office

Inner Temple gatehouse, September 7, 2013. (Courtesy of Creative Commons.)

Row. You stride their length. A generous green fronts them, spreading down to the water. You light on No. 2. This is Charles Lamb's birthplace. Until his family leaves the Temple seventeen years later, in 1792, Charles almost daily crosses back and forth through No. 17 Fleet, jolted from garden to mob and back again. He quickens to the turning. "What a transition for a countryman visiting London for the first time—the passing from the crowded Strand or Fleet-street, by unexpected avenues, into [the Temple's] magnificent ample squares, its classic green recesses!"[5]

If anyone ever needed openings through which to rush *elsewhere,* be it bustle or calm, Charles Lamb did. On September 22, 1796, Charles, twenty-one, was returning home from East India House, where he was an accountant. No longer living in the Temple—unfortunate circumstances had pushed them out—his family now crammed into a shabby dwelling on No. 7 Little Queen Street in Holborn. Things were tense. Charles's mother was an invalid who required constant care, as did his senile father. An aunt Sarah also resided; she bickered with Mother or sat sullen. Then there was Mary, Charles's beloved sister, a little over ten years his senior. She took care of their parents and pacified Sarah, on top of making complex dresses for a pittance and overseeing an unruly teenaged apprentice. She was strained near breaking, and she had a history of mental instability.

Charles could almost see the door. He heard a scream. He ran, the door was open, he burst in. There Mary stood, holding a kitchen knife high, and below her, slumped in a chair, was their mother, stabbed to death. Charles wrested the blade from his sister's hand before she could kill his father and his aunt.

This happens to you, and everything before, even six weeks in an asylum (which the young Lamb endured), feels unreal, and everything after, an aftershock. To ensure that his sister, clearly not in her right mind when she plunged the blade, would not go to prison—or worse, Bedlam—Lamb agreed to care for her for the rest of his life, at that moment in effect denying himself a wife and children. He also chained himself for the next decades to the accounting job he loathed; he would need a steady income to pay for the more comfortable private asylums Mary would inhabit off and on for the rest of her life. Now as well, after determining that Mary should stay in such an asylum as long as their father lived, he would have to care for an enfeebled parent. His time and energy lost, he finally had to accept he would never enjoy the leisure of his more literary friends. He would be no Coleridge, who could survive on his pen, oratory, and patronage.

How could Lamb *not* stagger from that "day of **horrors**" in search of escapes?[6] He was desperate for openings: portals, doors, holes, windows, grates, cracks, gates, brinks, chinks, gaps, fissures, fractures, breaches, interstices, rifts. More than most, that feeling of "This can't be all there is; there must be something else" haunted him.

This is why he was such a prodigious walker, sometimes covering up to twenty miles a day in his hallowed London, even into his fifties. Stepping at night among the shop lights, the fruit wagons, the bookstalls (where an old Robert Burton might be), the theaters, the decaying buildings and the forgotten alleyways, Lamb sought a sensation so strong it could tear time, and through the rip he would slip, in reverie, to fountains now bricked over, or lost literary conversations in an oaken pub, or, preferably, his childhood, when he thrilled to a garden in the Inner Temple or a witch in a book or a man with an iron hook for a hand or the green velvet curtain going up, and there is the play.

One reason Lamb was so popular during the Victorian Age was his love of childhood. "Why must every thing smack of man, and mannish? Is the world all grown up? Is childhood dead? Or is there not in the bosoms of the wisest and the best some of the child's heart left, to respond to its earliest enchantments?" (*W,* 2:85).

The "mannish" meant clocks, bricks, offices, as opposed to sundials, rambling, playing whist, or writing, like Cowper, "divine chit-chat."[7] Man-smack was also seriousness, sobriety, and consistency, versus the frivolity of punning, joking, gin, tobacco, or pretending to be someone else, as Lamb did with his literary personae: "Londoner," the inveterate city walker, "Pensilis," the man inconveniently hanged, or "Elia," for whom everything is whimsy, if also melancholy.

But Lamb knew his immaturity could encumber. In the guise of a "friend" of the "late Elia" (companion to Lamb's dead literary persona), he acknowledges that he "was too much of the boy-man. The toga virilis never sate gracefully on his shoulders. The impressions of infancy had burnt into him, and he resented the impertinence of manhood. These were weaknesses; but such as they were, they are a key to explicate some of his writings" (*W,* 2:153).

Lamb's youth was simply one place among several to which he might figuratively flee. Nostalgia grows boring, though, or painful, and the present calls, with its adult pleasures, such as philosophy or sophisticated prose. But lucubrating, too, becomes tiring, and so again the quest for the portal to yore.

Child/man, Temple/Fleet: these are but two of the many polarities energizing Lamb's work, in which each pole invites temporary liberation from the other. Seriousness is a prelude to silliness, and vice versa, and so mirth and spleen fringe each other, as do tragedy and fancy. Neither side signifies alone; each inspirits the other. The adult of sorrow and the dream's child, self-opposing Lamb thus lived what he loved, irony, the "dangerous figure" that says yes and no at the same time. Lamb confessed that on his day of death, he would most lament losing this engine of infinite reversal (*W,* 2:152).

Lamb's very body figured his dispositional doubleness. He was irony's allegory. While his mature mind spanned all of London, for instance, he was no bigger than a child, standing—like Hogarth, Keats, and De Quincey—only five feet in his shoes.

He wobbled as he walked, swaying as much as striding, perhaps because of his peculiar "plantigrade" footfall, as one schoolfellow described it. Leigh Hunt found the "side to side" gait to be a tension between "involuntary consciousness and attempted ease."[8] Lamb ambled this way, forward and lateral at once, when he conversed with friends.

As noticeable as Lamb's footfall—the "whole sole of his foot characteristically slapped the ground, like a turkey or a duck"—were his spindly legs, a result of childhood polio. One friend called them "immaterial," while another saw them as "remarkably slight." (He covered his meager shanks with knee breeches and gaiters, quaint for his day, and they, like his entire garb, were black. He liked saying, "I take [black] to be the proper costume of an author" [*W,* 2:241]). But Lamb's whole body was scant. It seemed as if a breath could knock him down. A "head of amazing fineness," however, "most noble and sweet," ballasted his paltry torso. This globe pulled him forward as he walked, like he had been reading. Prominent was a "large intellectual forehead." "Black and crisp hair" fell luxuriantly over the brow.[9]

One eye was hazel, according to a friend, and the other gray flecked with red, mixed "as we see red spots in the bloodstone." Or perhaps not. Another friend saw Lamb's eyes as brownish hazel, while yet another found them brown and bright, while still another observed grayish blue.[10] Regardless of color, Lamb's eyes were quick, variable, restless. They twinkled; they penetrated. Melancholia was the background, though, over which the flashes played, and into which they receded.

Lamb's face resembled "a chance specimen of the Chinese ware, one to the set, unique, quaint." But his "sallow and uniform complexion," his nose "large and slightly hooked," also suggested Jewish origin. He even looked "Rabbinical" to some. Ethnicity aside, crazy lines, "physiognomical quips and cranks," networked the face. This baroque merriment, however, corresponded to Lamb's eyes. It was "somewhat expressive of anxiety and pain."[11]

Without Lamb's agony, no comedy; without his mirth, no relief. Lamb's humor was appropriately dark and strange, composed of "ambiguities," "whim-whams," "hints and glimpses," "fragments and scattered pieces of Truth" (*W,* 2:59). Like Lear's Fool—to whom he was sometimes likened—he directs his nonsense toward the niceties that protect from life's hard facts. He reveals the terrified child behind the ermine robe. The little one he pities, but the rift between what we project and what we are is hilarious.

# CHAPTER I

⟨⊙⟩

## *The Temple*

Lamb's urban Eden, his spot of infinite jest, had been around since the twelfth century, when the Knights Templar built their round church on the Thames. Since 1312, when the Knights disbanded, the Temple had been devoted to legal training. It was divided into two societies, the Inner and the Middle. Along with Lincoln's Inn and Gray's Inn, these bodies prepared barristers. Ruling each inn was its own parliament, composed of judges and seasoned barristers called "benchers." About sixty benchers regulated the Inner Temple in Lamb's day.

Lamb adored the old buildings, especially the Elizabethan Inner Temple Hall, but he most loved the three-acre garden, his front yard and route to the river. In the Middle Ages, an apple orchard grew there, and in Shakespeare's time, roses. This is where the Wars of the Roses possibly began. Fine wrought-iron work forged in 1618 had enclosed the plot, but new iron work stood in Lamb's day—installed in 1730. The highlight of the garden was a sundial built in 1707 by Edward Strong.[1]

So delicious was the garden that Wordsworth, the great hater of cities, prized it. Lamb walked him through the portal at No. 17 Fleet, and Wordsworth found himself in a "sequestered nook, / Still as a sheltered place when winds blow loud!," a place of "privileged regions and inviolate, / Where from their airy lodges studious lawyers / Look out on waters, walks, and gardens green."[2]

*Part of the Inner Temple, 1800,* from a drawing in Mr. Crace's Collection, in George Walter Thornbury's *Old and New London: A Narrative of Its History, Its People, Its Places* (London, 1872). (Courtesy of Wikimedia Commons.)

Lamb grew up in the Inner Temple because his father John worked as a clerk for a bencher of the Inner Temple, Samuel Salt. In 1759, Salt inhabited chambers at No. 2 Crown Office Row. In the back room, he installed his clerk and family. Here Charles was born, and he was christened in the Temple Church.

John Lamb was more than a clerk for Salt. He was scribe, valet, fixer, motivator, organizer, counselor: a true Jeeves to Salt's Wooster. On paper, Salt was impressive. His legal training—he entered the Middle Temple in 1741 and the Inner in 1745—was extensive, and in 1753 he was called to the bar. In 1768, he was elected as a Whig to the House of Commons, and he remained in Parliament until 1790. In 1769, he was elected as a director of the South Sea Company, a post he filled until 1775, at which time he became deputy governor, a title he held until his death in 1792. Salt also served as a director of the East India Company and sat as governor on the boards of many hospitals. Meanwhile, in 1782, he was sufficiently accomplished as a lawyer to attain bencher status, and he later was elected to be a "reader," in which capacity he was expected to lecture on legal topics.

The reality of Salt was otherwise. In "The Benchers of the Inner Temple," Lamb in the guise of Elia (the literary persona in which he wrote his greatest essays) observes that Salt "had the reputation of being a very clever man, and of excellent discernment in the chamber practice of the law," but suspects "his knowledge did not amount to much." How Salt gained his "repute for talents" baffles Elia. Salt was such a "shy man" that "a child might pose him in a minute." He was also "indolent and procrastinating to the last degree." "He never dressed for a dinner party but he forgot his sword." "If there was anything which he could speak unseasonably, he was sure to do it.—He was to dine at a relative's of the unfortunate Miss Blandy on the day of her execution;—and L. [Salt's assistant, Lamb's father] who had a wary foresight of his probable hallucinations, before he set out, schooled him with great anxiety not in any possible manner to allude to her story that day. S. promised faithfully to observe the injunction. He had not been seated in the parlour, where the company was expecting the dinner summons, four minutes, when, a pause in the conversation ensuing, he got up, looked out of window, and pulling down his ruffles—an ordinary motion with him—observed, 'it was a gloomy day,' and added, 'Miss Blandy must be hanged by this time, I suppose'" (*W*, 2:86).

Salt "had the same good fortune among the female world—was a known toast with the ladies, and one or two are said to have died for love of him— I suppose, because he never trifled or talked gallantry with them, or paid them, indeed, hardly common attentions. He had a fine face and person, but wanted, methought, the spirit that should have shown them off with advantage to the women. His eye lacked lustre." "Not so," thought one Susan P——, who at sixty, after forty years of pining for Salt, was found, on the day her beloved died, crying hard (*W* 2: 86–87).

John Lamb was born in 1738 in Lincolnshire, probably in Stamford, the heart of fen country. His father was a cobbler; Charles suggests in a poem ("The Family Name") that more ancient Lamb generations might have wielded the shepherd's crook. About John's mother we know nothing. At some point the family, which included at least two girls in addition to John, moved to Lincoln, famous for its great Gothic cathedral. John likely got some education at Lincoln School, esteemed, as was his son's Christ's Hospital, for its rigorous curriculum and success rate in placing less fortunate boys in respectable positions. John did not graduate. If we can take seriously a poem John later wrote, "The Lady's Footman," he next served as a footman in the spa city of Bath. By 1756, he had journeyed to London and found employment under Salt, for whom he would work for almost the rest of his life.

A story Charles wrote is likely based on his paternal grandparents. In the tale of Susan Yates, included in *Mrs. Leicester's School*, Susan describes growing up with her parents "in the midst of that lonely tracts of land called the Lincolnshire fens." "In no very affluent circumstances," her father lacked horse and carriage. When the family required supplies, he walked the seven miles to the closest village, through a "sad miry way." Located in this village was the parish church, and sometimes, if the Sunday weather was dry, the father would rise early and hike to the place of worship. He wanted to "see how *goodness thrived*." But he returned exhausted. In these parts, "a mile is as good as four" (*W*, 3:326–27).

Susan appears a stand-in for John Lamb, and her father for Charles's grandfather. His joke about Sunday morning, Lucas observes, is "quite in the Lamb manner," and the church in the story, St. Mary's, points to a church of that name in Stamford.[3]

A closer tie between literature and history occurs in "Poor Relations." Lamb (as Elia) describes an incident from his father's childhood. Regularly a man named Mr. Billet dined with the family. He and the father were schoolfellows "a world ago at Lincoln." Elia's father was from the hill section of Lincoln, and so known as an "Above Boy," while Billet, a "Below Boy," hailed from the valley. When the two men conversed about this divide, old hostilities flared. "My father had been a leading Mountaineer; and would still maintain the general superiority, in skill and hardihood, of the Above Boys . . . over the Below Boys . . . , of which party his contemporary had been a chieftain. Many and hot were the skirmishes on this topic" (*W*, 2:161–62). The fury of the quarrel—which sounds specific enough to be true—suggests that the father, now, vocationally speaking, a "below" boy, covets his former ascendancy.

The gap between merit and position proved a painful irony for Lamb.[4] Salt the imbecile enjoys wealth and prestige; Lamb's father, clever, is powerless and poor. Lamb, again as Elia, emphasizes this contrast in "Benchers." Whatever his difficulty, Salt looks to John, here called "Lovel" ("Love L," Love Lamb), for guidance. "A quick little fellow," Lovel could "despatch [the problem] out of hand by the light of natural understanding, of which he had an uncommon share." Salt "did nothing without consulting Lovel, or failed in any thing without expecting and fearing his admonishing" (*W*, 2:88).

Lovel "is a man of an incorrigible and losing honesty." "He once wrested a sword out of the hand of a man of quality that had drawn upon him; and pommelled him severely with the hilt of it. The swordsman had offered insult to a female—an occasion upon which no odds against him could have prevented the interference of Lovel. He would stand next day bare-headed to the same person, modestly to excuse his interference—for L. never forgot rank, where something better was not concerned" (*W*, 2:88).

In theatrics, Lovel is worthy of the famous actor he resembles, David Garrick. He sculpts heads in clay or plaster of Paris. He fashions cribbage boards and little toys. He's good at quadrille and bowls. He makes an excellent punch. He concocts "the merriest quips and conceits," and is "altogether as brimful of rogueries and inventions as you could desire." Most important for Charles, the man of letters, Lovel is a polymath in livery, enjoying a "fine turn for humorous poetry—next to Swift and Prior" (*W*, 2:88).

Decades after first meeting the Lambs in the winter of 1794–95, poet Robert Southey recalled John's comic verse. During the visit, Lamb showed off his father's favorite creation, "The Sparrow's Wedding: A Fable." The poem appears in John's *Poetical Pieces on Several Occasions*, likely published between 1770 and 1780. Underwriting the publication was the Friendly Society for the Benefit of Their Widows, a charitable organization of which John was a member. He no doubt entertained the group with his poetry, as well as with his puns and jokes, during the annual meetings at Devil Tavern.

"The Sparrow's Wedding," which opens the collection, is a charming animal fable, composed in rhyming couplets and jaunty iambic tetrameter. Its style recalls the octosyllabic virtuosity of Matthew Prior, to whom Elia likens Lovel. The protagonist of John's narrative is a Don Juanian sparrow whose sundry amorous exploits appear to end when Cupid pierces his heart. He falls in love with a beautiful, innocent female sparrow, and she consents to marry him. John's description of the wedding preparations by other birds is winsome.

> The chatt'ring Magpye undertook
> Their wedding dinner for to cook
> He being properly bedight
> In a cook's cloathing, black and white;
>
> . . . . . . . . . . . . . . . . . . .
>
> The snipe acted the butler's part,
> Who lov'd good suction at the heart;

A rav'nous Hawk was purver made,
As being proficient in that trade.[5]

During the wedding, Hatred takes Cupid's place and spreads discord. The marriage turns sour. The male sparrow returns to his philandering, leaving his wife distraught. But a turtle dove lectures the male sparrow on being grateful for one's blessings. She praises her own marriage and flies away, but not before demanding that the sparrow seek forgiveness from his wife. The poem ends before we see him do it.

John's verse parodies the animal fable, hinting at ambiguities that this moralistic genre usually conceals. But if "The Sparrow's Wedding" is unclear in its views of matrimony, other poems in John's collection praise it. Two public addresses extol the virtues of marriage, as do a poem called "Matrimony" and a verse letter to country friend.

The portrait of Lovel—we have no equivalent one of Charles's mother—implies that Lamb adored his father. He certainly emulated the man, growing into a connoisseur of puns, punch, poetry, cards, theater, and domesticity.

But Charles inherited from his father a darker strain: the torment of being a servant to an inept master. Perceiving early on that worth has nothing to do with class, Charles wrote his greatest essays out of the gap, always ironical, between appearance and reality. The result proved an ongoing satire, bemused more than bitter, of the subterfuges the powerful use to maintain the status quo.

William Plumer, a Whig MP like Samuel Salt, owned a large country house near Widford, Hertfordshire. He called it Blakesware. His housekeeper was Mary Field (née Bruton), married to Edward Field, a gardener. Plumer and Salt were friends, and the Inner Temple man visited Blakesware often. He took his assistant, John Lamb, with him. During his off hours, John flirted with the daughter of the Fields, Elizabeth. They fell in love and married in London in 1761 at St. Dunstan's-in-the-Field on Fleet Street. John was around thirty-six, while Elizabeth was about twenty-four.

Youth and age were not the only contraries Elizabeth had to manage in her marriage to John Lamb. She was descended from yeomen and farmers, men competent in tools and soil who were a step above domestic servants. Growing up in Blakesware, Elizabeth was accustomed to an even higher class of living. Her mother, though a servant, lived as though she were an aristocratic equal to her employers. "Tall, graceful, [and] upright," Lamb as Elia wrote, "in some respects she might be said to be the mistress of [the mansion]" (*W,* 2:101). Like her mother, Elizabeth was tall, stately, graceful, and strikingly beautiful. With her dark features she resembled the famous actress Sarah Siddons. Now she had to reconcile her country upbringing and elegant habits with dirty London and her new husband's subordinate status. Worse, she had to take on a domestic job herself, keeping house for Salt. Elizabeth's willingness to make this harsh transition shows she really loved John, but the contrast between her world and his likely troubled the marriage—and her parenting.

Of her three surviving children, Elizabeth favored John, the oldest, most, much to Mary's detriment. As Charles wrote only weeks after the killing, their mother had "*never understood* [Mary] right. She loved her, as she loved us all, with a **Mother's Love**, but in opinion, in feeling, & sentiment, & disposition, bore so distant a resemblance to her daughter, that she never understood her right. Never could believe how much *she* loved her—but met her caresses, her protestations of filial affection too frequently with coldness and **repulse**,—Still she was a good mother, God forbid I should think of her but *most* respectfully, **most** affectionately. Yet she would always love my brother above Mary, who was not worthy of one tenth of that affection which Mary had a right to claim" (*M,* 1:52).

John, born in 1763 (and so one year older than Mary and twelve years older than Charles), was tall like Elizabeth, and exhibited the high spirits of a young lord. By contrast, the more diminutive and darkly featured Mary was bookish, solitary, anxious, and prone even at an early age to mental instability. Valuing elegance and grace, Elizabeth couldn't connect with her daughter. Chances are she wasn't close to Charles, either, for he was likewise small, swarthy, depressive, and studious. It was in fact Mary who taught Charles to read.

In addition to the differences between her and John, did Elizabeth's divided heart toward her children harm the marriage? Was John's mental state also a detriment to the union? Bryan Waller Procter, friend and biographer of Charles Lamb, claims there was a "hereditary taint of insanity in the [Lamb] family."[6] What about Elizabeth's own moods? Aside from feeling geographically and culturally dislocated, she endured the death of at least three of her infants: Elizabeth in 1762, Samuel in 1764, and another Elizabeth in 1768. (She may also have lost a child named William in 1772.) Though this was at a time when about half of London's children died before the age of five,

losing children, regardless of the numbers, is traumatic.[7] The grief must have
devastated Elizabeth. How must it have been for her to be married to a man
constantly joking?

Did the children sense the tension, and choose, barely conscious of their
choice, sides? Did the book-loving younger two hang onto their poet dad,
while the snobbish older one latched onto his refined mother?

John's fable about the philandering sparrow now appears in another light.
Maybe the story wasn't so much a lesson on the value of marriage as a fantasy
of flight. The purity of the bride could be boring beside the excitement of
perpetually new seductions, and the turtle dove espousing harmonious marriage really is a tedious scold.

Charles's lengthiest literary treatment of his mother appears in "Written on the Day of My Aunt's Funeral" from 1798, two years after Elizabeth's
death. After bidding his deceased aunt, presumably Sarah, to lie in the same
grave as his mother, Lamb's speaker breaks into grief.

> Oh my dear mother, oh thou dear dead saint!
> Where's now that placid face, where oft hath sat
> A mother's smile, to think her son should thrive
> Into this bad world, when she was dead and gone;
> And where a tear hath sat (take shame, O son!)
> When that same child has prov'd himself unkind. (*W*, 5:20)

The guilt is strong. Did Charles regret not loving his mother more? Did he
blame himself for the coldness between them?

In another poem from the same time, he again chastises himself for being
a negligent son. He laments that his mother didn't live longer, and regrets all
the nights he might have enjoyed her company. Then, the confession:

> A wayward son ofttimes to thee;
> And yet, in all our little bickerings,
> Domestic jars, there was, I know not what,
> Of tender feeling, that were ill exchang'd
> For this world's chilling friendships, and their smiles
> Familiar, whom the heart calls strangers still. (*W*, 5:22)

In a letter to Coleridge not two weeks after Elizabeth's death, Lamb once
more expresses guilt. Two days after the incident, Lamb writes, about twenty
people were eating and making merry in the same dwelling where the tragedy
had occurred. Some had come out of friendship, others from curiosity, still

others out of interest. Lamb was prepared to eat with them "when my recollection came that my poor dead mother was lying in the next room, the very next room, a mother who thro' life, wished nothing but her children's welfare—indignation, the rage of grief, something like remorse, rushed upon my mind in an agony of emotion,—I found my way mechanically to the adjoining room, & fell on my knees by the **side** of her coffin, asking forgiveness of heaven, & sometimes of her, for forgetting her **so soon**. Tranquility returned, & it was the only violent emotion that master'd me" (*M*, 1:48).

Lamb felt he had not done right by his mother, had not loved her enough. But perhaps his mother had not loved him as much as he would have liked, and he blamed himself for not being worthy of more of her affection.

If Lamb writes little of his mother, he has much to say of his aunt Sarah, his father's older sister, who began living with the family around the time he was born. She was eccentric, awkward, studious, gloomy, and ferociously devoted to her nephew. But it is Mary's description of Sarah that exposes a chronic strain in the Lamb household.

> My father had a sister lived with us, of course lived with my Mother her sister-in-law, they were, in their different ways the best creatures in the world—but they set out wrong at first. They made each other miserable for full twenty years of their lives—my Mother was a perfect gentlewoman, my Aunty as unlike a gentlewoman as you can possibly imagine a good old woman to be, so that my dear Mother (who though you do not know it, is always in my poor head and heart) used to distress and weary her with incessant & unceasing attentions, and politeness to gain her affection, The **Old woman** could not return this in kind, and did not know what to make of it—thought it all deceit, and used to hate my Mother with a bitter hatred, which, of course, was soon returned with interest, a little frankness and looking into each others characters at first would have spared all this, and they would have lived as they died fond of each other, for the last ten years of their lives when we grew up & harmonised them a little, they sincerely loved each other. (*M*, 2:123–24)

Twenty years of tension destroys a household. How could John Sr. not show favoritism to his more like-minded sister? Did Mary lean toward Sarah as well, rebelling against her mother's coldness? What about Charles? It would've been difficult for him not to support Sarah. She doted on him.

As Elia, he recalled her fondly. She had soured on the world and claimed that little Elia was "the only thing in it which she loved; and, when she thought [he] was quitting it, she grieved over [him] with mother's tears." She was addicted to Catholic devotional books, which she studied despite being "admonished daily concerning their Papistical tendency." "The only secular employment I remember to have seen her engaged in, was, the splitting of French beans, and dropping them into a China basin of fair water. The odour of those tender vegetables to this day comes back upon my sense, redolent of soothing recollections." And though endowed with "strong sense, and a shrewd mind," she remained mostly silent, except for an occasional repartee (*W,* 2:70–71).

One example remains of her "repartee." Mr. Billet, the "Below Boy" of "Poor Relations," is dining at the Lamb table. Sarah continually urges him to accept more food, exclaiming, "Do take another slice, Mr. Billet, for you do not get pudding every day." The gentleman replied nothing to this affront to his pride, but later in the evening, he pronounced, "with an emphasis that chilled the company," "Woman, you are superannuated" (*W,* 2:162).

Awkward among adults, Sarah turned to little Charles for affection. But she embarrassed him. In "Christ's Hospital Five and Thirty Years Ago," Elia, in the persona of Coleridge, remembers how "L." (Lamb) enjoyed a privilege denied to the other boys. While the others, far from home, were choking down disgusting food, L., whose family dwelt close by, dined on roasted veal or pork loin brought to him by his "maid or aunt." The aunt, "Coleridge" remembers, let her love overcome her pride, and she indelicately squatted "down upon some odd stone in a by-nook of the cloisters, disclosing the viands . . . and the contending passions of L. at the unfolding. There was love for the bringer; shame for the thing brought, and the manner of its bringing; sympathy for those who were too many to share in it; and, at top of all, hunger (eldest, strongest of the passions!) predominant, breaking down the stony fences of shame, and awkwardness, and a troubling over-consciousness" (*W,* 2:13).

Soon after his aunt died, Lamb recalled her clumsy charity. When she would "toddle" to school to bring him treats, he "only despised her for it, & used to be ashamed to see her come & sit herself down on the old coal hole steps as you went into the old grammar school, & opend her apron & brought out her bason, with some nice thing she had caused to be saved for me" (*M,* 1:96).

This uneasy interplay among pleasure, embarrassment, and shame appears in another account of the aunt offering the young scholar food. In "A Dissertation upon Roast Pig," Elia remembers that at the end of a school holiday, his "good old aunt" always stuffed into his pocket a "sweet-meat, or some nice thing." On one occasion, she gave her nephew a fresh, hot plum cake. As the boy crosses London Bridge, an old beggar asks his charity. The boy, lacking money to "console" the man, "in the vanity of self-denial, and the very coxcombry of charity, school-boy-like, [he] made him a present of—the whole cake!" After the "sweet soothing of self-satisfaction" fades, his "better feelings" return, and he weeps, "thinking how ungrateful I had been to my good aunt, to go and give her good gift away to a stranger, that I had never seen before, and who might be a bad man for aught I knew." He then imagines "the pleasure my aunt would be taking in thinking that I—I myself, and not another—would eat her nice cake—and what should I say to her the next time I saw her—how naughty I was to part with her pretty present . . . and I blamed my impertinent spirit of alms-giving, and out-of-place hypocrisy of goodness" (*W*, 2:125).

Lamb's vexed love for his aunt drives the poem "Written on the Day of My Aunt's Funeral." Young Charles prepares to leave his "childhood's play-place, and his early home" for Christ's, the "rude fosterings of a stranger's hand, / Hard uncouth tasks, and school-boy's scanty fare." The aunt peruses "him round and round" but "hardly" knows him, in his "yellow coats, / Red leathern belt, and gown of russet blue!" (*W*, 5:20). The aunt's effort to be intimate with her nephew fails. He leaves a stranger. At the poem's end, Lamb bids her go lie in the grave with his mother.

Aunt and mother blur. Both died without his loving them properly. But neither loved him to his satisfaction; if the mother didn't love enough, the aunt loved too much.

The young Charles's ambiguous relationship with his aunt is probably the basis for Lamb's tale in *Mrs. Leicester's School*, "The Witch-Aunt." The story's protagonist, Maria Howe, is "subject to fears and depressions," and thus "very different" from her pleasure-loving parents (*W*, 3:318). When her parents are out socializing, she shuts herself up and reads. Sometimes her solitude turns from fun to terror, and she flees to the lap of her aunt. Like Sarah, this aunt is addicted to devotional books, loves only her young relative, feels disrespected by the girl's parents, rarely speaks, behaves oddly. These last two habits scare the girl.

An image from a book fuels Maria's terror. The picture—which Lamb describes in "Witches, and Other Night-Fears"—is of Samuel and the Witch of Endor, and it causes nightmares. One night, Maria wakes up so scared she steals into the room where her aunt sits alone. "The old lady was not yet retired to rest but was sitting with her eyes half open, half closed; her spectacles tottering upon her nose; her head nodding over her prayer-book; her lips mumbling the words as she read them, or half read them, in her dozing posture; her grotesque appearance; her old-fashioned dress, resembling what I had seen in that fatal picture in Stackhouse; all this, with the dead time of night, as it seemed to me, (for I had gone through my first sleep,) all joined to produce a wicked fancy in me, that the form which I had beheld was not my aunt but some witch" (*W*, 3:332).

In 1816, Charles's older brother John attended one of his and Mary's weekly literature and whist parties. An avid collector of art, John held strong opinions about the medium. At the gathering was essayist William Hazlitt, formerly a painter and now one of London's leading critics. The socially awkward Hazlitt enjoyed these evenings especially. Even he could relax. "If a person liked anything," he wrote, "it was sufficient."[8] But this night was tense. John observed to Hazlitt that the coloring skills of Hans Holbein the Younger were superior to those of Van Dyck. Hazlitt vehemently differed: "If you don't hold your tongue, right now, I'll expose you in the newspapers!" "And if you do," John responded, "I'll pound *you* into a mortar!" Thereupon he punched Hazlitt in the eye. "Cards scattered as the table tumbled over, startling those in the room. Wary of escalation, an onlooker [Thomas Noon Talfourd] seized Hazlitt's arms—provoking the injured man to retort, 'By God, sir! You need not trouble yourself. I do not mind a blow, sir; nothing affects me but an abstract idea!'"[9]

This compelling event was unusual in John Lamb's life. To slug the pugnacious Hazlitt took backbone and panache. But otherwise, John lacked these virtues. Being Elizabeth's favorite child—tall, blond, and hardy—did not help his ethics. He was spoiled, and he grew into an egotist, as his behavior after the day of horrors reveals. Unlike Charles, who sacrificed everything to keep Mary from Bedlam, John wanted to commit her. He didn't want the trouble of caring for her; nor did he want to pay for the private madhouse, even though he earned a fine salary clerking at the South Sea House. Once Charles got his way concerning Mary, John withdrew from the family. He probably thought he was justified, since he got a "bad leg" (a stone fell on it) around the time of Mary's tragedy. Charles might secretly have been glad to have John out of the way; he feared that too much stress would cause his brother to go insane.

John was a mess of contradictions, as Lamb observes in Elia's "My Relations." He entertains a "fire-new project in his brain" but is "the systematic opponent of innovation." Even though he is "eccentric," he cautions others against doing "any thing absurd." He promulgates nonviolence but proves "courageous as Charles of Sweden" (as his blow to Hazlitt showed). He eschews laughter; he guffaws wildly (*W*, 2:71).

Lamb embraces John's orneriness in "Dream-Children: A Reverie." As Elia, he admits that John was "handsome and spirited a youth, and a king to the rest of us; and, instead of moping about in solitary corners, like some of us, he would mount the most mettlesome horse he could get, when but an imp no bigger than themselves, and make it carry him half over the county in a morning, and join the hunters when there were any out." The adult John carried Elia when he was "a lame-footed boy" (perhaps stricken by polio). John later on fell lame, too (the stone accident), but Elia was impatient with him. When John died, he felt guilty for not being kinder, and mourned his brother deeply. Elia "missed his kindness, and [he] missed his crossness, and wished him to be alive again, to be quarrelling with him . . . rather than not have him again" (*W*, 2:102).

Lamb's friends could not muster this tenderness. Henry Crabb Robinson called John "grossly rude and vulgar," while Procter found him "abrupt and unprepossessing in manner, as well as assuredly deficient in that courtesy which usually springs from a mind at friendship with the world."[10]

Outside of his brother's indifference, his mother's aloofness, his father's merriment, were the two presences that shaped young Charles the most: Mary and the Temple.

In "Old Benchers of the Inner Temple"—published in the *London Magazine* in September 1821—Elia yearns for the sundials of the Inner Temple, the urban Eden where he spent his childhood. Can he get back to the Garden? Elia at the outset describes his "oldest recollections"—a nod to Wordsworth's "Ode: Intimations of Immortality from Recollections of Early Childhood." Elia's memories, though, are not of the eternal. They are of city buildings and a city river.[11]

The young Elia, passing from Fleet—via No. 17—into the Temple, was happy to find himself in "classic green recesses." He relished the "antique air" of the sundials, "with their moral inscriptions, seeming coevals with that Time which they measured." These dials "take their revelations of [time's] flight immediately from heaven, holding correspondence with the fountain of light!" (*W,* 2:83).

Even if the dial doesn't tell time as accurately as a mechanical clock, it is useful morally and aesthetically, since it speaks "of moderate labours, of pleasures not protracted after sun-set, of temperance, and good-hours." The sundial was, after all, Eden's clock, "the horologe of the first world," construed by Adam and Eve in their days-not-days, a measure not of passing but of recuperation (*W,* 2:83).

Time on the dial: you can see it, in black, on the stone. You can touch it. But the dial's time is also shadow. Here and gone, present and absent, light and dark. Dial-time is alive. But a clock: "What a dead thing, with its ponderous embowelments of lead and brass, its pert or solemn dulness of communication" (*W,* 2:83). The tick-tick is mere repetition: this and this and this. If something is always the same, nothing is happening.

Lamb hated watches. When a friend noticed Lamb lacked one, he gave him a golden timepiece. Later asked what became of it, Lamb said, "Pawned."[12] Lamb often did not date his letters, and he was always late for work. When a superior at the East India office admonished him, Lamb replied, "I always arrive late at the office, but I make up for it by leaving early."[13]

Fountains are "fast vanishing," too. They are "esteemed childish." "Why not then gratify children, by letting them stand? Lawyers, I suppose, were children once. They are awakening images to them at least." Why must everything be about adults? Don't adults retain a "child's heart?" (*W,* 2:84).

If you brick over a fountain, replace dials, you erase particularity, which is childhood, and innocence. The child views *this* aquamarine fountain, and *that* one several streets over—it is made of marble—and still *another* near the red shop, composed of rough stone. Each is mesmerizingly itself.

The child, like the speaker of Marvell's "The Garden," which Elia quotes at length, can become so immersed in an experience that he can, if enjoying a garden, annihilate "all that's made / To a green thought in a green shade." When you give over to this instant's greenness, you are verdant.

Elia celebrates the child by seeing as a child: he remembers past benchers with extreme specificity. Recall Thomas Coventry, "whose person was a quadrate, his step massy and elephantine, his face square as the lion's, his gait peremptory and path-keeping, indivertible from his way as a moving column, the scarecrow of his inferiors, the brow-beater of equals and superiors, who made a solitude of children wherever he came, for they fled his insufferable presence, as they would have shunned an Elisha bear" (*W,* 2:85).

Remember Peter Pierson, who "had that in his face which you could not term unhappiness; it rather implied an incapacity of being happy." Daines Barrington "did pretty well, upon the strength of being a tolerable antiquarian, and having a brother a bishop." There was old Barton, a "jolly negation" who ordered food for the benchers. Then "Read," who possessed a "singular gait, which was performed by three steps and a jump regularly succeeding. The steps were little efforts, like that of a child beginning to walk; the jump comparatively vigorous, as a foot to an inch." And Twopenny, who, though thin himself, habitually joked about Read's "attenuated and fleeting" figure. But Read couldn't take a joke. He "would pinch a cat's ears extremely, when any thing offended him." Of this time, too, was Mingay, with the "iron hand" (*W,* 2:88–89).

Such are Elia's "imperfect recollections" of the benchers. No intimations of immortality, these "fantastic forms" have fled. The distance between the adult Elia and these "inexplicable, half-understood appearances" pains him, since these men created the "mythology of the Temple," and so the vitality of his childhood. But Elia can at least remember these men, and he can contemplate the *idea* of childhood, which flowers in adults when they enjoy the "wholesome superstition" that draws the "unknown and the uncommon" out of ordinary days. To experience this vision is to dwell briefly in "little Goshen" (*W,* 2:90).

"Old Benchers of the Inner Temple" is this Goshen. It transforms familiar men and objects into engagingly strange occurrences. The essay *is* what it's about: an eccentric essay about eccentrics.

In "Mackery End, in Hertfordshire," Lamb (Elia) describes life with Mary (Bridget): "Bridget Elia has been my housekeeper for many a long year. I have obligations to Bridget, extending beyond the period of memory. We house together, old bachelor and maid, in a sort of double singleness" (*W,* 2:75). If they are not married in the usual sense, they are joined aesthetically: they complement each other perfectly, to the point that Elia feels no need to "bewail his celibacy" (as Charles himself possibly did).

Charles hated to be away from Mary, by far the most significant person of his life—his sister, yes, but also mentor, friend, literary collaborator and, in effect, wife. Lamb's 1805 letter to Dorothy Wordsworth, written while Mary was confined in an asylum, demonstrates the scope and depth of his relationship to his sister. Though he has "every reason to suppose that this ill-ness, like all Mary's former ones, will be but temporary," he fears she will not return. Meantime, he laments,

> she is **dead** to me,—I miss a [prop]. All my strength is gone, and I am like a [fool, bere]ft of her co-operation. I dare not think, lest I [should think] wrong; so used am I to look up to her [in the least] & the big-gest perplexity. To say *all that* [I know of her], would be more than I think anybody could [believe or ever under]stand; and when I hope to have her well [again with me] it would be sinning against her feelings to go about to praise her: for I can conceal nothing that I do from her. She is older, & wiser, & better than me, and all my wretched imper-fections I cover to myself by resolutely thinking on her goodness. She would share life & death, heaven & hell with me. She lives but for me. And I know I have been wasting & teasing her life for five years past incessantly with my cursed drinking & ways of going on. But even in this up-braiding of myself I am offending against her; for I know that she has cleaved to me **for better, for worse**; and if the balance has been against her hitherto, it was a **noble trade**. (*M*, 2:169–70)

In a poem written not long after the killing, he howls over the absence of his sister: "I am a widow'd thing, now thou art gone!" So horrific is the pain, he can barely speak, as the next clause shows, a verbatim repetition of the pre-ceding: "Now thou art gone." She is his "familiar friend, / Companion, sister, help-mate, counsellor!" (*W*, 5:22). As he admitted later, when Mary was again committed, "my daily & hourly prop has fallen from me. I totter and stagger with weakness, for nobody can supply her place to me—" (*M*, 1:203–4).

Lamb finds joy in her presence. "It is no new thing for me to be left to my sister. When she is not violent her rambling chat is better to me than the sense and sanity of this world. . . . I could be nowhere happier than under the same roof with her."[14] Lamb celebrated their "hypostatical union." "When Mary calls, it is understood that I call too, we being univocal" (*L*, 2:443).

Friends celebrated their harmony. Such as De Quincey: "As, among cer-tain classes of birds, if you have one you are sure of the other, so, with respect to the Lambs . . . seeing or hearing the brother, you knew that the sister could not be far off."[15] Wordsworth saw them as "a double tree / with two collateral stems sprung from one root."[16]

They looked alike. Both were small and dusky and, as their friends Charles and Mary Cowden Clarke observed, both possessed "a countenance of sin-

gular sweetness, with intelligence." Mary's "brown eyes were soft, yet penetrating; her nose and mouth very shapely; while the general expression was
mildness itself. She had a speaking-voice, gentle and persuasive; and her smile
was her brother's own—winning in the extreme." Mary dressed like Charles,
too—"her apparel was always of the plainest kind; a black stuff or silk gown,
made and worn in the simplest fashion"—and adopted his tobacco habit, taking "snuff liberally." Her "small, white, and delicately-formed hand" hovered
above "the tortoise-shell box containing the powder so strongly approved by
them both, in search of the stimulating pinch." The two would dip "when
hanging together over their favourite books and studies."[17]

The sane Mary was charming, clever, sensible, comforting. Thomas Noon
Talfourd, a friend, believed "Miss Lamb would have been remarkable for
the sweetness of her disposition, the clearness of her understanding, and the
gentle wisdom of all her acts and words, even if these qualities had not been
presented in marvelous contrast with the distraction under which she suffered
for weeks, latterly for months, in every year. There was no tinge of insanity discernible in her manner to the most observant eye." Charles benefited:
more "placid," with a "sense of enjoyment more serene" than her brother's,
Mary was able "to guide, to counsel, to cheer him; and to protect him from
the depths of which she rose so often unruffled to his side."[18] The Clarkes
agreed, praising Mary's mind as at "once nobly-toned and practical, making
her ever a chosen source of confidence among her friends, who turned to her
for consolation, confirmation, and advice, in matters of nicest moment, always secure of deriving from her both aid and solace."[19] Henry Crabb Robinson said of Mary, "With her I can unbosom myself cordially."[20] According to
Talfourd, even the irascible Hazlitt liked her. The essayist said that he "never
met with a woman who could reason, and had met with only one thoroughly
reasonable—the sole exception being Mary Lamb."[21]

Even though Mary relied upon Charles for her freedom and well-being,
he was much more dependent upon her, emotionally and intellectually. If
Mary died before Charles, friends believed, he would be unable to function
alone.

Mary scolded Charles for drinking too much, and Charles bristled at her
reproaches. More darkly, Charles more than once confessed that he wished
Mary were dead, for both their sakes: so she could escape her recurring mental suffering and he could be free of managing her madness. Her insanity
hounded them. They were "marked"; the pair moved house over ten times
to avoid the gawking of the morbidly curious. And Mary could be scary,

regardless of her periods of generous sanity. She had killed her mother, after all. Her older brother John feared her, as did Sara Hutchinson, the sister of Wordsworth's wife. She was wary of falling asleep in the Lamb house. Frances Kelly, the actress to whom Lamb proposed late in life, rejected him because she couldn't imagine living with his troubled sister.

The plot where Wordsworth's "double tree" took root was the Inner Temple, where Mary, a little over ten years old and lonely and gloomy, welcomed into the world a brother whom she could love and who would love her back.

When Mary was four, her sister Elizabeth died in infancy. Over fifty years later, in a letter consoling a friend whose child had died, she wrote, "The image of a little sister I once had comes as fresh into my mind as if I had seen her lately. A little cap with white satin ribbon, grown yellow with long keeping, and a lock of light hair, were the only relics left of her. The sight of them always brought her pretty, fair face to my view, that to this day I seem to have a perfect recollection of her features" (*L*, 2:272).

Charles was the only child born after Mary to survive—at least three others died—and this partially explains Mary's devotion toward her younger brother. Another factor was her loneliness. She needed a companion.

As we have seen, Mary's mother rejected her, as did mother's favorite, John Jr. Aunt Sarah spent her energies hating Elizabeth or doting on Charles, and so likely had little time for her niece. John Sr. was frequently engaged by his inept employer. Mary might have found love with her maternal grandmother, with whom she spent months at a time in Blakesware. But it was not to be. The grandmother shared the mother's inability to understand the girl. Both scolded Mary for her "poor crazy moyther'd brains" (*M*, 1:52).

Mary's story "The Young Mahometan," from *Mrs. Leicester's School,* describes her loneliness. After her father's death, young Margaret Green moves with her mother to the country house of Mrs. Beresford. The mother will manage the home of this woman of large fortune, who also happens to be Margaret's godmother. Strangely, Mrs. Beresford speaks to Margaret only in the mornings—asking how she's doing—and just before bed, when she praises Margaret's reading. The mother follows this example, and almost stops talking to her girl. Margaret wanders through the cavernous house "scarcely ever [hearing] a word addressed" to her "from morning to night." If not for the servants greeting her from time to time, she "should have been the greatest part of the day in as perfect a solitude as Robinson Crusoe" (*W*, 3:308).

Mrs. Beresford is based on Mrs. Plumer, the owner of Blakesware mansion and employer of Mary's grandmother, who is represented in this story by Margaret's mother. But if Margaret is a stand-in for Mary, the mother in the story also represents Mary's actual mother.

Margaret discovers a locked door in the mansion. Since the neglect from her elders has left her bereft of moral guidance, she tries to open it. Unsuccessful for weeks, one day she finds it unlocked, and enters an immense library. Searching for an "entertaining" text, she lights on *Mahometism Explained*. Aside from convincing Margaret that she is a Mahometan, the book describes a terrifying vision of the afterlife. A silken thread stretches across an abyss. Only Muslims can walk safely across the string, while those unconverted plunge into the darkness below. When Margaret later sees Mrs. Beresford stumble, she fears for the souls of this old woman and her mother. She hesitates to warn them of their plight, however, because she has been in the library without leave. Her anxiety induces a fever. When her mother soothes her, Margaret confesses. The doctor arrives, concludes she has "read [herself] into a fever," and removes her to his house, where she recovers (*W*, 3:309–11).

No doctor soothed Mary. Charles did. Later in life, Mary advised a melancholy young woman to "devote herself to [her] younger brother . . . , in the same way that she had attended to her own brother Charles in his infancy, as the wholsomest and surest means for all cure."[22]

Little Charles needed Mary's nursing. In "New Year's Eve," Elia relates that at five he contracted smallpox, then one of the leading causes of death in Europe. Lamb probably got polio, too, which could cause paralysis or even death.

Charles required teaching, too, and so Mary taught him, as noted, how to read. One day the two wandered into a London churchyard. When Charles read the encomiums on the tombstones, he blurted his first quip: "*Mary, where do all the naughty people lie?*"[23]

Outside of Charles, reading was Mary's greatest pleasure. While Charles and John were off at Christ's Hospital, she "happily missed" formal schooling and "tumbled early, by accident or design, into a spacious closet of good old English reading, without much selection or prohibition, and browsed at will upon that fair and wholesome pasturage" (*W*, 2:76).

This closet was Salt's library, extensive and fine, and Mary's (and eventually Charles's) full access to it was a perk of living in the Temple. Children of their socioeconomic status would typically not enjoy such a large array of books. If the elite gardens and dials and fountains of the Temple would later on remind Charles and Mary of what they could not have, the books of their employer's library opened the siblings' minds to the immaterial wealth of the literary life.

One day while browsing in Salt's closet of good English reading, young Charles happened upon Stackhouse's *New History of the Bible,* from which Maria Howe of "The Witch-Aunt" learned of the Witch of Endor. Lamb's Elia also studied this book. He based his most anti-Wordsworthian of essays on it, "Witches, and Other Night-Fears."[24]

Wordsworth in the *Prelude* recounts his fostering by "beauty and fear." In the poem's opening books, fear consumes the beauty, especially when the young Wordsworth steals a skiff and rows out on Derwent Water. The nearby mountain seems to rise up in judgment; it harries the boy back to shore, and home. For days after, strange forms "that do not live like living men" disturb the boy's thoughts and dreams.[25] These moments Wordsworth calls "spots of time," electric with terror and joy. To recall these instants when one is dejected, renovates the spirits.

Elia also remembers childhood nightmares, but they are far from therapeutic. They will not leave the mind, however; nor can they be avoided. Even if Elia had never seen Stackhouse's witch, he would still have faced the phantoms. Images from books are only "transcripts, types—the archetypes" of innate fear. Even if a child has never experienced a scary image or story, he will suffer night terrors. His fears "date beyond his body" (*W,* 2:68).

If these dark archetypes (Jungian) are traumatic, they can also stoke poetry. Though the adult Elia dreams only of ordinary things, Coleridge channels the child's oneiric exotica: "icy domes, and pleasure-houses for Kubla Khan, and Abyssinian maids, and songs of Abara." Barry Cornwall (the pen name of Lamb's friend Bryan Waller Procter) also dreams fantastically, of "gamboling" nereids (*W,* 2:69).

After reading Cornwall's aqueous visions, Elia dreams: "Methought I was upon the ocean billows at some sea nuptials, riding and mounted high, with the customary train sounding their conchs before me, (I myself, you may be sure, the leading god,) and jollily we went careering over the main, till just where Ino Leucothea should have greeted me (I think it was Ino) with a white embrace, the billows gradually subsiding, fell from a sea-roughness to a sea-calm, and thence to a river-motion, and that river (as happens in the familiarization of dreams) was no other than the gentle Thames, which landed me, in

*Saul Consults the Witch of Endor,* engraving by J. Mynde, in Thomas Stackhouse,
*New History of the Holy Bible from the Beginning of the World to the Establishment of
Christianity* (London 1737). (Courtesy of the Wellcome Collection, Creative Commons.)

the wafture of a lucid wave or two, alone, safe and inglorious, somewhere at the foot of Lambeth palace" (*W,* 2:69–70).

This dream mocks the Romantic fancies it appears to validate. That Elia rides the waves at "*some* sea nuptials" (my emphasis) with the "customary" train sounding their conchs shows he is aware of the vague clichés that pass for the "poetic." Placing himself as the "leading god" ridicules such conventions. Neptune in the dream is but a projection of the dreamer's self. Jovially floating over the billows, Elia and his train reach where Ino should greet them. Or maybe not. Elia only thinks it *should* be Ino. It doesn't matter, since this sort of conventional myth can't be taken seriously. As he nears his everyday surroundings, Elia's language becomes more specific, his syntax slower. The rough sea becomes the calm sea becomes a river current becomes this particular river, "no other than the gentle Thames." The rare "wafture" strikingly contrasts with the vague language earlier, as does "a lucid wave or two." These currents bring Elia back to real life, to Lambeth, where ingloriousness, contrasted to the platitudinous grandeur of exotic oceans, is a virtue, and safety reminds us of its Latin origin, *salvus,* good health.

# CHAPTER 2

## ᎧᏲ

# *Christ's Hospital*

Lamb received some schooling before he entered Christ's Hospital, at the age of seven and a half, but we know little about it. Early on he had a schoolmistress, Mrs. Reynolds, daughter of one of Salt's clerks, a Mr. Chambers. She claimed to have known another famous Temple dweller, Oliver Goldsmith, and to have borrowed from him a copy of *The Deserted Village*. Charles and Mary felt an abiding affection for this woman. When grown, they invited her to their literary dinners, even after she was so "decay'd in her members" she no longer remembered "things as she once did." At one of these gatherings she looked "remarkably like an animated wax doll" and spoke as if by "an artificial apparatus."[1] Lamb yearly contributed £32 to Mrs. Reynolds.

Lamb next attended a school run by Mr. Bird on Fetter Lane, not far from Crown Office Row. Mary received instruction there as well. As an adult, after reading an account of a memoir by one of Bird's assistants, Mr. William Starkey, Charles wrote a reminiscence for William Hone's *Every-day Book*. Lamb missed Starkey by a year, but his merits lingered in the schoolroom, which looked out "into a discoloured dingy garden in the passage leading from Fetter Lane into Bartlett's Buildings." In Lamb's day, only "a little of our native English" was taught, as well as basic mathematics. Bird the headmaster "was a squat, corpulent, middle-sized man, with something of the gentleman about him, and that peculiar mild tone—especially while he was

23

inflicting punishment—which is so much more terrible to children, than the angriest looks and gestures." Though not a proponent of frequent whipping, Bird kept on hand the bastinado and the ferule. To make himself look more "formidable" for his beatings, "Bird wore one of those flowered Indian gowns, formerly in use with schoolmasters; the strange figures upon which we used to interpret into hieroglyphics of pain and suffering" (*W,* 1:299–300).

The first text Lamb copied was a discourse on the lesson "Art improves Nature" (an injunction on which the mature Lamb based his style), though he struggled to control his "truant looks side-long to the garden, which seemed a mockery of our imprisonment." Charles paid enough attention to win "the prize for best spelling." He dipped his ink from "little leaden" stands sunk into the desks and noted how his washed "morning fingers" darkened throughout the day (*W,* 1:300).

Between his time at grammar school and Christ's Hospital, on December 10, 1781, a bit before 5 p.m., six-year-old Charles Lamb and his "elders" walk upward from the Inner Temple onto Fleet, dreary and puddled, and slog west, until Fleet turns into the Strand, from which they turn right, after about half a mile, onto Catherine Street, which immediately bends northwest into Brydges Street. After walking about two hundred yards—just before reaching Russell Street—they stop before a stucco façade on their right. They pass through its entrance into a dark, narrow hallway. It leads to a building in the middle of the block, whose back rises up from the street running parallel to Brydges: Drury Lane. In the corridor, voices: excited, violent. This is the Royal Theatre.

The Lambs' tickets, given to them by a family friend, are for the pit. Luckily for them they have in hand their "orders," passes for reduced or free admission. Otherwise they would have had to force their way into the crowd frantic at the pit door and take their chances. Even though the theater seats two thousand, it can't accommodate everyone who wants in. Celebrity actors— the rock stars of the day—have made theatergoing more popular than ever. Sarah Siddons and John Philip Kemble, her brother, are the brightest stars.

Charles and his family walk to their seats on one of the benches covered in green cloth. They take in the "higgledy-piggledy" contingent of the pit: honest commoners, quality gentlemen, ladies of virtue, and "damsels that hunt for Prey"—the theater prostitutes, or spells. Some of this motley crowd attend to watch the drama, but others are there to "chatter, toy, [and] play." The boxes above, the most expensive in the house, seat the "persons of best

*The Pit Door/ La porte du parterre*, after Robert Dighton the Elder, November 9, 1784.
(Courtesy of the Elisha Whittelsey Collection, the Elisha Whittelsey Fund, 1969,
Wikimedia Commons.)

Quality," mostly women, and the two galleries above, the cheap seats, contain "ordinary People," albeit the ones most likely, from that height, to pelt actors with orange peels.[2]

The stage on which the young Charles expectantly gazes is forty-five feet wide and thirty feet deep. It is "raked," meaning it angles upward from front to back. (The higher actor, nearer the back, could thus "upstage" his fellow players, being more clearly in the audience's view.) There are trap doors in the stage's floor, and grooves for flats, or moving scenery. Spikes rise from the edge of the stage, their purpose to prevent riots, not infrequent in this rough-and-tumble atmosphere, as far from our modern genteel theater as an opera from a Sex Pistols concert. Not twenty years before the Lambs' visit this evening, a riot broke out in nearby Covent Garden in protest of a new policy disallowing half-price admission after a play's third act. The play was *Artaxerxes*. "The mischief done was the greatest ever known on any occasion of the like kind: all the benches of the boxes and pit being entirely tore up, the glasses and chandeliers broken, and the linings of the boxes cut to pieces. The rashness of the rioters was so great, that they cut away the wooden pillars between the boxes, so if the inside of them had not been iron, they would have brought down the galleries upon their heads. The damages done amount to at least 2000 *l*."[3]

The play young Lamb sees is also *Artaxerxes*. In December 1821, as Elia, he describes the experience in "My First Play." He crosses the portal into the Drury. He waits in the foyer. When will he be let in? He will never be such "an expectant" again. Behind the door are "more than Arabian paradises!" He passes the threshold and beholds another, the "green curtain." It veils a heaven and whips him into more intense anticipation (*W,* 2:98).

The curtain rises. Another boundary passed. *Artaxerxes*. Elia does not follow the plot. He loses himself in the place. "All feeling was absorbed in vision. Gorgeous vests, gardens, palaces, princesses, passed before me. I knew not players. I was in Persepolis for the time, and the burning idol of their devotion almost converted me into a worshipper. I was awestruck, and believed those significations to be something more than elemental fires. It was all enchantment and a dream" (*W,* 2:99).

Young Elia watched two more plays not long after. Then, from the age of seven to thirteen or fourteen, he saw none, since his school prohibited attending the theater. When he again entered a theater, the magic was gone. In the interval, "what had I not lost! At the first period I knew nothing, understood nothing, discriminated nothing. I felt all, loved all, wondered all." Where he had left the temple a "devotee," he "returned a rationalist. The same things were there materially; but the emblem, the reference, was gone!" The curtain was no longer a veil, but simply a "quantity of green baize." The lights only "clumsy machinery." Actors merely "men and women painted" (*W,* 2:100).

When fact exterminates fantasy, though, other epiphanies fire. The night the dream fled, Elia first enjoyed actress Sarah Siddons perform. Regret soon yielded to "the present attraction." The theater became to him, "upon a new stock, the most delightful of recreations" (*W,* 2:100).

Siddons is not a nameless figure hovering in eternal exotica. She is a historical being, born on one date and destined to die on another. Her talent is particular; no one acts the role as *she* does. Her unique presence attracts right now, no other time. This particularity, necessarily transient, generates a new sort of theater for Elia: one of re-creation. The adult attends Drury weary and broken, and the play composes him again. It transforms pain to power. The losses of childhood are recompensed abundantly by the adult experience. A play can be "first" not just temporally but emotionally: the foremost solace.

Outside of the day of horrors, Lamb's admittance to Christ's Hospital was the most important event of his life. Christ's, still in existence today—though it has moved from London to Horsham—is one of the oldest boarding schools in England. In 1552 King Edward VI, only fifteen (he would die one year later), established a school for the poor on Newgate Street, in buildings once inhabited by the Grey Friars, a Franciscan order. Within the Gothic walls and cloisters, the students would be clothed, fed, and instructed. In the early days, the school took in orphaned babies and trained students in a trade. Brighter students studied for Cambridge or Oxford. After 1673, when Charles II chartered the Royal Mathematical School, students could study navigation. (The navy still pays tuition for the children of its sailors.) After the Great Fire of 1666 nearly destroyed Christ's, Christopher Wren, the architect of St. Paul's, designed the school's south wall as well as Christ's Church, just beyond the walls. The nearby dome of St. Paul's loomed majestically. The great hall brought its own grandeur: a copy of Hans Holbein the Younger's painting of a youthful Henry VIII decorated the wall, as did Antonio Verrio's eighty-six-foot-long painting of the children of Christ's standing before James II. The Gordon Riots of 1780—incited by Papist Act of 1778 and possibly sweeping up, against his will, a twenty-three-year-old William Blake—threatened the school as much as the fire. Nearby Newgate Prison was overrun and burned. The prisoners broke free. Soldiers, unwilling to fire on Londoners, laid down their weapons. When the unchecked mob reached Christ's, William Wales, the mathematics master and former seaman (he had sailed with Captain Cook), stood them down.[4]

When Lamb matriculated on October 9, 1782, Christ's was still a charity school. It admitted bright children whose families lacked the means to educate them, as well as orphans. The high reputation of the school, however, attracted the notice of wealthier families, and an increasing number of rich folk schemed their way in, thus leaving fewer slots for the poor. (Lamb's first essay on Christ's, from 1813, responds to this controversial issue.) While these wealthier students ("Pay Scholars") could pay their own way, the poorer ones required a member of the Board of Governors to sponsor them.

But regardless of a wealthy boy here and there, Christ's proudly educated the poor, even if it specialized in the poor who had once not been poor. As Coleridge wrote, "The true and specific purpose of Christ's hospital . . . is to preserve, in the same rank of life in which they were born, the children of reputable persons of the middle class, who either by the death or overwhelming calamities of their parents must otherwise have sunk down to a state, which to them would be penury and heart-breaking, because alike unfitted to their bodily and their mental habits. To preserve, and not to disturb or destroy, the gradations of society; to catch the falling, not to lift up the standing, from their natural and native rank."[5]

But for the more liberal alumnus Leigh Hunt, Christ's was less about upholding hierarchy and more about defining what "Englishness" is, at least at its best: "something solid, unpretending, of good character, and free to all. More boys are to be found in [Christ's], who issue from a greater variety of ranks, than in any other school in the kingdom; and as it is the most various, so it is the largest, of all the free-schools."[6]

Unlike the pastoral, upper-crust Eton, plebeian Christ's served the city. It fed London's great beast of commerce. Every spring, the students—also known as "Blues," for their elegant blue robes—marched eastward to Mansion House on Poultry, where the lord mayor presented them with wine, buns, and shillings. The largest of Christ's three schools, the Writing School, trained students in the London trades, primarily clerking. By fourteen or fifteen, the boys could contribute to the urban economy, itself a supplier to England's rapacious global empire.

With its Mathematics and Drawing School, Christ's supplied this empire directly. The school trained navigators for the navy and the East India

*The Hall, Blue Coat School*, plate 10, in Rudolph Ackermann, *Microcosm of London* (London, 1810). (Courtesy of Wikimedia Commons.)

Company, the country's mercantile monopoly (and Lamb's future employer). The brightest students, such as Lamb, were chosen for the Grammar School. There they learned Greek and Latin as well as the English classics. These elite pupils were divided between the so-called deputy Grecians, destined for the law or the military, and the Grecians, groomed for Cambridge and Oxford. The Grecians were the school's royalty. Hunt remembers their aura. "When I entered the school, I was shown three gigantic boys . . . who, I was told, were going to the university. These were the Grecians. . . . The next class to these—like a college of cardinals to those three Popes (for every Grecian was in our eyes infallible)—were the deputy-Grecians."[7]

During the morning, the deputies studied Homer, Virgil, or Horace; the Greek Testament; and Greek or Latin grammar. In the afternoon, they took Hebrew grammar, mathematics, and geography. They also recited classical poetry. The Grecians followed a similar curriculum but at a more advanced level. Additionally, both tiers of Grecian learned Chaucer, Spenser, Shakespeare, Milton, Pope, Collins, and Gray.

The boys created their own, earthier canons, as Lamb describes in "Christ's Hospital Five and Thirty Years Ago." When his schoolmaster, the lenient Reverend Field (he bore his punitive cane "as if it was a lily") left the room, "our mirth and uproar went on. We had classics of our own, without being beholden to 'insolent Greece or haughty Rome,' that passed current among us—Peter Wilkins—the Adventures of the Hon. Capt. Robert Boyle—the Fortunate Blue Coat Boy—and the like" (*W,* 2:18).[8]

Lamb sat beside another Blue (was he handsome Robert Allen or pious Marmaduke Thompson?) reading, while Field was in the room, Homer. But when the teacher retired, Lamb produced from deep in his gown Robert Paltock's *The Life and Adventures of Peter Wilkins, a Cornish Man* (1752), and shared it with his mate. Wilkins, his ship wrecked near the South Pole, finds a passage to a subterranean world populated by glums and gawrys, men and women who can fly. To Wilkins they are beautiful, superior to humans, and he marries one of the women. During his tenure at Christ's, Hunt found this book, clearly influenced by *Robinson Crusoe,* to be a "mixture of sentiment and voluptuousness beyond all the bridals we [had] read."[9]

The other "classics" Lamb mentions are likewise adventurous journeys. *The Voyages and Adventures of Captain Robert Boyle,* by William Rufus Chetwood, is a picaresque tale of exotic locales, dangerous escapades, and open sexuality (the Blues read of two characters "playing Rantum Scantum"), while *The Fortunate Blue-Coat Boy; or, Memoirs of the Life and Happy Adventures of Mr. Benjamin Templeton, Formerly a Scholar in Christ's Hospital* describes the young Blue's push for success in gritty, greedy, violent London.[10]

Lamb as an adult writer drew creatively on classical sources as well as the English literary greats, mainly Shakespeare. But this more underground canon shaped his mature style, too. The picaresque adventure stories feature an exuberant parataxis, perfect for the essay—the "and this and that and this" of life, fresh experiences mercurially rising and gone. And the harsh realism of *The Fortunate Blue-Coat Boy* demonstrates the power of unadorned urban detail.

Perhaps because Salt had already sponsored two other boys—the quota for each governor—he could not officially sponsor Charles. He arranged for his friend Timothy Yeats to pledge the £100 to cover Lamb's possible damage to the school's property. On March 30, 1781, as part of the application process, John Lamb Sr. claimed he could maintain his wife and three children only with difficulty. He needed assistance. This is a little odd, considering that

John Lamb Jr. was by then making a steady salary clerking at the South Sea House, and Mary was bringing in money from her mantua making. But the goal was admission, not accuracy. Elizabeth signed the document, which is strange, too, since normally this was the father's job.

The school admitted Lamb in July, but he didn't enter until October. He donned the famous uniform still in use today: a long, coarse, navy-blue gown buttoned to the neck with gold buttons, under which, in winter, the students wore a yellow vest; a red leather belt inscribed with roses and stars; worsted knee-length canary-yellow stockings; and a worsted black cap.

Christ's was only a fifteen-minute walk from Crown Office Row (a right turn, once out of the Temple, onto Fleet, left onto Old Bailey, right onto Newgate Street), but it felt to Lamb like another world. Hunt described it: "Wards, sleeping rooms, are twelve, and contained in my time, rows of beds on each side partitioned off, but connected with one another, and each having two boys to sleep in it. Down the middle ran the bins for holding bread and other things, and serving for a table when the meal was not taken in the hall; and over the bins hung a great homely chandelier. To each of these wards a nurse was assigned, who was the widow of some decent liveryman of London, and who had the charge of looking after us at night-time, seeing to our washing, etc and carving for us at dinner."[11]

Like the military, the school deliberately severed the boys from their homes. Coleridge wept after returning to Christ's from a holiday. James Bowyer, the sadistic headmaster, screamed: "Boy! the school is your father; boy! the school is your mother; boy! the school is your brother; the school is your sister; the school is your first cousin, and your second cousin, and all the rest of your relations. Let's have no more crying!"[12]

The school was more prison than barracks. "It will be seen that the outlook of the boys on life must have been extremely restricted—literally cloistered. Cabin'd, cribb'd, confin'd amid the massive buildings, shut in by stout walls and iron railings, guarded by beadles watchful and greedy as Cerberus at the gates, they could not but feel that C.H. was their microcosm, that the outer world was an alien country which would not concern them until they left school."[13]

The wake-up bell sounded at 6 in the summer, 7 in the winter. After a quick cold wash, the students straggled to breakfast. Next, class until 11, then an hour of play. Dinner followed at noon, then, after brief play, more class, lasting until 5 in summer and 6 in winter. Supper at 6, then more playtime, in summer, until 8. In winter, it was straight to bed. Religion pervaded the week, with Bible readings and prayers before each meal and before bed. "We rivalled the monks," Hunt wrote, "in the religious part of our duties."[14]

What was Charles like at Christ's? To his friend and fellow student Valentine Le Grice, he "was an amiable gentle boy, very sensible and keenly observing, indulged by his schoolfellows and by his master on account of his infirmity of speech. [Lamb stuttered.] His countenance was mild; his complexion clear brown, with an expression which might lead you to think that he was of Jewish descent. . . . His walk [was] slow and peculiar, adding to the staid appearance of his figure. I never heard his name mentioned without the addition of Charles, although, as there was no other boy of the name of Lamb, the addition was unnecessary: but there was an implied kindness in it, and it was a proof that his gentle manners excited that kindness."[15] Based on accounts of others, Talfourd, who did not attend Christ's, adds: Lamb at Christ's was "constitutionally nervous and timid, he would seem unfitted to encounter the discipline of a school formed to restrain some hundreds of lads in the heart of the metropolis, or to fight his way among them. But the sweetness of his disposition won him favour from all; and although the antique peculiarities of the school tinged his opening imagination, they did not sadden his childhood."[16] This kind treatment from his fellows made Christ's a not unpleasant experience for Lamb. He was left alone to walk with "the self-concentration of a young monk" (*W,* 1:141).

Lamb's experience inspired him in 1813 to publish "On Christ's Hospital and the Character of the Christ's Hospital Boy." In this piece defending the school's policy of admitting wealthier boys, Lamb evokes an idyllic past. Spots of time shine:

> I must crave leave to remember our transcending superiority in those invigorating sports, leap-frog, and basting the bear; our delightful excursions in the summer holidays to the New River, near Newington, where, like otters, we would live the long day in the water, never caring for dressing ourselves, when we had once stripped; our savory meals afterwards, when we came home almost famished with staying out all day without our dinners; . . . our . . . festivities at Christmas, when the richest of us would club our stock to have a gaudy day, sitting round the fire, replenished to the height with logs, and the penniless, and he that could contribute nothing, partook in all the mirth, and in some

of the substantialities of the feasting; the carol sung by night at that time of the year, which, when a young boy, I have so often lain awake to hear from seven (the hour of going to bed) till ten, when it was sung by the older boys and monitors, and have listened to it, in their rude chanting, till I have been transported in fancy to the fields of Bethlehem, and the song which was sung at that season, by angels' voices to the shepherds. (*W,* 1:148)

When Coleridge and Hunt read the essay, they scoffed. Why no mention of the gruesome beef? The icy beds? The organized bullying? Above all, the flogging? In describing the Reverend James Bowyer, the upper-grammar master, Lamb washes white. Even if the "terrors of his rod" and "temper a little too hasty" made some boys nervous, this "excellent" man demonstrated an "unwearied assiduity" in attending to "the particular improvement of each of us" (*W,* 1:145).

Of Bowyer, Hunt writes: "He once . . . knocked out one of my teeth with the back of a Homer, in a fit of impatience at my stammering. The tooth was a loose one, and I told him as much; but the blood rushed out as I spoke: he turned pale, and, on my proposing to go out and wash the mouth, he said 'Go, child,' in a tone of voice amounting to paternal."[17] When Coleridge claimed he had become a skeptic, Bowyer flogged him "soundly."[18] Coleridge complained of this beating perennially and, according to Hunt—who also noted that Bowyer pinched chins and earlobes "till he would make the blood come"—Coleridge "dreamt of the master all his life, and . . . his dreams were horrible."[19]

In his second essay on Christ's, from November 1820, Lamb, as Elia, describes Christ's more accurately. That he remembers the school from the point of view of Coleridge, and not himself, is apt, given Coleridge's traumatic memories.[20]

Elia accuses "Mr. Lamb's" 1813 essay, "a magnificent eulogy on my old school," of contriving "to bring together whatever can be said in praise of [Christ's], dropping all the other side of the argument most ingeniously." "L." enjoyed advantages over the other boys. As a Londoner, he had friends nearby and could visit them often, through some "invidious distinction, which was denied" to the rest. No doubt the "sub-treasurer to the Inner Temple," Randal Norris, was responsible for this unjust privilege, as well as for the tea and hot rolls L. enjoyed each morning while his fellow students "were battening upon our quarter of a penny loaf—our *crug*—moistened with attenuated small beer, in wooden piggins, smacking of the pitched leathern jack it was poured from." Every day of the week, L. enriched with bread and butter, ginger, veal, or griskin the disgusting meals his fellows choked down unembellished: "milk porritch, blue and tasteless," "pease soup of Saturday, coarse and choking," a "mess of millet," "scanty mutton crags," "boiled beef . . . with detestable marigolds floating in the pail to poison the broth." Moreover, L. relished extra treats from his aunt (Sarah) (*W,* 2:12–13).

Elia (drawing on Coleridge's memories) was "a poor friendless boy." His parents were distant, and local acquaintances soon wearied of his visits. Of the six hundred students, only he was bereft of hospitality. He longed for his life before school in his home country, Calne in Wiltshire (Lamb's substitute for Ottery St. Mary in Devon, Coleridge's actual birthplace) (*W,* 2:13).

Though there were small pleasures at the school—like swimming trips to the New River—Christ's was torture. Daylong furloughs in winter submitted students to aimless wandering in freezing streets. Worse was the severity of the punishments, which L., because of his connections, avoided. Elia had been awakened on cold winter nights to be flogged, along with eleven other boys, just because the monitor heard talking somewhere within the dormitory. One monitor actually branded a student with a "red hot iron"; he also starved the entire dormitory by giving half the bread to a "young ass" (*W,* 2:15).

These cruelties are minor compared to those perpetrated on boys who really broke the rules. On Elia's first day, when he was a "tender" seven (Coleridge was actually nine when admitted), he saw a boy in fetters. Being a hypochondriac—as Coleridge was—he was overcome with terror. The boy had run away and this was the punishment for the first offense. A second offense merited time in the dungeons, "little, square, Bedlam cells, where a boy could just lie at his length upon straw and a blanket . . . with a peep of light, let in askance, from a prison-orifice at top, barely enough to read by." This confinement was solitary. The truant's only contacts were the porter, who brought bread and water, and the beadle, who came twice a week to upbraid the boy. For his third offense, the boy was expelled, but not before he was divested of his blue gown, clothed in the garb of London lamplighters, and brought before the student body and school officials. Then he was viciously scourged (*W,* 2:16–17).

Matching this systematic cruelty was the more arbitrary violence of the Reverend Bowyer. While those in the lower Grammar School, the deputy Grecians (including Elia), were taught by the easygoing Field, students in the higher one, the Grecians (Coleridge's level), were instructed by the hard-nosed Bowyer. Bowyer wore two wigs, "both pedantic, but of differing omen. The one serene, smiling, fresh powdered, betokening a mild day. The other, an old discoloured, unkempt, angry caxon, denoting frequent and bloody execution." Woe fell upon the school when Bowyer appeared in his *"passy,"* or *"passionate wig."* "I have known [Bowyer] to double his knotty fist at a poor trembling child (the maternal milk hardly dry upon its lips) with a 'Sirrah, do you presume to set your wits at me?'" He would rush into the classroom from his "inner recess," single out a student, and roar, "I have a great mind to whip you." Then he would vanish back into his "lair" before running back in minutes later, yelling, "and I WILL, too" (*W,* 2:19–20).

Still, L. admired Bowyer's instruction, and Coleridge in his *Biographia Literaria* praised the man for teaching him how to write:

> In our own English compositions he [Bowyer] showed no mercy to phrase, metaphor, or image, unsupported by a sound sense, or where the same sense might have been conveyed with equal force and dignity in plainer words. Lute, harp, lyre, muse, muses, and inspirations, Pegasus, Parnassus, and Hippocrene, were all an abomination to him. I fancy I can almost hear him now, exclaiming, *"Harp? Harp? Lyre? Pen and ink, boy, you mean!—Muse, boy, Muse? Your nurse's daughter, you mean!—Pierian spring? Oh, aye! the cloister-pump, I suppose"* Nay, certain introductions, similes, and examples were placed by name on a list of interdiction.[21]

The distinguished scholars Bowyer molded were many: most notably, Thomas Middleton, who edited the *Country Spectator,* published an important study of the Greek article, and became bishop of Calcutta; George Richards, who composed a "most spirited poem" called the *Aboriginal Britons* (Byron admired it); and Coleridge, about whom Lamb memorably reminisced.

> Come back into memory, like as thou wert in the day-spring of thy fancies, with hope like a fiery column before thee—the dark pillar not yet turned—Samuel Taylor Coleridge—Logician, Metaphysician, Bard!—How have I seen the casual passer through the Cloisters stand still, intranced with admiration (while he weighed the disproportion between the *speech* and the *garb* of the young Mirandula), to hear thee unfold, in thy deep and sweet intonations, the mysteries of Jamblichus, or Plotinus (for even in those years thou waxedst not pale at such philosophic draughts), or reciting Homer in his Greek, or Pindar—

while the walls of the old Grey Friars reechoed to the accents of the *inspired charity-boy*! (*W*, 2:20–22)

Other notable Grecians of Elia's day became friends of Lamb. Valentine Le Grice, who could match wits with Coleridge, a brisk English man-o'-war to Coleridge's bulky Spanish galleon. Robert Allen, admired for his good looks, "cordial smile, and still more cordial laugh," though he was dead by 1820, having been killed by apoplexy after serving as an army doctor in Portugal and then working as a journalist. Then the younger Le Grice, Samuel, and Robert Favell. Both became soldiers, Samuel because of his "roving temper," Robert because of his "too quick a sense of neglect." Both also died young, Samuel of fever in Jamaica, Robert of wounds in the battle of Salamanca. Finally, there were "fine frank-hearted" F. W. Franklin, who became master of the Blue Coat School in Hertford, and Marmaduke Thompson, the mild missionary to whom Lamb dedicated his novel *Rosamund Gray* (*W*, 2: 21–22).

Why did Lamb refute his earlier, 1813 essay on Christ's, why did he do so under the guise of Elia, and why did he blend Elia with Coleridge? Perhaps because Bowyer died between 1813 and 1820, and Lamb felt free to depict the grammar head master more realistically. Likewise, maybe hiding behind the mask of Elia made Lamb more comfortable stating the darker facts.

There is a more compelling reason. "Christ's Hospital Five and Thirty Years Ago" was only the third Elia essay, so the piece appeared when Lamb's persona was still experimental: flexible, barely tested, and brimming with potential. Maybe Lamb was seeing what his mask was capable of. He had already created a literary persona closely associated with his historical identity. Now he blended the literary identity with another historical self. Fact became fiction that turned into fact. Just when you assume Elia is Lamb, Elia is Coleridge. But not simply Coleridge, since Elia in the essay is a deputy Grecian, and so partly Lamb. The effect is unsettling: who is the author? where is the authority? But it is also liberating; freed from the consistency of one identity, the essay can metamorphose into virtually anything.

Identity is not stable and unified. It is shifting, multiple. You are not what you are, you are what you experience, and each minute is a new experience, and so the self is as fickle and fecund as a cloud.

Though Lamb's formal education ended when he was fourteen, it nourished him the rest of his life. His mature essay style in particular reflects his

Christ's curriculum. Like Montaigne, he animates his sentences with quotations from Latin and Greek classics. He also enlivens his diction with the archaic words he learned from Chaucer, Spenser, and Shakespeare.

More fundamentally, Lamb as Elia adapts to modern London the progymnasmata, Christ's classical model for teaching rhetoric. Progymnasmata, or preliminary exercises, is a list of prompts—narratives, maxims, refutations, commonplaces—designed to produce essays. Students might be given a "moral," such as "ambition," and be required to argue for or against it.[22] A poem Lamb wrote at Christ's, "Mille Viae Mortis," a "thousand ways to die," prompts a meditation on the vanity of earthly striving.

Thirty years later, Lamb employs this method while satirizing it. Elia's "A Dissertation upon Roast Pig" is a comically academic disquisition on the merits of roasting pigs, while "A Complaint of the Decay of Beggars in the Metropolis" mocks the commonplace notion that "beggars are a nuisance." "Two Races of Men" likewise sends up pedantic exercise; Elia argues for the virtues of being forever in debt and criticizes those who lend.

If Lamb's playful rhetoric originated in Christ's curriculum, a far more important element of his mature style came from the terrible Bowyer himself. As a deputy Grecian, Lamb received his lessons mostly from the gentle Reverend Field. But he almost certainly learned from Bowyer, too. His detailed description of the man in "Christ's Hospital Five and Thirty Years Ago" suggests firsthand contact, as does the inclusion of his work in one of Bowyer's notebooks reserved for student writing of high distinction. Lamb would have learned from Bowyer the same lesson Coleridge did: "In truly great poets . . . there is a reason assignable, not only for every word, but for the position of every word."[23] Bowyer added to this an argument for formal rigor and another for plain style: why say muse when you mean the nurse's girl?

The adult Lamb cherished formal unity. He argued that Shakespeare was better read than acted, because theatrical renderings miss the literary intricacy. In the Elia essays, Lamb's writing miraculously fuses baroque digressions and glossy logic. Lamb also valued the plain style (even if he equally lauded the gaudy), which he espoused in a series of letters to Coleridge in 1796. Reading his friend's early verse, he directed: cultivate simplicity.

Lamb was Grecian material. Why did he finish as a deputy? He stuttered, and this impediment precluded a career in the clergy, and only those boys from Christ's who might make suitable preachers were sent to university, the assumption being that Cambridge and Oxford would train them up as vicars.

Leigh Hunt also stammered. Leaving Christ's at fifteen with no prospect of university crushed him: "I put off my band and blue skirts for a coat and neckcloth. I was then first Deputy Grecian, and I had the honour of going out of the school in the same rank, at the same age, and for the same reason, as my friend Charles Lamb. The reason was, that I hesitated in my speech. . . . It was understood that a Grecian was bound to deliver a public speech before he left school, and to go into the Church afterwards; and as I could do neither of these things, a Grecian I could not be. So I put on my coat and waistcoat, and what was stranger, my hat; a very uncomfortable addition to my sensations." This was exile. "I had a vague sense of worldly trouble, and of great and serious change in my condition; besides which, I had to quit my old cloisters, and my playmates, and long habits of all sorts. . . . I took leave of my books, of my friends, of my seat in the grammar school, of my good-hearted nurse and her daughter, of my bed, of the cloisters, and of the very pump out of which I had taken so many delicious draughts, as if I should never see them again."[24]

Lamb limns this angst more pithily: "I don't know how it is, but I keep my rank in fancy still since school days. I can never forget I was a deputy Grecian! . . . Alas! what am I now? What is a Leadenhall clerk, or India pensioner, to a deputy Grecian? How art thou fallen, O Lucifer!" (*L*, 3:306).

Lamb's stutter helped cause his lifelong addiction to alcohol. In his 1813 essay "Confessions of a Drunkard," a model for De Quincey's 1821 confession about opium, Lamb describes his social group—"men of boisterous spirits, sitters up a-nights, disputants, drunken"—and its obsession: wit. More fanciful than his friends, Lamb became "a professed joker." But he struggled to quip, since "his natural nervous impediment [of] speech" hindered his ability to express himself quickly. The booze, however, enlivened his tongue into a worthy conduit for his "preternatural flow of ideas" (*W*, 3:134–35).

The stuttering was embarrassing. Once Lamb pursued, at the recommendation of a physician, sea bathing at Hastings. At the door of his bathing machine, Lamb spoke to his two assistants: "Hear me, men! Take notice of this—I am to be . . ." Then followed "a rolling fire of 'Di—di—di—di.'" When Lamb finally "descended a plomb upon the full word dipped," the two men plunged him into the ocean. Surfacing, Lamb "sobbed so much from the cold, that he found no voice suitable to his indignation." Once he calmed, he once more stumbled toward "dipped," and "down the stammerer went for the second time." Once more Lamb emerged cold and angry, and a brisk plunge concluded his stutter. "Oh limbs of Satan!" Lamb said this time, "it's now too late; I tell you that I am—no, that I was—to be di—di—di—dipped only once."[25]

The impediment had one virtue. Its "pleasant" rhythm encouraged auditors to "listen eagerly for his words, always full of meaning, or charged with a jest; or referring (but this was rare) to some line or passage from one of the old Elizabethan writers, which was always ushered in with a smile of tender reverence."[26] According to De Quincey, the stutter "was worth an annuity to him as an ally of [Lamb's] wit," since he was able to train "the roll of stammers into settling upon the words immediately preceding the effective one; by which means the key-note of the jest or sarcasm, benefiting by the sudden liberation of his embargoed voice, was delivered with the force of a pistol shot." The firing won him "triple execution." "In the first place, the distressing sympathy of the hearers with his distress of utterance won for him unavoidably the silence of deep attention; and then, whilst he had us all hoaxed into this attitude of mute suspense by an appearance of distress that he perhaps did not really feel, down came a plunging shot into the very thick of us, with ten times the effect it would else have had."[27]

Incidentally, Mary also had a charming idiosyncrasy to her voice. As Charles and Mary Cowden Clarke observed, "There was a certain catch, or emotional breathingness, in her utterance, which gave an inexpressible charm to her reading of poetry, and which lent a captivating earnestness to her mode of speech when addressing those she liked. This slight check, with its yearning, eager effect in her voice, had something softenedly akin to her brother Charles's impediment of articulation: in him it scarcely amounted to a stammer; in her it merely imparted additional stress to the fine-sensed suggestions she made to those whom she counselled or consoled."[28]

# CHAPTER 3

# East India

On November 23, 1789, Lamb left Christ's and childhood. Outside of Mary's murdering of their mother, this was one of the most tragic moments of his life. Once exiled to Eden's east, is there a portal back to the garden? This question inspires Elia's "New Year's Eve."

Adulthood is awful, Elia believes, and he mocks his grown self. He is "light, and vain, and humorsome; a notorious ***; addicted to ***: averse from counsel, neither taking it, nor offering it;—*** besides; a stammering buffoon; what you will." His evils are unspeakable (*W,* 2:28).

But the child Elia, that "other me," he can love. He can cherish the boy patiently suffering "small-pox at five." Notice the boy's "poor fevered head upon the sick pillow at Christ's and wake with [him] in surprise at the gentle posture of maternal tenderness hanging over it." Relish how he shrinks "from any the least colour of falsehood" (*W,* 2:28).

Why does Elia envision his earlier self, though, "as if it had been a child of some other house, and not of my parents?" He refers to the child as an "it," not an "I" or even a "he." Perhaps that little fellow is not really he. Maybe Elia is witnessing the memories of another man, as though he watches a movie of a boy that looks like him but isn't. From what glory has Elia fallen, if the child were a mere simulation produced by "some dissembling guardian?" A guardian who rules the alien boy's "unpractised self" and regulates its "moral being?" (*W,* 2:28).

Regardless of epistemology, Elia obsesses over his past. He plunges "into foregone visions and conclusions," encounters "pell-mell with past disappointments," defends against "old discouragements," even courts again the great love, Alice W., he lost. He does all this in "fancy. But he knows the past lacks the essence of hope: pliability. Former years resemble a "well-contrived novel," static (*W*, 2:28).

Perhaps the future will be happy. No. Since he is without a family, Elia can't cast himself into his offspring. He enjoys no forward-looking thoughts. He fears change: "A new state of being staggers" him (*W*, 2:29).

Maybe he should stake down in the now. Elia does love "this green earth; the face of town and country; the unspeakable rural solitudes, and the sweet security of streets." The "sun and sky," too, and "breeze, and solitary walks, and summer holidays, and the greenness of fields, and the delicious juices of meats and fishes, and society, and the cheerful glass, and candle-light, and fire-side conversations, and innocent vanities, and jests" (*W*, 2:29). This amorous embrace of ordinariness is a "cordial" against "puling fears of death" (*W*, 2:32). But don't fishes and jokes and wine also rush by, gone even before relished? Elia does not say, but he implies this transience of the present. Like the past and the future, this minute is gone.

Elia is not at home in any time. But his exile isn't despair. His irony turns it to gentle melancholy. The more distant the thing you love, the more vividly you imagine it. Water, Emily Dickinson says, is taught by thirst.

In 1789, Salt's health was deteriorating—he would die in three years—and Elizabeth probably added nursing to her housekeeping duties. Her own health wasn't the best. The arthritis that would debilitate her within a few years already troubled her. John Sr. still worked as Salt's clerk and waited tables in the hall. He was near seventy, though, and a stroke would hit him soon, senility its aftermath. Mary earned what she could from dressmaking. The younger John was probably out on his own now, clerking at South Sea House. His selfishness would not permit him to help the family cause.

It was time for Charles to contribute. Once more, the Temple came through. Salt's colleague Thomas Coventry, probably at Salt's behest, asked Joseph Paice, a merchant and a director of the South Sea Company, to find Charles a place. Paice said, "Let him have the run of my counting house until something better offers."[1]

And so Lamb learned business at 27 Bread Street Hill. More important, he talked literature. Paice loved books. He especially valued Elizabethan poetry and had memorized long passages of Shakespeare. Moreover, he had known Samuel Richardson, and he might have been acquainted with William Hayley, the biographer of Milton and temporary patron—and (imagined) enemy—of William Blake. Paice's studies required focus, since a "bevy of admiring female friends" made heavy demands on "his attention and correspondence."[2]

We don't know what Lamb did in Paice's offices (probably learned book-keeping), or how long he worked in them. We can imagine the teenaged Lamb, fresh from Christ's, passionately talking Shakespeare with his business mentor.

We do know that Lamb paid attention to Paice's treatment of women. In November 1822, Lamb as Elia published "Modern Gallantry," a remark-ably, for the time, feminist denunciation of England's patriarchy. The only man never unjust to women was Joseph Paice, who "had not *one* system of attention to females in the drawing-room, and *another* in the shop, or at the stall." "I have seen him tenderly escorting a marketwoman, whom he had encountered in a shower, exalting his umbrella over her poor basket of fruit, that it might receive no damage, with as much carefulness as if she had been a Countess" (*W*, 2:80). Lamb, according to De Quincey, shared this virtue: "The instinct of his heart was to think highly of female nature, and to pay a real homage . . . to the sacred idea of pure and virtuous womanhood."[3]

That Paice's fellow Englanders "are but just beginning to leave off the very frequent practice of whipping females in public, in common with the coarsest male offenders," outrages Elia. Women are still hanged as well, and actresses booed from the stage. Men do not give up their theater seats to exhausted women, nor do they take off their raincoats for women in bad weather (*W*, 2:79).

In listing these and other offenses, Elia upholds traditional gender differ-ences: women, because physically weaker, deserve gentleness. He turns pro-gressive, however, when he pronounces: "I shall begin to believe that there is some [real gallantry] influencing our conduct, when more than one-half of the drudgery and coarse servitude of the world shall cease to be performed by women" (*W*, 2:80).

Women must insist upon more just treatment. "What a woman should demand of a man in courtship, or after it, is first—respect for her as she is a woman;—and next to that—to be respected by him above all other women. But let her stand upon her female character as upon a foundation; and let the attentions, incident to individual preference, be so many pretty additaments

and ornaments—as many, and as fanciful, as you please—to that main structure. Let her first lesson be . . . to *reverence her sex*" (*W,* 2:82).

While Paice taught him gallantry, the fourteen-year-old Lamb witnessed
patriarchal oppression firsthand. Mary by this time was working from home
as a mantua maker. After her scant schooling at Bird's, she was apprenticed
in this trade, by which she could generate a little extra income for the family.
The work was grueling, often requiring fourteen hours a day just to make a
modicum of profit. Seeing his intellectually gifted sister toil perturbed the
young Charles.

Mary herself schooled him in the subject of her work not just by example
but with words. In 1815, in a letter to the *British Ladies' Magazine,* she ques-
tioned the menial tasks men expect of women. Writing under the pseudonym
of Sempronia ("continuously, always"), she claims that earlier in life she spent
"eleven years in the exercise of my needle for a livelihood" and she would like
to address "the state of needle-work in this country." She hopes to "lighten the
heavy burthen which many ladies impose upon themselves," but her "strongest motive is to excite attention towards the industrious sisterhood to which
I once belonged" (*W,* 3:176).

Why do the majority of woman do their own needlework, for no remu-
neration, when they could spend time improving their minds? If they would
devote more time to learning and less to sewing, then "so much more nearly
will woman be upon an equality with men as far as respects the mere enjoyment of life." Likewise, trained needleworkers, very much in distress, would
enjoy more opportunities (*W,* 3:177).

A man is considered industrious if he works until dinner. A woman is seen
the same only if she labors about the house constantly. If she could increase
her leisure time, she could be a more compelling wife. She would enjoy more
time to read, and so better prepare herself for diverting conversation.

Like her brother, Mary mixes progressive and traditional. Following Mary
Wollstonecraft, England's first great feminist, she laments division of labor.
Because they are educated, men get the most satisfying jobs. Bereft of learn-
ing, women are stuck with either low-paying drudgery or the requirement of
softening their husband's lives. But Mary doesn't lament this second option.
The woman thrives in the domestic sphere.

After his stint with Paice, Lamb landed at South Sea House, surely with
the help of Paice and Salt. John Jr. worked there as a deputy accountant.

On the morning of September 1, 1791, Lamb walked north from Crown
Office Row to No. 17 Fleet, then turned east toward St. Paul's, beyond which
he continued, still easterly, onto Cheapside, the birthplace of Milton and
Herrick and the great thoroughfare of markets, one every ten feet, where the
young man gawked at paternosters of amber, puce silks, frankincense, cocked
hats, and beef shanks. Cheapside became Poultry, an extension, like Milk
Street and Bread Street, of the market but also home to Poultry Compter,
a prison for homosexuals and drunks, as well as playwright Thomas Dekker
(for debt) and a man who took a bet to run naked from Cornhill to Cheapside (a half mile). Once Lamb passed the jail—it was on his left—he reached
St. Mildred's Church, designed by Christopher Wren. Lamb glanced up at
the seventy-five-foot tower, topped by a weather vane of copper shaped like
a ship, and then he veered slightly north, onto Threadneedle Street, the financial center of the city, site of the Bank of England, the London Stock
Exchange, and his destination, to his left, on the corner of Threadneedle and
Bishopsgate Street: the South Sea Company. There it was, neoclassically sym-
metrical and simple, with a smooth rectangular front, each of its four stories lined with uniform windows. Ruddy from his walk—one mile—Charles
crossed under the semicircular arch, flanked on either side by elegant Doric
columns. He reported for work.

In the early eighteenth century, the South Sea Company, a joint-stock
outfit, purchased the country's debt in return for exclusive rights to trade in
the South Seas. But Spain gained control of the waters, and the company
catastrophically collapsed in 1720, the year of the so-called South Sea Bubble.
The organization recovered from its massive loss, though by Lamb's time it no
longer traded. It received interest from the capital it loaned the government.
Lamb was to work in the Examiner's Office, maybe under his brother's eye.
He earned half a guinea a week. He worked there just shy of six months.

Charles might have learned important accounting skills on Threadneedle.
The great gifts, though, were his memories of the building and the odd men
who worked in it. Of these men, one offered Lamb the name for which he
would become famous: Elia.

After he had been attributing his essays to "Elia" for eleven months, Lamb
admitted to his publisher there was an "ELIA, the real": "A person of that
name, an Italian, was a fellow clerk of mine at the South Sea House, thirty
(not forty) years ago, when the characters I described there [in the first of
the Elia essays] existed, but had left it like myself many years; and I having a
brother [John Lamb] now there, and doubting how he might relish certain

Detail of *South Sea House, Dividend Hall,* plate 101, in Rudolph Ackermann,
*Microcosm of London* (London, 1810). (Courtesy of Wikimedia Commons.)

descriptions in it, I clapt down the name of Elia to it, which passed off pretty
well, for Elia himself added the function of an author to that of a scrivener,
like myself." This man was one Felix Augustus Ellia, a minor writer who died
of consumption right about the time Lamb took the name (*L,* 2:302).

In "South-Sea House" Lamb's Elia leads us from the London Bank to the
"magnificent portals" of "a melancholy looking, handsome, brick and stone
edifice . . . where Threadneedle-street abuts upon Bishopsgate." Through the
portals we spy "a grave court, with cloisters and pillars, with few or no traces
of goers-in or comers-out." The space is beyond the bank's getting and spending; it is also useless, a ruin (*W,* 2:1).[4]

As we pass into this frictionless house, we see a "few straggling clerks"
going through the motions of work. They move among "long worm-eaten
tables, that have been mahogany, with tarnished gilt-leather coverings, supporting massy silver inkstands long since dry . . . oaken wainscots hung with
pictures of deceased governors and sub-governors . . . huge charts, which
subsequent discoveries have antiquated . . . vast ranges of cellarage under

all, where dollars and pieces of eight once lay." All of this has "long since dissipated, or scattered into air at the blast of the breaking of that famous BUBBLE" (*W,* 2:2).

Such was the South Sea House forty years ago, when Elia knew it. (Lamb himself would have been five.) Now it has deteriorated more. The dust covering the house's surface for decades has accumulated new layers. It is a "superfoetation of dirt!" (*W,* 2:2). Superfoetation refers to the formation of a fetus when another fetus already grows in the uterus. In the analogy, the dust layers are fetuses of various ages, the oldest the deepest. The house is a uterus, and the dust holds living creatures not yet birthed.

The inertia of the house—in contrast with the nearby bank—is charming. Elia delights in its "cessation—a coolness from business—an indolence almost cloistral." Pacing at twilight the empty rooms, he senses the "shade of some dead accountant," "visionary pen" perched on his ear, "stiff as in life." The dead man comforts Elia, while "living accounts and accountants puzzle" him. Their numbers baffle, but not the "great dead tomes" of the house, "with their old fantastic flourishes, and decorative rubric interlacings—their sums in triple columniations, set down with formal superfluity of cyphers" (*W,* 2:2).

Most appealing to Elia are phantoms of the clerks of forty years ago. Like the house, they are unconcerned with actual work. They exist simply to be themselves: utterly eccentric.

Evans the cashier "wore his hair, to the last, powdered and frizzed out, in the fashion which I remember to have seen in caricatures of what were termed, in my young days, *Maccaronies.* He was the last of that race of beaux." Evans's deputy was Thomas Tame, whose "intellect was of the shallowest order. It did not reach to a saw or a proverb. His mind was in its original state of white paper. A sucking babe might have posed him." There was the accountant, John Tipp. He relieved his "vacant hours" by playing the fiddle. But at the desk the musical Tipp was quite "another sort of creature. . . . His actions seemed ruled with a ruler. His pen was not less erring than his heart." Tipp was afraid of everything. He "never mounted the box of a stage-coach in his life; or leaned against the rails of a balcony; or walked upon the ridge of a parapet; or looked down a precipice; or let off a gun; or went upon a water-party; or would willingly let you go if he could have helped it" (*W,* 2:3–7).

All these men are bachelors, a role to which Elia's creator was also destined. But while this condition didn't always please the actual Lamb, it is a virtue to Elia, since bachelors, free of the responsibilities of family, can polish their hobbyhorses and foster their obsessions. No one much cares.

For Philip Lopate, the "somewhat celibate bachelor" is the ideal persona for the essayist. He is "able to practice seeing—to perceive the little, uncommercial miracles in life." Ironically, this abiding bachelorhood is feminine, traditionally speaking, "in its appreciation of sentiment, dailiness, and the domestic."[5]

Elia could go on describing odd bachelors forever—so many "fantastic shapes rise up"—but he must close, since he feels "night's wheels rattling fast" over him: his own ruin. He will become, like these eccentrics, a phantom. But that doesn't mean he will no longer exist. All the names Elia has just conjured might be "fantastic—insubstantial"; it doesn't matter, though, if we can "be satisfied that something answering to them has had a being. Their importance is from the past" (*W,* 2:7).

If the adult Lamb can't go back to the gardens—the Temple, Christ's, childhood—he can at least imagine portals to where nothing happens, nothing matters. The South Sea House sits outside of instrumentality. Its only purpose is to continue being itself. It floats from *if* to *if* to *if.*

Such spaces appealed to Lamb because he could escape the pressures of a world that pushed him down. In frictionless spaces actual and imagined, he didn't have to worry about his stutter or his awkward walk or his big head or his grueling job or his sister's madness. He could wisp as he pleased, remember the odd dead.

Between February 8, 1792, when he left the South Sea House, and April 5, 1792, when he started working at the East India House, Lamb very likely traveled to Blakesware, in Hertfordshire, to visit his grandmother Field, stricken with the breast cancer she would soon die of. Everyone else in the Lamb family was grinding out a meager living and caring for the terminally ill Salt, and so could not be spared. Charles was probably sent to console his grandmother. Caring for his dying relative was grisly work for a seventeen-year-old—the unanesthetized pain, the stench—but Lamb admired his grandmother and loved the house she cared for, which he had been visiting during summers for the last many years.

When younger, Grandmother Field "was esteemed the best dancer . . . in the county." She could also be nurturing. She comforted young Elia (Lamb) when he was frightened at night. She told him she "used to sleep by herself in a lone chamber of the great lone house; and how she believed that an apparition of two infants was to be seen at midnight gliding up and down the great staircase near where she slept, but she said, 'those innocents would do her no

harm.'" She was good to "all her grand-children"—Mary might disagree—
though she favored John (*W,* 2:101–2).

His grandmother's majestic presence made her cancer seem especially
"cruel," since it "bowed her down with pain," even if it "could never bend her
good spirits, or make them stoop . . . because she was so good and religious"
(*W,* 2:101).

Tending to his grandmother in the spring of 1792 felt strange to Charles.
Like the Temple, Blakesware had been an Eden, a rural pastoral balancing the
urban idyll. But now Lamb verged on adulthood, with all its vexations. He
hovered between joyful retreat and painful reality. In his 1824 essay "Blakesmoor, in H——shire" (Lamb's fictional name for Blakesware), Elia explores
this limbo.

The mansion of his grandmother no longer stands. (Between 1798, Lamb's
last visit to the site, six years after Mrs. Field's death, and 1822, his next visit,
the house had been pulled down.) Elia is "astonished at the indistinction of
everything," the collapse of meaningful differences (windows and books) to
ruin. Such devastation hurts philosophically, since it reveals the tenuousness
of identity. If Elia had seen the demolitionists at their work, he would have
pleaded with them "to spare a plank at least out of the cheerful store-room,
in whose hot window-seat I used to sit and read Cowley, with the grass-plat
before, and the hum and flappings of that one solitary wasp that ever haunted
it about me." Elia counters the destroyers with his memory. Of the wasp buzz,
he lilts, "It is in mine ears now, as oft as summer returns; or a panel of the
yellow room" (*W,* 2:154).

This is remembering in "Blakesmoor, in H——shire": not a recovery of
lost innocence but an assertion of identity against indifference. Elia's memories focus on artifice. When younger (Lamb first started visiting the house in
1780), he adored the tapestries depicting scenes from Ovid—"Actæon in mid
sprout . . . and the still more provoking, and almost culinary coolness of Dan
Phoebus, eel-fashion, deliberately divesting of Marsyas." And then there was
the haunted room and the "tarnished gilt leather battledores, and crumbling
feathers of shuttlecocks in the nursery" (*W,* 2:155).

(In her story "The Young Mahometan," Mary also remarked Blakesware's
"old broken battledore and some shuttlecocks, with most of the feathers missing." They remind her character, Margaret Green, that "that there had once
been younger inhabitants here." Unlike young Elia, who relishes solitude,
Margaret misses other children, since her only company is "the old lady and
her gray headed servants" [*W,* 3:307]. Stuck in the house when Mrs. Plumer

was still alive, having only her distant grandmother and aloof older brother for company, Mary felt the same loneliness.)

Missing neither friends nor outdoor games, Elia as a child wandered the house alone, worshipping every inch. It was his "Eden." But how could this great house, owned by another, be his? Because true gentility has nothing to do with money. It is a nobility of sensibility, an appreciation of beauty, a robust inhabitation of a grand house. These being the standards, Elia is squire of this estate (*W*, 2:156).

"Was it for this, that I kissed my childish hands too fervently in your idol worship, walks and windings of BLAKESMOOR! for this, or what sin of mine, has the plough passed over your pleasant places?" (*W*, 2:157). Elia begins the essay's final paragraph thus, alluding, ironically, to Wordsworth's famous lines in *The Prelude*. But where Wordsworth inquires if he is a poet worthy of his natural childhood, Elia asks if his imaginative usurpation of an artificial Eden has resulted in the place's destruction.

It hasn't, of course, but his suggestion that his consciousness is causal optimistically lifts identity above nature's indifference. Nature doesn't inspire the poet but opposes him. His only weapons are memory and language. They empower him to transform death into hope, "a germ to be revivified" (*W*, 2:157). To call ruin a "germ" is aesthetic pragmatism. If you term the destroyed Blakesmoor a rubble and believe that memories of the place are annihilated with its collapse, you are left with "indistinction." But if you call the shambles a seed, you inspire in yourself active construction of the history that occurred in the site, and this construction is a new Blakesmoor, which is what Elia's essay is.

Elia also reminiscences about Blakesware in "Dream-Children: A Reverie." He tells his fantasy offspring about their great-grandmother Field and the great house she managed. He remembers with most fondness the "spacious old-fashioned gardens" and how "the nectarines and peaches hung upon the walls, without my ever offering to pluck them, because they were forbidden fruit, unless now and then" (*W*, 2:102). If in "Blakesmoor, in H——shire" Elia pretends to own the house, here he faces facts: the sweets are not his. He might occasionally pluck the fruit but mostly craves what he can't have. He is Adam in limbo. This is the plight of the domestic servant: titillation and deprivation.

Irony assuages the hunger. Earlier Elia pretends to own what he wants, knowing he doesn't. Here he conjures love for the thing lacked, though he loathes the pain. This double vision is terrible solace but it's better than the single vision—you go without, period.

In 1824, as Suspensurus, Lamb published "The Last Peach" in the *London Magazine*. Suspensurus ("about to suspend") fears being hanged. He is a banker, and since last autumn, he has fantasized forging signatures to steal money. When he intends to sign his name, he writes another's, or his own "in a counterfeit character" (*W*, 1:284). He is financially secure. So why does he do this?

He remembers Blakesware. As a child, he was allowed to roam "his Lordship's magnificent fruit-garden," but the fruit was forbidden. On the south wall was suspended the last peach. Suspensurus hates peaches, but he "was haunted with an irresistible desire to pluck" this one. "Against appetite," he pulled the fruit, and he felt "naked and ashamed" (*W*, 1:284). He was Adam just ousted. He dropped the fruit unbitten.

Now the cash is the peach. Suspensurus can't control his impulse to steal. Thievery taints his dreams. He awakens feeling his hand in another's pocket.

Unlike the children of the Elia essays on Blakesware, Suspensurus, straight out of Poe, can't be playful. He can't accept that he will never possess his taboo objects and then *choose* how he will view them: as pretend property or fantastical beloved. He believes he *can* own the forbidden things, and the desiderata become solely paths to perdition.

In a late letter, Lamb jokingly casts the upright Bernard Barton, a bank clerk, as Suspensurus. He imagines his friend obsessed with stealing. What makes Barton—and Lamb, for that matter—believe they aren't capable of transgression? Are they "unstrangulable?" (*L*, 2:447).

This riff on forgery appears on the page Thackeray placed to his forehead while exclaiming, "St. Charles!" The gap between Elian tomfoolery and such serious devotion is wide.

Between rounds in his grandmother's sickroom, Lamb fell in love with Ann Simmons. She lived with her mother and sister in Blenheims, a group of cottages near the Plumer mansion. Lamb might have known her as early as fourteen, the age Allan Clare met Rosamund Gray in Lamb's autobiographical tale of young romance. If we believe "Dream-Children," Lamb courted "Alice W——n" for seven years. In the "Blakesmoor" essay, Elia praises Alice's "bright yellow H——shire hair, and eye of watchet hue" (*W*, 2:157).[6]

Just as an Inner Temple musician had the "power to thrill the soul" of young Elia, so his "day-spring of . . . absorbing sentiment" for Alice W——n made him "glow, tremble, and blush with a passion." Even though her rejection of him pained him for the rest of his life, it was "better" that he should "have pined away seven of . . . his goldenest years, when [he] was thrall to the fair hair, and fairer eyes, of Alice W——n, than so passionate a love-adventure should be lost" (*W*, 2:28).

We know little else of Lamb's great love, other than Ann rejected him sometime before 1795, and by 1799 she had married John Thomas Bartrum (or Batrum), a silversmith and pawnbroker who owned a shop near Leicester Square. With him Ann had a son and two daughters. Hazlitt's grandson, W. C. Hazlitt, claims that his grandfather saw Lamb, before Ann married, wandering "up and down" outside the pawnshop, hoping to catch "a glimpse of his object of passion."[7] Though this particular observation isn't trustworthy—Lamb didn't meet Hazlitt until 1803—it might reveal what those in Lamb's circle knew: he remained obsessed with Ann even after she married, to the point that he might stalk her.

According to Robert Southey, Lamb actually continued to enjoy regular contact with his wedded beloved. In May 1799, Southey met Lamb at East India House, where Charles confessed that he had "dined last week twice with his Anna—who is married, and he laughed and said she was a stupid girl." "There is something quite unnatural in Lamb's levity," Southey complained. "If he never loved her why did he publish those sonnets? If he did why talk of it with bravado laughter, or why talk of it at all? . . . Lamb loves to laugh at everything."[8]

That Lamb made light of serious heartache isn't so strange. Laughter at the painful absurdities of life was his primary psychological defense and the basis of his literary aesthetic. But dining twice with his ex-sweetheart after she had married another man: this is odd. Especially since by that time Lamb had already published stormy love sonnets to "Anna" and a novel based on their courtship. What husband would welcome such a man into his house? Would Ann have entertained Charles without her husband there?

These unanswerable questions aside, we can conclude that Lamb loved Ann long after she was inaccessible, and that the smart of their breakup remained sharp. An anonymous reviewer in 1848 claims that Lamb was still in love with Ann on the day of horrors, and that in choosing to care for Mary, he "sacrificed love, marriage, everything."[9]

Why did Ann and Lamb break up? Lucas speculates that Grandmother Field "discouraged the intimacy on the grounds that there was insanity in Lamb's family."[10] Mental instability probably ran in the father's line, and

Mary had likely already suffered at least one breakdown. If this family history contributed to Ann's rejection of him, Charles had to imagine that such rejections would happen again. It's one thing to have a lover break up with you because of a quirk here or there, or a dissolution of romantic chemistry; it's quite another when she spurns you because you are an unsafe prospect.

Losing Ann, Lamb virtually lost hope for traditional domestic happiness. He sometimes pined for this state as his life ran down, knowing that, because of his care for Mary, he would almost certainly never have it.

Ann became more than Ann. She became the One. Lamb so easily could have gone down Poe's road, turning Ann into Virginia Clemm or Ligeia or Lenore: an ideal blighting all else to a source of sorrow. But Lamb's irony saved him, his darkly humorous sense that expectations exist to be undercut, and it's comical to see men forget this.

"Dream-Children: A Reverie," Poe in reverse, displays Lamb's saving irony at full power. The essay begins with Elia telling his son John and daughter Alice about their great-grandmother Field and their uncle John, both deceased. When he finishes, the children ask him to recount some tales about "their pretty dead mother," also named Alice, though obviously based on Ann Simmons. Elia tells them how he courted her for seven years, "in hope sometimes, and sometimes in despair, yet persisting ever" (*W,* 2:103).

The dead Alice appears in the eyes of the living one, with "such a reality of re-presentment" that Elia doubts who is who. Whose bright hair is it? Both children blur, and recede, and recede, until they are "nothing at last but two mournful features . . . in the uttermost distance, which, without speech, strangely impressed upon me the effects of speech" (*W,* 2:103).

They say they are not the issue of Alice, nor of Elia; they are not real children, not even of another Alice and a man named Bartrum. They are "nothing, less than nothing, and dreams." They are "what might have been, and must wait upon the tedious shores of Lethe millions of ages before we have existence, and a name" (*W,* 2:103).

Elia wakes up in his bachelor's armchair. His cousin Bridget—the stand-in for Mary—sits unaltered beside him. All that was real in the transient fantasy was John, the brother, who is dead.

Reading the essay is like watching a condensed version of David Lynch's *Mulholland Drive,* in which an engrossingly realistic narrative is revealed, abruptly, shockingly, to be the wish-fulfilling dream of a suicidal woman. But the nondream world that follows feels oneiric: fragmented, shivery, hallucinatory.[11] What saves the film from being a mere exercise in epistemological despair is the Club Silencio, a cabaret hovering between wakefulness and dream. Here singers lip-synch their own numbers, suggesting that nothing is authentic, but also that some artifices are more "real" than others, more powerful and playful and expansive. Rebekah Del Rio mouthing her Spanish version of Roy Orbison's "Crying" demonstrates the paradox: her mimicry is so sublime that solid objects seem inconsequential.

This is Lynchian irony—there is no reality, only varying degrees of liveliness, with art being the most electric—and it resembles Lamb's. In "Dream-Children," Lamb as Elia renders a dream so robustly it seems real, and then describes his reality so minimally it blanches in comparison to the dream. How does Lamb save his own work from self-erasure? In his enraptured depictions of his vanished arcadia. When we read, "In watching the dace that darted to and fro in the fish pond, at the bottom of the garden, with here and there a great sulky pike hanging midway down the water in silent state, as if it mocked at their impertinent friskings,—I had more pleasure in these busy-idle diversions than in all the sweet flavors of peaches, nectarines, oranges, and such like common baits of children" (*W,* 2:102), we care little for veracity. Just as we weep along with Del Rio's devastating song, we thrill to the sassy satellites of the grim pike.

But by the essay's end, we are more likely to cry with the bereft Elia than ride his mnemonic lilts. The tone of the essay, like that of Lynch's film, is melancholy, yearning for what never was and cannot be. But where Poe would stagger under the sorrow, Lamb and (strangely) Lynch imagine the longing as liberation. To want something you can't have can inspire you to question what you have been given, and to envision other ways of being, more vital, more loving. This irony, pining as creating, combines skepticism and generosity.

During the winter of 1804–5, Thomas De Quincey, not yet twenty, as yet only a novice in opium, and an ardent acolyte of Wordsworth, walks from Oxford Street, where he last saw his beloved friend Ann (not Simmons), to Leadenhall Street, where he finds East India House, two hundred feet wide, three stories high. He intends to meet Lamb, Wordsworth's friend. Whether the architecture is magnificent or gaudy, he can't decide. The company intends grandeur, having eight years earlier hired Richard Jupp to remodel the façade in aggressive neoclassical style. De Quincey stands before the portico, in front of which rise six Ionic columns. He eyes the middle two up to the pediment, which features a stone carving of King George III defending "Commerce of

*East India House Leadenhall Street*, by Thomas Malton the Younger, watercolor over etched outline, c. 1800. (Courtesy of the Paul Mellon Collection, Yale Center for British Art, Yale University, New Haven, CT, Wikimedia Commons.)

the East." From the top acroterium rises a statue of Britannia. On her right, Europa rides a horse, while on her left, Asia rides a camel. De Quincey thinks the structure is "pompous," and understands why the building is called "The Monster of Leadenhall."

De Quincey—whose opium visions and life as a runaway have made him accustomed to wonders—crosses the portico. He finds himself at the start of a corridor running the length of the first floor. Palladian flourishes persist; Corinthian pilasters and ornate moldings crowd the walls. De Quincey proceeds through this gauntlet of classical might. He notices a huge doorway to the left. It opens into the Sale Room. It is immense, luminous. Rows of seats face ornately carved horseshoe-shaped wooden tables and velvet chairs. These are for the chairman and his staff. Protruding plinths halfway up the walls support statues of the company's heroes, such as Warren Hastings and Sir Eyre Coote. Togas adorn them. De Quincey looks right. The Directors' Court Room. Its main door is paneled with images of East Indian ports, like Bombay and Calcutta. The room is a cube, thirty feet by thirty. Above the room's huge, caryatid-supported mantle is a bas-relief of Britannia. She sits on a globe near a seashore. India offers her jewels; Africa, a lion; Asia, spices.

De Quincey doesn't tarry. It's Lamb he wants. But if he were to stroll through the entire East India House, he could encounter extravagance everywhere, installed less for function than for "branding." He could find painted on the oval ceiling of the Revenue Committee Room *The East Offering Its Riches to Britannia*, by Spiridone Roma. Or he might wander into the museum, where he could gawk at golden Hindu idols, gauntlets from Lahore, the sword of an executioner from the kingdom of "Candy," or a piece of ship in which are stuck the horns of the "monodon" fish. If he had waited four years, he could have seen the eventual highlight of the collection, created for Tipu Sultan, who ruled Mysore: a painted wooden carving of a tiger devouring a man. Both are almost life-sized. Hardware inside moves the man's hand. He wails, too. The tiger grunts.

De Quincey inquires for the Accountants' Department. He climbs to the upper floors. Gaudiness turns to gloom. These are "labyrinthine passages" and "light-excluding, pent-up offices, where candles for one half the year [supply] the place of the sun's light" (*W*, 2:197). A servant leads De Quincey into "a small room, or else a small section of a large one, in which was a very lofty writing-desk, separated by a still higher ceiling from that part of the floor on which the profane—the laity, like myself—were allowed to approach the clerus, or clerkly rulers of the room." De Quincey finds himself among thirty clerks, divided by seven-foot-high partitions into groups of six. The six sit on very high stools and scribble with quills at the tall writing table. There are three of them on each side. De Quincey makes himself known by touching the arm of one of these clerks, "by way of recalling him from his lofty Leadenhall speculations to this sublunary world; and, presenting my letter, asked if that gentleman (pointing to the address) were really a citizen of the present room; for I had been repeatedly misled, by the directions given me, into wrong rooms. The gentleman smiled; it was a smile not to be forgotten. This was Lamb."[12]

A typically Lambian experience follows: wordplay mixed with slapstick. Lamb climbs down from his lofty seat. So high is the perch, though, it is like a ladder, and he must turn his backside to this unknown petitioner, as if "for a sudden purpose of flight." Lamb realizes the comedy and laughs heartily. He says to De Quincey that he "must not judge from first appearances."[13] This line and other quips quickly following raise a laugh from the other five clerks.

Lamb takes De Quincey's hand, but hesitantly, almost defensively. De Quincey realizes later that this is a habit with Lamb, "derived from his too great sensitiveness" to "people's feelings, which run through a gamut so infinite of degrees and modes as to make it unsafe for any man who respects himself, to be too hasty in his allowances of familiarity." Lamb has "a high self-respect," and he likely suspects this young "Oxonian" of "aristocratic tendencies." But once Lamb reads the letter of introduction, he invites De Quincey to spend the evening with him and etches himself in the young opium eater's mind as "positively the most hospitable man" he has ever known.[14]

(De Quincey praises Lamb despite the [ostensibly] brusque treatment he received from the older man once they had joined Mary at the Temple— where Lamb had returned to live—for tea. Lamb found De Quincey's fanatical admiration of Coleridge silly, and wasted no time in "throwing ridicule" on the subject of Coleridge's genius. After De Quincey had lauded *The Rime of the Ancient Mariner* to the high heavens, Lamb "seemed to question the entire value of the poem." Sweating and vehement, De Quincey demanded that Lamb offer an "instance" for his negative assessment. "Oh, I'll instance you," Lamb replied. How laughable that Coleridge would call the dead sailors "beautiful," when they had to be "a gang of Wapping vagabonds, all covered with pitch, and chewing tobacco." A horrified De Quincey covered his ears. Lamb—who of course admired Coleridge, too, but put no man on a pedestal—smiled sarcastically. This was De Quincey's first experience of Lamb's odd "propensity to mystify a stranger.")[15]

Far more absurd than high chairs and derriere quips (and feigned mockery of a genius poet), though, is the gap between the irreverent, sensitive Lamb and his working for the most brutal engine in London's imperialistic machine. By the time Lamb came to work for the East India Company, to which Queen Elizabeth in 1600 granted a full monopoly over Asian interests, the corporation's influence extended from Cape Horn to China. This now joint-stock company had colonized vast areas of the Indian subcontinent and Southeast Asia, owned ports in Singapore and Penang, and conducted lucrative trade with China and Japan. In India, it had its own army, 260,000 strong. It made its own gunpowder and built its own ships and manufactured the materials required to make the ships. Its London docks could hold 250 ships at a time, East Indiamen carrying tea, cotton, silk, spices, indigo, coffee, cocoa, porcelain, and opium around the globe. The company's warehouses, located on Cutler Street, took up five acres. Four thousand workers kept the products moving, while four hundred clerks recorded the transactions. The company was one of England's largest employers and substantially shaped British life. It even opened its own training college, the East India College, on sixty acres in Haileybury; its curriculum included history, law, and Eastern languages.

The East India Company was a colonizing army under the guise of a global business. To ensure profit, the company seized cities and lands, and it levied taxes. Regardless of the jingoism the company and the country fabricated to justify its imperialism—ranging from "We are a superior race" to "We are educating ignorant souls" to "We are saving the otherwise damned"—Brits knew the company committed atrocities. They were exposed in the impeachment trials of Warren Hastings that ran from 1788 to 1795. In 1772, Hastings was appointed by Parliament the first governor-general of Bengal. One of his primary responsibilities was collecting taxes. Colleagues accused him of pocketing money for himself as well as of using torture to motivate recalcitrant taxpayers. At his impeachment trial, he faced the formidable Edmund Burke. In his four-day opening statement, Burke accused Hastings of having "gorged his ravenous maw" by "feeding on the indigent, the dying and ruined." Those who could not pay taxes

were most cruelly tortured: cords were drawn tightly round their fingers, till the flesh of the four on each hand was actually incorporated, and became solid mass: the fingers were then separated again by wedges of iron and wood driven in between them. Others were tied two and two by feet uppermost; they were then beat on the soles of the feet, till their toenails dropped off. They were afterwards beat about the head till the blood gushed out at the mouth, nose, and ears; they were also flogged upon the naked body with bamboo canes and prickly bushes and above all with some poisonous weeds, which were of a most caustic nature and burnt at every touch. . . . [Hastings] frequently had father and son tied naked to one another by the feet and arms, and then flogged till the skin was torn from the flesh and he had the devilish satisfaction to know that every blow must hurt, for if one escaped the son, his sensibilities were wounded by the knowledge he had that the blow had fallen upon the father; the same torture was felt by the father. . . . The treatment of the females could not be described: dragged from the inmost recesses of their houses, which the religion of the country had made so many sanctuaries, they were exposed naked to public view: the virgins were carried to the Court of Justice, where they might naturally have looked for protection; but now they looked for it in vain; for in the face of the Ministers of Justice, in the face of the spectators, in the face of the sun, those tender and modest virgins were brutally violated. The only difference between their treatment and that of their mothers was, that the former were dishonoured in the face of the day, the latter in the gloomy recesses of their dungeon. Other females had the nipples of their breasts put in a cleft bamboo, and torn off.[16]

Hastings was acquitted, but his acquittal, like the accusations against him, was politically motivated. The truth was difficult to establish. But the trial nonetheless exposed the evils of British rule in India.

Lamb certainly knew of Burke's vivid accusations and the questionable acquittal. If Lamb believed that even a fraction of Burke's arguments was valid, how could he, so gentle and liberal, justify working for East India? Even taking Hastings's extremities out of the picture, the same question could be asked. The corporation at the very least profited hugely from the subjugation of other countries.

Imagine Jonathan Franzen, the passionate animal rights activist, writing ads for a drug company experimenting on animals. Or David Foster Wallace, satirist of global capitalism, joining Google's branding team. Neither writer's reputation would survive the contradiction. The two would be labeled hypocrites and NPR would shame them right out of Big Five Publishing.

Why no denunciation of the analogous Lamb, a reformer laboring for the oppressor? The same could be asked of John Stuart Mill, an even more committed champion of liberty. He was a colonial administrator at the East India Company from 1823 to 1859. (He overlapped Lamb, who retired in 1825.)

First of all, hard imperialism (as opposed to the softer, though no less pernicious, "global capitalism" of our times) was more deeply wired into the cultural consciousness than it is today. Only a fringe of reformers would have espoused the more democratic ideal of the contemporary Left: a vision of cultures, regardless of ethnicity and belief, being intrinsically equal. Working for the East India Company would not have carried the cultural stigma it would in our current climate. Lamb even found the East India Company "pretty, rather Poetical" (L, 2:228), in the abstract. That Lamb could be on easy terms with such radicals as William Godwin demonstrates that his vocation wasn't problematic even for the Far Left.

Second, clerking at East India was simply a good job in Lamb's day, steady pay for six hours of labor a day. (Though there were times when Lamb had to work ten to thirteen hours.) Jobs at the company were coveted, difficult to get, with applications considerably outweighing positions. Until 1800, the support of one of the governors and a £500 bond were required. (Joseph Paice was Lamb's patron, along with John Jr.; Peter Peirson, a bencher, pledged surety on the bond.)

Third, the job offered social distinction. As Jane Aaron puts it, "The skills required to fulfill a clerk's functions, such as numeracy, a clear 'hand' and a relatively high degree of literacy, were still rare enough in the late eighteenth century to bestow some social prestige on the profession."[17]

But what about Lamb himself, his conscience? Lamb was a master at mental compartmentalizing. He had to be, to survive the family trauma. He was probably morally disgusted at the brutal imperialism of his company, but he needed a steady job to take care of his family, especially Mary. Lamb viewed his job either as mindless labor producing a steady check, or as material for literary comedy.

Lamb began at the East India Company on April 5, 1792, not long after his return from Hertfordshire. He would clerk there for the next thirty-three years. For the first three, probationary, Lamb received no salary. He did, however, get a £10 tip per annum. His starting salary in 1795 was £40, about £5,520 today, or $7,300. Not much, though his wages did increase steadily until he retired. He made £240 in 1815, which grew to £700 in 1821, and to £740 in 1825, his last year.

Under the eye of William Richardson, the accountant general, Lamb sat on his high, backless stool and recorded numbers. What had arrived from the East that day? How much tea and cotton and porcelain and cocoa? On which ships? Who were the captains? Did the quantity of goods match the money paid out? And then what goods were shipping out? Again, what quantity? What price? What ship and captain? Did it all add up? But the work was even more tedious than this. Other amounts had to be accounted for, such as wages, warehouse rental, auction price in the Sale Room.

A ledger in Lamb's hand for December 1, 1800, begins, "To Andrew Lindegren." "For sundry disbursement at this place in the course of the present year. To cash paid postage of letters & carriage of parcels trips this month, 1.86." A long list of other entries follows, with prices recorded in a column to the right. "Sloopshire on board," "Sloopshire kings ships enquiring for company,"

"Sloopshire yachts of postages," and so on, totaling 17,313.11. On March 13, 1807, Lamb completed a ledger for the "account of the expense to be paid" by the "East India Company" for the "education of the gentlemen cadets in the year 1806." There follow thirty-five different names; their amounts are totaled at the bottom.[18] Lamb did this all day, six days a week, for thirty-three years. He had to spell each word correctly, record each price correctly, add it all up correctly. A mistake could gum up huge enterprises. The pressure, the tedium, the hours: this was Lamb's hell.

Lamb occasionally escaped his cage to record transactions on the rambunctious auction floor. But mostly he sat at his desk, copied and added, copied and added. He blotted his errors, legion, with his little finger.

Lamb wrote to Barton in September 1822, "I am, like you, a prisoner to the desk. I have been chained to that gally thirty years, a long shot. I have almost grown to the wood. . . . I am very tired of clerking it, but have no remedy" (L, 2:312). Earlier, he complained to Wordsworth, "I sit like Philomel all day (but not singing) with my breast against this thorn of a Desk, with the only hope that some Pulmonary affliction may relieve me" (L, 2:320). He had griped to the Lake Poet still earlier: "The nature of my work, too, puzzling & hurrying, has so shaken my spirits, that my sleep is nothing but a succession of dreams of business I cannot do, of assistants that give me no assistance, of terrible responsibilities" (M, 3:111). Perhaps Wordsworth's freedom brought out the immured Lamb's greatest bitterness. He grumbled to the poet yet once more:

> I should have written before, but I am cruelly engaged and like to be, on Friday I was at office from 10 in the morning (two hours dinner except) to 11 at night, last night till 9. My business and office business in general has increased so. I dont mean I am there every night, but I must expect a great deal of it. I never leave till 4—and do not keep a holyday now once in ten times, where I used to keep all red letter days, and some fine days besides which I used to dub **Natures** holydays. I have had my day. I had formerly little to do. So of the little that is left of life I may reckon two thirds as dead, for **Time** that a man may call his own is his **Life**, and hard work & thinking about it taints even the leisure hours, stains Sunday with workday contemplations—this is **Sunday**, and the headache I have is part late hours at work the 2 pre-

ceding nights & part later hours over a consoling pipe afterwds. But I find stupid acquiescence coming over me. (*M*, 3:141)

In an 1819 sonnet, "Work," Lamb summed up a lifetime of vocational frustration. Of all the jobs, the worst is the "dry drudgery of desk's dead wood." Who created this and other labor? "Sabbathless Satan! he whose un-glad Task ever plies 'mid rotary burnings, / That round and round incalcula-bly reel / For wrath divine hath made him like a wheel" (*W*, 5:312). Blake, for whom Satan was a miller out to shackle souls to his "same dull round," would have approved these lines.

Like most who grit their teeth through a hated job, Lamb viewed vacation as paradise. In his sonnet of 1821, "Leisure," he imagines "works and busi-ness" as the trappings of sin, and desires, through "silent meditation," to be absolved of the "fiend Occupation." Then time would convert from prison to possibility, a "rich cup" never emptying. Life would feel endless, long enough to forge the "gem" that "crown'd white top of Methusalem." Lamb would turn god, Atlas, though he would take on his "weak neck" not a crushing sphere but the "heaven-sweet burthen of eternity" (*W*, 5: 56).

Vulgar men burdened Lamb. In 1796, he asked Coleridge, "Is it not hard, this 'dread dependence on the low bred mind'"? (*M*, 1:36). (The allusion is to Coleridge's poem "Monody on the Death of Chatterton.") In 1817, af-ter mocking a Stamp Office official at a literary party hosted by Benjamin Robert Haydon, he vented, "I hate all such people—Accountants, Deputy Accountants" (*L*, 2:228). But Lamb had to keep his disdain to himself, and toe the line, as the story of Tommy Bye testifies. Tommy had worked at East India for thirty-six years, twenty-seven of them with Lamb. One morning he came to work soused. This was bad enough, but when he tried to freshen up by washing his face with a new piece of calico, blue dye stained his cheeks. He would not wash it off; "it was characteristic, for he was going to a sale of indigo." Then Tommy "set up a laugh which [Lamb] did not think the lungs of mortal man were competent to" (*L*, 2:246–47). The company cut Tommy's salary from £600 to £100.

In 1825, Lamb as Elia summed up his years at East India House in "The Superannuated Man." It has been his lot to "waste the golden years of [his] life—[his] shining youth—in the irksome confinement of an office." He has suffered in this "prison" from "middle age down to decrepitude and silver hairs, without hope of release or respite," and has lately not even enjoyed the small respites from his incarceration, holidays. (East India had cut work holidays down to two, Christmas and Easter.) At first the "melancholy" transition from "abundant play-time" to "the eight, nine, and sometimes ten hours' a-day attendance at a counting-house" tormented him, but time, which "reconciles us to anything," has made him "doggedly contented, as wild animals in cages" (*W,* 2:193).

There were Sundays, at least—one day a week of freedom. But not really. Sundays "are . . . the very worst adapted for days of unbending and recreation."

> I miss the cheerful cries of London, the music, and the ballad-singers—the buzz and stirring murmur of the streets. Those eternal bells depress me. The closed shops repel me. Prints, pictures, all the glittering and endless succession of knacks and gewgaws, and ostentatiously displayed wares of tradesmen, which make a week-day saunter through the less busy parts of the metropolis so delightful—are shut out. No book-stalls deliciously to idle over—No busy faces to recreate the idle man who contemplates them ever passing by—the very face of business a charm by contrast to his temporary relaxation from it. Nothing to be seen but unhappy countenances—or half-happy at best—of emancipated 'prentices and little trades-folks, with here and there a servant maid that has got leave to go out, who, slaving all the week, with the habit has lost almost the capacity of enjoying a free hour; and livelily expressing the hollowness of a day's pleasuring. The very strollers in the fields on that day look anything but comfortable. (*W,* 2:194)

Elia *is* his work. Before retirement, he "had grown to [his] desk, as it were; and the wood had entered into [his] soul" (*W,* 2:194). Like Melville in "Bartleby, the Scrivener," Lamb predicted a primary consequence of capitalism: a vision of identity as vocation. You *are* what you do for money; money getting is the shaper of personal time. You are either working, resting up for work, or recovering from work. That Lamb and Melville explore the plight of clerks is significant in this regard, since the copyist is the metaphor for the modern worker. Beyond the literal bureaucracy of most workplaces, where the recording of labor is as important as the labor itself, capitalist vocation reduces time to a copy of itself: measures, prices, sales, consumptions that merely simulate diurnal mysteries.

Lamb is not Lamb, but the desk he works at, and one desk is just like another. Since Lamb the moneymaker for his family cannot, like Bartleby, say, "I prefer not to," how can he assert his "Lamb-ness," his beloved eccentricity? As we saw in his interchange with De Quincey, through little disruptions of wit, just enough to keep experience fresh and possibility afoot. A department head, looking over Lamb's shoulder, asked, "Pray, Mr. Lamb, what are you about?" "Forty, next birthday." The head countered, "I don't like your answer." "Nor I your question."[19]

Lamb also challenged his employer with subterfuge. One day he was "observed to enter the office hastily and in an excited manner, assumed no doubt for the occasion, and to leave by an opposite door. He appeared no more that day." He explained the next morning "that as he was passing through Leadenhall Market on his way to the office he accidentally trod on a butcher's heel. 'I apologized,' said Lamb, 'to the butcher, but the latter retorted: 'Yes, but your excuses won't cure my broken heel, and—me,' said he, seizing his knife, 'I'll have it out of you.'" Lamb fled, and he couldn't risk remaining for the rest of the day at nearby India House. No one bought this outlandish tale, however. His fellow employees knew the story was "a humorous excuse for taking a holiday without leave."[20]

Lamb was the office wit. One Mr. Ogilvie, a fellow clerk, recounts meeting Lamb: "When I first entered the India House and was introduced to him, he seized my hand, and exclaimed with an air, 'Ah, Lord Ogleby! Welcome, Lord Ogleby! Glad to see you! Proud of the honor!'—and he never called me anything else, and that got to be my name among the clerks, and is yet, when I meet any of the few that are left."[21] Another colleague received similar ribbing. "There was a clerk named Wawd distinguished for his stupidity, whom [Lamb] hit off in his couplet: 'What Wawd knows, God knows; / But God knows what Wawd knows'!"[22]

The six subdivisions of the accounting department, the smaller rooms within the larger room, each containing six clerks, were termed "compounds." Asked the meaning of the word, Lamb replied, "A collection of simples."[23] On the flyleaf of the 1818 edition of Booth's *Tables of Simple Interest*, Lamb wrote three mock reviews. From the *Edinburgh Review*: "This is a Book of great interest, but does not much engage our sympathy." *Gentleman's Magazine*: "This is a very interesting publication." And the *British Critic*: "The interest of this book, unlike the generality which we are doomed to peruse, rises to the end."[24]

Lamb wrote a "skit" titled "Life at India House." These are the "rules and directions" Mr. Chambers is to observe while he, Lamb, is on vacation. "When the month is fairly over," he begins,

> Imprimo,
>
> Thank God you have lived to see another July.
>
> Secundo,
>
> Clap the letters into a corner of your desk, and let them settle themselves till I return.

And so on, all the way up to Quarto Decimo. Other directions include, "Leave reading this for a moment, and scratch yourself. There—now you are easier." "If you see Rice and Dodwell ready to cut each other's throats,—quietly wait the issue." "When you meet a Director in the passage, do not kick him, under pretence of not knowing who he was." "Love your enemies, hail your friends, stir your tea with a finger instead of a tea-spoon, put butter in your brandy and water, anoint yourself with steel shavings instead of brimstone and treacle . . . sign your name in the appearance book backwards (to make the Directors laugh), chalk your face (to look rosy), fall a-crying (to show you have good nerves), be always upon the giggle and broad grin, to prove that you have a sense of human infirmities."[25]

Lamb could be Lamb in India House by viewing the operation as a comic performance. If the empire is a drama, then it possesses no more ontological value than any other play, and is therefore, at least in theory, invalidated. Lamb's antics make subtle revolutions, brief portals of hope.

# CHAPTER 4

*Salutation and Cat*

On July 27, 1792, three months after Lamb entered the East India House, Samuel Salt died. The family could no longer live in Salt's Inner Temple chambers. Worse, with his primary employer dead, and with his poor health keeping him from serving as butler in the Inner Temple Hall, John Sr. lost his income. Since he could no longer use his left hand, future employment was not likely. Elizabeth, too, lost her small salary from her domestic service in the Temple. Luckily, Salt had bequeathed John £500 worth of South Sea stock, as well as annuities of £210 and £14, out of which John would receive £10 a year. To Elizabeth, Salt left two amounts of £100 each. But the family could add to these sums only the scant money Mary earned from her mantua making. John Jr. was probably not willing to share much, if any, of his South Sea House income, and since Charles was serving a three-year probationary period at the East India House, he would receive no salary until 1795. And now Charles and Mary could no longer escape their hardships in Salt's closet of "good old English reading," nor could they wander among the garden's sundials. Nor, since Grandmother Field died only four days after Salt, could they flee to the peach gardens in Blakesware.

By 1794, if not sooner, the family (minus John, who lived elsewhere) moved to No. 7 Little Queen Street in Holborn, about a half mile from the Temple. The neighborhood was seedy. It was close to a penal colony and the Clara Market, a notorious red-light district. Since the address no longer exists, we can't know the dwelling's dimensions. (The road vanished when Kingsway was built in the early 1900s.) But the family could not afford a roomy lodging, and the Lambs were especially cramped early on, when they shared space with a Mr. and Mrs. Weight, newlyweds. (Mary the experienced seamstress said that she should be allowed "to improve Mrs. Weight's caps"— a rare moment of kidding during this hard time).[1]

When Southey met the Lamb family at this address in the winter of 1794– 95, the Lambs "were evidently in uncomfortable circumstances. The father and mother were both living; and I have some dim recollection of the latter's invalid appearance. The father's senses had failed him before that time."[2]

When portals to the green world slam shut, you suffocate in your crowded rooms with four inmates, poor health, constant whining, hardly enough money to eat, your only escape long hours at a job you hate. If you are Charles, at least you get to leave the house for your job, even if you loathe it; more promisingly, you can meet Coleridge of an evening at the Salutation and Cat at No. 17 Newgate Street, close to your old school, and talk poetry. If you are Mary, No. 7 Little Queen is your prison.

Charles during this period did spend substantial time with Coleridge and his old Christ's classmates. Valentine Le Grice left this reminiscence:

> After he quitted school he kept up a constant intimacy with his con-
> temporaries whose companion he would have been if he had remained
> on the University List, spending his hours of recreation and his eve-
> nings with them. It was during this intimacy that he obtained the
> Sobriquet of Guy of which he was as familiarly known among them
> in after life, as by his real name. . . . He obtained his Nickname from
> the following circumstances: In the very first years of his clerkship he
> came one evening, the 5th of November, and spent the evening with
> some of his contemporaries. His hat happened to be of peculiar large
> brim, and his late schoolmates pinning up the sides of it to form a
> three cocked hat: instead of taking out the pins he walked home in it;
> and as he was going down Ludgate Hill in his usual slow pace some
> young men exclaimed Here is the veritable Guy Fawkes in propria
> persona—no man of straw—Guy himself: they took him up in their
> arms and carried him as far as St. Paul's Yard—sat him on a post—
> gave him three cheers . . . and left him. This was the story Lamb told

and so seriously that we believed it to be true, and he retained the name ever after.[3]

Lamb, liberated from Little Queen, would do anything for a laugh.

Hunt at Christ's also knew Lamb as Guy. "Lamb I recollect coming to see the boys, with a pensive, brown, handsome, kindly face, and a gait advancing with a motion from side to side, between involuntary consciousness and attempted ease. His brown complexion may have been owing to a visit in the country; his air of uneasiness to a great burden of sorrow. He dressed with a Quaker-like plainness. I did not know him as Lamb: I took him for a Mr. 'Guy,' having heard somebody address him by that appellative, I suppose in jest."[4] Hunt's melancholy Lamb is the obverse of Le Grice's ebullient one.

Possibly Lamb visited Christ's while Hunt was there, just after his grandmother died, or in the wake of Ann's rejection. Maybe he even stepped into Christ's after 1796 and the day of horrors, to escape the pain among youth's sweet memories.

But Lamb was perennially melancholy. He was also persistently silly. The sadness generated the solaces of drink and wit, while the hangovers exacerbated the melancholia. It would be facile to call this vacillation bipolar disorder. Lamb, like Coleridge, was overabundant, manifold in imagination, extreme in appetites, self-aware to the point of paralysis, witty to the point of not shutting up. Such extravagance stretches and rends personalities.

Hunt emphasized this generative duplicity. Lamb's "sensibility to strong contrasts is the foundation of his humour, which is that of a wit at once melancholy and willing to be pleased. He will beard a superstition, and shudder at the old phantasm while he does it. One could imagine him cracking a jest in the teeth of a ghost, and melting into thin air himself, out of a sympathy with the awful."[5] Lamb's comedy is thus that of Hamlet, the pitch of whose wit rises with the intensifying of his woe. As an anonymous reviewer of Edward Moxon's 1848 edition of Lamb's works wrote, Lamb made "humor the safety valve of a sad, earnest heart."[6]

Lamb's first extant letter, dated May 27, 1796, and addressed to Coleridge, exposes the ferocity of his stress. "Coleridge, I know not what suffering scenes you have gone through at Bristol,—my life has been somewhat diversified of late. The 6 weeks that finished last year & began this your very humble servant spent very agreeably in a **mad house at Hoxton**—." "I am got somewhat rational now," Lamb assures his friend, "& **dont bit any one**. But mad I was—& many a vagary my imagination played with me, enough to make a **volume** if all **told**—." (*M*, 1:3–4).

The London suburb of Hoxton encompassed several madhouses, including the Hoxton House, a huge brick building on Hoxton Street. It is almost certainly this madhouse that returned Lamb to his wits in late 1795 to early 1796. Built in 1695, Hoxton House was from its outset private. Private madhouses tended to be cleaner, gentler, and more personalized than public ones such as Bedlam. Private patients, as opposed to paupers or prisoners committed by the authorities, could even hire their own doctors. Perhaps Lamb used David Pitcairn, whom he sought, unsuccessfully, on that day of horrors.

When Lamb entered Hoxton, the facility was run by Jonathan Miles, a sheriff and alderman, and it housed navy men who had gone insane. Since the navy monitored the facility, we have good records of its conditions, at least from 1808 to 1818. During this time, Hoxton House actually *was* as hellish as Bedlam. Patients, about 450 of them, were half-clothed or naked. Urine soaked the floors. Inmates were shackled to benches and crowded into small beds. They ate with their hands. Some lacked bedding and sprawled on loose hay. Physical ailments went untreated, and there was no space for exercise.[7]

Was the Hoxton madhouse as horrific in 1795 as it was in 1818? From Lamb we learn nothing. His experience was not unpleasant. As he wrote to Coleridge in early June 1796, "At some future time I will amuse you with an account as full as my memory will permit of the strange turn my **phrensy** took. I look back upon it **at times** with a gloomy kind of **Envy**. For while it lasted I had many many hours of pure happiness. Dream not Coleridge, of having tasted all the grandeur & wildness of Fancy, till you have **gone mad**. All seems to me **vapid**; comparatively so" (*M*, 1:19).

Where did this ecstasy come from? The probable causes of Lamb's breakdown suggest an answer. We find one potential origin in that May 27 letter to Coleridge: "It may convince you of my regards for you when I tell you my head ran on you in my madness as much almost as on another Person, who I am inclined to think was the more immediate cause of my temporary frenzy" (*M*, 1:4). This other person is Ann Simmons. However long he courted her, they broke off before December 1794, when over egghot and tobacco Lamb and Coleridge complained to each other of heartbreak: "You came to Town, & I saw you at a time when your heart was yet bleeding with recent wounds. Like yourself, I was sore galled with disappointed **Hope**" (*M*, 1:18). Coleridge's

Ann was Mary Evans. He was crazy about her. But he didn't tell her, and now she was marrying Fryer Todd.

Adolescent heartbreak is a flimsy reason for six weeks in a hellish asylum. But if Ann's fear of Lamb's potential madness—or Lamb's wishing to protect her from it—caused the break, the severing was more than love trouble. It portended a lifetime of romantic loneliness. Such despair could devastate a nineteen-year-old.

Lamb would never enjoy requited romantic love. He also would never be Coleridge, though he wanted to be, at least at this time of his life. In Hoxton, Charles paired his insanity with the explosively manic mind of his friend. That the proprietor of the Salutation and Cat allowed Coleridge to board for free as long as he talked loudly enough for patrons to hear indicates the poet's power. Wordsworth compared Coleridge's conversation to "a majestic river," while Hunt likened Coleridge's voice to a "stream of music." John Taylor Coleridge, the poet's nephew, claimed that his uncle "astonishes you, he electrifies you almost as he goes on." Dorothy Wordsworth beheld in Coleridge Shakespeare's inflamed poet, eye "in fine frenzy rolling."[8]

The line between mesmerism and tedium, however, is fine, as this apocryphal story, allegedly from the lips of Lamb himself, suggests. Lamb ran into Coleridge as he hurried to work,

> and in spite of my assuring him that time was precious, he drew me within the door of an unoccupied garden by the road-side, and there, sheltered from observation by a hedge of evergreens, he took me by the button of my coat, and closing his eyes commenced an eloquent discourse, waving his right hand gently, as the musical words flowed in an unbroken stream from his lips. I listened entranced; but the striking of a church-clock recalled me to a sense of duty. I saw it was of no use to attempt to break away, so taking advantage of his absorption in his subject, I, with my penknife, quietly severed the button from my coat, and decamped. Five hours afterwards, in passing the same garden, on my way home, I heard Coleridge's voice, and on looking in, there he was, with closed eyes,—the button in his fingers—and his right hand gracefully waving, just as when I left him. He had never missed me![9]

An inspired Coleridge could incite madness. Charles Lloyd lived with the Coleridges (Samuel, his wife Sara, and their infant Hartley) in Nether Stowey

*Samuel Taylor Coleridge,* by Peter Vandyke, oil on canvas, 1795.
(© National Portrait Gallery, London.)

in November 1796. Pressed tight to Coleridge's intense talk and opium dosing (to alleviate a neuralgia attack), Lloyd erupted into fits, possibly epileptic.
After a brief break in London, where he stayed with Lamb, Lloyd returned
to the Coleridge home in February 1797. His fits flared again, followed by
"agonizing Delirium of five or six hours."[10]

Aware of Lloyd's reaction to Coleridge, Lamb knew to keep Mary away. In
the winter of 1798, in response to Coleridge's invitation for Mary to visit him
in Nether Stowey, Lamb wrote, "Mary is recovering . . . but I see no opening
yet of a situation for her—your invitation went to my very heart—but you
have a power of exciting interest, [o]f leading all hearts captive, too forcible
[to] admit of Mary's being with you—. I consider her as perpetually on the
brink of madness—. I think, you would almost make her dance within an

inch of the precipice—she must be with duller fancies, & cooler intellects" (*M*, 1:127).

We can't blame John Lamb Jr. for thinking Coleridge caused his brother's madness, to the extent that he wanted to seize the letters Coleridge had sent Charles. Lamb chafed at John's opinion and gave the letters to a friend for safekeeping. The friend lost them.

Lamb the weary clerk and nurse craved madness: the wild imagination, emotions on fire. These powers electrified Coleridge; they liberated him. He disdained a desk job. He wrote essays for newspapers. His poetry sold. He lectured for money. Lamb coveted such a life, which he would never have. Instead he entertained nightly at the Salutation and Cat. Other university Blues preened there, too: the Le Grice brothers, Robert Allen, George Dyer.

Nothing feels snugger than a convivial tavern. As Samuel Johnson said, "As soon as I enter the door of a tavern, I experience oblivion of care, and a freedom from solicitude. There is nothing which has yet been contrived by man, by which so much happiness is produced as by a good tavern or inn."[11] The tavern's pleasure increases, if the fire is hospitable, in winter, the season Coleridge held forth in such fine fettle. His choice of venue was happy, since the Salutation and Cat (a cat was a small snuff container on the head of a cane) had an illustrious artistic history. Christopher Wren sat there drinking as he watched his cathedral, ruined by the fire, make its slow way skyward again. In the 1730s, Samuel Richardson patronized the place, even though on one occasion he could not accept an invitation, composed in verse by the stewards Bowyer and Cave, to a feast there. Whether Coleridge and Lamb realized this history—they likely did—is immaterial. What mattered, in addition to the egghot, were the rare intimacies not to be found in the outside world of toil and loss: the closeness of the cozy wooden walls, the affections of familiar friends, and the sweet pressure of poetry made and in the making.

Lamb could stand his grind as long as Coleridge hailed him in the Salutation. But when his friend left for Bristol to marry and start fresh, Lamb had nothing. "When you left London, I felt a dismal **void** in my heart, I found myself cut off at one & the same time from two most dear to me. . . . In your conversation you had blended so many pleasant fancies, that they cheated me of my grief. But in your absence, the tide of melancholy rushd in again, & did its worst **Mischief** by overwhelming my Reason" (*M*, 1:18).

For Lamb, Coleridge in London is possibility; his going is prison. Lamb thought of Coleridge at Hoxton because Coleridge was a fellow partaker of frenzy's gifts, but Coleridge was also a reminder that the bounty he enjoyed would be scarce in Lamb's life.

Southey recalls Lamb in his madness believing he was Young Norval, the protagonist of *Douglas: A Tragedy*, a popular play by John Home.[12] Norval's mother, Lady Randolph, abandons him at birth because the child's father, Douglas, is the son of her father's enemy. She sends the baby off with her maid, but a storm hits, and maid and baby are given up for dead. It turns out that Norval was left in the elements to die, and a kind shepherd, Old Norval, finds him and raises him. Norval discovers his identity and is reunited with his mother, but only briefly. Through a series of tragic events, both Lady Randolph and her son end up dead, the lady by suicide, Norval by murder.

It's easy to see why the Norval story appealed to mad Lamb. A character brought up in poverty discovers he is actually of noble birth and heir to wealth, a plot sure to appeal to the impoverished but well-educated Lamb. Norval is pushed away by his mother. Lamb likely felt abandoned by his mother, who preferred John, and might have unconsciously wished his mother would realize her neglect and punish herself by suicide.

Lamb's mother managed her son's confinement. After Lamb entered Hoxton, he wrote a long letter—it is now lost—to Valentine Le Grice; it advised Le Grice to read David Hartley's *Observations on Man,* because Hartley "appears to . . . have had as clear an insight into all the [secrets] of the human mind."[13] The next day, Le Grice got a letter from Lamb's mother saying that her son had composed the missive to Le Grice in madness, he was now confined, and Le Grice should not reply.

The ironies are vicious. Lamb's mother does damage control when he wants her to love his eccentricity. Lamb extolls Hartley the necessitarian while he is shackled.

Hoxton freed Lamb from sanity. Once inside the asylum's door, he could indulge his imagination at leisure. The world required him back, however, and again he fit his parts into the machine. If Mary hadn't done what she did, he might have passed through the portal of lunacy again. But after she killed, he had to settle for smaller rebellions: gin, punning, poetry.

He also, reasonably, developed a different model for creativity. In an essay some thirty years later, he dismissed the idea that great wit is joined to madness. Part of his series Popular Fallacies, which he wrote for the *New Monthly Magazine,* and later titled "The Sanity of True Genius," this essay argues that "greatness of wit, by which the poetic talent is here chiefly to be understood, manifests itself in the admirable balance of all the faculties." The most brilliant writers, like Shakespeare, are the sanest. Their sanity is not smoothness, though; it is the ability to flourish amid the hurly-burly. Poetry is emotional turbulence channeled into cogent song. The "true poet dreams awake. . . . He ascends the empyrean heaven, and is not intoxicated" (*W*, 2:187).

By this time in his life, Lamb was sick of the shadows that harried his sister into madhouses. He was also weary of his own suicidal despair and blackout drinking. He knew the value of control. But not too much. His essays, if not drunk, are three gins into the evening: a bit woozy, loose-tongued, extra witty, somewhat outlandish, and flirting with falling apart.

When Coleridge hit London in the autumn and winter of '94, he was on the make. He had just barely, with his brother's intervention, escaped the military (he had fled his Cambridge debts by joining the Fifteenth Light Dragoons under the name of Silas Tomkyn Comberbache), and now he was raising money and men for the Pantisocracy, a utopian scheme he had dreamed up with Southey, then at Oxford. The two poets, along with wives (both, conveniently, recruited from the Fricker family), would set up their philosophical village on the banks of the Susquehanna in Pennsylvania.[14]

In June 1796, a year and a half after the wondrous evenings in the Salutation and Cat, and a few months after his release from Hoxton, Lamb grew nostalgic. After reading from Coleridge's recently released *Poems on Various Subjects,* which included four of his own sonnets, he writes to his friend, "When I read in your little volume your 19th Effusion. or the 28th. or 29th. or what you call the 'Sigh,' I think I hear *you* again. I image to myself the little smoky room at the Salutation & Cat, where we have sat together thro' the winter nights, beguiling the cares of life with Poesy" (*M*, 1:18).

These conversations were as much about evading depression as rhythm and rhyme. When they ended, Lamb went mad. Now he tries to substitute Coleridge's letters for his healing presence. "Thank you for your frequent letters. You are the only **correspondent** & I might add the only friend I have in the world. I go no where & have no acquaintance. **Slow of speech**, & reserved of manners, no one seeks or cares for my society & I am left alone" (*M*, 1:17).

Later in his life Lamb turned garrulous. But now he substitutes letters and memories for friends. And reenacts dead scenes: "I have been drinking egg-hot and smoking Oronooko (associated circumstances, which ever forcibly recall to my mind our evenings and nights at the Salutation); my eyes and brain are heavy and asleep, but my heart is awake; and if words came as ready as ideas, and ideas as feelings, I could say ten hundred kind things. Coleridge, you know not my supreme happiness at having one on earth (though counties separate us) whom I can call a friend" (*M*, 1:32).

Six months later, Lamb still pines for the disquisitions in the tavern. He has "no higher ideas of heaven" than Coleridge reciting the poet Bowles's "sweetest sonnets in your sweet manner, while we two were indulging sympathy, a solitary luxury, by the fireside at the Salutation" (*M*, 1:78). This communion was, in the words of Robert Burns, a "cordial in this melancholy vale." Lamb envisions friendship as a redemptive connection between two autonomous people. What connects is spontaneous "sympathy" and then cultivated feeling for one another.

This emphasis on feeling over thought informs the so-called sentimental novel of the eighteenth century. Emotion grounds morality. Many tears are shed. Richardson's *Pamela*, Laurence Sterne's *Tristram Shandy*, and Henry MacKenzie's *The Man of Feeling* are examples. Since feeling dictates the narrative more than action, these novels are not traditionally linear but series of sentimental scenes. The first-person narrator's tender associations determine the sequence.[15]

David Hartley philosophizes this literature. We most intensely remember those events that evoked the strongest feelings, and when an experience in the present recalls these events, the associated sentiments erupt and electrify the now—a "now" that will in turn become a "then" awaiting the charge of yet another "now," and so on. Thus emotional moments are, as Wordsworth proclaims in his Hartley-inspired "Tintern Abbey," "life and food / For future years."[16]

Adam Smith extends Hartley to morality: sympathy with another's feelings is essential for doing good. Smith's ideas circulated in radical circles of the late eighteenth and early nineteenth centuries. Convention, with its class hierarchies, should not dictate human relations. Sympathy, innate and autonomous and devoted to overcoming distinctions, should.

This vision informs Coleridge's and Lamb's sense of sympathy. In "Religious Musings," the poem Lamb admired most in *Poems on Various Subjects*, Coleridge proclaims: without God, man is a "sordid solitary thing"; but when he opens to the deity, he enjoys a "sacred sympathy" with the All.[17]

Joseph Priestley—student of Smith, discoverer of oxygen and photosynthesis, radical Unitarian, champion of private experience—endorsed this cosmic democracy. He especially supported the equal rights of religious Dissenters, who were barred from political office, the military, and Oxford and Cambridge. An anti-Dissenter mob harried Priestley from Birmingham in 1791. He settled in Pennsylvania, not far from where Coleridge envisioned his Pantisocracy. During the Salutation days with Lamb, Coleridge corresponded with Priestley about the suitability of America for his utopian scheme. The poet also published a sonnet describing the riot, the ensuing exile, and Nature's pleasure in her freedom-loving son.

This sonnet appeared in the *Morning Chronicle* on December 11, 1794. Two weeks later, Coleridge wrote a sonnet to William Bowles, famous for his *Fourteen Sonnets*, tender invocations of nature and heart. Coleridge praises Bowles's "soft strains" that "on the still air floating, tremblingly / Wak'd in me Fancy, Love, and Sympathy!"[18]

On December 9, Coleridge published a sonnet to Edmund Burke. It was the second poem in a series called *Sonnets on Eminent Characters*. When younger, Coleridge had admired Burke's intelligence and eloquence. Now he views the conservative Burke as an enemy of freedom.

Priestley, Bowles, Burke: these articulate the sympathy Lamb and Coleridge enjoyed at the Salutation. Priestley maps the political terrain of sentiment. Bowles relishes the pleasure of affectionate feelings. Burke, though opposed to Priestley, emphasizes the ties of family, a unit the young writers expanded to include companions beyond the connections of blood. In the words of Felicity James, this nexus "reflect[s] and help[s] shape the wholesale revaluation of relationships—political, social, familial—of the 1790s."[19]

In his early letters to Coleridge—in which he repeatedly alludes to Priestley and Bowles—Lamb treats Coleridge as a wise older brother. Or as a sort of spouse: "I shall half wish you unmarried (don't show this to Mrs C.) for one evening only, to have the pleasure of smoking with you, and drinking egg-hot in some little smoky room in a pot-house, for I know not yet how I shall like you in a decent room, and looking quite happy. My best love and respects to Sara not withstanding" (*M*, 1:33).

Coleridge ignited homoerotic energy in Wordsworth and Lloyd, too. His closest friends felt as if he were, during their most vital moments, inside them.

Coleridge opens his *Poems on Various Subjects, 1796*, which contains his first great poem, "Eolian Harp" (titled "Effusion XXXV" in the collection), with this preface: "The communication of our nature leads us to describe our own sorrows; in the endeavor to describe them intellectual activity is exerted;

and by a benevolent law of our nature from intellectual activity a pleasure results which is gradually associated and mingles as a corrective with the painful subject of the description."[20]

Bowles's influence is here—Coleridge values conveyance of powerful feelings—but Hartley's, too. To express sadness poetically requires intellectual exertion. This work is pleasing. The pleasure of transforming melancholia into art becomes associated with the darkness. The link lightens the mood. Over time, the bond grows permanent and causal: every time the pain, the pleasure.

Coleridge enjoys these affinities, as will the readers. They will sympathize with the poet's sorrow, experience his artistic elevation, and enjoy the therapeutic association in their own hearts. This communion saves the poet's confessions from egotism. As long he translates self to other, he is benevolent.

Coleridge encapsulates his argument: "'Holy be the Lay, / Which mourning soothes the mourner on his way!'"[21] In early June 1796, Lamb alludes to these lines in a letter to Coleridge: "You have 'many an holy lay, that mourning soothed the mourner on his way.' I had ears of sympathy to drink them in, & they yet vibrate pl[e]sant on the sense" (*M,* 1:18). Lamb plays Coleridge's ideal reader: listening to Coleridge artfully communicate his sorrows, he feels sympathy, and this sympathy gives pleasure.

But Lamb was a mourner himself—galled with "disappointed Hope"—and likewise expressed his dejection lyrically. He included four sonnets in Coleridge's volume, two of which lament the loss of Ann Simmons. The third pines for lost childhood. The fourth, partially written by Coleridge, praises the emotional acting of Sarah Siddons.

Unbeknownst to Lamb, his three other sonnets were likewise collaborations, though in these cases the brunt of the work was his. Between the time Lamb sent his sonnets to Coleridge and their publication, Coleridge revised them. Far from meddling egocentrically, Coleridge thought he was entering into the Salutation and Cat spirit, where the difference between one poet's lines and another's was blurred, productively and enthusiastically. But when Lamb saw Coleridge's revisions, he was taken aback. "I charge you, Col. spare my **Ewe lambs**" (*M,* 1:21). If his were an epic poem, alterations would be fine, but for a confessional sonnet, leave the few words, so personal, alone. So emphatic is Charles about preserving his words he repeats his imperative (now too late) twice.

Since Lamb printed his own versions of the poems in his 1818 *Works,* we know his intentions. To these poems we now turn, with occasional glances at Coleridge's revisions.

The first, "Effusion XI," begins

> Was it some sweet device of Faery
> That mock'd my steps with many a lonely glade
> And fancied wand'rings with a fair-haired maid? (*W,* 5:3)

"Device" suggests that fairies have created an artifice to trick the speaker, let's call him "Lamb," into despair. But Lamb really doesn't know who mockingly compelled him to walk lonely through glades while fancying a blond-haired woman. He speculates a supernatural cause—fairies—but the very outlandishness of the theory implies confusion, exasperation, or bitterness.

He is lost and lonely and pining for a girl. The forlornness has beclouded his sense of the real. Has he really lost her or not? If not, he asks, again, what supernatural agent—maybe witches in this case—impregnated "with delights the charmed air" and "enlightened up the semblance of a smile / In those fine eyes?" (*W,* 5:3). Lamb imagines sex—impregnating the air—but nefarious wisps do the inseminating. He desires enlightenment, but it is a semblance.

Coleridge revised the witches to "Merlin." The line becomes more concrete and the insemination more traditionally male, but the change loses Lamb's ambiguity and confusion.

Lamb thinks those eyes have spoken (note the category mistake, once more intimating confusion) to him "soft soothing things," so comforting they "might enforce despair / To drop the murdering knife / And let go his foul resolve" (*W,* 5:3). This odd statement applies to Lamb himself, who is despairing and, it seems now, murderous. Toward whom is unclear, though he likely wants to kill the source of his pain, whether it be fairies, witches, or the maiden herself.

Coleridge's revision is apt; he changes "foul" resolve to "fell" resolve, capturing the evil of the despair as well as its connection to being fallen in the biblical sense.

Lamb wonders if the maiden is still around. Do the "gales" of summer still "sigh" through her "locks?" (Coleridge makes the poem hauntingly ask, do the "west winds" want to sigh through her hair?) Wherever the maid is, Lamb continues to "forlorn" "wander reckless where, / And 'mid my wanderings meet no Anna there" (*W,* 5:3). Lamb uses adjectival forms of the adverbs "forlornly" and "recklessly"; this grammatical idiosyncrasy makes the verb they modify, "wander," static, not a motion but a state. The effect is hallucinatory: movement without progression. Lamb isn't wandering anywhere particular, just to the "where" that contains "no Anna."

The poem begins and ends with Lamb walking alone toward a woman he will never reach. It is about a romantic quest that is not really a quest, steps that seem different but are the same. The reason for stasis is that Lamb wanders through projections of his own fears and desires, as if a mirror hangs in front of his face. Far from a conventional sonnet of lovelorn youth, the poem betrays the solipsism of romantic love. To love an idealized woman is to love your own idea.

"Was it some sweet device of faery" is a surprise precursor to "La Belle Dame Sans Merci," Keats's spooky ballad. Lamb's poem also dwells in the uncanny terrain of Wordsworth's Lucy poems, melancholy quests for an elusive maiden.

Two other Lamb sonnets in Coleridge's 1796 volume also probe melancholy idealism. In "Effusion XII," "Methinks how dainty sweet it were, reclin'd," Lamb imagines how lovely it would be to lounge with Anna beneath "vast out-stretching branches." He would enjoy their telling stories, maybe of "true love," "faithful vows repaid by cruel scorn," or a "friend forgot." Why the rejection and loss? Because the stories would exemplify Lamb's lesson to Anna: "how to rail / In gentle sort, on those who practice not / Or love or pity, though of woman born" (W, 5:4). She will learn how to chastise those who lack love and pity. It is she who needs chastising, however, since she is not with Lamb in this scene.

Though "Effusion XIII," "Oh! I could laugh to hear the midnight wind," is not about Anna, it considers an escape from emotional pain. Lamb dreams of suicide. He imagines himself on a ship where, "wet and chilly," he "gazed upon the flood" until it seemed pleasant to die (W, 5:4).[22]

Lamb never wrote poems like this again. A woman fleshy and close and dependent and troubled and murderous—Mary—made romantic fantasy self-indulgent. Lamb, after the day of horrors, vowed to put all verse aside. (He didn't.)

# CHAPTER 5

# *Day of Horrors*

Chairs, crockery, peas, beef, and bread on the floor; mother, bloody from chest to waist, lifeless; father, forehead gashed, bellowing; Aunt Sarah flinching in the corner. Mary towers over the riot, her eyes animal-wild. She has a knife.

Charles springs, rips the blade from her grasp.

His sister's eyes humanize again. She shrinks, confused. And then it dawns: the darkness of grief and guilt that will never leave her.

She has stabbed her mother in the heart. She was hot to kill her father and aunt. Where's the apprentice? She started it all with her incessant complaining. She might have been the first victim. But she got away.

Now, here is Charles.

This was dinnertime, September 22, 1796. That morning, Charles had visited Dr. David Pitcairn. He had noticed erratic behavior in his sister and feared she verged on the madness that had unhinged him. Maybe time in Hoxton would do her good. But the doctor was out.

Since the Lamb family had moved to 7 Little Queen Street, Mary had taken on crushing responsibilities. While Charles could get out of the house, Mary got no relief. All day she sewed mantuas. Her hands were cramped; pins pricked her fingers.

The woman ordering the dress provided the fabric (silk, linen, or cotton) and expressed her preferences. Mary took measurements, then designed and sewed the dress. The popular styles were the robe à l'anglaise and the robe à la française. Both were composed of a bodice closely fitted to the torso, save for the front; sleeves, also fitted, and often flounced at their cuffs; a stomacher, covering the space left by the bodice; a skirt, attached to the bodice and reaching to the floor; and a petticoat, which showed in the open front of the skirt.

Sewing these demanding styles from scratch, Mary might complete one dress in seven days. She made very little money. In 1750, a mantua maker earned only about 8 shillings a week, less than half a pound. As if this wasn't humiliating enough, especially to a bright woman devoted to Shakespeare, mantua making was a euphemism for prostitution, since many prostitutes worked on the side as milliners and mantua makers. The image of the clothes maker "measuring" a man was a popular joke.

Mary's mother was almost fully paralyzed and therefore required perpetual care. Mary had to feed her, wash her, comfort her, cater to her smallest requests, sleep with her. Mary also had to tend to her father, who had no more sense than a small child. Aunt Sarah was healthy enough, and possibly willing to help, but she was in her eighties and moody to boot.

Then John Jr. showed up. He needed nursing, too. A piece of masonry had fallen on his foot, and it was infected. He was fevered, delirious, terrified of amputation.

The apprentice who lived with the Lambs required tending as well. From the poorhouse of the local parish, she was fourteen, prone to the surly attitudes and mistakes of her age.

That Mary wasn't a complainer only increased her strain. The repressed anger agitated her. She talked and moved rapidly; she was irritable. If she had expressed her frustration and resentment, at least to sympathetic Charles, the pressure might have lessened. But the violence escalated within.

If Charles had found Pitcairn, what would he have said? What would a psychiatrist today say? The consensus is that Mary suffered from bipolar disorder, though one dissenter argues for limbic lobe seizures. Applying twenty-first-century diagnoses to people living over two centuries ago is suspect. Our knowledge of their symptoms is incomplete.[1]

Here is what we do know about Mary Lamb's mental health. She was prone to "ramblings" of a strange sort. Her talk

> often sparked with brilliant description and shattered beauty. She would fancy herself in the days of Queen Anne or George the First; and describe the brocaded dames and courtly manners, as though she

had been bred among them, in the list style of the old comedy. It was all broken and disjointed, so that the hearer could remember little of her discourse; but the fragments were like the jeweled speeches of Congreve, only shaken from their setting. There was sometimes even a vein of crazy logic running through them, associating things essentially most dissimilar, but connecting them by a verbal association in strange order. As a mere physical instance of deranged intellect, her condition was, I believe, extraordinary; it was as if the finest elements of the mind had been shaken into fantastic combinations, like those of a kaleidoscope.[2]

That was Talfourd. Here is Charles. When Mary

is not violent her rambling chat is better to me than the sense and sanity of this world. Her heart is obscured, not buried; it breaks out occasionally; and one can discern a strong mind struggling with the billows that have gone over it. I could be nowhere happier than under the same roof with her. Her memory is unnaturally strong; and from ages past, if we may so call the earliest records of our poor life, she fetches thousands of names and things that never would have dawned upon me again, and thousands from the ten years she lived before me. What took place from early girlhood to her coming of age principally live again (every important thing and every trifle) in her brain, with the vividness of real presence. For twelve hours incessantly she will pour out without intermission all her past life, forgetting nothing, pouring out name after name . . . as a dream, sense and nonsense, truth and errors huddled together, a medley between inspiration and possession. (*L*, 3:401)

The rambling could turn violent. Coleridge got a dose of this in 1803. As he wrote to his wife, on the Thursday before last, Mary had met an "old friend and admirer of her mother." "The next day she *smiled* in an ominous way—on Sunday she told her Brother that she was getting bad, with great agony—on Tuesday morning she laid hold of me with violent agitation, & talked wildly about George Dyer / I told Charles, there was not a moment to lose / and I did not lose a moment—but went for a Hackney Coach, & took her to the private Mad-house at Hogsden [Hoxton]. She was quite calm, & said—it was the best to do so—but she wept bitterly two or three times, yet all in a calm way. Charles is cut to the Heart."[3]

In 1811, at a gathering at the Godwins', Coleridge heard Mary talk wildly again. The hosts were "greatly alarmed" by her "manner of conversation . . . she talked far more & with more agitation concerning [Coleridge]" than about the death of one of his friends. She told Mrs. Godwin "that she herself had written to William Wordsworth exhorting him to come to town imme-diately, for that [Coleridge's] mind was seriously unhinged."[4]

Rapid, grandiose, illogical, long-running talk is a symptom of mania, as are agitation, distraction, abrupt movement, intense feelings and impressions, risky behavior, disorientation in time and space, excitability, insomnia, and aggression. In some cases, psychosis erupts. One might hallucinate, or believe oneself to be someone else or to possess superhuman power.

In thrall to these symptoms, Mary might grab a knife to quieten a cause—her mother—of unbearable agitation.

Opposed to mania, depression is a feeling of worthlessness, emptiness, numbness, indifference. All moments are equally vapid, all endeavors point-less. You don't want to move, speak, do anything. You are exhausted, though you have slept. You feel like you have the flu, but you don't. Better to end it all. You have no gumption for that, though. In your skewed view, suicide is actually heroic.

In 1829, Charles reported that Mary was currently at Fulham (an asylum in southwest London), and though she looked healthy enough, she was de-jected, what we in our time would call depressed: "sadly rambling, and scarce showing any pleasure in seeing me, or curiosity when I should come again." When she did leave the asylum, Lamb hoped, her "old feelings will come back again, and we shall drown old sorrows over a game of Picquet again." She would again be "herself": melancholy, yes, but softly so, and calm (*L*, 3:224).

In 1806, Mary wrote to Dorothy Wordsworth that "my poor mind is so weak that I never dare trust my own judgement in anything: what I think one hour a fit of low spirits makes me unthink the next." To Sarah Stoddart in 1805, she confessed, "My spirits been so much hurt by my last illness that at times I hardly know what I do. . . . I have lost all self confidence in my own actions, & one cause of my low spirits is that I never feel satisfied with any thing I do—a perception of not being in a sane state perpetually haunts me" (*M*, 2:186).

Another characteristic of bipolar disorder is genetic transfer. Lunacy ran on the father's side. Charles of course broke down not much over a year be-fore Mary, and Charles implied that his brother John was mentally unstable.

When Mary wasn't manic or depressed, she was preternaturally calm. Talfourd, comparing her to the rambunctious Charles, found her "temper more placid" and the "spirit of her enjoyment more serene." He celebrated her ability to rise from the depths of her "mysterious calamity" "unruffled."[5]

Lamb's bare account of the tragedy appears in the first letter he wrote in its wake, to Coleridge. "My poor dear dearest sister in a fit of insanity has been the death of her own mother. I was at hand only time enough to snatch the knife out of her grasp. She is at present in a madhouse, from whence I fear she must be moved to an hospital" (*M*, 1:44).

To get from snatching the knife to installing his sister in a madhouse was complicated and courageous. First Lamb had to calm Mary. He was the only one who could; she trusted him, loved him most, and he was not agitated. As he wrote to Coleridge five days later: "Thank God I am very calm and composed, and able to do the best that remains to do" (*M*, 1:44). Once he placated her, Lamb had to move her. Perhaps he asked the landlord to order a coach while he was talking his sister down, and when the man returned, the two escorted her to the conveyance. Maybe she needed restraining; a man's coat could serve as a makeshift straitjacket. Since he had been confined recently, Charles knew the facility best for her. It was not crazed Hoxton but a smaller asylum, still private: Fisher House in Islington.[6]

A man stares placidly—no, it's vacancy in his face, idiocy. He is bald, like a baby, and he lies prone, lifted up on his right elbow, with his right leg, the top one, raised fetus-like toward his distended belly. The left leg rests on the ground at a slighter bend. He wears only linens over his loins. If they are soiled, we don't know, since this is a statue crowning the left arch of the gateway leading into Bethlem Royal Hospital. He is *Melancholy*. It is 1796. The piece has been here since 1676, when Caius Gabriel Cibber completed it. Topping the right arch is Cibber's *Madness*. His face contorts in torment, and his entire body is tense. He lies on his side, supported by his right elbow, and his right hand is shackled to his left. His legs, bending slightly upward, are spread, his penis and testicles exposed.

Of a Sunday, if you strolled in Moorfields, a public green just north of London's center and the site of the hospital, these men would beckon as much as repel. They are the silent ushers to a palatial structure, 550 ornate feet long, designed in 1676 by a colleague of Christopher Wren, Robert Hooke. If this

*Statues of "Raving" and "Melancholy" Madness, Each Reclining on One Half of a Pediment,*
*Formerly Crowning the Gates at Bethlem [Bedlam] Hospital,* engraving, 1784, after
C. Cibber, 1680. (Courtesy of the Wellcome Collection, Creative Commons.)

were not the turn of the nineteenth century but a few decades earlier, you
could, for a fee, enter and amble along the vast corridors, gawking into the
cages of the inmates and relishing the theater of human extremity. During
Easter week, 1753, "a hundred people at least . . . having paid their two pence
apiece, were suffered, unattended, to run rioting up and down the wards,
making sport and diversion of the miserable inhabitants."[7]

Built over a massive trash ditch, the hospital reeks. Its floors nauseatingly
dip and rise over shaky foundations. Little light reaches the inmates, or air.
Some are chained to the wall. The women wear loose cotton gowns; the men
go naked. A group of inspectors in 1814 likened the place to a dog kennel.
Aside from being shackled and shamed and smeared in feces, patients endure a horrendous litany of "therapies": bloodletting, or suffering an arm vein
(usually) to be sliced and drained sufficiently to leave the patient faint; purga-
tives, to induce diarrhea and vomiting; blistering, or vesiculation, caused by
the application on the skin of irritants (such as cantharides and verdigris) or
hot glass cups; forced immersion in icy water. Hair, which could overheat the
brain, is shorn. Doctors terrify patients, hoping to scare the madness out of
them; they coerce, cajole, restrain, sequester, deprive.[8]

Add hunger, cold, heat, harassment from paying visitors, and the threat,
if you are a woman, of sexual abuse, and you see what would have been Mary

Lamb's hellish life had Charles had not taken charge and arranged for his sister to come under his perpetual care.

An entry in the *Times* of September 24, 1796, reads:

> On Friday afternoon the Coroner and Jury sat on the body of a Lady, in the neighbourhood of Holborn, who died in consequence of a wound from her daughter the preceding day.
>
> It appeared by the evidence adduced, that while the family were preparing for dinner, the young lady seized a case-knife laying on the table, and in a menacing manner pursued a little girl, her apprentice, round the room. On the calls of her infirm mother to forbear, she renounced her first object, and with loud shrieks approached her parent. The child, by her cries, quickly brought up the landlord of the house, but too late. The dreadful scene presented to him the mother lifeless, pierced to the heart, on a chair, her daughter yet wildly standing over her with the fatal knife, and the old man her father weeping by her side, himself bleeding at the forehead from the effects of a severe blow he received from one of the forks she had been madly hurling about the room.
>
> For a few days prior to this, the family had observed some symptoms of insanity in her, which had so much increased on the Wednesday evening, that her brother, early the next morning, went to Dr. Pitcairn, but that gentleman was not at home. It seems the young lady had been once before deranged. The Jury of course brought in their verdict, Lunacy.

Two days later, the *Morning Chronicle* added that the "young Lady" apparently became deranged earlier because of "the harassing fatigues of too much business." The current breakdown erupted from the "increased attentiveness" she showed her parents, whose "infirmities called for" care "day and night." The young woman had always been "towards her mother . . . affectionate in the extreme." A report that "she has an insane brother also in confinement" was "without foundation."

The *Whitehall Evening Post* carried a similar article, adding that this "unfortunate young person is a Miss Lamb, a mantua-maker, in Little Queen-Street, Lincoln's-inn-fields. She has been, since, removed to Islington mad-house."

Possibly as early as 1765, five years into his reign, King George exhibited manic symptoms similar to Mary's. Whether he had bipolar disorder or, as some think, porphyria, by 1788 he suffered an intense breakdown. He foamed at the mouth and rambled for hours at a time. More strikingly, he engaged in hypergraphia, writing sentences of some four hundred words, composed in a vocabulary more sophisticated than his usual one. This was the first of the king's several breakdowns. Unable to rule, he retired to Cheltenham Space.[9]

The king's insanity made mental illness a hot subject in the newspapers and fostered an attitude of pity toward lunacy. This cultural atmosphere especially benefited criminally insane people like Mary.

A more specific event helped Mary even more. Sometime before 1783, Margaret Nicholson, a domestic servant born in Stockton-on-Tees, was dismissed from her position for having an affair with another servant. Soon after she was sacked, her lover left her, and she earned a meager living, like Mary, from needlework. She was now living on Wigmore Street in Marylebone. She had previously shown no signs of mental illness and had in fact worked in some of the most distinguished households in England. But on August 2, 1786, she watched King George's carriage pull up at St. James's Palace. Then, walking calmly toward the conveyance as the footmen opened the door, she found herself face-to-face with the king. She said she was bearing a petition; would the king look at it, please? He took the paper. Before he understood that the page was blank, Nicholson feebly thrust at his chest, twice, with a dessert knife. She was detained. The king recognized her condition immediately. "The poor creature is mad!—Do not hurt her! She has not hurt me."[10]

An investigation revealed she had written delusional letters claiming her right to the throne. Authorities deemed her insane, and so she was not tried for treason. She avoided the gallows or prison; instead she was committed to Bethlem, where she lived out the remaining forty-two years of her life. The public lauded the king for his compassion.

On May 15, 1800, King George was seated in his royal box at Theatre Royal, Drury Lane, waiting for the curtain to rise on Colley Cibber's comedy *She Would, and She Would Not*. Before the performance began, the audience prepared to sing "God Save the King." The orchestra played the strain, and everyone stood, including the monarch himself. James Hadfield, a former soldier who had fought bravely and sustained many wounds in the battle of Tourcoing, turned from his position in the orchestra pit, withdrew a pistol, and fired toward the king. He missed. He was apprehended by authorities and removed from the theater. The king insisted that the show go on. (It did, but it was not to the king's liking. He fell asleep in his box.)[11]

Unlike Nicholson, Hadfield stood trial for treason. But he was not in his right mind when he fired. He believed that if the state killed him as punishment for assassinating the king, Christ would return. Thomas Erskine defended Hadfield; he won acquittal on the grounds of lunacy. Acquittal by insanity meant that Hadfield could be released once he regained his wits. But this was a dangerous man; he needed to be kept off the streets. Parliament rushed through the Criminal Lunatics Act, which stipulated that those who committed treason, murder, or felony while insane were to be retained until his "Majesty's pleasure be known." Hadfield was remanded to Bethlem where he, too, lived out his days, save for a brief escape attempt that got him all the way to Dover.

If Mary had stabbed her mother a few years later, after passage of the Criminal Lunatics Act, she would have suffered the fate of Hadfield. But she had more options. The main concern of the authorities was whether the insane person could be cared for. One possibility for care was the lunatic's family. Another was placing the patient, at a cost, in a private madhouse. The final choice was Bethlem.

Charles chose the first route, against his brother's wishes. Barely a week after the tragedy, Charles wrote to Coleridge of Mary's terror of going to Bethlem, since "one of her brother's [John] would have it so," and since her other brother, Charles, though he "would wish it Not," would "go with the stream." Charles needed enough money to keep Mary in a private madhouse for the present, when she could not reasonably live with her father and aunt, and enough to fund, in perpetuity, periodic confinements in asylums. Aunt Sarah, now moving out of 7 Little Queen to live with "an old Lady, a cousin of my father & Aunts," donated the interest from her small annuity to Mary's cause, money formerly paid to Charles's father for board. Adding this sum to his current capital, Charles figured he and his father would have £170 or £180 a year, sufficient to cover their expenses, pay a servant (to look after John Sr. when Charles was out), and keep Mary at Islington. There was more coming in—£100 at Christmas, presumably part of the Salt legacy, and another £20, a gift from a "Gentleman brother to my Godmother" (*M*, 1:49–50).

By October 3, Charles had visited Mary in Islington. "My poor dearest sister . . . is restored to her senses; to a dreadful sense & recollection of what has past, awful to her mind & impressive (as it must be to the end of life) but temper'd with religious resignation, & the reasonings of a sound judgment, which in this early stage knows how to distinguish between a deed committed

in a transient fit of frenzy, & the terrible guilt of a **Mother's** murther." She
was now "calm & serene," and "she has a most affectionate & tender concern
for what has happened." Charles was not surprised, since he all along had
"confidence . . . in her strength of mind, & religious principle, to look forward to a time when *even* **she** might recover tranquility" (*M,* 1:47).

Not all facilities for the mentally ill were as hellish as Bethlem or Hoxton.
Private madhouses could be kind and understanding. The private facility of
the Reverend Dr. Francis Willis, located in Greatford, Lincolnshire, was exemplary. A visitor saw "almost all the surrounding ploughmen, gardeners,
threshers, thatchers, and other labourers, attired in black coats, white waist-
coats, black silk breeches, and stockings, the head of each bein poudree, frisee
et arrange. These were the doctor's patients; and dress, neatness of person
and exercise being the principle features of his admirable system, health and
cheerfulness conjoined towards the recovery of every person attached to that
most valuable asylum."[12]

Fisher House appeared to give Mary good care. As Charles reported to
Coleridge, "The good Lady of the Mad house, & her daughter, an elegant
sweet behaved young Lady, love her & are taken with her amazingly, & I
know from her **own** mouth [Mary] loves them, & longs to be with them as
much." Mary was being treated like a family member there, and Charles himself liked the lady and her daughter "exceedingly." The lady—who has been
identified as Ann Holmes—even helped Charles save money, assuring him
that he didn't need his current doctor and apothecary but could use the "less
expensive establishment in the house" (*M,* 1:49).

Did Mary receive any of the current treatments—bloodletting, berating,
and so on—at Fisher? It seems not; Mary would have had a difficult time loving a woman who subjected her to cruel correctives, and surely Charles would
have perceived signs of abuse. But if Fisher were uniformly gentle and fair
to its inmates, it would have been the exception. Many private madhouses,
because unregulated, were as horrendous as Bethlem. Remember Charles's
Hoxton.

In 1815, J. W. Rogers published *A Statement of the Cruelties, Abuses, and
Frauds, Which Are Practiced in Mad-houses.* Rogers was the visiting physician
at Whitmore House, a private facility also known as Warburton's. There he
saw "a combination of evils, moral and physical, sufficient to overpower the
soundest intellect." Keepers force-fed patients by jamming spoon handles
into their gums. They gagged inmates who talked too much. They chained
and beat their charges, too; they stripped them and doused them with icy

water; they left them dead in their bunks. Those abused were not only poor patients paid for by the parish. A tradesman's wife was beaten and force-fed salt. The wounded gums of a young married lady got infected. Her teeth fell out and she died.[13]

John Mitford, in his 1822 *A Description of the Crimes and Horrors in the Interior of Warburton's Private Mad-house,* also exposed crimes against wealthier patients. Keepers stuffed feces into the mouth of a former Irish MP. They prostituted a Miss Rolleston, daughter of the chief clerk in the Secretary of State's Office. They robbed Mrs. Wakefield, an author of children's books, of her clothes. They told her family she had destroyed them.[14]

Like Mary Lamb, Mrs. Wakefield fell into periodic fits of madness. Her family members checked her into Whitmore until her senses returned. How could they subject her to such cruelty, which probably included more than being stripped? When the family visited, or when Mrs. Wakefield was temporarily released to their care, she was cleaned up. If she did report any horrors, the keepers would have dismissed them as a madwoman's hallucinations. But she probably remained mute. She feared disbelief, or that the keepers would punish her.

Until 1817, when Mary boarded with female keepers during her fits, she was periodically confined in Whitmore House. How could she have avoided the cruelty? At the very least, she would have seen the violence or heard the screams. But maybe she was insensible when confined. Later in life she often fell into catatonia. This seems unlikely, though, since Charles often visited and conversed with her. Did she remain silent out of fear?

And how could Charles not know to what terrors he was subjecting his sister? Was he deceived by the madhouse officials? Had he been aware of the cruelties, surely he would have protected Mary from that hell. The lacunae are alarming.

CHAPTER 6

☙☙

*Unitarian*

In a letter of October 3, 1796, Lamb asks Coleridge not to judge the stingy John too harshly. Coleridge can be generous since he is a "necessarian" and therefore can "respect a difference of mind" (*M,* 1:50). Coleridge and Lamb became necessarians after studying Joseph Priestley. Coleridge had fallen under Priestley's sway at Cambridge, where he supported one of Priestley's Dissenting colleagues, William Frend. In "Religious Musings" Coleridge designated Priestley a "patriot, and saint, and sage," and the poet moreover wrote a laudatory sonnet about the philosopher.[1] Coleridge had even hoped that Priestley might join the Pantisocracy.

What excited Coleridge most about Priestley was his blending of natural philosophy and political vision. In December 1794, when he conversed almost daily with Lamb, Coleridge claimed, "I am a compleat Necessitarian—and understand the subject almost as well as Hartley himself—but I go further than Hartley and believe in the corporeality of *thought*—namely, that it is motion."[2] Coleridge the "library-cormorant" ("*deep* in all out of the way books") had probably read Priestley's edition of Hartley's *Observations on Man,* where Priestley in his preface explains that all phenomena are vibrations of energy, and this energy is divine, and so all events are manifestations of God's force.[3] This materialistic determinism of Priestley and Hartley is profoundly Christian. Good will triumph, and the good, for Priestley and the young Coleridge, is democratic. The French Revolution happened for a reason, and the powers opposing its freedoms—England's oppressive regime—will be overturned in a great apocalypse of equality.

"There is one Mind, one omnipresent Mind, / Omnific. His most holy name is LOVE." To understand ourselves as "parts and proportions of [this] one wondrous whole" is to comprehend our "noontide Majesty." Consent to God's "moral . . . cohesion," and you will rise to blissful fellow feeling, the joy of sentiment.[4] So Coleridge intoned in "Religious Musings."

In May 1796, Lamb declares to Coleridge that in reading "Religious Musings" he "**felt** a transient superiority," since he has "**seen priestly**." "I love to see his name repeated in your writings. I love & honor him **almost profanely**. You should be charmed with his *sermons*, if you never read em,— You have doubtless read his books, illustrative of the doctrine of **Necessity**. Prefixed to a late work of his, in answer to **Paine**, there is a preface given an account of the Man & his Services to **Men**, written by Lindsey, his dearest friend" (*M,* 1:12).

The generally unphilosophical Lamb was poring over Priestley. Maybe it was he who influenced Coleridge's understanding of the philosopher, not the other way around. In addition to the sermons, Lamb studied Priestley's *The Doctrine of Philosophical Necessity, Illustrated* (1777) as well as *An Answer to Mr. Paine's Age of Reason* (1794), edited by Theophilus Lindsey, the first Unitarian in England and the founder of the Essex Street Chapel. Since Lamb worshipped at Essex Street, he had no doubt listened to Lindsey preach. Lamb had heard Priestley, too, in the Gravel Pit Chapel in Hackney.

Lamb read Priestley and Lindsey out of the deep Unitarian piety he had inherited from Aunt Sarah. The ethics of these theologians excited him. Both connected determinism and the good. Priestley argued that necessity doesn't free us from moral choice. When we understand that God's "presence and energy" overrule "all things," we should humble ourselves to his will and embrace "his goodness and providential care."[5] Lindsey celebrates Priestley's own morality. Far from a "monster who delights in blood and confusion," as the Birmingham mob saw him, Priestley "from early youth devoted" himself to "virtuous pursuits."[6] Through his joy in God's will, he views the cold seas of exile as "new scenes of nature" that might inspire fresh experiments.

A day after the killing, Lamb thanks God he is calm, suggesting a Priestley-like fortitude in the face of adversity, and he requests his sympathetic friend Coleridge to write a letter of consolation.

About a week later, in the letter of October 3, 1796, Lamb informs Coleridge the letter was "an inestimable treasure" and again emphasizes God's providence. He calls Mary "the unhappy & unconscious instrument of the Almighty's judgments on our house." But he resigns himself to the doom: "I have never once been otherwise than collected, & calm; even on the dreadful day & in the midst of the terrible scene I preserved a tranquility, which bystanders may have construed into indifference, a tranquility not of despair." A "religious principle most supported" him. Though his aunt was insensible from the trauma, his father wounded in the head, and his mother dead, he felt "wonderfully supported." He passed the first night "without terrors & without despairs." He reached this calm by striving for a "comprehension of mind" and by refusing to "rest" in the "things of sense" (*M*, 1:47–48).

Two weeks later, on October 17, Lamb writes Coleridge again. Leaving aside his own torment, he wonders why Coleridge, constantly hatching new projects (such as the Pantisocracy) and moving to new locations (most recently from Bristol to Clevedon), is so restless. Why do you "[veer] about from this hope to the other, . . . settling no where?" he asks. Are these mercurial shiftings products of fate, "an untoward fatality?" Or does the poet's aimlessness grow from a "fault" in his "mind?" (*M*, 1:51).

Maybe events are not necessary—human agency causes them. Returning to his troubles, Lamb considers this possibility. After reporting on Mary's nights—she suffers no bad dreams and awakens to feel the spirit of her mother, whom she believes she will see in heaven—Lamb recalls how his mother rejected Mary. Though he quickly defends his mother, he has raised the question: what caused Mary to kill? Not God's judgment in this instance, but perhaps Mary's unconscious resentment toward an unloving parent.

Charles does not pursue this proto-Freudian possibility. But in his next letter to Coleridge, October 23 or 24, he deepens his skepticism. Maybe we can't know the reasons for events; we must simply accept them with humility. Lamb questions Coleridge's notion that God has given "a portion" of "His Omnipresence" to "finite spirits." Is there not a "distance between the Divine Mind and [human intellect], which makes such language blasphemy?" (*M*, 1:53).

Coleridge blasphemes similarly in his consolatory letter to Lamb, when he says that Charles is a "temporary sharer in human misery" so that he may be "an eternal partaker of the Divine Nature." Far from divine, man for Lamb is "a weak and ignorant being, 'servile' from his birth 'to all the skiey influences' [Lamb alludes to *Measure for Measure*], with eyes sometimes open to discern the right path, but a head generally too dizzy to pursue it" (*M,* 1:54). To angels, man is laughable. Rather than speculate on the nature of God, we should accept that we will never understand God, and submit to the darkness of ignorance. If we do think of God, we should imagine him as our loving father, or our best friend, an image of God that suits Lamb's, and Priestley's, sense that morality is sociability.

Lamb turns Priestley's ideas into powerful tools for managing life at its most horrific. He cultivates stoicism: what happens is fated to happen, so I might as well affirm it. But he can't deny the skepticism of this resignation: I can never understand God's will, and proper humility dictates that I never try. Humility is essential to community, open-ended conversation about what ideas work—make you happy—and what ones don't. This is the sort of conversation Lamb relishes in his letters to Coleridge and his tipsy talk at the Salutation and Cat.[7]

# CHAPTER 7

# Mention Nothing of Poetry

Lamb valued Priestley more for personal than political reasons, but he was still ardently attuned to his hero's democratic vision. In addition to explorations of the heart, those evenings with Coleridge during the winter of 1794–95 were informal seminars on Priestley's political brilliance. The old Blues nightly expounded upon the conflict Coleridge so eloquently described in his sonnet: between the "King-bred rage" that harried Priestley to America and the "halls of brightness" the man created in his exile.[1]

Priestley was lucky to be alive. After establishing the Constitutional Society in Birmingham, he arranged the Gallic Commemoration on July 14, 1791, the second anniversary of the storming of the Bastille. For Priestley, the overthrow of monarchy was not a cataclysm but a manifestation of cosmic necessity. But for the British government, the French Revolution signaled potential anarchy on British shores. Any whisper of dissension should be silenced, violently. When conservative forces got wind of Priestley's celebration, they condemned it in pro-government periodicals. So vehement were the attacks that Priestley withdrew from the event. But the damage had been done. A government-incited mob torched his home, laboratory, and library. Over the next three days rioters burned four Dissenting churches and twenty-seven houses. Eight rioters were killed, along with one constable. Many others were injured. Government agencies supported the violence as a just response to the (unproven) treason of the supporters of the French.

This Birmingham catastrophe was only one of many during Lamb's lifetime, a hell of reactionary brutality. England was a police state. Armed press gangs burst into coastal taverns and forced drunken men into military servitude; a young William Hazlitt witnessed this happen in Liverpool.[2] Spies were everywhere. Tom Poole of Nether Stowey—tanner, republican, patron of Coleridge—had his mail secretly opened by government officials. After Coleridge moved to be near him, and took philosophical walks along the coast with Wordsworth, a Home Office spy described the poets as "a mischievous gang of disaffected Englishmen." He wondered at their strange practice of carrying "Camp Stools" around the countryside and entering "observations" in a "Portfolio." John Thelwall, who visited Coleridge in Stowey, was tried for treason in 1794 for lecturing against the arrests of other radical activists. He was acquitted, but not before serving time in gruesome Newgate.[3] Leigh Hunt wasn't so fortunate. He and his brother were convicted of libel for mocking the Prince Regent, King George's son, in the paper they edited, the *Examiner*. The siblings spent two years behind bars.[4]

A week before the Hunts printed their libelous piece, Lamb published in the same paper a verse satire of the regent. He was lucky to avoid the fate of the brothers. That he did take such a risk is but one of many emphatic demonstrations of Lamb's commitment to the most radical principle of Priestley's Unitarianism: human sympathy, not the rules (selfish or whimsical) of a monarch, should guide our lives.

Unlike Coleridge, Lamb rarely trumpeted his politics. Such uncharacteristic taciturnity from the gabby Lamb has led many readers to assume he wasn't interested in politics. Talfourd wrote that "no one could be more innocent than Lamb of political heresy," while Lucas observed that Lamb's writings were as far "removed" from radical politics as they were from "bimetallism." As late as 2000, literary historian Michael Alexander claimed that Lamb was "indifferent to ideas, to politics."[5]

On the contrary, Lamb believed in the difference-making power of ideas and their political applications, as his deep, nuanced reading of Priestley shows. When the king monitors your most private, intimate affairs and punishes you if you don't conform to his despotic rules, how can you not, Lamb surely reasoned, be political? To choose to be apolitical in the king's panopticon *is* a political act, a tacit "yes" to the system.[6]

Lamb and the Blues confided such ideas to one another in the Salutation and Cat. Caution was essential. They no doubt knew of William Hodgson, a member of the radical London Corresponding Society. In September 1793,

Hodgson and his friend Charles Pigott were drinking at the New London Coffee House. When the two got going with republican toasts, this bothered the proprietor. He listened more closely, and he thought he heard Hodgson denounce the king as a "German Hog Butcher." He called the authorities. The two men were arrested. Pigott was acquitted, but Hodgson, a physician, got two years in Newgate and a £200 fine.[7]

In the weeks following the day of horrors, Lamb lacked the elasticity required for nuanced political thinking. With Mary confined in Islington, and Aunt Sarah staying with a relation, Lamb lived alone with his senile father. Between calculating for East India and caring for his demanding parent, Lamb was exhausted.

Luckily, he had help. For the first few days after the tragedy, his Christ's friend Sam Le Grice gave up "every hour of his time, to the very hurting of his health & spirits, in constant attendance & humoring my poor father" (*M*, 1:48–49). Sam chatted with John Sr., read to him, played cribbage with him. John's mind was so clouded that his wife's death hardly registered. Randal Norris, a sub-treasurer and librarian at Christ's Hospital, supported Lamb as well, as did Mrs. Norris.

Lamb visited Mary frequently. She recovered her wits and found her character. "Of all the people I ever saw in the world my poor sister was most & thoroughly devoi[d] of the least tincture of **selfishness**—. . . . If I mistake not in the most trying situation that a human being can be found in, she will be found . . . uniformly great & amiable." She is "serene & cheerful" (*M*, 1:50). And her accommodations were comfortable. The "people of the house are vastly indulgent to [Mary]; she is likely to be as comfortably situated in all respects as those who pay twice or thrice the sum. They love her, and she loves them, and makes herself very useful to them" (*M*, 1:56).

The visits could turn dark, though. By November, almost two months after the calamity, Lamb was lamenting the terrible fortunes of his sister and regretting his "little asperities of temper" that gave his father's "gentle spirit pain." "Cultivate the filial feelings!" Lamb admonished Coleridge (*W*, 1:64).

The first Christmas without his mother makes Lamb lonely. The geographically distant Coleridge seems his only friend. "I never met with any one, never shall meet with any **one**, who could or can compensate me for the top of your **Society**—I have no one to talk all these matters about too—I lack friends, I lack books to supply their absence." What he does have is a grueling job. "I am starving at the India house, near 7 oClock without my dinner, &

so it has been & will be almost all the **week**." He gets home faint with exhaustion but finds no rest. His father must be playing cribbage all the time; when Charles asks for a break, John exclaims, "If you wont play with me, you might as well not come home at all!" (*M*, 1:65–66), Outside the family, Lamb has contact only with colleagues. They are as disappointing, as interlocutors, as his father is. "Not a soul loves Bowles here; scarce one has heard of Burns. . . . They talk a language I understand not: I conceal sentiments that would be a puzzle to them" (*M*, 1:79).

Even the well-read Mary can't stimulate Lamb intellectually since, as Lamb writes, "our reading and knowledge [are] from the self-same sources, our communication with the scenes of the world alike narrow: never having kept separate company, or any 'company' '*together*'—never having read separate books, and few books *together*—what knowledge have we to convey to each other." On top of all this, Lamb has a "stupefying" toothache (*M*, 1:79).

Coleridge is his "Brother" and his "Friend," and he loves Coleridge's writing as he adores the "Confessions of Rousseau, and for the same reason: the same frankness, the same openness of heart, the same disclosure of all the most hidden and delicate affections of the mind: they make me proud to be thus esteemed worthy of the place of friend-confessor, brother-confessor, to a man like Coleridge" (*M*, 1:59). The very act of writing Coleridge elevates Lamb: "I love to write to you. I take pride in it—. It makes me think less meanly of myself. It makes me think myself not totally disconnected from the better part of Mankind" (*M*, 1:59).

Part of the joy of writing Coleridge was the exchange of poems. Before the catastrophe, Lamb had included in letters some of the poems that appeared in Coleridge's *Poems on Various Subjects* and *Poems, 1797,* including two of the Anna sonnets, and he had commented in detail on Coleridge's verses. But now, after the event, he will no longer versify. "Mention nothing of poetry. I have destroyed every vestige of past vanities of that kind," as well as "a little journal of my foolish passion" for Ann (*M*, 1:45).

But Lamb can't stop thinking about his verse. He gives Coleridge leave to publish his work in the *Poems* of 1797, and barely a month after the tragedy, he agrees with Coleridge that "Was it some sweet device of faery" should be included in the volume. He also sends Coleridge some other verses (he calls them "Fragments" or "Sketches"—anything but "Love Sonnets"), just to get rid of them. And even if he believes that versifying "is unprofitable to [his] soul," and even if he relishes parting from the "weakness" of poeticizing," he is committed to getting the title page to his poems just right. It should read,

**"Poems, Chiefly Love Sonnets**, by Charles Lamb, of the India House." Then, after an epigraph by Philip Massinger (on youth and love), he dedicates the poems to "**Mary Ann Lamb**, The author's best friend and sister" (*M,* 1:63).

He wants the dedication to be a surprise to Mary, since "there is a monotony in the affections, which people living together or, as we do now, frequently seeing each other, are apt to give in to: a sort of indifference in the expression of kindness for each other, which demands that we should sometimes call to our aid the trickery of surprise" (*M,* 1:62.)

In late November, Lamb asks that Coleridge include in the volume "Laugh all that weep." (This poem did not make it, and it is now lost.) Two weeks later, Lamb sends Coleridge two new poems for inclusion: "To a Young Lady, Going out to India" (which wasn't included) and "The Tomb of Douglas" (which was). By December 10, he admits to Coleridge, "with regard to leaving off my versifying, you have said so many pretty things, so many fine compliments, ingeniously decked out in the garb of sincerity, and undoubtedly springing from a present feeling somewhat like sincerity, that you might melt the most un-muse-ical soul" (*M,* 1:77). In January, he mails a sonnet to his sister, later titled "Sonnet to a Friend" and a verse to his new friend Charles Lloyd, "To Charles Lloyd."

This back-and-forth on poetry, with verse winning out, shows Lamb's struggle between two visions. Before the tragedy, Lamb viewed poetry as yearning for lost beauty. The style corresponded to this escapism: Shakespearean diction and form. After Mary plunged the knife, no escape. The world is dark and horrible, and to pine for romance worsens the pain. Lamb bitterly renounces his sonneteering. But he doesn't want to stop writing poetry; he desires to make verse of another kind. From the fall of 1796 to the summer of 1798, Lamb did this, resulting in *Blank Verse,* a collaborative effort with Charles Lloyd that stands as a grisly twin of Coleridge's and Wordsworth's *Lyrical Ballads.*

In *Blank Verse,* Lamb realized the poetics he had been prescribing to Coleridge. Throughout the mid- to late 1790s, Coleridge sent Lamb his poetry, and Lamb responded with line-by-line feedback. His insights are striking, original. Most remarkably, he reaches the same groundbreaking conclusions as Wordsworth, a year before Wordsworth does.

In May 1796, Lamb said of Coleridge's "Religious Musings," "I hesitate not to pronounce it sublime." But he then qualified: "If there be any thing in it approachg. to tumidity (which I meant not to infer in elaborate (I meant simply labord)) it is the Gigantic hyperbole by which you describe the Evils of existing Society. Snakes Lions hyenas & behemoths, is carrying your resentment beyond bounds" (*M,* 1:10). Lamb grew increasingly uneasy with the "tumid" in Coleridge's poetry, in all poetry, by which he meant language convoluted, conventional, and abstract.

Opposed to tumidity is simplicity, as Lamb meant the term in a letter of November 1796. He had read Coleridge's "To a Friend, Who Asked How I Felt When the Nurse First Presented My Infant to Me," and especially liked the conclusion: "So for the Mother's sake, the Child was dear / And dearer was the Mother for the Child."[8] These lines are "simple, tender, heart-flowing," a model for all verse: "Cultivate simplicity, Coleridge, or rather, I should say, banish elaborateness; for simplicity springs spontaneous from the heart, and carries into daylight its own modest buds and genuine, sweet, and clear flowers of expression. I allow no hot-beds in the gardens of Parnassus" (*M,* 1:60–61).

Lamb had intimated this poetic ideal in his first letter praising "Musings," back in May, when he also lauded the poem Coleridge published as "Effusion XXXV." (The poem later bore the title "Eolian Harp.") A man, obviously based on the newly married Coleridge himself, reclines on a cot with his beloved, Sara. He talks philosophy, then he erupts into a pantheistic rhetorical question: "What if all of animated nature / Be but organic Harps diversely framed / That tremble into thought" according to a spirit "plastic and vast," "the Soul of each, and God of all?" "Pensive Sara" reproves this metaphysical reaching. She reminds her husband he is "sinful and miserable," and ill-equipped to speculate so confidently on the nature of God. He should "walk humbly."[9]

Lamb finds the poem "charming, admirable, exquisite," not for its ideas but for its simple, direct conversation between husband and wife (*M,* 1:12). Sensing the magnetism of intimate talk, Lamb identifies what will become the most original contribution of early Romanticism: the conversation poem. This sort of poem, which Coleridge quickly mastered, features a speaker engaged in sympathetic talk with an interlocutor. The interaction shifts the speaker's self-understanding, propelling him from alienation to community, from despair to hope.

"Eolian Harp" exemplifies this structure, breezily awakening the speaker from hubris to humility. But Coleridge puts more at stake in later verse conversations, such as this "This Lime-tree Bower My Prison," which includes Lamb himself as "gentle-hearted Charles" (the moniker Lamb most loathed).

"Well," the poem casually begins, "they are gone, and here must I remain, / This lime-tree bower my prison!" Because of a foot injury (pensive Sara spilled hot milk), Coleridge in this autobiographical poem can't join Charles, William, and Dorothy on a hike in the Quantocks. Coleridge's fear of missing out gets the best of him. He laments the loss of the sublime experiences he could have enjoyed. But he imagines what his friends are seeing, and he is there, virtually. He addresses Charles, believing that his London friend—imprisoned in the city as he is in the bower—feels exactly as he does. The bower no longer imprisons, and he and Charles, because "no sound is dissonant which tells of Life," connect.[10]

Lamb did not cultivate the simplicity he recommended for Coleridge. Most of his ten new poems in Coleridge's *Poems, 1797* rely on staid Shakespearean diction.

Of these ten, three are of a piece with the "Anna" sonnets; they are wistful for a lost past. All were written in the summer of '95, back when a twenty-year-old's greatest fears were the responsibilities of adulthood and romantic heartbreak. "We were two pretty babes" is a straightforward sonnet on the vanishing of innocence. The speaker outgrows his childhood companion "Innocence," laments the loss, and searches for "delicious Eden" (*W*, 5:8).

"When last I roved these winding wood-walks green," is more sophisticated. When the speaker (based on Lamb) roamed the forest, "Anna" would shroud "her beauties in [her] lone retreat." Now he hears her "footsteps in the shade no more." Only her "image" meets him where they once conversed. He walks by the cottage she once lived in. "It spake of days which ne'er must come again." He turns away, sighing (*W*, 5:7). Like the earlier Anna sonnets, this one is epistemological as much as romantic. Longing so consumes Lamb, he has lost orientation in space—he perceives his beloved's image only—and time. He rewalks the same ground, seeking signs of her.

The sonnet "A timid grace sits trembling in her eye" is similar. This grace sheds a "delicious lunar light" that "steeps / The care-crazed mind" in "oblivious ecstasy." The beauty is a narcotic, though. It disconnects the mind from care, and from the concrete world. But then the light turns away from the speaker, and he pines. These are his options: blissed-out obliviousness or retrospective longing (*W*, 5:7).

These three poems are the sort Lamb wanted to burn, along with the four from the 1796 volume. His other contributions to the new volume explore other emotions, however. In "If from my lips some angry accents fell," a sonnet he wrote in Hoxton, he regrets being angry, judgmental, and peevish toward Mary. He behaved this way out of a "sickly mind," and he wants this poem to atone. Having endured without criticism his "lovesick lays" (his Anna sonnets), she especially deserves an apology (*W,* 5:8).

Though this poem is Elizabethan in form, it expresses a vulnerability that Lamb will explore two years later in *Blank Verse.* Another transitional poem is "The Sabbath Bells." Its blank verse approaches conversational rhythms and it lives in the concrete world. The solipsistic seekers of Anna would benefit from bells that "salute / *Sudden!*" (*W,* 5:9).

Another transitional poem is "To Charles Lloyd," addressed to Lamb's new friend, whom he met in January '96. The poem's emotional specificity is far from the generalized yearning of the sonnets. Lloyd is lonely, longing for Coleridge's Nether Stowey, whence he has come, and Lamb is "alone, obscure . . . cheerless" in London. A random meeting brings them together for a joyful evening. The pleasure is transient. Both will return to their solitude, even if it is lightened by the memory (*W,* 5:11).

Otherwise, Lamb's contribution to Coleridge's volume are oddities, poetic modes he never developed. "A Vision of Repentance" reminds one of "Kubla Khan," which it probably influenced, as well as of Keats's "La Belle Dame Sans Merci" and *Hyperion: A Dream.* It is a dream vision of a garden, through which wanders a sad, penitent Psyche. "The Tomb of Douglas" narrates the story of Young Norval, the character Lamb adopted while mad. "Fancy Employed on Divine Subjects" allegorizes Fancy, a truant wanderer in search of Eden.

CHAPTER 8

*Divine Chit-Chat*

On December 9, 1796, Lamb was "perplexed & at times cast down," and now more physical hardship was exacerbating his emotional struggle. Aunt Sarah had returned to 7 Little Queen Street. The "old Hag of a wealthy relation" found Sarah "'indolent & mulish'" and sent her home. Though Charles loved his aunt, she was another high-needs person to care for (*W,* 5:73).

Lamb could not fully relish a gift from Coleridge: Charles Lloyd's *Poems on the Death of Priscilla Farmer,* which included Lamb's "The Grandame," and Coleridge's own *Sonnets from Various Authors,* containing four of Lamb's already published sonnets.

Lloyd had met Coleridge in Birmingham in late August.[1] Lloyd, only two days younger than Lamb, lived there with his family of wealthy Quaker bankers. Imaginative and sensitive, he eschewed the family business and sought the life of the mind. Since his religion excluded him from Oxford and Cambridge—both still admitting only Anglicans—he needed a tutor. Coleridge was staying with Thomas Hawkes in nearby Moseley. He was returning home to Bristol from Derbyshire, where he had discussed a tutoring position. Deeply in debt from his failed periodical the *Watchman* and awaiting the birth of his first child, Coleridge needed money. Coleridge and Lloyd met, Coleridge mesmerized Lloyd, and Lloyd's father offered Coleridge £80 a year for instruction plus room and board. The poet agreed.

Lloyd had told Coleridge he wished to be a physician, and so Coleridge developed a curriculum. But Lloyd most craved intellectual companionship. "My Coleridge!" he wrote, "take the wanderer to thy breast, / The youth who loves thee, and who, faint, would rest / . . . In the long sabbath of subdued desire!"[2] Coleridge understood the young man's emotional needs; he knew Lloyd's "colloquial powers" would "open" only in a "tete a tete with one whom he love & esteems."[3] The two men were soon celebrating each other's genius.

One reason for Coleridge's early pleasure in Lloyd was his student's sophistication. Lloyd had already published a collection of poems in 1795; was read deeply in democratic politics; and had developed an enlightened view of religion. As Lloyd wrote to his younger brother Robert, "I am convinced that nothing tends so much to narrow the mind as sectarian and confin'd notions of religion and morality. The pure ardour of universal benevolence does not abate at the sight of a Lutheran or a Quaker, or Catholic, or an Unbeliever."[4]

During his first month in the Coleridge household, Lloyd started having violent seizures. They took the form, in Coleridge's baffled words, of "either Somnambulism, or frightful Reverie, or *Epilepsy from accumulated feelings*." Whatever the diagnosis, Lloyd would fall into "a kind of Night-mair," and the external world would "mingle with, and form part of, the strange Dream."[5] Coleridge, forced to sleep with Lloyd because the house was so small, was soon exhausted. By December 4, he gave up tutoring Lloyd. He decided to move to a farm in Nether Stowey.

Lloyd joined the Coleridges in Somerset in February 1797. The seizures erupted again, three times in seven days. Coleridge was up with him from midnight until 5 a.m., during which time Lloyd "remained in one *continued* state of *agoniz'd Delirium*."[6]

Lloyd's seizures exacerbated his already nervous sensibility. He was extremely insecure. His desperate need for affection actually made him a good friend—early in a relationship. But trouble came fast. He required constant shows of affection, and if he didn't get them, he grew paranoid and melancholy. Such sorrow might generate powerful poetry; it might equally crack sanity.[7]

On January 16, 1797, Lloyd, during his hiatus from Coleridge, appeared at the door of lonely Charles Lamb. The two men found themselves in perfect sympathy. They were virtually the same age; acolytes of Coleridge (though

Lamb was more the great man's equal); aspiring poets; melancholy and insecure; passionate about the radical Protestantism of Priestley and its ideal of
sacred friendship.

"I do so love him!" Lamb exclaims to Coleridge. Lamb and Lloyd spend
their evenings enjoying "Anglice, Welch rabbits, punch, & poesy" at the Bull
and Mouth Inn in St.-Martens-le-Grand, where Lloyd is staying; the "Cat &
Salutation," Lamb notes, "would have had a charm more forcible for me" (*M*,
1:93). They discuss Coleridge's poetry and Quaker theology. When Lloyd goes
to Nether Stowey, Lamb wants Coleridge to tell him "I have had thoughts of
turning Quaker, and have been reading, or am rather just beginning to read,
a most capital book, good thoughts in good language, William Penn's 'No
Cross, no Crown;' I like it immensely" (*M*, 1:103).

Soon after Lloyd left, Lamb was again bereft, but at least he had made
another intimate literary friend, someone he could perhaps rely on if one of
his worse fears were realized. What if Coleridge pulled away?

In early February Lamb could still fire off exhilarating passages to Coleridge, such as this sketch that perhaps sparked *The Rime of the Ancient Mariner*: "I have a dim recollection, that when in town you were talking of the
**Origin of Evil** as a most prolific subject for a Long Poem—why not adopt it,
Coleridge? there would be **room** for imagination. Or the description (from a
vision or dream, suppose) of an Utopia in one of the planets, (the Moon for
instance)—. Or a five day's dream" (*M*, 1:97).

But Lamb remained mostly depressed, and now a new tragedy struck:
Aunt Sarah died. She never recovered from "the shock she received on that
our **evil** day" (*M*, 1:96). Though the woman was hearty until the tragedy,
she ended, Lamb wrote to Coleridge, "a mere skeleton" and "looked more
like a corpse that had lain weeks in the grave, than one fresh dead." With all
the pain in life, why go on "after all the strength and beauty of existence are
gone?" (*M*, 1:103).

Coleridge did not answer. April came, and Coleridge still had not written.
Lamb was hurt. "Your last letter was dated 10th February; in it you promised
to write again the next day. At least, I did not expect so long, so unfriendlike,
a silence." Lamb has not heard from Lloyd, either. How is his health? How is
Hartley, who was earlier ill? These are not idle questions, since the Coleridges
and Lloyd "are all very dear and precious to" him. You can "hurt and vex me
by your silence, but you cannot estrange my heart from you all" (*M*, 1:105).

At least there is some good news. Mary is well enough to leave the asylum in Islington, and Charles has found rooms for her in Hackney, a London borough just to the northeast of Regents Park. Charles spends his Sundays and holidays with her and relishes her as an "ever-present and never-alienable friend" (*M*, 1:106)—qualities Coleridge seems now to lack.

A week later Lamb finally gets a letter from Lloyd. Its hypersensitivity is "truly alarming." Lloyd confessed to leaving the last letter Lamb sent unopened for three weeks, ostensibly afraid that the epistle criticized him for not writing. (The letter in fact replied to one Lloyd had sent earlier, confessing that an illness had kept him from writing Lamb.) Lamb sees in this irrational fear another side of Lloyd, the mentally unstable one Coleridge had already struggled with. As Lamb writes Coleridge, their mutual friend quavers into an "exquisiteness of feeling" that "must border on derangement." Lamb still loves Lloyd "more & more," though, and asks that God "shield us from insanity, which is 'the sorest malady of all'" (*M*, 1:109).

The quote on insanity is Lamb's, from his poem "To the Poet Cowper, on His Recovery from an Indisposition," written in July 1796, when Lamb's own fit of madness still haunted him. The poem, which Lamb published in the *Monthly Magazine*, celebrates Cowper's emergence from a period of "Lunacies." In the letter to Coleridge in which he includes the poem, Lamb asks, do you love Cowper as much as I? Probably not, even though the just-healed man should be pitied, loved, admired. A very odd clause follows: "it goes hard with **People** but they **lie**!" (*M*, 1:41). Society is not truthful with the insane. Instead of engaging authentically with odd behavior, people hide behind saccharine gestures. (In light of what will happen two months later, Lamb's attack is eerie, since he will find himself having to choose between lying to Mary and embracing her troubling uniqueness.)

Like Mary, Cowper fought insanity his whole life. After a difficult childhood—he was bullied so frequently in boarding school he recognized his oppressor "by his shoe-buckles better than any other part of his dress," and his mother died when he was five—he studied at Westminster School, then trained for the law in the Middle Temple before residing in the Inner Temple itself.[8] In 1763, he was offered a prestigious clerkship in the House of Lords, but a family rival challenged the appointment. The stress pushed Cowper into a devastating depression. He attempted suicide three times.

In 1767, mentally stable again, he published *Adelphi*, an autobiographical poem on his madness, sinning, and salvation. John Newton, once a captain of slave ships and now an impassioned abolitionist, asked Cowper to write hymns for the *Olney Hymns*. Cowper produced "Light Shining out of Darkness," which opens: "God moves in a mysterious way / His wonders to perform." In 1773, Cowper exploded into lunacy again. The sentence "It is all over with thee, thou hast perished" would not leave his head.

He recovered, and in 1783, began his masterpiece, *The Task*. He had met the clever Lady Austen in 1781 and, as Cowper explained in a brief preface to the poem, she "demanded a [blank verse] poem . . . from the author, and gave him the SOFA for a subject. He obeyed; and, having much leisure, connected another subject with it; and, pursuing the train of thought to which his situation and turn of mind led him, brought forth at length, instead of the trifle which he at first intended, a serious affair—a Volume!" In 1796, Cowper collapsed again, more or less for good. He pulled out of his dug-in madness for brief stints only. During one of these periods, he composed "The Castaway," a harrowing portrait of loneliness.[9]

It was to one of these rare seasons of stability that Lamb referred in his letter to Coleridge. Recently recovered from madness himself, Lamb was intrigued by a poet who fell in and out of sanity. In his poem to Cowper, Lamb goes against a Romantic commonplace (one he himself embraced earlier in celebrating his Hoxton phrensy): madness weds genius. Where Blake and Byron worshipped the muse of mental disorder, Lamb holds that brilliance and lunacy are opposed, a thesis he will later develop, as noted, in "The Sanity of True Genius." Lamb thanks God for healing Cowper, whose strings might quiver again into Miltonic song.

Lamb did not include this piece in the second volume of Coleridge's poems; he ultimately wasn't interested in the "epic" Cowper. *The Task* intrigued him more, for here he could track Cowper's "divine chit-chat," a Coleridge phrase Lamb adored.

When Cowper published *The Task* in 1785, there was no poem like it. It draws from the mock epic, the pastoral, the diatribe, and the religious conversion, but it is ultimately about nothing but itself. The poet's task is to write a poem about a sofa. He composes a comic history of furniture before recalling he needed no sofa when a boy in the woods. He praises the rural life, and then pretty much tells any story that comes to mind. Through the poem's six books, Cowper talks about nature's joys, the cruelty of blood sports, the pomp of Handel's music, snow ("the downy flakes / Descending, and, with never-ceasing lapse, / Softly alighting upon all below"), cucumbers, slavery, the ills of cities and factories, France, farming, a paralytic, tepid clergy, and so on.[10]

Cowper's essayistic verse encouraged Lamb to break from the Bowles sonnet and forge the more confessional, varied, conversational style that came to early fruition in *Blank Verse* and fully bloomed in the Elia essays.

# CHAPTER 9

## Nether Stowey

In early June 1797, after a four-month silence, Coleridge wrote Lamb. Charles was thrilled: "I stared in wild wonderment to see thy well-known hand again. It revived many a pleasing recollection of an epistolary intercourse, of late strangely suspended, once the pride of my life." Lamb planned to store the letter in a "little drawer" where he kept his treasures (*M,* 1:110). Coleridge invited Lamb to Nether Stowey, but Lamb couldn't come, though he wanted to. There is the expense, and fifty other things he does not mention, including his father and Mary.

That Charles about-faced three weeks later, leaving London for Somerset, can be attributed to his deep melancholy. He wrote to Coleridge on June 24, "I am ashamed of what I write. But I have no topic to talk of. I see nobody, and sit, and read or walk, and hear nothing. I am quite lost to conversation from disuse; and out of the sphere of my little family, who, I am thankful, are dearer and dearer to me every day, I see no face that brightens up at my approach. My friends are at a distance; worldly hopes are at a low ebb with me, and unworldly thoughts are not yet familiarized to me." In this mood, why come to Stowey? What conversation could he offer to a man of Coleridge's "knowledge and fancy?" (*M,* 1:112–13).

If Lamb sounds like a jilted, self-pitying lover, he is. He senses that Coleridge has cooled to him, and this has drained his confidence. He appears to be fishing for compliments, too. Look how stupid I am, he is saying. I will never be able to keep up with you. He hopes that Coleridge will disagree.

Five days later, Lamb announces he is coming. "I long, I yearn, with all the longings of a child do I desire to see you, to come among you—to see the young philosopher [Samuel and Sara's son Hartley] to thank Sara for her last year's invitation in person—to read your tragedy—to read over together our little book—to breath fresh air—to revive in me vivid images of 'Salutation scenery.' There is a sort of sacrilege in my letting such ideas slip out of my mind & memory" (*M*, 1:114).

What Lamb desired from his visit to Stowey he had expressed a year earlier, just after he had reluctantly declined Coleridge's invitation to come to Bristol. (His mother was too ill for him to leave the family.) The day after sending his regrets, July 5, 1796, he passed along a poem to Coleridge, "Lines, Addressed, from London, to Sara and S.T.C. at Bristol, in the Summer of 1796." Lamb likens his disappointment to that of a steer who has labored all the sweltering day, only to be denied cool water. The pleasures Lamb will miss are the summer winds hitting the high banks of Clifton (a Bristol suburb through which the Avon flows); the Avon waters themselves (Lamb erroneously connects these Bristol currents with Shakespeare's Stratford-upon-Avon); and the tower of the St. Mary Redcliffe, where Thomas Chatterton's imagination was shaped before he traveled to London, composed his Rowley poems, and killed himself. All that stops Lamb from complaining over such losses is that another poet rises from Avon, Coleridge (*W*, 5: 15).

Coleridge in Stowey also offers sublime vistas, salubrious currents, poetic inspiration. And, it turns out, a gift more strange: the Wordsworths, the reasons Coleridge did not write Lamb for so long. He had found another, and stronger, literary love.

Lamb traveled to Nether Stowey by coach; he arrived on July 7. Coleridge had moved to this Somerset village from Clevedon in December 1796 to be near the tanner Thomas Poole, a friend and patron. He had met Poole two years earlier on a walking tour in Somerset, and now looked to this politically radical, philanthropic, and intellectually ambitious merchant for financial and emotional support. Coleridge also harbored Edenic fantasies. The Pantisocracy might have fallen apart, but he could combine farming and poetry on his own. He settled in with Sara and the infant Hartley. "From seven till half past eight I work in my garden; from breakfast till 12 I read & compose, then read again—feed the pigs, poultry, &c., till two o'clock—after dinner work again till Tea—from tea till supper *review*. So jogs the day; & I am happy."[1]

Though he called this damp, mouse-infested cottage a "miserable hovel"—thus justifying Lamb's ribbing, "You are not in arcadia when you are in the west of England" (*M*, 1:58)—he thrived in Somerset, not least because of its natural beauty. The village of Nether Stowey rests just east of the Quantock Hills, undulations of heather, gorse, whortleberry, buttercups, hyacinths, and poppies. From every combe you stride out of, you find yourself on a knoll whose northward horizon is the Bristol Channel. As you continue west into the Exmoor region, the terrain becomes rockier. Fossil-ridden cliffs plunge into the channel.

Coleridge tramped enthusiastically along the Exmoor coast, regularly covering the forty-five miles from Stowey to Lynton. Many places he made famous: Ash Farm, near Porlock, where he likely dropped opium and rose to "Kubla Khan"; the nearby Culbone Church, the smallest parish church in England and possibly the model for the Hermit's dwelling in *Rime of the Ancient Mariner*; and Watchet, the harbor, apparently, from which the Mariner embarks.[2]

William Wordsworth and his sister Dorothy joined the most significant of Coleridge's walks, which Wordsworth recalled in the final book of his *Prelude*: "That summer, under whose indulgent skies / Upon smooth Quantock's airy ridge we roved / Uncheck'd, or loitered 'mid her sylvan combs." Coleridge on these ranges did "chaunt the vision of that Ancient Man, / The bright-eyed Mariner, and rueful woes / Didst utter of the Lady Christabel," while Wordsworth murmured "of him who, joyous hap! was found," the idiot boy.[3]

Coleridge had spent much of June with the siblings in Racedown in Dorset. He had met the poet briefly in Bristol in 1795, and now he wanted a friendship. He walked fifty miles from Bridgwater (he had delivered a sermon there) to Racedown. Upon glimpsing the Wordsworths' cottage, he "did not keep to the high road, but leaped over a gate and bounded down a pathless field by which he cut off an angle."[4] He reached Dorothy in the garden, and verbally seduced her and her brother. Dorothy's description still electrifies:

[Coleridge] is a wonderful man. His conversation teems with soul, mind, and spirit. Then he is so benevolent, so good-tempered and cheerful, and, like William, excites himself so much about every little trifle. At first I thought him very plain—that is, for about three minutes. He is pale, thin, has a wide mouth, thick lips, and not very good teeth; longish, loose-growing, half-curling, rough, black hair. But if you hear him speak for five minutes, you think no more about them. His eye is large and full, and not very dark, but grey—such an eye as would receive from a heavy soul the dullest expression; but it speaks every emotion of his animated mind. It has more of the "poet's eye in fine frenzy rolling" than I ever witnessed. He has fine dark eyebrows and an overhanging forehead.[5]

William Wordsworth was straight man to the frenzied Coleridge. Hazlitt remembered him as

> gaunt and Don Quixote-like. . . quaintly dressed . . . in a brown fustian jacket and striped pantaloons. There was something of a roll, a lounge in his gait, not unlike his own "*Peter Bell.*" There was a severe, worn pressure of thought about his temples, a fire in his eye (as if he saw something in objects more than the outward appearance), an intense, high, narrow forehead, a Roman nose, cheeks furrowed by strong purpose and feeling, and a convulsive inclination to laughter about the mouth, a good deal at variance with the solemn, stately expression of the rest of his face. . . . He sat down and talked very naturally and freely, with a mixture of clear, gushing accents in his voice, a deep guttural intonation, and a strong tincture of the northern *burr*, like the crust on wine.[6]

Dorothy carried her own charge, as Coleridge perceived: "She is a woman indeed!—in mind, I mean, & heart—for her person is such, that if you expected to see a pretty woman, you would think her ordinary—if you expected to find an ordinary woman, you would think her pretty!— But her manners are simple, ardent, impressive—." He most admired her eyes, "watchful in minutest observation of nature—and her taste a perfect electrometer—it bends, protrudes, and draws in, at sublest beauties & most recondite faults."[7]

After these three had galvanized one another for two weeks, Coleridge convinced the siblings to visit him in Nether Stowey. The two arrived in early July, probably about the same time Lamb showed up, on the seventh.

But regardless of arrival times, Charles was late for the party. Coleridge had transferred his affection to the Wordsworths, and they adored him back. Their shared passion was for what we now call "Nature"—landscape dimming and shimmering into forms emotionally charged. Within months,

*William Wordsworth*, by Robert Hancock. (© National Portrait Gallery, London.)

William and Samuel, during one of their many rambles, turned this nature love into a moneymaking scheme: *Lyrical Ballads*, the Ur-text of British Romanticism.[8]

By the time Lamb was sent out on his immortal hike with Dorothy and William—Coleridge, hobbled after Sara spilled the boiling milk, could not join—did he feel excluded from the intimate group? Coleridge was no doubt happy for his old friend to visit, and subsequent correspondence shows that William and Dorothy both admired Charles. But Coleridge's "This Lime-tree Bower My Prison" suggests that he wasn't really viewing Charles as Charles so much as reducing his friend to a symbol of his own yearnings.

Coleridge sentimentalized Lamb, calling him "gentle-hearted," but Lamb saw *himself* as a "drunken dog, ragged head, seld-shaven, odd-ey'd, stuttering" (*M*, 1:224). He demanded that Coleridge never call him "gentle-hearted" again.

Coleridge also pictured Lamb as a hater of London. But it was Coleridge the nature poet who saw the city (at least at this point in his mercurial life) as a penitentiary. Lamb didn't; he cherished his London and didn't care if he ever saw a mountain again.

If Lamb felt excluded at Nether Stowey, he didn't let on, at least not in the letter he sent Coleridge a few days after his return to London. The loss of his friends pains him, especially their conversation, which had improved him. He loved Wordsworth's "Lines Left upon a Seat in a Yew Tree," and wants a copy. What's going on there now? Has John Thelwall, the famous radical, arrived? Have the Wordsworths departed? Please post the coat I left behind, and remember the poem, since "it will recall to me the tones of all your voices—and with them many a remembered kindness to one who could and can repay you all only by the silence of a grateful heart" (*M,* 1:117–18).

Lamb's own voice was not much heard. "I could not talk much, while I was with you, but my silence was not sullenness, nor I hope from any bad motive; but, in truth, disuse has made me awkward at it. I know I behaved myself, particularly at Tom Poole's, and at Cruikshank's, most like a sulky child; but company and converse are strange to me. It was kind in you all to endure me as you did" (*M,* 1:117–18).

It is telling that of all the exuberant talk of verse, Lamb most remembered Wordsworth's lines on the yew seat. The poem describes a man the world has beaten into solitary despair. He sits under the tree for days, all alone, his "only visitants a straggling sheep, / The stone-chat, or the glancing sand-piper." He stares at the surrounding empty rocks, randomly stained "with juniper, / And heath, and thistle." The scene is his morbid pleasure, since he gleans from the barrenness an "emblem of his own unfruitful life."[9]

Even though he was among like-minded folk, Lamb gazed around the crags of the Quantocks and saw—contrary to Coleridge's lime-tree fantasy of rook-blessing unity—his isolation. Where the nature poets sensed connection—between nature and emotion, feeling and thought—Lamb encountered bareness, roughness, fixity: the lineaments of his life.

But Lamb blamed only himself for his loneliness. One of his great virtues—one Coleridge didn't much share—is that he refused victimhood. This quality is on display in this letter. He never suggests that the two poets excluded him. He criticizes himself for not finding his place in the conversation—to some extent justly, since his silence sprang as much from his shyness or melancholy as it did from Coleridge and Wordsworth having ears *only* for each other.

Lamb never recovered from his loss of Coleridge's intimacy. But as the door to Coleridge's deepest interiors closed, other portals opened. He cultivated William and Dorothy, who would later become very close friends. He deepened his friendship with Jem White, a fellow Blue. He developed the friendship with Lloyd, and with him wrote his own volume of verse.

CHAPTER 10

## Blank Verse

In mid-August 1797, about two weeks after Lamb had returned to London, "poor Charles Lloyd" once more rushed into his life. He had become engaged to Sophia Pemberton, nineteen, of Birmingham. He had doubts about the engagement, though, and had traveled to London to buy time and get advice. Lamb had none to give. He was relieved when Lloyd proposed they go to Southey in Burton (*M,* 1:118–19). The two took the seventy-mile trip to Burton, and Lamb returned the next day. Lloyd had planned to leave with him but decided to write an "explicit letter" to Sophia and to stay on with the Southeys. The letter proposed a quick, clandestine marriage (*M,* 1:118–19).

The next time Lamb heard from Lloyd, the beleaguered man was in Bath, on his way, with Southey, to Birmingham. There Lloyd hoped to persuade Sophia to a "Scotch" wedding, a declaration, in front of witnesses, of a desire to be married. Lamb didn't believe Sophia would be amenable, and he feared, as did Coleridge, for Lloyd's sanity.

A month later, on September 20, as the anniversary of the day of horrors nears, Lamb is alarmed by more than Lloyd who, it turns out, did not convince Sophia to marry him in a hugger-mugger way. In a letter to Coleridge on this day, Lamb sets the scene. He is sitting in his East India office. The terror of twelve months earlier overtakes him, like a post-traumatic flashback, and out of him, with "unusual celerity" (*M,* 1:123) surges a poem unlike any he has ever written before: a stark confession of desperate personal sorrow, penned in rugged blank verse and impassioned diction. Lamb immediately recognizes the poem as one of his best.

In this letter to Coleridge, Lamb calls the poem "Written a Twelvemonth After the Events." "Alas!" it opens,

> how am I chang'd! where be the tears,
> The sobs, and forc'd suspensions of the breath,
> And all the dull desertions of the heart,
> With which I hung o'er my dear mother's corse? (*M*, 1:120)

The torqued syntax ("how am I chang'd!") and the blurring of moods (is he asking or stating how he's changed?) betray a twisted, baffled soul. His problem: I am not grieving *enough* for my dead mother. Where are the lamentations? He is numb, misses the violent weeping and the relief afterward. Yet these calms are God's grace, and to be indifferent to the rhythm between devastation and tranquility is brutish ingratitude.

As a verse of regret and desired renewal, the poem should properly stop here. But Lamb now oddly shifts from first-person singular to third-person plural.

> O keep not now, my Lord,
> Thy servants in far worse, in spiritual death,
> And darkness blacker than those most feared shadows
> O' the Valley, all must tread. (*M.* 1:121)

Lamb aims to escape his individual plight and view himself as one of a mass, all needing the same grace. His subsequent transition to first-person plural— "Lend us thy balms / Thou dear Physician of the sin sick soul"—compromises between the "I" and the "they" (I am part of a group that shares my inmost concern) but still distances Lamb from his personal crisis. He craves, with other sick souls, "new flesh, new birth," "**Salvation**" (*M*, 1:121).

Lamb dramatizes his struggle to accept his own shortcomings. A year after his mother was killed, he no longer suffers sufficiently, nor does he appreciate the grace that eases the pain. He can admit this, but instead of exploring the reasons why he has fallen numb, he places himself in a grand Christian narrative of sin and redemption.

Lamb jerks again to the personal, as if remembering why he is writing in the first place. "Thou and I, dear friend, / With filial recognition sweet, shall know / One day the face of our dear mother in heaven." He and his friend—Mary, one assumes—share a hopeful future. They will see their mother in heaven. She will greet her children—one of whom killed her—with love, and her "placid" smile will correspond to their likewise tranquil smiles, and "her hand" will be wetted with their "drops of fondness." A spirit has a hand. Lamb can't keep the physical out of his heaven. In proclaiming that he and his friend need not "**fear repulse**" from this maternal hand, he evokes the repulsing it did on earth—Elizabeth was cold toward Mary—and implies the hand could do the same in the hereafter (*M,* 1:121). This is not unjust, since Mary did kill the body from which the mother's soul is free.

The fear of repulsion pulls Lamb away from this potentially bright reunion, back to his troubled past, even before the terrible day. He does not wish to return to his "days of vanity," composed of "vain loves" and fanciful poems to the blond-haired Ann (*M,* 1:121). His grief prods him to these idolatrous days, and he wants God's forgiveness for worshipping the maid more than him. But Lamb can't stop recalling the past. Before he fell for the "fair haird maid," he enjoyed his mother's "fondness." Now that is no more, and no more his childhood companions: all Lamb possesses is "unavailing grief"—for one parent dead, and another alive but joyless (*M,* 1:122).

The poem ends where it began, in loss, sorrow, and regret. The only difference is that Lamb does have one friend (Mary, not God) who remains and who can lead him out of "**black . . . morning storms**" to the "not unpeaceful Evening of a Day" (*M,* 1:122). This is a strangely secular conclusion for a pious poem. But it is one of many abrupt shifts in the piece, which runs from guilt to beseeching to fantasy to reminiscence to nostalgia to resignation. The perspectives are just as varied. We move from an earth-rooted personal point of view to a communal spiritual one to a vision of the afterlife to a child's perception and then back to the adult Lamb. This circularity suggests the poem's drama is moot. Nothing happens. But the presence of the faithful friend intimates otherwise. Lamb enjoys one blessing, ironically from the woman who killed his mother.

A poem about overcoming grief oddly lacks a lesson. This lack of discursive moralizing will prove an integral part of Lamb's mature poetics, which encourage an *experience* of linguistic richness, not rational pursuit of a meaning.

In the same September 20 letter to Coleridge, Lamb followed this poem with another like it, an agonized portrait of his own loneliness and the mental

vexations of Lloyd. This poem would appear within weeks in *Monthly Magazine* under the title "To a Friend," and later in *Blank Verse* as "To Charles
Lloyd."

Lloyd was much on Lamb's mind. He had been spending time with his
new friend, who was as usual agitated. Lamb chastised Coleridge for neglecting to write Lloyd and reminded his old friend that Lloyd "is not a mind
with which you should play tricks. He deser[v]es more tenderness from you"
(*M,* 1:123).

Lamb could have been speaking of himself. Coleridge was neglecting him
again. "If you don't write to me now,—as I told Lloyd, I shall get angry, & call
you hard names, Manchineel, & I don't know what else." Lamb wanted more
than a letter; he had left his coat in Nether Stowey, had already asked Coleridge to post it, and now requested it again, as London was moving toward
high autumn: "I wish you would send me my Great coat—the snow & the
rain season is at hand & I have but a wretched old coat, once my fathers, to
keep'em off." Coleridge's failure to send the coat marks a dying companionship: "I shall remember where I left my coat—meek Emblem wilt thou be,
old Winter, of a friend's neglect—Cold, cold, cold" (*M,* 1:123).

Lamb's allusions harshly criticize Coleridge. The "hard name," Manchineel, means "poison tree." Ironically, Coleridge used this very word in his
dedication to the 1797 edition of his poems. There the poison tree stands for
"false and fair-foliag'd friends." The failure to send Lamb's coat as an "Emblem . . . of a friend's neglect" refers to Coleridge's "To an Old Man," where
Coleridge's speaker gives an old man his coat. Coleridge doesn't do the same
for his friend. And so Lamb is "cold, cold, cold"—like Edgar on the freezing
heath in *King Lear,* or like Desdemona after she has been strangled.[1]

Lamb was half kidding, but if he'd known how seriously Coleridge had
chilled on him, even he would have put joking aside. In November 1797,
Coleridge, under the comical moniker Nehemiah Higginbottom, published
in the *Monthly Magazine* three "Sonnets Attempted in the Manner of Contemporary Writers." He intended them to parody three common errors of
young writers: melancholy egotism, overemphasis on simplicity, and "the in-
discriminate use of elaborate and swelling language." But a letter to publisher
Joseph Cottle suggests Coleridge had goals beyond exciting a "good-natured
laugh." The poems "may do good to our young bards."[2]

These young bards were himself, Lamb, and Lloyd, the three authors of
*Poems, by S. T. Coleridge, Second Edition, to Which Are Now Added Poems by*

*Charles Lamb and Charles Lloyd.* The book had been published in October. One reviewer discovered in the volume a "Coleridgean School," claiming that the three poets resemble one another in "manner" and "sentiment." Coleridge likes rhyming "ess" and "ness," as do his friends. Lloyd and Lamb are also guilty of "a turgescence of style not very remote from affectation." The reviewer surely had in mind Lamb's Anna sonnets which, taken straight— as opposed to psychological explorations of excess—come off as overblown longing. And the reviewer definitely was thinking of Lloyd's "The Melancholy Man" and "The Maniac," emotionally turgid idealizations of a mental disorder.[3]

Now under the sway of Wordsworth, champion of plain language and authentic (versus affected) feeling, Coleridge wanted to dissociate himself from his less poetically brilliant friends. And not only aesthetically; he was annoyed at Lloyd for destroying his peace, and probably for seeking marital advice from Southey, not him. Coleridge was not on a good footing with Southey. As their Pantisocratic vision evaporated in the winter of 1795–96, the two men broke. Their very different dispositions would have led to a severing anyway; the precise, responsible Southey could never quite accommodate the improvisational brilliance of Coleridge, just as Coleridge of the flashing eye could not long endure Southey's consistency.[4] In an ungenerous moment, Wordsworth mocked Southey for seldom feeling "his burthened breast Heaving beneath th' incumbent Deity."[5]

When it came to Lloyd and Southey at this time, Coleridge didn't know the half of it. Even though the fastidious Southey didn't much care for Lloyd's character, his "contemptible frivolities" and "fickleness," he did not plug his ears when Lloyd started bad-mouthing Coleridge.[6] The mudslinging was in earnest: it wasn't enough for Lloyd to toss off the flaws of Coleridge—his heavy opium taking, his indolence—over a pint or two of ale; Lloyd had to write them up, in a novel called *Edmund Oliver.*

Coleridge's irritation with Lloyd is justified, but what about Lamb? Lamb signified the poetry of sensibility, the London literary scene, friends who were not Wordsworth—all of which Coleridge wished to abandon. Wordsworth, in Coleridge's own words, "descended" upon him like "the Gnothi seauton [the daimon telling Socrates to "know thyself"] from Heaven; by shewing to him what true Poetry was, he made him know, that he him self was no Poet."[7] This dysfunctional infatuation pressed Coleridge to inaccurate self-assessment: Wordsworth was "a very great man—the only man, to whom *at all times* & in *all modes of excellence* I feel myself inferior."[8] When Coleridge saw an awkward and depressed Lamb at Nether Stowey, and compared him to his new god, his Christ's friend looked pretty shabby.

The Higginbottom sonnets resemble *Spinal Tap*: they are such subtle parody that some might think they are not parody. The first sonnet might have actually been written by the lachrymose Lloyd. Nehemiah is "pensive at eve," and "on the *hard* world" he mused, and his "*poor* heart was sad," and so "at the MOON" he "gazed and sighed, and sighed." The second sonnet, a paean to "meek SIMPLICITY," might have been by Lamb. Same with the third, where the character Jack sees a woman like Anna haunting the glade.

Those in the know recognized these poems as Coleridge's. Southey thought the satire was directed at him, even though Coleridge denied it. Southey nonetheless responded with verses satirizing Coleridge, the *Amatory Poems of Abel Shufflebottom* (1799). Though Southey wearied of Lloyd throughout the fall of 1797—"Our living together was unpleasant"—he appeared with him in London in November. By this time, Lloyd was deep into writing *Edmund Oliver*.[9]

We possess no letter of Lamb from September 20, 1797, when he sent Coleridge the two blank verse confessionals, to January 1798, at which time he sent his Christ's friend Marmaduke Thompson "The Old Familiar Faces." During this time, Lamb was deep in collaboration with Lloyd. They were completing *Blank Verse*. They published the volume in early summer 1798, a whole season ahead of *Lyrical Ballads*, which came out in early October.

Did Coleridge know Lamb and Lloyd were collaborating? If so, did this sting, that his two former disciples (Lloyd more than Lamb) were moving ahead without him? Did he know that Lloyd and Southey were backbiting him, and Lloyd rushing his satirical novel toward completion?

Whatever Coleridge's feeling toward Southey and Lloyd, as late as January 1798, he and Lamb were solid. Lamb apologizes for not responding to Coleridge's "many kind letters," especially since he owes so much to his Christ's friend, whose conversation back in the Salutation and Cat days "won me to the better cause, and rescued me from the polluting spirit of the world." "I might have been a worthless character without you." Lamb's recent "afflictions"—Mary's insanity and his father's fast-declining health—have kept him from writing. Unlike in the past, when tragedy softened his spirit, these misfortunes have turned him irascible, "full of little jealousies and heartburnings." He has argued with Lloyd, "for no other reason, I believe, than that the good creature did all he could to make me happy—. The truth is, I thought he tried to force my mind from its natural & proper bent, he continually wished me from home, he was drawing me *from* the consideration of my poor Mary's situation, rather than assisting me to gain a proper view of it, with religious consolations." Lamb wanted to hurt alone, and this injured Lloyd, who called Lamb "jaundiced" toward him. The bad feelings have passed. Mary is at least recovering, but Lamb sees "no opening yet of a situation for her," probably meaning a private asylum, where she can get care, as opposed to her lodgings in Hackney, where she cannot. Coleridge has kindly invited them to Somerset, but Coleridge's personality is too powerful; it will overexcite Mary. Lamb doesn't mention here the Higginbottom poems, which suggests either that he didn't yet know they were by Coleridge or that they simply didn't bother him (*M*, 1:126–27).

The insecure Lloyd, however, didn't take kindly to the sonnets. In March, he conveyed to Coleridge via publisher Joseph Cottle that he wished to have his poems removed from the third edition of *Poems*, which Coleridge was preparing for the press. Coleridge replied, "It is curious that I should be applied to ... in hope that I might 'CONSENT TO GIVE UP' a number of poems which were published at the earnest request of the author. . . . I have no objection to any disposal of C. Lloyd's poems except that of their being published with mine."[10]

In May, Lloyd published *Edmund Oliver*. Those who knew Coleridge recognized him in Edmund, who possessed a "large glistening eye," "dark eyebrows," and "dark hair," and described himself thus: "I have at all times a strange dreaminess about me, which makes me indifferent to the future, if I can by any means fill the present with sensations. With that dreaminess I have gone on here from day to day; if at any time though troubled, I have swallowed some spirits, or had recourse to my laudanum."[11]

Coleridge considered Lloyd's disclosure of such personal details an inexcusable betrayal. But what stung him just as much was the book's dedication: to Charles Lamb.

Lamb was much with Lloyd that spring. It seems impossible that Lamb hadn't read all or some of *Edmund Oliver*, and that he didn't give his permission for Lloyd to dedicate the book to him. Does this mean Lamb shared Lloyd's embittered views of Coleridge? Allegedly, Lloyd told Charles that Coleridge had defined himself as a genius, but Lamb only as talented. And Lloyd told Charles that Coleridge also said, "'Poor Lamb . . . if he wants any *knowledge*, he may apply to me'" (*M*, 1:130). Add to this "sad" tattling—as Lamb would later call it—his displeasure at Coleridge for not writing Lloyd, and his own pain over Coleridge not writing him, and we can see how Lamb might resent his old friend.

On the other hand, in the January letter to Coleridge, Lamb was annoyed with Lloyd. He even felt that Lloyd was trying to block him from Mary.

Lamb's position was complicated. Coleridge's was not. He immediately recognized himself in "Edmund Oliver's love-fit, debaucheries, leaving college & going into the army." He felt "calumny & ingratitude from men who have been fostered in the bosom of my confidence!"[12] He was further angered by more of Lloyd's tattling. Lloyd had told Dorothy that Lamb was on his side and was no longer going to write Coleridge. In May, Coleridge opened a letter to Lamb by announcing that Dorothy had told him of Lamb's position. Then he attacked:

> I have been unfortunate in my connections. Both you & Lloyd became acquainted with me at a season when your minds were far from being in a composed or natural state & you clothed my image with a suit of notions & feelings which could belong to nothing human. *You* are restored to comparative saneness, & are merely wondering what is become of the Coleridge with whom you were so passionately in love. *Charles Lloyd's* mind has only changed its disease, & he is now arraying his ci-devant angel in a flaming Sanbenito—the whole ground of the garment a dark brimstone & plenty of little Devils flourished out in black. O me! Lamb, "even in laughter the heart is sad"—My kindness, my affectionateness he deems wheedling, but if after reading all my letters to yourself & to him you can suppose him wise in his treatment & correct in his accusations of me, you think worse of human nature than poor human nature, bad as it is, deserves to be thought of.[13]

Only Coleridge, a psychologist whose subtlety is matched only by his neediness, could have written this. You and Lloyd, not in your right minds, have projected onto me superlatives beyond what any man can embody, and so when I behaved in a merely human way, you found me a failure and attacked me out of disappointment. Lloyd will never now see me as anything other than Satan himself, though you, Lamb, have returned to sanity, and wonder what happened to the Coleridge you loved so much. Why is he not as close to you as he once was? Both of you, to draw from Proverbs 14, have made my heart sad even in laughter. I need not remind you that this chapter contains the lines, "An honest witness does not deceive, but a false witness pours out lies."

Coleridge foregoes responsibility. He also asserts his superiority over Lloyd and Lamb. He might not be the saint the younger men want him to be, but he does not deny he is a man whose virtues inspire idealizing.

Lamb's riposte is pained, bemused, witty, insulting, accurate. Writing from Birmingham, where he was visiting the Lloyds, he opens with "Certain Theological Propositions." These eight questions respond to Coleridge's implication that Lamb has been a false friend. The first asks, "Whether God loves a lying Angel better than a true man?" Aside from parodying the kind of theological question that will soon subsume Coleridge, the inquiry implies that the "angelic" Coleridge is delusional, while Lamb, though spiritually inferior, is a "true" man. The same theme emerges in the second question: "Whether the Archangel Uriel could affirm an untruth? & if he *could* whether he *would*?" Can the angelic Coleridge, like the perfect Uriel, discern falsehood? If he were so capable, would he choose to exercise that ability? Is Coleridge in his self-righteousness able to see clearly, and, if he is, might he choose, out of vanity, not to? Is honesty angelic? Do angels sneer? Can "pure Intelligences" love? Do "Seraphim Ardentes" express virtues via theory, since practice might be human and beneath them? (*M*, 1:128).

Number seven is especially pointed: "Whether the Vision Beatific be anything more or less than a perpetual representation to each individual Angel of his own present attainments & future capabilities, somehow in the manner of mortal looking-glasses, reflecting a perpetual complacency & satisfaction?" (*M*, 1:128).

After this biting mockery, Lamb addresses Coleridge as "Learned Sir, my Friend," and says he will now take Coleridge up on his offer for Lamb to apply to him for knowledge. (An alleged offer, remember, passed to Lamb from Lloyd.) He wants Coleridge to address these questions while in Germany. (The poet would depart England for Göttingen in December.) Lamb looks forward to the consolation he will receive if "thro' the channel of [Coleridge's] wished return [from Germany] . . . may be transmitted to this our Island, from those famous Theological Wits of Leipsic & Gottingen, any rays of illumination, in vain to be derived from the home growth of our English Halls and Colleges. Finally, wishing Learned Sir, that you may see Schiller, & swing in a wood (*vide* Poems), & sit upon a Tun, & eat fat hams of Wesphalia" (*M*, 1:128–29).

Lamb did not write to Coleridge again for two years, nor did Coleridge write him.

CHAPTER 11

*Pentonville*

At the end of 1796, Lamb and his father had moved three miles northeast to No. 45 Chapel-Street, in Pentonville, a newly developed suburb in the large meadows north of Clerkenwell. Not yet ten years old, this nondescript area offered father and son a kind of tabula rasa, devoid of personal and city history. This is exactly what they wanted. The impetus for the move from No. 7 Little Queen was almost certainly to avoid enduring the one-year anniversary of the tragedy on the site where it occurred. Charles also wanted to be near Islington's Fisher House, where Mary, during her time in Hackney, recovered from periodic attacks, and 45 Chapel-Street was only a short stroll from the asylum (but a three-mile walk westward to Hackney).[1]

At least Charles wasn't as lonely during the fall of 1797 and the winter and spring of 1798. He had Lloyd and Southey to socialize with in the autumn, and Lloyd and his old Christ's friend Jem White in the spring. (Lloyd lived with White at the time; Southey observed, "No two men could be imagined more unlike each other. Lloyd had no drollery in his nature; White seemed to have nothing else.")[2]

Still, as Mary vacillated between relative mental health at Hackney and fits of madness in Fisher, and as his father continued senile, Lamb fell into abysmal melancholy, and he frequently wanted to be alone. Out of this darkness flamed Lamb's most brilliant and terrifying poem.

It is January 1798. Lamb has been carousing with Lloyd and White. Lloyd plays the pianoforte. The music inspires in Lamb feelings "wrought too high not to require vent." He leaves Lloyd "suddenly & rushe[s] into ye Temple," where he was born. In "ye state of mind that followed," he composes the stanzas. "They pretend to little like Metre," but they show the "Disorder" he is in (*M*, 1:124). The poem is "The Old Familiar Faces." It is Lamb's most direct response to the day of horrors.[3]

This poem opens, "Where are they gone, the old familiar faces?" Each stanza is a harrowing nonanswer: an invocation of all who have vanished, with no attempt to grasp where they have gone or if they are coming back. If there is any progression in the poem, it's from "worst" to "almost worst." After the question, the poet confesses, "I had a mother, but she died, and left me, / Died prematurely in a day of horrors—/ All, all are gone, the old familiar faces" (*M*, 1:124). Lamb removed this raw revelation in his reprinting of the poem in his 1818 *Works*, and it didn't appear in the more prominent anthologies in which the poem prospered, *The Oxford Book of English Verse* and *Palgrave's Golden Treasury*.

That Lamb included such an intimate disclosure at all in the days before Ginsberg, Lowell, Sexton, and Plath is remarkable. His rhythm is similarly, for his day, striking. It reads, as Lamb himself said, as if it lacks meter. The first four lines feel like free verse. Iambic hexameter predominates, but the first line opens and closes with a trochee. The second line is more regular, though it ends with a trochee. The third line, though, is very irregular. Three trochaic feet open it, then two iambs, followed by one unstressed syllable. (The extra syllable makes the line hypercatalectic.) The fourth line begins with a spondaic foot ("All, all"), proceeds with four iambs, before closing with a trochee. Strangely, the most regular feature of these opening lines, aside from the repetition of "faces" at the ends of the first and fourth lines, is the unstressed, or "feminine," ending. This technique is rare in "serious" verse, especially in combination with end-stopped lines. The effect is apt: lines that desire the clarity and confidence of end stops but lack the verbal gumption to achieve it. The lines trail off into a whisper, a mumble. But such is the effect of the overall stanza: an aspiration toward a reassuring pattern but a failure to establish it.

The subsequent stanzas similarly describe what the poet—we can call him Lamb—has loved and lost. The language remains rough, verse more free than blank, and each stanza ends with the lament: "All, all are gone, the old familiar faces."

"I have had playmates, I have had companions," Lamb laments in the second stanza, and they are gone. In the next stanza, he shifts from present perfect tense to present perfect continuous, "I have been laughing, I have been carousing" (*M*, 1:124). This change makes the activities feel more immediate—we can imagine them going on as Lamb speaks—but the more dynamic tense only highlights what the poet does not have: continuous joy.

The rift between the conviviality he wants and his agony over its absence: this pushes Lamb back, in the next stanza, to past tense. Best to keep what's gone where it belongs. "I loved a love once." She "closed" her "doors" (*M*, 1:125).

In the next stanza the poet leaps to the present tense: "I have a friend, a kinder friend has no man." But like "an ingrate, I left my friend abruptly; / Left him, to muse on the old familiar places" (*M*, 1:125). This jump to the present isn't the only change. This is the first instance where the poet shows agency. The familiar faces in this case aren't taken from him; he abandons the familiar himself. Whether this friend is Charles Lloyd, whom Lamb did abandon at the piano to brood over his sorrows, or someone else, the gist of this stanza, right in the middle of the poem, is this: lost loved ones alienate you from present friends.

The next stanza develops the idea that brooding over loss distances instead of connects. When the poet ungratefully left his friend, he paced alone "round the haunts of my childhood," perhaps the Temple Courts (*M*, 1:125).

The next stanza also emphasizes choice. Just as Lamb can decide to stay close to his friend or be an ingrate, he can also connect, or not, to another friend, a friend of his "bosom," more "than a brother" (*M*, 1:125).

In addition to highlighting Lamb's power to choose, the last three stanzas discussed break the pattern established by the first four, each of which ends with "All, all are gone, the old familiar faces." That each of the three subsequent stanzas concludes differently suggests, as does Lamb's agency, that change—maybe healthy change—is possible. But the last stanza returns to the earlier pattern, concluding with "All, all are gone, the old familiar faces." Though change might be possible, Lamb will not realize it.

This poem depicts the repetition compulsion of inconsolable grief. If there is any hope in the poem, it is the possibility that we can choose how to mourn, and some forms of mourning are more soothing than others. There is nothing you can do about the darkness, but you can decide to whistle or not, and some tunes sound better.

Lamb's other contributions to *Blank Verse* are also shockingly dark contraries to the luminous organicism of *Lyrical Ballads*, as well as to the communal hopes (though hesitant) of Lloyd's contributions, such as "To ******. Written in Worcestershire, July 1797" and "London: A Poem."

"To Charles Lloyd," Lamb's opening verse and a direct response to "This Lime-tree Bower My Prison," describes the absence of his beloved friend. The first draft of the poem, contained in a letter to Coleridge before their break, exposes the wound at its rawest. Lamb is a "stranger and alone" as he passes the scenes he once experienced with his companion. So overwhelming is his pain, he can't articulate it; his heart feels "something like desertion." Nor can he keep his senses straight. When he looks around, it is not his friend's appearance but his voice that is absent. The friend is Lloyd, and he is gone. All that remains for Lamb is "to mingle with a world impure / With men who make a mock of holy **things**, / Mistaken, & of man's best hope think scorn." Lamb has sometimes even joined in the world's "ideot laugh" himself. "Of this I now complain **not**." This jarring inversion slightly prepares us for the abrupt imperative: "Deal with **me**, / Omniscient Father! as thou judgest best; / And in *thy* season tender thou my heart" (*M*, 1:122).

For God to "deal" with Lamb, means that he will take competent action with respect to Lamb's condition. But "deal" also suggests the tossing of cards. Does Lamb want God to flutter him to a happenstance landing? God "tendering" Lamb's heart is also disturbing. "To tender" means to make tender or, archaically, to treat tenderly. But tender also means to offer formally, especially money, language that echoes "deal" in a third sense, to sell. Toss me in a game of chance, offer me up as a good to be bought.

Lamb doesn't care about himself. He is praying for Lloyd, whose "soul is sore perplex'd." "Shine on him," Lamb demands of God, and "make plain his way." This generous imperative resembles Coleridge's in "This Lime-tree Bower My Prison," where he asks the sun to sink and the heather to shine and the clouds to burn, all for the benefit of "gentle-hearted Charles." But Lamb is not invoking nature to do what it already does; he asks God to alter the landscape, make the dark light, to help his be-dimmed friend. He requests further reversals: don't let Lloyd think his "**own** thoughts," nor allow him to pursue "his own ends" (*M*, 1:122). Don't let Lloyd, in other words, be Lloyd. The only way for Lloyd not to be woefully befuddled is to become an identity-less vessel for God. How can a poem be titled "To Charles Lloyd" when Lloyd has vanished by the end?

This poem would remind us of Hopkins's "Terrible Sonnets," but it lacks the verbal mania of those vertiginous cries. It is Beckett. Words wind down to meaninglessness but keep on sounding.

Look at the poem following "To Charles Lloyd": "Written on the Day of My Aunt's Funeral." The opening is Poe, a repetition compulsion of mourning. "Thou too art dead,. . . . .!" it opens. The "thou" is obviously the aunt. It is the "too" that horrifies. Knowing Lamb's biography, we conclude that the other deceased is the mother. But who else? Taking the poem as a poem, and not simply Lamb's confession, we can ask of this speaker: how many have died before this aunt? Could be one, could be scores. So strong is the grief, it threatens to overwhelm the poem before it even gets going. The initial burst of sadness—the absence of commas after "thou" and "too" imply a rush of emotion—overpowers speech. The six suspension points mark a silence so intense an exclamation punctuates it. The poet musters great verbal will to continue. With "very kind" he ends the first line, followed by a description of how kind the aunt was to him. But he can't sustain this dirge for his aunt. Sixteen lines into the thirty-three-line poem, another grief silences his mourning for his aunt, a grief seemingly over the person he refers to in the first line. Go to your "grave-bed," the poet says to the aunt, where you will lie with "the dead mother." The use of the definite article over the possessive here chills. The flesh festering in the ground can't be "his" mother, since a mother to be a mother must be alive, but yet remains "the" mother, the reminder of the mother he had but has now lost. The poet laments the loss of this mother for the next several lines, before leaving her behind, as he did the aunt, and turning to the father who, though he remains alive, is now a "palsy-smitten, childish, old, old man / A semblance forlorn of what he was."[4]

"Written on the Day of My Aunt's Funeral" opens a triad of poems bluntly acknowledging the mother's terrible death. Following the dirge for the aunt is "Written a Year After the Events," which laments the loss of Lamb's parent and his distance from his sister. Next is "Written Soon After the Preceding Poem," where Lamb admits his inadequacy as a son but also his "tender feeling."[5]

If "To Charles Lloyd" is a somber antithesis of "The Lime-tree Bower," the final poem of Lamb's *Blank Verse*, "Composed at Midnight" (coming just after "The Old Familiar Faces") negates Coleridge's "Frost at Midnight."[6] From a fitful sleep, Lamb's poet wakes into despair. A dying man drowns the sounds that might relieve him, those of the watchman or the reveler. The man will die. Does he go to heaven? It is "darkness and conjecture" to consider what's beyond. Don't speculate. Just give God his "due."[7] But if our conjectures regarding the afterlife are erroneous, how can we imagine what we owe God?

# CHAPTER 12

⟨⟨⟨⟩⟩⟩

# *Frog and Toad*

Lamb has just written Coleridge a mocking good-bye letter and seen his collaboration with Lloyd enter the public arena. His poems, like his tiff with Coleridge, are terrifically personal, indecorously raw.

Not so all of Lloyd's. His first poem in *Blank Verse* praises the Pantisocratic vision of his new friend Southey, to whom he dedicates the volume, and his estranged friend Coleridge. Ambiguously titled "To ******. Written in Worcestershire, July 1797," the poem is clear in its argument. The everyday world is a "prison-house of man, where Power / And loathlier Wealth inflict on trembling Slaves / The rackings of despair." Praised then be the "noble souls / Who deem'd it wise, e'en in the morn of youth, / To quit this world!" These souls, we learn in a footnote, are "S. T. Coleridge and Robert Southey," who planned to establish a society in America, "in which all property was to be abandoned." Lloyd regrets that he could not live in "high-soul'd fellowship" with his "best friend" (apparently Coleridge, but possibly Southey), and laments that his friend's hopes were "blasted." Luckily the "godlike scheme" will rise again, and those who have struggled against the greedy, power-hungry world will join the "elect of Heaven."[1]

In a footnote, Lloyd asserts that "elect" referenced in the book have nothing to do with the "arbitrary dogma of Calvinism"; the authors intend the term to express the "doctrine of philosophical necessity," which will result in "the final happiness of all mankind."[2] Contemporary readers would have recognized Priestley here. But the doctrine of necessity could just as easily have come from William Godwin, also essential to the Pantisocratics. In his 1793 *Enquiry concerning Political Justice*, Godwin, whose youthful Tory views were reversed when he met Priestley, explained that "he who affirms that all actions are necessary, means, that, if we form a just and complete view of all the circumstances in which a living or intelligent being is placed, we shall find that he could not in any moment of his existence have acted otherwise than he has acted. According to this assertion there is in the transactions of mind nothing loose, precarious and uncertain." Perfectibility is "one of the most unequivocal characteristics of the human species, so that the political, as well as the intellectual state of man, may be presumed to be in a course of progressive improvement."[3] The abolition of government will bring about this improvement. No longer oppressed, men and women will reason their way to communal harmony.

Lloyd aligns with radical England. He had done so earlier in contributing sonnets to the *Monthly Magazine,* which actively supported revolutionaries such as Coleridge, William Blake, George Dyer, and Mary Wollstonecraft (Godwin's deceased wife). Joseph Johnson, the publisher, had devoted his life to reformers, for whom he held weekly dinners. He spent six months in prison in 1799 for seditious libel.

Lloyd should not have been surprised when he appeared as one of the butts of a satirical cartoon in the *Anti-Jacobin*, George Canning's conservative weekly. For Canning and his ilk, such as poet William Gifford, Dissenters like Godwin and Southey were British versions of the French Jacobins, the most radical faction of the French Revolution. A small political club at the beginning of the revolution, this group—called Jacobins because they met in a Jacobin monastery—rose to power under Maximilien Robespierre. By 1793, when the new French government warred with England, Austria, and Prussia, Robespierre purged perceived treasonous threats by instituting the Terror. From September 1793 to July 1794, he arrested and executed thousands.

The *Anti-Jacobin*, fearing similar chaos on home soil, wished to eradicate those, like Godwin and Southey, who sympathized with the ideals of the French Revolution: distrust of government and the religions supporting it, commitment to equal rights, validation of private experience, faith in the morality of sympathetic feelings, celebration of the universal citizen.

The *Anti-Jacobin* of July 9, 1798, featured a poem called "The New Morality," by Canning himself, a diatribe against all perceived threats to the empire,

Detail of *New Morality;—or—The Promis'd Installment of the High-Priest of the Theophilanthropes, with the Homage of Leviathan and His Suite*, by James Gillray. (© National Portrait Gallery, London.)

ranging from radical poets to Whig politicians to Dissenting ministers to liberal newspapers.

A cartoon illustrating the poem appeared the next month. It was by James Gillray, the Hogarth of his time, robustly attuned to surrealistic extremes. Godwin is a donkey holding *Political Justice*. Thomas Holcroft, a dramatist, is a crocodile. Coleridge and Southey are also donkeys. The "Cornucopia of Ignorance" vomits their poems. Squatting just to the left of this cornucopia are a toad and a frog. They are reading *Blank Verse*. So they are Lloyd and Lamb, though it is hard to tell one amphibian from the other.

How did Lamb find himself in Gillray's satire? As we know, many have concluded that Lamb was not political; he simply associated with those who were. According to this line of thinking, his friendships with Lloyd, Southey, and Coleridge, as well as his publications in the *Monthly Magazine*, are what landed him in the middle of an anti-Jacobin attack. Even Southey was surprised to see Lamb in the image. "I know not what poor Lamb has done to be croaking there. What I think the worst part of the anti-Jacobin abuse is the lumping together of men of such opposite principles: this was stupid."[4]

But Lamb, as we now realize, was eminently worthy of the anti-radical satire. Lamb was friends with Coleridge, Southey, and Lloyd because he staunchly shared their views. And Lamb published in *Monthly Magazine* because he espoused its ideals. Add Lamb's subtle understanding of Priestley, Unitarianism, and sensibility, and you have a man avidly concerned with liberal politics.[5]

Lamb was no Godwin, though, or Blake—a fiery radical. (Nor were, soon enough, Coleridge and Southey, who migrated toward the Right; nor Lloyd, who pulled back from the Left after the Gillray cartoon.) Lamb's politics were complicated by his employment for the East India Company as well as his love of domesticity and nationalism. Lamb, aware of these tensions, dramatized them in his mature work.

About three weeks after Lamb wrote Coleridge the breakup letter, in early July 1798, he started a close epistolary relationship with Southey. Lamb had met Southey in the winter of 1795–96, when Southey had traveled from Bristol to London to retrieve his fellow Pantisocrat Coleridge from the Salutation and Cat. But Lamb didn't get to know him until the late summer and fall of 1797, through their mutual dealings with Lloyd.

When Southey met Coleridge at Oxford in 1794, he was the straight man to his new friend's hyperbolic passion and manic wit.[6] The two shared a thirst for reform, and Southey looked the part of the young rabble-rouser. He was tall, longhaired and, when Coleridge met him, bearded. Henry Crabb Robinson said he resembled Shelley, the poster child of radical idealism.[7] (Just as Shelley was expelled from Oxford for writing "The Necessity of Atheism," so Southey was ousted from Westminster for editing the *Flagellant*, opposed to flogging and other pedagogical oppressions.) Byron found Southey the "best-looking bard" he had "seen for some time": "To have that poet's head and shoulders, I would almost have written his Sapphics. He is certainly a prepossessing person to look on, and a man of talent."[8] Duncan Wu saw in Southey's "luxuriant mane of hair, his large brown eyes and long face" an image of an "exceedingly well-bred Afghan hound."[9] The young Southey cultivated a heart as fiery as his appearance. He was rarely without Goethe's *Werther*, about a young man so lovelorn he kills himself. Southey didn't shy away from traditionally feminine behaviors. His friendship with Coleridge was very weepy, and Southey once sashayed through Bristol wearing women's clothes.[10]

But the over-long nose gave Southey's face a workmanlike quality, and his work ethic is what he is largely remembered for, aside from his relationship to Coleridge and his being the first to print the *Three Bears*. When Wordsworth mocked Southey for being unused to inspired panting, he had in mind Southey's breakneck composing pace. Even before Coleridge met him, Southey had already written ten thousand lines of his epic *Joan of Arc*. Coleridge found the poem overly methodical: Southey "does not possess opulence

*Robert Southey*, by Robert Hancock. (© National Portrait Gallery, London.)

of Imagination, lofty-paced Harmony, or that *toil* of thinking, which is necessary in order to plan *a Whole*."[11]

By this time, December 1796, Coleridge needed this definition of Southey to justify his part in the severing of the friendship. On his side, Southey found Coleridge too volatile. Southey was simply more pragmatic and more pleased with domesticity. He enjoyed his marriage with Edith Fricker in a way Coleridge never could with Edith's sister Sara. Southey's stability served Coleridge well later on, when he took care of Coleridge's wife and children while Coleridge was careening from Germany to Malta to the Lakes to London.

History has not been kind to Southey. Aside from being crowded out of the canon by gigantically talented friends, he faltered politically as he aged. After being named poet laureate in 1813, he wrote to the prime minister, Lord

Liverpool, that reforming journalists, if they attacked the crown too aggressively, should be transported.

In June 1796, after he had met Southey briefly the winter before, Lamb wrote to Coleridge of his admiration for *Joan of Arc*: "I have been delighted, amazed. I had not presumed to expect of any thing of such excellence from Southey. Why the poem is alone sufficient to redeem the character of the age we live in from the imputation of degenerating in Poetry. . . . The subject is well chosen. It opens well. . . . On the whole, I expect Southey **one** day to rival Milton" (*M,* 1:15–16).

Young men emit such exaggeration of their friends' genius in hopes of elevating themselves through the association, and Lamb was not immune. In his correspondence with Southey, he quickly became a more accurate assessor of Southey's poetic talent.

In his response to Southey's "The Ruined Cottage," a Wordsworthian tale of rural suffering, Lamb praises "picture-work and circumstances," strong imagery and particular detail, while chafing at clichéd plotting and sentimentality. He finds Southey's depiction of Joanna, a young woman cruelly seduced, "too trite," and wearies of Southey's overuse of "the tale of ruined Innocence" (*M,* 1:137). Lamb discovers similar fault in Southey's "The Wedding," another tragic pastoral. The poem is "defective in pathos" (*M,* 1:140). "The Last of the Family" Lamb also finds stiff, aside from one passage: "And when he came to shake me by the hand, / And spake as kindly to me as he used, / I hardly knew his voice——" (*M,* 1:142). Lamb notes in these lines the uncanniness Wordsworth is so good at, capturing those enigmatic moments that baffle but define us.

Southey misses this intense strangeness in his review of *Lyrical Ballads* in the *Critical Review.* In a letter from November 1798, Lamb accuses his friend of discussing a minor passage in *The Rime of the Ancient Mariner* and thus overlooking "fifty passages as miraculous as the miracles they celebrate." "A spring of love gush'd from my heart, / And I bless'd them unaware" is profoundly "pathetic" to Lamb; it stings him into "high pleasure through sufferings." Southey is "too correct" in his "taste" (Lloyd, by contrast, is "too metaphysical") to sound these psychological depths of Coleridge, as profound as those of Christopher Marlowe, who potently mixes "the ludicrous & the terrible" (*M,* 1:139, 142–43).

Lamb develops this aesthetic in March 1799, in another letter to Southey. He criticizes Southey for concluding his poem "Metrical Letter Written from London" (later titled "To Margaret Hill. Written from London, 1798") with a "cold moral." Southey's dogmatism converts "Religion into mediocre feel-ings," which properly "should burn & glow & tremble." If a poem has a moral, it should be "wrought into the body and the soul, the matter and the tendency . . . not taggd to the end" (*M*, 1:163). Ideas should grow out of the work from the messy ground up, never be imposed from above. "I never judge system-wise of things," Lamb proclaims, "but fasten upon particulars" (*M*, 1:163). Latching onto the concrete becomes Lamb's mature aesthetic: writing that bores into *this* feeling, and no other.

During the summer and fall of 1798, Lamb cultivated simplicity and com-pleted his first and only novel, *A Tale of Rosamund Gray and Old Blind Mar-garet*.[12] The book returns to the world of the Anna sonnets, pastoral Blakes-ware. Lamb got the story from an old folk ballad, "'An old woman cloathed in grey, Whose daughter was charming & young, and she was deluded away By Roger's false flattering tongue'" (*M*, 1:137). The title he borrowed from Lloyd's 1795 poem *Rosamund Gray*.

The tale reminds one of Wordsworth's spare ballads of violated innocence. The sweet, Bible-reading Rosamund, fourteen, lives with her old blind grand-mother in Widford, Hertfordshire. The girl's father fled to another country to escape his debts, and her mother died of a broken heart. In order to pay the father's debts, Grandmother Margaret had to sell everything. She and her granddaughter now live in poverty.

Like Ann Simmons, Rosamund has yellow hair. She is beautiful, "artless, and innocent, meaning no harm," as "affectionate as a smiling infant—play-ful. . . as a weaned lamb." The melancholy caused by her losses deepens her features. "Everybody loved her" (*W*, 1:7).

Allan Clare, possibly a stand-in for Lamb the young suitor, loves her most. Though two years older, and from a family of higher status, Allan is just as "virginal" as Rosamund, and his "temper had a sweet and noble frankness in it." Aside from age and gender, all that separates Allan from Rosamund is complexion. Where hers is fair and melancholy, his expresses "fire and enthu-siasm," and his hair, chestnut, is darker, as are his cheeks, which, like Lamb's, were "ruddy, and tinged with brown" (*W*, 1:10).

Like Lamb, Allan was raised by an older sister, and his mother is dead. (Allan's father is dead, too, as Lamb's soon would be; all three young charac-ters in the book—Rosamund, Allan, and the narrator—are orphaned.) The sister's name is Elinor. She takes a maternal interest in Allan's affection for Rosamund.

One night, Elinor visits Rosamund without Allan. He cannot accompany her because he must meet with an old friend home from school. Allan is so preoccupied with Rosamund, though, that he shows no interest in his friend's life. When Allan departs, the friend is hurt, and sits "down to compose a doleful sonnet about a 'faithless friend'" (*W*, 1:11).

In the wake of Lamb's falling-out with Coleridge, the biographical parallel is strong. Lamb had friendship much on his mind, in particular sympathetic friendship. As the first-person narrator explains, one of life's noblest gifts can be "Friendships of Sentiment," which occur when "two persons of liberal education, like opinions, and common feelings" enjoy a "Variety of Sentiment." So deep is their pleasure, they decide "to look upon the other as the only being in the universe worthy of friendship, or capable of understanding it" (*W*, 1:29). Coleridge and Lamb shared this ideal—and the result was not happy. If your goal is perfection, you fall into a wearisome either/or: either your life is exactly what you want, or it is not. Since life is never exactly what you want, you will be frustrated.

The narrator—who, it turns out, is the hurt friend—explains this flaw in idealized friendship. While the two like-minded idealists are imagining one another as the "solitary receptacles of all that is delicate in feeling, or stable in attachment," "the odds are, that under every green hill, and in every crowded street, people of equal worth are to be found, who do more good in their generation, and make less noise in the doing of it" (*W*, 1:29).

*Rosamund Gray* is more than sentimental pastoral longing. It dramatizes Lamb's transition from his youthful idealism to a generous skepticism. In questioning the friendship of sentiment, his narrator doesn't dispel its worth; he suggests that there are other ways to appreciate others.

The night after Rosamund visits with Elinore, and Allan is cool toward the narrator, a tragedy, as starkly random as Mary Lamb grabbing a knife and stabbing her mother, happens. Electrified with her love for Allan and new friendship with Elinor, Rosamund sneaks out of her cottage after dark. She crosses paths with one Matravis, of whom we have heard only one insignificant mention. He rapes Rosamund. Margaret dies during the night, out of worry for her lost granddaughter. Trauma kills Rosamund soon after. Then Elinor dies.

By the standards of a traditional plot, *Rosamund Gray* fails. To bring in a minor character near the end of the story to cause a major conflict constitutes a perverse deus ex machina as jarring as it is nondramatic. But if we view the brutal intrusion of Matravis as a correlative of Mary's violent eruption, the narrative aptly renders a psyche shaken and terrified.

Years after the terrible events, the narrator returns to his childhood village to brood over his losses. He runs into Allan, melancholy over his own bereavements. They renew their friendship. Not as Friends of Sentiment, but as two sad and abandoned men needing companionship. The book closes with the two witnessing the death of Matravis. His repentance, on the verge of his expected death and so many years after his horrific act, feels meaningless.

In admiring *Rosamund Gray*'s "knowledge of the sweetest, and deepest parts of our nature!" Shelley misses the point.[13] The novel might delve into the "deepest parts" of our being, but it does not find them sweet. The novel depicts Lamb's lost idealism and his struggle with a dark, broken, excruciating world.

# CHAPTER 13

# Quakers

In his encomium to *Rosamund Gray*, Shelley declares that Lamb reinforces his own aspirations toward "higher objects" than "fame."[1] In mid- to late August 1798, not long after the publication of the novel, another young man admired Lamb's nobility. This was Robert Lloyd, Charles's younger brother.

Lamb probably met Robert in Birmingham in March 1798. Charles Lloyd was called from London to his home city to tend to his brother James, stricken with paralysis, and Lamb accompanied him. On the way, the two probably stopped in Bristol, where Lamb discussed literary business with Joseph Cottle, publisher of Coleridge and Southey. Through Cottle's arrangement, Lamb sat for his first extant portrait, by Robert Hancock. The artist chalked Lamb's profile in red, brown, and black. Lamb's large, hooked nose dominates his face, and his one eye showing is neutral, looking not to look. Coleridge believed the portrait accurate.

Upon reaching the Lloyd family mansion in Birmingham, known as Bingley House, Lamb became intimate with Charles's many siblings, as well as with their Quaker religion. After Charles, the next oldest was James. Two years later he recovered movement and joined the army, only to be extricated by his anxious parents, whereupon he became a dandy. Robert followed; his parents hoped he would thrive in the drapery trade. Then there was Thomas, sent to America for business. Plumsted next; Lamb liked his impetuousness

*Charles Lamb*, by Robert Hancock. (© National Portrait Gallery, London.)

and love of Shakespeare. Six girls, all younger than the boys, completed the sprawling family. The oldest was Priscilla, who married Wordsworth's brother Christopher. Lamb liked Priscilla enough to send her poems, and he socialized with her when she visited London. The next oldest sister was Olivia, whom Lamb kiddingly said he'd like to marry. The other daughters were young children.[2]

The Lloyd Lamb liked most after Charles was Robert, twenty. Like his brother Charles, Robert wanted to escape getting and spending. Charles said no to the bank; Robert wanted to reject the draperies. When Lamb got to know Robert, he was an apprentice at Day and Green, located in Saffron Walden, Essex. The young man looked up to the twenty-three-year-old Lamb, but he also found in Lamb a kindred spirit, someone, like him, prone to melancholy and in need of confession.

Lamb's first extant letter to Robert, from August 1798, reveals their intimacy. Another "calamity" has struck Charles. Mary is "unwell again," "one of her old disorders." But even in this crisis, Lamb has been "thinking about [Robert] with the warmest affection." He is among Lamb's "very dearest friends," and Lamb knows that the younger man will "feel deeply" over Lamb's current difficulty (*M*, 1:133–34).

Robert brings out the philosopher in Lamb, in the sense that Plutarch and Emerson were philosophers: not systematic thinkers, like Priestley, but soul doctors. In his correspondence with Coleridge, Lamb lacked this authority. He might offer literary advice or quibble with a theological point, but he played protégé to the ponderously learned Coleridge. Lamb felt intellectually equal to Southey; however, their somewhat formal relationship didn't invite disclosures of private pains.

Lamb writes to Robert that he will not sink under this latest "misfortune" with Mary. He has been "season'd to such events," and believes he can bear "anything tolerably well" because he has reasonably set his expectations; terrible things have happened, and they will again, so why hope otherwise or be devastated when they occur? Lamb adds to this Stoic sensibility a Kantian one: his sense of duty helps him weather calamity. In making duty itself his "object," he can remove disappointment from the equation. No matter what happens to Mary, it is his duty to care for her. Robert needs to discover his own duty: only this will address his current condition, one Lamb himself knows too well—"the painfulness of vacuity, all its achings, & inexplicable longings—." Lamb recommends religious study, which will discipline Robert's mind "to wait with patience for duties that may be your lot in life." When Robert embraces his duty, he will not "expect too much" from himself (*M*, 1:134). He will conform desire to reality.

Lamb's moral realism breaks from Priestley. Priestley leaned toward utilitarianism: morality is the greatest happiness for the greatest number of people. God directs the universe toward this perfection. We should conform to this plan, and foster happiness. The vision is consequentialist. Good actions issue good results.

Lamb cares little about consequences; the performance of duty is paramount. While Kant founded this deontological morality, the idea also informs the religion Lamb was studying and the Lloyds themselves were practicing: Quakerism. As Quaker theologian Jackie Leech Scully observes, George Fox implored his followers to recognize "God in everyone," and behave accordingly.[3] This statement expresses the essence of Kant's categorical imperative: treat everyone not as a means (to your happiness) but as an end: an intrinsically valuable being. John Woolman, the Quaker theologian Lamb was reading, agrees. We have a moral obligation to abolish slavery because slaves are children of God, not because our good actions might generate more happiness.

In his next letter to Robert, Lamb applies his philosophy of duty to friendship. Lamb suggests a friend might calm Robert, but not necessarily. Friendship can be dangerous, since it can encourage egotism. "We love our friend because he is like ourselves. . . . Say, you love a friend for his moral qualities,—is it not rather because those qualities resemble what you fancy your own?" True friendship occurs when two companions "propose to become mutually of benefit to each other in a moral or religious way." But even this more unselfish form is frequently not "pure," since we value our friend because he is "*ours*," just as we value money or wit or knowledge. "Wherever this sense of appropriation and property enters, so much is to be subtracted from the value of that friendship or virtue." The path to a virtuous friendship is the duty to "do good," expecting nothing in return. Only then can we "bear with contrary dispositions," "be candid and forgiving." This friendship opposes the Friendship of Sentiment, which induces a craving for "communication of . . . feeling" (*M,* 1:134–35).

Lamb fears Robert is now blinding himself to his, Lamb's, faults, and so setting himself up for disappointment. "I know you have chosen to take up an high opinion of my moral worth, but I say it before God, and I do not lie, you are mistaken in me. I could not bear to lay open all my failings to you, for the sentiment of shame would be too pungent." "Friends fall off, friends mistake us, they change, they grow unlike us, they go away, they die" (*M,* 1:135).

Rely on God, who "is everlasting & uncapable of change, and to him we may look with cheerful, unpresumptuous hope, while we discharge the duties of life in situations more untowardly than yours." If you follow God, you will set aside your ego, do as much good as you can, "never be easy to neglect a duty tho' a small one," and "praise God for all, & see his hand in all things, & he will in time raise you up *many friends*—or be himself in stead an unchanging friend—" (*M,* 1: 135).

Lamb's next letter of guidance is a remarkable apotheosis of this deontological vision. To Robert, the world is drained "of all its sweets." Lamb, whose tragedies have given him every reason to agree, bristles.

O Robert, I do'nt know what you call sweet,——Honey & the honey
comb, roses & violets, are yet in the earth. The sun & moon yet reign
in Heaven, & the lesser lights keep up their pretty twinklings——
meats & drinks, sweet sights & sweet smells, a country walk, spring &
autumn, follies & repe[ntan]ce, quarrels & reconcilements, have all a
sweetness by turns— . . . good humor & good nature, friends at home
that love you, & friends abroad that miss you—you possess all these
things, & more innumerable, & these are all sweet things————.
You may extract honey from every thing; do not go a gathering after
gall—. the bees are wiser in their generation than the race of sonnet
writers & complainers, Bowless & Charlotte Smiths, & all that tribe
who can see no joys but what are past, and fill peoples' heads with notions of the Unsatisfying nature of Earthly comforts—. I assure you I
find this world is a very pretty place————. (*M*, 1:144)

Lamb might have included himself in the tribe of sonneteers who long for
an ideal past now irretrievably gone. Now Lamb strives to take the world as
it is, right now, in its glory (honey and the moon) and meanness (quarrels
and follies). Though Lamb had abundant rationale for nostalgic escapism, he
chooses gracious Stoicism, a celebration of life's "is-ness."

Lamb continued to mentor Robert, even if sister Priscilla did not approve.
When Robert was contemplating living with Lamb—a prospect Lamb himself did not favor—Priscilla counseled that Lamb "would not I think by any
means be a person to take up with. He is too much like yourself—he would
encourage those feelings which it certainly is your duty to suppress. Your sta-
tion in life—the duties which are pointed out by that rank in society which
you are destined to fulfill—differ widely from his."[4]
    Priscilla's remarks would have stung Lamb had he known of them. He not
only liked the Lloyds, he also fancied their religion. From the time he wrote
to Coleridge in 1797 that he "had thoughts of becoming a Quaker," to 1822,
when he admitted to Barton that he was "half a Quaker," Lamb remained fascinated by the religion. In his black garb, he looked the part. Lamb admired
the Quaker's ethical integrity and elegant piety, qualities to which he aspired.[5]
But he found the religion strange in its emphasis on characteristics he decidedly lacked: silence and restraint.[6]
    He expresses his contradictory feelings in "A Quaker's Meeting," an Elia
essay from April 1821. Come with "me into a Quaker's meeting," if you wish

to know "what true peace and quiet mean," and "enjoy at once solitude and society," singularity "yet not without some to keep thee in countenance," simplicity in a "composite" (*W,* 2:45).

In praising the noble silence of the Quaker meeting, Elia is ironically hyperbolic. "What is the stillness of the desert, compared with this place? what the uncommunicating muteness of fishes?—here the goddess reigns and revels.—'Boreas, and Cesias, and Argestes loud,' do not with their inter-confounding uproars more augment the brawl—nor the waves of the blown Baltic with their clubbed sounds—than their opposite (Silence her sacred self) is multiplied and rendered more intense by numbers, and by sympathy. She too hath her deeps, that call unto deeps. Negation itself hath a positive more and less; and closed eyes would seem to obscure the great obscurity of midnight" (*W,* 2:45).

We are inside a quiet building of simple worshippers, and Elia jerks our minds out into the desert and deep into the ocean. These comparisons are easy—Quaker meetings are very quiet —next to those that follow. We imagine extremely loud events, only to negate them into extremely quiet events. The wind gods roaring and the wind-whipped Baltic do not louden the brawl, anymore than many silent people in sympathy quieten the silence. Elia then pushes beyond logic: negation, a concept that cannot be qualified (something is either negated or it isn't), he qualifies. Dark negates the light, but closed eyes negate the light more. Silence negates sounds, but Quakers negate it more.

There are two Quaker meetings: the one Elia describes in "A Quaker's Meeting" and the essay itself. The former, Elia tells us, is profoundly silent; the latter, he implies, is symphonic exaggeration. The form is at odds with the content. Which is better? The content, it would seem: the silence of a Quaker meeting is exemplary, since it blends individual and collective. A desert hermit enjoys silence, but the silence of a group of hermits is more powerful. Similarly, the silent reading of a book is enhanced when a friend or spouse sits near.

Elia makes this point repeatedly, not shutting up, challenging content with form. Walking alone in an old cathedral is vulgar compared to several people in the same space choosing to be silent. Holy inscriptions on the walls of Westminster Abbey are inferior to the "naked walls" of the Quaker meeting. The sublimity of ancient ruins themselves are but "insolent decays of mouldering grandeur" when compared to shared silence (*W,* 1:46).

How many ways can Elia say the same thing and still be interesting? His appositive virtuosity is stunning, as if he owns a magical thesaurus that endlessly generates fresh conceptual parallels. If sound, compared to silence, is ignoble, it sure is an exhilarating meanness.

Have the current Quakers retained the nobility of George Fox? Elia has witnessed "a sample of the old Foxian orgasm."

> It was a man of giant stature. . . . I saw him shake all over with the spirit—I dare not say, of delusion. The strivings of the outer man were unutterable—he seemed not to speak, but to be spoken from. I saw the strong man bowed down, and his knees to fail—his joints all seemed loosening. . . . The words he uttered were few, and sound—he was evidently resisting his will—keeping down his own word-wisdom with more mighty effort, than the world's orators strain for theirs. "He had been a WIT in his youth," he told us, with expressions of a sober remorse. And it was not till long after the impression had begun to wear away, that I was enabled, with something like a smile, to recall the striking incongruity of the confession—understanding the term in its worldly acceptation—with the frame and physiognomy of the person before me. . . . By *wit*, even in his youth, I will be sworn he understood something far within the limits of an allowable liberty. (*W,* 2:48)

Here is a witty description of a man, and perhaps a religion, lacking in wit, and with this deficiency comes a deficiency in self-knowledge.

"The Quaker Meeting" covertly celebrates the wisdom of wit. Hyperbole, contradiction, creative repetition: these are exuberant expressions of the intricacy and abundance of the humming human mind, and so throw stolid Quakers in a negative light.

But look at heroic Quaker James Naylor: "What dreadful sufferings, with what patience, he endured even to the boring through of his tongue with red-hot irons without a murmur; and with what strength of mind, when the delusion he had fallen into, which they stigmatised for blasphemy, had given way to clearer thoughts, he could renounce his error, in a strain of the beautifullest humility, yet keep his first grounds, and be a Quaker still!" (*W,* 1:47).

This language is as pellucid, understated, and elegant as Elia's explosions are surreal, over-the-top, and bewildering. Piety and wit tensely sit together. They don't cancel each other out. They invite us to contemplate why they would be together in the first place.

# CHAPTER 14

ⲟⲟⲟ

# *George Dyer*

Throughout the fall of 1798 and the winter of 1799, Lamb debated literature with Southey. He guided Robert Lloyd. He also studied the emblem books of Jacobean poets George Wither and Francis Quarles. He would soon deepen his affection for other British writers of the seventeenth century: the freakish prose stylists Robert Burton and Thomas Browne, the dramatist Fulke Greville. Lamb was working on a drama of his own, titled *Pride's Cure*.

Lamb also completed a theological poem, "Living without God in the World." It is the last of Lamb's tortured spiritual laments. From this time on, his vision grows increasingly comic. Published by Southey in his *Annual Anthology* of 1799, the poem opens with the rugged piety of Hopkins, and the Jesuit poet's vexed syntax.

> Mystery of God! thou brave and beauteous world!
> Made fair with light, and shade, and stars, and flowers;
> Made fearful and august with woods and rocks,
> Jagg'd precipice, black mountain, sea in storms;
> Sun, over all, that no co-rival owns,
> But thro' heaven's pavement rides in despite
> Or mockery of the Littleness of Man!

God made a world dark and light, treacherous and pleasurable. No one knows why. The vertiginous syntax—"Sun, over all, that no co-rival owns / But thro' heaven's pavement rides in despite"—expresses befuddlement (*W,* 5:17).

Lamb discerns a "mighty Arm," by others unseen, that guides the world. Why does man trust in "his mortal strength" to sustain him? Why does he lean on "a shadowy staff . . . of dreams?" (*W,* 5:17).

Lamb is one of these shortsighted men. "We consecrate our total hopes and fears / To idols, flesh and blood, our love (heaven's due), / Our praise and admiration." To worship man instead of God can be glorious, since we acknowledge the glory of God's handiwork. But fealty to man results in more pride. Some men don't worship at all; they affect "Godhead" themselves. These men, like Godwin, overvalue reason and believe mind determines fate. Worse are atheists. Thy reduce "heav'n's roof" to "a painted ceiling hung with lamps." God will destroy these unbelievers (*W,* 1:17).

This poem recalls Lamb's Unitarian conversations back at the Salutation and Cat. He even borrows his title from Priestley's *Letters to a Philosophical Unbeliever.* The lines might be Lamb's response to the *Anti-Jacobin*'s attack.

But the poem is also a personal exploration of the dangers of intellectual pride. When Lamb was completing the poem in November 1798, he was still smarting from the dark fruits of this kind of arrogance. Pride had severed his friendship with Coleridge. It had distanced him from God. He spoke to Robert with the authority of experience: to elevate the self over the universe leads to despair. Only a humble affirmation of what is, which is God, redeems us from solipsistic agony.

Few needed saving more than Lamb, still caring for his senile father, exhausting himself at the office, worrying about whether his sister would go mad and not come back.

If we can accept for a moment Lamb's metaphysical assumptions, that God guides every instant, we should thank the deity for sending George Dyer. In a letter to Southey in which he mentions "Living without God in the World," Lamb describes the night before. He showed Dyer "The Witch" and "The Dying Lover," extracts from the play he was working on. Dyer "could not comprehend how that could be poetry, which did not go upon ten feet, as George & his predecessors had taught it to do; so George read me some lectures of the distinguishing qualities of the Ode, the Epigram, & the Epic, & went home to illustrate his doctrine by correcting a proof sheet of his own Lyrics." George "writes odes, where the rhimes, like fashionable man & wife, keep a comfortable distance of 6 or 8 lines apart, & calls that observing the

**Laws** of **verse**—. George tells you, before he recites, that you must listen with great attention, or you'll miss the rhymes—I did so, and found them pretty Exact—." Dyer also admires his own metaphorizing. "George speaking of the **Dead Ossian** exclaimeth, 'Dark are the Poet's eyes'—. I humbly represented to him that his own Eyes were dark, & many a living Bard's beside—& recommended '**Clos'd** are the Poet's eyes'—. But that would not do—I found there was an antithesis between the darkness of his Eyes, & the splendor of his Genius—& I acquiesced" (*W,* 1:151).

This is the first of many gently comic portraits of Dyer, a Christ's alum and Cambridge classics scholar twenty years Lamb's senior. To Lamb, Dyer was an unwittingly entertaining eccentric whose blend of absentmindedness, poor eyesight, pedantry, poor hygiene, benevolence, and naïveté was irresistible. Though he was a respected political radical and generous supporter of younger firebrands such as Coleridge and Southey, Dyer is largely remembered as a humorless, over-composing poet of middling talent with a genius, though he didn't know it, for slapstick.[1]

Dyer was once "seen in Fleet Street without his stockings, and he took off his inexpressibles to give them to a poor man who was wretchedly clad." At a party he "took up a coal-scuttle instead of his hat, and its contents fell into his neck and down his back." At "his own table [he] put his fingers into the mustard-pot, mistaking it for the sugar basin."[2] Dyer was halfway home from a dinner at Leigh Hunt's when he realized he was only wearing one shoe. He returned to the Hunts' after midnight to retrieve the other. He found it under the dinner table and went on his way.[3]

Of a day you might witness Dyer "with a classical volume in his hand, and another in his pocket, walking slowly along Fleet Street or its neighborhood, unconscious of gazers, cogitating over some sentence. . . . You might meet him murmuring to himself in a low voice, and apparently tasting the flavor of his words."[4] Dyer possessed a "gaunt, awkward form, set off by trowsers too short, like those outgrown by a gawky lad, and a rusty coat much too large for the wearer, hanging about him like those garments which the aristocratic Milesian peasantry prefer to the most comfortable rustic dress; his long head silvered over with short yet straggling hair, and his dark eyes glistening with faith and wonder."[5]

Lamb once "taxed" Dyer's "bland unconsciousness of evil" to "the utmost by suddenly asking what he thought of the murderer Williams, who, after destroying two families in Ratcliffe Highway, had broken prison by suicide, and whose body had just before been conveyed in shocking procession to its cross-road

*George Dyer*, by Elizabeth Cristall, after J. Cristall.
(© The National Portrait Gallery, London.)

grave?" This "desperate attempt to compel the gentle optimist to speak ill of a
mortal creature produced no happier success than the answer, 'Why, I should
think, Mr. Lamb, he must have been rather an eccentric character.'"[6]

Lamb prized Dyer's eccentricity but knew enough of the older man's political work of the 1790s to admit to Coleridge in 1800 that the "oftener"

he saw Dyer, the "more deeply" he "admire[s] him." While at Cambridge, to which he gained entrance as a Christ's Grecian, Dyer met the radical reformer William Frend, who lost his residency when he converted from the Church of England to Unitarianism. (Coleridge was at Cambridge during Frend's university trial and was an ardent defender of the man; in Frend's London lodgings Wordsworth met William Godwin, as well as Dyer.) Under Frend's influence, Dyer became a radical himself, and after a stint tutoring the children of Robert Robinson (a Dissenting friend of Priestley), he moved to London and joined the radical circles there. He was among the Salutation and Cat group (Lamb met him at the pub in 1796), funded Coleridge after his paper the *Watchman* went under (though he had little money himself), and wrote *Dissertation on Benevolence*, which argues that goodness is best propagated through small communities, like his own at the Salutation and the proposed one of the Pantisocracy.

Dyer's great contribution to classical studies was his edition of Dr. James Valpy's 143-volume collection of Latin classics, which took him eleven years—1819–30—to complete. In contributing all that "is original" to that famous Valpy collection, he deprived himself of sight. Moreover, he published a biography of Robert Robinson—Wordsworth considered it one of the finest in that genre—and he completed a definitive history of Cambridge University.

Dyer appears prominently in Elia's essay from October 1820, "Oxford in the Vacation."[7] This is the second of his Elia essays, following "The South-Sea House." In the opening of the Oxford piece, he assumes that readers want to know "*Who is Elia?*" Perhaps, since his last essay described an "old house of business," the reader might think he is "one of the self-same college—a votary of the desk—a notched and cropt scrivener—one that sucks his sustenance, as certain sick people are said to do, through a quill." Elia does "agnize something of the sort" (*W,* 2:7). (Note the pun in "agnize": "agnes," or Lamb.)

Ironically, his job, the contemplation of "indigos, cottons, raw silks, piece-goods, flowered or otherwise," is a muse. Daytime labor

in the first place ******* and then it sends you home with such increased appetite to your books **** not to say, that your outside sheets, and waste wrappers of foolscap, do receive into them, most kindly and naturally, the impression of sonnets, epigrams, *essays*—so that the very parings of a counting-house are, in some sort, the settings up of

an author. The enfranchised quill, that has plodded all the morning
among the cart-rucks of figures and cyphers, frisks and curvets so at
its ease over the flowery carpet-ground of a midnight dissertation.—It
feels its promotion. **** So that you see, upon the whole, the literary
dignity of *Elia* is very little, if at all, compromised in the condescen-
sion. (*W,* 2:8)

Elia composes in the interstice between his work periods, when most employees rest. He transforms his daily grind into preparation for his passion. The
indigos become raw material for the "flowery carpet-ground" of his essays;
scribbling in ledgers is practice for the literary quill. The odd gaps in the passage, signaled by asterisks, make concrete the gaps in which Elia writes. That
they come in seemingly random places suggests the unpredictability of the
muse's visitations.

Since Elia writes best in the "in-between" times, with work behind and
ahead, he values holidays, and therefore he laments the recent "abolition" "of
those consolatory interstices, and sprinklings of freedom, through the four
seasons." These were once "*red-letter days,*" when writings pumped blood, and
now they are "*dead-letter days,*" cadaverous prose (*W,* 2:8).

Elia is not the man to decide when holidays should take place, since he is
no archbishop, though he is right now where such men study, the Bodleian
Library of Oxford. Here, just as he transforms his labor into his fancy, he
converts from clerk into university man. He "can . . . play the gentleman,
enact the student" (*W,* 2:9). Elia turns the iron "is" into the pliable "perhaps."
Elia is a scribe; he *might* be a writer. He is a vacationer at Oxford; he *could*
be a student. In both cases, the transmutation occurs in a jocund interstice
between the rule-driven worlds of conventional life.

Elia loves the libraries at Oxford, "repositories of mouldering learning."
He doesn't wish to touch the old pages, though. Such tactility would ground
his imagination. He would rather walk among the shelves and "inhale [the]
learning" (*W,* 2:10). Such breathing in of the immaterial vitality of the imagined past: this is Eden.

Who is the opposite of Elia, a "Herculanean raker" among the actual objects of the past? "G.D.," George Dyer himself, whom Elia glimpses among
the shelves. Unlike the unmoored Elia, slipping through gaps, transforming
actual into possible, G.D. hovers in one nook, "busy as a moth over some
rotten archive, rummaged out of some seldom-explored press." "He is grown
almost into a book" (*W,* 2:10).

D. is the inverse of Elia. While Elia moves between one state and another, D. is static. But since both men value the interior over the exterior, they are both free of the stresses of the workday world. Where Elia transforms work into preparation for play, D. lives so vividly inside his own head that he is oblivious to his surroundings. Back in London's Clifford-Inn, "like a dove on the asp's nest, he has long taken up his unconscious abode, amid an incongruous assembly of attorneys, attorneys' clerks, apparitors, promoters, vermin of the law, among whom he sits, 'in calm and sinless peace'" (*W,* 2:10).

When Elia greets him at the Oxford library, "D. started like an unbroke heifer." But he would have done the same anywhere, since all locales are identical to a man who dwells inside his own head. So "absent" is he in relation to externals that he "made a call the other morning at our friend *M.'s* in Bedford-square; and, finding nobody at home, was ushered into the hall, where, asking for pen and ink, with great exactitude of purpose he enters me his name in the book . . . and takes his leave with many ceremonies, and professions of regret." Then, "some two or three hours after, his walking destinies returned him into the same neighbourhood again, and again the quiet image of the fire-side circle at *M.'s* . . . striking irresistibly on his fancy, he makes another call . . . and disappointed a second time, inquires for pen and paper as before: again the book is brought, and in the line just above that in which he is about to print his second name (his rescript)—his first name (scarce dry) looks out upon him like another Sosia, or as if a man should suddenly encounter his own duplicate!" (*W,* 2:11).

D.'s "absenteeism" is not trifling. Distant from matter, he is close "with the Lord." He walks down the street recognizing no one. Inside he "is on Mount Tabor—or Parnassus—or cosphered with Plato" (*W,* 2:11).

D.'s is the true vacation in Oxford. He vacates space and time, negates them, to visit the spiritual presences in his head. He turns his own noggin into the kind of interstice that fascinates Elia, where a thing becomes its opposite.

# CHAPTER 15

## *Manning*

As Lamb emerged from the serious, nature-based Romanticism of Coleridge and Wordsworth (the "Two Noble Englishman" who split as soon as they reached "german Earth"), he migrated toward a more urban and comic vision. The catalyst for this shift, however, was not Dyer. It was Thomas Manning, the Cambridge math tutor and sinologist whom Lamb first met in December 1799.

Between this time and November 1798, when Lamb first humorously described Dyer, a major event lightened Lamb's mood: he reunited with Mary. The death of his father made this possible. Lamb doesn't mention his father's dying in an extant letter; nor does he describe Mary's homecoming. We do learn in a letter to Robert Lloyd, dated April 23, 1799, that Lamb's parents are no longer alive. (If they were, Lamb tells his protégé, he would "do more things to please them.") Lamb also remarks that it is a holiday (St. George's Day), so he and Mary will dine early, and "have a long walk afterwards" (*M*, 1:169).

In addition to reuniting with Mary, Lamb moved to new lodgings, 36 Chapel Street, only a few doors from where he had lived with his father. The old place carried bad memories, and he wanted a fresh start with Mary. He got it. Mary was her old self again, and had been since January, when Lamb wrote Southey that "Mary was never in better health or spirits than now"

(*M*, 1:160). Perhaps to celebrate her return, in October they took a trip to Hertfordshire, the stomping ground of their youth.

As long as he and Mary shared a roof—just the two of them, with no others to care for—Lamb never had to worry about the terrible loneliness that hollowed him during the months before and after his mother's death. But now Lamb had friends, too. There was his growing friendship with Dyer, and he and Southey were becoming more intimate, at least in their correspondence.

In March 1799, Lamb let his bizarre wit loose on the serious Southey. Commenting on Southey's poem to a spider, he veers into other verses on animals. Pindar "apostrophised a fly," Burns "hath his mouse and louse," and Coleridge "hath made overtures of intimacy to a jackass." Lamb half-seriously proposes that Southey write poems "to a rat, to a toad, to a cockchafer, to a mole." But, as Southey might have learned from Lamb's animal-loving brother, moles are treated terribly; people bake them "alive by a slow oven-fire to cure consumption." It's okay, though, to mistreat rats, since they are "the most despised and contemptible parts of Gods earth. I killed a rat the other day by punching him to pieces." But this was not guiltless after all: I "feel a weight of blood upon me to this hour." Now that he is thinking of cruelty to animals, Lamb revises his proposal. Southey should compose poems to mistreated animals, and could accompany the verses "with plates descriptive of animal torments, cooks roasting lobsters, fishmongers crimping skates, &c, &c." (*M*, 1:165). No wonder Southey, chasing such ambiguous riffs, said to his wife that Lamb likes to laugh at everything.

Around this time, unbeknownst to any but his closest friends, Lamb fell in love. But he didn't risk having his heart broken. He loved from afar, never even conversing with the object of his passion, Hester Savory, the daughter of Joseph Savory, a goldsmith. She was a Quaker two years Lamb's junior. We would know nothing about her, quite likely, had Lamb not written a poem about her in the spring of 1803, a month after she died, of fever, after having married Charles Stoke Dudley eight months earlier. He sent this poem on the "death of a young Quaker" to Thomas Manning, explaining she was a woman he was in love with while he lived in Pentonville, "tho' I had never spoken to her in my life" (*M*, 2:107). Hester had "a bright-eyed gypsy face such as we know so well from the canvas of Reynolds."[1]

Lamb first published "Hester" in his 1818 *Works*. Unlike the nostalgic Anna sonnets, this poem about lost love is vibrant and hopeful, perhaps because the love remained virtual. So vivid was Hester that Lamb cannot think about her lying cold in a "wormy bed." He sees the "springy motion in her gait / A rising step" that "did indicate / Of pride and joy no common rate, / That flush'd her spirit." Though brought up as a "cool" Quaker, she was warm.

> A waking eye, a prying mind;
> A heart that stirs, is hard to bind;
> A hawk's keen sight ye cannot blind;
>      Ye could not Hester's! (*W,* 5:30)

Hopefully Lamb will meet his "sprightly neighbor" on death's "unknown and silent shore" as he once encountered her during a summer morning on Chapel Street.

> When from thy cheerful eyes a ray
> Hath struck a bliss upon the day,
> A bliss that would not go away,
>      A sweet forewarning? (*W,* 5:30)

If this poem imagines the "might be" of meeting Hester in the afterlife, an essay of February 14, 1819, "Valentine's Day," speculates on what "could have been" had Lamb actually expressed his love to the pretty Quaker. On this day celebrating romantic love, young men and women fixate on their doors: "Not many sounds in life, and I include all urban and rural sounds, exceed in interest a *knock at the door*," and of all knocks, the "welcomest in expectation is the sound that ushers in, or seems to usher in, a Valentine" (*W,* 2:56).

Lamb imagines a young man in love, one E.B., certainly a stand-in for himself. The man lived across from a young maiden, "all joyousness and innocence." They were not known to one another, but E.B. had admired her "kindly face" for a while. To repay her for simply passing him in the street, he decided to make her an anonymous Valentine. An accomplished artist, he fashioned a gorgeous card and sent it by common post. Without the woman knowing, he watched her receive his romantic missive. "She danced about, not with light love or foolish expectations, for she had no lover; or, if she had, none she knew that could have created those bright images which delighted her. It was more like some fairy present; a God-send, as our familiarly pious ancestors termed a benefit received, where the benefactor was unknown" (*W,* 2:57).

This wistful Lamb fantasy shows the ecstasy of breaking the expected connection between giving and receiving. Here the man gives, but with no hope of getting back; the woman receives, but she has no way to reciprocate. In this rift in conventional causality—I do this; thus, that follows—thrives possibility. There are a thousand ways the beloved might feel upon receiving the valentine; the lover will never know. There are multitudes of lovers who might have sent the card; the beloved will never learn.

This secret Valentine functions like an Elia essay. It is a text from an unknowable source (we can't "know" Elia because he doesn't really exist); its import is ambiguous (Elia's prose is agile to the point of blurriness); and it resists final analysis (and so leaves readers entertaining scores of interpretations).

When Lamb sent his verse on Hester to Manning in 1803, the mathematician had replaced Coleridge as his closest friend and most frequent correspondent.[2] Manning served as the math tutor of Charles Lloyd, who matriculated at Caius College, Cambridge, in 1798. Lloyd became friends with this brilliant polymath only three years his senior, and he wanted Lamb to meet him. Lloyd was now emotionally stable. He was finally, and happily, married to Sophia Pemberton. (In the end the two did elope, though she had to marry Charles by proxy, with Southey standing in.) She was now pregnant. After the visit, Lamb wrote to Robert Lloyd, "No husband & wife can be happier, than Sophia & your Brother appear to be in each other's company" (*M*, 1:176). Sophia and Charles lived in the house of Mr. Styles on Jesus Lane. Here they watched Lamb meet Manning.

Born in 1772, Manning was the second son of the rector of Diss. After being educated in Norfolk, in 1790 he matriculated at Cambridge, in particular to Gonville and Caius Colleges, where he studied mathematics. The young Manning bristled at subscribing to the Thirty-Nine Articles of the Church of England, then a requirement for graduation. (As it would be until 1856.) Affecting, like Lamb, "the plain dress of Quakers, and with it adopting their strong repugnance to oaths and tests," Manning refused to sign the articles, and so he did not graduate.[3] He remained in Cambridge, however, setting up as a tutor above Mr. Crisp's barbershop on St. Mary's Passage. Between his sessions preparing students for their math exams, he composed a two-volume introduction to arithmetic and algebra.

Fashion and irreverence weren't the only things Manning shared with Lamb. He also had dark features, a taste for the odd, a love of drink, and a penchant for quirky wordplay. (Among his papers—recently discovered in a bookseller's cupboard—are epigrams on the conditions of the Cambridge toilets.) But Manning was much more than a convivial and eccentric wit. In addition to mathematics, Manning had a scholarly interest in China. At a time when most Britons interacted with the East in the service of pecuniary

*Portrait of Thomas Manning,* oil on canvas, c. 1805.
(Courtesy of the Royal Asiatic Society.)

interests, Manning's interest was free of greed—and of prejudice. He thought
he might find in China valuable lessons for the English. He hoped to understand "a moral view of China; its manners; the actual degree of happiness
the people enjoy; their sentiments and opinions, so far as they influence life;
their literature; their history; the causes for their stability and vast population,

their minor arts and contrivances; what there might be in China to serve as a model for imitation, and what to serve as a beacon to avoid."[4]

After studying Chinese and medicine in Paris, Manning sailed to Asia, where he resided from 1807 to 1817. He lived in Canton, Macao, Calcutta, and Beijing. In 1811–12, Manning became the first Englishman to travel to Lhasa. There he met the seven-year-old ninth Dalai Llama, whose "beautiful and interesting face engrossed" all of Manning's "attention." He found it "poetically and affectingly beautiful." The Englishman also admired this "well-educated princely" child's "simple and unaffected manners."[5]

The linguistic virtuosity required to negotiate so many different Asian regions—Manning was said to know fifteen languages—is remarkable enough. But Manning's courage and resourcefulness are stunning. In one instance, after having served as a doctor to Lhasa's Chinese rulers, he fell under suspicion and imagined his execution: "I put myself in imagination in the situation of the prisoner accused; I suppose myself innocent; I look around; I have no resource, no refuge; instruments of torture [and] . . . of execution are brought by florid, high-cheeked, busy, grinning, dull-hearted men. . . . The friendlessness, this nothingness of the prisoner is what sickens me to think of." Will he be able to submit to his own death with "firmness and manliness?"[6]

Manning obviously escaped his own execution, but not without first intensely imagining, as a poet might, what it would feel like to face certain death. Manning possessed a talent for this sort of Keatsian empathy, and he didn't express it only in Asia. Around the time he met Lamb, his perception was as sensitive as his new friend's, Wordsworth's, or Coleridge's. In the summer of 1799, spending time in Penrith with the newly married Lloyds, he is alert to nuance. He admires Charles's "ardent, warm, & generous disposition" but balks at his "excessive & morbid sensibility." Priscilla shares her brother's ardor; her talent for restraint and understanding, though, grant her a simplicity he lacks. These qualities have emerged during a "tour of the lakes."[7]

With the Lloyds, Manning ascends Mount Skiddaw, a favorite climb of Wordsworth. On the way up, though, Manning observes people more than scenery. Priscilla's endurance impresses him but he relishes the "pleasure" he has in "giving her that support, without which I believe she could not have" reached the peak.[8]

Manning and the Lloyds walk to Ambleside by way of Windermere. They run into rain and find themselves "enveloped with mountains & clouds which sometimes descended & blew across us. But at last . . . the sky cleared

& it became a beautiful evening." When they reach Ambleside, they find Mrs. Lloyd, Charles and Priscilla's mother, "ill from her apprehensions about us. She is not sufficiently romantic perhaps for such strangely acting people as we are." Though he appreciates nature's authentic power, Manning is aware that he and the Lloyds are performing a kind of "poetic" behavior, perhaps a bit tongue-in-cheek.[9]

Manning admits he is "impelled unswervingly to strange things." However, he has "nothing, absolutely nothing, in [his] constitution of what is called crack-brained."[10] An anecdote from Sir John Davis, a noted sinologist who was working for the East India Company when Manning was in Canton, reveals Manning's mix of the weird and the wily. "One day roused by a strange shouting I went out and discovered it was Manning, who, wishing to cross [a river] and finding nobody who would attend to him, commenced a series of howls like a dog, supplemented by execrations derived from the Chinese vernacular. This led our attendant mandarins very naturally to infer that he was mad, and they lost no time in conveying him over the river to the other side, which was all he wanted." Davis found that Manning "was seldom serious, and did not often argue any matter gravely, but in a tone of banter in which he humorously maintained the most monstrous paradoxes, his illustrations being highly laughable."[11]

There was another side of Manning, however, that linked him more with the mesmerizing Coleridge than the nonsensical Lamb. Thomas Allsop—radical, stockbroker, and disciple of Coleridge—described this lyrical Manning: "Once, and only once, did I witness an outburst of his unembodied spirit, when such was the effect of his more than magnetic, his magic power." In Manning's presence, Allsop and others at a social gathering were "rapt and carried aloft into seventh heaven. He seemed to see and to convey to us clearly . . . what was passing in the presence of the Great Disembodied ONE. I am unwilling to admit the influence this wonderful man had over his auditors, as I cannot at all convey an adequate notion or even image of his extraordinary and very peculiar powers."Allsop also noted of Manning that "few persons had so great a share of Lamb's admiration, for to few did he vouchsafe manifestations of his very extraordinary powers."[12] Lamb found Manning to be "a man in a thousand," and "far beyond **Coleridge** or any other man in **power of impressing**—when he gets you alone, he can act the wonders of Egypt" (*M*, 1:271).

Part of Manning's charm, a friend observed, was the "beauty in his face." Lamb saw it differently. He liked Manning's "fine, *dogmatical, sceptical* face," most flattered by "punch-Light" (*M*, 1:221). He also relished Manning's lazy streak. If Manning had "put forth his full strength," no "man of genius" would be at "all comparable to him" (*M*, 1:271). But he would not have been as funny.

Lamb's first meeting with Manning at the Lloyd abode went well. Upon returning to Chapel Street and Mary (she apparently did not accompany him to Cambridge), he wrote his new friend. Might they begin a regular correspondence? Would Manning visit him in London? His tone is demure. Lamb doesn't feel comfortable letting loose his outlandishness. Manning's reply, which was slow to arrive, is at first perfunctory. But he shatters convention at the close and sets the zany pattern for the remainder of the correspondence. May God keep you "from all evil things, that walk upon the face of the Earth—I mean Night-mares, Hobgoblins, & Spectres." This catalogue inspires a wonderfully odd postscript: "(*Here is a page of drawings of queer beasts.*). I wish I could draw. It will not do."[13]

Unfortunately, the drawings have gone missing, but they inspired Lamb's own absurdities. "Do you continue to bewilder your company with your thousand faces, running down thro' all the Keys of Ideotism . . . from the smile and the glimmer of half-sense, and quarter-sense, to the grin and the hanging lip of Betty Foy's own Johnny. ?—" If Manning's impersonations are good, his beasts, alas, are not: "How unlike the great originals were your petty terrors in the Post-[s]cript, not fearful enough to make a fairy shudder, or a Lilliputian fine lady, eight months full of child, miscarry." To this surrealism, Lamb adds, and then subtracts, a pun: "I long to see your own honest Manning-face again—I did not mean a pun,—your *man's* face, you will be apt to say, I know your wicked will to pun—" (*M*, 1:177).

Lamb would have evolved his bizarre wit on his own, but Manning evoked a comic energy from Lamb that he wasn't aware he possessed. Over the next twenty years, Lamb intensified this vigor until it condensed into the essays of Elia. Lamb's letters to Manning are test runs for his mature style, in some cases serving as first drafts for Elian essays.

Lamb's development as a writer depended on the post. Part of the impetus for Lamb's epistolary virtuosity was his historical moment, when letter writing provided more than information. The genre had risen to confession, the more vulnerable the better.

In 1720 Ralph Allen of Bath signed a seven-year contract to manage the Cross and Bye Posts. The business was barely breaking even. Allen made

it profitable through a more rigorous system for documenting recipients'
payments. By removing the requirement that all mail go through London,
he made the post more efficient. Allen—a model for Fielding's Squire All-
worthy—inaugurated a golden age of letter writing. A new genre emerged:
the familiar letter, composed with an eye toward a larger readership than one,
and possibly publication. Pope, Swift, Lady Montagu, and Samuel Johnson
produced epistles of sophisticated common sense.[14]

By the time of Lamb's first extant letters, 1796, the post was even more
reliable. The mail coach had been introduced in 1784. As for the Augustans,
the letter for Lamb was art, but Lamb, like the other great epistolary writers
of the Romantic age, valued sensibility more than reason. The most powerful form of feeling was the raw monologue, best if modeled on the vertigo of
drunk-talk.

On August 21, 1800, Lamb writes Manning of their mutual friend George
Dyer. I have been studying best how to beg, Lamb exaggerates, by studying
Pliny, but find no example in this ancient sufficient to my purposes, so I must
proceed barbarically. He requires an algebra text, not for himself but for Dyer.
Dyer has been diverted from his literary pursuits by a paradox stated by William Frend. Frend claims that the "negative quantities" of mathematicians
are "merae nugae" (mere nonsense), "scarcely" among "rerum naturae" (the
things of nature), and thus too mysterious for a rational Unitarian theologian
(*M*, 1:228).

> However the dispute, once set a-going, has seizd violently on Georges
> Pericranic, and it is necessary for his health that he should speedily
> come to a resolution of his doubts—. He goes about teasing his friends
> with his new mathematics—. He even frantically talks of purchasing
> **Manning's** Algebra, which shews him far gone, for, to my knowl-
> edge, he has not been master of seven shillings a good time. George's
> Pockets &. . . . 's brains are two things in nature which do not abhor
> a vacuum. . . . Now, if you could step in, in this trembling suspense of
> his reason, and he should find on **Saturday** morning, lying for him at
> the **Porter's Lodge Clifford's Inn**—his safest address—M'g's Algebra,
> with a neat manuscription in the blank leaf, running thus, "**From the
> Author!**"—it might save his wits and restore the unhappy author to
> those studies of Poetry & Criticism which are at present suspended, to
> the infinite regret of the whole Literary World. (*M*, 1:228–29)

Dyer is a Shandyean hobby-horseman, whose sudden obsession with a mathematical riddle causes him to toss aside literature. He will purchase an algebra book even though he has no money. Nature might hate a vacuum but Dyer's pockets, empty, do not, nor do the brains of . . . who? Perhaps Lamb, suggesting that his words are nothings. If so, the lacuna where his name should be is apt, an erasure of his "I"; but the statement, if intended, is also ironic, since Lamb's words are anything but vacuous. Lamb imagines Manning toting his book to the inn where Dyer sometimes stays. Though Dyer desires a math book devoted to no-nonsense problem solving, his own reason is tremblingly suspended, and his life is so chaotic he lacks a stable address. To restore Dyer to his wits and literary pursuits is not really the worthiest goal, since the absence of Dyer's poetry and criticism would decidedly not cause much pain.

Two days later, Lamb extends his Dyer routine. This math-hankering literary critic is now an Archimedes as well as a Zoroastrian priest of high magic. He is also a Tyco Brahe and a Copernicus. In contrast, Manning the mathematician is "the darling" of the nine muses, and midwife "to their wandring babe," Orpheus, son of Calliope. But perhaps Manning is also capable of birthing another babe of the muses, Dyer himself, who still needs to be returned to his literary pursuits.

> If thou couldst contrive to wheel up thy dear carcase on the **Monday**, and after dining with us on **Tripe**, Calves' kidneys, or whatever else the Cornucopia of St. Clare may be willing to pour out on the occasion, might we not adjourn together to the **Heathen's?**—thou with thy Black Backs, and I with some innocent volume of the Bell Letters, Shenstone, or the Like——it would make him wash his old flannel gown, (that has not been washed, to my knowledg, since it has been *his*,—O the long time!)—with **Tears** of joy—. Thou shouldst settle his Scruples, and unravel his cobwebs, & spunge off the sad stuff that weighs upon his dear wounded Pia Mater—thou shouldst restore light to his Eyes, and him to his friends and the Public. . . Parnassus should shower her civic crowns upon thee for saving the wits of a Citizen— (*M*, 1:230–31)

Lamb compares the humble repast he can offer Manning to the similar fare in the nunnery of Clara of Assisi and her charges. After the meal, he and Manning will visit Dyer, now a heathen, since he has broken with poetry, his true religion, and also because he aspires to the dark arts of mathematics. Manning with his math texts, and Lamb with his literary ones, will inspire such gushes of tears that Dyer's filthy gown will be cleansed. This baptismal imagery—we are still in mock epic, the high blended with the low—raises Lamb to biblical diction (notice his uses of "thou) and a pun conflating the physical (pia mater is the brain's most delicate part) and the spiritual (pia mater, via etymology, is also tender mother). This cleansing of Dyer will restore him to his rightful home, the abode of the muses.

Lamb concludes this letter by admitting it is "Nonsense." Lamb's purpose is the comedian's: I want to make you laugh, and this desire dictates content and form. But Lamb's letters to Manning are nonsensical in a more serious way, in the same way that Beckett's work is, and that of the Dadaists and Marcel Duchamp. Call it hyperbolic parody, a mockery of stultifying convention through exaggerating those conventions in the extreme. Vladimir and Estragon parody the devotional abiding of the faithful. Duchamp's wine rack exposes the arbitrariness of aesthetic standards. Hugo Ball's sound poetry at the Cabaret Voltaire reveals the meaning of words beyond the Meaning of Words.

Take away the existential torments of the twentieth century, and add some constitutional gentleness, and you have Lamb exciting the same subversive nonsense. When Lamb refers to Dyer's brain as Pia Mater, and his skull as his "pericranics," his diction is not meant to communicate so much as to mock the semantic fantasies of scientists. To address Manning as "thou" is a similar move, a send-up of overly formal speech. And why inflate Dyer's quibbles into a profound crisis of faith, and Manning's mathematic texts into hermetic scrolls, if not to suggest that all belief systems are games?

But Lamb's transgressions retain a sweetness lacking in twentieth-century avant-garde. If his "thou's" parody high rhetoric, they express his love for Quaker diction. His Latinate phrasing arises as much from his nostalgia for Christ's as his tendency to make fun of intellectualism. Lamb finds zealousness comical, but he was no nihilist.

Lamb mocks himself. In August 1800, he implores Coleridge no longer to call him gentle-hearted, since he is drunk, dirty, stammering, with crazy eyes. He proves his drunkenness: "My head is playing all the tunes in the world, ringing such peals! It has just finished the "merry Xt Church Bells,' and absolutely is beginning 'Turn again, Whittington.' Buz, buz, buz, bum, bum, bum, wheeze, wheeze, wheeze, feu, feu, feu; tinky, tinky, tinky, *craunch*.

I shall certainly come to be damned at last. I have been getting drunk two days running. I find my moral sense in the last stage of a consumption, my religion burning as blue and faint as the tops of evening bricks" (*M*, 1:224).

A few weeks later, Lamb admits to Coleridge he lied while paying a visiting to Joseph Cottle, who was mourning the death of his brother Amos. To distract Cottle from his grief, Lamb had mentioned the man's poem "Alfred." Cottle turned to Lamb, eyes suddenly dry, and asked Lamb's opinion of the work. Though Lamb thought the poem less than stellar, he succumbed to his pity, and "went to work and beslabberd Alfred with most unqualified praise . . . or only qualifying my praise by the occasional polite interposition of an exception taken against trivial faults, slips, & human imperfections, which, by removing the appearance of insincerity, did but in truth heighten the relish" (*M*, 1:239).

Lamb's self-effacements could turn serious. To Southey in May 1816, he admits, "I have a timid imagination, I am afraid; I do not willingly admit of strange beliefs or out-of-the-way creeds or places. I never read books of travel, at least not farther than Paris, or Rome. I can just endure Moors, because of their connection as foes with Xtians; but Abyssinians, Ethiops, Esquimaux, Dervises, & all that tribe, I hate. I believe I fear them in some manner." Does this admission of parochialism mock Southey's faux exoticism? The admission feels earnest, especially in light of Lamb's remarks a few sentences on: "I am a Christian, Englishman, Londoner, *Templar*, God help me when I come to put off these snug relations, & to get abroad into the world to **come**—" (*M*, 3:155).

If this complex tonality wavers between the satirical racism in "Imperfect Sympathies" and the celebration of local imagination in "Witches, and Other Night-Fears," Lamb's letter to Bernard Barton in December 1822 is more direct. Lamb remarks that Southey is not the right historian for the Society of Friends, because the poet "will put in some Levity." But then Lamb himself has been inappropriately comical toward the Quakers. He regrets his lightness; he will reform (*L*, 2:356).

Lamb goes too far in his comedy. This is his most consistent criticism of himself, humorously (he can't stop himself) embodied in a letter to Sara Hutchinson, the sister of Wordsworth's wife Mary and the flame of tortured Coleridge. In April 1823, he criticizes Mary's inkblots for lacking boldness. They are "but poor smears, half left in and half scratched out, with another smear left in their place." His blots are robust, as he shows by inserting a large blot into the letter. He also chides Mary's handwriting. It is too nice, with its carefully dotted "i's" and crossed "t's." He favors a flourishing hand. While Mary couldn't even "make a corkscrew if she tried," he will whip one up right in the middle of a letter, as he does in this epistle, and finds it one of the best "he ever drew." But Lamb catches himself in his nonsense. If he is going to write a proper letter to Miss Hutchinson, he says he should begin again, and not "stand flourishing like a fencer at a fair." "Dear Miss H.," he decorously writes, "It gives me great pleasure [the letter now begins] to hear that you got down so smoothly, and that Mrs. Monkhouse's spirits are so good and enterprising" (*L,* 2:381).

CHAPTER 16

*Godwin*

To begin the nineteenth century, Lamb reconciled with Coleridge. In June 1799, Coleridge had returned from Germany to Nether Stowey. There he made up with Southey. After a trip to Sockburn, where he met Sara Hutchinson, he spent the autumn walking the Lakes with Wordsworth. As the year ended, he returned to Sockburn. He fell in love with Sara, henceforth referred to in his notebooks as Asra, and set himself up for a life of romantic disappointment. He also was hired to write for the *Morning Post*, and so moved to London, and on December 27, he settled at 21 Buckingham Street. About three weeks later, Lamb wrote Coleridge a gently mocking letter of praise for the "very novel and exquisite manner in which you combined political with grammatical science, in your yesterday's dissertation on Mr. Wyndham's unhappy composition. It must have been a death-blow to the ministry" (*M*, 1:180). The kidding suggests a return to ease, as does as Lamb's invitation to come to his house to meet Manning, who was to travel down from Cambridge in the evening.

Lloyd was at it again. One night Lloyd and his friend Stephen Weever Browne, a prodigious talker, had gone out with Mary Hays, friend of Godwin and feminist philosopher. Browne had worn the already depressed Hays down with his incessant talk. After Browne departed, Hays broke into tears. Lloyd comforted her in person and then, the next day, in a letter. Soon enough, Lloyd told friends that Miss Hays was in love with him and that she had arranged for Browne to leave so that she could be alone with him. This got back to Hays. She accused Lloyd of vanity. Lloyd apologized for sullying her character, though he attempted to justify his behavior by claiming that he thought her principles questionable, since she chose to remain unmarried and live alone. But only a "fool or a villain," he conceded (obsequiously?), could doubt her excellence. Southey, who reported the incident to Edith, commented, "She thinks him one or the other."[1] Coleridge thought his old nemesis's behavior "atrocious" and claimed that "Lamb himself confessed to me, that during the time in which [Lloyd] kept up his ranting sentimental Correspondence with Miss Hays, he frequently read her Letters in company as a subject for *laughter*."[2]

In a February letter to Manning, Lamb corroborates. Lloyd's actions have been "shockingly & nauseously indelicate," and he has shown poor judgment as well in asking his younger sister Olivia to transcribe his apology letter (*M*, 1:182). Lamb softens toward Lloyd pretty quickly, however—"I am still desirous of keeping on kind terms with Lloyd"—and he is likewise gentle toward Coleridge, who apparently lied to a former classmate about his work for the newspaper. Coleridge has a habit of "quizzing the world by lyes most unaccountable & and most disinterested **fictions**." No matter. He will still sup at Coleridge's tonight (*M*, 1:183).

Like Keats, Lamb could remain friends with both parties in a feud. He could also be generous toward flaws in others. And he was alert to his own faults. Rather than make him defensive, his self-awareness inspired tolerance. "I am determined to lead a merry Life in the midst of Sinners. I try to consider all men as such, and to pitch my expectations from human nature as low as possible. In this view, all unexpected Virtues are God-sends & beautiful exceptions" (*M*, 1:183).

Gossip aside, in February Lamb also met the "Atheist" William Godwin. He told Manning that at his dinner with Coleridge would be Godwin, whom he was curious to know, even though he had attacked him in "Living without God in the World." Perhaps Coleridge's "roof" would "fall and crush the Atheist" (*M*, 1:183).

Godwin was forty-four. His popularity had peaked in the mid-1790s, when he had published *Political Justice*, his radical philosophical treatise, and *Caleb Williams*, a novel illustrating his philosophy. By 1800, he was under attack by the conservative press, and he was a widower.[3]

He and Mary Wollstonecraft had married in March 1797. What first peaked Godwin's romantic interest in Wollstonecraft was her narrative of her time in Scandinavia, of which Godwin wrote, "If ever there was a book calculated to make a man in love with its author, this appears to me to be the book."[4] The two began their courtship in 1796. Wollstonecraft became pregnant. Even though Godwin had argued against marriage, the two wed and moved into adjoining houses. Their servants carried notes between them. The relationship was happy.

Mary Shelley was born in late August 1797. Her mother died weeks later of complications. William, who had never raised a child, was now left with an infant daughter of his own, as well as three-year-old Fanny Imlay, Wollstonecraft's daughter from her former lover, the American explorer Gilbert Imlay. Wollstonecraft's death wrecked him. When he paid tribute to her in *A Memoir of the Author of the "Vindication of the Rights of Women,"* he candidly wrote of her love affairs, her illegitimate child, her suicide attempts. The press attacked him and friends spurned him.

This was the Godwin Lamb met: beaten down by tragedy, responsibility, pillory. He had given up philosophy and fiction and was at work on a drama, *Antonio.* He was also very much in want of a wife to help him with the children and assuage his loneliness. He was not too far away, though he didn't know it, from putting most of his efforts into publishing, a decision that would benefit Charles and Mary mightily.

Godwin was still a hero to many, though. Coleridge and Southey admired him deeply, as Wordsworth had earlier. Shelley would later idolize him. Henry Crabb Robinson, though he resented Godwin's making him feel "inferior," confessed that "I saw none but remarkable persons [at his house]."[5]

On Friday evening, February 7, 1800, Lamb walked southwest from Chapel Street down to Coleridge on Buckingham Street. Coleridge welcomed him, and there was Godwin, a very short man with a large head and a big nose. In attendance was Basil Montagu, a handsome twenty-nine-year-old who had until very recently ardently supported Godwin. He and the philosopher had taken a walking tour together, and the younger man had been a help to Godwin when Mary was dying. But now Montagu rejected Godwin's thought. Why Coleridge had invited someone whose presence would hurt Godwin is odd—perhaps a slight taint of the Oedipal was to blame. Coleridge had veered from Godwin as well, and maybe it was satisfying to watch his former philosophical master stumble. With Montagu came two other younger men:

*William Godwin*, by James Northcote. (© National Portrait Gallery, London.)

John Frederick Pinney, who allowed Wordsworth and Dorothy to live for free in Racedown, his family's country house; and James Weebe Tobin, a close friend of Wordsworth who introduced Coleridge to Tom Wedgewood, the poet's future patron.[6]

Lamb shook hands with the Atheist Godwin, and the roof did not cave in. Lamb, hypersensitive, would have picked up on the vibe in the room, observing that Coleridge and his three young friends were vaguely antagonistic toward Godwin. Always relishing a good intellectual scrimmage, the more booze-fueled the better, Lamb likely jumped into the mix immediately—awkwardly at first, his stutter thwarting his talk, but then more elegantly as the drink flowed. We imagine him prodding Godwin on his atheism one minute, poking Coleridge on his German abstractions the next.

At some point, Lamb went too far with Godwin. Southey, years later, described the scene: "Lamb got warmed with whatever was on the table, became disputatious, and said things to Godwin which made him quietly say, 'Pray, Mr. Lamb, are you toad or frog?' [Godwin was referring to the Gillray cartoon of two years earlier] . . . But the next morning S. T. C. called on Lamb, and found Godwin breakfasting with him, from which time their intimacy began."[7]

A week later Lamb provided Manning his own positive report on Godwin. "Godwin I am a good deal pleased with—. He is a well-behaved decent man, nothing very brilliant about him or imposing as you may suppose; quite another Guess sort of Gentleman from what your Anti Jacobins Christians imagine him—. I was well pleased to find he has neither horns nor claws, quite a tame creature I assure you. A middle-sized man both in stature & in understanding—whereas from his noisy fame, you would expect to find a **Briarcus** Centimanus or a Tityus tall enough to **pull** Jupiter from his Heavens! I begin to think you Atheists not quite so tall a species" (*M*, 1:185–86).

Manning objected to Lamb calling him an atheist, but that Lamb thought him one yet still sought his friendship shows the theist Lamb expanding his intellect. His ecumenical stance was not simply theoretical. As he became more social during the early years of the nineteenth century, he increasingly relished difference, to the point of eccentricity. After the drudgery of his days at East India House, he craved anything *not* predictable. Alcohol certainly helped him to feel pleasantly disoriented—it also loosened his tongue—but friends emphatically different from him did as well.

## CHAPTER 17

CHAPTER 17

# Anatomy of Melancholy

In February and March 1800, Lamb was pushing on Manning a strange book by his old Christ's friend James, or Jem, White called *Falstaff's Letters*, a "bundle of the sharpest, queerest, profoundest humours, of any these juice-drained latter times have spawned" (*M,* 1:187). Even though White published the book under his name, Southey claimed that Lamb and White coauthored it, and John Matthew Gutch, a friend of both men, asserted that Lamb provided "incidental hints and suggestions."[1]

Published in 1796, officially titled *Original Letters, etc, of Sir John Falstaff and His Friends,* the book purports to be the letters of Shakespeare's most famous comic creation, discovered in an archive of the heirs of Mistress Neil Quickly, the proprietor of the Boar's Head Tavern, where Falstaff and his raucous companions drank away their time.

Here is a typical letter, addressed, as many are, to Prince Hal:

I squander away in drinkings monies belonging to the soldiery. I do deny it—they have had part—the surplus is gone in charity—accuse the parish-officers—make them restore—the whoreson wardens do now put on the cloak of supplication at the church doors, intercepting gentlemen for charity, forsooth—! Tis a robbery, a villainous robbery! To come upon a gentleman reeking with piety, God's book in his hand, brimful of sacrament! Thou knowst, Hal, as I am but man,

I dare in some sort to leer at the plate and pass, but as I have the body
and blood of Christ within me, could I do it? An I did not make an
oblation of a matter of ten pound after the battle in Shrewsbury, for
thy humble safety, Hal, then I am the veriest transgressor denounced
in God's code.—But I'll see thee damned ere I be charitable again. Let
'em coin the plate—let them coin the holy chalice.[2]

Lamb admired this not-much-loved book because he saw in it his own literary preoccupations. First of all, the irony. Falstaff is up to double business,
denouncing the church for taking the money that he himself has pilfered for
his drink. That the audience knows this gives another level of irony to the
passage, dramatic irony (where Falstaff's is verbal). We know Falstaff is lying,
while he thinks he is getting away with it.

A second reason Lamb liked White's book is its ventriloquism. Soon
Lamb will attempt his own historical impersonation, of Robert Burton. This
extreme mimicry—Lamb must write in an archaic, convoluted style foreign
to his time—is practice for the more subtle character of Elia, who blends
seventeenth-century baroque, the crazed ironies of Sterne, and Lamb's own
wacky nostalgia.

Another reason Lamb hailed White's book was it dizzying conceits. Here
is Falstaff speaking of Robert Shallow, the vain and wealthy justice of the
peace in *Henry IV, Part 2* and *The Merry Wives of Windsor*: "By the Lord, this
uncomb'd hemp-stalk doth breed more convulsive propensities in man, than
is in a whole fry of stricken Finsmen; and yet is it all unwittingly:—though his
Countenance be as sharp as the tweak of a bully, his wit is benumbing too."[3]
The thin, disheveled Shallow, compared to a frizzy stalk of hemp, is capable
of causing such spasms in his auditors that they feel like an unruly gathering
of small terrified fish. But somehow Shallow's wit, though his face features a
nose so sharp it resembles a bully's strike, benumbs as well. White's imagery
vertiginously rushes Shallow from plant to prod to blow to anesthesia.

Lamb escaped to historical pasts as much as fictional ones. In early March
1800, he confessed to Manning that "public affairs—except as they touch
upon me, & so turn into private—I cannot whip my mind up to feel any
interest in . . . I cannot make these present times present to me." The past he
can make present, though, even when the past seems trifling compared to the
momentous current events, such as England's war with France. He is reading
Gilbert Burnet's *History of His Own Times, 1724–1732*, a firsthand account of

the English Civil War and the founding of the Commonwealth. Lamb values the history for being "garrulous" and "pleasant." Burnet "tells his story like an old man, past political service, bragging to his sons, on winter evenings, of the part he took in public transactions, when 'his old cap was new.' Full of scandal, which all true history is. No palliatives, but all stark wickedness, that actually gives the momentum to national actors. Truth & sincerity staring out upon you perpetually alto relieve.—Himself a party man, he makes you a party man. None of the Damned Philosophical Humeian indifference, so cold & unnatural & unhuman" (*M*, 1:187–88).

If White's ironic playfulness stokes one side of Lamb's imagination, Burnet's unapologetic subjectivity fires another. For Lamb, the writer should always be honest about his prejudices and idiosyncrasies. The personal, the more immediate and vulnerable the better, makes writing alive.

Lamb's spring began with three weeks of Coleridge. In early March, Sara and Hartley had gone to Gloucestershire and Bristol to visit friends, and Coleridge moved in with the Lambs. The friendship was rekindled. "The more I see of [Coleridge] in the quotidian undress and relaxation of his mind, the more cause I see to love him and believe him a *very **good** man*, and all those foolish impressions to the contrary fly off like morning slumbers—" (*M*, 1:189).

Coleridge left in April "to go into the North, on a visit to his God, Wordsworth" (*M*, 1:191). Lamb filled the emptiness with Robert Lloyd, his sisters Olivia and Priscilla, and their mother. He also cultivated his friendship with Godwin. Moreover, he found himself serving as proxy for Coleridge to the poet's admirers. One "Miss Wesley and her friend, and a tribe of authoresses that come after you here daily . . . hive and cluster upon us." After shaking off Miss Wesley, Mary and Charles are beset by "one Miss Benje," who berates the reluctant Lambs into having tea with her. They endure her holding forth for hours on philosophical matters about which they know and care nothing. The evening ends with her insisting the Lambs come next week to meet her friends the Porters, "who . . . have heard much of Mr. Coleridge, and wish to meet *us*, because we are *his* friends. I have been preparing for the occasion. I crowd cotton in my ears. I read all the reviews and magazines of the past month against the dreadful meeting, and I hope by these means to cut a tolerable second-rate figure" (*M*, 1:199–200).

On May 9 Hetty, the Lambs' longtime servant, died, and "in consequence of fatigue and anxiety," Mary fell ill and two days later had to be confined. Charles was now alone with "nothing but Hetty's body to keep [him] company." "My heart is quite sunk and I dont know where to look for relief—. Mary will get better again, but her constantly being liable to such relapses is dreadful,—nor is it the least of our Evils, that her case & all our story is so well known around us. . . . We are in a manner *marked*" (*M*, 1:202).

Mary's madness would hound her forever. Charles had to keep her (and others) safe, find a humane asylum, pay for it. Just as terrible as Mary's relapses were the morbidly curious gawks. "I am completely shipwreck'd," he wrote Coleridge, and "my head is quite bad." "I almost wish that Mary were dead" (*M*, 1:203).

Coleridge was compassionate and generous. He wrote Godwin, "My poor Lamb!—how cruelly afflictions crowd upon him! I am glad, that you think of him as I think—he has an affectionate heart, a mind sui generis, his taste acts so as to appear like the unmechanic simplicity of an Instinct—in brief, he is worth an hundred men of *mere* Talents. Conversation with the latter tribe is like the use of leaden Bells—one warms by *exercise*—Lamb every now & then *eradiates*, & the beam, tho' single & fine as a hair, yet is rich with colours."[4]

This is the Coleridge who could put aside his Wordsworth worship as well as his lyrical petulance to see clearly Lamb's luminous intellect. For his part, Lamb always accurately took Coleridge's measure: his brilliant yet self-indulgent friend was "an Arch angel a little damaged" (*M*, 3:215).

On May 17, Lamb told Manning the empty house was too much for him. He was sleeping at White's and intended to stay there until he could find new lodgings. Mary would get better, he trusted, but he felt as if his "daily & hourly prop [had] fallen away." He "totter[ed] and stagger[ed] with weakness" (*M*, 1:203–4).

Lamb is a melancholy man. Today we would call him clinically depressed. His spirits sink regardless of circumstance. Mary's breakdowns darken his moods, but he battles despair even when she is sane. He drinks heavily, a futile effort to ease the pain. More promisingly, he socializes, jokes, and makes literature.

Robert Burton, whose tomb in Oxford reads, "Melancholy gave him life and death," is therapy for Lamb. The deeper the despair, the more potent the hope. Only the strongest light can penetrate the deepest darkness. When a melancholy man laughs, he laughs hard. When he writes, desperate energy crackles. Essential to Burton's jesting are his "out-of-the-way humours and opinion," the "diverting twist" to them, the "oddities" of his authorship (*W*, 2:75).

These were the qualities Lamb mimicked in his "forgeries" of Burton, encouraged by Coleridge and completed in the spring of 1800. Lamb called them "Curious Fragments, Extracted from a Common-place book, Which Belonged to Robert Burton, the Famous Author of the *Anatomy of Melancholy*." The *Morning Post*, despite an introductory letter from Coleridge, rejected them. Lamb eventually published them as addenda to his play *John Woodvil.*

(Nothing shows Lamb's own "out-of-the-way humours and opinion" like his galley proofs of Thomas Holcroft's 1804 *Travels in France and Italy*. Lamb came by these pages when he saw the book through the press for his friend. The large margins and empty pages were inviting, and Lamb filled them with passages from his favorite works, either by copying or gluing. Some are now well known—Coleridge's "Kubla Khan," De Quincey's "On the Knocking at the Gate in Macbeth," Blake's "The Chimney Sweeper"—and others, now vanished, were familiar in Lamb's day: Shelley's "Lines to a Reviewer," Lord Thurlough's "To a Bird, That Haunted the Waters of Lacken, in Winter," and Barry Cornwall's "Sings; Who Sings." But the majority of the entries in this odd commonplace book are obscure, idiosyncratic. Extract from the *Letters of Anna Seward,* in which a French prisoner tells Miss Seward of his release: "Ah madam! I am too happy to eat & sleep no more me. I go to bed, and fall asleep one hours; dream see my wife, my children wake, find so much better than dream—am so glad cannot drowsy." *Extracts from the Correspondence of Joseph Highmore, Esq:* "There lived in Wyld-street, about fifty years ago, a Dutch Painter of Landscapes, whose name was Vanderstraaten; he was perhaps the most expeditious painter that ever lived; it is said of him that he has painted 30 landscapes in a day, of the size commonly called a three-quarter, that is, such as contains a head." Thomas Fuller's *The Church History of Britain:* "Man's life, O King, is like unto a little sparrow . . . altogether ignorant." Epitaph on Sir T. Smith, at Hone Church, Kent: "Betwix this place and our Antipodes—/ He got intelligence what might be found / To give contentment through this massy Round." Parson's gerundial pun: "When Dido found Aeneas would not come, / She wept in silence, and was di do dum." "On a Lady Who Beat Her Husband": "Come hither, Sir John, my picture is here / What say you, my love, does it strike you?" "I can't say it does just at present, my dear / But I think it soon will, it's so like you." Extract from James Barry: "I could be happy on my going home to find some corner where I could sit down in the middle of my studies, books, and casts after the antique, to paint this work and others, where I might have models of nature when necessary, bread and soul, and a coat to cover me. I should care not what became of my work when it was done.")[5]

Burton's *Anatomy*, a book Samuel Johnson so adored that he would get up two hours early to read it, was first published in 1621, and revised five times before Burton's death in 1640. Though a mathematician by training, Burton ranged widely in his massive volume, drawing mightily from personal experience, medicine, literature, philosophy, and theology. Though a doorstopper, the book reads as an experimental essay. Under the guise of Democritus Jr., Burton questions almost every argument he makes and digresses so prodigiously that mainstream and drift are indistinguishable. The book is as much about the writing of the book as it is about its subject. As Democritus Jr. announces in the preface, "I writ of melancholy, by being busy to avoid melancholy." This endless writing—to which the book's six editions are a testament—did not challenge Democritus Jr., since he possessed a "giddy disposition." This disposition generates his "running wit, . . . unconstant, unsettled mind," and his desire to express "some smattering in all, to be Somebody in everything, Nobody in anything." Such is Democritus Jr.'s "roving humor." He shares it with Montaigne, and it makes him like "a ranging spaniel, that barks at every bird he sees."[6]

The *Anatomy* teems with nimble similes. Democritus Jr. admits that he did not spend too much time crafting his book but spilled it out as he would everyday speech. He did not have "time to lick it into form," like a bear brings forth her "whelps," as "confused lumps."[7]

The *Anatomy* mocks society's overemphasis on artifice. But all we have is artifice. When Burton claims that he "shrouds" himself under Democritus's name, he admits that his actual self is a corpse covered for burial.[8] Nothing alive, nothing significant, is behind the shroud. There is only the veil.

This is the melancholy of the world. We are incapable of establishing durable selves and yearn for a continuity we will never achieve. But melancholy also liberates. It invites perpetual creation of new roles, new scripts.

Lamb enters this play in his "Curious Fragments." Just as Burton wrote under the guise of Democritus Jr., so Lamb dons the mask of Burton himself. The most immediate reason was to "pick up a few guineas" from an editor who might publish the forgery (*M*, 1:190). A more significant reason was to reconnect with Coleridge after their break. Even though Coleridge was weighed down by "his own worrying and heart-oppressing occupations," he cultivated Lamb's dormant literary talent "as a gardiner tends his young *tulip*—" (*M*, 1:189). He recommended that Lamb forge Burton, as Chatterton had forged medieval verse and as MacPherson copied Celtic epic. An even deeper rationale for the Burton extracts was aesthetic experimentation. After the yearnings of the Anna sonnets and the resignations of *Blank Verse*, Lamb through Burton finds a new literary voice whose impetus is not confession but play.

The first extract considers melancholy and love. "My fine Sir is a lover, an *inamorato*, a Pyramus, a Romeo; he walks seven years disconsolate, moping because he cannot enjoy his miss, *insanus amor* is his melancholy, the man is mad; *delirat*, he dotes; all this while his Glycera is rude, spiteful, not to be entreated, churlish, spits at him, yet exceeding fair, gentle eyes, (which is a beauty,) hair lustrous and smiling, the trope is none of mine, *Aeneas Sylvius* hath *crines ridentes*—in conclusion she is wedded to his rival, a boore, a *Corydon*, a rustic, *omnino ignarus*, he can scarce construe *Corderius*, yet haughty, fantastic, *opiniatre*" (*W*, 1:32).

The man loves a beautiful woman who does not love him back and has married another much less worthy than he. The lusty style makes up for the loss of love. Notice the excessive use of *scesis onomaton*, the illumination of an idea through a series of more or less synonymous words or phrases. The effect is excess, suggesting abundance if done well, repetition if not. The man described is a lover (in English), in love (in Latin), a Pyramus, a Romeo. The beloved Glycera (suggesting "courtesan") is hostile in five similar ways. The lack of conjunctions among the synonymous elements (asyndeton) makes the sentences feel rushed, spontaneous. The allusions, however, as well as the Latin, counter the casualness. Alliteration intimates craft, too: "man is mad"; "*delirat* [deranged], he dotes." As does irony. After describing the beloved's hair as smiling (synesthesia), "Burton" disowns the phrase.

Similar panache enlivens Lamb's other two Burton extracts. Like his letters to Manning, the extracts show Lamb distancing himself from his recent tragic past. He is no longer the Charles Lamb who suffered love-loss and mother-death and religious doubt and the near crippling of his friendship to Coleridge. He is Burton. He laughs at everything. Don't take this botched cosmos seriously. It will only kill you.

# CHAPTER 18

## 27 Southampton Buildings

After Mary's breakdown and her consequent confinement, Lamb bordered on his own mental collapse. Confessions to Coleridge and Manning, socializing with Godwin and the Lloyds, pretending to be Burton: these helped him cope. But he needed something more concrete. He needed to escape Chapel Street, haunted with dead aunts, fathers, and servants, with madness and loneliness.

Help came from another Christ's friend, John Mathew Gutch. Gutch, one year Lamb's junior, was a law stationer living at 27 Southampton Buildings in Holborn. He would later become a printer, publisher, and journalist in Bristol. His one book is the irresistibly titled *Narrative of a Singular Imposture Carried out at Bristol by One Mary Baker, Styling Herself the Princess Caraboo*, from 1817. It was Gutch who hired F. S. Cary to paint Lamb's portrait just before Lamb's death. Gutch also possessed the famous notebook of Coleridge (now known as "Gutch Memorandum Book") that contains the poet's first jottings on "Kubla Khan" and *The Rime*.

Gutch offered Lamb rooms at his Southampton Buildings address. Lamb is relieved to be quitting "a house & neighborhood where poor Mary's disorder, so frequently recurring, has made us marked sort of people," and he relishes living in town, meaning the *city* of London (versus the then suburban Pentonville), where he and Mary can be more "*private*" (*M,* 1:207). The bustle of the new location reminds him of his brighter days in the Temple. From the lodging, he can walk south on Chancery Lane and reach Fleet in about six minutes. Covent Gardens, teeming with markets, bookstores, theaters, and prostitutes, lies twenty minutes to the west. And he and Mary will be little noticed on their new street, peopled with young bachelors in the legal trade who have eyes only for their own advancement.[1]

But Lamb's optimism is short-lived. Two weeks after Gutch's good news, Mary is no better. Lamb finds himself more "wretched" than ever. Luckily, he has some days off from work, and he travels to Hertfordshire. He will be "very much alone" on the trip, and he is glad, since the solitude "revives" him (*M,* 1:208).

When Lamb returns to London four days later, Mary has "perfectly recover'd." She will join him in a week (*M,* 1:208).

But six weeks later, on July 22, Lamb is depressed again, even though Mary is with him and well. As he writes to Robert Lloyd, "My mind has been so barren and idle of late, that I have done nothing. I have received many summons from you, and have repeatedly sat down to write, and broke off from despair of sending you anything worthy your acceptance. I have had such a deadness about me. Man delights not me nor woman neither" (*M,* 1:213).

A recent trip to Oxford did not lift his spirits as the Hertfordshire excursion did. One reason is that he witnessed there the happy Gutch family—"a **numerous** assemblage of young men & women, all fond of each other to a certain degree, & all happy together" (*M,* 1:214)—and probably lamented the sadness of his own, even though he noted that the largeness of the group made intimacy such as he enjoyed with Mary challenging.

Recent news of Coleridge didn't help his mood. His friend moved to Greta Hall in Keswick to be close to Wordsworth in Grasmere. A brisk half-day's walk, and the two men could be together. So intimate are they now, Lamb (jealously?) realized, that they would seek each other's company even in landscapes conducive to solitude, such as the Hebrides or the mythical Thule (*M,* 1: 214).

At least Charles and Mary have now settled into 27 Southampton Buildings. The rent is reasonable, and the rooms come with a servant. Such a great bargain is all the more extraordinary, since Gutch knows of "the perpetual liability to a recurrence in my sister's disorder, probably to the end of her life" (*M,* 1:215).

But while Gutch treats Mary as he would anyone else, not everyone does—in particular Gutch's family in Oxford. Lamb tells Coleridge that this was "not a family, where I could take Mary with me"—either because the family feared her potential violence, or because Lamb wanted to protect Mary from embarrassment (*M*, 1:215). Lamb feels guilty traveling without Mary, and for enjoying pleasures in which she can't partake. But at the same time, he is bitter over the guilt, and partially blames her for it.

Before the dreadful summer of 1800 and the move to Holborn, Lamb had from time to time celebrated tipsiness in his letters. He longed for his buzzed riffing with Coleridge at the Salutation and Cat, and he tried to reproduce the fun by writing while drunk.

But now drink appears more frequently, less happily. Lamb can still muster to Manning a lyrical catalogue of booze: when you come to London, "you shall drink Rum, Brandy, Gin, Aquavitae, Usquebagh, or Whiskey a nights——& for the after-dinner-Trick I have 8 Bottles of Genuine Port which mathematically divided gives 1 1/7 for every day you stay, provided you stay a **week**" (*M*, 1:223). But then he admits to Coleridge the aftereffects: "I am suffering from the combined effect of two days drunkenness, & at such times it is not very easy to think or express in a natural series" (*M*, 1:226).

The effects of drink have worsened by February 1801, right around the time Charles and Mary are preparing to move again. "Last Sunday was a fortnight as I was *coming to town* from the Professor's [Godwin's], inspired with new **Rum**, I tumbled down and broke my **nose**" (*M*, 1:276–77).

It's one thing to hurt yourself while soused, something else to injure another, which is what Lamb did in August 1801. He and some friends, including his East India House colleague Walter Wilson, took a boat to Richmond. Upon their return, a drunken Lamb fell into his "accustomed gambols." They would have proven funny enough on land but were ill suited for boat travel. Lamb's "bodily movements" put the boat "within a hair's-breadth of being upset," and thus placed the group in "imminent peril." The boat didn't capsize, but the "contemplation" of Lamb's shenanigans after the event was "anything but satisfactory." Wilson took it upon himself to write Lamb "a letter of remonstrance upon his conduct" that day.[2]

Lamb's reply satisfied Wilson, though it falls just short of a full apology. "I am extremely sorry that any serious difference should subsist between us on account of some foolish behavior of mine at Richmond." But "you knew me well enough before" to realize that "a very little liquor will cause a considerable alteration in me" (*M*, 2:11). The gist is, I apologize, but you should let me off the hook, since you were well aware what a little liquor could do, and you should have kept me from drinking in the first place. And it is the drink that should offend you, not I, since the drink alone is responsible for my conduct.

Lamb goes too far, and not just in ignoring decorum: he can drown you. Suddenly Carlyle's nasty portrait of Lamb doesn't seem so egregious:

> Charles Lamb I sincerely believe to be in some considerable degree insane. A more pitiful, ricketty, gasping, staggering, stammering Tom fool I do not know. He is witty by denying truisms, and abjuring good manners. His speech wriggles hither and thither with an incessant painful fluctuation; not an opinion in it or a fact or even a phrase that you can thank him for: more like a convulsion fit than natural systole and diastole.—Besides he is now a confirmed shameless drunkard: asks vehemently for gin-and-water in strangers' houses; tipples until he is utterly mad, and is only not thrown out of doors because he is too much despised for taking such trouble with him. Poor Lamb! Poor England where such a despicable abortion is named genius![3]

This is over the top, but Lamb was a shameless enough drunk to land himself, at age thirty-four, in the stocks for public drunkenness, in Barnet, a village outside of London.[4]

As Anya Taylor has shown, Lamb's biographers have tended to defend Lamb from the accusation of alcoholism. Lamb was placed in the stocks not for drunkenness but because of his low social status. Lamb's regular employment demonstrates his freedom from alcohol addiction. Lamb could not tolerate much alcohol because of his nervous dyspepsia, brought on by a poor diet and too much walking. Lamb himself denied his dependence on drink, even though he wrote a ferociously frank confession of alcohol dependence in "Confession of a Drunkard," first published in 1813.[5]

The essay is one of the first to treat alcohol addiction as something more insidious than a failure of will. The "sturdy moralist" can scream, "Abstain!" all he wants, but the drunkard, unlike the thief or the liar, cannot stop. To expect the drinker to cast off his addiction as easily as a liar can hold his tongue is to "trample . . . on the ruin of a man." For the drunkard to go sober, he must walk through fire, or flay his skin, or "undergo a change violent as that which we conceive of the mutation of form in some insects. The drunkard is not a man with drink added. His very being is drink. Without it, he feels as if nothing" (W, 1:133).

Lamb is this man. The comfort others feel in society, he lacks, and thus he requires alcohol. Twelve years ago, he spent his hours soberly, with books.

But he took up with men "of boisterous spirits, sitters up a-nights, disputants, drunken." Wit was their game, and he finds himself more skilled than his companions. But he suffers "a natural impediment in [his] speech"—a stammer—and requires spirits to free his tongue. The booze becomes his comic muse. But over time, the causality reverses. Just as the gin inspires wit, so the prick of wit—"the tickling relish on your tongue disposing you" to joking—makes him want "bottle and fresh glasses" straightaway (W, 1:135).

Eventually all occasions are for drinking. And for drinking more—from "malt liquor" to "thin wines" to "stronger wine and water" to "small punch" to "mixed liquors" to brandy mixed with water to brandy unmixed (W, 1:136).

The drunkard drops these false friends who seek him only when he is witty. But the habit is ingrained. The drinking is not circumstantial; it is wired into his sinews. Recovery seems impossible. Why not just drink more moderately? For the drunkard, that is not an option—he must either stay drunk or abstain. But how to abstain when the drunkard is most himself—indeed, paradoxically at his best—when he is soused? "The drinking man is never less himself than during his sober intervals. Evil is so far his good" (W, 1:138). Rational when deranged, well when poisoned, finding day a range of dark mountains, and night a bright buzz, the drunk loses logic, unity, integrity.

Lamb's essay itself embodies this disintegration. Its ending paragraphs crack into brief, jittery discharges of pain.

Nine years after Lamb published "Confessions of a Drunkard," an author in the *Quarterly Review* treated the essay as a true account of Charles Lamb. Lamb responded vigorously that the essay was not about him but a description of someone else, in the same way that "Edax on Appetite," from 1812, is about a glutton, emphatically not the actual author, who is slim. The *Quarterly* obviously has Lamb the nondrunkard confused with a drunken contemporary. Regardless, the essay, like those of Elia, is ironic, characterized by "mock fervor and counterfeit earnestness" (W, 1:429–32).

We think of the stocks, and we understand why Lamb might be ashamed of his drinking and distance himself from this harrowing portrait of addiction. But the drunkard is Lamb, who drank to overcome his stutter, fashioned himself (justifiably) a wit and, as Henry Crabb Robinson claimed, felt best when tippling, tending to fall ill when not drinking. Robinson, who often watched Lamb get tight, concluded that "Confessions of a Drunkard" accurately depicts Lamb.[6] Lamb himself conceded that a "portion of his own experiences may have passed into the picture." Who has not, after all, "felt the after-operation of a too-generous cup?" (W, 1:432).

As Lamb aged, he had to apologize more and more for drunken behavior. In 1834, after an evening at the home of Henry Francis Cary, a clergyman and translator of Dante, he cringed at the thought that he was seen "deliberately" going out "of the house of a clergyman drunk," and regretted "the shameful violation of hospitality" (*L*, 3:405). Four years earlier, he apologized to Jacob Vale Asbury, a doctor who attended Charles and Mary's adopted daughter Emma Isola. Lamb was so drunk at the doctor's he had to be carried home, like Ariel, "on a bat's back" (*L*, 3:265). In 1828, he described to Cary the undulation between hangover and high: "There is a necessity for my drinking too much . . . at and after dinner; then I require spirits at night to allay the crudity of the weaker Bacchus; and in the morning I cool my parched stomach with a fiery libation. Then I am new aground in town, and call upon my London friends, and get new wets of ale, porter, etc.; then ride home, drinking where the coach stops, as duly as Edward set up his Waltham Crosses" (*L*, 3:167). After drinking with John Taylor, then editor of the *London Magazine*, he blacked out. "Is it to you, or to some other kind unknown, that I owe my safe arrival home on Friday night? I confess I have no knowledge of the manner how, or time when. Between ourselves, I am not much better this morning" (*L*, 2:307).

Lamb strove unsuccessfully for sobriety. To Wordsworth he wrote, "I write with great difficulty & can scarce command my own resolution to sit writing an hour together. I am a poor creature, but I am leaving off Gin" (*M*, 3:125). This was in 1814. That the spirits were doing noticeable harm at this point we know from an 1811 letter from Coleridge to John Rickman. Coleridge chastises himself for being a too-eager drinking buddy for Lamb, before noting that porter is fine with Lamb until he fires up his pipe. The tobacco ignites an "unconquerable Appetite for Spirit."[7]

*John Woodvil*, which Lamb began writing in 1798 but did not publish until 1802, is a tragedy about alcoholism.[8] During this four-year period, Lamb sent the play around to his friends for comments, and he revised it substantially. He changed the title from *Pride's Cure*, and he decided to have characters narrate an important scene in the play instead of dramatizing it directly. He sent the play to John Kemble of the Theatre Royal, who rejected it, but he recommended that Lamb try George Colman of the Haymarket. If Lamb did so, Colman rejected it, too. Lamb published the play at his own expense.

The play resembles *As You Like It* in plot and style. The time is 1660, just after the Restoration. With other victorious Cavaliers, John Woodvil carouses in Woodvil Hall, the family home, while his father Walter, a Cromwellian, hides, a traitor, in Sherwood Forest. With Walter is his son Simon, who is loyal to him. Eventually he is joined by the virtuous Margaret, whom he took in as an orphan. At the beginning of the play Margaret is at Woodvil Hall, since she is in love with John. He once seemed to be in love with her, too, but he now neglects her. All he does his drink; all anyone does in Woodvil Hall is drink. She endures "fresh insult from the scorn / Of Woodvil's friends, the uncivil jests, / And free discourses, of the dissolute men" (*W,* 5:138). They haunt the mansion, make her their mirth. Fearing for her safety, she flees, disguised (like Rosalind) as a boy.

In the play's scary Bacchic overture, three servants swill prodigiously while boasting of how, since John has taken over from Walter, they can drink all day and night, even though drink takes "away the understanding," "makes the eyes red," causes the tongue to "stammer" and "to blab out secrets." Men reveal secrets while drunk because they can't discern between enemy and friend. Why drink? The servant Martin explains: because he begins to "be melancholy." But he is melancholy because of drinking too much, which means that his "cure" for melancholy will only cause more melancholy, and so on (*W,* 5:133). This is the alcoholic's logic: I am depressed, so I must drink; drinking makes me more depressed, so I must drink more.

Deep in his cups, John proves his servants right. Lonely and desperate, he befriends one Lovel. To show his affection, he reveals the whereabouts of his father and brother. This leads to their capture. When Walter realizes his son has betrayed him, he dies.

If Lamb's play is about the dangers of his own excessive drinking, it also reflects his troubled friendships with Coleridge and Lloyd. Like John, he craved a friend in the dark periods just before and after Mary's death. He confided in these two men and felt betrayed by both.

Through the relationship between John and Margaret, the play explores Lamb's blend of affection and guilt toward the sister he is bound to care for. Surely Charles felt that his drinking disappointed Mary and jeopardized his ability to care for her. But he also resented her, since her presence encouraged him to curb his drunken socializing and his convivial travels. Lamb felt guilty for this resentment—and then resented the guilt.

The play has a happy ending. Margaret returns from the forest to redeem her brother-lover. John repents, and they will be together. Lamb believed this abrupt and solacing ending was a great virtue. As he wrote to Rickman, "The whole ends with Margaret's Consolation, where it *should* end, without any pert incident of surprise & trick to make a catastrophe" (*M*, 2:37). Southey disagreed, asserting that Lamb's play will "please you by the exquisite beauty of the poetry and provoke you by the execrable silliness of the story."[9] Thomas Holcroft, an actor and playwright, held the same view. The play was "full of poetry—but the plot" was terrible.[10] Dorothy Wordsworth concurred. "The language is often very beautiful, but too imitative in particular phrases, words, etc. The characters, except Margaret's, unintelligible, and, except Margaret, do not show themselves in action."[11]

Margaret remains one of Lamb's finest straightforward, as opposed to ironic, creations. Though she loves John, she flees him for her life; and though she hates his traitorous ways, she returns. This tension between affection and disgust gives her a nuanced psychological realism lacking in the other one-dimensional characters of the play. William Hazlitt believed Margaret is "perhaps the finest and most genuine female character out[side] of Shakespeare."[12]

Lamb admitted he had no talent for plotting, but he was brilliant at putting together a short sequence. When Margaret asks Simon what he loves, he answers as the pantheistic Coleridge might have.

> Simply, all things that live,
> From the crook'd worm to man's imperial form,
> And God-resembling likeness. The poor fly,
> That makes short holyday in the sun beam,
> And dies by some child's hand. The feeble bird
> With little wings, yet greatly venturous
> In the upper sky. The fish in th' other element,
> That knows no touch of eloquence. What else?
> Yon tall and elegant stag,
> Who paints a dancing shadow of his horns
> In the water, where he drinks. (*W*, 5:153)

Margaret, more Lamb-like, replies: "I myself love all these things, yet so as with a difference:—for example, some animals better than others, some men rather than other men; the nightingale before the cuckoo, the swift and graceful palfrey before the slow and asinine mule. Your humour goes to confound all qualities" (*W*, 5:153).

Simon's next speech responds to Margaret's question about how he spends his days in the forest. Sometimes,

To see the sun to bed, and to arise,
Like some hot amourist with glowing eyes,
Bursting the lazy bands of sleep that bound him,
With all his fires and travelling glories round him.
Sometimes the moon on soft night clouds to rest,
Like beauty nestling in a young man's breast,
And all the winking stars, her handmaids, keep
Admiring silence, while those lovers sleep. (*W,* 5:153)

Godwin remembered the phrase "hot amourist," but couldn't place it. He looked in the Elizabethans, and, not finding it, inquired among his friends. He eventually lighted on Lamb.[13]

*John Woodvil* stands as a major moment in Lamb's literary development. It showed him what he was good at, and what he wasn't. He excelled in writing striking, lush, euphonious sentences, as well as in playing with different literary genres. He wished his play to be a "medley" of "laughter, & tears, prose & verse & in some places rhime, songs, wit, pathos, humour, & if possible sublimity." "Discordant atoms" might be the result (*M,* 1:152). Ideally, though, this mix of elements would be a dynamic conversation among diverse perspectives and expressions, always ironic, since the tragic moments would be qualified by the comic and vice versa, and the whole blend would feel less like literature, often consistent in genre and voice, and more like life: messy, contradictory, bizarre.

Near the end of August 1800, while Lamb was still waiting to hear from Kemble about his play, Mary produced her first extant poem, "Helen Repentant Too Late." Empathetically, she creates a speaker who resembles her brother much more than herself. The male lover has pined for a "high-born Helen" for twenty years. He has "pac'd in vain" around her "dwelling," while she has gloried in his pain. But one day she relents, and the lover need no longer complain. But it is too late. Outside his role as pining lover, he has no identity. He loved the "'scorn in her eye.'" Now that her sighs match his, the thrill is gone. He rejects the living Helen. He hangs a portrait of her at his bedside, and to this inanimate image he now sings his "mournful lays." His true love is masochism (*W,* 5:26).

Poe could have written this poem, which first appeared in 1802, included in the volume containing *John Woodvil* and the Burton extracts. It expresses the solipsism of romantic love, which is more about the intense feelings of the lover than the beloved. The beloved is valuable only as an ideal onto which the lover projects his desires. When she behaves as a warm woman would, he recoils. The last thing he wants is a real relationship, which would require him to empathize with another. As is true of all romantic lovers, he is in love with death: an actual woman so indifferent to his pleadings that she seems artificial or, better, an artificial woman, as in a painting, who is incapable of returning his love.

Why would Mary, who had never been in romantic love (as far as we know), write this poem? Maybe she was exploring her brother's complex romantic feelings toward Ann Simmons. But why at that time, after Charles had ostensibly gotten over her? Charles had seen Ann again fairly recently, though. Did this contact incite his passion again?

Maybe Mary wrote the poem to poke gentle fun at her brother. Perhaps she was bitter over Charles wasting so much of his affection on a cold idol. Was she tired of his (childish) melancholy? The sonnet Lamb wrote in Hoxton suggests that he owed Mary an apology for enduring his "lovesick lays."

Possibly the poem expresses Mary's pain. While confined, she might have pined for her brother as a lover desires a beloved. But upon living with him and putting up with his drinking and depression and punning, she felt disappointed. Did she prefer the brother she imagined, locked up in her asylum, as her savior?

Through the fall of 1800, Lamb socialized with Manning and Godwin. He also fraternized with Ralph Fell, a prodigious drinker and raconteur who inspired quaffing and punning. Fell later wrote *A Tour through the Batavian Republic during the Latter Part of the Year 1800* and a biography of Charles James Fox. Lamb also befriended John Fenwick, another extravagant drinker and, apparently, a borrower. He was the model for "Bigod" in Elia's essay "The Two Races of Men," and he edited a newspaper, the *Albion*, for which Lamb would soon write.

One evening Lamb and Fell were with Godwin. The philosopher fell asleep after supper—as was his habit—and while he was napping, Lamb and Fell carried "off his rum—brandy—sugar—picked his pockets of every thing—& made off in triumph."[14]

Godwin admired Lamb now. He asked him to contribute the epilogue to his first play *Antonio; or, The Soldier's Return*.[15] The play, at which Godwin had been at work for about two years, is a Shakespearean tragedy, down to the blank verse, of vow breaking and revenge. Antonio loves his sister Helena, who is betrothed to his best friend Roderigo. While the two men are off at war, Helena marries Don Gusman. When Antonio returns, he is furious, and tries to have the marriage annulled. Failing, he kills his sister.

Lamb's epilogue, which he completed only a few days before the play's debut on December 13, 1800, at Drury Lane, has little to do with the play, and it is far from tragic. He sent it to Manning only hours before the play was to open. After some statements about the play's promise breaking, it tells the faintly humorous story of Jack, a hatter who falls so deeply in love with the theater that he squanders all his earnings on the stage, putting him and his family on the brink of financial ruin. He promises his wife to amend his ways but breaks his vow.

The play failed. Twenty years later, in the Elia essay "The Old Actors," Lamb described the debacle. He sat in a box between Godwin (G.) and Godwin's friend and assistant James Marshall (M.). In the beginning, Godwin "sate cheerful and confident, but "in his friend M.'s looks, who had perused the manuscript," Lamb "read some terror." By the end of the play, during which there was virtually no applause, the "whole house rose up in clamorous indignation demanding justice." The audience was angered by Antonio's murder of his sister. "The feeling rose far above hisses I believe at that instant, if they could have got him, they would have torn the unfortunate author to pieces. . . . M., I believe, was the only person who suffered acutely from the failure; for G. thenceforward, with a serenity unattainable but by the true philosophy, abandoning a precarious popularity, retired into his fast hold of speculation" (*W*, 2:293).

But because of this failure, Lamb loved Godwin all the more, as well as Marshall. As Lamb wrote to Manning, "The **Professor** has won my heart by this *his* mournful catastrophe. . . . You remember Marshall, who dined with him at my house!—I met him in the lobby immediately after the damnation of the Professor's play, and he looked to me like an angel: his face was lengthen'd, and **all over sweat**; I never saw such a care-fraught visage; I could have hugg'd him, I loved him so intensely—'From every pore of him a Perfume fell'" (*M*, 1:259).

Godwin got the play into print quickly, by December 22, after Lamb suggested detailed revisions. The result did not improve Godwin's reputation as a dramatist. (Though he did try the stage again in 1807, with *Faulkner*, for which Lamb wrote a brief prologue.) Three days later, Lamb invited Godwin to Christmas dinner in the Southampton Buildings. George Dyer was also there, along with Lamb's new friend John Rickman.

All of Lamb's supping in Godwin's London and Manning's Cambridge inspired in him a great appetite for, and appreciation of, food. After returning from Cambridge, he praises Manning's "fine hare and fine birds," saying he now looks forward to eating more, to help him combat a hangover.

> Foh! how beautiful and strong those buttered onions come to my nose! For you must know we extract a divine spirit of Gravy from those materials, which duly compounded with a consistence of bread & cream (y'clept bread sauce) each to each giving double grace, do mutually illustrate and set off (as skillful gold-foils to rare jewels) Your partridge, pheasant, woodcock, snipe, teal, widgeon, and the other lesser daughters of the **Ark**. . . . My friendship, struggling with my Carnal & **fleshly** prudence (which suggests that a bird a man is the proper allotment in such cases) yearneth sometimes to have thee here to pick a wing or so. (*M*, 1:237)

This bachelor's culinary writing reaches its erotic apotheosis in the Elia essay on roast pig.[16] The piece opens with a wacky account of the origin of roasting, gleaned, Elia claims, from a Chinese manuscript his friend M. (Manning) translated for him. For their "first seventy thousand ages," the Chinese "ate their meat raw." Fortunately, an accident occurred. Bo-bo, the oldest son of the swineherd Ho-ti, liked to play with fire, and one day he inadvertently set the house ablaze, along with "a fine litter of new-farrowed pigs." As he was fretting over how to explain this calamity to his father, "an odour assailed his nostrils, unlike any scent which he had before experienced." His mouth watered. As he felt the flesh of a dead pig, the heat burned his fingers; he put them in his mouth to cool them. For the "first time in his life (in the world's life indeed, for before him no man had known it) he tasted—crackling!" Bo-bo began cramming the roasted flesh "down his throat in his beastly fashion" (*W*, 2:121).

Soon the father discovers the gustatory ecstasy of roast pig. Wishing to duplicate the tasty meal, he and his son rebuild the house, put piglets inside, burn it down, and relish the crackling. This they do repeatedly but secretly, fearing that they are breaking a taboo. Their "terrible mystery" is found out, however, and they are brought before a judge. Once the court tastes the burned pig, Ho-ti and Bo-bo are acquitted. Everyone in the entire village then roasts pigs by burning down their homes, until a sage, "like our Locke," realizes that the flesh of swine, or indeed of any "other animal, might be cooked . . . without the necessity of consuming a whole house to dress it" (*W*, 2:122–23).

Elia admits that we shouldn't place "too implicit faith" in this account. This is an understatement. Through Elia, Lamb parodies the sort of exotic travel narratives his friend Coleridge once consumed like a cormorant. The East India employee understood the imperialistic impulse behind Englishmen reducing the lore of foreign cultures to domestic terminology. Lamb also criticizes imperialism by suggesting that there is little difference between Elia and Bo-bo, colonizer and colonized. Both are gluttons.

The remainder of the essay depicts Elia in an increasingly negative light. He might be his typical whimsical self—of "all the delicacies in the whole *mundus edibilis*, I will maintain [crackling] to be the most delicate—*princeps obsoniorum*"—but his attitude toward piglets is disturbing. Slaughter the pigs young, he proclaims, when they are "tender," "under a moon old—guiltless as yet of the sty—with no original speck of the amor immunditiæ, the hereditary failing of the first parent, yet manifest—his voice as yet not broken, but something between a childish treble, and a grumble—the mild forerunner, or præludium, of a grunt" (*W*, 2:123).

We picture a human baby burning. In Elia's sadistic fantasy, the infant pig *enjoys* getting cooked. The fire seems "a refreshing warmth" rather than "a scorching heat." Even more unsettling: the pig's "tender age" is expressed by its crying, as a baby would, but the tears are the "radiant jellies" exuded by his boiled eyes. When the pig is finally dished, he lies in his "second cradle" (*W*, 2:124).

This monstrous vision is not the apex of Elia's cruelty. He wonders if the "tender" victim would taste even better if its flesh were whipped prior to slaughter. Though he is aware that this practice sounds horrendous, he feels justified in considering its efficacy in "a philosophical light merely" (*W*, 2:125). But rather than soften Elia, this intellectual distancing shows him psychopathically removed, picturing infant whipping in a mental game.

After envisioning the baby pig scourged and burned and cradled, Elia turns it into an object of sexual desire. The cooked pig is the "best of Sapors," and pineapple intensifies the flavor: the fruit, which Lamb refers to as a "she," "is indeed almost too transcendent—a delight, if not sinful, yet so like to sinning, that really a tender-conscienced person would do well to pause—

too ravishing for mortal taste, she woundeth and excoriateth the lips that approach her—like lovers' kisses, she biteth—she is a pleasure bordering on pain from the fierceness and insanity of her relish" (*W,* 2:124).

Dish and relish drive Elia into an erotic frenzy. He is part Petrarch—so ferocious is his love for Laura he feels he might go mad—and part Poe: the acme of amour is for a dead thing. But all of this . . . for a roasted animal. The sweet Elia of "New Year's Eve" has become a cannibal in love with his victim, as unhinged as Hannibal Lecter.

Lamb's extravagantly creepy Elia reveals the psychosexual roots of imperialism.[17] The colonizer in this portrait lusts after those he subjugates but expresses this lust through cruelty. That the lust is directed toward an infant suggests pedophilia: the imperialist desires to violate innocent victims unable to defend themselves.

It is not difficult to interpret "Dissertation upon Roast Pig" more lightly—as a joke at the expense of the kind of sentimentalism the vegetarian Shelley held toward creatures great and small. This is the comically anti-sentimental Lamb who, when asked how he liked children, responded, "B-b-boiled."[18] The essay could also simply be satirizing the capitalistic culture of consumption, in which all things are reduced to commodities to be engulfed. Certainly Lamb criticizes gluttony in his Elia essay "Grace before Meat."

But these readings miss the ferociousness of Lamb's attack on the perverse values of the company he worked for, as well as his country's leaders and their supporters. While Lamb in his indictment of injustice glances back at Swift in "A Modest Proposal," his surreal conjoining of power, sex, and addiction looks ahead to William Burroughs's *Naked Lunch.*

Lamb pushed Elia this far away from himself only one other time, in "Imperfect Sympathies," a satire of prejudice. His habit was to keep his alter ego close. He didn't want to sacrifice Elia's likability.

If Elia allowed Lamb to explore ideas he himself found repellant, Elia also enabled Lamb to articulate desires he otherwise, most likely, would not have. For instance, Elia in the pig dissertation expressed erotic feelings Lamb himself would probably not reveal. Elia also expresses romantic, if not erotic, longings in "Valentine's Day" and "Dream-Children."

In an Elia essay especially autobiographical—about his relationship with his cousin (sister) and their relatives in Hertfordshire—Lamb admits that he "find[s] in [him]self no sort of disposition to go out upon the mountains, with the rash king's offspring, to bewail [his] celibacy" (*W,* 2:75). Does this mean that Lamb never had sex? Even though he never married, he could have found outlets for his sexuality that were not socially unacceptable. There in the "bustle and wickedness of Covent Garden" that Lamb so adored were the "very women of the Town," the prostitutes (*M*, 1:267). Of Lamb's literary friends and acquaintances, several did more than verbally celebrate London the city "with-the-many-sins . . . abounding in whores" (*M*, 1:248). Coleridge, Shelley, Keats, and Hazlitt (especially Hazlitt) all partook of London's bustling sex market. In 1817, some 360 brothels operated in London, containing about two thousand prostitutes. No laws prohibited the practice; it was a regular part of city life.[19]

Lamb's letter to Wordsworth of June 26, 1806, hints at an outing to a brothel. Hazlitt was in town, and the two of them went out one evening to "see a very pretty girl professedly, where there were two young girls—the very head & sum of **Girlery** was two young girls—they neither laughed nor sneered nor giggled nor whispered—but they were young girls—and he [Hazlitt] sat and frowned blacker & blacker indignant that there should be such a thing as Youth & Beauty, till he tore me away before supper in perfect misery & owned he could not **bear** young girls" (*M*, 2:233). Duncan Wu, Hazlitt's biographer, believes that these girls were almost certainly prostitutes. If so, it appears that the exchange of money for love did not happen on this occasion, owing to Hazlitt's mood, frequently sullen around women he desired.[20]

If this letter does describe a visit to a brothel, it's the only time in all of Lamb's known letters when he even nods at participating in the sex trade. We simply don't have enough information to say if Lamb had a sex life or not. If he did join his fellow writers in frequenting London's "dirtiest drab-frequented alley[s]" (*M*, 1:277), he remained remarkably discreet about his escapades. If he didn't, it was perhaps because his Unitarian beliefs encouraged him to keep his bodily urges in check.

Or maybe he didn't buy sex because he simply wasn't a very sexual being, at least in the traditional sense. Even if he approached food and drink with an erotic gusto, perhaps Lamb simply didn't think in terms of sexuality. This possibility seems odd in our post-Freudian age.

Language was just as sensual to Lamb as pheasants and Fleet, and in his letters of this fall of 1800, he continued to create lush comedy. To Manning he sent a masterpiece of slapstick. He hates that Manning missed in London "an exhibition quite uncommon in Europe": "**A Live Rattle Snake 10 feet in Length**, and of the thickness of a big **Leg**." Lamb saw it last night, "by candlelight," in "a room very little bigger than [theirs] at Pentonville," where a man, woman, and four boys live with nine snakes so poisonous, there is no known antidote for their bites.

> We walked into the middle, which is formed by a half-moon of wired boxes, all mansions of **Snakes**,—Whip snakes, Thunder-snakes, Pig nose-snakes, American **Vipers**, and this *monster*.— He lies curled up in folds; and immediately a stranger enters (for he is used to the family, & sees them play at cards) he set up a rattle like a watchman's in London, or near as loud, and reared up a head, from the midst of these folds, like a **Toad**, and shook his head, and showed every sign a snake can show of irritation.— I had the foolish curiosity to strike the wires with my finger, and the devil flew at me with his Toad-mouth wide open.— the inside of his mouth is quite white. I had got my finger away, nor could he well have bit me with his big mouth, which would have been certain death in five minutes. But it frightened me so much that I did not recover my voice for a minute's space. I forgot in my fear that he was secured. You would have forgot too, for 'tis incredible how such a monster can be confined in small gauzy-looking wires.— I dream'd of snakes in the night.— I wish to Heaven you could see it. He absolutely swelled with passion to the bigness of a large **thigh**.— I could not retreat without infringing on another box, and just behind, a little devil, not an inch from my back, had got his nose out, with some difficulty and pain, quite thro the bars! He was soon taught better manners—— All the Snakes were curious & objects of Terror. But this monster, like Aarons serpent, swallowed up the impression of the rest—. He opened his damned mouth, when he made at me, as wide as his head was broad.— I hollooed out quite loud—. And felt pains all over my body with the fright—— (*M*, 1: 241–42)

The vivid language galvanized by striking imagery—"reared up a head, from the midst of these folds, like a **Toad**," "the inside of his mouth is quite white"—brings the scene cinematically to life. Harold Lloyd—more Lamb's type than Chaplin or Keaton—might do this bit—or, more recently and with sound, John Cleese.

# CHAPTER 19

## *Flâneur*

Manning replaced Coleridge as Lamb's closest friend. Lamb remained fond of Coleridge, though. He thrilled to Coleridge's living with him in the spring of 1800, he helped his old friend see his translation of Schiller through the press, and he continued to write him warm letters.

Still, Lamb was hurt by Coleridge's favoring of the Wordsworths over him. The pain shows in a letter to Manning in August 1800. "Coleridge is settled with his Wife (with a child in her Guts) and the young philosopher at **Keswick** with the Wordsworths." Lamb's rough description of pregnancy is uncharacteristic of this paragon of gallantry. It indicates aggression. Lamb continues: "They have contrived to spawn a new volume of **Lyrical** Balads, which is to see the Light in about a month, & causes no little excitement in the *Literary World*" (M, 1:221–22). These men make their book with artifice, not the organicism they philosophically value. If there is organicity, it is unseemly: they birth the book as frogs or fish their eggs. The litotes modifying "excitement" suggests that *Lyrical Ballads* causes not much excitement at all. It will only stimulate the "literary world," which takes itself more seriously than it merits.

A letter to Coleridge is also tinged with bitterness. Lamb reminds the poet that he promised to send him Wordsworth's play *The Borderers*, and Lamb would be happy if he would do so. Manning is with him, and the two want to read it together. That is an understatement. If he were "alone in Cold Bath Prison, or in the Desert Island, just when Prospero & his crew had set off, with Caliban in a cage, to Milan, it would be a treat to me to read that play" (*M*, 1:234). Manning has read it already, and Charles Lloyd, and all of Lloyd's family, so why not me?

These epistles contextualize the November 23 letter to Manning. Charles and Sophia Lloyd, now with a child and settled in Ambleside, have invited Lamb to visit. He has the means to accept and is bent on escaping his office anyway. Please don't be offended, Manning, if I back out of my proposed visit to you in Cambridge. Surely you can understand my desire to go, since, having been "pent up all my life in a dirty city," I imagine release in the Lakes. "Consider Grasmere! Ambleside! Wordsworth! Coleridge!" (*M*, 1:247). Lamb has become his character in "This Lime-tree Bower My Prison": the gentle-hearted urban inmate desperate for mountains and lakes. This is the Lamb who could fit in with Coleridge's new circle, who would not be silent and awkward among the landscapers.

**"Hills, woods, Lakes, and mountains, to the Eternal Devil**. I will eat snipes with thee, Thomas Manning." Thus Lamb exclaims, after the sentence ostensibly praising "Wordsworth! Coleridge!" He was mocking the nature fanaticism of the Lake Poets. He will keep his promise to Manning. "With reference to my friends northward, I must confess that I am not romance-bit about *Nature*."

The earth, and sea, and sky . . . is but as a house to dwell in. If the inmates be courteous, and good liquors flow like the conduits at an old coronation, if they can talk sensibly and feel properly, I have no need to stand staring upon the gilded Looking-glass . . . , nor his five-shilling print over the mantel Piece of old Nabbs the Carrier. . . . Just as important to me (in a sense) is all the furniture of my world. Eye-pampering, but satisfies no heart. Streets, streets, streets, markets, theatres, churches, Covent Gardens, Shops sparkling with pretty faces of industrious milliners, neat sempstresses, Ladies cheapening, Gentlemen behind counters lying, Authors in the street with spectacles, George Dyers (you may know them by their gait) Lamps lit at night, Pastry-cooks' & Silver smith shops, Beautiful Quakers of Pentonville [like Hester], noise of coaches, drousy cry of mechanic watchman at night, with Bucks reeling home drunk if you happen to wake at midnight, cries of fire & stop thief, Inns of court (with their learned air

and halls and Butteries, just like Cambridge colleges), old Book stalls,
Jeremy Taylors, Burtons on melancholy, and Religio Medici's on every
stall—. These are thy Pleasures O London with-the-many-sins—O
City abounding in whores—for these may Keswick and her giant
brood go hang (*M,* 1:248)

Nature is no better nor worse than a city. Both are houses to dwell in, and
they are best inhabited by good conversation and booze. If Lamb can enjoy
vibrant talk, he has no need to gaze at aesthetic objects, artificial or natural.
But if Lamb is to look at beautiful things, he will choose the city, with its
whirl of the sordid and the sweet, books and thieves, sexy women and cries
of fire.

Lamb establishes himself as a writer separate from the Lake Poets, and not
just separate—opposed. His is an urban Romanticism.

Lamb elaborates his opposition to the Lake Poets three months later, in
his first known letter to Wordsworth. Until this time, Lamb's contact with
Wordsworth had been minimal. Aside from enduring Coleridge's worship of
the man, Lamb had been in Wordsworth's presence only once, during his visit
to Nether Stowey in 1797. He took a hike with him; he admired "Lines Left
upon a Seat in a Yew Tree."

In his January 30, 1801, letter, Lamb acknowledges an earlier correspondence from Wordsworth. It included the second edition of *Lyrical Ballads,*
recently published. Lamb has already perused the second volume, and he
appreciates the "Song of Lucy," by which he means "She dwelt among the
untrodden ways." He also commends "To a Sexton" (which made him cry)
and "To Joanna" (where the "mountains and all the scenery seem absolutely
alive"). And he extols "the delicate and curious feeling in the wish for the
Cumberland Beggar, that he may ha[ve] about him the melody of Birds,
altho' he hear them not.— Here the mind knowingly passes a fiction upon
herself, first substituting her own feelings for the Beggar's, and, in the same
breath detecting the fallacy, will not part with the wish" (*M,* 1:265). This
striking observation grows from the sort of moment only Wordsworth could
illuminate: a feeling so specific it feels weird, yet, once described, so common
as to seem universal.

Wordsworth at his strangest suits Lamb. What about the dogmatic Wordsworth? Lamb chafes at "The Poet's Epigraph," Wordsworth's crude satire of
narrow-minded lawyers, preachers, statesmen, philosophers, physicians, and

the like. Such didacticism also shows up in the otherwise fine "Beggar," near the end when Wordsworth lectures readers on what to feel. Ideas in poems should "slide into the mind of the reader," not be foisted upon him. Intelligent readers are insulted by "being told, I will teach you how to think upon this subject." This fault appears in Sterne and other modern novelists, "who continually put a sign post up to shew **where you are to feel**." These writers assume their readers are "stupid." How much more powerful are those "beautiful bare narratives" of *Robinson Crusoe, The Vicar of Wakefield,* and *Roderick Random*. In these works, there "is implied an unwritten compact between Author and reader; I will tell you a story, and I suppose you will understand it" (*M,* 1:265–66).

Lamb leaves off his criticisms of Wordsworth's verse—"I have written so much only that you may not think I have passed over your book without observation"—and turns to the poet's misunderstanding of Coleridge. In this edition of *Lyrical Ballads,* Coleridge's *The Rime of the Ancient Mariner* is subtitled "A Poet's Reverie." To Lamb, this is as bad as Wordsworth telling readers what to feel, since it sets up expectations that could limit a reader's experience of this unearthly poem, far weirder than a mere reverie. Unlike Wordsworth, who thinks the old sailor should have a "character and a profession," Lamb holds that the ballad's power originates from the Mariner's trials being so horrendous they "bury all individuality or memory of what he was" (*M,* 1: 266–67). Lamb also disagrees with Wordsworth's conclusion that the Mariner gains supernatural powers from spiritual forces. The Mariner may have strange powers simply because he has strange powers.

Aside from the poetry, Lamb has another problem with the volume. The now-famous preface is the same as Coleridge's subtitle and Wordsworth's poetic lessons: it is reductive, boiling possibility down to one option. Even if the "dogmas are true and just," the poems are diminished when Wordsworth asserts they were written as an "Experiment on the public taste." Surely, the poems were up-gushes from "living and daily circumstances" more than exploration of a hypothesis (*M,* 1:267). While the Lake Poet when relaxed conjures eldritch lyricism, he tends toward a dogmatic, top-down poetic in which his verses are "examples of" arguments. Lamb values the bottom-up: literature springing from curious, delicate feelings.

Instantly Lamb writes the way he has just advocated. After refusing Wordsworth's "very kind invitation" to the Lakes (he and Mary can't afford it), he asserts that, although he would value the Wordsworths' company, he doesn't care if he never sees a mountain again. Then: the best piece of early writing from Lamb, a casual prose poem (akin to the one he wrote Manning) praising the city and the proper way to experience the city—wander loose and ready. London is "the Lighted shops of the Strand and Fleet Street, the innumerable trades, tradesmen and customers, coaches, wagons, playhouses, all the bustle and wickedness round about Covent Garden, the very women of the Town, the Watchmen, drunken scenes, rattles;—life awake, if you awake, at all hours of the night, the impossibility of being dull in Fleet Street, the crowds, the very dirt & mud, the sun shining upon houses and pavements, the print-shops, the **old Book** stalls, parsons cheap'ning books, coffee-houses, steams of soups from kitchens, the pantomimes, London itself, a pantomime and a masquerade." "All these things work themselves into my mind and feed me without a power of satiating me. The wonder of these sights impels me into night-walks about her crowded streets, and I often shed tears in the motley Strand from fulness of joy at so much **Life**. All these emotions must be strange to you. So are your rural emotions to me" (*M*, 1:266–67).

Here is Wordsworth's essence urbanized and contained in a paragraph. Like Wordsworth, Lamb values dynamic interactions between mind and environment. London stokes Lamb's mind, and in turn his mind imbues the city with fresh intensity. Lamb also favors the local as the locus for poetry. You grow up in Grasmere, you write nature verse. If London is your origin, street lit is your genre. (Hazlitt wrote of Lamb's awkwardness in the country. When his city friend visited in Winterslow, he "was 'like the most capricious poet Ovid among the Goths.'")[1]

But beyond these similar methods (in vastly difference environments), Lamb's style is as unlike Wordsworth's as London differs from the Lakes. Lamb promotes a paratactic openness to novelty that the rock-loving Wordsworth would never try. Literature for Wordsworth increasingly became a kind of religion of which he was priest, and a series of symbols—wind, mountain, moon, lake. For Lamb, the opposite: the literary is a way of participating in an urban world resistant to stable signs, where to live is to move.

Lamb's urban Romanticism glances back at the London ramblings of Addison and Steele but, more interestingly, looks ahead to the flâneur: Baudelaire, Woolf, Walter Benjamin.

Lamb's city pleasure is the ecstasy of the et cetera, each street a whirligig, perpetually different from itself.[2] All that brings the assorted events together is the walker's gaze. It catalogues the sights into ever-shifting sequences. Unlike maps, designed to coordinate long stretches, these lists temporarily arrange the immediate surrounding. They become obsolete the instant the stroller veers to a new scene.

As Baudelaire describes him, the flâneur, the "passionate spectator" who sets up "house in the heart of the multitude," loves the list. He throbs in "the ebb and flow of movement, in the midst of the fugitive and the infinite." Though he is unmoored, blowing where the crowd drifts, he is also firmly staked, since his consciousness organizes the currents into personal patterns. He is like a "mirror as vast as the crowd itself," or a "kaleidoscope gifted with consciousness, responding to each one of its movements and reproducing the multiplicity of life and the flickering grace of all the elements of life."[3]

In the current—it is electric—the flâneur strangely blends voyeurism and empathy, watching the world without being watched, loving what he sees. He is, like Whitman in "Song of Myself," in the game and out of the game, a deliberate loafer. He is, as with Poe's London narrator in "The Man of the Crowd," a pursuer of the city's most idiosyncratic creatures, attuned to their inscrutability.

Walter Benjamin thought the flâneur embodied the struggle of the modern urban man, between numbing overstimulation and ecstatic alertness. It is the ecstasy that draws Woolf into London in "Street Haunting," where twilight phantasmagoria frees her from her room's well-apportioned memories. Later, New York's Frank O'Hara records the city's glinting accidents during his breaks from MOMA. More recently, in *Open City*, Teju Cole turns New York's streets into arcades of loss.

# CHAPTER 20

## *Journalism*

Right after sending his flâneur's creed to Wordsworth, Lamb described his urban affection to Robert Lloyd: "I have lent out my heart with usury to such scenes from my childhood up.—and have cried with the fullness of joy at the multitudinous scenes of Life in the crouded streets of ever dear London." Lamb wishes Robert could move to London. Depend upon it, if you understand my "low Urban taste," you will see that "**a mob of men is better than a flock of sheep**——and a crowd of happy faces jostling into the playhouse at the hour of six is a more beautiful spectacle to man than the shepherd driving his **'silly' sheep to fold**——" (*M*, 1:271).

The Lake Poets were displeased, Lamb reported to Manning. His "opinion" of *Lyrical Ballads* has set all "the North of England . . . in a turmoil." Wordsworth produced "a long letter of four sweating pages . . . the purport of which was, that he was sorry his 2d vol. had not given me more pleasure (Devil a hint did I give that it had *not pleased me*), and 'was compelled to wish that my range of **Sensibility** was more extended, being obliged to believe that I should receive large influxes of happiness & happy Thoughts' (I suppose from the L.B.—)" Wordsworth audaciously compared himself to Milton, claiming that he and the author of *Paradise Lost* shared a "certain **Union of Tenderness & Imagination**" that is "the highest species of Poetry," a species higher than Shakespeare attained. Lamb finds Wordsworth's claims absurd: "After one has been reading Shaksp. twenty of the best years of one's life, to have a fellow start up, and prate about some unknown quality, which Shakspeare possess'd in a degree inferior to Milton and somebody else! !" (*M*, 1:272–73).

Coleridge, who had not written in months, roused from his sickbed to "reprove" Lamb for his "hard presumption. "Four long pages, equally sweaty and more tedious, came from him: assuring me that, when the works of a man of true genius such as W. undoubtedly was, do not please me at first sight, I should suspect the fault to lie 'in me & not in them'" (*M*, 1:273).

"What am I to do with such people?" Write them a "very merry Letter" (*M*, 1:273). (If Lamb did write this letter, it is lost.)

Almost two weeks later, on February 27, 1801, in another letter to Manning, Lamb provides a definition of imagination appropriate to his taste for invigorating ambiguity. Opposed to Wordsworth, who views imagination as the capacity to imbue ordinary events with extraordinary meaning, Lamb thinks imagination is the power to generate multiple interpretations of the same event. The power is exhilarating, like riding a "good blood mare," but also dangerous, since it opens "too many paths" over which the horse might run (*M*, 1:275).

As winter turned into spring, Lamb invoked a champion of his kind of imagination, Bishop Jeremy Taylor. In a letter to Robert Lloyd, Lamb claimed that this seventeenth-century divine has "more, & more beautiful, imagery and (what is more to a Lover of Willy [Shakespeare]) more knowledge & description of **human life** and manners, than any prose book on the language." He moreover has "more **delicacy, & sweetness**, than any mortal, the 'gentle' Shakespear hardly excepted,—his similes and allusions are taken, as the bees take honey, from all the youngest, greenest, exquisitest parts of nature, from plants, & flowers, & fruit, young boys & **virgins**, from little children perpetually, from sucking infants, babies' smiles, roses, gardens,—his imagination was a spatious Garden where no vile insectae could crawl in." Lamb most admires Taylor's 1651 *The Rules and Exercises of Holy Dying*, a manual for understanding death. Lamb recommends that Robert read the first chapter, paying special attention to the first paragraph of section 2, which features, in Lamb's summary, "for a simile . . . a rose, or more truly many similes within simile, for such were the riches of his fancy, that when a beauteous image offered, before he could stay to expand it into all its capacities, throngs of new coming images came up, and justled out the first, or blended in disorder with it, which imitates the order of every rapid mind" (*M*, 2:4–5).

In the passage, Taylor (now in his own words) likens the "mighty change" death makes in a person—from "fair cheeks" to "dead paleness"—to a "rose newly springing from the clefts of its hood." "First, [the rose] was fair as the morning, and full with the dew of heaven, as a lamb's fleece; but when a ruder breath had forced open its virgin modesty, and dismantled its too youthful and unripe retirements, it began to put on darkness, and to decline to softness and the symptoms of a sickly age; it bowed the head, and broke its stalk; and at night, having lost some of its leaves and all its beauty, it fell into the portion of weeds and outworn faces."[1]

Images birth images. The "dew of heaven" resting on the morning petals is "lamb's fleece." Metaphor ("dew" is literal, but "heaven's dew" is not) begets a simile. The innocent "lamb's fleece" metamorphoses into virginal flesh being forced open by the "ruder breath" of mortality. This is rape, of innocence by experience. The "mantles" of the innocent—the clothing but also the walls, as of a fortress—can't defend against time. Denuded and violated, the rose must put on another vestment, "darkness." The weight of the shadow pushes the rose downward, breaks its stalk, and night pushes the flower down into weeds and "outworn faces," human faces, which remind readers why Taylor fashioned the image in the first place.

A new path had just opened for Lamb's imagination. He and Mary planned to move on the day of "our Lady's next feast," March 25, 1801. The rooms, Lamb writes Manning, are "delectable," and they "look out (when you stand Tip toe) over the Thames & Surrey Hills; at the upper end of King's Bench walks in the **Temple**." The lodging, 16 Mitre Court Buildings, is in Lamb's old domain, the pastoral Inner Temple. "I shall have all the privacy of a house without the encumbrance, and shall be able to lock my friends out as often as I desire to hold free converse with my immortal mind." But if his new lodging is hidden and cozy, it is also bright and vibrant. Located on the fourth floor, it is as "airy" as if it were in the country, and gardens surround it (*M*, 1:277). Lamb can see from his bed in the morning "the white sails glide by the bottom of King's Bench walks" (*M*, 2:3). Still, Lamb would not trade the "dirtiest drab-frequented alley, and her lowest bowing Tradesman" for any natural scene, including the "Skiddaw" and "Helvellyn" of the Lakes (*M*, 1:277).

With this new lodging came a new vocation: journalism. Lamb needed more money. He and Mary had to sell their guest bed to pay for the move, and the rent in the Inner Temple was probably higher than in Holborn. They could not afford a maid. Lamb was also lending money to Coleridge, and he knew that at any time, he might have to pay for Mary's confinement.

Whereas his connection with Coleridge had failed to land him newspaper work (Coleridge had unsuccessfully recommended Lamb to the *Morning Post*), his relationship with Godwin did. Through Godwin he met Fenwick, who, in addition to being a drinker and borrower, was also a reformer. He wrote the first biography of Godwin, and he might well have been a part of the Philomaths, a distinguished conversation club that included, among others, Godwin, John Thelwall, and Thomas Holcroft. After the owner of the *Albion* was jailed for libel against the Prince of Wales, Fenwick took over the enterprise, sometime in the spring of 1801. By June of that year, he had hired Lamb.

The spendthrift Fenwick couldn't afford to run the paper himself. He got help from wealthy aristocrats, such as Lords Stanhope and Petre, who shared the paper's radical values, especially its commitment to Catholic emancipation. But even with this funding, the paper's headquarters—located at 197 Fleet, former location of Rackstrow's Museum of anatomical oddities—were shabby compared to those of the *Morning Post*. While the *Post* was housed in "a handsome apartment" with "rose-wood desks, and silver-inkstands," the *Albion* worked out of a "den" "just redeemed from the occupation of dead monsters, of which it seemed redolent." "This murky closet" of "vulgarity and sedition" was cramped, "inadequate from its square contents to the receipt of the two bodies of Editor, and humble paragraph-maker" (*W*, 2:244).

Even though the paper was a "hopeless concern" when Fenwick took over, he envisioned his pages pulling "down the Government" in addition to making a fortune for him and Lamb. For seven weeks, kept barely afloat by the patronage of the likes of Stanhope and Fenwick's borrowing, Lamb and his editor wrote "treason." But the treason was rather tepid, based more on "recollections of feelings" of boyish fervor for the French Revolution "than any tendency . . . to Republican doctrines." And to avoid libel, the paper had to "insinuate, rather than recommend, possible abdications." "Blocks, axes, Whitehall tribunals, were covered with flowers of so cunning a periphrasis . . . that the keen eye of an Attorney General was insufficient to detect the lurking snake among them" (*W*, 2:225).

Writing for the *Albion* threw Lamb into his country's turmoil. England was still at war with France, Catholic emancipation was fiercely debated in Parliament, the country was falling deeper into debt, wheat was scare because of a blockade. The *Albion* reported on these events of great import, but also covered more sensationalist fare, like abortion pills and lightning strikes and a man whose skin turned from black to white. Lamb's probable pieces, identified by his heavy use of italics, were primarily philosophical satire. In one of his "paragraphs," he mocks how England dehumanizes its enemy the French, not even allowing that the Frenchman is a man. A poem by one of Lamb's favorite poets, Marvell, is a corrective, asserting that every man mixes good and bad. In another paragraph, Lamb chastises conservative writers who twist Burke's "splendid political sophisms." These men resemble the *"crooked man"* described by a "facetious Greek professor" who "swallowed a *threepenny nail*, and voided it out a cork-screw!"[2]

Lamb's longest piece in the *Albion* is "What Is Jacobinism?" A parrot calls everyone who walks by a "Jacobin." Men are the same. They indiscriminately call men better than themselves "Jacobin," with no thought toward the particular nature of these men. These parrot-men pin "Jacobinism" on any man whom they believe evil. This Manichean reduction is philosophical laziness. It is easier "violently to force into *one class*, modes and actions, and principles *essentially various*, and to disgrace that *class* with one ugly name" than to think about things themselves, nuanced and complex. Lamb ties the word to things. "Jacobin" refers to a group of men who desired, in the wake of the French Revolution, to improve the world by destroying the oppressive practices of "ancient usage." Eventually the word cut free from this historical context and became a general term for everything Anti-Jacobins disliked. Now the word condemns factions "foreign to politics," such as Unitarian Christianity and Sunday newspapers.[3] "What Is Jacobinism?" demonstrates Lamb's continuing commitment to democratic causes. More important, the essay predicts Lamb's stance in the Elia essays: a suspicion of ideas and an embrace of quirky, pell-mell particulars.

By August, Lamb's peculiar writing lost him his job, and not only that—he shut down the paper. He wrote an epigram on Sir James McIntosh that offended Stanhope, and the lord pulled his funding. Lamb included the offending epigram a letter to Manning dated August 22. This epigram, "one of the last I *did* for the Albion," mocks McIntosh for being an apostate:

> Tho thou'rt like Judas an apostate black,
> In the resemblance one thing thou dost lack;
> When he had gotten his ill-purchas'd pelf,
> He went away, & wisely hang'd himself:
> This thou do at last; yet much I doubt,
> If thou hast any **Bowels** to gush out! (*M*, 2:13)

Lamb believed the barrister McIntosh a Judas-like traitor because of his political flip-flopping. In 1791, McIntosh had attacked the conservative Burke's
*Reflections on the French Revolution*. But after meeting Burke, he accepted his
former opponent's views. Lamb connected this turn with McIntosh's desire
for a post in India, more likely to be granted if his opinions corresponded to
those of the government.

Fenwick moved on to edit the *Plough*, funded by the Duke of Northumberland. Lamb did not follow. With the help of Dyer, he received an offer to
write for the more prestigious *Morning Chronicle*. As he wrote to Manning
at the end of August, he knew he would need to "rise a peg or so, be a little
more decent and less abusive," if he were going to thrive at the *Chronicle*
(*M*, 2:16). This stint didn't last a month. Three-fourths of what he produced,
Lamb reported to Rickman, the "Lordly Editor of the Great Whig Paper"
"superciliously rejected." For a man who had enjoyed the privilege of printing
any "nons[en]se current" in the *Albion*, this was a blow. Lamb planned to give
up newspaper writing and compose a book (*M*, 2:21).

But in December, with the help of Coleridge, Lamb again sought employment from the *Morning Post*. This time he was hired by the editor Daniel
Stuart—"frank, plain, and English all over"—to write theatrical reviews and
the same sort of paragraph "jokes" he composed for the *Albion* (*W*, 2:220).
Rickman thought this pairing of Lamb and the *Post* would be especially
happy. In "this time of no intelligence, where can such an aid be found as
Lamb? I have heard wit from him in an evening to feed a paper for a week."[4]

Lamb's first piece, published January 4, 1802, was a review of George Frederick Cooke's portrayal of Richard III. Lamb admired the fire and passion
Cooke brought to the role, which had become frozen in a staid declamatory
style. But he criticized Cooke for missing the subtlety of Richard, reducing
him to a "vulgar villain, rejoicing in his being able to overreach, and not possessing that joy in silent consciousness, but betraying it, like a poor villain,
in sneers and distortions of face, like a droll at a country fair" (*W*, 1:398). As
Lamb had written to Robert Lloyd back in June, Shakespeare's Richard was
not a monster but a "Man" possessed of a "genius" and "mounting spirit,
which no consideration of his cruelties can depress" (*M*, 2:8). By 1812, in his
famous essay on Shakespeare, Lamb will argue that Cooke's limitations are
not the fault of his acting but of the theater in general: actors are simply incapable of embodying the nuances of the Bard's characters.

Lamb's other substantial essay for the *Post* was "The Londoner," printed
February 1, 1802. In the persona of "the Londoner"—a sober precursor to

Elia—Lamb channels the urban prose poems he had sent to Manning and Wordsworth. The Londoner was born in a crowd, and this "has begot in [him] an entire affection for that way of life, amounting to an almost insurmountable aversion from solitude and rural scenes." He veered from this devotion when he fell for a "charming young woman," most certainly Ann Simmons. His amorousness addicted him "to groves and meadows and purling streams." The fit having passed, he now enjoys "ten thousand sincerer pleasures" over "a mob of happy faces crowding up at the pit-door of Drury Lane Theatre," "than [he] could ever receive from all the flocks of silly sheep that ever whitened the plains of Arcadia or Epsom Downs" (*W,* 1:39–40).

The London mob uplifts. Only the most melancholy of men can be "dull in Fleet Street." This Londoner knows, since he is prone to hypochondria, and the city cures his "ills." He rushes into the crowd, forgets his own moods, weeps over "unutterable sympathies with the multitudinous moving picture" (*W,* 1:40).

The depressive Lamb himself understood the therapy of crowds, how contact with the crush can temporarily free you from dark moods. He also knew how prejudice can induce melancholia in the first place. Standard taste, chopping existence into what's acceptable and what's not, alienates. Maximum connection, the kind the melancholic craves, requires a grasp of the bizarre. Lamb's Londoner finds the "abnormal" does not displease him; nor do the "gauds and toys," the smoke, the dirty boxing ring, the pickpocket (*W,* 1:40).

Aside from these essays, Lamb printed light bits in the *Post.* The material for these jokes was "the chat of the day, scandle, but, above all, *dress.* . . . The length of no paragraph was to exceed seven lines. Shorter they might be, but they must be poignant" (*W,* 2:63). Lamb earned sixpence a joke. One was comical poem about a wife who made her husband renounce his beloved pipe, and two others satirized political figures.

The grueling schedule of the newspaperman tested Lamb. He struggled to review plays the same night they were performed. "I ca'nt do a thing against time." The jokes also pressured. To produce several jokes daily was hard enough, but impossible after nine hours of work and several glasses of gin. The only time to joke was the morning, while hungover. "O those headaches at dawn of day, when at five, or half-past-five in summer, and not much later in the dark seasons, we were compelled to rise, having been perhaps not above four hours in bed" (*W,* 2:222).

Stuart proved "wonderfully polite and civil at first," perhaps because Coleridge had recommended Lamb. But pretty soon Stuart treated his new writer coldly. Maybe Coleridge was instrumental here, too, since his "ill health & unsettlement" had disappointed Stuart and disinclined him toward Coleridge's friend (*M*, 2:52). Stuart didn't much like Lamb's writing. As "for good Charles Lamb, I never could make any-thing of his writings. Coleridge often and repeatedly pressed me to settle him on a salary, and often and repeatedly did I try; but it would not do. Of politics he knew nothing; they were out of his line of reading and thought; and his drollery was vapid, when given in short paragraphs fit for a newspaper." Stuart at least appreciated the Elia essays for their "tone of humour and kind feeling" rendered in "a quaint style" that is "amusing to read, and cheering to remember."[5] Whatever the cause, Stuart began to reject Lamb's "paragraphs" in earnest, taking only about "one in five" (*M*, 2:52).

Lamb felt unappreciated. Moreover, the brutal routine was depriving him of his "pleasures of walking, reading, idling, &c.," pleasures as necessary to him as "the 'golden vapour' [to call on Spenser] of Life itself." Without these diversions, Lamb felt his health "suffered bitterly" (*M*, 2:52). He resigned.

While negative at its close, Lamb's first newspaper experience proved valuable. It required him to imagine a broad and varied audience, and to figure out what would pique readers' interest, an exercise that served Lamb well as he matured into Elia, who was, despite his baroque style, popular. His journalism, too, taught him how to stay close to London society, but not too close. To write his paragraphs and essays, he had to capture London life, its bustling streets and political scandals and raucous theaters, but he needed to remain distant enough to comment humorously. This double vision is irony, that "dangerous figure." Finally, Lamb's journalism produced two of his essential ideas: abstraction alienates, and Shakespeare is too subtle for the stage.

Throughout 1801 and 1802, as Manning prepared for China, Lamb addressed the bulk of his letters to John Rickman, then in Ireland. Lamb had met Rickman back in November 1800, through George Dyer. Rickman lived across the street from Lamb's Southampton Buildings address and proved "the finest fellow to **drop** in a nights about nine or ten oClock, cold bread & cheese time, just in the *wishing* time of the night, when you *wish* for somebody to come in, without a distinct idea of a probable anybody." Rickman is "a fine *rattling* fellow, has gone through Life laughing at solemn apes." He is "hugely literate, oppressively full of information in all stuff of conversation from matter of fact to Zenophon and Plato—can talk Greek with Porson,

politics with Thelwall, conjecture with George Dyer, nonsense with me, &
any thing with anybody." (Porson was the Regius Professor of Greek at Cambridge—brilliant, handsome, unkempt, drunken.) Rickman is moreover a
"great farmer," and edits an agricultural magazine. He "reads no Poetry but
**Shakspeare**," is intimate with Southey (even if he does not read his poetry),
"relishes George Dyer," "thoroughly penetrates into the ridiculous wherever
found," "understands the first time . . . you need never twice speak to him,"
does "not want **explanations**, translations, limitations, as Professor Godwin
does when you make an assertion." This new friend is "*up* to any thing," and
"*down* to every thing." He is a "new Class," an "exotic" who is nonetheless
clear-headed. He is, above all, a "*pleasant hand*" (*M*, 1:243–44).

Among Lamb's close friends, Rickman is in the same class as Manning: a
nonliterary man alert to the pulses of the quotidian and brimming with high
mockery. Like Manning, Rickman was a university man. In 1792, he took his
degree from Lincoln College, Cambridge. By 1797, he was living in Hamp-
shire with his father, a retired clergyman, and it was then he met Southey,
then residing in Burton. Southey found Rickman "a sensible young man,
of rough but mild manners, and very seditious."[6] Perhaps Southey evoked
in Rickman higher intellectual ambitions. Rickman wrote to his new friend
around this time that he was "almost tired of staying in this obscure place
so long" and that he believed he "was born for better purpose than to veg-
etate at Christchurch."[7] He traveled to London in 1800, carrying a letter from
Southey recommending him to Dyer. Possibly Dyer arranged his lodging near
Southampton Buildings. He definitely helped Rickman land the editorship of
the *Commercial, Agricultural, and Manufactures' Magazine*. In 1800 Rickman
published a pamphlet called "On Ascertaining the Population," based on his
1796 article "Thoughts on the Utility and Facility of a General Enumeration
of the People of the British Empire." When Rickman made this argument for
census taking, no count of the population had ever been conducted in the
United Kingdom, and the government of a country at war needed to know
how many people might be enlisted to fight, as well as the country's food requirements. In the wake of Robert Malthus's *Essay on the Principle of Population*, published in 1798, the food supply was an especially dire concern. Rickman's work came to the attention of Charles Abbot, Speaker of the House of
Commons. He named Rickman his secretary and, on December 30, 1800,
presented his ideas before Parliament. The Population Act was passed. Abbot
enlisted Rickman to oversee the first census, which occurred in March 1801,

and then recruited Rickman to move to Dublin to become chief secretary for Ireland. By 1814, Rickman had become the second clerk assistant at the table of the House of Commons, and in 1820, he rose to chief clerk.

This "sterling man," as Coleridge called him, never let his genius for calculation crowd out his passion for literature.[8] He offered to underwrite Lamb's publication of *John Woodvil*, served as Southey's agent when Southey was in Portugal, and helped Coleridge arrange a ship for Malta. Rickman furthermore got census work for George Burnett, friend of Lamb and Coleridge, and a foundering former Pantisocrat.

Rickman's rapid move to Ireland, not even a year after Lamb met him, deprived Lamb of a madcap London friend. But there were letters. Lamb's letters to Coleridge are wit; to Manning whimsy; to Robert Lloyd paternal; those to Rickman are journalistic. They display the sharp eye Lamb had honed working for the papers.

Writing from Margate in September 1801—he and Mary were on holiday there—he sketches Burnett, who has just finished an essay asserting that subversive statements should not be "rashly vented in every company." Before critics call this view "Commonplace," they should realize "how much brain-sweat" the piece caused Burnett, now living with a young surgeon while he awaits publication of the piece. Burnett was evicted from his earlier lodging because "he wanted too much attendance. He used to call up the girl, and send her down again, because he had forgot what he wanted; and then call her again, when his thought came back, to ask what a Clock it was" (*M*, 2:21).

(Burnett, here depicted as a Dyer-like absentminded and naïve aspirant to literary fame, later descended into terrible sufferings that Dyer was able, somehow, to avoid. After failing to thrive as a Unitarian minister, surgeon in the army, tutor to the rich, and writer of history and literary criticism, he became addicted to opium and died penniless in a workhouse. His death in 1811 so shocked Mary Lamb that she suffered another mental breakdown that kept her confined for two months. As Coleridge's biographer Richard Holmes noted of Burnett, he was "a curious version of Coleridge's life as a real failure."[9] Interestingly, in 1804, Coleridge ran into Burnett in Lincoln's Inn Fields, and witnessed his monstrous double: "I met G. Burnett the day before yesterday . . . so nervous, so helpless, with such opium-stupidly-wild eyes.")[10]

In this same Margate letter to Rickman, Lamb describes the latest shenanigans of Godwin. The "**Professor** . . . is *Courting*. The Lady is a Widow* with green spectacles & one child, and the Professor is grown quite juvenile. He bows when he is spoke to, and smiles without occasion, and wriggles as

fantastically as Malvolio, and has more affectation than a canary bird plum-
ing his feathers when he thinks somebody looks at him. He lays down his
spectacles, as if in scorn, & takes 'em up again from necessity, and winks
that she may'nt see he gets sleepy about eleven oClock. You never saw such
a philosophic coxcomb, nor any one play Romeo so unnaturally." At the letter's end, Lamb glosses the asterisk superscripted to "Widow": the lady is "a
very disgusting woman" (*M*, 2:22). His opinion didn't change after Godwin
married her in December 1801. As he wrote Manning, "The Professor's Rib
has come out to be a damn'd disagreeable woman, so much as to drive me
& some more old **Cronies** from his House. If a man will keep **Snakes** in his
House, he must not wonder if People are shy of coming to see him **because
of the Snakes**" (*M*, 2:55).

(This woman was Mary Jane Clairmont, who brought two children to
her marriage with Godwin, each from a different man, neither of whom she
had married. Mary Jane had begun the courting herself by leaning over her
balcony and calling to Godwin below, "Is it possible that I behold the immortal Godwin?" When they married, Mary Jane was already pregnant by
Godwin. Within a few years she would be managing, with Godwin's help, a
very successful line of children's books, the Juvenile Library, and Lamb would
be one of her star writers. Mary Jane's daughter Clair became Byron's lover,
and together they had a child, Clara Allegra.)

In a later October or early November letter to Rickman, Lamb again
found gentle humor in the other George, Dyer. "'Twas on Tuesday week the
poor heathen scrambled up to my door about breakfast time. He came thro'
a violent rain with no neckcloth on, and a *beard* that made him a spectacle to
men and angels, and tap'd at the door. Mary open'd it, and he stood stark still
and held a paper in his hand importing that he had been ill with a fever. He
either wouldn't or couldn't speak except by signs. When you went to comfort
him he put his hand upon his heart & shook his head & told us his complaint
lay where no medicines could reach it." Dyer sent Lamb for William Frend,
who would be executor of his estate, and a Dr. Dale, who would attend his
last hours. When Frend arrived, Dyer arranged for his final works to be published and lay down to die. But food and drink rallied him, as did the doctor's
"little white powders" (placebos), even though Dyer had concluded that the
doctor actually meant the powders "to hasten his departure that he might
suffer as little pain as possible." Dyer recovered. His niece, who had arrived
to witness his last minutes, told the Lambs that if her uncle neglected to dine
out, all he took tea and gruel. He was not sick, just very hungry (*M*, 2:28–29).

Good-natured mockery aside, the Lambs cared about Dyer's welfare, as their rapid response to his ill health shows. They also tried to set Dyer up with a female companion. Right around the time Dyer thought he was dying, Southey wrote to Rickman: "Mary Lamb and her brother have succeeded in talking [Dyer] into love with Miss Benjay or Bungay or Bungay; but they have got him into a quagmire and cannot get him out again, for they have failed in the attempt to talk Miss Bungay or Bungey or Benjey into love with him. This is a cruel business, for he has taken the injection, and it may probably soon break into sonnets and elegies."[11] This Miss Benjey (or Bungay or Bungey or Benjay) we have met before; she was the admirer of Coleridge who subjected the poor Lambs to a dreadfully long one-sided conversation.

Lamb in January reports to Rickman on Fenwick. His old boss at the *Albion* has now started the *Plough*, and he gives "routs & balls & suppers (not balls)" in honor of the paper's "first fruits." The money funding these entertainments comes from "some hundreds of pounds **from** unthinking Nobility." Part of these monies has been extended, Lamb hopes with "no breach of Charity," to "magnificent Hats" for Fenwick's wife and children. Mary has "waggishly . . . christen'd" this headwear "Northumberland Hats," since Fenwick's patron is the Duke of Northumberland (*M*, 2:43).

Lamb created a particular mode of discourse for each of his friends: spirited character sketches to Rickman, philosophical guidance to Robert, virtuoso erudition to Coleridge, absurdist humor to Manning. His friend Procter observed this habit: "It was curious to observe the gradations in Lamb's manner to his various guests, although it was courteous to all. With Hazlitt he talked as though they met the subject in discussion on equal terms; with Leigh Hunt he exchanged repartees; to Wordsworth he was almost respectful; with Coleridge he was sometimes jocose, sometimes deferring; with Martin Burney fraternally familiar; with Manning affectionate; with Godwin merely courteous; or, if friendly, then in a minor degree."[12] Lamb's generous ventriloquism was not adopted for the purpose of pleasing people. On the contrary, he developed a persona for each of his closest friends out of empathy for that friend's specific disposition. It turned out that these epistolary masks were good practice for forming his character Elia, an amalgamation of observer, teacher, scholar, and comedian.

But, as was the case with Elia, Lamb remains firmly Lamb, despite his playful varieties. Whatever his audience, Lamb expresses the same cheeky humor, emotional candor, wordplay, and decency. This tension between consistency and variation gives the letters and the essays their perpetual attraction.

CHAPTER 21

❦

# *Bartholomew Fair*

Lamb spent the fall, winter, and spring of 1801–2 complaining about money but socializing mightily. He found Coleridge and Manning in town at the same time, and his brain became "overwrought with variety of worldly-intercourse" (*M*, 2:35). He continued to enjoy Godwin, Fell, and Dyer. (Frend made Lamb promise to feed Dyer "constantly.")

By late summer of 1802, he and Mary needed a break. Surprisingly, given Charles's recent celebrations of London over mountains, they traveled to the Lakes. This was in early August. Charles had found himself overwhelmed with "a strong desire 'to visit' remote regions" (*M*, 2:68). He and his sister showed up unannounced at Coleridge's Keswick residence, Greta Hall.

Finally he grasped what Coleridge and Wordsworth had been raving about. Arriving at Coleridge's in the evening from Penrith, Lamb witnessed "a gorgeous sunset which transmuted the mountains into all colours, purple, &c." He felt like he was in "Fairy Land." He and Mary entered Coleridge's study "just in the dusk when the mountains were all dark with clouds upon their heads." "Such an impression" Lamb had "never received from objects of sight before." He found the mountains, such as Skiddaw, to be "glorious creatures, fine old fellows." He would never "forget them" (*M*, 2:68–69).

The couple stayed three weeks. They visited, in addition to Keswick, Grasmere, Ambleside, Ulswater, Patterdale, and Helvellyn. Most notably, the two climbed Skiddaw. Though "Mary was excessively tired, when she got about half-way up Skiddaw . . . we came to a cold rill (than which nothing can be imagined more cold, running over cold stones) and, with the reinforcement of a draught of cold water, she surmounted it most manfully.—Oh its fine black head! & the bleak air atop of it, with the prospect of mountains all about & about, making you giddy, & then Scotland afar off & the border countries so famous in song & ballad—.It was a day that will stand out, like a mountain, I am sure, in my life" (*M*, 2:69).

Meanwhile, William and Dorothy Wordsworth were on their way home from France. (The Lambs had called on the Wordsworths in Grasmere and were disappointed not to find them at home.) The siblings had traveled there to settle financial terms with Annette Vallon and Wordsworth's daughter with her, Caroline, conceived when the young and radical poet was touring post-revolutionary France. Wordsworth wanted to make an arrangement with Annette and Caroline before marrying Mary Hutchinson.

On August 31, back on English soil, the northbound Wordsworths stopped in London. They stayed in the rooms of Basil Montagu in the Inner Temple. The nature lovers found themselves urban neighbors of the Lambs.

Had the Wordsworths been at their Lake District home when the Lambs called, they would have been surprised, since Lamb had very recently shared with William his tepid views of nature. But when the Wordsworths arrived in London, Lamb was more sympathetic to the natural sublime than before, and so more open to Wordsworth's sensibility. Even days after returning to the city, Lamb was still buzzing from his draughts of the northern Lakes. As he wrote to Coleridge, "I feel that I shall remember your mountains to the last day I live. They haunt me perpetually. I am like a man who has been falling in Love unknown to himself, which he finds out when he leaves the Lady" (*M*, 2:65–66).

(If Lamb's only overt nature poem is any indication, we can be glad his affair with the green world petered out soon. In "On the Sight of Swans in Kensington Garden," a sonnet first printed in his 1818 *Works*, Lamb begins with promise, observing how the mother swan, "Queen-bird that sittest on thy shining nest," must waddle carefully, to avoid stepping on her "young cygnets," whom she hatched "without sorrow." But this brisk description quickly fatigues into allegory. The mother swan's chicks, "shrined" "in a chrystal cradle, / Brighter than Helen's ere she yet had burst Her shelly prison," are born "Strong, active, graceful, perfect," while we poor humans are in "grief brought

forth, both outwardly and in / Confessing weakness, error, and impurity"
[*W*, 5:40].)

This was the first time Wordsworth had seen Lamb with Mary. Intimate
with his own sister, he appreciated Charles's affection for his sibling and
warmed to this man who'd criticized his verse several months back. And William and Dorothy alike took to Mary, and the Lambs adored Dorothy.

Wordsworth gained a fresh perspective on London, a positive one. Within
days of arriving, Wordsworth wrote "Composed upon Westminster Bridge,
September 3, 1802," in which he gazes out over the London dawn and concludes "Earth has not anything to show more fair." Only the "dull" soul could
miss a "sight so touching in its majesty." The city dons the morning's beauty
as a garment, and all the skyward structures, like ships and temples, aspire
brightly into the "smokeless air." The sun shines more gorgeously on this city
than it ever lighted on "valley, rock, or hill." Never did this son of nature see
or feel a "calm so deep." The Thames glides by; the houses seem asleep.[1]

It is difficult to imagine the Wordsworth of the *Lyrical Ballads* writing this
poem. In the preface to the second edition of that collection, he laments "the
increasing accumulation of men in cities, where the uniformity of their occupations produces a craving for extraordinary incident, which the rapid communication of intelligence hourly gratifies." Overstimulation causes a "savage
torpor."[2] In the Westminster Bridge sonnet Wordsworth recognizes in the city
what he loves about nature: the splendor, the grace. These qualities shimmer
more intensely in London, like light when it cuts through blackness.[3]

The Lambs took William and Dorothy to Bartholomew Fair, an ancient
event occurring every September in Smithfield and notorious for its debauch-
ery. This was the sort of spectacle Lamb would love, and Wordsworth likely
hate. But as his description of the event three years later shows, Wordsworth's
attitude toward this serious "din" is ambiguous, perhaps because he experienced the scene with an ardent Lamb. Though the freakishly vertiginous
whirl of the fair disgusts the poet, it also exhilarates him, as a test: if he can
imagine a harmony underlying this chaos, he can discern concord anywhere.[4]

The Lambs and the Wordsworths bonded. Lamb was soon sending William letters filled with poetry and jesting, and Mary was writing Dorothy her
most intimate feelings: "I have been in better health and spirits this week past
than any since my last illness—I continued so long so very weak & dejected
I began to fear I should never be at all comfortable again, I strive against low
spirits all I can, but it is a very hard thing to get the better of" (*M*, 2:117).

CHAPTER 22

*Mary's Letters*

In July 1802, just before leaving for Keswick, the Lambs met Sarah Stoddart, the sister of barrister John Stoddart, whom Lamb knew from at least the winter of 1801, when he mentioned him as the translator of Schiller. Sarah was bookish, eccentric, funny, independent—just like Mary, save that Sarah actively pursued romance. The women took to each other; a lively friendship began. They took long walks, talked literature, gossiped, and quaffed brandy—Mary preferred "three parts" to one of water (*M,* 2:213). It is to Sarah, who would later marry (with no little encouragement from Mary) William Hazlitt, that Mary wrote her first extant letter.[1]

Mary was as skilled as her brother in letter writing. A study of her early correspondence shows her to be thoughtful, candid, empathetic, vulnerable, curious, nostalgic, and self-effacing, but also nervous, depressed, skittish, and self-loathing.

Mary admits to Sarah that she is "a miserable letter writer." She also says she is "lazy." But she feels great affection for Sarah, so much so that she will lie on her behalf if need be (she is joking) to get her to London next winter. "I will protest you are the most amusing, good-humoured, good sister, and altogether excellent girl I know, or any other fibs you will please to dictate me." Mary would like to see Sarah so much she wishes "balloons were a common and a cheap conveyance." Then she would "come over and make a list'ner of your party, now and then of an evening when I had a few hours to spare" (*M*, 2:63–64).

After this charming first letter, Mary did prove a lax correspondent, not writing to Sarah again until December 1802. She has an excuse. She has been "very ill," depressed, so much so that her head is too "dull" to describe any circumstance from the trip to the Lakes. She can recall, though, her walks with Sarah down the Strand, "so fast (lest the scotch broth should be spoiled in our absence) we were ashamed of showing of red faces at your friend's in westminster, or bustling down Fleet-Market-in-all-its-glory of a saturday night, admiring the stale peas and co'lly-flowers and cheap'ning small bits of mutton and veal for our Sunday's dinner's, returning home in all haste, to be scolded for not laying the cloth in time for supper (albeit it being nine o'clock) and then chidden for laughing in an unseemly manner" (*M*, 2:90). This writing has a rush Lamb's more deliberate language doesn't—a mania even, the joy of running all flushed down Fleet.

Mary's next letter, from September 1803, approves of Sarah's plan to accompany her brother to Malta, where he will serve as chief justice and justice of the vice admiralty court. (Coleridge would live with the Stoddarts in Malta before quarreling with John and moving on to become public secretary to Alexander Ball, the British minister.) Sarah should take this measure to free herself from love trouble. "The terms you are upon with your Lover does (as you say it will) appear wondrous strange to me, however, as I cannot enter into your feelings, I certainly can have nothing to say to it, only th[a]t I sincerely wish you happy in your own way, however odd that way may appear to me to be. I would begin now to advise you to drop all correspondence with William [the lover], but, as I said before, as I cannot enter into your feelings and views of things, *your ways not being my ways*, why should I tell you what I would do in your situation. So child, take thy own ways and God prosper thee in them!" (*M*, 2:123–24).

Mary the life-long maiden has never experienced the travails of courting, and so humbly refrains from offering advice. Her admission that she *can't* feel what Sarah does is a delicate form of empathy: an acknowledgment that it would be arrogant to assume she can know what Sarah knows, and an understanding of how her misguided advice might make Sarah feel. (Sarah is capacious in her courting, currently juggling two suitors.)

If Mary were to offer advice, she would say, "Use as little *Secresy* as possible, and as much as possible make a friend of your sister-in-law." She doesn't want Sarah to go through the problems of her mother, who struggled bitterly with her own sister-in-law Sarah. As an aside almost, Mary adds, "You will smile when I tell you I think myself the only woman in the world, who could live with a brothers wife, and make a real friend of her. partly from [e]arly observation of the unhappy example I have just given you, and partly from a knack I know I have of looking into peoples real characters, and never expecting them to act out of it—never expecting another to do as I would do in the same case" (*M*, 2:124–25).

Here again is Mary's negative capability. She allows Sarah to act on her own terms and accepts those terms, without expectation or judgment. Still, Mary can admit that Sarah's secrecy is her "grand failing," as it is her brother John's. She and Charles tell each other everything.

It is March 27, 1804. Sarah is in Malta. Coleridge is on his way. He is ill, but he "will talk, & talk, and be wondrously admired." Please be kind to him, Mary begs her friend, treat him as you would Charles and me, if we came to you sick. Not much is going on here, but Charles is undertaking a project (his farce *Mr. H.*) that he hopes will bring a little money. "I sit writing here and thinking almost you will see it tomorrow, and what a long, long, time it will be before you receive this—. When I saw your letter I fancy'd you were even just then in the first bustle of a new reception, every moment seeing new faces, & staring at new objects, when at that time every thing had become familiar to you, and the strangers, your new dancing partners had perhaps become gossiping fire-side friends." Tell me, Mary continues, "of your gay, splendid doings, tell me likewise what manner of home-life you lead—is a quiet evening in a Maltese drawing room as pleasant as those we have passed in Mitre Court?" (*M*, 2:134).

Mary's curiosity is intense, specific, her sense of the strangeness of writing to distant friends acute. Charles was fascinated by this phenomenon as well, in his letters to Manning in China and in an Elia essay, "Distant Correspondents."

By mid-June, Mary offers her thoughts on femininity. She wishes Sarah would return from Malta to be a "comfortable English wife" before bemoaning the "vexatious Tyranny that woman have no business to exercise over men, which merely because *they having a better judgment* they have the power to do." The italicized section Mary intends ironically, as the next sentence shows. Men do not practice better judgment; women possess a "kind of intuition" allowing them to perceive the "right way" at once (*M*, 2:143). In this patriarchal society, they are not allowed to express their intuitions. They must wait silently, until men at last come around. Men do make mistakes; women should not badger them.

In this complicated view on gender—recall the same mix of feminism and traditionalism in Mary's essay on needlework—we see an iconoclastically intelligent woman struggling with male strictures. We also get a candid glimpse into the workings of the Lamb household, where Mary humors her brother's whims rather than criticize him. In the end he will do the right thing. This dynamic sometimes has its humor—a bemused Mary watches her brother act out his harmless petulance—but also its pains. Charles fretted over their poverty, only to go on spending sprees. He swore off drink, then went on dangerous binges.

After over a year not writing, Mary exposes her dark parts. On September 18, 1805, she explains: thoughts of writing Sarah during the past months only brought "troubles" to her mind. There is another reason: her "banishment" in an asylum, during which time she longed for Sarah's presence to "chear my drooping heart." Her spirits are still low (*M*, 2:174). Wit and excitement are gone.

Two weeks later, Mary is worse. She addresses a quarrel between Sarah and her John. He wishes Sarah to practice more etiquette, "nicely correct maidenly manners." Mary flippantly recommends that she and Sarah find a "demure Lady" to imitate. The brother isn't Sarah's only trouble, though. Her mother is suffering mental illness. Don't let this "malady affect you too deeply. I speak from experience & from the opportunity I have had of much observations in such cases that insane people in the fancy's they take into their head do not feel as one in a sane state of mind does under the real evil of poverty the perception of having done wrong or any such thing that runs in their heads." Think as little as you can of your mother, who isn't hurting as much as you think. When you do attend to her, let it be with "*tenderness*," the quality the insane require the most (*M*, 2:184–85).

Only days later, Mary has fit of regret. She wrote the last letter after "a very feverish night." She fears she has treated Sarah's troubles with her brother "too lightly" and that she has implied that Sarah has not treated her mother's illness properly. Her own mental malady compelled her to share her opinion. She now retracts it, saying her "spirits have been so hurt by my last illness" that I "at times . . . hardly know what to do."

I do not mean to alarm you about myself, or to plead an excuse that I am very much otherwise than you have always known me—I do not think anyone perceives me altered, but I have lost all self-confidence in my own actions, & one cause of my low spirits is that I never feel satisfied with anything I do—a perception of not being in a sane state perpetually haunts me. I am ashamed to confess this weakness to you, which, as I am so sensible of I ought to strive to conquer. But I tell you that you may excuse any part of my letter that has given offence, for your not answering it, when you are such a punctual correspondent, has made me very uneasy. (*M,* 2:185–86)

This is depression. You are unsure of every single action; you regret everything. You live in constant fear of alienating those close to you. You blurt words sure to push them away.

# CHAPTER 23

*Long and Rueful Faces*

Mary's breakdown of March 1803, the one spurred by the "old friend and admirer" of her mother, was especially violent. Luckily Coleridge was there to help get her to a Hoxton asylum.[1]

In June 1805, Mary broke down again. Her absence ravaged Charles. He felt as though she were dead, and he regretted his persistent teasing of her and his heavy drinking. But he knew that she would never leave him. She would cling to him like a wife.

Mary succumbed yet again in June 1807. She and Charles were journeying home from Bury St. Edmunds, where they had visited their friends the Clarksons. All was calm until they reached Chelmsford. There Mary "began to be very bad." With the help of some friends of the Clarksons, Lamb managed. "Among other acts of great attention they provided me with a waistcoat to confine her arms, by the help of which we went through the rest of our journey. But sadly tired and miserably depressed she was before we arrived at Hoxton. We got there about half past eight; and now 'tis all over, I have great satisfaction that she is among people who have been used to her." Mary would likely remain in confinement a few months. Her last illness had required ten weeks. If she did recover (that Charles had to consider "if" horrified him), Lamb would be mindful of trip distances in future. The episode taxed him, "for she talked in the most wretched desponding way conceivable, particularly the last three stages, she talked all the way" (*M*, 2:257).

Mary's fits explode in part from the siblings' intense relationship. Mary falls into low spirits. Charles's mockery and drunkenness exacerbate her depression, harrying her to the asylum. While she is away, Charles suffers awful guilt, and realizes his deep affection and dependence. She returns; he is ecstatic. But Mary's post-mania malaise dampens his joy, and he falls into low spirits himself, which he battles with drink and nonsense. The cycle starts again. For her part, Mary knows how her periodic attacks burden her brother, and so she endures her own guilt. She also knows she is dependent upon Charles financially and emotionally. She loves him for his tenderness but resents that she lacks freedom. Charles's own mental illness and its corollary nonsense also irritate her.

In a letter to Sarah, Mary describes their painful interdependence best: "When I am pretty well his low spirits, throws me back again [into dejection] & when he begins to get a little cheerful then I do the same kind of office for him." You should see us, she continues, "looking at each other with long and rueful faces, & saying how do you do? & how do you do? & then we fall a crying & say we will be better on the morrow—[Charles] says we are like tooth ach & his friend gum bile, which though a kind of ease, is but an uneasy kind of ease, a comfort of rather an uncomfortable sort" (*M*, 2:183).[2] Each causes pain only the other can comfort, but the comfort they give causes more hurt.

The strain both endured of living always on the edge of a breakdown was tremendous. They had to be ready at all times. So Charles would not have to depend on an overcoat, the two bought their own straitjacket. Procter recalls their routine. "Whenever the approach of one of her fits of insanity was announced, by some irritability or change in manner, Lamb would take her under his arm, to Hoxton Asylum. It was very affecting to encounter the young brother and his sister walking together (weeping together) on this painful errand; Mary herself, although very sad, very conscious of the necessity for temporary separation from her only friend. They used to carry a strait jacket with them."[3]

In the early years of the nineteenth century, the strain of caring for Mary, intensified by poverty and no prospect for alleviating it, hurled Charles into a hole almost as dark as Mary's. He looked at the straitjacket himself, thinking he might be wearing it next. Repeatedly, either he or Mary mentions his sickness or low spirits. He is "quite out of spirits" (*M*, 1:203); he "is very unwell"(*M*, 2:155); his "health and spirits are so bad" and his "nerves so irritable" that if he continues to review a book by Godwin, he will "teaze" himself into a "fever" (*M*, 2:126); he is "so unwell" Mary fears he will not be able to write a letter for two weeks (*M*, 2:183). Lamb's poor spirits could have been symptoms of hangovers, intense depression or, most likely, a combination of the two.

Whatever the causes of the malady, Lamb tried heroically to quit his vices. After he returned from the Lakes, he wrote to Manning that he was going sober.

> My habits are changing, I think; i.e., from drunk to sober: whether I shall be happier or no, remains to be proved. I shall certainly be more happy in a morning, but whether I shall not sacrifice the fat and the marrow & the kidneys, i.e., the Night, glor[iou]s, care-drowning night, that heals all our wrongs, pours wine into our mortifications, changes the scene from indifferent and flat to bright & brilliant—. O Manning, if I should have formed a diabolical resolution, by the time you come to England, of not admitting any spirituous liquors into my house, will you be my guest on such shame worthy terms? Is life, with such limitations, worth trying.—The truth is, that my liquors bring a nest of friendly harpies about my house, who consume me.— (*M*, 2:70)

This sobriety was short-lived, but Lamb persisted in trying to quit his habit. He sometimes stayed sober for a spell. As Mary wrote to Dorothy in July 1803, "Charles is very well and very *good* I mean very sober" (*M*, 2:118). He stayed dry for a whole month while visiting Hazlitt and his new wife Sarah Stoddart in Winterslow.

But Lamb always fell off the wagon. In 1809, he got so drunk the coachman had to carry him up to his and Mary's rooms. "I got home tolerably well, as I hear, the other evening," he wrote to Robinson. "It may be a warning to any one in the future to ask me to a dinner party. I always disgrace myself" (*M*, 3:10). Soon after, Mary reported to Sarah that "Charles was drunk last night, and drunk the night before, which night before was at Godwins," where Charles got "brimfull of Gin & water & snuff" before returning home to drink more with Robinson by the fire. "Charles could not speak plain for tipsyness" (*M*, 3:49–50).

Socializing with other big drinkers who waffled on their sobriety vows didn't help. Take Coleridge, for instance. As Lamb wrote Dorothy, "He has powdered his head, and looks like Bacchus, Bacchus ever sleek and young. He is going to turn sober, but his Clock has not struck yet, meantime he pours down goblet after goblet, the 2d to see where the 1st is gone, the 3d to see no harm happens to the second, a fourth to say there's another coming, and a 5th to say he's not sure he's the last" (*M*, 3:62).

When Charles wasn't trying to kick alcohol, he was swearing off smoking. Sometimes he tried to quit both at once. In September 1805, he wrote to Dorothy that he had bid "farewell" to his " Sweet Enemy' Tobacco," and written a long poem to say good-bye (*M*, 2:177). He reported to Hazlitt in February 1806, "I, going to leave off smoke. In mean time am so smoky with last nights' 10 Pipes, that I must leave off" (*M*, 2:209). A few months later, Mary reported that "Charles has been very good lately in the matter of *Smoking*" (*M*, 2:243). But he couldn't leave the leaf alone. "*One* pipe is wholesome, *two* pipes toothsome, *three* pipes noisome, *four* pipes fulsome, *five* pipes quarrelsome; and that's the *sum* on't.— But that is deciding rather upon rhime than reason" (*M*, 2:109).

# CHAPTER 24

⌒⊙⌒

# *Puns*

Drinking and smoking soothed Charles's perturbed spirit, but writing did more so, in particular "crammed, and very funny" letters to Manning. When Manning was in Paris studying Chinese and medicine, Lamb chastised him for refusing to leave his rooms until he knew French. "You cannot stir from your rooms until you know the Language? what the Devil! are men nothing but word-trumpets?, are men all tongue & ear? have these creatures, that you & I profess to know *something about*, no faces, gestures, gabble, no folly, no absurdity, no induction of French education upon the Abstract Idea of Men & Women, no similitude nor dissimilitude to English! Why, thou *damned* **Smelfungus**!" (*M*, 2:55).

Lamb is most interested in Manning's plan to travel to China. In February 1803, he wonders why Manning would want to travel to Tartary. Isn't he afraid of all the mythical dangers the West has historically attributed to the East? "My dear friend, think what a sad pity it would be to bury such *parts* in heathen countries, among nasty, unconversable, horse-belching Tartar people! . . . The Tartars, really, are a cold, insipid, smouchey set. You'll be sadly moped (if you are not eaten) among them." Furthermore, Manning should "have a care . . . of Anthrophagi! their stomachs are always craving. But if you do go among [them] pray contrive to *stink* as soon as you can that you may [not (?)] hang [on (?)] hand at the Butcher's" (*M*, 2:95–96).

Beyond a plea for his close friend not to leave England, this is an early instance of Lamb satirizing imperialistic prejudices. He lists the clichés Englanders deploy to reduce exotic cultures to comfortable stereotypes. The clichés are projections of fear of the unknown and desire for control.

Behind Lamb's antic hyperbole is epistemological analysis: in attempting to understand what we don't know, we project ideas and images that will *ensure* that we don't know. We trade lenses for walls. Lamb disdains this wrenching of the unfamiliar into the familiar. He looks cock-eyed at the near and contorts it to the far.

Lamb discerned another epistemological problem in Manning's travels, already noted by Mary: how the distance a letter travels affects its ability to signify. On May 10, 1806, Lamb replies to Manning's letter notifying him that he has reached Portsmouth, from which he will sail to China. Shaking hands with Manning before he left for Portsmouth was like shaking hands with a "**wretch** on the scaffold & when you are down the ladder you can never strech out to him again." Why send newsy letters to a man so far away he might as well be dead? "By the time you've made your escape from the **Kalmuks**, you'll have staid so long I shall never be able to bring to your mind **who Mary was**, who will have died about a year before, nor who the Holcrofts were; **me** perhaps you will mistake for Philips, or confound me with Mr. **Daw** because you saw us together" (*M*, 2:225–26). The narratives in London will be dead by the time you learn of them, because you will have forgotten the characters. You will be living in two time zones, increasingly difficult to reconcile. Eventually, the China one—months behind the England one—will take precedence, and the dated events from London will be meaningless. Lamb will become just one blank face among many.

By December, Manning had reached China. Lamb's mind still boggled. "China—Canton—bless us—how it strains the imagination and makes it ache! I write under another uncertainty whether [this letter] can go tomorrow by a ship, which I have just learned is going off direct to your part of the world, or whether the dispatches may not be sealed up & this have to wait— for if it is detained here, it will grow staler in a fortnight than in a five months voyage coming to you." Lamb wants his letters to go out immediately, while the news is fresh, so that although Manning might receive the information five months later, it will be new to him (*M*, 2:244). This is the reverse of Lamb's complaint in the May letter. Here he considers the possibility that a letter sent out hot with gossip will strike Manning six months later just the way it currently stimulates Lamb.

These letters sublimate pain into wit. Manning's absence hit Lamb hard. He wanted to understand how the distance would affect their correspondence. If his words could no longer convey vibrant meanings to Manning, what would become of their friendship? Would they become dead to each other? Insofar as their narratives were alienated, yes, since Lamb's words to Manning would be like the talk of one deceased to one alive. But if Lamb could keep his letters close to his "now," they would hum in Manning's hands.

By the time he published "Distant Correspondents" in March 1822, Lamb had seen Manning return safely, and so he could explore his ideas on meaning and time in a purely comical way. The essay appears as a letter addressed to one "B.F. Esquire at Sydney New South Wales," Lamb's friend Barron Field, in 1816 named judge of the supreme court in New South Wales. Lamb worries over how immense distances negate the ingredients of a good letter: "news, sentiment, and puns." News is obsolete, feelings are dead. Puns require "extremely circumscribed" spheres to thrive. They "are so far from a capacity of being packed up and sent beyond sea, they will scarce endure to be transported by hand from this room to the next. Their vigour is as the instant of their birth. Their nutriment for their brief existence is the intellectual atmosphere of the bystanders. . . . A pun hath a hearty kind of present ear-kissing smack with it; you can no more transmit it in its pristine flavour, than you can send a kiss" (*W*, 2:104).

Why write at all? Don't aspire to be newsy, emotional, or linguistically clever. Write a letter that is an essay, as Elia does to Field, an essay about nothing but itself. Its style is its substance. Original images (the pun with its "ear-kissing smack") electrify, as do wild Elian allusions ("I see Diogenes prying among you with his perpetual fruitless lantern") and outlandish conceits ("Conceive [a sentiment] pawed about and handled between the rude jests of tarpaulin ruffians—a thing of its delicate texture—the salt bilge wetting it till it became as vapid as a damaged lustring") (*W*, 2:107). Though no language can convey the present moment out of which it was uttered—words mark absence—some sentences feel more alive than others, more like walloping puns at a party, or a gut-cramping joke. Elia gives his letters this gas. They blast in a wink over any abyss. When we read them now, two hundred years later, they pulsate.

Lamb's favored form of conversational wit was the pun, "arising," in Addison's good definition, "from the use of two words that agree in sound, but differ in the sense."[1] Puns, according to Lamb, can become "twinkling corpuscula" only in an immediate "sphere of action." Unlike published jests, "their vigour is as the instant of their birth," and dependent upon the "intellectual atmosphere of the bystanders." If sympathetic, these auditors relish the pun as they would a hearty kiss, which exists only, contrary to the love letter, as the touching of flesh. In a successful smooch, kisser and kissed are inseparable. So the punster and his hearers enjoy "coinstantaneous" pleasure (*W*, 2:107). If this galvanic relay—the speaker is lightning, the listeners thunder—is broken, the pun dies. The farther the distance between the utterance and its consumption, the staler the joke. How tedious to hear a play summarized. The same is true of yesterday's pun. It is a mirror's image coming back to you hours after you gazed in the glass.

The farther beyond analysis the pun, the more "entertaining" it is. The best pun is so palpable its blurs word and thing. It is "a pistol let off at the ear" (*W*, 2:257). It bangs, booms, crashes, whams, pops, smacks, thumps, rattles.

Think of the laugh above the throat we emit over Oscar Wilde's epigrams. After deliberating for some seconds, we go "Ah," raise an eyebrow, and chuckle. Better the belly laugh, spontaneous as a sneeze, cough, hiccup. You might chortle over Geoff Dyer's *Out of Sheer Rage*. But conversing with those gifted in the ridiculous shivers your ribs.

Keats distinguishes between these two sorts of laughter. He writes of a recent dinner where wits were on display. Their ingeniousness is mere mannerism, and only makes one "start," with no feeling. This wit resembles "disquisition," overly ideological argumentation, in which the speaker knows his end before the beginning. Opposed to wit is "humour," the instinctive belly laugh, and different from disquisition is "disputation," the unpredictable and generative back-and-forth of a good conversation. These ideas dovetail in Keats's mind. In the interlacing he chances on negative capability, that virtue of all geniuses, especially Shakespeare, who can rest in "uncertainties, Mysteries, doubts, without any irritable reaching after fact & reason."[2]

To pun requires the poet's mix of confidence and humility: the humility to suspend personal dogma before this particular absurdity and the self-assurance to assert, "This is hilarious!" Lamb says as much. The pun is "a noble thing per se," "entire," filling the mind as perfectly as a "sonnet." At the same time, though, the pun "limps ashamed, in the train and retinue of humour."[3] This statement balances the ethic of the pun—Lamb observes, "I never knew an enemy to puns who was not an ill-natured man"—and its ludicrousness. An "antic which does not stand upon manners, but comes bounding into the presence," a pun is more likely to induce groan than guffaw (*W*, 2:257).

The best puns are the worst. Take an Oxford scholar meeting a porter toting a hare down the street. The learned man asks, "Is that thy own hair or a wig?" There is no "excusing this" violation of good taste, and "no resisting it" (*W,* 2:258). Lamb could have produced this pun. A Lamb pun was often "startling" in "its own demerit," more apt to be a "catastrophe" than a climax.[4]

Once, at a dinner party, after the group expounded on the uses and abuses of the word *nice,* Lamb flared, "Now we have held a council of Nice."[5] When he learned a man had "lampooned him," Lamb retaliated, "Very well . . . I'll Lamb-pun him."[6] A friend, preparing to introduce the bashful Lamb to a new group, asked, "Now will you promise, Lamb, not to be as sheepish as usual?" Lamb replied, "with a rustic air, 'I wool.'"[7] A farmer by chance sat by Lamb on a coach, and he asked the essayist a litany of boring questions about crops. When the man inquired, "How go turnips?" an exasperated Lamb stammered, "Why, that, sir, will depend upon the boiled legs of mutton."[8] Lamb heard how the Duke of Cumberland had hindered the duchess from embracing her son, whom she had not seen in ages. After the narrator censured the coldness of this act, Lamb stuttered, "Yes, but you know he is the Duke of Cu-cum-ber-and."[9] On a chilly, wet day, a beggar approached Lamb, hand outstretched, whining, "I have seen better days." "So have I," Lamb returned. "This is a very bad day indeed."[10]

Summarized, these puns aren't very funny. If they cause any laughter at all, it is above-the-throat chuckling. In the moment, however, through Lamb's gestures, expressions, intonations, mood, timing—perhaps they were howlers.

What is the difference between a good pun and bad? Recent researchers claim that unfunny puns are less semantically ambiguous than funny ones. "What was the problem with the other coat? It was difficult to put on with the paint-roller." This is unfunny, because the ambiguous word—*coat*—points to only one meaning. In a funny pun, both meanings are true, as in "Why were the teacher's eyes crossed? Because she couldn't control her pupils."[11]

Brain imaging suggested this conclusion. So-called funny puns inspire more neuron activity than nonfunny ones.[12] But does the activity really result from humor? Perhaps the brain brightens at puns because of cognitive challenge. According to other research, puns threaten our meaning-making capacities, since they reveal "the arbitrariness of meaning, and the layers of nuance that can be packed onto a single word."[13] This is why many, going back to Samuel Johnson, don't like puns.

Lamb cares less about a pun's funniness, which can't be measured outside of the conversational context of its creation, and more about its transgressive qualities. The best puns are the "most far-fetched and startling" and so the "worst" to good taste. The pun involving the Oxford scholar asking the hare-carrying porter if the animal is his own hair or a wig: that would make most groan. But take in the wholeness of the scene. Imagine the pert scholar leisurely stopping and the bafflement of the rushing porter, the utilitarian atmosphere of the street, the initial class satire (what porter owns the hare he carries?) and then the more subtle one (what porter wears an aristocratic wig?) and the hurrying man beginning to understand the quip before descending again into confusion. This is a scene worthy of Hogarth.

In this case the pun goes beyond semantic acrobatics—a hare as a rabbit is hair as head growth is a wig is a sign of status the porter lacks—to a metaphysical category: revelation of a heightened order of being where oppositions are momentarily balanced. Spontaneity and art, ambiguity and clarity, the destruction of language and the elevation of it. Think of Shakespeare's puns in this regard—Polonius is at supper not "where he eats but where he is eaten"—as well as those of Dadaist Marcel Duchamp, whose candy wrappers for Bill Copley's 1953 Parisian show read, "A Guest + A Host = A Ghost."

Drinking, witty epistles—these distracted Lamb from his darkness during the first decade of the nineteenth century, as did his socializing. To his social circle during these years he added Hazlitt, whom he met at Godwin's in 1803. At that time, Hazlitt was still considering a career as a painter, and he completed a portrait of Lamb in 1804, one of his last.

Perhaps because of Lamb's swarthy complexion, Hazlitt painted him wearing the garb of Velázquez's Philip IV, a black tunic with ten brass buttons, from which rises a high gray collar. Lamb sits in half profile, looking studiously into the distance to his left. His right eye is brown, while the left is hazel, and the hair is thick and black. A red velvet curtain slants from the top right to the bottom left. Behind are shadows. De Quincey found the painting "far from being a good likeness" of Lamb and suggested it looked like John Hamilton Reynolds.[14] The portrait eventually went to Coleridge. It now hangs in the National Portrait Gallery.

Hazlitt abandoned painting for philosophy—his theory of "disinterestedness" in *On Human Action* influenced Keats's poetics—and then philosophy for essay writing. In pieces like "My First Acquaintance with the Poets," "On Going on Journey," "The Fight," "On the Pleasures of Hating," and "The Indian Dancers," he developed a direct, vigorous, improvisational style, belting his essays out in one breathless sitting. If Lamb is the freewheeling,

William Hazlitt, *Charles Lamb*. (© National Portrait Gallery, London.)

ever-ironical Bob Dylan, Hazlitt is Springsteen: spleen or love full-on. Or: where Lamb resembles trickster Muhammad Ali, Hazlitt is Joe Louis, punching with brutal precision.[15]

Hazlitt describes a fight between the "Gas-Man" and Bill Neate: "After making play a short time, the Gas-man flew at his adversary like a tiger, struck five blows in as many seconds, three first, and then following him as he staggered back, two more, right and left, and down he fell, a mighty ruin. There was a shout, and I said, 'There is no standing this.' Neate seemed like a lifeless lump of flesh and bone, round which the Gas-man's blows played with the rapidity of electricity or lighting, and you imagined he would only be lifted up to be knocked down again."[16]

Here's Hazlitt on hating:

> There is a spider crawling along the matted floor of the room where I sit . . . ; he runs with heedless, hurried haste, he hobbles awkwardly towards me, he stops—he sees the giant shadow before him, and, at a loss whether to retreat or proceed, meditates his huge foe—but as I do not start up and seize upon the straggling caitiff, as he would upon a hapless fly within his toils, he takes heart, and ventures on with mingled cunning, impudence and fear. As he passes me, I lift up the matting to assist his escape, am glad to get rid of the unwelcome intruder, and shudder at the recollection after he is gone. A child, a woman, a clown, or a moralist a century ago, would have crushed the little reptile to death—my philosophy has got beyond that—I bear the creature no ill-will, but still I hate the very sight of it.[17]

In addition to his explosive essays (he thought "slow, inert, speculative" reason "no match for power and prejudice, armed with force and cunning") Hazlitt also produced brilliant Shakespeare criticism, in particular reaching the insight that later ruled Keats's poetics: "The striking peculiarity of Shakespeare's mind was its generic quality, its power of communication with all other minds—so that it contained a universe of thought and feeling within itself, and had no one peculiar bias, or exclusive excellence more than another. He was just like any other man, but that he was like all other men. He was the least of an egotist that it was possible to be. He was nothing in himself; but he was all that others were, or that they could become."[18]

He excelled at art criticism, too, mainly in his analysis of the "gusto" of Titian: "There is a gusto in the colouring of Titian. Not only do his heads seem to think—his bodies seem to feel. This is what the Italians mean by the *morbidezza* of his flesh-colour. It seems sensitive and alive all over; not merely to have the look and texture of flesh, but the feeling in itself. . . . The blood circulates here and there, the blue veins just appear, the rest is distinguished throughout only by that sort of tingling sensation to the eye, which the body feels within itself."[19]

But the gusto of Hazlitt's own personality repelled his companions. As he himself wrote in "On the Pleasures of Hating," "I have quarreled with

*William Hazlitt*, by J. Hyatt, after John Hazlitt. (© National Portrait Gallery, London.)

almost all my old friends."[20] Hazlitt turned against Coleridge, the idol of his youth, for going conservative and for not reaching his potential as a poet and philosopher. He called his former mentor "the sleep-walker, the dreamer, the sophist, the word-hunter, the craver after sympathy."[21] He also mocked Coleridge's famous talk: "C.—is the only person who can talk to all sorts of people, on all sorts of subjects, without caring a farthing for their understanding one word he says—and *he* talks only for admiration and to be listened to, and accordingly the least interruption puts him out."[22] Coleridge retorted: Hazlitt's "manners are 99 in 100 singularly repulsive; brow-hanging, shoe-contemplative, *strange*." (Coleridge continued to admire Hazlitt's writing, however: "well-headed and well-feathered Thoughts straight forwards to the mark with a Twang of the Bowstring.")[23]

Hazlitt offended Wordsworth in print (he said *The Excursion* repeats the same conclusions until they become "flat and insipid" and "fell still-born from the press") and in his actions.[24] In 1803, on a visit to the Lakes to paint Wordsworth, Coleridge, and Coleridge's son Hartley, Hazlitt went too far with a Keswick maiden. A mob pursued him. Wordsworth had to harbor him as he would a criminal before sneaking him out in the middle of the night.[25] Almost fifteen years after the event Wordsworth confided "with great horror" to his friend Benjamin Robert Haydon "Hazlitt's licentious conduct to the girls of the Lake & that no woman could walk after dark for 'his Satyr & beastly appetites.' Some girl called him a black-faced rascal, when Hazlitt enraged pushed her down '& because, Sir,' said Wordsworth, 'she refused to gratify his abominable & devilish propensities, he lifted up her petticoats & smote her on the bottom.'"[26]

Hazlitt's marriage with the Lambs' beloved Sarah Stoddart ended, after fourteen years, in divorce. What precipitated the split was likely Sarah's loathing of their 19 York Street address in London. The couple had moved there in May 1813. Though the dwelling was dilapidated, faced a filthy street, and required a hefty rent, it had once housed John Milton, and Hazlitt loved the idea of composing where England's champion of liberty once did. By 1819, however, Sarah was sick of the house, and probably of Hazlitt's stubborn refusal to move, as well as of his poor management of the place. She was spending substantial time in her brother's large London home and showing up at parties by herself. In the summer, she moved to Winterslow, along with William Jr.[27] If there was any hope of a reconciliation, it was destroyed on August 16, when Hazlitt met a barmaid named Sarah Walker, twenty years his junior. He became obsessed with her. After stringing him along for three years, she dropped him for a man named Tomkins. Out of Hazlitt's agony gushed *Liber Amoris*, a shockingly raw confession of his romantic torment. Robert Louis Stevenson refused to write a biography of Hazlitt, otherwise his hero, because he was so disgusted by this book.

(Now we can hear Sarah Walker's side of the story, at least fictionally, in Anne Haverty's novel *The Far Side of a Kiss*, where Sarah says of Hazlitt, "He has put me in a book. He had but a frail steel nib for his weapon but he has destroyed me by it as clean as if he used a blade and impaled me on its point. There was a time when he called me his queen and by other fancy titles and next I am become no more than a juicy bone for him to throw to the scribblers in the newspapers for a right good chew.")[28]

Hazlitt married again in 1823, to the widow Isabella Bridgwater, who enjoyed £300 a year. The money might have been more attractive to Hazlitt than the love. They lived together only three and a half years.

Prejudices gave Hazlitt's prose power; they ruined his life. He viewed Napoleon as a revolutionary champion of egalitarianism long after the dictatorial general proved himself otherwise. After Napoleon fell at Waterloo in 1815, Hazlitt went on a weeks-long drunk. He staggered the streets unshaven and unwashed.

To work off his pains, Hazlitt became a serious player of the game of fives, similar to modern handball or, when played with a racquet, racquetball. He was a "furious" player of the game. He competed against players much younger. He played for six hours at a time, diving, screaming, sweating, grunting. He once whacked a better player in the head with his racquet. That was the only way he could win.[29]

Lamb was the only friend Hazlitt, who thought man was a "toad-eating animal," did not lose. This was because Lamb valued Hazlitt's friendship higher than anyone's except Coleridge's and Manning's. There is, he wrote Wordsworth in 1816, "something tough in my attachment to H——, which all these violent strainings cannot quite dislocate or sever asunder. I get no conversation in London that is absolutely worth attending to but his" (*M*, 3:225). Lamb's praise was even more effusive later on, in 1823, in an essay in the *London Magazine*.

> I stood well with [Hazlitt] for fifteen years . . . and have ever spoke my full mind of him to some, to whom his panegyric must naturally be least tasteful. I never in thought swerved from him, I never betrayed him, I never slackened in my admiration of him, I was the same to him (neither better nor worse) though he could not see it, as in the days when he thought fit to trust me. . . . Judging him by his conversation which I enjoyed so long, and relished so deeply; or by his books, in those places where no clouding passion intervenes—I should belie my own conscience, if I said less, than that I think W. H. to be, in his natural and healthy state, one of the wisest and finest spirits breathing. So far from being ashamed of that intimacy, which was betwixt us, it is my boast that I was able for so many years to have preserved it entire; and I think I shall go to my grave without finding, or expecting to find, such another companion. (*W*, 1:234)

Lamb, Hazlitt wrote, "is shy, sensitive, the reverse of every thing coarse, vulgar, obtrusive, and commonplace. He would fain 'shuffle off this mortal coil,' and his spirit clothes itself in the garb of elder time, homelier, but more durable. He is borne along with no pompous paradoxes, shines in no glittering tinsel of a fashionable phraseology. . . . His style runs pure and clear, though it may often take an underground course, or be conveyed through old-fashioned conduit-pipes. Mr. Lamb does not court popularity, nor strut in gaudy plumes, but shrinks from every kind of ostentatious and obvious pretension into the retirement of his own mind."[30] Furthermore, Lamb was "the most delightful, the most provoking, the most witty and sensible of men. . . . His serious conversation, like his serious writing, is his best. No one ever stammered out such fine, piquant, deep, eloquent things in half a dozen half-sentences as he does. His jests scald like tears: and he probes a question with a play upon words. What a keen, laughing, hair-brained vein of home-felt truth! What choice venom!"[31]

Lamb's early letters to Hazlitt exhibit the same crazed verve as those to Manning. In his first extant one, from November 10, 1805, Lamb admits that what he is about to write is "beneath the dignity of epistolary communication." There is "something about" Rickman's new wife (John married Susanna Postelthwaite on October 30): she is very tall and "she visits prank'd up like a **Queen of the May** with green streamers." She is "good natured" enough, "which is as much as you can expect from a friend's wife, whom you got acquainted with a bachelor." (Here is the seed of the Elian essay "A Bachelor's Complaint of the Behaviour of Married People.") Manning is in town, "in spectacles, and studies physic: is melancholy and seems to have something in his head, which he do'nt impart." Lamb has been to an Oxford gallery, where his mouth watered for the Leonardos. He now appreciates the artist—he was too Gothic in his taste earlier—relishing "the small head, the [here Lamb draws the shape of a long narrow eye] long Eye—that sort of peering curve, the wicked Italian mischief, the stick-at-nothing Herodia's daughter-kind of grace." After comparing the Sampson of painter George Dawe to Milton's, he laments the recent death of Lord Nelson, killed on October 21, in the battle of Trafalgar. Lamb thought he looked "just as a **Hero** should look," was the only "pretence of a Great Man we had," and Lamb is "**cut**" about his demise. Nelson's secretary died by his side. Was this the same man whom Hazlitt met at his friend Joseph Hume's? Mrs. Hume says no. "What other news is there, Mary?" Lamb asks, turning from page to his sister by the fire. "What puns have I made in the last fortnight? You never remember them. You have no relish of the Comic." Mary says, "O! tell Hazlitt not to forget to send [de Crèvecoeur's] American Farmer" (*M,* 2:187–89).

Lamb made other life-long friends during the early years of the nineteenth century. At Rickman's house, he met Admiral James Burney and his wife Sarah, with whom he and Mary took a holiday to the Isle of Wight in July 1803.[32] Burney had forged a distinguished naval career. He had sailed with Captain Cook on his second and third voyages. After the captain died on the latter—he was killed while kidnapping a Hawaiian chief, part of a plan to recover a stolen cutter—it was Burney who took command of the *Discovery's* voyage home. He was named commander in 1780 and captain in 1782. His brilliance for leadership was widely noted, even reaching Samuel Johnson, who wrote, "I question if any ship upon the ocean goes out attended with more good wishes than that which carries the fate of Burney."[33]

Brother of the novelist Fanny Burney (whose masterpiece is the epistolary novel *Evelina*), James, once he returned from sea, took to writing himself. He wrote a six-volume history of the South Seas, a history of the *Discovery's* northeastern voyages and, of most interest to Lamb, *An Essay by Way of Lecture, on the Game of Whist.* Lamb was a fiend for this card game, but no one played it more intensely than Admiral Burney's wife Sarah, the model for Mrs. Battle in Elia's "Mrs. Battle's Opinions on Whist."

The Lambs loved the Burneys' fifteen-year-old son Martin as much as the parents. Lamb describes James and Sarah's indulgent parenting style: "A volume might be made of Martins blunders which parental tenderness omits. Such as his letting the packet boat's boat go without him from the quay at Southampton, while he stood hiatusing, smit with the love of a Naiad; his tumbling back over a stone twice the height of himself, and daubing himself; his getting up to bathe at six o Clock, and forgetting it, and in consequence staying in his room in a process of annihilation &c. &c." (*M,* 2:122). As Lamb suggested in a poem dedicating volume 2 of his 1818 *Works* to Martin, the Burneys' parenting resulted in "caprices wild." Beneath the "humorous clouds that flit o'er brightest days," though, Martin's adult character was "free from self-seeking, envy, [and] low design" (*W,* 5:42). Lamb has not found a purer soul.

Charles and Mary now socialized with the Burneys and the Rickmans regularly. (Manning was mostly away from London during these years.) Mary's letter of March 14, 1806, pictures one of these many social evenings. "We have been visiting a little to Norris's to Godwins and last night we did not come home from Captain Burneys till two O Clock, the *saturday* night was changed into *friday* because Rickman could not be there tonight.—We had the best *tea things*, & the litter all cleared away, and every thing as handsome, as possible Mrs Rickman being of the party. Mrs. Rickman is much *encreased in size*, since we saw her last, and the alteration in her strait shape wonderfully improves her. Phillips [Molesworth Phillips, married to James Burney's sister Susan and a lieutenant colonel in the Marines] was there, and Charles had a long batch of Cribbage with him. & upon the whole we had the most cheerful evening I have known there a long time" (*M*, 2:219).

In 1806, the Lambs formalized these gatherings. They inaugurated the "Wednesday Evening" gathering at 16 Mitre Court. (The event later moved to Thursdays.) As Lamb wrote to Manning, "Rickman & Burney are well—they assemble at my house pretty regularly of a Wednesday, a new institution, like other great men, I have a public day; cribbage & pipes, with Phillips & noisy Ma[rtin] [the Burney's son]" (*M*, 2:247). The evenings became famous. As late as 1848, an anonymous writer in the *British Quarterly* observed that these meetings in the Lambs' "very humble quarters of the Temple" were more exhilarating than "any dozen conversaziones which London could offer." In this modest, "dimly lighted" room, one could find gracing the walls "an engraving or two," and "a famous head of Milton, the possessor's pride." Guests quietly played whist, the solemnity "relieved" "from time to time" by witty remarks and antic shenanigans. Plain clay pipes elevated their smoke, bread and cheese and "perhaps oysters" were the simple fare, and to drink "a foaming tankard of porter; a glass of ginger wine, and a glass or so of grog." The "champagne" of the evening, the spirit of privilege, "was in the talk,—and to hear them was worth the sacrifice of any entertainment."[34]

Hazlitt was a regular. Though awkward in most social settings because he struggled "to express the fine conceptions with which is mind was filled," he was "thoroughly understood" at the Lambs', "dexterously cheered by Miss Lamb, whose nice discernment of his first efforts in conversation, were dwelt upon by him with affectionate gratitude, even when most out of humor with the world."[35]

Feeling at home, Hazlitt could enter into "lively skirmishes" without fear of creating real conflict. (Aside from the night Lamb's brother socked him.) The blend of literary talk and gustation was heady. "How often did we cut into the haunch of letters, while we discussed the haunch of mutton on the table! How we skimmed the cream of criticism! How we got into the heart of controversy! How we picked out the marrow of authors!" The writers—

"the old everlasting set"—were so fully present, they were as guests them-selves: "Milton, Shakespeare, Pope and Dryden, Steele and Addison, Swift and Gay, Fielding, Smollet, Sterne, Richardson. The Hogarth prints on the walls, Claude's landscapes, too, and the Cartoons at Hampton Court: these images enlivened the evenings, too."[36]

What mattered were "wit and good fellowship." "When a stranger came in, he was not asked, 'Has he written anything?'—we were above that ped-antry; but we waited to see what he could do." Could he play piquet, a trick-taking card game? He was welcome. "If a person . . . took snuff heartily, it was sufficient. He would understand, by analogy, the pungency of other things beside Irish blackguard or Scotch rappee. A character was good anywhere, in a room or on paper." What the group abhorred was "insipidity, affectation, and fine gentlemen."[37]

The most vivacious guests were full-on eccentrics. Rickman might have been a nationally famous statistician but at Lamb's he typically "asserted some incredible matter of fact as a likely paradox, and settled all controversies by an *ipse dixit*, a fiat of his will, hammering out many a hard theory on the anvil of his brain—the Baron Munchausen of politics and practical philosophy." "Captain [Burney] . . . had you at an advantage by never understanding you." William Ayrton, a music critic and impresario, was "Will Honeycomb," the *Spectator's* expert in women's fashion. The Burneys' boy Martin was present as well. Lamb thought he was begotten "upon a mermaid," for he "is the queer-est fish out of water."[38]

Still other nonliterary folk joined, as Leigh Hunt put it, "humanity's tri-umph." There was Thomas Alsager, who reported on music for the *Times* and contributed £10 to Lamb's fund to help an impoverished Godwin. Charles Cowden Clarke borrowed Alsager's folio edition of Chapman's translation of Homer in 1816. He recited passages with Keats. Alsager lived across the street from Horsemonger Prison, where Hunt served time for libel. Alsager brought his incarcerated friend dinner on the first day of the sentence. Hunt thought Alsager "the best of neighbors," "especially if you happen to be confined to your room."[39]

Thomas Allsop was also present. He was a silk merchant and radical who sent game to Lamb and Coleridge and gave Coleridge £100. Lieutenant Colo-nel Phillips was there, too. He had sailed "round the world . . . when a boy, and had challenged his lieutenant for not standing closer to his captain."[40] Phillips killed the Hawaiian who shot Captain Cook. You might find James

Kenney there as well. He was a successful playwright who got to see John Lamb smite Hazlitt and who housed Charles and Mary in Versailles during their 1822 trip to France.

Others dropped in and out. Charles Lloyd, Thomas Holcroft, Charles Kemble, Frances Kelly (the actress to whom Lamb would propose in 1819), Basil Montagu, the poet Bryan Procter, Barron Field, the diarist Henry Crabb Robinson, Catherine Stephens (the actress and singer), and Elizabeth Reynolds, Lamb's schoolmistress before he entered Christ's, whom Lamb supported with £32 a year and who, according to Hazlitt, "being of a quiet turn loved to hear a noisy debate."[41]

In addition to Hazlitt and Hunt, other literary royalty would occasionally show up: Godwin, Wordsworth, and Coleridge. Talfourd imagines Lamb playing whist with "the author of 'Political Justice,' (the majestic expression of his large head not disturbed by disproportion of his comparatively diminutive stature)." Godwin regards his hand "with a philosophic but not a careless eye." When Wordsworth appeared, happy was the young disciple "to be admitted to the presence of the poet who had opened a new world for him in the undiscovered riches of his own nature, and its affinities with the outer universe." Sometimes the acolyte might persuade the Lake Poet to "speak of his own poetry—to hear him recite its noblest passages." When Coleridge came, "argument, wit, humor, criticism were hushed; the pertest, smartest, and the cleverest felt that all were assembled to listen; and if a card-table had been filled, or dispute begun before he was excited to continuous speech, his gentle voice, undulating in music, soon

> 'Suspended whist, and took with ravishment
> The thronging audience.'"[42]

But out of this brilliant array of weekly visitors, Lamb might have been most fascinated by Sarah Burney, the captain's lively wife. As we learn in the Elia essay "Mrs. Battle's Opinions on Whist," in the midst of the boozy irony and casual grazing, Sarah, the model for Mrs. Battle, played whist with the concentrated fierceness of an elite warrior. For her, the game was the most important activity on earth. To those who held that cards are trivial, even when played for money, she retorted, "Man is a gaming animal. He must always be trying to get the better in something or other" (W, 2:37).

This fanaticism Elia finds amusing, and oddly charming, even though Mrs. Battle's feelings about cards are exactly the opposite of his own. Elia enjoys cards when he is playing "*for nothing*." "When I am in sickness, or not in the best spirits, I sometimes call for the cards, and play a game at pi-quet *for love* with my cousin Bridget—Bridget Elia." The last game he played with Bridget—Mary—he wished "might have last forever, though we gained nothing, and lost nothing, though it was the mere shade of play: I would be content to go on in that idle folly for ever" (*W*, 2:37).

Mrs. Battle's goal-oriented obsession gives Elia occasion to celebrate the delight of merely passing the time, especially with a beloved companion. And what else are Lamb's essays but his casual attempts to make a small period en-tertaining, for himself and his reader? His verbal drifts aren't going anywhere in particular. Whim is the guide. But when the final punctuation presses, you realize, oh, I didn't know I wanted to be here, in this mood or this idea, but I don't desire to be anywhere else. And like any brilliant improviser, in jazz, say, or acting, Lamb might have known he was getting there all along; he found the impeccable time to stop. If so, this is Lamb's equivalent to Mrs. Battle's winning the prize: getting out of the game, which is fun if you take it in the right spirit, before it gets ugly.

# CHAPTER 25

## Sweeps and Beggars

Valorize uniqueness. Redeem individual from system. Lamb as Elia follows both imperatives, especially in his essays on London oddities. One such work is "The Praise of Chimney-Sweepers."

Charles Lamb walked the same London streets as Blake and witnessed similar horrors. Chimneys in London were narrow, eighteen inches wide. The smaller the sweep, the better. Impoverished parents apprenticed their boys to a master sweep as early as age four. The boys shimmied up the chimney, holding their brushes high. The loosened soot fell over their heads and shoulders. The master bagged the soot and sold it. Sometimes an impatient master lighted a fire below to speed his charge along. The narrow shafts, poor nutrition, and lack of light stunted the boys' growth. The contortions of their not-yet-developed bodies deformed their ankles. Smoke and soot infected their lungs, swelled their eyes. The boys were filthy and cold and hungry. They slept on bags of soot. Some got stuck in chimneys and died. Others contracted cancer in the scrotum. Sweeps were lucky to live until puberty.[1]

Lamb loved Blake's poem on sweeps from *Songs of Innocence*. In 1824, he chose it for James Montgomery's anthology *The Chimney Sweeper's Friend, and Climbing Boy's Album*, intended to improve sweepers' lives. Lamb called it the "flower of the set," but he didn't have much hope for the volume. Montgomery's cause had made few converts "these twenty years," but Lamb wished "the little Negroes all the good that can come from it" (*L*, 2:425).

Conflating chimney sweepers with African slaves was common in reform circles. That Lamb would express this analogy suggests he had an interest in liberating the sweepers from their suffering. How, then, to account for his casual opening to his essay on sweeps? "I like to meet a sweep—understand me—not a grown sweeper—old chimney-sweepers are by no means attractive—but one of those tender novices, blooming through their first nigritude, the maternal washings not quite effaced from the cheek—such as come forth with the dawn, or somewhat earlier, with their little professional notes sounding like the *peep peep* of a young sparrow; or liker to the matin lark should I pronounce them, in their aerial ascents not seldom anticipating the sun-rise?" (*W,* 2:108).

Elia seems to overlook the suffering of the sweep, to reduce him to an object for his own pleasure. Perversely, so it appears, he prefers to encounter the tenderest sweeper he can, one that will be most sensitive to the pains of his vocation. To Elia, these most innocent sweeps, blooming in their first "nigritude" (blackness and slavery), resemble the sun with which they rise; the sparrow, whose notes their cries—weep, weep—mimic; and the lark, which the boys copy in their morning ascents.

But the style of this essay reveals a mind groping. After the confident opening clause, dashes break the flow, implying doubt's jaggedness. "Understand me" suggests that Elia knows he might not be understood, by readers or himself. He then falls into confusing pleonasm ("tender novice") and contradiction (blackness blooming) and punning (efface is to erase as well as to become shy).

The following sentences also undercut Elia's apparent insensitivity. Through scesis onomaton, he questions the ability of his language to convey meaning at all. "I have a kindly yearning toward these dim specks—poor blots—innocent blacknesses." The dashes again signal the hesitation. The difference between a "dim speck" and a "poor blot" is scant. Repetition can imply abundance; it can also signal linguistic entropy (*W,* 2:109).

These tensions presage Elia's progress from connoisseur of extremity to compassionate admirer of the outcast's resilience. Essential to this move from general to particular is Elia finding his own language to refer to the sweeps, as opposed to the language of the popular press. Early in the essay, he likens the sweeps to "Africans," and he also compares them to the "clergy," a common association for cartoonists satirizing priests.

Elia turns these tired analogies into terms of endearment. Sweeps as priests might mock the clergy, but the boys, emerging each morning from "their little pulpits" (the tops of chimneys), also preach, wordlessly (*W*, 2:109). Their sermon: be patient in the pain. This pain justifies the analogy with African slaves: both groups have been cruelly stripped of agency and reduced to tools of middle- and upper-class whites.

Pushing through cliché, Elia nears the sweeps. He remembers seeing them when a child. He observed their similarity to him. He appreciated their magic-seeming virtuosity. He pursued a "chit no bigger" than himself in imagination, "as he went sounding on through so many dark stifling caverns, horrid shades!" he shuddered "with the idea that 'now, surely, he must be lost for ever!'" and he revived "at hearing his feeble shout of discovered day-light." What joy to witness this Lazarus miracle, to feel the "fulness of delight" of "running out of doors . . . just in time to see the sable phenomenon emerge in safety, the brandished weapon of his art victorious like some flag waved over a conquered citadel!" (*W*, 2:109).

Closer now to the sweep, Elia approaches the reader, as though the delight of empathy with one promises similar pleasure with the other. "Reader, if thou meetest one of these small gentry in thy early rambles, it is good to give him a penny. It is better to give him two-pence. If it be starving weather, and to the proper troubles of his hard occupation, a pair of kibed heels (no unusual accompaniment) be superadded, the demand on thy humanity will surely rise to a tester" (*W*, 2:109).

Elia describes particular boys with specific tastes. The sweeps relish saloop, a mixture of hot water and the powdered root of orchids to which sugar and milk are added. If you wish to aid one of these boys, buy him a cup.

The sweeps are jocular.

In the last winter but one, pacing along Cheapside with my accustomed precipitation when I walk westward, a treacherous slide brought me upon my back in an instant. I scrambled up with pain and shame enough—yet outwardly trying to face it down, as if nothing had happened—when the roguish grin of one of these young wits encountered me. There he stood, pointing me out with his dusky finger to the mob, and to a poor woman (I suppose his mother) in particular, till the tears for the exquisiteness of the fun (so he thought it) worked themselves out at the corners of his poor red eyes, red from many a previous weeping, and soot-inflamed, yet twinkling through all with such a joy, snatched out of desolation. . . . I could have been content, if the honour of a gentleman might endure it, to have remained his butt and his mockery till midnight. (*W,* 2:111)

The scene is cinematic. Elia strolls westward. Medium shot of him walking right to left. Then a point-of-view shot: we see what he sees. Back to medium shot. He goes down hard on the street, hops back up, hoping no one has seen. Cut to a medium shot of a be-sooted boy. Close-up: through the grime, roguish mockery. A long shot, taking in the larger scene. The sweep points Elia out to the mob. The camera pans into the mass, focuses on one woman, maybe the mother who sold the sweep, in the center.

Jem White held a feast every May in honor of the sweeps. Hence Lamb's initial subtitle of the essay in the *London Magazine*, "A May-Day Effusion." At the north end of Bartholomew Fair, Elia and one Bigod (Fenwick) helped White serve the boys meat, bread, and small ale.

After Jem White's death Lamb dropped "Effusion" from the subtitle when he published the essay in a book. The piece is more autumnal than vernal. With White's death, so end the suppers. White "carried away with him half the fun of the world when he died—of my world at least. His old clients look for him among the pens; and, missing him, reproach the altered feast of St. Bartholomew, and the glory of Smithfield departed for ever" (*W,* 2:114).

Lamb published his essay on chimney sweeps in the *London Magazine* in May 1822. He followed it the next month with another piece on London unfortunates: beggars. The immediate context for "A Complaint of the Decay of Beggars in the Metropolis" was very likely the establishment of the Society for the Suppression of Mendicity in 1818. An 1816 parliamentary report on beggars mobilized the group. Mendicants were a terrible problem in the city, the report went, not only because of their numbers but also their activities. Their "gross and monstrous frauds" supported their "vice, idleness, and profligacy." Rather than address the factors causing the destitution, the society simply wanted the beggars gone. It gave charity to the unfortunates in exchange for their vacating the city.[2]

Others found the city's beggars worth keeping around. The vagabonds were quite colorful, after all, and one could gain a sentimental "glow" by pitying their plight.[3] In *Vagabondiana; or, Anecdotes of Mendicant Wanderers through the Streets of London*, published in 1817, John Thomas Smith charmingly sketches particular beggars, in both word and image. That Smith terms the city's homeless "wanderers" demonstrates his romantic spin; his characters aren't people forced into suffering by bad governance but adventurers by choice.

Elia also finds beggars worth his attention, but not because he wants to remove or sentimentalize them. He wants to represent them accurately, with an eye toward revealing their virtues. He highlights the problem of fair representation in his opening paragraph:

> The all-sweeping besom of societarian reformation—your only modern Alcides' club to rid the time of its abuses—is uplift with many-handed sway to extirpate the last fluttering tatters of the bugbear Mendicity from the metropolis. Scrips, wallets, bags—staves, dogs, and crutches—the whole mendicant fraternity with all their baggage are fast posting out of the purlieus of this eleventh persecution. From the crowded crossing, from the corners of streets and turnings of allies, the parting Genius of Beggary is "with sighing sent." I do not approve of this wholesale going to work, this impertinent crusado, or *bellum ad exterminationem*, proclaimed against a species. Much good might be sucked from these Beggars. (*W,* 2:114)

Here is classic Elian disjunction between hyperbolic rhetoric and ordinary subject matter. The rare words *besom* and *purlieus*; allusions to Greek mythology (Alcides) and Milton ("with sighing sent"); Latin phrasing; scesis onomaton (repetition of synonymous phrases, remember, suggesting superabundance): all this machinery in play just to say that reform groups are trying to remove beggars from the city. The gap between form and content is comical, but it also a serious dramatization of the difficulty of representing experience with language.

Clearly the language of reform doesn't even come close to the beggars' lives. To do-gooders, beggars are simply pests, like rats, who need to go. Smith with his lively anecdotes and pictures might come closer to their existence, but his goal is to transform the sordid into the sweet.

Elia takes another tack: irony. The significance of beggars is this: they transcend signification. The beggar "is not in the scale of comparison. He is not under the measure of property. He confessedly hath none, any more than a dog or a sheep." Since he has nothing, "no one twitteth him with ostentation above his means. No one accuses him of pride, or upbraideth him with mock humility. None jostle with him for the wall, or pick quarrels for precedency. No wealthy neighbour seeketh to eject him from his tenement. No man sues him. No man goes to law with him" (W, 2:116).

Again Elia's rhetoric outsizes his semantics. The anaphora—reminiscent of the Bible—is excessive for simply saying that the beggar escapes the petty conflicts generated by the desire for possessions. But the rhetoric here isn't simply a comical riff on the gap between words and things. The repetition of "No" at the beginning of each sentence emphasizes the beggar's true value: nothing, nil, zero.

One is more than zero, and less than two. But zero is neither more nor less than anything. It bears no quantity. Zero, moreover, is outside of linear succession, the increasing amounts as the number line moves right, the decreasing ones to the left. So the beggar: he doesn't organize his life according to a narrative of accumulation or loss. In this way, he, like zero, is outside of capitalistic causality, the "if . . . then" required for working one's way toward financial goals.

Aptly, the beggar's garb transcends set value as well. He doesn't wear his rags to impress, mourn, reflect fashion or affiliation. "He is the only man in the universe who is not obliged to study appearances. The ups and downs of the world concern him no longer. . . . He is the only free man in the universe" (W, 2:116).

Existing outside of conventional measures, the beggar remains a mystery. Even a beggar with a very concrete history is an enigma. Elia vividly remembers a beggar with no legs—he lost them in the Gordon Riots—who rolls himself around the city. What he lacks below, he makes up for above: "He was of a robust make, with a florid sailor-like complexion, and his head was bare to the storm and sunshine. . . . The common cripple would despise his own pusillanimity, viewing the hale stoutness, and hearty heart, of this half-limbed giant." Everyone knew of this "Anteus." (His name was possibly Samuel Horsey, known as the "King of Beggars.") Nonetheless, he is a "grand fragment" in Elia's mind, an incomplete ruggedness who hints at a smooth whole irrevocably lost. The lack, though inscrutable, is full. He is as "good as an Elgin marble" (W, 2:118).

This man did not agree to enter a poorhouse, so he was imprisoned. Those supporting projects to remove beggars begrudge such a man getting his money without a job. Why should he get away with doing nothing and still support his (supposed) child, or enjoy a hot meal of a night with other cripples? But no one really knows if this man funded a child or enjoyed tasty dinners. The miserly reformers concoct such stories to turn citizens against beggars. Reformers also cast doubt on the sad tales the beggars recount to inspire pity.

How can you ever know, though, Elia asks, if the beggar is lying or not? His ambiguous appearance conceals his history. Even if you were able to ascertain his honesty, however, why would you? Charity is indifferent to veracity. If the beggar's distress is "painted," then perform charity anyway. In fact, why not just assume that all beggars are acting? Then you can treat him as a "player" and reward him for his craft. You would pay a comedian for his fakery (*W*, 2:120).

Elia is a comedian. Is he faking in the essay? Can we take him seriously? If we are looking for research-driven analyses of beggars or glow-inducing moralizing on their plight, the answer is no. But if we are looking for a way to find clarity in an indecipherable situation, then Elia is our man. When in doubt, give your halfpenny. The worst that can happen? You are duped. The best that can happen—you gave a man a gift briefly lifting him from his suffering.

We are all actors, the essay implies, and so should shift our values away from truth and falsehood and toward wit, panache, verve, gusto.

# CHAPTER 26

# Shipwreck

Though Lamb was rarely around Wordsworth, whose visits to London were not frequent, and though he was in Coleridge's presence only occasionally, he stayed in close touch with both men. He bought books for the poets in the city and sent them northward, and he saw Coleridge's 1803 *Poems* through the press at Longman.

Both friends brought sadness into the Lambs' life. In August 1806, Coleridge returned to England after his two-year stint in Malta. On the 17th, he landed at Stangate Creek, Lower Halstow, Kent, barely alive. His voyage had been horrific. "Both the Captain and my fellow-passenger were seriously alarmed for my Life—and indeed such have been my unremitting Sufferings from pain, sleeplessness, costiveness, loathing of food, & spirits wholly despondent, that no motive on earth short of an awful duty would ever prevail on me to take any sea-voyage likely to be longer than three or four days. I had rather starve in [a ho]vel; and if Life thro' disease become worthless, will choose a Roman Death."[1] Now on land, he was "shirtless & almost penniless," weak in body and mind. He was dangerously depressed, addled by opium. He had lost his trunk.[2]

Coleridge showed up at the Lambs' door a few days later. They witnessed a worse version of what Dorothy Wordsworth saw in October: "Never did I feel such a shock as the first sight of him. We all felt the same way. . . . He is utterly changed; and yet sometimes, when he was in animated conversation concerning things removed from him, I saw something of his former self."[3]

The Lambs took care of Coleridge. They gave him sympathy, a good bed, food and drink. But within about ten days, he wore on them. As Mary wrote to Dorothy, she was in "low spirits, brought on by the fatigue of Coleridge's conversation and the anxious care even to misery which I have felt since he has been here that something could be done to make such an admirable creature happy" (*M,* 2:238–39).

Mary had written to William and Dorothy the day before, August 28, urging them to arrange a separation between Coleridge and Sara. Ever since his arrival, Coleridge had complained about the difficulty of his marriage and how it goaded his addiction. He might have mentioned he was in love with Sara Hutchinson. Separation was best, Mary thought, for the sake of both Coleridge and his wife.

But she had second thoughts, as she often did when depressed. ("What I think one hour a fit of low spirits makes me unthink the next.") She remembered a letter she received from Mrs. Coleridge telling her "as joyful news, that her husband is arrived." Burn this letter, she implores Dorothy, and the one I sent yesterday, "because Charles will either blame me for having written something improper or he will laugh at me for my foolish fears about nothing" (*M,* 2:239).

Soon after, Mary made Coleridge write his wife, with whom he had not communicated since his return. When Coleridge finally made it to Keswick in late October, a separation was arranged.

Compared to the horror of the winter of 1805, getting pulled into a marital imbroglio was minor. On February 1, 1805, Captain John Wordsworth, the poet's younger brother, launched the ship he commanded, the *Earl of Abergavenny,* from Portsmouth.[4] An employee of the East India Company— he had served in its navy since the age of sixteen—he was setting out to India and China, with high financial hopes. The ship, an East Indiaman built in 1796, was one of the largest vessels ever made, and John's launch was the company's richest ever. The ship contained some £200,000 worth of cargo, including £70,000 in silver dollars. The coins, whose weight totaled 275,000 ounces, were reserved for purchasing tea in Bengal and opium in China. John had invested £20,000 in this venture—he had lost money on his first two eastern voyages on the ship—and had encouraged Dorothy and William to invest as well, and they did, handsomely and riskily, putting up £3,000, virtually all the money the family had recently received from a long-awaited settlement from the Lowther estate. The ship's massive cargo was matched in scale by the number of people it carried, somewhere between 386 and 402.

John was thirty-three and had proven himself an honest, courageous, just, competent commander. His family placed high hopes in him. They loved him, too, especially William and Dorothy. William wrote, "We were not Brother sister with him in blood only but had the same pleasures the same loves in almost everything."[5]

On February 5, the *Earl of Abergavenny* and the six sister ships in its convoy reached waters off the shore of Portland Bill. The commander of the fleet ordered the ships to sail to safe harbor, since the group had become separated from its naval escort, essential for safety during this time of war with the French. A local pilot led the *Earl* to shore. He was inept. He ran Captain Wordsworth's vessel into the Shambles, a three-mile-long sand and shingle bank submerged about two miles from shore. The collision knocked the ship on its side. Icy water flooded it. The ship righted but stayed stuck on the Shambles. The waves bashed the hull, ripped away the planks. Those on board endured this beating for two hours. The *Abergevanny* broke free of the sand. But the boat was so waterlogged it could not sail. After seven hours, at around 11 p.m., the ship sank into sixty-five feet of water. The mate said to Captain Wordsworth, "We have done all we can, Sir—she will sink in a moment." To which the captain replied, "It cannot be helped. God's will be done." The even distribution of cargo, along with its weight, kept the vessel from rolling as it went down. It rested upright on the ocean's bottom, its masts raised slightly above the waves. Some passengers clung to the rigging. Others grabbed planks and flopped into the sea, hoping to float to land. Some piled into a rescue boat, but their weight capsized it. Two hundred and sixty-six people died. Among them was the captain.[6]

Newspapers and liability investigators blamed Captain Wordsworth. He was accused of indecision and suicidal passivity. Drunkenness was proposed but dismissed.

The loss stunned Dorothy and William. As William wrote, "Our loss is one which never can be made up; had it come earlier in life or later it would have been easier to bear; we are young enough to have had hope of pleasure and happiness in each others company for many years, and too old to outgrow the sorrow."[7] The rumors of incompetence scalded them. They wanted answers, so they wrote to the only man they knew who could get them—Charles Lamb of the East India Company.

On February 18, 1805, Lamb responded to a letter sent by the Wordsworths seeking more information about their brother's death. His tone is guilty. We (he and Mary) should have written to you sooner to find out about your situation, but "it never seemed the time." We "felt all your situation," and knew how much you'd want Coleridge (still in Malta) to comfort you. Lamb then tries to muster affection for John. We "loved & honoured your Brother, & his death always occurs to my mind with something like a feeling of reproach, as if we might have been nearer acquainted, & as if there had been some incivility shewn him by us, or something short of that respect we now feel: but this is always a feeling, when people die, and I should not foolishly offer a piece of refinement, instead of sympathy, if I know any other way of making you feel how little like indifferent his loss has been to us" (M, 2:151–52). Lamb fears that the Wordsworths believe he *is* indifferent to John, since he has not written. Lamb hints at why this thought might be present; perhaps he was not as well acquainted with John as he felt he should have been (why else would he mention that possibility?), and maybe there was some incivility (why else mention it?). But Charles reveals the strongest reason he has not written: he has been extremely depressed—"wretchedly ill and low." He will make appropriate inquiries but he "can hardly express [himself], [he is] so really ill." For now, Mary is crying by his side, as they both remember John's "noble person, & his sensible manly modest voice, & how safe & comfortable we all were together in our apartment." Again, though, as if he hasn't said this enough, he is "seriously unwell" and will conclude from "utter inability to write any more (M, 2:152–53).

This is not the Lamb Thackeray hailed as "St. Charles." This Lamb is so depressed he has been indifferent to a friend's tragedy and how me might relieve the pain. And when he tries to bring forth reasons for his lack of feeling, he deals in meaningless abstractions—the "time" wasn't right for writing—or feebly explains that really *did* care for John and wishes he had known him better. But what Lamb cares most for right now is his depression, which he mentions three times, claiming that his sickness is so overwhelming he can barely write.

Here we see how Lamb's own dark moods might have precipitated Mary's. His "sad depression of spirits" and "most unaccountable nervousness" (M, 2:155)—as he termed his February 1805 condition to Manning—could easily set Mary off. "I get so irritable & wretched with **fear**," he wrote Dorothy around this time, "that I constantly hasten on the disorder. You cannot conceive the misery of such a foresight" (M, 2:169).

But Charles rallied for the Wordsworths, as he did for Mary. The next day, February 19, he wrote Wordsworth again, admitting that his letter from the day before was "very unsatisfactory." He has since interviewed Thomas Gilpin, the ship's fourth mate, and discovered that John did not "in any absence of mind" neglect his own safety. On March 4, Lamb sent the Wordsworths the full transcript of Gilpin's testimony to East India House Court of Directors. He apologizes for having mentioned his "ill health" earlier. He is getting better, now having persisted in a "course of **regular living**," an admission that suggests that Charles's low spirits were exacerbated, if not caused by, alcohol (*M*, 2:159).

Soon, before March 21, Lamb received a list of detailed questions from Wordsworth. He wanted more particulars about his brother's final hours. It is as if the poet wished to visualize the tragedy minute my minute. Lamb submitted the queries to midshipman Benjamin Yates, who survived the wreck. He had the answers by April 2. Why were all the lifeboats not released and used? The lowering would have taken the men away from pumping and bailing. Where was Captain Wordsworth when the ship sunk? "The fore part of the Poop between the Mizzen and th[e] ladder close into the starboard side which leads down on the quarter deck." Did you see the captain when the ship sank? Yes. Was the captain composed? Yes. Why was the captain not saved? I don't know, but I believe he "never had a wish to survive the loss of his property" (*M*, 2:162–63).

To this last answer, which hints at suicide, we have no response from Lamb or Wordsworth.

# CHAPTER 27

## Hogsflesh

Lamb's circumlocution to Wordsworth in 1804 characterizes his first decade of the nineteenth century: "I am not plethorically abounding in Cash at this present" (*M*, 2:146). His salary from the East India Company, even though it had grown from £40 to £130 from 1796 to 1802, was still not enough to cover the Lambs' expenses comfortably, mainly because of the cost of private asylums. Charles's heavy smoking and drinking, and the siblings' frequent holidays, didn't help.

Lamb needed extra money. When Coleridge backed out of reviewing Godwin's new biography of Chaucer, Lamb took it on. But on November 7, 1803, Lamb confesses to Godwin that he has been strangely "hindered in the review." He promises to complete it soon. But the next day though he admits he can "produce nothing but absolute flatness and nonsense." Part of the problem is his depression. His "health and spirits are so bad, and [his] nerves so irritable," that if he persists in trying, he will "teaze" himself into a fever. If you knew how "sore and weak a brain I have," you would "allow for many things in me, which you set down for whims" (*M*, 2:126–27).

In passing, Lamb had a conversation about the book with Godwin's new wife. He told her he delighted in the book generally, but he did find a fault. He didn't wish to go into particulars but preferred to discuss his opinions with Godwin in person. But Mary Jane rushed to her husband and told him

Lamb did not favor the book. This angered Charles. He wrote to Godwin on November 10. Yes, he does believe that the book's "one considerable error" is a tendency to be too conjectural about Chaucer's life. But he is "greatly delighted" on the whole. As for the review—Godwin should be more patient. "You, by long habits of composition, & a greater command gained over your own powers, cannot conceive of the desultory and uncertain way in which I (an author by fits) sometimes cannot put the thoughts of a common letter into sane prose. Any work which I take upon myself as an engagement will act upon me to torment." Reviewing is especially difficult. My "**head** is so whimsical a head, that **I** cannot, after reading another man's book, let it have been never so pleasing, give any account of it in any methodical way, I cannot follow his train.— Something like this you must have perceiv'd of me in conversation. Ten thousand times I have confessed to you, talking of my talents, my utter inability to remember in any comprehensive way what I read. I can vehemently applaud, or perversely stickle, at *parts*: but I cannot grasp at a whole" (*M,* 2:128).

In "Old and New Schoolmaster," an Elia essay from May 1821, Lamb expounds upon his reading habits, versus those of a polished teacher. "My reading has been lamentably desultory and immethodical," Elia admits. "Odd, out of the way, old English plays, and treatises, have supplied me with most of my notions, and ways of feeling. In every thing that relates to science, I am a whole Encyclopædia behind the rest of the world. I should have scarcely cut a figure among the franklins, or country gentlemen, in king John's days" (*W,* 2:49).

The modern schoolmaster is the opposite. His learning is wide. "The modern schoolmaster is expected to know a little of every thing, because his pupil is required not to be entirely ignorant of any thing. He must be superficially, if I may so say, omniscient. He is to know something of pneumatics; of chemistry; of whatever is curious, or proper to excite the attention of the youthful mind; an insight into mechanics is desirable, with a touch of statistics; the quality of soils, &c. botany, the constitution of his country" (*W,* 2:52).

The schoolmaster's life is dully repetitive, however. Every experience, even a coach ride with a stranger, is another excuse for gaining information that he can deposit in his students' heads.

Elia's life, by contrast, is varied and exciting. If you don't go looking for facts—the average cost of calico at the Saturday auction—you can enjoy eccentrics: the azure cloth just in the corner reminds you of the blue that stained the face one morning of a drunken colleague named Tommy Pye.

Here is one of the many instances where Lamb turns his limitation into virtue. By the time he wrote this essay, he had transformed his inability to think methodically into digressive essays flashing with unexpected particulars.

Lamb wrote to Hazlitt in February 1806 that he had taken a room so he could work on a farce between 5 and 8 every evening. He could get no work done at home, since he had too many "*knock-eternal* visitors." The play was to go to Richard Wroughton, the manager of Drury Lane, the next day (*M*, 2:209).

Lamb's boisterous social life wrecked work habits. He once lamented, "I never have an hour for my head to work quietly in its own workings; which as you know is as necessary to the human system as **Sleep**" (*W*, 2:201). On another occasion, he said, "It is not of guests that we complain, but of endless, purposeless visitants; droppers in, as they are called. We sometimes wonder from what sky they fall" (*W*, 2:265).

Only a week after completing the farce, titled *Mr. H.*, Lamb decided he missed Mary too much and moved back into Mitre Court full-time. By June he had a response from Drury Lane: the play was accepted. It was to open December 10. If it succeeded, Lamb might earn as much as £300. He would get nothing if it flopped.

The play is about a "coxcomb appearing at Bath vastly rich—all the Ladies dying for him—all bursting to know who he is—but he goes by no other name than Mr. H." This mystery creates great curiosity about the man, which turns into "vehement admiration." His "true name comes out, *Hogsflesh*." Now all "the women shun him, [av]oid him & not one can be found to change their name for him—that's the idea" (*M*, 2:246).[1]

The plot is obviously ridiculous, but it reflects one of Lamb's most favored modes of comedy, the eighteenth-century comedy of manners. As he writes in his 1823 Elia essay "On the Artificial Comedy of the Last Century," this kind of theater has now fallen into disrepute, since audiences find the characters too unrealistic to "stand the moral test" (*W*, 2:286). But Elia enjoys the farcical comedies of the last century precisely because they allow him for "a season to take an airing beyond the diocese of the strict conscience—not to live always in the precincts of the law-courts—but now and then, for a dream-while or so, to imagine a world with no meddling restrictions—to get into recesses, whither the hunter cannot follow me." He returns to his "cage" and his "restraint" "more healthy for it" (*W*, 2:142). What Congreve does in his plays, Elia practices in his essays.

But Lamb was no Congreve.

When he attended opening night with Mary, Hazlitt, and his new friend Henry Crabb Robinson, his hopes were high—for good reason. According to Hazlitt, "the streets filled with the buzz of persons asking one another if they would go to see Mr. H—, and answering that they would certainly."[2] The house was full. Many from Charles's wide circle of friends were there, as well as colleagues from his and his brother John's respective offices.

The prologue, Lamb reported to Wordsworth, "was received with such shouts as I never witness'd to a Prologue. It was attempted to be **encored**" (*M*, 2:250). Robinson in his *Diary* concurred. "The prologue was very well received. Indeed, it could not fail, being one of the very best in the language."[3]

At the request of the theater's manager, Lamb had penned this opening at the last minute. It is a jaunty, clever riff on initials. Here are its first lines.

> If we have sinn'd in paring down a name,
> All civil well-bred authors do the same.
> Survey the columns of our daily writers—
> You'll find that some Initials are great fighters.
> How fierce the shock, how fatal is the jar,
> When Ensign W. meets Lieutenant R.
> With two stout seconds, just of their own gizard,
> Cross Captain X. and rough old General Izzard
> Letter to Letter spreads the dire alarms,
> Till half the Alphabet is up in arms. (*W*, 5:180)

So popular was the prologue with the audience, Lamb believed it would appear in most of the morning papers. He found himself laughing at his own wit.

With the prologue's end, so ended the cheers. As Robinson put it, "The squeamishness of the vulgar taste in the pit on the disclosure of the name showed itself in hisses."[4] A reviewer elaborated. When the name associated with the H. was revealed, "all the interest vanished, the audience were disgusted, and the farce went on to its very conclusion almost unheard, amidst the contending clamours of Silence! Hear! Hear! And off! off! off!"[5] For Lamb, the infectiousness of the hissing was the most brutal part. After the prologue, the audience "yielded at length to a few hissers," then exploded into a "hundred hisses." "Damn the word. I write it like **kisses**—how different—a hundred hisses outweigh a 1000 **Claps**. The former come more directly from the Heart" (*M*, 2:251).

Over two years later, Lamb still felt the shame. The hissing felt like

a sort of a frantic yell, like a congregation of mad geese, with roaring
something like bears, mows & mops like ap[e]s, sometimes snakes,
that hissed me into madness. 'Twas like St. Anthony's temptations.
Mercy on us, that God should give His favourite children **men**,
mouths to speak with, to discourse rationally, to promise smoothly, to
flatter agreeably, to encourage warmly, to counsel wisely, to sing with,
to drink with, and to kiss with, and that they should turn them into
the mouths of adders, bears, wolves, hyenas, and whistle like tempests,
and emit breath thro them like distillations of aspic poison, to asperse
and vilify the innocent labours of their fellow creatures who are desirous to please them! (*M*, 2:272–73)

According to Robinson, Lamb—whose identity would be unknown to
many in the audience, since his name was not on the playbill—joined the
hissers vigorously. Either he didn't want the audience to know he was the
author—who would hiss down his own work?—or he was simply doing his
Lamb thing, ironic nonsense. Probably both.

The play failed. Mary took the play's "ill success" more to heart than
Charles. She couldn't even write about it for two weeks. When she did give
her take, she said the failure rested on Charles—as opposed to the actors. His
"ignorance of stage effect" kept the play from succeeding—just as it had hindered *John Woodvil*. Charles would learn from his errors and apply his lessons
to another farce (*M*, 2:253).

CHAPTER 28

 ⟨♥⟩

# Tales from Shakespear

On November 18, 1805, a little book was released by one "Tho⁸. Hodgkins, Hanway St." Called *The King and Queen of Hearts,* it announced on its title page that it would show how the queen made her tarts and how the knave stole them. The first page featured the nursery rhyme, which ends with the king beating the guilty knave "full sore," and the thief returning the tarts, vowing "to steal no more." The remainder of the book was composed of six-line verses glossing each of the nursery rhyme's twelve lines, plus two more of these brief poems to end the book. Illustrations appeared on every page.

The text was by Charles Lamb (as we know from a February 1, 1806, letter to Wordsworth), and the images by William Mulready. Hodgkins was the manager of a new bookshop and publisher on Hanway Street, the City Juvenile Library, which opened in March 1805. The owners were William and Mary Jane Godwin. Hodgkins appeared as publisher of *The King and Queen of Hearts* because Godwin thought his own name, anathema in many circles, would hurt sales.

The first title of the Juvenile Library Godwin wrote under the name of Edward Baldwin: *Fables Ancient and Modern, Adapted for the Use of Children from Three to Eight Years of Age*. Mulready—whose biography would be Godwin's second title (*The Looking-Glass: A True History of the Early Years of an Artist*, by "Theophilus Marcliffe")—provided the thirty-six illustrations for the book. "Baldwin" in the preface proclaimed that "if we would benefit a child . . . we must make our narrations pictures, and render the objects we discourse about, visible to the fancy of the learner."[1]

*The King and Queen of Hearts* fulfills this requirement. Mulready's images strikingly tell the story. We barely need Lamb's words. Artist and poet transform the original nursery rhyme from a moral tale—do not steal—into a subversive scene. Mungo, a character not in the original, tells the king and queen that Pambo has stolen from them. When Pambo finds out, he prepares to beat the "little Tell-Tale" "black and blue." What will the king and queen do? Nothing. They are drunk—another detail absent from the original. If there is a lesson, it is "Don't be a snitch."

The ever-impoverished Godwins got into publishing to make money, but also to express political dissent. Their Juvenile Library de-emphasized moral didacticism and encouraged imaginative freedom.

(The books, luckily, didn't reflect Godwin's own failures with children. Back in December 1799, three-year-old Hartley Coleridge "gave the philosopher such a Rap on the shins with a ninepin that Godwin in huge pain *lectured* Sara on his boisterousness." Coleridge knows his boy "is somewhat too rough & noisy," but he'll take the hellion any time over "the cadaverous Silence of Godwin's Children," which is "quite catacomb-ish.")[2]

Godwin knew from the days of the Gillray cartoon that Lamb was amenable to dissenting politics and thus would make a fine author for the Juvenile Library. Lamb was also a vehement critic of the didactic children's tale, as his letter to Coleridge from October 1802 demonstrates.

> Goody Two Shoes is almost out of print. Mrs Barbauld['s] stuff has banished all the old classics of the nursery; & the shopman at Newbery's hardly deigned to reach them off an old exploded corner of a shelf, when Mary ask'd for them. Mrs B's & Mrs T's nonsense lay in piles about. Knowledge insignificant & vapid as Mrs B's books convey, it seems, must come to a child in the *shape* of *knowledge*, & his empty noddle must be turned with conceit of his own powers, when he has learnt that a Horse is an Animal, & Billy is better than a Horse, & such like, instead of that beautiful Interest in wild tales, which made the child a man, while all the time he suspected himself to be no bigger than a child. Science has succeeded to Poetry no less in the little walks of children than with Men.———: Is there no possibility of averting this sore evil? Think what you would have been now, if instead of

being fed with Tales & old wives fables in childhood, you had been crammed with Geography & Natural History? **Damn them**. I mean the cursed Barbauld crew, those **Blights & Blasts** of all that is **Human** in man & child.—(*M*, 2:81–82)

John Newbery's *The History of Goody Two-shoes* (1765) is about an orphan named Margery Meanwell whose exceedingly virtuous behavior is rewarded with wealth. Anna Laetitia Barbauld's *Early Lessons for Children* (1778), though revolutionary in its conversational style and typographical simplicity, focuses on pedagogy and correct behavior. In *Easy Introduction to the Knowledge of Nature* (1782), Sarah Trimmer portrays a mother teaching her two children about God in nature. These didactic narratives miss what children crave: wild tales.

Coleridge was the right man for this letter. Five years earlier, he expressed the same idea: "From my early reading of Faery Tales, & Genii &c &c—my mind had been habituated *to the Vast*—& I never regarded *my senses* in any way as the criteria of my belief. I regulated all my creeds by my conceptions not by my *sight*—even at that age. Should children be permitted to read Romances, & Relations of Giants & Magicians, & Genii?—I know all that has been said against it; but I have formed my faith in the affirmative.—I know no other way of giving the mind a love of 'the Great,' & 'the Whole.'"[3]

Lamb's *The King and Queen of Hearts* might not have habituated the mind to the "Vast," but it was a wild tale, and it established Lamb's credentials to write imaginatively stimulating tales for the Godwins. But it was to Mary, not Charles, that William and Mary Jane turned for a more substantial project: a summary of Shakespeare's plays for children. How this came about isn't clear. Perhaps Mary simply expressed to the Godwins an interest in writing. She and Charles were socializing with them regularly in the winter of 1806—they had put their differences over the aborted Chaucer review aside—and one can imagine many conversations about the Juvenile Library and the need for authors.

While Charles was away in the evenings writing *Mr. H.*, Mary held "solitary consultation" over how she might employ herself. "Writing plays, novels, poems, and all manner of such-like vapouring and vapourish schemes are floating in my head" (*M*, 2:210). In March she was still considering writing projects, but Charles's presence in the evenings hindered her progress. He has given up the lodging, Mary lamented, since he "could not endure the solitariness." He was as "unsettled and as undetermined as ever." He had not begun a new farce, as she had hoped, and had developed no other literary work. Mary was trying to avoid his procrastination; she resolved to "turn over a new leaf with [her] own mind." She wanted a more "calm & quiet" temper (*M,* 2:220).

By early May, she had signed on with the Godwins. As Lamb wrote to the departing Manning, Mary "is doing for Godwins Bookseller 20 of Shakespears plays to be made into Childrens tales" (*M,* 2:225). Six were done, all comedies or romances. Charles would handle the tragedies, and he had already completed *Othello* and *Macbeth.* The books were likely to be popular among the children, but more important, the job would bring in 60 guineas.

"I go on very well," Mary wrote Sarah in June, "& have no doubt but I shall always be able to hit upon some such kind of job to keep going on." She trusted her consistent writing would bring in at least £50 a year. Charles's progress was not as smooth. "You would like to see us as we often sit writing on one table (but not on one cushion sitting) like Hermia & Helen in the Midsummer Night's Dream, or rather like an old literary Darby and Joan. I taking snuff & he groaning all the while & saying he can make nothing of it, which he always says till he has finished and then he finds out he has made something of it" (*M,* 2:228–29).

Mary composed fourteen tales, Charles six, but the work was a collaboration. As Lamb wrote to Manning, "Mary is just stuck fast in All's Well That Ends Well. She complains of having to set forth so many female characters in boy's clothes. She begins to think Shakespear must have wanted Imagination.—I to encourage her, for she often faints in the prosecution of her great work, flatter her with telling her how well such a play & such a play is done. But she is stuck fast & I have been obliged to promise to assist her" (*M,* 2:233). He was helpful. By the next day, Charles was praising her summary. Surely Mary performed the same service for Charles.

The siblings were so busy with the *Tales* they skipped their annual holiday trip. The book was published in January 1807. Like Charles's "Modern Gallantry" and Mary's essay on needlework, the book stretches between progressive (Shakespeare's "wild poetic garden") and conservative (traditional cultural hierarchies). "Beautiful bare narratives," stories as stories, the tales are largely free of moral or interpretive comment.

Mary's narratives are simpler than Charles's. But they are not simplistic. Her spare prose has the lean authority of the Bible, paratactic "is-ness" that feels as inevitable as it does authoritative. Here is her opening paragraph to the volume, from *The Tempest*: "There was a certain island in the sea, the only inhabitants of which were an old man, whose name was Prospero, and his daughter Miranda, a very beautiful young lady. She came to this island so young, that she had no memory of having seen any other human face than her father's" (*W,* 3:3). This is proto-Hemingway, as is this passage from *A Midsummer Night's Dream*: "The fairy king, who was always friendly to true lovers, felt great compassion for Helena; and perhaps, as Lysander said they used to walk by moonlight in this pleasant wood, Oberon might have seen Helena in those happy times when she was beloved by Demetrius" (*W,* 3:14). This is from *As You Like It*: "In the summer they [the duke and his followers] lay along under the fine shade of the large forest trees, marking the playful sports of wild deer; and so fond were they of these poor dappled fools, who seemed to be the native inhabitants of the forest, that it grieved them to be forced to kill them to supply themselves with venison for their food" (*W,* 3:38).

Contributing to Mary's success is her ability to translate Shakespeare's dialogue into conversation a child can understand. After Prospero tells Miranda of how he saved her as an infant from his evil brother, she says, "O my father . . . what a tremendous trouble I have been to you then!" To which Prospero replies, "No, my love . . . you were a little cherub that did preserve me. Your innocent smile made me to bear up against my misfortunes" (*W,* 3:5).

But Mary's restraint at strategic times eases, and her language leaps—simply to stoke the imagination. Ariel flies into focus: "When Caliban was lazy and neglected his work, Ariel (who was invisible to all eyes but Prospero's) would come slyly and pinch him, and sometimes tumble him down in the mire; and then Ariel, in the likeness of an ape, would make mouths at him. Then swiftly changing his shape, in the likeness of a hedgehog he would lie tumbling in Caliban's way, who feared the hedgehog's sharp quills would prick his bare feet. With a variety of such-like vexatious tricks Ariel would often torment him, whenever Caliban neglected the work which Prospero commanded him to do" (*W,* 3:3). This is Puck:

> [He] was a shrewd and knavish sprite, that used to play comical pranks in the neighbouring villages; sometimes getting into the dairies and skimming the milk, sometimes plunging his light and airy form into the butter-churn, and while he was dancing his fantastic shape in the churn, in vain the dairy-maid would labour to change her cream into butter: nor had the village swains any better success. . . . When a few

good neighbours were met to drink some comfortable ale together, Puck would jump into the bowl of ale in the likeness of a roasted crab, and when some old goody was going to drink he would bob against her lips, and spill the ale over her withered chin; and presently after, when the same old dame was gravely seating herself to tell her neighbours a sad and melancholy story, Puck would slip her three-legged stool from under her, and down toppled the poor old woman, and then the old gossips would hold their sides and laugh at her, and swear they never wasted a merrier hour. (*W,* 3:13)

Charles's style in the tragedies is more complex in syntax and diction, and he mostly forgoes dialogue, relying more on telling than showing. His narration is still brisk, however. A street brawl in *Romeo and Juliet*:

Romeo wished to avoid a quarrel with Tybalt above all men, because he was the kinsman of Juliet, and much beloved by her; besides, this young Montague had never thoroughly entered into the family quarrel, being by nature wise and gentle, and the name of a Capulet, which was his dear lady's name, was now rather a charm to allay resentment, than a watchword to excite fury. So he tried to reason with Tybalt, whom he saluted mildly by the name of good Capulet, as if he, though a Montague, had some secret pleasure in uttering that name: but Tybalt, who hated all Montagues as he hated hell, would hear no reason, but drew his weapon; and Mercutio, who knew not of Romeo's secret motive for desiring peace with Tybalt, but looked upon his present forbearance as a sort of calm dishonourable submission, with many disdainful words provoked Tybalt to the prosecution of his first quarrel with him; and Tybalt and Mercutio fought, till Mercutio fell, receiving his death's wound while Romeo and Benvolio were vainly endeavouring to part the combatants. Mercutio being dead, Romeo kept his temper no longer, but returned the scornful appellation of villain which Tybalt had given him; and they fought till Tybalt was slain by Romeo. (*W,* 3:164)

Charles's lyrical eruptions are also denser than Mary's, and more ambitious. See the weird sisters in *Macbeth,* making their "dreadful charms."

Their horrid ingredients were toads, bats, and serpents, the eye of a newt, and the tongue of a dog, the leg of a lizard, and the wing of the night-owl, the scale of a dragon, the tooth of a wolf, the maw of the

ravenous salt-sea shark, the mummy of a witch, the root of the poisonous hemlock (this to have effect must be digged in the dark), the gall
of a goat, and the liver of a Jew, with slips of the yew tree that roots
itself in graves, and the finger of a dead child: all these were set on to
boil in a great kettle, or cauldron, which, as fast as it grew too hot,
was cooled with a baboon's blood: to these they poured in the blood
of a sow that had eaten her young, and they threw into the flame the
grease that had sweaten from a murderer's gibbet. By these charms
they bound the infernal spirits to answer their questions. (*W,* 3:96)

But Charles's interpretations of the action sometimes normalize his narratives, making them psychologically safe. "Iago was artful, and had studied human nature deeply, and he knew that [of] all the torments which afflict the mind
of man (and far beyond bodily torture), the pains of jealousy were the most
intolerable, and had the sorest sting. If he could succeed in making Othello jealous of Cassio, he thought it would be an exquisite plot of revenge, and might
end in the death of Cassio or Othello, or both; he cared not" (*W,* 3:187).

Other times Charles's commentary is conservatively didactic. Lady Macbeth is a "bad ambitious woman" (*W,* 3:477). While the surface of this phrase
is self-evident—of course Macbeth's wife is villainous—its hidden assumption is that an ambitious woman is bad.

Mary faced her own struggles with patriarchy.[4] The "problem" play *All's
Well That Ends Well* was especially difficult for her to simplify. The play is
about a "low-born" woman, Helena, trying to win the love of a haughty libertine, Bertram. The king forces him to marry Helena, but he will love her only
if she wears his family ring and bears his child. After the wedding, he goes
off to war. Helena secretly follows him and convinces his recent love interest,
Diana, to steal Bertram's family ring and give it to her. Helena takes Diana's
place in bed. Bertram impregnates her without knowing it. Helena returns
home, fakes her death, and Bertram, glad to be free of his unwanted wife, also
comes home, where he gets engaged. Helena reveals that she still lives. From
now on, Bertram will love her.

How to make this sexually dark play acceptable to children? Mary relied
on traditional morality. Instead of describing Helena's grim contrivance to
have intercourse with Bertram, Mary writes that she wins her husband's affection with the "simple graces of . . . [her] lively conversation and the endearing
sweetness of her manners" (*W,* 3:107). Traditional female virtues, sweetness
and good conversation, are paramount. Mary also ignores the ambiguous

conclusion—which features a marriage based on desperation and subterfuge—and announces that Helena will be happy as a "beloved wife" (*W*, 3:111).

The book came out in two volumes, duodecimo, blue boards and green
back-strip, 520 pages. Like *The King and Queen of Hearts*, its title page listed
Thomas Hodgkins as printer. The stories, the page further announced, were
"embellished with copper plates." Charles did not like these plates, most of
which were by Mulready, but some of which were created by William Blake.
(The magnificent image of Prospero and Miranda gazing out over the sea, it
should be noted, is most certainly Blake's.) Lamb's primary reason for dislik-
ing them was not their quality but their placement. The "**bad baby**," as he
derisively called Mary Jane, did not match image and event (*M*, 2:256).

The book sold well. The Godwins released a second edition in 1809 in
which they reprinted the famous review of the book from the *Critical Review*
of May 1807: "We have compared these little volumes with the numerous
systems which have been devised for riveting attention at an early age, and
conquering the distaste for knowledge and learning which so frequently opposes itself to the instruction of children; and we do not scruple to say, that
unless perhaps we except Robinson Crusoe, they claim the very first place,
and stand unique, without rival or competitor."[5]

The book is still in print today and has been translated into forty languages.

# CHAPTER 29

# Specimens of English Dramatic Poets

The Lambs missed their 1806 holiday trip in order to complete their *Tales*. They had enjoyed recent trips to Margate (1801), Keswick (1802), the Isle of Wight (with the Burneys, 1803), Sadler's Wells (with Southey and Rickman, 1803), and Richmond (1804). (They did not travel in 1805, because Mary was ill the entire summer; Charles took trips without Mary to Cambridge in 1801 and to Sadler's Wells in 1806.)

After seeing their book released, they were eager to travel again. In early summer, they journeyed to Bury St. Edmunds to visit the Clarksons. They had met Thomas and Catherine in August 1802, in the Lake District. The Clarksons were keeping Dove Cottage, the Wordsworths' home, while the poet and his sister were in France. The Lambs passed a "very pleasant little time" with the couple (*M*, 2:66). (But on the way home Mary had her terrifying breakdown.)

Thomas had been educated at Cambridge, where in 1785 he entered into a Latin essay contest a piece on the unlawfulness of slavery. In researching the essay, he studied firsthand accounts of the slave trade and interviewed people with direct experience of slavery. That he won the prize was secondary to what happened just after. As he was riding from Cambridge to London, he brooded so ardently on the essay that "it almost wholly engrossed my thoughts." "I became at times very seriously affected while upon the road.

I stopped my horse occasionally, and dismounted and walked. I frequently tried to persuade myself in these intervals that the contents of my essay could not be true. The more, however, I reflected upon them, or rather upon the authorities on which they were founded, the more I gave them credit. Coming in sight of Wades Mill, in Hertfordshire, I sat down disconsolate on the turf by the roadside and held my horse." An epiphany: "Here a thought came into my mind, that if the contents of the essay were true, it was time some person should see these calamities to their end."[1]

Clarkson wanted to be that person. After publishing the essay, he was introduced into abolitionist circles, and soon helped found the Committee for the Abolition of the Slave Trade. Clarkson traveled to slave ports in Britain to collect data for his cause. In Liverpool he was almost murdered by paid assassins. He presented his facts to the MP William Wilberforce, who was sympathetic, and he lectured all around England to gather support. He used artifacts to make his arguments more vivid: the slavers' leg shackles, thumbscrews, branding irons; elegant handcrafts and artwork made by slaves. He lectured throughout the 1790s and published heartrending antislavery tracts. In 1791, Wilberforce presented to Parliament a bill to abolish slavery. It did not pass. Wilberforce persisted over the next sixteen years. When the Lambs met Clarkson in 1802, he had retired from his work. He would later take up his cause again. In 1807 the Slave Trade Act ended slavery in Britain.

Thomas married Catherine in 1796. She shared his radical views and intellectual energy. Her childhood friend Henry Crabb Robinson called her "the most eloquent woman I have ever known, with the exception of Madame de Staël. She had a quick apprehension of every kind of beauty and made her own whatever she learned."[2]

The Lambs' friendship with the Clarksons shows yet another link between Charles and democratic politics. In 1802, when they first met, Charles's interest in the Quakers was high, and he was spending quite a lot of time with Godwin. Charles and Thomas, and the clever women with them, were in sympathy.

It was through the Clarksons that the Lambs met Henry Crabb Robinson in 1806, right around the opening (and closing) of *Mr. H.* Robinson, Lamb's exact contemporary, was a notable barrister, journalist, traveler, literary socialite, and diarist. Catherine was Henry's first mentor: "She lent me books, made me first acquainted with the new opinions that were then afloat, and was my oracle, till her marriage with the then celebrated Thomas Clarkson, the founder of the society for the abolition of the slave trade. . . . Our friend-ship never ceased."[3]

Robinson shared his friend's and her husband's dissenting views, and for this reason was unable to attend an English university. He trained in the law, but soon after coming into money in 1798, he traveled around Germany, where, like Coleridge, he met the leading lights of the German Romantic movement, including Goethe, Schiller, Herder, and de Staël. He returned to England in 1805 before heading to Spain in 1808 to cover the Peninsular War for the *Times*. In England a year later, he took up his legal studies and was admitted to the bar in 1813.

Robinson's travels, as well as his keen mind and curiosity, made him a valuable party guest. Because he was an avid lover of literature and the theater, he circulated among the literati. After meeting Lamb, he acquainted himself with Wordsworth, Coleridge, Blake, Hazlitt, Southey, and Leigh Hunt. The *Diary* he began in 1811 is an intimate window into the everyday lives of these writers, their magnificence and blindness, awkwardness and generosity.

Mary spent most of the summer of 1807 in a madhouse, following her breakdown on the return from the Clarksons'. Charles studied in the Brit-ish Museum; he was at work on a new project on Elizabethan drama. When we next hear from Mary, in November, we learn that her best friend Sarah has fallen in love again, this time with Hazlitt, from whom she is receiving odd letters. Three weeks later, Mary refers to the relationship as a "match" (*M,* 2:262). She no doubt felt deep satisfaction. After watching her Sarah go through one unworthy suitor after another, she could now enjoy a union—one she certainly urged—between two of her closest friends.

Meanwhile, Lamb was enjoying some epistolary nonsense with his and Hazlitt's mutual friend Joseph Hume, a clerk at the Victualling Office in Somerset House. On December 29, Lamb sent Hume a mock obituary of Hazlitt: "Last night Mr. H . . . put an end to his existence by cutting his throat in a shocking manner. It is supposed that he must have committed his purpose with a pallet-knife, as the edges of the cicatrice or wound were found besmeared with a yellow consistence, but the knife could not be found. The reasons of this rash act are not assigned, an unfortunate passion has been mentioned, but nothing certain is known. The deceased was subject to hypo-chondria, low spirits, but he had lately seemed better, having paid more than usual attention to his dress and person" (*M,* 2:265).

(This comically morbid language presages a terribly morbid event. In June 1846, Lamb and Hazlitt's friend Benjamin Robert Haydon, a painter of massive historical canvases, wrote, "Stretch me no longer on this tough world," and shot himself.[4] The bullet didn't work. Haydon cut his throat. That killed him.)

Lamb's bizarre mock obit, where humor bleeds into horror, was his way of saying that the engaged Hazlitt would be ending his life as "Hazlitt," as Rickman and Godwin, upon marrying, had ended their bachelor selves, upon marrying. When Hazlitt read of his own death, he wrote to Hume eight reasons proving he was indeed not dead, one of which read, "He [Hazlitt] has twice attempted to read some of his own works, but has fallen asleep."[5] For the next two weeks, the state of Hazlitt's mortality was merrily debated among the three men.

But the cicatrix smeared with yellow: this image goes beyond male banter to something else, a sort of wit that hovers between the comically quirky, yellow paint covering an artist's wound, and the outright Gothic: paint as pus, art as death. This awkward mix of charm and charnel vexes Lamb's wit, which his friend P. G. Patmore noted: "The fact is, that in ordinary society, if Lamb was not an ordinary man, he was only an odd and strange one."[6] The strangeness was more David Lynch than Lewis Carroll, drawing-room routines making guests wonder: should I laugh or cringe? Hazlitt biographer Stanley Jones believes that Lamb's perverse joking "served his fissured personality as a protective device, an amateurish psychiatric homeopathy, following his mother's terrible death."[7]

Apotropaic or not, Lamb's humor often challenged auditors as much as entertained them. One Reverend N. P. Willis, an American, came to pay Lamb his respects. When this guest pulled up an armchair for Mary, Charles said, with mock gravity, "Mary, don't take it; it looks as if you were going to have a tooth drawn." Mary's hearing had deteriorated. Lamb told Willis she was so deaf that she "hears all of an epigram but the point." When Mary asked what Charles had said, he replied that Mr. Willis "admires your 'Confessions of a Drunkard' very much," adding, "and I was saying it was no merit of yours that you understood the subject." Then, after comically (?) trying to reimburse Willis for the money he paid for the Elia essays, insisting that his works weren't the kind that sell, Lamb sat down to eat. But he ate nothing. He "inquired anxiously for some potted fish, which [one] Mr. R—— used to procure for him." None being in the house, Lamb requested to see the lid of the pot that once contained the fish. "It was brought, and on it was a picture of the fish. Lamb kissed it, and then left the table, and began to wander about the room, with an uncertain step, &c."[8] Willis didn't know how to react. There is cruelty to this sort of wit, epistemological cruelty, since the joke calls into question the distinction between fun and discomfort.

At a dinner party, a woman lectured Lamb on his "irregularities." After a while, noticing that he paid no attention, she said she feared her words were having no effect on him. Lamb assured her that, on the contrary, her words were quite useful, since they had gone into one of his ears and out the other, and so had "done incalculable good to the gentleman standing on the other side of him."[9]

An admirer, the Reverend J. Fuller Russell, observed that rum loosened Lamb's tongue early in his visit. "He would throw out a playful remark, and then pause a while. He spoke by fits and starts, and had a sight impediment in his utterance which made him, so to say, grunt once or twice before he began a sentence." When Lamb and the reverend agreed that the poetry of Thomas Moore was "akin to rich plum-cake," Lamb quipped that the cake was very nice, but too "much of it made one sick." Lamb began attributing his literary opinions to Mary. She was used to the routine and submitted to it wearily. "Mary, don't you hate Byron?" "Yes, Charles." "That's right." And then he slapped her "playfully" on the back.[10]

Lamb retired to the parlor after a dinner. A guest bent over, maybe to tie his shoe or adjust his stocking. Lamb leapfrogged over the man's back.

Lamb's kind of wit is baroque: freakishly extravagant. His hero Sir Thomas Browne mastered this mode. In *Religio Medici* Browne rolls out, "The world that I regard is my selfe, it is the Microcosme of mine owne frame, that I cast mine eye on; for the other, I use it but like my Globe, and turne it round sometimes for my recreation. Men that look upon my outside, perusing onely my condition, and fortunes, do erre in my altitude; for I am above Atlas his shoulders."[11] I look outside my skin to the physical world; paradoxically, it is a microcosm of myself. It is but a pumpkin-sized globe. Sometimes I play with it. If you think my frame is my body, you are wrong. My soul is my identity. It is the macrocosm, continuous with the cosmos. I rise above the shoulders of Atlas. Just as Browne's body contains boundlessness, his text is inexhaustible. The small and large vertiginously reverse, as do the unseen and seen, reality and appearance, self and universe.

Lamb's most Brownian essay is "A Chapter on Ears." "I have no ear," it begins. Elia has been cropped. No, he does not lack "those exterior twin appendages, hanging ornaments, and (architecturally speaking) handsome volutes to the human capital." What does he possess? Natural outgrowths, yes, but also hanging (*appendage*'s origin is "to hang") ornaments, which are artificial. Artificial, too, are the spirals capping classical columns, even if they protrude from the human head, or capital, which derives from *caput,* "head" (*W,* 2:38).

As if emphasizing the glory of vision over sound, these images fly from the organic to the artificial to a bizarre blending of the two. The onrush suggests Elia could go on creating aural appositives forever, an infinite progression of analogy. Or he could erase it all. It would have been better that he had never been born, he writes, if he were without physical ears. This possibility of nonexistence tempts us to unimagine the bristling appendages, ornaments, and volutes. Words can unmake as much as they fashion. One instant an ear is a nautilus spiraling in the sound. The next, nothing.

Elia chooses meaning over muteness. He expands his ears. Though they aren't large—they are delicate—they are suitable "conduits" through which sound flows. He therefore is not disposed to "envy the mule for his plenty, or the mole for her exactness." Mules and moles are now surreally connected to Elia's ears, which suitably he now calls "ingenious labyrinthine inlets," a phrase that also describes his own writing and the sort of ear we need to absorb his intricacies. We need flanking our skulls "those indispensable side-intelligencers," Elia's final image for his ears in this opening to his essay (*W,* 2:38). Spies are alert readers of arcane signs. They are models for how properly to read Elia's whacked-out text.

On May 1, 1808, Sarah and William married in Saint Andrew's Church, Holborn. Outside, in the cemetery, rested the remains of Elizabeth Lamb. Mary was Sarah's bridesmaid, and Charles was in attendance. The siblings were too poor just then to offer a wedding present, and probably wouldn't be able to give anything to the first child at christening (*M,* 1:282). Charles's imp of the perverse, probably drunk, almost broke up the ceremony. "I was at Hazlitts marriage & had like to have been turned out several times during the ceremony. Any thing awful makes me laugh. I misbehaved once at a funeral. . . . The realities of life only seem the mockeries" (*M,* 3:181). In "The Wedding," Lamb as Elia similarly mocks nuptials as "something ludicrous" (*W,* 2:241).

"There is love a-both sides" (*M,* 2:272), Lamb wrote to Manning, as much out of hope as anything, since now he and Mary could enjoy two of their closest friends at the same time. The siblings had reasons to believe the couple would thrive.

Mary knew the deepest interiors of Sarah, and so would know if her friend really loved Hazlitt or not, despite Sarah's careful financial negotiations. (The money talks had held up the marriage. Sarah had "somewhere around £80 a year, to be £120 when her mother dies." Hazlitt, however, had "no settlement, except what he [could] claim from the parish" [*M*, 2:272]. One can't blame Sarah for protecting her interests.)

And Lamb knew Hazlitt. He would not have been surprised to read from Hazlitt's only extant love letter to Sarah: "I never love you so well as when I think of sitting down with you to dinner over a boiled scrag-end of mutton, and hot potatoes."[12] (In 1822, when William and Sarah were working on another settlement, the heart-sickening one of divorce, Sarah alluded to this passage bitterly, describing William's new love obsession, Sarah Walker, "as thin and bony as the scrag end of a neck of mutton.")[13]

The Lambs had had been hard at work. By February 1 (four months before the wedding), Lamb had completed *The Adventures of Ulysses*, another title for the Godwins' Juvenile Library, and *Specimens of English Dramatic Poets*, which he had researched in the British Museum during the summer of 1807. As for Mary, she was completing the Juvenile volume she had started in 1806, *Mrs. Leicester's School*, stories for young girls.

Of his adaptation of Homer's *Odyssey* for children, Lamb wrote, "It is done . . . not from the Greek . . . nor yet from Pope's Odyssey, but from an older translation of one Chapman" (*M*, 2:272). That Lamb chose the Chapman translation suggests he wrote his *Ulysses* in the same spirit in which he composed his Shakespeare: as a wild tale that would stoke the child's imagination.

George Chapman's 1614 translation of the *Odyssey* is a neglected source of the Romantic vision of literature as energy more than argument. In 1802, Lamb wrote Coleridge, "I have just finished Chapman's Homer. Did you ever read it? It has *most* the continuous power of interesting you all along, like a rapid original, of any. . . . Chapman gallops off with you his own free pace" (*M*, 2:82). Six years later, Lamb again emphasizes Chapman's vigor: "His Homer is not so properly a Translation as the Stories of Achilles and Ulysses re-written. The earnestness and passion which he has put into every part of these poems would be incredible to a reader of mere modern translations." Chapman's passion electrifies the language, "raising the low, dignifying the mean, and putting sense into the absurd. [Chapman] makes his readers glow, weep, tremble, take any affection which he pleases, be moved by words or in spite of them, be disgusted and overcome their disgust" (*W*, 4:83).[14]

Coleridge largely agreed—though he, like Lamb, criticized the translation for its "quaintness." Coleridge found the translation to be "exquisite," enjoying an "almost unexampled sweetness & beauty of language, all over spirit & feeling. In the main it is an English Heroic Poem, the *tale* of which is borrowed from the Greek."[15]

Coleridge and Lamb treat Chapman not as a translator but as a poet in his own right, who simply chose Homer's story as the matter for his powerful meter. Keats in his first poem of note does the same. After Cowden Clarke read to him Chapman's description of Ulysses as "soaked to the very heart," he observed Keats's "delighted stare." Reaching home later that night, Keats wrote "On First Looking into Chapman's Homer" in one sitting. He sent it over to Clarke. When Clarke sat down to breakfast, he saw on his table Keats's amazement turned into verse.[16]

Compare Pope's opening to the poem to that of Chapman. Pope:

> The man for wisdom's various arts renown'd,
> Long exercised in woes, O Muse! resound;
> Who, when his arms had wrought the destined fall
> Of sacred Troy, and razed her heaven-built wall,
> Wandering from clime to clime, observant stray'd,
> Their manners noted, and their states survey'd,
> On stormy seas unnumber'd toils he bore,
> Safe with his friends to gain his natal shore.

And Chapman:

> The man, O Muse, inform, that many a way
> Wound with his wisdom to his wished stay;
> That wandered wondrous far, when he the town
> Of sacred Troy had sack'd and shivered down;
> The cities of a world of nations,
> With all their manners, minds, and fashions,
> He saw and knew; at sea felt many woes,
> Much care sustained, to save from overthrows
> Himself and friends in their retreat for home.

Pope's Odysseus is "renowned," or valued by others. He is passively lauded. Not Chapman's, who "wound" through diverse paths to reach his destination. Pope's muse "resounds," or echoes. Chapman's "informs," shapes. Pope's hero "razes" Troy, Chapman's "sacks" and "shivers" it down. Pope's Ulysses suffers "unnumbered toils," while Chapman's "felt many woes." Pope's heroic couplets are elegant. Chapman's alliterations—"man," "muse," "many"; "wound," "wisdom," "wished," "wandered," "wondrous," "when"—clang against the iambs.

Lamb's prose opening of his *Adventures* channels Chapman:

> This history tells of the wanderings of Ulysses and his followers in their return from Troy, after the destruction of that famous city of Asia by the Grecians. He was inflamed with a desire of seeing again, after a ten years' absence, his wife and native country, Ithaca. He was king of a barren spot, and a poor country in comparison of the fruitful plains of Asia, which he was leaving, or the wealthy kingdoms which he touched upon in his return; yet, wherever he came, he could never see a soil which appeared in his eyes half so sweet or desirable as his country earth. This made him refuse the offers of the goddess Calypso to stay with her, and partake of her immortality in the delightful island; and this gave him strength to break from the enchantments of Circe, the daughter of the Sun. (*W,* 3:208)

Lamb's earthy Homer ran him afoul of Godwin. The anarchist had become a practical publisher, and he feared offending his readership, especially young females. He asked Lamb to remove three passages. One, a description of the Cyclops vomiting, Lamb removed readily, since it was "perfectly nauseous" (*M,* 2:279). But the other two he did not. First, a scene where the Cyclops eats two of Ulysses' men: "He replied nothing, but gripping two of the nearest of them, as if they had been no more than children, he dashed their brains out against the earth, and, shocking to relate, tore in pieces their limbs, and devoured them yet warm and trembling, making a lion's meal of them, lapping the blood" (*W,* 3:211). Godwin felt the blood lapping would offend the "squeamish."

He thought the same of Ulysses gouging out the Cyclops's eye:

> Ulysses watched his time, while the monster lay insensible, and, heartening up his men, they placed the sharp end of the stake in the fire till it was heated red-hot, and some god gave them a courage beyond that which they were used to have, and the four men with difficulty bored the sharp end of the huge stake, which they had heated red-hot, right into the eye of the drunken cannibal, and Ulysses helped to thrust it in with all his might, still farther and farther, with effort, as men

bore with an auger, till the scalded blood gushed out, and the eye-ball smoked, and the strings of the eye cracked, as the burning rafter broke in it, and the eye hissed, as hot iron hisses when it is plunged into water. (*W,* 3:212)

To Godwin's objections to these passages, Lamb replied, if you wish to omit these passages, you might as well cut many more, including the description of the Scylla devouring six men, the most exhilarating in the book:

She [the Charybdis] did not show herself as yet, and still the vessel steered closer by her rock, as it sought to shun that other more dreaded; for they saw how horribly Charybdis' black throat drew into her all the whirling deep, which she disgorged again, that all about her boiled like a kettle, and the rock roared with troubled waters; which when she supped in again, all the bottom turned up, and disclosed far under shore the swart sands naked, whose all stern sight frayed the startled blood from their faces, and made Ulysses turn his to view the wonder of whirlpools. Which when Scylla saw, from out her black den, she darted out her six long necks, and swoopt up as many of his friends; whose cries Ulysses heard, and saw them too late, with their heels turned up, and their hands thrown to him for succour, who had been their help in all extremities, but could not deliver them now; and he heard them shriek out, as she tore them, and to the last they continued to throw their hands out to him for sweet life. In all his sufferings he never had beheld a sight so full of miseries. (*W,* 3:229)

Lamb invokes his earlier argument about the importance of "wildness" in children's tales to justify this and the other questionable passages. If you want a book that does not "shock," why choose the *Odyssey*, which is "so full of Anthropopagi & monsters?" The most "shocking" passages are examples of the "*terrible*," not the "*nauseous*," and are "*fine*" rather than "*disgusting*" (*M,* 2:279).

Godwin listened to Lamb. Maybe he shouldn't have. The book flopped. One reviewer cringed at Lamb's violence and denounced the book as "almost too low for criticism."[17]

In the letter to Manning—February 26, 1808—in which he announces the publication of *Specimens of English Dramatic Poets, Who Lived about the Time of Shakespeare,* Lamb says, "Specimens are becoming fashionable. We have

Specimens of Ancient English Poets. Specimens of Modern English Poets. Specimens of Ancient English Prose Writers, without end." Longman—the distinguished publisher of works by Wordsworth, Southey, and Coleridge—will print the book as its own expense, and Lamb will "pocket what they please to tell me is due to me." Regardless of potential profit, Lamb likes the book very much. "It is done out of old plays at the Museum & out of Dodsley's collection, & c. It is to have Notes" (*M*, 2:272).

Lamb is referring to Robert Dodsley's twelve-volume *Select Collection of Old Plays* (1744). This anthology inspired similar collections at the turn of the nineteenth century, three of which Lamb alludes to: George Ellis's *Specimens of the Early English Poets* (1790), George Burnett's *Specimens of English Prose Writers* (1807), and Southey's *Specimens of the Later English Poets* (1807).

In compiling his collection, Lamb drew from Thomas Hawkins's *Origins of English Drama*, from 1773, as much as from Dodsley. He also extracted from plays he found in the British Museum and "some scarce private libraries." Instead of simply presenting "single passages and detached beauties," he cites "entire scenes, and in some instances successive scenes." Where the poetry in the scenes had "better never" been "written," he "expunges" it "without ceremony." His critical criteria are "passion, sometimes of the deepest quality, interesting situations, serious descriptions, that which is more nearly allied to poetry than to wit, and to tragic rather than comic poetry." These elements illustrate the "moral sense of our ancestors," showing "in what manner they felt, when they placed themselves by the power of imagination in trying situations, in the conflicts of duty and passion, or the strife of contending duties; what sort of loves and enmities theirs were; how their griefs were tempered, and their full-swoln joys abated." Lamb hopes that his specimens will reveal how much of Shakespeare "shines in the great men his contemporaries, and how far in his divine mind and manners he surpassed them and all mankind." Another aim is to excavate dramatists we have "slighted"—like Heywood, Webster, and Ford—by praising out of "all proportion" one or two favorites (*W*, 4:xii).

Almost twenty years later, Lamb claimed that in his *Specimens*, he "was the first to draw the Public attention to the old English Dramatists" (*W*, 1:320–21). Lamb was to a certain degree correct. Several of his specimens had not been in print since the seventeenth century—the four Ford plays, for instance, as well as Dekker's *Old Fortunatus* and Marlowe's *Doctor Faustus*. But many other plays from which he extracts had been more recently in circulation, primarily through Dodsley and Hawkins. But even if the plays were available, they were not presented as works of a particular kind of dramatic genius, the sort of genius Lamb found in Chapman: an aptitude for expressing the sublimities—the terrors and ecstasies—of desire. Lamb was the first to draw the public's attention to this quality in non-Shakespearean Elizabethan and Jacobean dramatists.

Lamb's commentary on the final speech of *Doctor Faustus* invokes this imaginative wildness. "Marlowe is said to have been tainted with atheistical positions, to have denied God and the Trinity. To such a genius the history of Faustus must have been delectable food: to wander in fields where curiosity is forbidden to go, to approach the dark gulf near enough to look in, to be busied in speculations which are the rottenest part of the core of the fruit that fell from the tree of knowledge." Barabas the Jew and the conjuror Faustus "are offsprings of a mind which at least delighted to dally with interdicted subjects. They both talk a language which a believer would have been tender of putting into the mouth of a character though but in fiction" (*W,* 4:34).

In his gloss on Thomas Middleton and William Rowley's *A Fair Quarrel*, Lamb turns his empathetic description of *Faustus* into a prescriptive poetics: "The insipid levelling morality to which the modern stage is tied down, would not admit of such admirable passions as these scenes are filled with. A puritanical obtuseness of sentiment, a stupid infantile goodness, is creeping among us, instead of the vigorous passions, and virtues clad in flesh and blood, with which the old dramatists present us. Those noble and liberal casuists could discern in the differences, the quarrels, the animosities of men, a beauty and truth of moral feeling, no less than in the everlastingly inculcated duties of forgiveness and atonement" (*W,* 4:114).

Uninterested in soothing viewers, Cyril Tourneur in *The Revenger's Tragedy* expresses "reality and life." Every time Lamb reads the scene he extracted, which shows "the passion of shame truly personated," his "ear tingle[s]," and he feels "a hot blush spread through [his] cheeks" (*W,* 4:114).

Webster in *Duchess of Malfy* surpasses even Tourneur in his ability to enflame terror and dread: "To move a horror skilfully, to touch a soul to the quick, to lay upon fear as much as it can bear, to wean and weary a life till it is ready to drop, and then step in with mortal instruments to take its last forfeit: this only a Webster can do" (*W,* 4:179).

If Lamb didn't rediscover all the dramatists in *Specimens,* he definitely awakened important readers to their sublimities. When William Hazlitt in 1819 was preparing his lecture series on Elizabethan drama, he found he knew little of the subject, except for Shakespeare. And so, according to Procter, "he spoke to Charles Lamb, and to myself, who were supposed by many to be well acquainted with those ancient writers."[18] Hazlitt retired to the country, appropriate volumes in tow. Among them must have been *Specimens*. After six weeks, having mastered his topic, he returned to town.

Just before sailing to his death in Italy, Keats gave his copy of Lamb's *Specimens* to his beloved, Franny Brawne. The only other volumes he gave her were his folio Shakespeare, Cary's translation of Dante, and *The Cenci* of Shelley. He had annotated his *Specimens*. Of Lamb's comment on Heywood's *A Woman Killed with Kindness*, he wrote: "This is the most acute deep sighted and spiritual piece of criticism ever penned."[19]

Melville's annotated copy of *Specimens*, discovered only in 1993, was likely the source of this passage of 1850, when the American writer was deep into *Moby-Dick*: "Let anyone, hitherto little acquainted with those neglected old authors, for the first time read them thoroughly, or even read Charles Lamb's Specimens of them, and he will be amazed at the wondrous ability of those Anaks of men, and shocked at this renewed example of the fact, that Fortune has more to do with fame than merit,—though, without merit, lasting fame there can be none."[20] In his *Specimens*, Melville underscored Lamb on Faustus and Barabas; like Ahab, these characters speak words too dangerous to exist outside of ficton.

T. S. Eliot drew from *Specimens* in forming his canon of neglected Early Modern writers. For Eliot, "Lamb set in motion the enthusiasm for the poetic drama [of the Elizabethan age] which still persists. . . . All modern opinion of the Elizabethans seems to spring from Lamb."[21] "Oh keep the Dog far hence, that's friend to men, / Or with his nails he'll dig it up again!": we owe this, from *The Wasteland* via Webster's *White Devil*, to Lamb.

CHAPTER 30

Mrs. Leicester's School

*Specimens* didn't sell, though it made up in influence what it lacked in profit. Soon after it was released, Charles and Mary published *Mrs. Leicester's School*. Mary wrote seven stories, Charles three.[1] Ten young girls arrive for their first day at Amwell School, a charity school for girls. That evening, the teacher, M.B., gathers the students in a circle around the fire, and asks each girl to tell "some little anecdotes of [their] own lives" (*W*, 3:274).

Mary's stories benefit from the same clean, immediate style of her Shakespeare narratives, and they draw heavily on her own childhood. Here is the opening of the first story of the book, Elizabeth Villiers's "The Sailor Uncle":

> My father is the curate of a village church, about five miles from Amwell. I was born in the parsonage-house, which joins the church-yard. The first thing I can remember was my father teaching me the alphabet from the letters on a tombstone that stood at the head of my mother's grave. I used to tap at my father's study-door; I think I now hear him say, "Who is there?—What do you want, little girl?" "Go and see mamma. Go and learn pretty letters." Many times in the day would my father lay aside his books and his papers to lead me to this spot, and make me point to the letters, and then set me to spell syllables and words: in this manner, the epitaph on my mother's tomb being my primmer and my spelling-book, I learned to read. (*W*, 3:276)

Aside from recalling Mary's instruction of Charles among the tombs, this passage is charming and haunting, a child's simple words floating over corpses.

Other stories draw more substantially from Mary's childhood. "The Farm House," Louisa Manners's tale, is based on Mary's summer visits to Mackery End. Margaret Green's "The Young Mahometan" depicts—as we have seen—Mary's alienation from her mother and grandmother.

Charles's three stories, as was the case with his Shakespeare tales, are more complex in style, and just as prone to interpret as to narrate. He channels his childhood as well, especially in Maria Howe's "The Witch Aunt," which originates in his relationship with Aunt Sarah. Here is Maria describing her aunt: "There was an oddness, a silence about my aunt, which was never interrupted but by her occasional expressions of love to me, that made me stand in fear of her. An odd look from under her spectacles would sometimes scare me away, when I had been peering up in her face to make her kiss me" (W, 3:319).

The remarkable quality of these stories, especially Mary's, is that they are not overtly moralistic. The tales are guidebooks for life's tragedies. Elizabeth's "The Sailor Uncle" teaches how to mourn. Ann Withers's "The Changeling" meditates on maintaining identity when the "self" you were born into is ripped away. Margaret Green's "The Young Mahometan" delves into the challenges of encountering cultural "otherness."

The stories are morbid. We encounter several literal deaths of relatives ("The Sailor Uncle," "The Young Mahometan," "The Sea Voyage," "My Father's Wedding Day") and the figurative deaths that occur when familiar identities are ripped away ("The Changeling," "The Young Mahometan"). Vexed relationships between mothers and daughters also appear throughout the tales ("The Young Mahometan," "The Changeling," "The Father's Wedding Day"), as do the struggles between upper and lower classes ("The Changeling," "The Merchant's Daughter").

Mary and Charles turn the loss, madness, and poverty of their own lives into a melancholy yet sturdy vision of how a young girl might live—not by fleeing inevitable catastrophe but by owning the sorrow and expanding hearts and habits to accommodate it.

Like Blake's *Songs of Innocence and Experience*, *Mrs. Leicester's School* attunes to emotional complexity. Innocent children might be free of neurotic self-consciousness, but they are ignorant of danger. Experienced youths might worry like adults; however, their awareness inspires moral agency.

The Lambs' tales and Blake's poems do what Charles most admired about the Early Modern dramatists: reject easy moralizing and dive into the craters of the heart.

Like *Tales from Shakespear*, *Mrs. Leicester's School* succeeded. From 1809— when the book was published with no author listed—to 1825, the Godwins put the book through eight more editions. One reviewer captured the book's appeal: these "elegant and most instructive Tales . . . are delightfully simple, and exquisitely told."[2]

Ironically, these successful authors of books for children had no children themselves. Charles, in fact, appeared to loathe little ones. As we have seen, when a woman asked Charles how he liked babies, he said, boiled.[3] He once encountered a horde of children at a social event; he stuttered out a toast to the "m-m-much ca-calumniated good King Herod."[4] As Elia, he asserted that he could not for the life of him "tell what cause for pride there can possibly be" in one's children. They "are so common" (*W*, 2:128). Children "are unwholesome companions for grown people," Elia says elsewhere (*W*, 2:53). More disturbingly, one might argue, Elia is indifferent to the suffering of chimney sweeps; he uses them for their poetic value but doesn't help them. The only "child" Elia is capable of loving is himself, as an adult shunning the *toga virilis*.

But Lamb could interact beautifully with children. Elizabeth Hunt recalled him visiting her school, Goddard House, in Widford. He took the children to the "little general shop" and bought them a huge hunk of rock candy, so formidable the shop owner had to break it up with a hammer. Lamb stuck his head into the classroom during a lesson. The children laughed. Nothing more was learned that day. He created with the children playful versions of the catechism, and he encouraged Lizzy Hunt's talent for reciting the Lord's Prayer backward.[5]

These tales of Charles and children share one characteristic: lack of sentimentality. A man who can half-seriously imagine a group of unruly children slain by a crazed ancient king, or who can spur little blasphemies in girls: this man is as far from Wordsworth, praising the child as a "Philosopher Blest," as you can get.

# CHAPTER 31

# No. 4 Inner Temple Lane

Just before the Hazlitt-Stoddart wedding in May 1808, Lamb introduced Wordsworth to Robinson. The meeting occurred over breakfast, since Wordsworth's evenings were taken up in caring for Coleridge, then very ill. Wordsworth had arrived in London from the Lakes on February 24 to find his friend depressed and opium-wrecked. His stomach was sick—a side effect of opium—and the poet was dosing himself with, in addition to laudanum, henbane, rhubarb, and magnesia. Wordsworth believed he could swoop in and remove Coleridge to the healing Lakes. His confidence at this time was high.[1]

Lamb found it funny. "Wordsworth, the great poet, is coming to town. He is to have apartments in the Mansion House. He says he does not see much difficulty in writing like Shakspeare. . . . Even Coleridge is a little checked by this hardihood of assertion" (*M,* 2:274–75).

With the Hazlitts living in Winterslow, the Lambs were bereft of the "glory" of their Wednesday night dinners. They especially missed William, "the most brilliant, most ornamental" "wednesday-man" (*M,* 2:286). As compensation, Charles and Mary saw Robert Lloyd. Their absence from him had been long, during which time, in August 1804, he had married Hannah Hart. Robert visited the Lambs in March 1809. He wrote to Hannah that Charles and Mary's "union of affection is what we conceive of marriage in Heaven. They are the World *one* to the *other.*"[2]

Just after Robert left, the Lambs moved again. Their landlord wanted to live in the Mitre Court residence himself. On March 25, 1809, while their new rooms in the Temple were being prepared, Charles and Mary inhabited 34 Southampton Buildings. On June 3, they settled into 4 Inner Temple Lane. Charles hoped this would be their last dwelling. As he wrote to Manning on March 28, he has "such horror of **moving**. . . . What a dislocation of comfort is comprised in that word 'moving'!"

> Such a heap of little nasty things, after you think all is got into the cart, old drudging boxes, worn out brushes, gallipots, vials, things that it is impossible the most necessitous person can ever want, but which the Women, who preside on these occasions, will not leave behind if it was to save your soul, they'd keep the cart ten minutes to stow in dirty pipes and broken matches, to show their economy. Then you can find nothing you want for many days after you get into your new lodgings. You must comb your hair with your fingers, wash your hands without soap, go about in dirty gaiters, was I Diogenes, I would not move out of a kilderkin into a hogshead though the first had had nothing but small beer in it, and the second reeked Claret. (*M*, 3:4)

This destination might be worth the trouble. It is a return to Lamb's birth-place. It "looks out upon a gloomy churchyard-like court, call'd Hare Court, with three trees and a Pump in it." He used to drink at the pump when he was six. Now he mixes the water with brandy (*M*, 3:4).

The rooms themselves "are delicious." They open to a view of the court and the pump, which is "always going." "It is like living in a garden." Lamb can enjoy two sitting rooms on the third floor, and five more above, for "sleeping, cooking, & c," with an "inner staircase" all to himself. The dwelling is freshly painted, too, and only £30 a year (*M*, 3:12–13).

Only two days after she and her brother had settled in, Mary fell ill. She had to check into an asylum, and now Charles was all alone, save for a maid, a stranger. The rhythm of sanity and madness is tedious, he writes Coleridge. Worse, Mary's fits deprive her of a normal life. "What sad large pieces" her madness "cuts out of life—our her life, who is getting rather old." Charles realizes they "may not have many years to live together!" He "is weaker," and bears her fits "worse than [he] ever did." He will not be able to say he properly lives in this address until Mary returns. "No hearth" has yet blazed on the rooms. He asks Coleridge, always a desultory correspondent, to write, for he is "desolate" (*M*, 3:12–14).

Some solace comes from the books he let Coleridge borrow while the poet was living in London over the spring. Of these books, Lamb has recovered all but one, a third volume of the "old plays" containing Webster's *The White Devil*, among others. He found the first two volumes of these plays, containing *Arcadia* and *Daniel*, "enriched with [Coleridge's] manuscript notes." "I wish every book I have were so noted. They have thoroughly converted me to relish Daniel. . . . Your notes are excellent" (*M*, 3:13).

This throwaway remark seeded one of Lamb's greatest Elia essays, "The Two Races of Men," published in the *London Magazine* in December 1820. "The human species, according to the best theory I can form of it, is composed of two distinct races, *the men who borrow*, and *the men who lend*." All opposing groups are not really at odds over race or property but borrowing and lending. Borrowers are "the *great race*," "trusting and generous," possessed of a "certain instinctive sovereignty." Lenders "are born degraded"; they are "lean and suspicious" (*W*, 2:23).

The borrower is free from causality. If the lender gives out his money, then he expects it back, with interest. The borrower cares nothing for this "if . . . then." He takes money from another without earning it, and he does he not pay it back. He squanders it. He trusts he will borrow again, and again, and again. Like the lilies of the field, he flourishes in the present, no worries over past contracts or future poverty. Beyond causality, outside of time, the borrower escapes logic itself, based on the principle of noncontradiction: something can't be both "A" and "not A" at the same time. For him, the distinction between mine and yours is meaningless, like the difference between earning and spending.

One of the great borrowers in Elia's life is Ralph Bigod, based, as we know, on John Fenwick, who spent newspaper funds on entertainment, ended up in debtors' jail twice, fled to Canada, and died in 1820. Bigod borrowed so much money from so many people, it "was a wonder how he contrived to keep his treasury always empty. He did it by force of an aphorism, which he had often in his mouth, that 'money kept longer than three days stinks.'" He drank it away, gave it away, literally threw it away "into ponds, or ditches, or deep holes—inscrutable cavities of the earth" (*W*, 2:24).

Elia cares little for money. His treasures are books, and the Bigod who borrows his volumes is one "Comberbatch," Coleridge himself. In Elia's study, Coleridge, by not returning Elia's books, has created "that foul gap in the bottom shelf . . . like a great eye-tooth knocked out . . . with the huge Switzer-like tomes on each side (like the Guildhall giants, in their reformed posture, guardant of nothing)." That shelf "once held the tallest of my folios, *Opera*

*Bonaventuræ*, choice and massy divinity, to which its two supporters (school divinity also, but of a lesser calibre—Bellarmine, and Holy Thomas), showed but as dwarfs—itself an Ascapart!" Comberbatch is unapologetic, however. He holds a theory that "'the title to property in a book (my Bonaventure, for instance), is in exact ratio to the claimant's powers of understanding and appreciating the same.' Should he go on acting upon this theory, which of our shelves is safe?" (*W*, 2:25).

When "C," returns, at long last, the book, he does so no longer as a borrower, but as a lender himself. Since he understands the book better than the lender, it is his. He marks his property with his brilliant annotations, and so invests the book with more value than it originally possessed. "Shut not thy heart, nor thy library, against S.T.C." (*W*, 2:27).

"The Two Races of Men" is about essay writing. Elia values in borrowers what he embodies in this essay. It disdains causality, linearity, logic. The piece upends a hierarchy essential for a healthy economy. If borrowing is better than lending, and if everyone improves himself into a borrower, no one will earn money any longer. Elia doesn't consider the consequences of his "argument." Instead he extols borrowing as grace. You can do whatever you want and will always be forgiven. This graced state encourages superfluity. Elia's essay revels in surplus. The section on Bigod is superfluous to the book's conclusion, which is "If you borrow, return with value." Elia's characteristic archaisms—"cometh," "troubleth," "applieth"—are not necessary for communication. They are brio, gusto. So too Elia's Latin phrases—"lene tormentum," "cana fides"—and bizarre allusions—likening a folio to Ascapart—and use of out-of-the-way words like "obolary" and "visnomy."

On July 5, 1809, at 8:30 a.m., the son that William and Sarah Hazlitt had barely six months earlier welcomed to the light died. His name was William. When the father's sister Peggy rushed to the couple to help them through their mourning, she saw on her brother a look of "anguish" she would never forget. Only in 1822 could the essayist bring himself to write about the tragedy: "I have never seen death but once, and that was in an infant. It is years ago. The look was calm and placid, and the face was fair and firm. It was as if a waxen image had been laid out in the coffin, and strewed with innocent flowers." "It was not like death," Hazlitt continues, "but more like an image of life. . . . While I looked at it, I saw no pain was there; it seemed to smile at the short pang of life which was over: but I could not bear the coffin-lid to be closed—it almost stifled me; and still as the nettles wave in a corner of the churchyard over his little grave, the welcome breeze helps to refresh me and ease the tightness at my breast."[3]

Lamb's comments on the sick infant about two months before his death are baffling, if not cruel. In a letter of March 28, in which Mary writes to Louisa Martin that the Hazlitts' child is likely to die, Charles adds this in a footnote: "J. Hazlitt's child died of swallowing a bag of white paint, which the poor little innocent thing mistook for sugarcandy. It told its mother just two hours before it died, that it did not like soft sugar candy, and so it came out, which was not before suspected. When it was opened several other things were found in it, particularly a small hearth brush, two golden pippins and a letter which I had written Hazlitt from Bath" (*M*, 3:8).

Is this J. Hazlitt "John Hazlitt," William's brother? Or did Lamb mean to write "W?" We can't know, but we can recognize that this is an odd note to include in a letter about your close friend's terminally ill child. Did Lamb believe Hazlitt's child wasn't really in danger, and so assume that one of his surreal jokes would fly? But Mary in the letter is clear: death is expected. So Lamb riffs on real tragedy, one that will devastate his friend. Maybe we can excuse the insensitive comedy, though, by remembering that one of Lamb's primary coping mechanisms was his peculiar wit. For a decade now, he had deployed jokes to deflect the pain from his own trauma. In this case, perhaps he was protecting himself from sorrow over his friend's impending catastrophe. But all this is to forget that Lamb's whimsy sometimes possessed him, and he stammered out whatever popped into his outlandish head, which could be sinister as much as silly. His footnote to Mary's letter seems an extremely unsettling version of the disarming comedy he perpetrated on the Reverend Willis (before whom he kissed the fish picture) and the Reverend Russell (at whose visit he attributed his opinions to Mary).

The same Lamb who could turn a sick infant into an occasion for macabre humor could also compose, along with Mary, verse for children. Over the spring and summer of 1809, Charles and Mary had been at work on two volumes of juvenile poetry titled *Poetry for Children*. By June, they completed the project. They did it, once more, for money, and now they were no longer interested in writing children's books. "Our little poems are but humble, but they have no name, You must read them, remembering they were task-work, & perhaps you will admire the number of subjects, all of children, pick'd out by an old Bachelor & an old Maid" (*M*, 3:14).

Robert Lloyd hinted at why the siblings had chosen this genre: it was already established, and so the book had a ready-made audience.[4] A recent title in the genre was *Original Poems for Infant Minds* (1804, 1805), by Ann and Jane Taylor. (The sisters wrote "Twinkle, Twinkle, Little Star.") The collection was violently moral. A boy who fishes without permission gets caught in a meat hook. A girl plays with matches, and she is burned to death.

The Lambs' collection is gentler, and perhaps this is why the book didn't sell as well as the Godwins had hoped. William and Mary Jane released this small, two-volume book in 1809, listing the author as the "author of 'Mrs. Leicester's School.'" Though the book sold out within three years, the Godwins did not reprint it. Instead they included the poems they deemed best in an anthology called *The First Book of Poetry*, published in 1811. By 1827, Lamb was hard pressed to find a copy for himself.

Which sibling wrote what in this work of "minor poetry," as Lamb termed it, is difficult to ascertain. Lamb sent a copy to Robert in which he marked the poems he wrote. That volume has been lost, so all we have to go on is what Lamb comically wrote to Manning: "The best you may suppose mine; the next best my coadjutor's; you may amuse yourself guessing them out; but I must tell you mine are but one-third in quantity of the whole. So much for a very delicate subject" (*M*, 3:35). Lucas took Lamb's invitation, deciding which of the eighty-four poems were Charles's, and which Mary's. He did so "at a venture, except in a few cases, with no exact knowledge" (*W*, 3:491). Fifty-eight he believed to be Mary's, twenty-five Charles's. The remaining one, "The Beggar Man," John Lamb the younger wrote.

The range of the poems is impressive. Some are outright moral parables. In "Envy," "envious persons" are like "a blind and senseless tree" (*W*, 3:353). "Cleanliness" teaches that this virtue is indeed "next to Godliness," and that it is the "easiest, cheapest, needful'st duty" (*W*, 3:364).

The animal tales are lessons. In "The Rook and the Sparrows," a child feeds a rook crumbs he had been giving to sparrows. The little birds go hungry. The boy in "The Two Bees" stomps on two bees, killing them. He gets lost in the woods, falls into a fever, and his aching limbs make him aware of the pain he caused the insects.

Many poems are dialogues. In "The Butterfly," a sister convinces her brother not to kill this "finest gentleman of all / Insects," since it "has a form and fibres fine" that were "temper'd by the hand divine." Robert and Jane quarrel; their mother steps in; they reconcile. In "What Is Fancy?" a brother and a sister collaborate on a poem about the subject. The sister writes three lines, and the brother composes three more lines that respond to and rhyme with hers. She responds in kind, and so on. At one point the sister asks what fancy is. She answers her own question: it's what "comes in our head when we / Play at 'Let's make believe,' / And when we play at 'Guessing.'" The brother ominously replies, "And I have heard it said to be / A talent often makes us grieve, / And sometimes proves a blessing" (*W*, 3:374). The poem is a charming picture of siblings composing as Charles and Mary themselves almost certainly did. The verse also explores the kind of ambiguity that made *Tales from Shakespear* and *Mrs. Leicester's School* so compelling.

A handful of other poems transcends simple moralizing. In "Conquest of Prejudice" a "Negro youth" named Juba is sent to a Yorkshire school. Henry Orme, the head boy, insults Juba, and intends to turn all the other boys against him. To remove prejudice from Orme, the headmaster locks Orme and Juba in a room for a week. For three days they don't speak, until Orme talks, and then each boy tells his life story and they become good friends. The students now "contend who most shall make amends / For former slights to Africa's son" (*W*, 3:420). Though the poem concludes harmoniously, the schoolmaster's exercise is pure Beckett, and implies the psychological violence required to shock one out of prejudice.

"Parental Recollections" examines the strangeness of parenting. "A child's a plaything for an hour," it begins. After enjoying its "pretty tricks," we "lay it by." This is not the Romantic cult of childhood. The child is interesting only briefly, and then distanced into an "it," a thing, and put away. But the speaker transposes perspective: "I knew one, that to itself / All seasons could control." Notice the power shift. Now the child controls time, and so how long the parent will play with it. This child can "mock" the "sense of pain / Out of a grieved soul." How does this child comfort? Is it through playful mocking, or something more embittered? Regardless, the adult appears to be a grieved soul. The speaker next addresses the child: you are a "straggler into loving arms," a "young climber up of knees." If I forget "thy thousand ways, / Then life and all shall cease" (*W*, 3:398). The child controls time and so, the logic goes, to alienate the child would be to end time. The parent seems depressed, thinks of death often, and imagines the child as a savior.

The most disturbing poem is "Nurse Green," a dialogue between a scared little girl and a comforting mother. The girl can't sleep because she knows there's a corpse in the next room, that of Nurse Green. The mother attempts to talk the child out of her fear of death, but seems not to succeed, since she ends her speech by asserting that "if no endeavour your terrors can smother," then "Come, bury your fears in the arms of your mother; / My darling, cling close to me, I am alive" (*W*, 3:403). The biographical connection here is obvious and chilling, but the more general meaning is, too. Conventional solace for fear of the dead is impotent, and all the girl can do is cry in her mother's arms, simply because her mother is alive.[5]

Once Mary recovered from her breakdown after the move to No. 4 Inner Temple Lane, during the fall of 1809 she and Charles embarked on a long-anticipated visit to the Hazlitts' in Winterslow. Sarah owned a cottage in this small Wiltshire village, located some eighty miles southeast of London and six miles northeast of Salisbury. Though as citified as Lamb, William adored this pastoral retreat: "I look out of my window and see that a shower has just fallen: the fields look green after it, and a rosy cloud hangs over the brow of a hill; a lily expands its petals in the moisture, dressed in its lovely green and white; a shepherd-boy has brought some pieces of turf with daisies and grass for his young mistress to make a bed for her sky-lark, not doomed to dip his wings in the dappled dawn." He did some of his best writing in Winterslow. If London sometimes "cramp[ed] and dried" his style, in Winterslow, his words "flow[ed] like a river" and overflowed "its banks."[6]

Charles and Mary enjoyed Winterslow's expansiveness, too. "The Country," Charles announced, "has made us whole." "Nothing but sunshiney days & daily walks from 8 to 20 miles," as well as tours of Wilton, Salisbury, and Stonehenge (M, 2:26).

Mary agreed. "I never passed such a pleasant time in the country in my life, both in the house & out of it—the card playing quarrels, and a few gaspings for breath, after your swift footsteps up the high hills excepted, and those drawbacks are not unpleasant in recollection" (M, 3:31).

Hazlitt remembered the visit fondly. "I used to walk out at this time with Mr. and Miss Lamb of an evening, to look at the Claude Lorrain skies over our heads melting from azure into purple and gold, and to gather mushrooms that sprung up at our feet, to throw into our hashed mutton at supper."[7]

Mary and Charles tried to keep the healthy habits of the country alive in the city—they ate "salt butter" on their toast and "meat suppers"—but soon the "pipe and the gin bottle" came out (M, 3:30).

Petty vices aside, the siblings happily returned to their new lodgings. As Charles wrote to Coleridge on October 30, 1809, they loved their "Hogarth Room" and their library. "You never saw a bookcase in more **true** harmony with the contents than what I've nailed up in a room which though new has more aptitudes for growing old than you shall often see—as one sometimes gets a friend in the middle of life who becomes an old friend in a short time" (*M,* 3:27).

Lamb's contemporaries cherished his eclectic, ragtag book collection. Hunt observed that Lamb's library, "though not abounding in Greek or Latin . . . is anything but superficial." "The depths of philosophy and poetry are there, the innermost passages of the human heart." The library harbors "a handsome contempt for appearance. It looks like what it is, a selection made at precious intervals from the book-stalls; now a Chaucer at nine and twopence; now a Montaigne or a Sir Thomas Browne at two shillings; now a Jeremy Taylor; a Spinoza; an old English Dramatist, Prior, and Sir Philip Sidney; and the books are 'neat as imported.'" The organization is hodge-podge: "The very perusal of the backs is a 'discipline of humanity.' There Mr. Southey takes his place again with an old Radical friend: there Jeremy Collier is at peace with Dryden: there the lion, Martin Luther, lies down with the Quaker lamb, Sewell."[8]

Bryan Procter admired Lamb's knowledge of his books. "He had more real knowledge of old English literature than any man whom I ever knew. He was not an antiquarian. He neither hunted after commas, nor scribbled notes which confounded his text. The *Spirit* of the author descended upon him; and he felt it! With Burton and Fuller, Jeremy Taylor and Sir Thomas Browne, he was an intimate. The ancient poets—chiefly the dramatic poets—were his especial friends. He knew every point and turn of their wit, all the beauty of their characters; loving each for some one distinguishing particular, and despising none."[9]

In "Detached Thoughts on Books and Reading," an Elia essay of 1822, Lamb describes his love of books: "I must confess that I dedicate no inconsiderable portion of my time to other people's thoughts. I dream away my life in others' speculations. I love to lose myself in other men's minds. When I am not walking, I am reading, I cannot sit and think. Books think for me" (*W,* 2:172).

So addicted is he to the page he cares little for outward appearance. In fact, the greatest of books require the least of bindings, and look best worn.

A Shakspeare, or a Milton (unless the first editions), it were mere foppery to trick out in gay apparel. The possession of them confers no distinction. The exterior of them (the things themselves being so common), strange to say, raises no sweet emotions, no tickling sense of property in the owner. Thomson's Seasons . . . looks best (I maintain it) a little torn, and dog's-eared. How beautiful to a genuine lover of reading are the sullied leaves, and worn out appearance, nay, the very odour . . . of an old 'Circulating Library' Tom Jones, or Vicar of Wakefield! How they speak of the thousand thumbs, that have turned over their pages with delight!—of the lone sempstress, whom they may have cheered (milliner, or harder-working mantua-maker) after her long day's needle-toil, running far into midnight, when she has snatched an hour, ill spared from sleep, to steep her cares, as in some Lethean cup, in spelling out their enchanting contents! Who would have them a whit less soiled?

The only books that benefit from "durable and costly covers" are the ones both good and rare, like the life of the Duke of Newcastle, and the works of Sydney, Bishop Taylor, Fuller, and Burton (*W,* 2:173).

As important as the form of the book is the context for its perusal. Milton, for instance, "almost requires a solemn service of music to be played before you enter upon him. But he brings his music, to which, who listens, had need bring docile thoughts, and purged ears." Winter nights are the time for Shakespeare, maybe *The Tempest* or *A Winter's Tale*. Regardless of the atmosphere, both these poets should be read aloud—as opposed to newspapers and "books of quick interest," which "are for the eye to glide over only" (*W,* 2:175).

Reading outside won't do, though Elia admires a certain "class of street-readers," the "poor gentry, who, not having wherewithal to buy or hire a book, filch a little learning at the open stalls—the owner, with his hard eye, casting envious looks at them all the while, and thinking when they will have done. Venturing tenderly, page after page, expecting every moment when he shall interpose his interdict, and yet unable to deny themselves the gratification, they 'snatch a fearful joy'" (*W,* 2:176).

Mary enjoyed the library and the Hogarths, too, and she also relished the "beautiful green curtains" hung in November 1809, soon after she and Charles returned from Winterslow, as well as the "green baize" striping the doors. "Four new boards" were "put to the coal hole," and "fastening hasps put to the windows and . . . dyed Manning-silk cut out" (*M,* 3:31). The Lambs could afford new Hogarth prints and handsome household amenities now, since Charles had recently received a raise of £20 a year. (He also—inexplicably—was writing, at the encouragement of Jem White, "more lottery puffs," handbills advertising the lottery [*M*, 3:31].) Charles and Mary's money worries were over. From this point on, the East India House paid Lamb well. The company doubled his salary in 1815, bringing it to £480 a year. By 1821, he was earning £700.

These two offspring of domestic servants were now middle class. If you've been poor all your life, and then you are not poor, you ask, who am I? You wonder if your identity is defined by economics, if money, quite literally, makes you.

In "Old China," an Elia essay from 1823, Lamb considers this rise in status. Elia has cultivated a passion for old chinaware. Bridget longs for the former days when she and Elia were not as rich. They were happier then. When buying is easy, purchases have little value. When money was scare, exchanges were dear. Elia forewent a much-needed new suit to purchase a folio of Beaumont and Fletcher. He and Bridget eyed the book for weeks—it was for sale at Barker's in Covent Garden—before choosing to buy it. They decided about 10:00 one Saturday night. Elia rushed to the bookseller, afraid the shop would close. Bridget reminds him: "When the old bookseller with some grumbling opened his shop, and by the twinkling taper (for he was setting bedwards) lighted out the relic from his dusty treasures—and when you lugged it home, wishing it were twice as cumbersome—and when you presented it to me—and when we were exploring the perfectness of it (*collating* you called it)—and while I was repairing some of the loose leaves with paste, which your impatience would not suffer to be left till day-break—was there no pleasure in being a poor man?" (*W*, 2:249).

Didn't you enjoy a print of Leonardo more when you could barely pay for it? What about a walking trip, when you carried simple food and spread your fare in a humble pub? Didn't you relish the drama more when you sat in the 1-shilling gallery?

Elia concedes the point— he and Bridget were happier when poorer. But their youth was probably as much a cause for contentment as poverty. Whatever the origin, Elia urges, we should accept our new status. As older people, we need to ride instead of walk, lie soft instead of hard. Sitting in the shilling gallery at the theater was dangerous.

Elia directs Bridget's attention to a piece of China he recently purchased, a teacup on which is painted a "merry little Chinese waiter holding an umbrella, big enough for a bed-tester, over the head of that pretty insipid half-Madona-ish chit of a lady in that very blue summer-house" (*W*, 2:252).

Pictures like these so enthrall Elia, he can't take his cousin's complaints seriously. The china figures are "little, lawless, azure-tinctured grotesques, that under the notion of men and women, float about, uncircumscribed by any element, in that world before perspective—a china tea-cup." He especially loves the images on his cups. They figure "up in the air (so they appear to our optics), yet on *terra firma* still—for so we must in courtesy interpret that speck of deeper blue, which the decorous artist, to prevent absurdity, has made to spring up beneath their sandals." If Elia enjoys violations of the laws of space—his people defy while depending upon gravity—he also relishes transgressions of time: men who have somehow developed women's faces, and women who have evolved into more "womanish" women (*W,* 3:248).

"Here is a young and courtly Mandarin, handing tea to a lady from a salver—two miles off. See how distance seems to set off respect! And here the same lady, or another—for likeness is identity on tea-cups—is stepping into a little fairy boat, moored on the hither side of this calm garden river, with a dainty mincing foot, which in a right angle of incidence (as angles go in our world) must infallibly land her in the midst of a flowery mead—a furlong off on the other side of the same strange stream!" (*W,* 2:248).

The disproportionately long tray places server and lady impossibly far off, yet somehow close. And this same lady—though maybe not—has her leg angled in such a fashion that she is both stepping into the boat and a furlong beyond it. How can this lady be the same as the one receiving the tea? Time is parallel. One person exists simultaneously in two narratives. But the boater might not be the same woman at all.

No wonder Elia is bored with Bridget's reasoning. She exists in a causal world. If I struggle to buy this book, then it is of higher worth than if I did not struggle. Surreal violations of the "if-then" exhilarate Elia. If a man hands a woman a cup of tea, she is two miles off. If a woman places her dainty foot into a boat, she steps over the boat and the stream into a meadow two hundred yards beyond.

As in the essay "The Two Races of Men," Elia extols the acausal, the nonlinear, the alogical. These characteristics imply an aesthetic, an aesthetic, it turns out, of the Elian essay. In the case of "Old China," Elia begins the essay as an appreciation of the spatiotemporal baroqueness of china; Bridget breaks in with her long speech on struggle and value; Elia returns to gazing at his china as if she had never spoken. Elia's china reverie does not seem a legitimate "cause" for Bridget's speech, which in turn does not cause in Elia the reaction she wants. Instead of linear development, we experience two different visions pressed awkwardly together. That the essay is one thing and another at the same time—a decadent lyricism redolent of Wilde, a moral vision that reminds of Thoreau—should not surprise us, when we remember the first sentence of the piece: "I have an almost feminine partiality for old china." Elia is male and female, as double as his essay is, as the china figures are.

Is there something pernicious behind this whimsy?[10] Lamb acquired his china because of the British Empire, whose major engine of oppression was Lamb's employer. In dreaming over the exotic Chinese images, is Elia benefiting from the Orientalism that defined the empire, a reduction of another culture to arousal and curiosity? This is the dark side of distorting time and space, a necessity for empire. The imperialist imposes his narratives and objects onto the colonized region, trying to turn other into same. He also imports the myths and artifacts of his colony into his own markets, transforming same into other.

If Elia plays the imperialist, Lamb does not—at least here. Bridget's emphasis on labor counters Elia politically irresponsible idleness. Value arises only by earning one's own keep, not relying on the labor of others. The best work is locally directed, toward *this* book in *this* shop on *this* corner. The book is most valuable when its purchase creates shortage, not the surplus that empire desires.

"Old China" dramatizes Lamb's own struggle between decadence and rigor, "as if" and "is." The tension generates his abiding ironic aesthetic: pleasure is danger; joyful is the grind.

By January 1810, the Lambs had settled in their new dwelling. As Lamb wrote to Robert Lloyd, "When you come to London, you find us at **No. 4** Inner Temple Lane, with a few old Books, a few old Hogarths round the room, and the **Household** Gods at last establish'd. The feeling of **Home**, which has been slow to come, has come at last. May I never **move** again, but may my next Lodging be my **Coffin**" (*M*, 3:34).

Lamb began the year with a newsy letter to Manning. Hazlitt is writing a life of their friend Thomas Holcroft, who had died last spring. Hazlitt is also making, for the Godwins, an English grammar. Godwin progresses on his own treatise on language, but the "*gray mare is the better horse.*" This isn't the only pun Lamb sends across the oceans. "A constable in Salisbury Cathedral was telling me that eight people, dined at the top of the spire of the cathedral; upon which I remarked, that they must be a very sharp-set" (*M*, 3:35).

In February, John Lamb, strangely, appeared in Lamb's life. He had written a book, *A Letter to the Right Hon. William Windham, on His Opposition to Lord Erskine's Bill, for the Prevention of Cruelty to Animals.* The volume, published by Maxwell and Walter Wilson, luridly describes human cruelty to animals in hopes of garnering support for Lord Erskine's bill. Eels are forked in their eyes, skinned alive, coiled on a skewer, and thrust into boiling water. Lobsters are immersed in cold water and boiled alive. The best way to avoid such cruelty is to become a vegetarian. All this seems reasonable, especially in the twenty-first century, but John's idiosyncrasy, fully appreciated by Charles, perhaps thwarted the book's purpose. Can you take seriously a man who argues that the worm on the hook is the same as Christ on the cross? Or who claims that God never intended for creatures to eat one another?

Charles asked Robinson to find reviewers for the book. I am the last person to help, Lamb asserts, since he and the reviewers loathe each other. He "would willingly consign them all to Hell flames & Megaera's snaky locks" (*M*, 3:40).

By March, Lamb's good Winterslow intentions were awash. According to a frustrated Mary, "Charles was drunk last night, and drunk the night before; which night before was at Godwin's." There, we finished "at twelve o'clock, Charles . . . brim full of gin and water and snuff, after which Henry Robinson spent a long evening by our fireside at home, and there was much gin and water drunk, albeit only one of the party partook of it, and H. R. professed himself highly indebted to Charles for the useful information he gave him on sundry matters of taste and imagination, even after Charles could not speak plain for tipsiness. But still he swallowed the flattery and the spirits as savourily as Robinson did his cold water" (*W*, 3:49–50).

Perhaps with another cleansing in mind, Charles and Mary returned to Winterslow in July. Martin Burney and Molesworth Phillips accompanied them, and they visited Oxford on the return trip.

But traveling was becoming difficult for the siblings. "No more night travelling. My head is sore . . . with that deduction from my natural rest, which I suffered coming down. Neither Mary nor I can spare a morsel of our rest. It is incumbent on us to be misers of it. Travelling is not good for us—we travel so seldom" (*M*, 3:53),

When Mary became overly fatigued—from moving, traveling, too much visiting—she almost always broke down. Charles and Mary still wanted to travel—it was so restorative for them—but they must do so in a less fatiguing way. If they can't travel anymore, they will be exhausted by their hectic London schedule. Which could make Mary ill. But in touring, they weary themselves on the return. Which could make Mary ill.

Immediately upon the return from Winterslow, Mary broke down, and had to go once more to Hoxton. This was early August 1810. By September 18, she was improving, and Lamb expected her home within a week. He was looking forward to a visit from Dorothy Wordsworth, who would stay with him and Mary. He was also dreaming of Dorothy's region. As he wrote to Mrs. Clarkson, the mountains of the north returned to him in a repeated dream, "which is that I am in Cumberland, that I have been there some weeks, & am at the end of my Holydays, but in all that time I have not seen Skiddaw &c—the Hills are all vanished, & I shall go home without seeing them. The trouble of this dream denotes the weight they must have had on my mind, while I was there, which was almost oppressive, & perhaps is caused by the great difficulty I have in recalling any thing like a distinct form of any one of those great masses to my memory" (*M*, 3:55).

This anti-Wordsworthian dream—Lamb finds the northern mountains either absent or oppressive, and he cannot remember them well regardless—hints at why Lamb loved the city so much. London jerks him perpetually into the present (this street, that face, those prostitutes and books and beggars) and makes memory seem insignificant or confining.

But the dream is about loss—of past and present experiences. Mary's periods of madness were heavy on Charles's mind. He was either enduring Mary's absence, managing her low spirits upon her return, or bracing for the next fit. Or worse—terrified that this cycle, though vicious, would stop, and his sister would disappear into an asylum forever. Obsessed with these dark thoughts, Lamb regrets lost opportunities for happiness and laments a memory incapable of reliving past joys.

By October 19, Mary was back with Charles in the Temple, but she remained, as Charles wrote Wordsworth, "very weak and low spirited" (*M*, 3:57). Dorothy had just been visiting them, and their time was delightful. "The kindness of Charles Lamb and his sister were unbounded," Dorothy herself wrote. "I never was a hundredth part so comfortable in London and I should have stayed at least a fortnight if all had gone on well at home."[11] But the poet's sister had to rush back to the Lakes on October 22. William and Mary's daughter Catherine, only two, was ill, and she was needed at home.

(Catherine would die in June 1812. Though polio lamed her, her mix of sweetness and wildness captivated the adults around her. Dorothy found her "a sweet creature—very fair, very bonny, but not beautiful in spite of her blue eyes"; she also observed in her niece a "perfectly comic" face and an "uncommonly quick and lively" manner.[12] After learning of her death, De Quincey, twenty-seven, wrote Dorothy that Catherine was his beloved. "Nobody can judge from her manner to me before others what love she shewed to me. . . . On the night when she slept with me in the winter, we lay awake all the middle of the night—and talked oh how tenderly together: When we fell asleep, she was lying in my arms. . . . Many times on that night . . . she would lock her arms with such passionateness round my neck—as if she had known that it was to be the last night we were ever to pass together."[13] De Quincey likely equated her death with the even more traumatic one of his sister Elizabeth, when she was nine and he was seven. Robinson recorded De Quincey's reaction to Catherine's death: "Mr. De Quincey burst into tears on seeing Wordsworth and seemed to be more affected than the father." Wordsworth exhibited a stoic calm "that became a man both of feeling and of strength of mind.")[14]

Lamb concludes his October 19 letter to Wordsworth by praising the poet's essay "Upon Epitaphs." He offers his own example of the form. In the churchyard of Ditton-upon-Thames, a poet "for Love or Money, I do not well know which, has dignified every gravestone for the last few years with brand new verses, all different and all ingenious, with the Author's name at the Bottom of each. This sweet Swan of Thames has so artfully diversified his strains & his rhymes that the same thought never occurs twice. More justly perhaps, as no thought ever occurs at all, there was a physical impossibility that the same thought should recur." This poet can generate such diversity in his epitaphs because his understanding of death is so abstract. "Of Death, as it consists of **dust** and worms, and mourners and uncertainty, he had never thought; but the word 'death' he had often seen separate, & conjunct with other words, till he had learned to speak of all its attributes as glibly as Unitarian Belsham will discuss you the attributes of the **word God** in a Pulpit" (*M*, 3:58)

Extreme grief eludes the truisms of epitaph and pulpit. Worms and uncertainty and pains too intense for words: these are the matters of real poets, who try to say what can't be said, and fail, but with mesmerizing desperation. Lamb, and Wordsworth, would know.

On November 13, Mary and Charles composed a letter to Dorothy addressing one Charles had written to her earlier. In this unrecovered epistle, Charles had informed Dorothy of Mary's terrible mental state in order to excuse his sister from some favor Dorothy had requested of her. Dorothy's mention of this letter in a November 6 correspondence to Robinson hints at the severity of Mary's condition and expresses Dorothy's regret over not being more sensitive. "I am much afraid that Miss Lamb is very poorly.—I have had a letter from Charles, written in miserably bad spirit. I had thoughtlessly . . . requested her to execute some commissions for me; and her Brother writes to beg that I will hold her excused from every office of that sort at present, she being utterly unable to support herself under any fatigue either of body or mind." Dorothy reproaches herself for not being more perceptive of Mary's illness and for putting Charles in the awkward position of having to refuse her request. Dorothy now understands why Charles struggles to keep away taxing visitors (like Mrs. Godwin). Mary requires "absolute quiet." It is fitting for Charles to turn away all visitors except those who make Mary feel better. Please keep me informed on the Lambs, Dorothy asks Robinson. "There is nobody in the world out of our own house for whom I am more deeply interested."[15]

Mary in her part of the November 13 letter expresses her extreme regret over being unable to help her friend Dorothy. "It is a great mortification to me to be such an useless creature, and I feel myself greatly indebted to you for the very kind manner in which you take this ungracious matter" (*M,* 3:60–61). She is not so ill now and is at present under the care of Dr. George Leman Tuthill. (Tuthill studied at Cambridge with Manning, found himself in Paris when England declared war on France, was imprisoned in Verdun, and released only after his wife appealed to Napoleon himself.) Tuthill has prescribed medicines beneficial to Mary, and advised her to drink only water, a habit that agrees well with her. Mary hopes Dorothy enjoyed her visit, especially the "many pleasant fireside hours together," but she fears her "stupid dispirited state made me seem a very flat companion" (*M,* 3:61).

Charles jumps in with a lengthy postscript devoted to "nonsense." Mary has taken to water like a "hungry otter," and he has decided to "limp" after her in "lame imitation." He has been on the water for four days, and he is "full of cramps & rheumatisms, and cold internally so that fire wo'nt warm me, yet I bear all for virtues sake. . . . Damn Temperance & them that first invented it" (*M,* 3:62).

Ten days later, the Lambs are still on water—easy for Mary by now, but not Charles—and they are dealing with a problematic new maid, "a stupid big country wench" (*M,* 3:65). But Mary continues poorly, as Charles reports to Hazlitt on November 28. It pains him to say this, but since Mary lives always "with a kind of fever upon her," she can no longer entertain overnight company. The contact might overexcite her and cause a fit. This means that her best friend Sarah can see Mary only during the day. As of now, Mary never leaves the house, and Charles is trying to keep troublesome visitors away, ever since that night Mrs. Godwin, "that damn'd infernal bitch," came and stayed so late, that Mary could not sleep, and it was only by a "miracle that she escaped a very bad illness" (*M*, 3:68).

Charles persisted in his campaign to protect his sister from overexcitement. In December, he wrote to Godwin that Mary could have no visitors in the "forenoon." He hopes this rule won't offend Godwin or his wife. It has already cost him "more than one friendship" (*M*, 3:70).

# CHAPTER 32

# *The* Reflector

Remarkably, during this exhausting period, Lamb was writing in a genre he had not undertaken since he had completed "The Londoner" for the *Morning Post* eight years earlier: the essay. In late 1810, Hunt founded, with his brother John, a radical newspaper called the *Reflector*. Leigh invited distinguished fellow Blues to contribute. He asked Lamb, as well as Dyer, Thomas Barnes, Thomas Mitchell, and James Scholefield. He planned to contribute himself. In the second number of the paper, from March 1812, he published an essay called "A Day by the Fire." Simon Hull has called this essay the origin of the so-called Cockney School, of which Lamb became a major part.[1]

The piece celebrates "a day's enjoyments by the fireside." Hunt sits in his easy chair by the fire. He enjoys "a little hoar-frost upon the windows, a bird or two coming after the crumbs, and the light smoke from the neighboring chimneys brightening up into the early sunshine. Even the dustman's bell is not unpleasant from its association; and there is something absolutely musical in the clash of the milk-pails suddenly unyoked." This meditation on the ordinary meanders into speculation on how the ancient poets experienced their own fires. "Would Homer, the observer of character, the panegyrist of freedom, the painter of storms, of landscapes, and of domestic tenderness,—aye, and the lover of snug house-room and a good dinner,—would he have complained of our humours, of our liberty, of our shifting skies, of our

ever-green fields, our conjugal happiness, our firesides, and our hospitality?"
No. Homer's experiences are little different from ours. The moon shining
through the window at this moment—the essay has moved at a leisurely pace
from morning to night—is the "same identical planet that enchanted . . . all
the great men and geniuses that have existed."[2]

As Lamb learned when he wrote his own such familiar essays in the early
1820s, whimsical meditations on what's right in front of you are powerfully
political. The fire Hunt loves the great men of history also loved. The divi-
sions between high and low, elite and ordinary are arbitrary. My personal
experience is just as important as anyone else's.

Hunt carried his democratic vision into the next paper he and his brother
founded, the *Examiner,* likewise robustly devoted to liberal reform. (The *Reflector* ran for only four numbers.) The paper attacked the current regime,
headed by George IV, the Prince of Wales, who had become Prince Regent in
his insane father's stead. The Prince Regent upheld his father's Toryism, which
favored continued war with France while opposing Catholic emancipation
and parliamentary reform. He was also a gambler, womanizer, begetter of
bastards, and fat.

In the *Examiner* of March 22, 1812, in an article called "The Prince on
St. Patrick's Day," Leigh and John accused the Prince Regent of being "a
violator of his word, a libertine over head and ears in debt and disgrace, a
despiser of domestic ties, the companion of gamblers, and demireps, a man
who has just closed half a century [his father began his reign in 1760] without
one single claim on the gratitude of his country or the respect of posterity!"[3]
(The week before, Lamb published his most political work ever, a poem called
"The Triumph of the Whale," in which he likened the Prince Regent to this
sea creature.) The Hunts went too far. They were charged with libel. On the
trial's opening day, a crowd of ten thousand supported the brothers. But they
were convicted on December 9, 1812, and sentenced to two years in prison.
Hunt was remanded to Horsemonger Lane Gaol. He was twenty-nine and
had a wife and two children.

Through well-placed bribes and blandishments, Hunt convinced the bailiff to house him in a suite of rooms in the infirmary. He hired decorators,
transforming his prison into a bower. "I papered the walls with a trellis of
roses; I had the ceiling coloured with clouds and sky; the barred windows I
screened with Venetian blinds; and when my bookcases were set up with their
busts, and flowers and a pianoforte made their appearance, perhaps there was

*Leigh Hunt,* by Benjamin Robert Haydon. (© National Portrait Gallery, London.)

not a handsomer room on that side [of] the water."[4] Lamb, who visited often, likened the cell to a fairy bower.

Hunt also arranged for his family to live with him and eventually planted a garden in the prison yard. Soon he was editing the *Examiner* again; entertaining Jeremy Bentham, Byron, and Hazlitt; and feasting on produce he'd planted in the prison yard.

Hunt's conversion of prison into parlor and publishing house is easy to mock, as is Hunt himself, who relied on the charity of friends to fund his papers and his (eventual) ten-children family. (This Hunt is the original for Dickens's Skimpole, from *Bleak House,* a father of a large brood who shamelessly takes charity in lieu of an actual job and whiles away his time doing diletanttish art projects.) But, according to Simon Hull, Hunt "triumphantly re-imagine[s]" an "unpromising" surrounding as "otherworldly, exotic" space.[5] Doing so, Hunt engages in a political act akin to "A Day by the Fire." He turns government oppression into domestic comfort. This is the man Lamb called "one of the most cordial-minded men I ever knew" and "a matchless fireside companion" (*W,* 1:232).

In February 1815, Hunt was released. He settled in the Vale of Health in Hampstead, and became the center of a thriving literary circle that included Keats and Shelley. (Keats lived with him for extended periods and took up Hunt's challenges to see who could write the best sonnet in fifteen minutes; one such bout produced Keats's famous line "The Poetry of earth is never dead.") After Hunt published an essay praising Keats and Shelley as members of a "new" school of poetry—as opposed to the "Lake" school of poetry—*Blackwood's Magazine*, one of the most conservative papers of the day, printed a series of articles attacking the "Cockney School." The articles were written by John Gibson Lockhart, soon to be the son-in-law of Sir Walter Scott. Ironically, the qualities that Lockhart derided became, with a shift in perspective, powerful virtues of a novel literary movement, one not only new in its time but largely overlooked, until recently, by students of Romanticism. The Cockney School grew out of the rising London lower-middle class and expressed the particular urban concerns of this group: social mobility, flexible selfhood, the aesthetics of the city and its suburbs, suspicion toward hierarchy, and love of middle-brow entertainment, including, most notably, magazines like the *Examiner* and soon enough the *London.* Out of this world sprang the urban Romanticism of Lamb (versus the pastoral one of Wordsworth), who proclaimed himself a "pure" Cockney.[6]

No isolated egos brooding over stones, the Cockneys were a community. Hunt knew everyone. He introduced Keats to Benjamin Robert Haydon, who introduced Keats to Wordsworth, who joined Keats and Lamb at Haydon's "Immortal Dinner." Hunt presented Keats to Shelley, who encouraged Keats to question Hunt's influence, and who invited the consumptive Keats to stay with his family in Italy; Keats refused and died in Rome with Joseph Severn.

Shelley wrote a pastoral elegy on Keats, *Adonais*. Soon after, he drowned off the coast of Lerici. When his shark-mauled corpse washed up, the volume of Keats in the pants pocket identified him. Hunt, who had traveled to Livorno to start a new paper with Byron's funding—the *Liberator*—was present at the funeral. He was the reason Shelley had undertaken his voyage in the *Don Juan* in the first place. The poet wanted to confer with Hunt on the paper. Edward Trelawney, Shelley's friend, decided to cremate the poet, pagan style. He built a pyre on Viareggio's shore. Before igniting it, he and Byron had to search for Shelley's remains, which they had buried to prevent further decay. The August heat was brutal, the stench of cooking flesh unbearable. Hunt retired to his coach. Byron dove into the ocean for a swim. The heart did not burn; perhaps it was calcified because of tuberculosis. Trelawney recovered it from the ashes. Hunt had returned from his coach, and Trelawney presented the organ to him. He wanted to keep it, but thought better of it. He proffered it to Mary Shelley, who had not attended the service.[7] She kept it the rest of her life, part of which she spent corresponding enthusiastically with Charles Lamb.

We owe much to Hunt for inviting Lamb to contribute to the *Reflector*. If he had not, perhaps Lamb never would have become an essayist. He had completed "The Londoner," a familiar essay, in 1802, and he had written many letters with essayistic verve, but in 1810, he was a writer of children's books who did not want to write any more children's books, a glosser of literature by other writers, and a failed dramatist. He had hit a dead end, and his personal life, wrecked by Mary's periodic attacks and his own drinking and depression, held little promise.[8]

Lamb contributed four essays to the second number of the *Reflector*, released in July 1811. Of the four, he reprinted two in his 1818 *Works*, "On the Inconveniences Resulting from Being Hanged" and "On the Danger of Confounding Moral with Personal Deformity"; incorporated one, "On the Probable Effects of Gunpowder Treason," into a longer essay on Guy Fawkes in 1823; and simply let the fourth, the brief "On the Ambiguities Arising from Proper Names," see the light just this once.

The two pieces he preserved in his *Works* exhibit techniques Lamb will perfect in the Elia essays. Both are authored by a character. "Pensilis" composed the article on hanging, which appeared as a letter to the editor. The second article was also a letter to the editor, written by "Crito." Like the name

"Elia"—which suggests "A Liar," among other meanings—these names are comically ironic. Pensilis is Latin for "hanging," but suggests "penis." Crito recalls Plato's famous dialogue on justice while hinting at "critic."

That the pseudonyms are self-contradictory is apt. Both essays explore phenomena that appear to have only one meaning, but in reality have others. "On the Inconveniences Resulting from Being Hanged" is about a man hanged for a crime he didn't commit, only to be cut down just before he expired. This "rebirth" has not been successful. He is embarrassed by what has happened, and so wears a cravat to hide his scar. He moves to "the metropolis, as the place where wounded honour . . . could lurk with the least danger of exciting inquiry, and stigmatised innocence had the best change of hiding her disgrace in a crowd" (*W,* 1:57). But his cover is blown when he runs into a countryman who publicizes his unfortunate past. His urban friends desert him. Even though he is innocent, they imagine only his guilt, and they are disturbed by the freakishness of his near-death experience. Pensilis then falls in love, but when his beloved discovers his secret, she breaks off the engagement. She explains that she could never see him in a nightcap, since she would always imagine the hood the hangman pulls over the heads of the condemned.

The unhanged man is no Lazarus. He is emotionally castrated. Proven innocent, he appears guilty. Although his neck wound is healed, his mark, Cain-like, remains. And while he seems a perfectly eligible suitor, his beloved's vision of him swinging limply destroys her passion.

These isn't inconvenience; it is Kafka.

"On the Danger of Confounding Moral with Personal Deformity" likewise hinges on situational irony. Crito claims we erroneously attribute physical ugliness to those we suspect of immorality. Look at a "wanted" poster. When someone has committed a crime against us, we paint him demonically, projecting our negative opinion onto his features. Ironically, this attribution hinders our ability to apprehend the criminal, since the face we paint is not the actual face. A man who has borrowed money of you and fled is really handsome and honest-looking. Otherwise you wouldn't have lent him money.

As with the essay on hanging, this piece weighs the difficulty of discerning between our psychological projections and the objects we hope to understand. This gap between appearance and reality generates the reversals. Pensilis, though raised, is still viewed as hanged, and so is dead and alive at once. Crito believes that physiognomy is a legitimate form of detecting criminals, but that projecting ugliness onto faces is not. But aren't both modes efforts to discover the invisible through the visible? How is one better than the other?

These essays lack the play and subtlety of Elia's forays, where irony isn't simply reversal but proliferation, and the persona is not double but multiple. Still, both pieces present the ideas Elia will dramatize: there is an unbridgeable gap between interpretation and reality; what we want in life, we get the opposite of; and we are all flawed—guilty, criminal, punished—in ways we barely understand.

Lamb published three more pieces in the *Reflector*, no. 3, published in October 1811. Two are "letters" to the editor. The first is "On the Custom of Hissing at the Theatres, with Some Account of a Club of Damned Authors." Written by "Semel-Damnatus," "Once-Damned," the piece comically compares an audience's hissing to the sounds of actual snakes. For instance, "there is the Common English Snake.—That is that part of the auditory who are always in the majority at damnations, but who, having no critical venom in themselves to sting them on, stay till they hear others hiss, and then join in for company" (*W,* 1:90). (Lamb, of course, hissed like this snake at his own play.) All who have been hissed at are members of a literary club, the Damned, whose tenets are: "That the public, or mob, in all ages, have been a set of blind, deaf, obstinate, senseless, illiterate savages. That no man of genius in his sense would be ambitious of pleasing such a capricious, ungrateful rabble. That the only legitimate end of writing for them is to pick their pockets, and, that failing, we are at full liberty to vilify and abuse them as much as we think fit" (*W,* 1:91).

Moriturus, "about to die," authors the second letter in the *Reflector*, no. 3, "On Burial Societies; and the Character of an Undertaker." The piece recalls Sir Thomas Browne, whom Moriturus quotes: "Man . . . is a noble animal, splendid in ashes, and pompous in the grave" (*W,* 1:93). Moriturus applies Browne's irony to burial societies that guarantee an elegant burial to anyone who can pay a shilling up front and 2 pence per week for the next six months. Those who join pitifully believe that an ostentatious funeral will elevate their death, when the coffins of rich and poor alike are inconsequential to the corpses within. The essay ends with a sketch of an undertaker, apparently from the time of Richard Steele. We grant great power to this "bed-maker to the dead," even though we won't care what he does to us when it is time for his work.

These essays, like those on hanging and ugliness, entertain on the surface, but dark currents flow underneath: the self-loathing of authors, our pitiful attempts to invest death with meaning. But neither of these pieces, nor the earlier ones, display the scope and depth of Lamb's third essay in the *Reflector*, no. 3: "On the Genius and Character of Hogarth."

Head shaved, one ankle shackled, naked save for ragged underpants, his ass on the black floor where he has just fallen or is getting up from (he supports himself with his right hand; with his left he presses his head), a man stares down. There is nothing to look at. A woman in a light-brown dress trimmed in white, her head covered with a white dormeuse cap, sits at his back. She seems to be supporting him. A man wearing a puce overcoat stands behind her. He rests his right elbow on the top of her head, as though she is high table or a post. Behind this man is another—dim, as though only a shadow. He holds a rolled-up piece of paper to his eye like a telescope. Another huddles in the far left corner. Naked, he grips his hands together as if praying and looks upward, agonized. In the center is another naked man. He wears a crown, holds a scepter, and stares imperiously to the right. In front of him a gaunt old woman kneels. She appears to be conjuring a spell on the bald man. To the crone's left, on the far right of the room: a man wearing an open book for a hat plays a fiddle, and a woman dons a dunce hat and extends upward a stick crossed at the top by three bars, each shorter than the one below. She is a moronic pope.

This teeming scene is from Hogarth's eighth and final panel of his engraving of *The Rake's Progress*. Our rake through his profligacy has now lost everything, including his sanity, and he languishes in Bedlam. Hogarth's brutally realistic depiction of the horror is enthralling.

Hogarth's ability to see everyday details, no matter how sordid, with intense specificity: this is what Lamb admires in the artist. He finds in the painter a talent for acquainting us "with the everyday human face" and so empowering us "to detect those gradations of sense and virtue (which escape the careless or fastidious observer) in the countenances of the world about us." Attuned to myriad expressions, ranging from aristocrat to pauper, dandy to lunatic, we lose "that disgust at common life . . . which an unrestricted passion for ideal forms and beauties is in danger of producing" (*W*, 1:86). So Lamb concludes in "On the Genius and Character of Hogarth." For Lamb, Hogarth is to painting what Shakespeare is to literature: an artist whose morality isn't (as Wordsworth's could be) sententiousness but rather a generosity

*A Rake's Progress,* by William Hogarth, etching and engraving.
(Courtesy of the Metropolitan Museum of Art. Gift of Mrs. Carl Joseph Ulmann, 1929.)

(more Keatsian) toward the quotidian, a love, rare in a world ruled by ought-
ness, of the unadorned *is.*

Lamb first appreciated Hogarth as a child visiting his grandmother at the
Blakesware house near Widford. Later, when not poring over a Burton or a
Browne, Lamb studied his collection of Hogarth prints, especially during the
period from 1809 to 1817, when he and Mary lived at 4 Inner Temple Lane.
When the Lambs moved to Russell Street in 1817, and Charles could not find
a room large for his Hogarths, he removed the prints from their frames and
bound them in a book. Mary wrote to Dorothy about making the best of a
diminished thing: the prints "were sent home yesterday, and now I have them
all together and perceive the advantage of peeping close at them through
my spectacles. I am reconciled to the loss of them hanging round the room,

which has been a great mortification to me—in vain I tried to console myself with looking at our new chairs and carpets" (*L,* 2:217–18).

Hogarth's teeming details challenge audiences. In *Gin Lane,* for instance, the artist places three small dark figures at the very back of the scene, beyond a gap in a decaying wall. They are hardly noticeable. They appear "to make a part in some funeral procession which is passing on the other side of the wall, out of the sphere of the composition." This "extending of the interest beyond the bounds of the subject could only have been conceived by a great genius" who believes "the spectator must meet the artist in his conceptions halfway" (*W,* 1:74).

Ironically, Hogarth's clarity is ambiguous, because it doesn't easily fit into a Theory of Life. A Hogarth image is not an "example of" Idea X. It *is* X. We might mistakenly call this luminous obscurity "difficult" or "slight," and favor lesser pieces made by artists who "require an object to be made out to themselves before they can comprehend it" (*W,* 1: 74). This reduction of particular to general Coleridge calls the allegorical, while the emphasis on the particular as infinitely momentous is symbolic. Interpreting the former is easy. Crack the code. The latter resists conclusion but generates perpetual pleasure. You find "matter for the mind of the beholder to feed on for the hour together,— matter to feed and fertilize the mind" (*W,* 1:75).

Hogarth's work "is too real to admit one thought about the artist who did it" (*W,* 1:75). Because he empathizes so fully with the diverse subjects, he is not there. He *is* the work. He is, like Keats's ideal poet, the most "unpoetical" of figures. He delights in dark and light, rich or poor, villain and victim. He knows that in the "drama of real life," there is "no such thing as pure tragedy." Rather, "merriment and infelicity, ponderous crime and feather-light vanity, like twi-formed births, disagreeing complexions of one intertexture, perpetually unite to shew forth motley spectacles to the world" (*W,* 1:77).

In the fourth number of the *Reflector,* released in March 1812, Lamb published "On the Tragedies of Shakespeare, Considered with Reference to Their Fitness for Stage Representation."

Like Coleridge, Hazlitt, and Keats, Lamb valued Shakespeare as a psychological poet. Lear's greatness is "intellectual: the explosions of his passion are terrible as a volcano; they are storms turning up and disclosing to the bottom that sea, his mind, with all its vast riches. It is his mind which is laid bare." Hamlet's grandeur is mental, too. His "transactions between himself and his moral sense," the "effusions of his solitary musings," the "silent meditations with which his bosom is bursting," his "profound sorrows," "light-and-noise-abhorring ruminations, which the tongue scarce dares utter to deaf walls and chambers": these, not "the gesticulating actor," fascinate (*W,* 1:100).

The actor hinders the character. His elocution and gesturing simply cannot capture the subtlety of Shakespeare's poetry. The actor's Lear is a blustery old fool. But when you read *Lear* in your garret, words crackle and explode and reconfigure.

That the play "is beyond all art" producers seem to know. Why else would they tamper so freely with the plot? The version of *Lear* most performed in Lamb's day was Nahum Tate's 1681 adaptation, *The History of King Lear,* wherein Cordelia and Edgar marry, and the old king is restored to sanity and throne. This is perverse, "as if the living martyrdom that Lear had gone through—the flaying of his feelings alive, did not make a fair dismissal from the stage of life the only decorous thing for him" (*W,* 1:107).

Lamb's *Reflector* essays explore deformity: the mangled neck of Pensilis, the hideous traits we project onto alleged criminals, the serpentine contortions of disgruntled theatergoers, monstrous fantasies of how gaudiness might cheat death, Hogarth's depictions of London's broken souls, Shakespeare's acute renderings of distorted minds. Certainly Lamb's experiences of Mary's own mental impairments can account for this fixation, not to mention his repeated encounters with the disturbed inmates of Mary's asylums. But we can't forget that Lamb composed these essays during the Napoleonic Wars.[9] Though England's war with France was waged abroad, the fighting impacted Lamb's London. As the war drained England's economy, beggars, derelicts, and drunkards teemed. Husbands perished on the fields, and their widows and children back home descended into indigence. Soldiers who did return were maimed, physically or psychologically. Add to these factors the chronic threat of an enemy invading the homeland, and the paranoia of a government terrified of rebellion, and we can glimpse another context for Lamb's obsession with trauma.

CHAPTER 33

*Mania*

Lamb completed other pieces for the *Reflector*, no. 4. Three resemble the earlier letters by eccentrics, such as the one by Pensilis on being hanged: "Edax on Appetite," about one "Edax," "I eat," cursed with an appetite he can never sate; "Hospita on the Immoderate Indulgence of the Pleasures of the Palate," on the difficulty of serving a man like Edax; and a satire by "L.B." on the unreasonable expectations employers place on clerks. (Lamb would know.) Another essay in this style—a character addressing a particular problem—was "A Bachelor's Complaint of the Behaviour of Married People." Lamb republished it in 1823 as one of Elia's. Lamb also contributed a poem to Hunt's paper, "A Farewell to Tobacco," which took its first form in a letter to Dorothy Wordsworth in 1805. In addition, Lamb included specimens from Thomas Fuller, the seventeenth-century church historian. "The Pyramids themselves, doting with age, have forgotten the names of their founders." Mr. Perkins, the Divine, "had a capacious head, with angles winding and roomy enough to lodge all controversial intricacies." "A generous creature a horse is, sensible in some sort of honour; and made most handsome by that which deforms men most—pride" (*W,* 1:112).

During the year and a half over which he wrote his *Reflector* pieces, Lamb didn't keep to his plan to curtail his and Mary's socializing. Though he complained of social exhaustion, he desperately needed the escape of gin-lubed witty chitchat.

Not a month after asking the Godwins not to call as often, the Lambs are having a party. It is January 8, 1811. Robinson is there and Lamb, though not feeling well, is talking of Southey's *Curse of Kehama*, which he admires more than his friend's other long poems. The conversation turns to Coleridge and Wordsworth, who are just now having a falling-out. Lamb, to Robinson's surprise, claims Coleridge "to be the greater man." *The Ancient Mariner* is better than anything from Wordsworth. The problem with Wordsworth is that he is "too apt to force his own individual feelings on the reader, instead of, like Shakespeare, entering fully into the feelings of others." Lamb's wit on this night matches his critical acumen. When someone at the party says that Shakespeare commits an anachronism in having Hector speak of Aristotle, Lamb replies, "That's what Johnson referred to . . . when he wrote—And panting Time toils after him in vain."[1]

Twelve days later, Robinson enjoyed a "long tete a tete with Mary Lamb. A confidential gossiping."[2] Three days after that, Robinson found himself at the Lamb's again, along with Coleridge, Rickman, and John Morgan, an attorney and graduate of Christ's Hospital, with whom Coleridge was now living. Coleridge was not in "good form" that night, Robinson thought. "Very wordy."[3]

A month later, February 24, Robinson attended a "very large party to supper," whose guests included the Lambs.[4] On March 6, Robinson called on the Lambs after dinner. Hazlitt and Coleridge were there. Lamb reported the death of their friend George Burnett. He "had died wretchedly in a workhouse."[5]

This death, as we know, unnerved Mary. But it was probably Coleridge's own mania that precipitated her attack. On March 8, Hazlitt confided to Robinson that "poor Miss L. as well as her brother [are] injured by Coleridge's presence in town, and their frequent visits and constant company at home, which keep their minds in a perpetual fever."[6]

On March 14, Robinson agreed. "Poor Mary Lamb has been attacked again by her shocking malady. It has been, I fear, precipitated by Coleridge's company, which I think has a dreadful effect upon her nerves and shatters her frame. The conversation of such a man, whose eloquence is full of passion and mystical philosophy, a compound of poetry, metaphysics, plaintive egotism and diseased sensibility, continued for hours to a late hour in the night, is enough to disorder a sane but susceptible frame, much more rouse a dormant disease of imagination."[7]

Coleridge's sensibility was diseased in the extreme just then. In late October 1810, he had arrived in London. He had come at the invitation of Basil

Montagu, with whom he planned to spend the winter. The poet looked forward to socializing and literary prospecting, but something wasn't right. Montagu didn't put him up at his swanky townhouse at 4 Gray's Inn Place, Holborn. Instead he installed Coleridge at No. 55 Frith St, Soho, markedly less posh. (The home might have been Mrs. Montagu's family home.) The next night, over spirits, Coleridge asked Montagu why he wasn't staying with him in Holborn. According to Coleridge, Montagu told him that Wordsworth had "commissioned" Montagu to tell him that he, Wordsworth, "has no hope of you," that you have been an "ABSOLUTE NUISANCE" in "[his] Family," that you are a "rotten drunkard" or a drunkard "rotting out his entrails by intemperance," that you run "into debt at little Pot-houses for Gin."[8] Wordsworth's advice to Montagu: don't let Coleridge live with you.

Coleridge worshipped Wordsworth and loved Wordsworth's family. He had no idea they felt like this. "Whirled about without a centre—as in a nightmair—no gravity—a vortex without a centre."[9] He left Soho and checked into Hudson's Hotel in Covent Garden. He felt "a compressing and strangling Anguish, made up of Love, and Resentment, and Sorrow."[10] He wandered the streets until he found his way to No. 4 Inner Temple.

Charles was still at East India House, but Mary was home. She saw the "wildness & paleness" in her friend and begged him to tell her what was wrong. He opened his mouth to speak. Only an "agony of weeping followed," until he "convulsively" got out the words, "Wordsworth—Wordsworth has given me up. He has no hope of me."[11]

Around this time Lamb was writing to Dorothy Wordsworth, the Hazlitts, and the Godwins that Mary needed as little stimulus as possible. A desperate, depressed Coleridge daily in her presence was the last thing she needed. Incredibly, she held it together until March. That Charles allowed Coleridge into his life while Mary was at high risk shows how much he loved his old Christ's classmate.

(A reconciliation between Coleridge and Wordsworth did not occur until May 1812, aided by the diplomacy of Lamb and Robinson. The treaty was icy.)

With Mary confined by mid-March 1811, Charles was alone. Socializing now became even more urgent, but also a burden, since Lamb felt he should pretend to be merry when his spirits were low. On March 16, he called on Robinson, and they went for a walk. "C.L. was seemingly very merry—his sister's illness I dare say leaves him in no other state than outward affliction or violent and false spirits which he works himself into to subdue his real feeling."[12]

By May 15, Mary was back home with Charles in the Temple. Robinson called on them and enjoyed a pleasant evening, part of which was spent reading Charles's new poem for children, the tale of Prince Dorus, "the long-nosed king." Lamb likely completed his verse rendering of this ancient tale—often called "The Enormous Nose" or "The Prince with the Nose"—around March, while Mary was away. Soon after, the Godwins published it in their Juvenile Library as *Prince Dorus; or, Flattery Put out of Countenance. A Poetical Version of an Ancient Tale, Illustrated with a Series of Elegant Engravings.*

Mary and Charles resumed their spirited social schedule. Robinson found them with Godwin in late May, and in early June called on them himself. On June 13, he visited the Lambs and found John Jr. there. He got to hear Charles recite two of his favorite puns, one of which we have heard: the compounds in East India House, composed of six clerks, are made of simples.[13] A week later, with the Lambs again, Robinson observed Lamb was "very merry"— meaning very drunk. He was punning more numerously than wittily, Robinson observed. Though Charles did fire off one good one. "[Barron] Field had said, 'Who ever puns will steal—I always button my pockets when in company of a punster.' Someone said, 'Punsters have no pocket.' 'No,' said C.L., 'they have no pockets, they carry only a ridicule.'"[14]

On July 10, the Lambs resumed their Wednesday evening parties. Two weeks later, they probably had to cancel, since one of Lamb's colleagues, H. Wawd, had thrown a pen full of ink into Lamb's eye and nearly put it out. Did Lamb rib Wawd one joke too far?

In August Robinson called again at the Lambs', and found Lamb serious—a rarity—and therefore "very interesting."[15] What brought out the sobriety was his affection for Coleridge, who was falling apart right in front of literary London. Robinson at one point exclaimed, "Poor Coleridge!" Lamb "corrected me," Robinson recorded, "not angrily, but as if really pained. 'He is,' he said, 'a fine fellow, in spite of all his faults and weaknesses. Call him Coleridge; I hate poor, as applied to such a man. I can't bear to hear such a man pitied.'" Lamb might have been talking more of himself than Coleridge. He was weary of being called "poor Charles Lamb" on account of his drinking. "You get drunk—and the heartless and the selfish and the lewd crave the privilege of pitying you, and receiving your name with an odious smile."[16]

The Lambs' social schedule was more crowded this summer because they didn't travel. They didn't want to risk another attack. Charles spent his month at home, and by October he was getting on Mary's nerves. As she wrote to Sarah, "He is always in my way." His holiday was to end in five days—and then hers could begin. She planned to travel to Richmond to spend a week with her old friend Mrs. Burney. She would "read Novels & play at Piquet all day long" (*M*, 3:77).

The big news this autumn was the birth of the Hazlitts' son, also William, on September 26. By mid-January, William Sr. and Sarah had moved to London—19 York Street, Milton's former residence—so that William could earn some money lecturing.

Hazlitt gave talks on the history of philosophy at the Russell Institute, located at No. 55 Great Coram Street in Bloomsbury. The talks were not successful. According to Robinson, Hazlitt "seems to have no conception of the difference between a lecture and a book. What he said was sensible and excellent, but he delivered himself in a low monotonous voice, with his eye fixed on his MS, not once daring to look at his audience; and he read so rapidly that no one could possibly give to the matter the attention it required."[17]

In April 1812 the Hazlitts threw a christening party for their boy. Like many, Benjamin Robert Haydon had reservations about Hazlitt's character but believed the essayist's "parental affections" to be "beautiful," and so he accepted Hazlitt's invitation to the occasion. Haydon arrived on time, at 4:00. Hazlitt was out. Sarah was there, "ill by the fire in a bed gown." "Nothing [was] ready for the guests," and everything wore "the appearance of neglect and indifference." Hazlitt was out looking for a parson, Sarah said. Had he not thought of doing this before? No. Haydon set off to find Hazlitt and came upon him striding in a rage through Queen's Square. No parson. When the two men returned to York Street, no food had been set out, and no guests had come. Eventually, company arrived, namely, "Charles Lamb and his poor sister" followed by all sorts of "odd, clever people." Finally a maid set the table and brought "a dish of potatoes, cold, waxy, and yellow. Then came a great bit of beef with a bone like a battering-ram toppling on all its corners. Neither Hazlitt nor Lamb seemed at all disturbed, but set to work helping each other; while the boy, half clean and obstinate, kept squalling to put his fingers into the gravy. Even Lamb's wit and Hazlitt's disquisitions, in a large room, wainscoted and ancient, where Milton had meditated, could not reconcile me to such violation of all the decencies of life."[18]

On October 26, 1811, Robert Lloyd died. Two weeks later, Lamb published an obituary in the *Gentleman's Magazine* candidly stating that Robert's "constitutional misfortune was an excess of nervous sensibility" that "produced too great a spirit of self-abasement." But Robert was also unselfish, able to recognize good in others, and capable of great continuance of "esteem and love." "It seemed as if the affectionate part of his nature could suffer no abatement." Though not necessarily in possession of "shining talents," Robert "oftentimes let fall, in his familiar talk, and in his letters, bright and original illustrations of feeling, which might have been mistaken for genius, if his own watchful modest spirit had not constantly interposed to recall and substitute for them some of the ordinary forms of observation, which lay less out of that circle of common sympathy, within which his kind nature delighted to move" (*W*, 1:130–31). (Robert's death was only one of three tragedies to hit the Lloyd family that fall. Thomas Lloyd died on September 12, and Caroline on October 15.)

After Lamb sent the obituary to Charles Lloyd, the older brother sent it to Robert's widow Hannah, along with this commendation of Lamb: "If I loved him for nothing else, I should now love him for the affecting interest that he has taken in the memory of my dearest Brother and Friend."[19]

Lamb could distract himself from his grief by hearing Coleridge lecture. Beginning on Monday, November 18, Coleridge was to lecture on Shakespeare and Milton every Monday and Thursday evening at 7:30, until January 27, 1812. On various nights during this series, Lamb headed north on Middle Temple Lane, took a right on Fleet Street, and then a left onto Fetter Lane, where he found the Philosophical Institution. At any given lecture, he might see Godwin (perhaps accompanied by the fourteen-year-old Mary), Hazlitt, Robinson, Dyer, Rickman, Morgan, and the brilliant scientist and friend of Coleridge, Humphry Davy. It is possible that Lamb was comped extra tickets, since he sent three to his and Mary's friend Matilda Betham, the miniaturist painter and poet.

Coleridge's digressive, provocative, scintillating lectures held the attention of Lamb, sometimes to Coleridge's detriment. On December 5, after Robinson claimed that in one lecture Coleridge ran from "topic to topic without any guide whatever," Lamb responded, "This is not so much amiss. C. said in his advertisement he would speak about the Nurse in Romeo and Juliet, and so he is delivering the lecture in the character of the Nurse."[20]

Five days later, Lamb was more serious. He was dining at Robinson's with Mary and Mrs. Fenwick. Robinson disagreed with Coleridge's claim that

Shakespeare "became everything except vicious." Lamb retorted that "Shake-speare never gives characters wholly odious and detestable." Iago and Rich-ard III, though they are horrible, are nonetheless "interesting" because they are not simply malevolent. The same is true of Lady Macbeth, whose "sleep-walking does not suit so hardened a being," and Edmund in *Lear,* whose malice is "the result of provocation on account of his illegitimacy."[21]

In Robinson's January 17, 1812, diary entry, we find Charles again defend-ing Coleridge, this time against Hunt. Charles "soon became tipsy, [and] in his droll and extravagant way abused every one who denied the transcendent merits of Coleridge's writing."[22]

But the new year darkened. At a card party at Captain Burney's, Mary showed Robinson and the other guests the *Quarterly Review*'s notice of Henry William Weber's *The Dramatic Works of John Ford.* Weber had cited Lamb's remarks on Ford, and the reviewer, William Gifford, condemned them as "the blasphemies of a maniac."[23] Aware of the damage this insult would do the Lambs, Southey explained to Gifford the Lamb family history. Had he known the facts, Gifford responded, he would rather lose his right arm than call Lamb a "maniac." Three weeks later Mary was ill.

Lamb had other reasons to dislike Gifford. Like Lockhart, who viciously attacked Hunt and the Cockney School, Gifford was an aggressive Tory critic. He used the *Quarterly Review*, which he edited, to hack away at radicals, including Hunt, Hazlitt, Shelley, and Keats. It was the *Quarterly* that pub-lished a review of Keats so harsh that Byron and Shelley thought it killed him. (Keats "is a copyist of Mr. Hunt; but he is more unintelligible, almost as rugged, twice as diffuse, and ten times more tiresome and absurd than his prototype, who, though he impudently presumed to seat himself in the chair of criticism, and to measure his own poetry by his own standard, yet generally had a meaning.")[24]

Gifford and Lockhart were right-wing cultural warriors who believed that their journalism helped hold the center in place. They, along with the mad king and the corrupt Prince Regent they supported, had good reason to fear the crumbling of the old orders. Economically, England was in terrible shape. The cost of the long Napoleonic Wars had drained the government's coffers, and thousands of demobilized soldiers were unemployed. Whigs and radicals were pushing for Catholic emancipation and the reform of Parliament. So afraid was the government of a revolution that habeas corpus had been sus-pended since 1799.

But jailing alleged traitors without reading them their rights didn't squelch rebellion. In 1811, textile workers in Nottingham, Yorkshire, and Lancashire, already struggling under the brutal economy, feared that new machines would make their manual labor obsolete. Over the next two years, many of these workers, calling themselves Luddites, destroyed factory machinery. The British Army engaged the Luddites several times. In January 1813, authorities rounded up sixty men in Yorkshire for a mass trial. When some found guilty were sentenced to be executed, the movement slowed.

On May 11, 1812, at 5:15 p.m., the Tory prime minister Spencer Perceval stepped into the lobby of the House of Commons. He had arrived for the Inquiry into the Orders in Council. Just as he crossed the threshold, a man strode toward him, drew a pistol, and shot Perceval in the chest. He went down, saying as he fell, "Oh my God," or maybe "murder." He died minutes later. This was the first and last time a British prime minister was assassinated. The killer was John Bellingham, a merchant who believed the government should compensate him for the time he had been imprisoned in a Russian jail.

(The day of the assassination, Robinson rushed to Coleridge's. He found Lamb there. Coleridge was "shocked" "exceedingly," while "C.L. was apparently affected, but could not help mingling with humour his real concern at the event, for he talked of loving his Regent.")[25]

On November 15 and December 2, 1816, followers of the radical Thomas Spence, who believed in common property, gathered at Spa Fields, Islington. About ten thousand Spenceans gathered the first day, twenty thousand the second. They were there to petition the regent to relieve the country's distress. During the second gathering, a breakout group marched toward the Tower of London. Troops met the protestors at the Royal Exchange and arrested some of them. One protestor was stabbed in the incident, and one man who stole a gun was sentenced to death. After the Spa Fields Riots, Parliament passed the Seditious Meeting Act, making it illegal for over fifty people to gather for a meeting.

The greatest threat to the stability of the regency occurred on August 16, 1819, at St. Peter's Field, Manchester. A crowd of some seventy thousand had gathered to demand reform in parliamentary representation. Local authorities enlisted the Manchester and Salford Yeomanry to arrest the leaders. The yeomanry galloped into the crowd. Before reaching the protestors, the riders knocked a woman down and killed a child. Next the Fifteenth Hussars charged into the people, injuring over four hundred and killing fifteen. The papers ironically compared this "battle" to Waterloo; thus the event became known as Peterloo. Instead of heeding the unrest of the masses, and working for reform, the government passed the so-called Six Acts, designed to silence protest.

This was the dangerous political climate into which the ridiculous Charles Lamb, who would do anything for a laugh, released his devastating satire of the Prince Regent, "The Triumph of the Whale." Did Gifford the Tory spur Lamb to enter the political arena and fight back? The poem mocks the prince's corpulence ("blubber"), womanizing ("mermaids delight his fancy"), drunkenness, and susceptibility to flattery. "Is he the Regent of the Sea?" What should naturalists call the oily bulk? The "PRINCE OF WHALES" (W, 5:43).

On March 16, 1812, the day after the poem was printed in the *Examiner*, Lamb was with Robinson, who found Charles "in his best humour—very good-humoured, but at the same time solid." His poem encouraged the conversation to "take more a political turn than usual with Lamb." Hunt was there, "an enthusiast, very well-intentioned, . . . prepared for the worst." The editor said, "pleasantly enough, 'No one can accuse me of not writing a libel. Everything is a libel, as the law is now declared, and our security lies only in their shame.'"[26]

Once Hunt was incarcerated in Horsemonger Lane in February 1813, Charles and Mary called frequently. Hunt said to other visitors, "But what return can I make to the L.s, who came to comfort me in all weathers, hail or sunshine, in day-light or in darkness, even in the dreadful frost and snow of the beginning of 1814? I am always afraid of talking about them, lest my tropical temperament should seem to render me too florid."[27]

Lamb expressed his own love in a poem to Hunt's four-year-old son, Thornton Leigh Hunt, in jail with his father.

> Guileless traitor, rebel mild,
> Convict unconscious, culprit child!
> Gates that close with iron roar
> Have been to thee thy nursery door. (W, 1:42)

About six months earlier, in August 1812, Lamb inherited property. Francis Fielde—Lamb's godfather, a successful oil merchant, a lover of Latin phrases, and the procurer of the tickets to Lamb's first play—left his wife three-quarters of an acre in West Hill Green, Buntingford, Hertfordshire. A cottage stood on the grounds. Mrs. Fielde bequeathed the property to Lamb, who rented it to one Mr. Sargus. Lamb might have named the property Button Snap. He sold it in February 1815 for £50.

Lamb didn't need a financial windfall to feel generous. A couple of months later, he showed Hazlitt the same kindness he would exhibit to Hunt. On October 4, he wrote a letter to John Dyer Collier, a friend and the foreign editor of the *Morning Chronicle*, recommending Hazlitt as a parliamentary reporter (*M*, 3:85–86). The plan worked. Collier persuaded the paper's editor, James Perry, to interview Hazlitt, who got the job, thus entering a rare stretch of steady, salaried employment.[28]

Lamb opened 1813 with the harrowing "Confessions of a Drunkard." He published it in January in the *Philanthropist*, edited by William Allen, a Quaker, whose associate was James Mill, father of John Stuart. Lamb's friend Basil Montagu, a contributor, probably connected Lamb with Allen. The piece was published anonymously, probably because Lamb didn't wish to be seen throughout London as a drunkard. But it is hard to imagine Lamb's friends not recognizing him as the author. Robinson, for one, remarked the striking closeness of Lamb and the drunkard: it "will hardly be thought so near a correct representation as it really is."[29]

Why would Lamb publish such a raw, vulnerable, potentially scandalous essay at this point in his life? Compared to what he'd written before, it appeared to come out of nowhere. But look at Lamb's life in 1813. He is thirty-eight. When male life expectancy is about forty, this is decline. What has he accomplished? He began well enough, at twenty-three publishing accomplished verse and a not unsuccessful novel. By twenty-seven, he was writing for two of the leading newspapers in London, and he completed a promising sketch of urban experience, "The Londoner." But then his play *John Woodvil* was rejected, and soon after, his journalism was discontinued. Then *Mr. H.* failed. Lamb enjoyed some success with his children's books but he felt this genre was beneath him, and not likely to call forth his true talent: comedy. (He complained to Robinson of his writing for juveniles: "Sense for humour . . . is extinct.")[30] By 1811, he was done with the genre. His *Specimens* did not sell well; indeed, it was barely noticed. Moreover, it was not an original work, just a gathering of passages from greater literary men. His essays for the *Reflector* showed immense potential—especially the ones on Shakespeare and Hogarth—but the magazine went under after only four numbers, and it was associated with a notorious radical doing jail time. And now a prominent reviewer had called Lamb a maniac in print.

Mania had taken over his life. Mary's attacks of madness had sent her away for about a month in seven of the past twelve years. Out of the last six years, she had fallen ill during four. While Mary was confined, Lamb was extremely lonely. But he battled guilt, too; he wished Mary dead. Even when Mary was around, the two languished in low spirits. Charles's moods darkened to Mary's pitch, and the man who spent six weeks in Hoxton in 1795 staggered toward another collapse.

Then there was work. In 1814, he wrote Wordsworth that "puzzling & hurrying, [it] has so shaken my spirits, that my sleep is nothing but a succession of dreams of business I cannot do, of assistants that give me no assistance, of terrible responsibilities" (*L*, 2:136). Lamb was desperate, reckless. He had already risked prison in publishing "The Triumph of the Whale" a few months earlier, and now he was releasing a thinly disguised portrait of a devastating addiction.

But "Confessions of a Drunkard" isn't so aberrant. It's an intensification of the primary theme of "On the Inconveniences Resulting from Being Hanged," "On the Danger of Confounding Moral with Personal Deformity," "On the Custom of Hissing at the Theatres," "On Burial Societies," and "Edax on Appetite": the craving to escape a life of torture, and the impossibility of doing so.

It is too easy to say that the personae of these essays are versions of the historical Charles Lamb: cursed by family tragedy into alcoholism, fantasy, nonsense, and playacting. While these essays grow from Lamb's own experience, they express a more general vision of identity. A self, these essays say, is what you *can't* do. There is a limit imposed upon you by society. But this social determinism, though strong, is not final. If the speakers of the essays are fated, the writer of the essays is not. Lamb creates different personae through which he expresses possibilities society denies him. He proliferates identities, and even if common concerns unite these selves, each persona is distinct to the point of eccentricity. There is no one like a man who's been hanged within seconds of death, and lived, or a man who never gets full, or a man so obsessed with hissing, he anatomizes it. If each character voices despair and longing, he does so from a different angle, with a different mood, and allows Lamb to express his own melancholia in more than one way, and so, even if he can't cure the condition, he can at least enjoy the temporary relief of variety. Burton says that to ease melancholy, you might travel. The motion and the newness pull you out of the solipsism that depression is: I am sad, I am sad that I'm sad, I am sad that I am sad that I am sad, and so on, the infinite self-pitying self-regard of hopelessness. Traveling might break through this fierce concentricity, because it forces you to pay attention to objects outside yourself. Playing other roles, wearing masks, might do the same. What is a mask but a brief portal to another life?

By the time Lamb creates Elia, he has settled on one mask, a mask that is closer to his historical existence than the *Reflector* personae. But if the *Reflector* masks offer different perspectives on the same theme, Elia is a more unified view of different phenomena. There are themes that run through the Elia essays (longing for childhood, relish for the outlandish, affection for the everyday) that manifest in a wide array of contexts: the South Sea House, whist, pork, old china, witches, ears, valentines, Hertfordshire, gallantry, schoolmasters. When Elia pays attention to these things, he does so playfully, ironically, making each experience manifold, dynamic, engrossing, expansive. Perhaps Lamb without the mask of Elia could do the same, but the latitude offered by his fictional alter ego—not limited by societal expectations or personal history—generates possibilities for being that no historical entity can reach.

Lamb republished "Confessions of a Drunkard" in August 1822. This time he was clearer—only somewhat—about the relationship between the drunkard and himself. From August 1820 until that time, Lamb had been publishing his Elia essays every month in the *London Magazine*. Since Lamb was in Paris over the summer of 1822, he was unable to write a new essay for August of that year, and so the editors, John Taylor and J. A. Hessey, decided to print some of Lamb's older writings, but under the name of Elia. They first chose "Confessions of a Drunkard." (Which actually had appeared two times—in the *Philanthropist* in 1813, as we know, but also in Basil Montagu's 1814 teetotaler tract, "Some Enquiries into the Effects of Fermented Liquors," by a Water Drinker.) To the essay, the editors attached a note. After explaining the reasons for publishing the reprint, the note states, "We have been induced . . . to reprint a Thing, which he [Elia] put forth in a friend's volume some years since, entitled the Confessions of a Drunkard, seeing that Messieurs the Quarterly Reviewers have chosen to embellish their last dry pages with fruitful quotations therefrom; adding, from their peculiar brains, the gratuitous affirmation, that they have reason to believe that the describer (in his delineations of a drunkard forsooth!) partly sate for his own picture."[31]

The note, obviously by Lamb, refers to an article in the *Quarterly Review* by Dr. Robert Gooch, who introduces a quote from "Confessions of a Drunkard" in this way: "In a collection of tracts 'On the Effects of Spiritous

Liquors,' by an eminent living barrister, there is a paper entitled the 'Confessions of a Drunkard,' which affords a fearful picture of the consequences of intemperance, and which we have reason to know is a true tale" (*W*, 1:433n).

The *London Magazine* note objects to the idea that the essay is true, and thus an account of an actual person's life—Lamb's. The truth is, Elia "had been reading among the Essays of a contemporary who has perversely been confounded with him, a paper in which Edax (or the Great Eater) humorously complaineth of an inordinate appetite; and it struck him, that a better paper—of deeper interest, and wider usefulness—might be made out of the imagined experiences of a Great Drinker." Elia wants to make up a drinker as Edax portrayed an eater. And so Elia "set to work, and with that mock fervor, and counterfeit earnestness, with which he is too apt to over-realise his descriptions, has given us—a frightful picture indeed—but no more resembling the man Elia, than the fictitious Edax may be supposed to identify itself with Mr. L., its author" (*W*, 1:432). Just as Lamb created the fictional Edax to write a humorous essay on overeating, so Elia fashioned a fictional drunkard to paint an interesting portrait of drinking. But Elia is the drunkard no more than Lamb is Edax.

Elia is treated as if he were as "real" as Charles Lamb but different from Charles Lamb, although Elia is a fiction of Charles Lamb just as Edax is a fiction of Charles Lamb. That's clear enough.

But then the note—by Lamb—dizzies. Elia's essay, not a factual account, is really "a compound extracted out of his long observations of the effects of drinking upon all the world about him; and this accumulated mass of misery he hath centered (as the custom is with judicious essayists) in a single figure." However, "we deny not that a portion of his own experiences may have passed into the picture, (as who, that is not a washy fellow, but must at some times have felt the after-operation of a too generous cup?)—but then how heightened! how exaggerated!—how little within the sense of the Review, where a part, in their slanderous usage, must be understood to stand for the whole!" (*W*, 1 432).

Some of Elia's personal experience probably did inform the essay. How much? We don't know. We do know that the essay is true and not true of Elia, and so it is true and not true of Lamb. But since Elia is Lamb, how much of Lamb is in Elia? And since Elia is a character created by Lamb, how much of Elia is in Lamb? Where do fact and fiction break?

Does it matter? What does matter—to return to Lamb's sense of the imagination, borrowed from Jeremy Taylor, among others—is that Elia imbues

"Confession of a Drunkard" with more semantic energy than it had when anonymous. Now the drunkard might be Elia and might not. If he is Elia, what does this tell us about this character we've come to know over the past two years? If he isn't, what does this tell us about Elia's powers of imagination? If the drunkard is an amalgamation of Elia and not-Elia, then how are we to understand the "I" of the piece? How does his ambiguous nature affect our understanding of the narrative? And how are all these questions impacted when we know that Elia himself is a fiction? Questions proliferate, answers proliferate. This is the mind alive, and not, for a time, melancholy.

CHAPTER 34

֍

# The Melancholy of Tailors

On January 23, 1813, soon after "Confessions of a Drunkard" appeared in the *Philanthropist*, Coleridge's *Remorse* opened in the new Drury Lane Theatre (the older one had burned down in 1809). Lamb wrote the prologue. He emphasized how the spacious, well-equipped theatrical space far surpassed the stages of Shakespeare and other great dramatists of the past, so if the play fails, the author can't blame it on the theater. The play was successful.

By springtime Coleridge was still much on Lamb's mind, mainly because of the poet's continuing feud with Wordsworth. On May 9, Lamb told Robinson that he was skeptical of a concord, because Wordsworth, then in London, standoffish toward his old friend. Lamb also thought Coleridge feared Wordsworth's presence in the city. He was afraid the poet's negative views of him might hurt attendance at his lectures. (He was then lecturing at the Surrey Institution on belles lettres, mostly to Robinson's displeasure.)

In June Lamb published "On Christ's Hospital and the Character of the Christ's Hospital Boys," which he retitled "Recollections of Christ's Hospital" for his 1818 *Works*. The piece appeared in *Gentleman's Magazine*.

Lamb's only other work in this year was a series of brief "Table Talks" for the *Examiner*. He provided brief notes on, among other topics, "Reynolds and Leonardo Da Vinci" (da Vinci's *John the Baptist* has a "more than mortal majesty in the brow and upon the eyelid—an arm muscular, beautifully formed—the long graceful massy fingers compressing, yet so as not to hurt, a lamb more lovely, more sweetly shrinking, than we can conceive that milk-white one which followed Una" [*W,* 1:151]); "The New Acting" ("[Frances Kelly's] judicious attention to her part, with little or no reference to the spectators, is one cause why her varied excellencies, though they are beginning to be perceived, have yet found their way more slowly to the approbation of the public, than they have deserved" [*W,* 1:152]); "Books with One Idea in Them" ("Montaigne is an immense treasure-house of observation, anticipating all the discoveries of succeeding essayists. You cannot dip in him without being struck with the aphorism, that there is nothing new under the sun" [*W,* 1:153]); and "Play-House Memoranda" ("The sitting next a critic is contagious. Still now and then, a genuine spectator is to be found among them, a shopkeeper and his family, whose honest titillations of mirth, and generous chucklings of applause, cannot wait or be at leisure to take the cue from the sour judging faces about them" [*W,* 1:159]).

Not much more of Lamb's activities in 1813 is known, save that Mary suffered another attack, and recovered in Windsor.

The year 1814 proved to be Lamb's year of Wordsworth. On July 3, Robinson and Lamb are walking, via Southgate, to Enfield (where the Lambs would move in 1827). After taking tea there with Unitarian minister Anthony Robinson (no relation to Henry Crabb) and his wife, the men return. "The whole day delightfully fine," Robinson writes, "and the scenery very agreeable. Lamb cared for the walk more than the scenery, for the enjoyment of which he seems to have no great susceptibility. His great delight, even in preference to a country walk, is a stroll in London. The shops and the busy streets, such as Thames Street, Bankside, &c. are his great favorites. He, for the same reason, has no relish for landscape painting." Lamb's "peculiarities are very interesting. We had not much conversation. He hummed tunes, I repeated Wordsworth's 'Daffodils,' of which I have become very fond."[1]

Lamb wrote to Wordsworth about a month later, on August 9. He had just received a copy of *The Excursion* and found it "the noblest conversation poem I ever read. A day in heaven" (*M,* 3:95). (This long narrative poem features several conversations between a poet and a wanderer, a solitary, and a pastor.) Lamb especially enjoyed Wordsworth's description of how it feels to walk into Harrow Church after "a hot & secular day's pleasure." One feels the "instantaneous coolness and calming, almost transforming, properties of a country church just entered—a certain fragrance which it has—either from its holiness, or being kept shut all the week, or the air that is let in being pure country—exactly what you have reduced into words but I am feeling that which I cannot express." Wordsworth's lines about this emotion fixed in Lamb's mind "a monument in Harrow Church . . . with its fine long spire, white as washed marble, to be seen, by vantage of its high site, as far as Salisbury spire itself almost—" (*M*, 3:96–97).

This is the Wordsworth Lamb loves, who sets his didacticism aside and captures the witchy particularities of the everyday, the little shifts, shivers, jostles, clashes we all sense but cannot name. Such ephemeral moments will quicken Lamb's mature essays.

Still, Lamb, with Mary's support, can't help but rib Wordsworth, very gently, about his mountain adoration. Harking back to his great letters of 1801—when he strenuously traded mountains for streets—Lamb admits there is "a deal of noble matter about mountain scenery, yet not so much as to overpower & discountenance a poor **Londoner** or Southcountry man entirely, though Mary seems to have felt it occasionally a little too powerfully, for it was her remark during reading it that by your system it was doubtful whether a Liver in Towns had a Soul to be Saved. She almost trembled for that invisible part of her" (*M*, 3:96).

The Lambs would never trade their London for the Lakes, but they do love their urban parks, particularly Hyde Park, which had recently been ruined by celebrations over the Treaty of Paris, which took place on May 30. A recent celebration, proclaimed by the Regent, has left Hyde a "dry crumbling sand . . . not a vestige or hint of grass ever having grown there, booths & drinking places go all around it for a mile & half I am confident . . . the stench of liquors, *bad* tobacco, **dirty people & provisions**, conquers the air & we are stifled & suffocated" (*M*, 3:96).

When Lamb writes Wordsworth again—September 19—he confesses that Hazlitt has been in possession of his copy of *The Excursion* until two days ago. In the August letter Lamb had noted that he had not been able to read the poem a second time because Martin Burney had borrowed the book. It turned out that Burney passed the book to Hazlitt, who was planning to review the book for the *Examiner*. Hazlitt wouldn't ask Lamb for the poem himself, because the two men had had a misunderstanding about six months back, when Hazlitt "blowed" Lamb up, over what we don't know. The two had not spoken since, so Hazlitt sneakily and rather shabbily enlisted Burney to borrow the book. Now Lamb has the copy back and knows that Hazlitt's comments have "some vigor in them . . . [and wear] a slovenly air of dispatch and disrespect" (*M*, 3:112). Wordsworth would already have known Hazlitt's opinion of the poem, at least partially, since Hazlitt had already published the first two parts of the three-part review in the August 21st and 28th numbers of the *Examiner.* Though the review at this point was far from negative, Wordsworth wanted a resoundingly positive notice, and thought Lamb was the man for the job. Lamb agreed but said his work schedule wouldn't allow him to get to the review for two weeks. Then he would take it on.

Wordsworth enlisted Southey to arrange for Lamb's review to appear in the *Quarterly Review,* an odd choice, given Gifford's earlier attack on Lamb. By October 20, the piece was done. Lamb spent all but ten days of his vacation completing it. He complained to Southey, "I am afraid it is wretchedly inadequate. Who can cram into a strait coop of a review any serious idea of such a vast & magnifict. poem as Excursn—?" (*M,* 3:115).

Lamb could. His review communes with the Miltonic sublime he thrills to in Wordsworth. Nature for Wordsworth isn't simply symbol or emblem. "To a mind constituted like that of Mr. Wordsworth, the stream, the torrent, and the stirring leaf—seem not merely to suggest association of deity, but to be a kind of speaking communication with it. . . . In his poetry nothing in Nature is dead. Motion is synonymous with life. To such a mind . . . the visible and audible things of creation . . . [are] revelations and quick insights into the life within us, the pledge of immortality" (*W,* 1, 163). Lamb believes that the fourth book, "Despondency Corrected," is the best. "For moral grandeur; for wide scope of thought and a long train of lofty imagery; for tender personal appeals; and a *versification* which we feel we ought to notice, but feel it also so involved in the poetry, that we can hardly mention it as a distinct excellence; it stands without competition among our didactic and descriptive verse" (*W,* 1:167). So elevated is the poem, so morally serious, that "those who hate the Paradise Lost will not love this poem. The steps of the great master are discernible in it; not in direct imitation or injurious parody, but in the following of the spirit, in free homage and generous subjection" (*W,* 1:171).

Two months after completing the review, Lamb confessed to Wordsworth that he had written it under duress. He was depressed—a "poor creature"—and hitting the bottle—"I am leaving off Gin." He also struggled to be objective, not simply to write all "Panegyreck" (*M,* 3:125). Still, as Lamb asserted about a week later, on January 7, 1815, the review was, "in point of composition," "the prettiest piece of prose" he had ever written—at least Mary thought so. Sadly, Gifford butchered the essay before printing it in his magazine. What appears is a "spurious" review that Gifford "palm'd upon it for [Lamb's]." "I never felt more vexd in my life than when I read it. I cannot give you an idea of what he has done to it out of spite at me because he once sufferd me to be called a lunatic in his **Thing**" (*W,* 3:128–29).

Lamb needed a good editor, and he found one, though he did not then know it, soon after Gifford wrecked his review. On November 28, 1814, he wrote to John Scott, offering him an essay he originally wrote for Hunt's *Reflector* but could not publish, "owing to the stopping of that work." If Scott were amenable to paying for "occasional trifles of this sort," Lamb would perhaps "trouble" him sometimes (*M,* 3:120).

Scott was the editor of the *Champion*, launched on January 2, 1814. Inaugurated a year earlier and originally called *Drakard's Paper*, the *Champion* positioned itself as a moderate voice. Where the *Edinburgh Review* reflected Whig positions, *Blackwood's* Tory ones, and Hunt's *Examiner* more radical ones, the *Champion* aspired to "a temper of impartiality and a desire to reconcile the various claims of the different orders of society for the common interest of all." For Scott, valid writing must rise "far above the heavy vapors of arbitrary doctrine and the turbulent storms of party spirit."[2]

Scott was born in Aberdeen in 1783 and attended the grammar school there, as did Byron, five years his junior. (Byron and Scott became acquaintances. In Venice in 1819, the two reminisced about their school days, and Scott observed in the *London Magazine* in 1821 that though "Lord Byron's compositions do not entitle him to be called the best of our present poets," "his personal character, and the history of his life have clearly rendered him the most interesting and remarkable of the persons who now write poetry."[3] After Scott's death, Byron, under the initials N.N., contributed £30 toward helping the widow and children.) Not long after school, Scott traveled to London to make his way, and he turned to journalism. Before editing *Drakard's Paper*, he founded the *Censor* and edited the *Statesman*. While editing the *Champion*, he roamed Europe, which triggered *A Visit to Paris in 1814* and *Paris Revisited in 1815 by Way of Brussels, Including a Walk over the Field of Battle at Waterloo*. Thackeray found these books "famous good reading," and Wordsworth said of the second, "Every one of [the] words tells."[4] In June 1815, Scott breakfasted with Wordsworth while the poet was in London. Robinson was in attendance, as was Haydon. Robinson observed of Scott, "He is a little swarthy man" who "talked fluently on French politics." Also, like Haydon (who did not say much but expressed "an animated countenance"), Scott "seemed to entertain a high reverence for the poet."[5] In the end, Haydon did not hold Scott in high reverence, but rather found him an "unhappy man" who "ill used" everyone he knew and beat his wife.[6]

At such a gathering Scott and Lamb probably met, and they discussed Lamb sending Scott some work. In late November 1814, Lamb submitted "On the Melancholy of Tailors." Scott published it, and requested more from Lamb, who wrote to the editor in December asking how much payment he could expect for submitting work quarterly, starting in March. But on December 12, Lamb shut down the deal, since "very particular circumstances have happened to hinder my fulfillment of it at present" (*M*, 3:123).

These circumstances were another of Mary's attacks. On December 11, Robinson observed that Mary had "undergone great fatigue" in completing her essay "On Needlework," published in the *New British Lady's Magazine and Monthly Mirror on Literature and Fashion* in April 1815. She had spoken of "writing as a most painful occupation, which only necessity could make her attempt." Remarkably, she had "been learning Latin merely to assist her in acquiring a correct style."[7] (Robinson was surprised to hear her complain about difficulty composing, since she had demonstrated such "grace and talent" in *Mrs. Leicester's School*, & c.") Between this day and April 20, Mary once again had to be confined, and Lamb was left forlorn. On the 20th, he called on Robinson, late. He sat and smoked his pipe. The night before, Robinson had visited Lamb, who "seemed absurdly grateful for the visit." Robinson had delicately "abstained from inquiring after" Mary.[8]

"On the Melancholy of Tailors" resembles the *Reflector* pieces. It is authored by a fictional character who paints a black mood. But unlike the earlier essays, this one doesn't want to escape the melancholy. The tailor stoically accepts the sorrow of his labor. Also distinct from the *Reflector* work, Lamb employs a third-person narrative, as though the stoicism requires distance between author and subject.

Tailors are "professional" melancholics. "Observe," Burton Jr. (Lamb revived his old pseudonym) writes, "the suspicious gravity of their gait. The peacock is not more tender, from a consciousness of his peculiar infirmity, than a gentleman of this profession is of being known by the same infallible testimonies of his occupation." Have you ever seen a tailor whistle like a "carman" or "brush through a crowd like a baker, or go smiling to himself like a lover?" (*W*, 1:172). The tailor is melancholy because he sits fourteen hours a day in an awkward position, "with his legs crosswise, or decussated," which "among the ancients [is] the posture of malediction." He is also a great eater of cabbage, which "causeth troublesome dreams, and sends up black vapors to the brain." Moreover, he is "sore at being misprized, undervalued, and made a word of scorn" (*W,* 1:175).

If Lamb's *Reflector* essays are psychological portraits of eccentrics, this piece parodies the very idea that we can understand the causes of moods. To attribute the tailor's melancholy to sitting, cabbage, and shame is absurd.

The essay suggests that our theories (even those of Burton and Browne) aren't subtle enough to explain feelings. This is unfortunate if you are low-spirited. If you can't know the cause of your sorrow, you can't know the cure. You must resign yourself to your fate, as tailors do: they keep on sewing regardless of how they feel.

Lamb might as well be a tailor. He is melancholy, and he sits all day. He feels shame over his family's manias. He makes textiles, texts. He does his job despite his chronic depression.

"On the Melancholy of Tailors" signifies a major development in Lamb's essay writing. To the confessional personae of the earlier essays, he adds a more distanced, satirical mask. Burton Jr. reveals nothing about himself, and this lack of personal implication allows him to stand to the side and mock intellectual arrogance.

Six years later, when John Scott, as editor of *London Magazine,* reaches out to him again, Lamb will combine these two forms of mask—the confessional and the satirical—into Elia, who vacillates between raw expression and bemused mockery, and who sometimes, when he is at his most vital, combines the two, making readers wonder if they should cry or laugh—or both at once.

# CHAPTER 35

# Which Is the Gentleman
# We Are Going to Lose?

One night back in the autumn of 1814, Charles and Mary "were distressed by the cries of a cat." They seemed to originate from garrets adjoining their rooms at No. 4 Inner Temple. But wait—the sound was coming from behind a locked door in Charles's bedroom. The lock was broken open, and "poor puss" scampered out from "behind a panel of the wainscot" (*M,* 3:117). She became a pet. Charles and Mary were thankful to her for revealing four secret rooms.

The siblings put up clothes-drying lines in one. Charles moved his bed into one larger than his current bedroom. And he turned another of these rooms into a writing space, sufficiently tucked away to where he would not be so frequently interrupted by "friends who were more at leisure than himself." He would not be able to hear the knock on the door, or himself "denied to be at home," which was sure to make him call "out and convict the poor maid in a fib." He could now, as Mary put it, be home and not at home. She "put in an old grate, and made him a fire in the largest of these garrets, and carried in his own table and one chair, an[d] bid him write away and consider himself as much alone as if he we[re] in a n[e]w lodging in the midst of Salisbury Plain, or any other wide, unfrequented place where he could expect few visitors to break in upon his solitude" (*M,* 3:117).

Though Mary left Charles "quite delighted with his new acquisition," "in a few hours he came down again, with a sadly dismal face. He could do nothing, he said, with those bare whitewashed walls before his eyes. He could not write in that dull unfurnished prison!" (*M*, 3:117).

The next day, before Charles returned from the office, Mary "gathered up various bits of old carpeting to cover the floor; and to a little break the blank look of the bare walls [she] hung up a few old prints that used to ornament the kitchen." She showed Charles her decorating after dinner (*M*, 3:117).

Her choices inspired them both. They got busy covering the walls with prints that Charles cut from print books in his "old library." He had to ask Mary's permission for each cutting, though, as she was the "older sister." "There was such pasting, such consultation upon these portraits, and where the series of pictures from Ovid, Milton, and Shakspeare would show to most advantage, and in what obscure corners authors of humble rank should be allowed to tell their stories." "The poor despised garret is now called the print room, and is become our most familiar sitting-room" (*M*, 3:118).

In January 1815, William Evans, a colleague of Lamb's at East India House and the owner of the *Pamphleteer*, held a dinner to which he invited his friend Thomas Noon Talfourd, a law student in the Temple. Talfourd greatly admired Lamb, and the supper was set so he could meet his hero. But Talfourd's responsibilities detained him, and he couldn't make the event. He trudged to Evans's in the snow anyway, arriving at 10:00, just as Lamb was leaving. Lamb remained, half out of kindness, before accompanying Talfourd to their "common home, the Temple." Lamb "stammered out fine remarks as they walked; and when we reached his staircase, he detained me with an urgency which would not be denied, and we mounted to the top story . . . [and] we were soon seated beside a cheerful fire; hot water and its better adjuncts were before us." Lamb smoked, both men drank, and they "discoursed . . . of life and death, and our anticipation of the world beyond the grave. Lamb spoke of these themes with the simplest piety, but expressed his own fond cleavings to life—to all well-known accustomed things—and a shivering (not shuddering) sense of that which is to come."[1] They finally parted at 2 a.m.

Talfourd didn't see Charles again for a few months, even though he lived only the next staircase over from the Lambs. When the two did meet again, Wordsworth was present, to whom Lamb said, "Give me leave to introduce to you my only admirer."[2]

Talfourd and Lamb remained close, and Talfourd, who became a judge as well as a successful writer, was Lamb's literary executor. He published the first biography of his hero in 1837. To him we owe substantial firsthand material.

The disciple whitewashed, however. Little of Lamb's bitter melancholy comes through, and none of his alcoholism.

Robinson, who saw Lamb frequently during this same time, is a much surer source. January 23: "I went to Lamb; he was glad to see me. He complained of his solitary evenings and that he was harassed by the business of his office, which, with the affliction his sister's illness caused him, renders his life wretched. He is indeed unhappy."[3] February 7: "At 9 I sat with Lamb. He was low-spirited. Miss Lamb's protracted illness and the difficulties in the business of his office almost distract him."[4]

Best to listen to Lamb himself. In early October 1815, he confesses to a friend, "My head is in such a state from incapacity for business, that I certainly know it to be my duty not to undertake the veriest trifle in addition. I hardly know how I can go on. I have tried to get some redress by explaining my health, but with no great success. No one can tell how ill I am, because it does not come out to the exterior of my face, but lies in my skull, deep and invisible. I wish I was leprous, and black-jaundiced skin-over, or that all was as well within as my cursed looks" (*M,* 3:200).

About two weeks later, he reports to another friend that Mary has been in confinement for about five weeks. "She has left me very lonely and very miserable. I stroll about, but there is no rest but at one's own fireside, and there is no rest for me there now. I look forward to the worse half being past, and keep up as well as I can." Fortunately, she "has begun to show some favourable symptoms." But overall the situation is dire. "The return of her disorder has been frightfully soon this time, with scarce a six months' interval. I am almost afraid my worry of spirits about the E. I. House was partly the cause of her illness; but one always imputes it to the cause next at hand; more probably it comes from some cause we have no control over or conjecture of." Her absence in the asylum "cuts sad great slices out of the time, the little time we shall have to live together. I don't know but the recurrence of these illnesses might help me to sustain her death better than if we had no partial separations. But I won't talk of death. I will imagine us immortal or forget that we are otherwise" (*M,* 3:202–3).

Lamb wrote nothing except letters for the remainder of this year; the same was true of the next two years. These three gloomy durations were pretty much the same. Lamb is beat down by work, he collapses into low spirits, his atrabiliousness exacerbates Mary's fragile moods, the stress incites an attack, Lamb is alone and even lower, Mary returns, feels better, the two muster a trip, which often causes Mary's condition to flare. Meanwhile, Lamb drinks, tries to stop, drinks more—the cycle aggravates his melancholy. He socializes to distract himself. He writes letters, most of them quotidian, except for an occasional literary burst, usually for Manning or Wordsworth.

In May 1815, the Lambs visited Mackery End, Hertfordshire, along with Barron Field. Mary was overjoyed to visit the farmhouse where she had spent summers with her great-aunt, back when Charles was an "urchin of three or four years" and she had full control over him, not like now, when he is her "lord & master" and she is no longer an innocent girl escaping her cold mother by going to the great green English country (*M*, 3:159).

That Mary was in rare good spirits during this time is charmingly demonstrated in a letter Charles wrote to Wordsworth three weeks earlier: after referring to Wordsworth's "The Force of Prayer," whose first line is "What good is bootless bene?" (meaning what good is an ineffectual blessing?), he says to Mary, "as if putting a riddle 'What is good for a bootless bean?' to which with infinite presence of mind (as the jest book has it) she answered, a **'shooless pea.'** It was the first joke she ever made" (*M*, 3:148–9).

In August 1815, the Lambs took a Cambridge vacation, at whose conclusion Mary lamented: "Returning home down old Fetter Lane I could hardly keep from crying to think it was all over——Jesus College where Coleridge was——the barbers shop where Manning was—the house Lloyd lived in—the rooms where Charles was with Franklin. I peeped into the window the room was deserted, old chairs standing about in disorder they seemed to have stood there ever since they had sat in them.——I write sad nonsense about these things" (*M*, 3:186).

Soon after returning, the Lambs acquired three black kittens.

In December, Lamb roused himself to write one of his best letters, to Manning, once again on the dizzying difference between the time frames of Europe and Asia:

> Empires have been overturned, crowns trodden into dust, the face of the western world quite changed: your friends have all got old—those you left blooming—myself (who am one of the few that remember you) those golden hairs which you recollect my taking a pride in, turned to silvery and grey. Mary has been dead and buried many years—she desired to be buried in the silk gown you sent her. Rickman, that you remember active and strong, now walks out supported by a servant-maid and a stick. Martin Burney is a very old man. . . . St. Paul's Church is a heap of ruins; the Monument isn't half so high

as you knew it, divers parts being successively taken down which the ravages of time had rendered dangerous; the horse at Charing Cross is gone, no one knows whither,—and all this has taken place while you have been settling whether Ho-hing-tong should be spelt with a—— or a——. For aught I see you had almost as well remain where you are, and not come like a Struldbug into a world where few were born when you went away. Scarce here and there one will be able to make out your face; all your opinions will be out of date, your jokes obsolete, your puns rejected with fastidiousness as wit of the last age. (*M*, 3:204–5)

The Lambs traveled extensively in summer and autumn of 1816. They spent June and July in Calne with John and Mary Morgan. Coleridge had lived with this couple from 1814 until recently, when he moved back to London, where he eventually settled in Highgate with Dr. James Gillman, who would assist Coleridge in managing his opium intake for the remainder of the poet's life. The Morgans, who had known Coleridge from his Bristol days, had kindly housed the broken, homeless man, estranged from his wife and children, on tense terms with the Wordsworths, and enfeebled by opium. Calne, a small pastoral village about ninety miles east of London and thirty miles northwest of Winterslow, suited the damaged genius. It was there that he rallied to dictate, in 1815, his *Biographia Literaria*.

After leaving the Morgans, the Lambs spent two months in Dalston, a rural area of East London, since the time in Calne had restored Charles and Mary to such a degree that they "could not stomach" the city air and required "rusticating" (*M*, 2:224).

At some point during 1816, Hunt introduced the Lambs to the esteemed musician Vincent Novello and his family, with whom Charles and Mary became close friends. The siblings attended many of the musical gatherings the Novellos held at their home at 240 Oxford Street. Other celebrated writers often showed up as well, including Keats and Shelley. Mary Cowden Clarke also frequently listened to the concerts, and she left behind this lovely description of the scene:

The walls simply coloured of a delicate rose tint, and hung with a few choice water-colour drawings by Varley, Copley Fielding, Havell, and Cristall . . . the floor covered with a plain gray drugget bordered by a tastefully designed garland of vine-leaves drawn and embroidered by Mrs. Novello; toward the center of the room a sofa-table strewed with books and prints; and at one end, a fine-toned chamber organ, on which the host preluded and played to his listening friends, when they would have him give them "such delights, and spare to interpose them oft" between the pauses of their animated conversation. Keats, with his picturesque head, leaning against the instrument, one foot raised on his knee and smoothed beneath his hands: Leigh Hunt, with his jet-black hair and expressive mouth; Shelley, with his poet's eyes and brown curls, Lamb with his spare figure and earnest face; all seen by the glow and warmth and brightness of candlelight, when the young musician and his friends assembled in that unostentatious informal fashion which gave zest to professional social intercourse at the then period.[5]

If Lamb's face was earnest, it was because he was trying to maintain composure. In his "Chapter on Ears," he, as Elia, describes his fear of being as overwhelmed by music as the melancholic is by depression. Music assaults his ears and routs his head until there is nothing else and he is no longer *he,* so he must rush from the concert out into the "noisiest places of the crowded streets, to solace myself with sounds, which I was not obliged to follow, and get rid of the distracting torment of endless, fruitless, barren attention." "I take refuge in the unpretending assemblage of honest common-life sounds" (*W,* 2:39).

Aside from rushing into the streets, which stimulate his mind to wander as it will, Elia's best defense against music is his own imagination. At a concert at the Novello's, like the one Mary Cowden Clarke so lyrically conjured,

I stagger under the weight of harmony, reeling to and fro at my wit's end;—clouds, as of frankincense, oppress me—priests, altars, censers, dazzle before me—the genius of [Novello's] religion [Catholicism] hath me in her toils—a shadowy triple tiara invests the brow of my friend, late so naked, so ingenuous he is Pope, and by him sits, like as in the anomaly of dreams, a she-Pope too—tri-coroneted like himself!—I am converted, and yet a Protestant;—at once *malleus hereticorum,* and myself grand heresiarch: or three heresies centre in my person:—I am Marcion, Ebion, and Cerinthus—Gog and Magog—what not?—till the coming in of the friendly supper-tray dissipates the figment, and a draught of true Lutheran beer (in which chiefly my friend shows himself no bigot) at once reconciles me to the rationalities of a purer faith;

and restores to me the genuine unterrifying aspects of my pleasant-countenanced host and hostess. (*W,* 2:41)

The Catholic music inundates Elia's Protestant brain. His language pushes back. He transforms Novello into the pope, and Mrs. Novello into a dreamy female pontiff. Elia himself feels converted to the older Christian faith but somehow remains a disciple of his own newer religion, and so is both converted and not. He is subject to the Catholic pope as well as a kind of pope himself—of his pope-less religion. As heretic to the Catholics, he resembles Marcion, a Gnostic heretic to all Christians, since he believed that the God of the Old Testament is not a real God. But if being a Protestant heretic to Catholics is a positive for this Protestant, then the Marcion to whom he compares himself is positive, too: it is good to rebel against a God overly legal. Elia is Ebion, too, who allegedly believed Jesus to be only a man; and he is Cerinthus, another Gnostic. As these heretics, Elia resembles in the eyes of his Catholic friends Gog and Magog, great enemies of the Hebrews, and so demonic, but also the foes the Hebrews will defeat before the reign of the Messiah, and thus symbols of salvation. Just as Gog and Magog signal apocalypse, the end of natural time and the advent of the divine, so Elia's passage reaches its own ironic (reverse) Armageddon, as his battle between holy music and divine allusion ends, and the profane returns: solid Protestant beer appears, and Elia quaffs; popes and heretics fade and now he appreciates the sweet faces of his familiar hosts.

In the summer of 1817, the Lambs traveled to Brighton, the seaside resort some fifty miles south of London. Mary loved walking among the eldritch hills of the Downs. Mrs. Morgan accompanied the siblings.

In October, Charles and Mary moved from No. 4 Inner Temple Lane to No. 20 Russell Street, Covent Garden, since their Temple dwelling, in need of renovation, had become "inconvenient." They weren't happy about this move. An "ugly wrench," Charles called it. But after the move happened, it felt like the aftermath of a tooth being pulled: relief and ease (*L,* 2:18).

Charles and Mary quickly came to love their new address. From their perch above a brazier's shop at the corner of Bow Street, they are perpetually stimulated by this "place all alive with noise and bustle," where they can enjoy, as Mary reports, "Drury Lane Theatre in sight of our front, and Covent Garden from our back windows." Charles decides that "we are in the individual

*Covent Garden Piazza and Market 1737, Looking West toward St. Paul's Church,*
by Balthazar Nebot. (Courtesy of Wikimedia Commons.)

spot I like best in all this great city. The theatres with all their noises; Covent
Garden dearer to me than any gardens of Alcinous, where we are morally sure
of the earliest peas and 'sparagus; Bow Street, where the thieves are examined,
within a few yards of us. Mary had not been here four and twenty hours before she saw a Thief. She sits at the window working, and casually throwing
out her eyes, she sees a concourse of people coming this way, with a constable
to conduct the solemnity. These little incidents agreeably diversify a female
life." The market is nourishing and sordid, its stalls brimming with fruits
and vegetables, its narrow, labyrinthine passageways, its donkeys braying and
its quarrelsome vendors, its flower girls, some selling primrose bundles at a
penny, others peddling another kind of flower, especially after dark, when the
theatergoers crowd out the market folk (*L*, 2:217–19).

On December 28, 1817, Lamb enjoyed the company of his new friend
John Keats, Leigh Hunt's protégé, at Benjamin Robert Haydon's dinner party,
and asked a question yet unanswered: did British explorer and surgeon Joseph Ritchie "fling" a copy of Keats's *Endymion* into the "midst" of the "great
desert of Sahara?"[6] We will never know. Two years after Ritchie dined with
Lamb, Keats, and Haydon, he died in that desert, succumbing to illness in
Murzak, the capital of Fezzan. That night he had talked of his soon-to-come
quest to discover Timbuktu and had promised, in his drunkenly jovial mood,
to offer Keats's lush verse to the sand.

Lamb was the drunkest man at this gathering, now famous, since it brought together Lamb, Keats, and Wordsworth. Haydon was then esteemed as a painter of grand historical incidents. His *Death of Dentatus* (1808) and *Judgment of Solomon* (1814) had already garnered positive attention, and now, on December 28, 1817, he was finishing his masterpiece, *Christ's Triumphant Entry into Jerusalem*, thirteen feet high by fifteen wide. The fiercely ambitious Haydon viewed his painting as a sublime example of the epic art he championed, as opposed to the portrait painting then au courant. But Haydon did not simply idealize the past. He wanted past and present mutually to energize each other. How better to do this than to paint the faces of luminous contemporaries into ancient scenes? In *Christ's Entry*, Haydon placed Wordsworth to the right of the donkey-riding Christ. The poet stares broodingly down, instancing what Hazlitt called the poet's "drooping weight of thought and expression." [7] Keats appears further to the right and back of the older poet. Every bit the "Fiery Particle," as F. Scott Fitzgerald called him, he is conversing heatedly with a bystander. To the left of Jesus, close to the savior's elbow, is Lamb himself, stunned, as the ironist rarely was in actual life.

Haydon had called his friends to his home in Lisson Grove to celebrate his gigantic canvas. Haydon had known the young Keats, ten years his junior, for a little over a year. (Haydon was thirty-one.) The two rhapsodized over the Elgin Marbles. So impressed was Haydon by the eager poet he cast a life mask for him. Haydon had known Wordsworth a bit longer, since the spring of 1815. Like many of his age, he worshipped the Lake Poet. He cast a mask of him around the time they first met, and later, in 1842, painted Wordsworth on Helvylln. Lamb Haydon had known since 1812, when the two began moving in Hunt's circle. Haydon relished Lamb's "quaint incomprehensibilities." [8] The two found each other funny. As one observer noted, they "were often like boys, so boisterous in their mirth and hilarity." [9]

In his winsome account of the "Immortal Dinner" in his *Autobiography*, Haydon plays the absurd Lamb against the dignified Wordsworth. [10] "Wordsworth was in fine cue and we had a glorious set-to, on Homer, Milton and Virgil. Lamb got exceedingly merry and exquisitely witty; and his fun in the midst of Wordsworth's solemn intonations of oratory was like the sarcasm and wit of the fool in the interval of Lear's passion."

Amid the worshipful attitude toward the solemn Lake Poet, absurdity is a relief, and Lamb knows it. He stares at the poet. "Now . . . you old lake poet, you rascally poet, why do you call Voltaire dull?" The group defends

Wordsworth, perhaps only half seriously, everyone conceding they have all fallen into a mood that would make the philosopher boring.

Lamb sarcastically hails Voltaire as "the Messiah of the French nation," beyond reproach. Then, "in a strain of humour beyond description," he mocks Haydon for putting the head of Newton into *Christ's Entry*. "The fellow . . . believed nothing unless it was as clear as the three sides of a triangle." Keats agrees, and the two rehearse a conceit Keats will make famous in *Lamia*: Newton "has destroyed all the poetry of the rainbow by reducing it to the prismatic colours." The group now sides with Lamb, drinking to "Newton's health, and confusion to mathematics."

The fool is breaking up the king. The dignified Wordsworth is "giving in to all our frolics without affectation and laughing as heartily as the best of us."

Ritchie arrives. Haydon introduces him as the man bound for Timbuktu. Lamb takes no notice, or seems not to, then roars, "Which is the gentleman we are going to lose?" All drink to Ritchie's health.

The group is taking tea when another man joins the party. Earlier in the day he had visited Haydon and, expressing his admiration of Wordsworth, asked if he could attend the party and meet the poet. He had already been in correspondence with Wordsworth in his capacity as the comptroller of stamps. Haydon neglects to tell Wordsworth the man's name. The man asks Wordsworth if he thinks Milton was "a great genius." Keats glances at Haydon, Wordsworth at the comptroller, and Lamb, drunkenly dozing near the fire, turns to the man and asks if he said Milton was a genius. No, the man replies, I asked Wordsworth, and Lamb says, "Then you are a silly fellow." (Or, as Haydon wrote in his more immediate diary, "Sir, I say, hiccup, you are—you are a silly fellow. This operated like thunder!")[11]

Lamb subsides again. The man, after an "awful pause," asks Wordsworth if Newton is a genius. Haydon, Keats, and Ritchie can't conceal their laughter. Wordsworth is bewildered. Lamb pops up, puts a candle to the poor comptroller's head, and says, "Sir, will you allow me to look at your phrenological development?" Lamb then turns his back to the man, and every time the man asks a question, Lamb chants, "Diddle diddle dumpling, my son John Went to bed with his breeches on."

The man tries to recover his dignity. When he realizes that Wordsworth doesn't know who he is, he smugly remarks that he has "had the honour of some correspondence" with the poet. Wordsworth doesn't remember any such correspondence.

"Don't you, sir? I am a comptroller of stamps." As the distributor of stamps for Westmorland (more a sinecure than a job), Wordsworth is actually in this man's employ!

"A dead silence." Into this awkwardness—it had a "visible effect on Wordsworth"—plunges Lamb. "Hey diddle diddle, The cat and the fiddle."

"My dear Charles!" Wordsworth says.

"Diddle diddle dumpling, my son John." Lamb stands again. "Do let me have another look at that gentleman's organs."

Keats and Haydon shuffle Lamb into the painting room, shut the door, and erupt into laughter. They return to the parlor.

The comptroller, whose name is Kingston, is "irreconcilable," wounded, and aloof. But the guests placate him, asking him to stay to supper. By the party's end he has eased, and leaves in "good-humour."

Which is surprising, since throughout dinner Lamb has been hollering from the painting room, "Who is that fellow? Allow me to see his organs once more."

For Haydon, Lamb achieves the "quaint sparkle of lambent humour." It glows over "Wordsworth's fine intonation as he quoted Milton and Virgil" and "Keats' eager inspired look."

This evening remained a high point of Haydon's life, redolent of Elizabethan erudition and wit, and reminiscent of the Last Supper itself, as the men caroused under the artist's colossal vision of Christ.

But when Haydon describes the event some twenty-four years later, it is elegy. "Poor Ritchie went to Africa, and died, as Lamb foresaw, in 1819. Keats died in 1821, at Rome. C. Lamb is gone, joking to the last. Monkhouse is dead, and Wordsworth and I are the only two now living (1841) of that glorious party."

Haydon himself—bedeviled by debt as well as, to quote Stanley Plumly, "the difference between [his] outsized sense of his large-scale ambitions . . . and the reality of the size of his actual talent"—committed suicide five years later.[12] "When a man is no longer anxious to do better," Haydon had written, "then, well, he is done for."[13]

You can find *Christ's Entry* at Mount St. Mary's Seminary in Cincinnati, Ohio.

CHAPTER 36

Works

In December 1823, Lamb as Elia published "Amicus Redivivus," a friend revived, in the *London Magazine*.

The epigraph is from *Lycidas*: "Where were ye, Nymphs, when the re-
morseless deep / Clos'd o'er the head of your loved Lycidas?" In this pastoral elegy, Milton mourns the death of his noble friend Edward King, who
drowned off the Irish coast in 1637. Heroically, the poet finds solace in Christianity. The death of the body is the spirit's life.

George Dyer is as far from Lycidas as you can get: "I do not know when
I have experienced a stranger sensation, than on seeing my old friend G.D.,
who had been paying me a morning visit a few Sundays back, at my cottage
at Islington, upon taking leave, instead of turning down the right hand path
by which he had entered—with staff in hand, and at noon day, deliberately
march right forwards into the midst of the stream that runs by us, and totally
disappear" (*W*, 2:209).

If the heroic mode showcases protagonists transcending bodily limitations—sadness, hunger, sickness, fatigue—the slapstick reveals humans for
what they really are: units of matter that gravity knocks about. Dyer doesn't
rise from a fatal shipwreck in the abysmal sea; he falls into the river outside
Elia's Islington house because he is absentminded and does not look where he's
going. He vanishes swiftly into the brown water. He can't even put up a fight.

As Elia witnesses "such an unreserved motion towards self-destruction in a valued friend," he loses "all power of speculation" (*W,* 2:209). Why speculate before brute gravity? It has no meaning, just as the objects it pushes and pulls have no meaning.

But the random can be liberating. Just as Elia's speculative powers go dark, "some spirit, not [his] own, whirled [him] to the spot" where he needs to be to save his friend. He hoists G.D. onto his back and finds himself "freighted with a load more precious than his who bore Anchises" (*W,* 2:209). He is like the epic hero Aeneas—which really signifies, in this satire, that he is not like Aeneas at all, but the opposite.

Elia finds heroism impossible. "Sundry passers by," "too late to participate in the honours of the rescue," come "thronging in philanthropic shoals," variously prescribing remedies (*W,* 2:209). People are no different than a crowd of fish and, like fish, are unable to revive a nearly drowned man.

But out of the "stifle of conflicting judgments" about remedies, a "bright thought" arises: get the doctor. He appears, "MONOCULUS," the one-eyed, Elia calls him, recalling the Cyclops with whom epic hero Odysseus battled. He is "a grave, middle-aged person, who, without having studied at the college, or truckled to the pedantry of a diploma, hath employed a great portion of his valuable time in experimental processes upon the bodies of unfortunate fellow-creatures, in whom the vital spark, to mere vulgar thinking, would seem extinct, and lost for ever." His "occupation tendeth for the most part to water-practice; for the convenience of which, he hath judiciously fixed his quarters near the grand repository of the stream mentioned, where, day and night, from his little watch-tower, at the Middleton's-Head, he listeneth to detect the wrecks of drowned mortality— partly, as he saith, to be upon the spot—and partly, because the liquids which he useth to prescribe to himself and his patients, on these distressing occasions, are ordinarily more conveniently to be found at these common hostelries, than in the shops and phials of the apothecaries." This worthy physician "passeth by the name of Doctor, and is remarkable for wanting his left eye. His remedy . . . is a simple tumbler, or more, of the purest Cognac, with water, made as hot as the convalescent can bear it." When he finds that his patient is not keen on imbibing the brandy, he drinks it himself. "When the doctor swalloweth his own draught, what peevish invalid can refuse to pledge him in the potion?" This "humane, sensible man" plies the near-drowned with brandy in return for "a slender pittance, scarce enough to sustain life" (*W,* 2:211).

If the essay opens with slapstick undercutting Miltonic grandeur, this section moves in the opposite direction: ostensibly heroic language (archaic diction, Homeric allusion) reveals, through its overstatement, sordid reality: the "doctor" is a half-blind alcoholic conman. In both cases, Elian irony says and unsays at once.

The brandy brings the "dear absentee" back to his senses, and "G.D." rests on Elia's couch. He drunkenly catalogues his various "providential deliverances" from death in the course of his "long and innocent life," and he sings fragments of "deliverance hymns" forgotten since childhood. These bits of song rise up now because G.D.'s heart has become a child's again, since "in the retrospect of a recent deliverance, as in a case of impending danger, acting upon an innocent heart, will produce a self-tenderness, which we should do ill to christen cowardice" (*W,* 2:211).

Elia compares the recovered Dyer to Shakespeare's "good Sir Hugh" Evans from *The Merry Wives of Windsor.* While the ordinary Welsh parson waits to fight a duel, he nervously sings a love song intermixed with scripture. The fear of death returns Evans to his childhood and the music that informed his innocence.

The essay has changed moods. The mock-heroic world indifferent to human suffering has given way to a little friendly recovery room where extreme fear and then relief almost magically lift men from their sad adulthood to childhood, when all was possible, when the cruel "if-then" of experience had not yet hardened. Though the source of the terror or relaxation might be random, and though the saving from death might be accidental, too, the result is redemptive.

This is a deeper irony: in a world mostly meaningless, instances intensely significant still occur, sometimes in the most inopportune situations—such as when one is half drowned and scammed.

Lamb enjoyed a virtually unprecedented late revival, anticipating George Eliot (who published her first novel, *Adam Bede,* at forty) and Raymond Chandler (who released *The Big Sleep,* his first book, at forty-four) as a writer who found his voice past his prime. At the age of forty-three, in the wake of his *Works* being published, Lamb discovered a literary vitality he didn't know he had.

The artist George Francis Joseph uncannily saw this, even if Lamb could not. In 1819, just as Lamb was on the rise, his colleague and friend William Evans, brother of Coleridge's old flame Mary and the man who introduced Charles to Talfourd, envisioned a unique literary project. He would collect miniatures of the writers satirized in Byron's *English Bards and Scotch Reviewers* and interleave the images near where the matching author was named. The image Evans requested from Lamb is radically unlike Hancock's bland profile and Hazlitt's melancholy stare. Joseph in his watercolor displays a ruddy Lamb, his head turned halfway to the right. The nose is smaller, more proportional, and sideburns extend below the ear, trimmed to a point. The earnest gaze reaches into the middle distance. Lamb looks like the virile Byron at forty—if Byron had reached that age. Lamb would never be painted this way again, for the good reason that he lacked the optimism he had at this time.

Lamb's keeping company with Hunt catalyzed his rejuvenation. On April 24, 1818, Hunt wrote to Shelley, "We go to plays, to operas, and even to concerts, not forgetting a sort of conversazione at Lamb's, with whom, and Alsager, I have renewed the intercourse, with infinite delight, which sickness interrupted. One of the best consequences of this is that Lamb's writings are being collected for publication by Ollier, and are now, indeed, going through the press."[1]

Hunt might have encouraged Lamb to publish his *Works* on a night like this, on April 18, when Robinson showed up at Lamb's. "There was a large party,—the great part of those who are usually there, but also Leigh Hunt and his wife. . . . He, tho' a man I very much dislike, did not displease me this evening. He has improved in manliness and healthfulness since I last saw him last, some years ago. There was a glee about him which evinced high spirits, if not perfect health, and I envied his vivacity. He imitated Hazlitt capitally, Wordsworth not so well."[2]

Hunt knew the publisher Charles Ollier well. Along with his brother James, Charles had published Hunt's *Foliage, Hero and Leander,* and the second edition of *The Story of Rimini.* The Olliers met Keats through Hunt and brought out his first collection of poems in 1817. (The book sold poorly, and Keats and his brother George blamed the publishers. The young poet and the Olliers parted company; Taylor and Hessey published the remainder of Keats's poetry books.) The Olliers published most of Shelley's works, too. The brothers were among the primary publishers of the Cockney School.

*Charles Lamb*, by George Francis Joseph. (Courtesy of British Museum Images.)

They released Lamb's *Works* in the summer, in a gorgeous two-volume
sextodecimo with olive-green covers. Lamb dedicated the books to Coleridge, candidly, elegiacally. "It would be a kind of disloyalty to offer to anyone
but yourself a volume containing the *early pieces*, which were first published
among your poems, and were fairly derivatives from you and them." But
then Lloyd came along, and Lamb wrote a volume with him. How did the
connection among Coleridge, Lloyd, and himself break? Lamb doesn't know,
but "wanting the support of [Coleridge's] friendly elm (I speak for myself),
my vine has, since that time, put forth few or no fruits; the sap (if ever it had

any) has become, in a manner, dried up and extinct; and you will find your old associate, in his second volume, dwindled into prose and *criticism.*" As we age, life loses its poetry. "We transcribe but what we read in the great volume of Nature; and, as the characters grow dim, we turn off, and look another way. You yourself write no Christabels, nor Ancient Mariners, now" (*W,* 5:1).

This is less a dedication than a farewell to creation. Lamb likely thought this publication would be his last. He had much to be proud of: poems like "The Old Familiar Faces" and "Hester" and the terrifying lines of *Blank Verse,* and essays such as the ones on Hogarth and Shakespeare, "The Londoner," and "On the Melancholy of Tailors." But Lamb's quality and quantity were far from Coleridge's and Wordsworth's respective outputs, and already a younger generation of writers was showing more talent and energy than he—Shelley and Byron, namely (neither of whom Lamb liked), as well as Hazlitt and Keats.

The first volume contained Charles's miscellaneous verse, such as "Hester," "A Vision of the Repentance," "A Farwell to Tobacco," and "To T.L.H. a Child"; sonnets, including the Anna sonnets, "The Family Name," and "To John Lamb, Esq, of the South-Sea-House"; *Blank Verse*; *John Woodvil*; the Burton "Curious Fragments"; *Rosamund Gray*; "Recollections of Christ's Hospital"; and poetry by Mary, like "Helen." In the second volume, Charles placed his criticism, including his essays on Shakespeare's tragedies, Shakespeare's contemporaries, and Hogarth's genius. He added his "letters," or pieces he wrote under another identity, such as "The Londoner," "On the Inconveniences Resulting from Being Hanged," "On the Melancholy of Tailors," and "Edax on Appetite." Lamb ended his works with *Mr. H.——, a Farce, in Two Acts.*

Writing in his own *Examiner,* Hunt praised the criticism: it is "obviously of a most original cast, and directly informs the reader of a number of things which he did not know before."[3] Lamb's new friend Talfourd lauded the two volumes in the *Champion.* He emphasized Lamb's gentleness. In opposition to "mere strength" in writing, Lamb delights with "glimpses of new and fresh beauty."[4] In *Gentleman's Magazine,* Dyer celebrated the volumes, too, as did anonymous reviewers in the *Monthly Review* and the *European Magazine.*

William Jerdan in the *Literary Gazette* likewise commended Lamb, but he qualified his praise: Lamb holds himself back by remaining close to the Lake Poets. The *British Critic* was similarly mixed, though leaning toward the positive. The same was true, remarkably, of the review from the *Blackwood's* critic, John Wilson, from whom a pan would seem most likely.

The only savaging came late, in 1822, from Lamb's old enemy William Gifford, who had called Lamb a lunatic and a drunkard.

Though not glowing, these reviews were enough to jump-start Lamb. Within two years, he would be sounding reservoirs of genius he didn't know he had, and he would elevate himself to the top level of the Romantic pantheon, right up there with Wordsworth and Coleridge.

CHAPTER 37

᷀᷀᷀

*Fanny*

Gifford's insults didn't surface until Lamb had recovered his energy for writing. Perhaps because the reviews tended to praise the prose over the poetry, Lamb returned to that genre, in particular to criticism. Hunt invited Lamb to write drama criticism in the *Examiner*. This was a genre for which this lover of the theater, well situated across from Drury Lane, was perfectly suited.

Lamb's first piece, unsigned, reviews actress Frances Kelly, whom he had already praised back in 1813, also in the *Examiner*. Then he hailed her ability to immerse herself so deeply into a character that she paid no attention to the audience. Here he does the same, emphasizing how her acting is so natural it doesn't seem to be acting. Her craft is "the joy of a freed spirit, escaping from care, as a bird that had been limed; her smiles, if I may use the expression, seem saved out of the fire, relics which a good and innocent heart had snatched up as most portable." The source of her "fervid, glowing" acting is her "wonderful force of imagination," which liberates her from the constraints of gentility, and enables her to forget herself in her part (*W,* 1:186). We would call this method acting.

Next Lamb reviews Richard Brome's *Jovial Crew,* an opera. Kelly appears in this as well, as a beggar, and about her Lamb writes: "Her gabbling lachrymose petitions; her tones, such as we have heard by the side of old woods, when an irresistible face has come peeping on one on a sudden; with her

349

full black locks, and a *voice*—how shall we describe it?—a voice that was by nature meant to convey nothing but truth and goodness, but warped by circumstance into an assurance that she is telling us a lie . . . her face, with a wild out-of-doors grace upon it." After reporting that an audience member sitting beside him praised Miss Kelly, Lamb, with sexual innuendo, confesses, "We longed to drip a tester in her lap, she begged so masterly" (*W,* 1:187).

The following review also boosts Kelly. Her part as the artificial Charlotte in Isaac Bickerstaff's *Hypocrite* is beneath her, since her "cue is to be natural; she cannot put on the modes of artificial life, and play the coquet as it is expected to be played. . . . She is in truth not framed to tease or torment even in jest, but to utter a hearty Yes or No; to yield or refuse assent with a noble sincerity" (*W,* 1:189).

In his final theater review, Lamb covers recent plays at the Lyceum. Again he singles out Kelly. He has been accused of "flattering her," but "truth is, this lady puts so much intelligence and good sense into every part which she plays that there is not expressing an honest sense of her merits, without incurring a suspicion of that sort" (*W,* 1:190).

Lamb favored two other works, nondramatic, in 1819—those of his friends Jem White (*Falstaff's Letters*) and Charles Lloyd (*Nugae Canorae*)—but not to the extent he praised Kelly. Her acting embodies Lamb's twofold aesthetic, articulated in his essays on Shakespeare and Hogarth. She so fully immerses herself into her roles, her ego disappears. Escaping her identity, she expresses the "drama of real life," not pure comedy or tragedy but the "merriment and infelicity, ponderous crime and feather-light vanity [that] . . . perpetually unite to shew forth motley spectacles to the world" (*W,* 1:77).

Lamb didn't praise Kelly only in prose. In his *Works* he reprinted the sonnet "To Miss Kelly," which had appeared in the *Examiner* in July 1818. Kelly doesn't pander to the audience but retains her "native dignity of thought" by *becoming* her characters: "Your tears have passion in them, and a grace / Of genuine freshness, which our hearts avow" (*W,* 5:40). In the *Examiner* of November 1819, Lamb published another sonnet on Kelly. She had recently played a blind boy. Without using her eyes, "expression's throne," she pressed "powerful'st meanings on the heart" and lent to "blank deformity a grace" (*W,* 1:459).

If Fanny fulfills Lamb's aesthetic ideals—unwittingly, no doubt—Lamb models his mature writing style on Fanny's relaxed, realistic acting. He inhabits his character Elia with the same unaffected vigor, and so blurs the line between reality and artifice, face and mask. The result is great theater: that giddy sense that at any moment the mask might crack and accident gush through, or the wonder of the crazed heart falling into euphonious rhythm.

The older he got, the more Lamb relied on actors as models for his writing. In February 1822, in an Elia essay called "The Older Actors," he admired James William Dodd's ability to dramatize dynamic thinking.

> You could see the first dawn of an idea stealing slowly over [Dodd's] countenance, climbing up by little and little, with a painful process, till it cleared up at last to the fulness of a twilight conception—its highest meridian. He seemed to keep back his intellect, as some have had the power to retard their pulsation. The balloon takes less time in filling, than it took to cover the expansion of his broad moony face over all its quarters with expression. A glimmer of understanding would appear in a corner of his eye, and for lack of fuel go out again. A part of his forehead would catch a little intelligence, and be a long time in communicating it to the remainder. (*W*, 2:136)

In his Elia essays, Lamb attempts a similar revelation of thought. His ideas expand not linearly but multidimensionally, as air slowly fills a balloon, or as water ripples out concentrically from a dropped pebble.

What generates Elia's fanning-out cognition are less thoughts than things: what he looks at—a portal to an old building, a picture in a book, an ear— and how the mind responds. He learned this technique from comic actor Joseph Shepherd Munden, whose eye transforms stuff to splendor. "Who like [Munden] can throw, or ever attempted to throw, a preternatural interest over the commonest daily-life objects? A table, or a joint stool, in his conception, rises into a dignity equivalent to Cassiopeia's chair. It is invested with constellatory importance. . . . The gusto of Munden antiquates and ennobles what it touches. His pots and his ladles are as grand and primal as the seething-pots and hooks seen in old prophetic vision" (*W*, 2:149).

Charles Lamb knew Frances Kelly personally. He was in love with her. Charles and Mary got to know "Fanny" soon after their move to Covent Garden. They met her through Robinson, who found her "an unaffected, sensible, clear-headed, warm-hearted woman."[1] Before this meeting, the siblings had admired her for her craft but also for her courage.

*Miss Frances Maria Kelly*, 1811, Harry Beard Collection.
(© Victoria and Albert Museum, London.)

In the winter of 1816, Fanny started receiving letters from George Barnett, a lawyer's clerk who loathed seeing women wear men's clothes.[2] Fanny
and other actresses often donned male clothing, usually to play young boys.
Audiences enjoyed the comic possibilities of these gender switches, and men
likely relished a rare opportunity to witness the contours of a woman's body.
Men also probably felt their masculinity threatened: the performances suggested that maleness is not inherent, but an act. Barnett feared Fanny, and at
the same time he found her arousing. In one letter, he claimed he loved the
female sex, and had once "esteemed" Fanny "as an ornament to it." Now he

hated her "impertinence and scandalous abuses." She had better not dress as a man anymore, or he would punish her for her "temerity."

Fanny ignored such lunatic epistles. This made Barnett angrier. On February 15, he accused Fanny of "trifling" with his affections. He had a claim to her. She should marry him. If she did not, he would duel with her. His weapon of choice was pistols.

Fanny walked onstage in Drury Lane two days later to act her role in *Modern Antiques*. The play began. The audience settled in; all went smoothly. But then a ruckus in the back broke out. Everyone turned around. There was Barnett aiming a pistol at Frances Kelly. He fired, she dropped, Barnett was subdued, arrested, and removed, and Kelly was carried into the wings. Barnett had missed; the bullet ricocheted and landed in the lap of Mary Lamb. Kelly recovered and returned to the stage. The crowd cheered. Barnett spent the rest of his life in Bedlam.

Lamb appreciated Kelly's more longer-lived acts of bravery. Her apothecary father was a drunkard who abandoned the family. The talented Fanny took to the stage at eight to support her mother and three siblings. Her honesty trumped comfort. As she reported to Lamb, and as he recorded in his Elia essay "Barbara S.———," when her manager once inadvertently added an extra half a guinea to her salary, she returned the surplus, even though the family needed the money desperately. She was horrified when the manager pocketed the money nonchalantly, as if it meant nothing.

As an adult, Fanny continued to work hard at a profession that offered few rewards. Actresses didn't make much money—even less than their not-well-paid male counterparts—and struggled with an image problem. They were not much higher on the social scale than prostitutes.

Sketches of Fanny reveal a woman of calm intelligence. If her face is not traditionally beautiful, it is pert and smart, ringed by black curls. Charles admired her "divine plain face" (*L*, 2:225). Another contemporary found "her face . . . round and pleasing, though not handsome; her eyes are light blue; her forehead is peculiarly low . . . her smile is peculiarly beautiful and may be said to completely *sun* her countenance" (quoted in *W*, 1:159).

In the commonplace book he made out of the two volumes of Holcroft's *Travels*, Lamb glued on page 403 of volume 2 a professional drawing of Fanny. Her expression is an intriguing mix of intelligence and smugness. She looks like she could handle Lamb's wit and give back as good. The portrait is attached to a notice: Miss Kelly the famous actress is traveling to Bath to ply her craft.

When did Charles fall in love with Fanny? Did he express his affection for her, or flirt with her, during their many shared social outings? Did he ever mention his affection to Mary? We can't know.

Nothing prepares for the letter he wrote Fanny on July 20, 1819. After praising her performance in last night's play and acknowledging how grueling her life is, he exclaims, "Would to God you were released from this way of life; that you could bring your mind to consent to take your lot with us, and throw off forever the whole burden of your profession. I neither expect nor wish you to take notice of this which I am writing, in your present over occupied and hurried state—but to think of it at your leisure." "I have quite income enough if that were all, to justify for me making such a proposal, with what I may call even a handsome provision for my survivor. What you possess of your own would naturally be appropriated to those, for whose sakes chiefly you have made so many hard sacrifices." He acknowledges that he might not be a worthy match for her, but he has long held her as a "principal object" in his mind. He has loved her in her characters but loved her better as "F. M. Kelly." "Can you quit these shadows of existence, and come and be a reality to us? Can you leave off harassing yourself to please a thankless multitude, who know nothing of you, and begin at last to live to yourself and your friends?" Please answer me, and if you refuse, I will not be aggrieved, and I will never speak of the matter again. But he hopes there will be a time when "our friends might be your friends; our interests yours; our book knowledge, if in that inconsiderable particular we have any like advantage, might impart something to you, which you would every day have it in your power ten thousand fold to repay by the added cheerfulness and joy which you could not fail to bring as a dowry into whatever family should have the honor and happiness of receiving *you*, the most welcome accession that could be made to it" (*L*, 2:254).

Fanny replied quickly to this odd proposal, which offers a brother-sister team—note the use of first-person plural pronouns—more than a husband, and financial security and book learning more than love. Her refusal, though well mannered, is candid—and conclusive. "An early and deeply rooted attachment has fixed my heart on one from whom no worldly prospect can well induce me to withdraw it, but while I thus *frankly* and decidedly decline your proposal, believe me, I am not insensible to the high honour which the preference of such a mind as yours confers upon me." But here this thing ends: "Let me, however, hope that all thought upon this subject will end with this letter, and that you will henceforth encourage no other sentiment towards me than esteem in my private character and a continuance of that approbation of my humble talents which you have already expressed so much and so often to my advantage and gratification" (quoted in *L*, 2:225).

Surely Charles did not think he had a great chance. This was an attractive, vivacious, sexy, famous woman who could court most any man she wanted. The married Earl of Essex implored her to be his kept mistress. What would she see in a man fifteen years her senior who, though witty and kind, had a well-known drinking problem and chronic low spirits? Then there was Mary, with whom a wife would have to live, and whose attacks she would have to manage.

The latter factor definitely influenced Fanny's decision. As she wrote to her sister later, she was "sorry to refuse" Lamb, since "he shows the most tender and loyal affections." But even though she might cause him "great despondency," she had no choice but to say no. "I could not give my assent to a proposal which would bring me into that atmosphere of sad mental uncertainty which surrounds his domestic life. Marriage might well bring us both added causes for misery and regrets in later years."[3] She could not imagine living with Mary's fits. Perhaps she feared bearing children who might inherit the Lamb madness. Maybe she was afraid of getting stabbed.

Charles took the rejection stoically. The same day Fanny refused, he assured her that her injunctions never to speak of the matter "*shall be obeyed to a tittle*." He falls back, rather pitifully, on his comic persona, trying to distance himself from the pain. "I had thought to have written seriously, but I fancy I succeed best in epistles of mere fun: puns & *that* nonsense." Will you still be glad to be friends with "us"? he asks. "Let what is past 'break no bones' between us. You will not refuse us them next time we send for them?" (*L*, 2:255).

The pun is offbeat even for Lamb. "Bones" refers to ivory tickets given out by cast members to friends. Lamb is saying he hopes Fanny will continue to give him these tickets so he can see her act. But "bones" also refers to Fanny's skeleton, which Lamb hopes will visit when he invites her. Lamb intends this playfully, but to equate Fanny with her bones suggests both an untoward intimacy with her interiors and a wish that she were dead.

This was not the first time Lamb punned on bones and Fanny. Eleven days before his proposal, he invited her to his house by saying, "If your Bones are not engaged on Monday night, will you favor us with the use of them?" If you will come, "you will break no bones of it." He lists other women whose bones he cannot get. If you can't come, "God rest your bones." He puns on his pun: he is at "the end of [his] bon-mots" (*L*, 2:253).

Charles never stopped loving Fanny. Ten years later, she wrote that even strangers noted "the great attention he paid to every word she uttered." Fanny clearly appreciated this abiding attention; she continued to socialize with the Lambs, exuberantly. As late as 1834, on a visit to Mary and Charles out in Edmonton, she expressed "a child's delight in wild flowers" and a "passion for little frogs."[4]

# CHAPTER 38

☙❦☙

# *The* London Magazine

Despite his revival as a writer, Lamb was weary of being Lamb, and one reason he proposed to Fanny is that being the "husband of Frances Kelly" would have given him a new identity.

In February 1818, he wrote to Dorothy Wordsworth that he can't compose letters from home—this one he pens in East India House—since he is "never alone," "except my morning's walk to the office." "I cannot walk home from the office but some officious friend offers his unwelcome courtesies to accompany me. All the morning I am pestered. I could sit and gravely cast up sums in great books, or compare sum with sum, and write 'paid' against this, and 'unpaid' against t'other, and yet reserve in some corner of my mind 'some darling thoughts all my own,'—faint memory of some passage in a book, or the tone of an absent friend's voice—a snatch of Miss Burrell's singing, or a gleam of Fanny Kelly's divine plain face." He can mentally multitask until "amateurs of the Belles Lettres . . . come to me as a sort of rendezvous, putting questions of criticism, of British Institutions, Lalla Rookhs, &c.—what Coleridge said at the lecture last night—who have the form of reading men. . . . These pests worry me at business, and in all its intervals, perplexing my accounts, poisoning my little salutary warming-time at the fire, puzzling my paragraphs if I take a newspaper, cramming in between my own free thoughts and a column of figures, which had come to an amicable compromise but for them." He can't escape these hangers-on at home. Just as he sits down to eat, there is a knock,

357

and "in comes Mr.——, or Mr.——, or Demi-gorgon, or my brother, or somebody, to prevent my eating alone—a process absolutely necessary to my poor wretched digestion. O, the pleasure of eating alone!—eating my dinner alone!" (*L,* 2:225). "I am never C.L., but always C.L. & Co" (*L,* 2:226).

Lamb doesn't harbor animosity toward these "good creatures" who are so "anxious to drive away the harpy solitude from me." "I like 'em, and cards, and a cheerful glass." He simply wants to let Dorothy and William know how "little time I can call my own" (*L,* 2:227).

Lamb wishes he could escape all this by accepting Dorothy's invitation to the Lakes—she "haunts him with visions of seeing the lakes once more"— but he can't. The distance between the Wordsworths and the Lambs—geographical and psychological—is too great. But this gulf is not "inexplicable moral antipathies and distances, as there seemed to be between me and that gentleman concerned in the Stamp Office that I so strangely recoiled from at Haydons" (*L,* 2:227–28).

Lamb "hate[s] all such people—accountants' deputy accountants. The dear abstract notion of the East India Company, as long as she is unseen, is pretty, rather poetical; but as she makes herself manifest by the persons of such beasts," "I loathe and detest her as the scarlet what-do-you-call-her of Babylon" (*L,* 2:228). Moreover, the company has cut back on holidays, and no longer allows workers to leave early, at 1:00, on Saturday.

In this same year, Lamb will write to a colleague, John Chambers, that "the Committee have formally abolish'd all holydays whatsoever—for which may the Devil, who keeps no holydays, have them in his eternal burning workshop." Worse, the company now polices workers when they are at the office. "We are . . . to sign our names when we go as well as when we come, and every quarter of an hour we sign, to show that we are here" (*L,* 2:231). Lamb did not dare break these rules; the consequences could be dire. It was around this time that Lamb's colleague Tommy—"a pleasant, gossiping, half-headed, muzzy, dozing, dreaming walk-about, inoffensive chap; a little too fond of the creature"—got his salary viciously reduced by five-sixths because he came to work drunk (*L,* 2:246–47).

The Lambs tried to fix the problem of too much London society by living part of the year in Dalston, far enough away for tranquility, but close enough for Lamb to walk to work. Perhaps for a time they alternated weeks between "quiet rest and dear London weariness" (*L,* 2:273).

Mary never took to Dalston, regardless of its pastoral calm. "Flowers are flowers still, and I must confess I would rather live in Russell Street all my life, and never set my foot but on London pavement, than be doomed always to enjoy the pleasures I now do" (*L*, 2:273).

Perhaps Fanny appeared to the petulant Charles as a potential source of stability. What had given him pleasure in life no longer did, and what else was there except more of the deadening same or else a radical change? But Fanny, whom he likely saw as his last chance for deliverance from the same dull round, had said no, and now what was there?

Deliverance for Charles came in the summer of 1820 in the person of his old acquaintance John Scott, in whose magazine, the *Champion*, he had published "Confessions of a Drunkard."

The end of 1819 boded well. William and Mary Wordsworth's nine-year-old son Willy stayed with the Lambs, and he delighted them. The boy adored Waterloo Bridge, and "remarked that if we [in London] had no mountains, we had a fine river at least." He was sorry that the lion in the menagerie near the Exeter 'Change didn't meet his "ideal standard." ("So impossible it is," Lamb observed, "for Nature in any of her works to come up to the standard of a child's imagination.") Willy also lamented the deaths of the lioness's cubs, as well as the poor-looking "Ouran Outang," who had "gone the way of all flesh also." Willy's cheeky humor compensated for these disappointments. Lamb saw "the future satirist in him, for he hath a sub-sardonic smile which bursteth out upon occasion, as when he was asked if London were as big as Ambleside, and indeed no other answer was given, or proper to be given, to so ensnaring and provoking a question" (*L*, 2:265).

The year 1820 began with clarity, with Lamb finally perceiving—as he wrote to Coleridge—that Charles Lloyd is a "sad Tattler" who "twenty years ago . . . estranged one friend [Coleridge] from me quite" (*L*, 2:267). By May he was happily anticipating seeing Dorothy Wordsworth in London with her new false teeth, which would enable "Eating, Talking, Biting," but hopefully not "gnashing" (*L*, 2:278). Her brother joined her in the city in June, much to Lamb's pleasure. And in July Charles and Mary traveled again to their beloved Cambridge.

In August Lamb breaks into a new life. He announces to Barron Field that the world will soon have something fresh, "a tissue of truth and fiction impossible to be extricated, the interlacings shall be so delicate, the partitions perfectly invisible, it shall puzzle you till you return, & [then] I will not explain it" (*L*, 2:282). Thus Lamb describes Elia, on the threshold of his electrifying debut in the *London Magazine*.

After taking a hiatus from publishing to travel in France, John Scott accepted from Robert Baldwin the editorship of the *London Magazine*. The publishers wanted to revive the famous *London Magazine* of the eighteenth century, which ran from 1732 to 1785. Like the earlier publication, which opposed the Tory *Gentleman's Magazine*, Scott's would antagonize the conservative *Blackwood's*.

In his prospectus, Scott proclaims that he and the publishers have been "induced to revive the title of the once well-known but discontinued magazine and to appropriate it to our new undertaking, in consequence of its occurring to us as singular, that, while secondary towns of the Kingdom give name and distinction to popular Journals, the Metropolis should remain unrepresented in the now strenuous competition of Periodical Literature. This circumstance has induced us to enter the lists under the auspices of LONDON. And one of the principal objects of the LONDON MAGAZINE will be to convey the very 'image, form, and pressure' of that 'mighty heart' whose vast pulsations circulate life, strength, and spirits throughout this great Empire." Scott's primary goal is to "catch, condense, and delineate" the "present time." To that end, his magazine will be a "miscellany" "conspicuous for its alertness to noticing matters of immediate interest" and the entertaining "variety of its contents."[1]

The first number, published in January 1820, was true to this vision. You could find articles on the state of Italy in 1818–19, on two of its greatest cities, Rome and Venice, and on tombstones in Paris. There were critical essays on John Clare and Sir Walter Scott, as well as a piece on how religion influences "Patriotic Feeling in Literature." There were poems—"The Traveller" and "Farewell to England"—and there were notices of recent plays, discussions of fine art, gleanings from foreign literature, public documents from Parliament, takes on public manners, and descriptions of new books and books in process.

Scott dove hard into the rough-and-tumble world of London magazines. He acknowledged the competition—he would be going toe-to-toe with *Blackwood's,* the *Quarterly Review,* the *Examiner,* and the *Edinburgh Review*—and he was ready for a fight. He recruited writers whose charged urban prose would explode the columns of his rivals.[2]

The writers Scott published in the *London Magazine*—among them Lamb, Hazlitt, and De Quincey—were required to see themselves as *magazine* writers. Their essays would most likely be transient, never reaching the more permanent form of a book. Moreover, they would be *about* ephemeral subjects: what's hot in London this minute, what's not.

Lamb seems wrong for this kind of writing. He adored books *because* they described eccentric worlds of yore. He was antiquarian through and through, with his old-fashioned black suit, aged fountains and sundials, affection for London's odd forgotten past. In *Spirit of the Age*, Hazlitt highlights Lamb's unsuitability for the faddish magazine world. Lamb "has none of the turbulence or froth of new-fangled opinions." He is "the very soul of an antiquarian . . . shy, sensitive, the reverse of every thing coarse, vulgar, obtrusive, and commonplace." But Lamb's contrariness to the present actually makes him a powerful contemporary voice. His taste for the past inspires love for the local London spots that informed his childhood: "With what a gusto Mr. Lamb describes the inns and courts of law, the temple and Gray's-Inn, as if he had been a student there for the last two hundred years. . . . The streets of London are his fairy-land, teeming with wonder, with life and interest in his retrospective glance, as it did to the eager eye of childhood: he has contrived to weave its tritest traditions into a bright and endless romance."[3] Lamb captures the spirit of the *London Magazine* because he doesn't. His lack of interest in the ruckus of the "now" frees his consciousness to delve into the city's abiding peculiarity and touch its deepest heart.

The *London Magazine* in fact would not have been the *London Magazine* without Lamb. Scott praised "our ELIA" as "the pride of our magazine," and backed his appreciation by making Lamb his highest-paid writer. Lamb received 20 guineas per sheet, two to three times more than the other writers, and overall earned £170 for his *London Magazine* essays. Those Lamb surpassed, at least according to Scott's measure, were among the best writers of the age: Hazlitt, De Quincey, John Clare, Bryan Waller Procter (also known as Barry Cornwall), and T. G. Wainewright (who wrote under the pseudonym Janus Wethercock; he was a dandified art critic, a painter whom Blake admired, a lover of Lamb's literature and art, and later a forger and probable murderer who lived his final years as a convict in Van Dieman's Land). These colleagues acknowledged Lamb's ascendancy in the pages of the magazine. Bernard Barton (the Quaker poet and banker to whom Lamb would write, "Keep to your bank and the Bank will keep you" [*L*, 2:364]) penned a sonnet in Elia's honor, as did John Clare. Wainewright mourned the "death" of Elia. Procter published two essays overtly indebted to Elia, while Hazlitt lauded Lamb as Lamb in his essay on literary conversation.[4]

But without the *London Magazine*, Lamb would not have been Lamb. His greatest and most lasting literary creation, the character of Elia, he fashioned specifically for his *London Magazine* essays. And the *London*'s primary charge—to capture the "image, form, and pressure" of the city's "mighty heart"—inspired Lamb to attend to his beloved environs more imaginatively than before, and this alertness generated his quaintly mind-blowing essays.

CHAPTER 39

# Elia

Say it as "El-i-*a*," and it sounds like "a liar." Then try "El-*i*-a," and you hear "Elijah," the biblical prophet, messenger of divine truth. "*E*l-i-a." Hallelujah? El, Hebrew for God? Or, as one reader of Lamb heard echoed, "elegist"? Another student of Lamb proposed "Eelya," rhyming with "Celia."[1]

Look only at the letters. "Elia" is an anagram for "A lie."

Lamb relished this clever arrangement of letters. He said the name should be pronounced "*Ell*ia," after the Italian clerk at the South Sea House. But a contemporary rhymed "Elia" with "aspire," suggesting that the word indeed sounded like "a liar." Lucas regrets this rhyme, however, and asserts that "modern usage" dictates that "Elia" should rhyme with "Celia." He bases this claim on a letter from John Taylor, who knew Lamb, which says, "We think Mr Lamb pronounces the word Elià."[2] George L. Barnett claims that Lucas wrongly transcribed the letter, and that Lamb's own personal directive for pronunciation, "*Ell*ia," is authoritative.[3]

These sonic and semantic ambiguities, before we even see Elia breathe in the essays, aren't surprising. Lamb refers to his persona as a "phantom cloud" (*W,* 2:29) and observes Elia's affinity for that "dangerous figure," irony (*W,* 2:152). The name is self-canceling. It is a statement of identity and an erasure.

The origin of the name seems simple. Writing to Taylor in 1821, Lamb claims he borrowed the name from an old Italian clerk at the South Sea House during the days Lamb himself worked there, 1791–92. He took the name for his *London Magazine* essays because he wanted to hide his identity from his brother John, who might dislike "certain descriptions" (*L*, 2:302).

The subterfuge worked fairly well, since the "real" Elia was an author. Though now, as Lamb notes, a dead one, having passed away about a year earlier of consumption. Talfourd claims Lamb took the name by accident. His initial submission to the magazine was "The South-Sea House," and he just happened to recall the "name of a gay, light-hearted foreigner, who fluttered there at that time, [and] he subscribed his name to the essay."[4] David Chandler has proposed that Lamb's appropriation was more than accidental, since Felix Ellia, in addition to being a published author (of the 1799 novel *Norman Banditti; or, The Fortress of Coutance*), "was a colourful, eccentric, memorable character" exhibiting an "odd self-importance," "schoolboyish humour," "moral earnestness," and a "capacity for self-delusion." Such traits "may very well have contributed to the cocktail of whimsy, pathos and irony that is the 'Elian' manner."[5]

Throughout the nineteenth century, readers equated Elia with the historical Lamb, thus simplifying the relationship between author and pseudonym, as well as blotting out Felix Ellia. In the early part of the twentieth century, however, Lucas distanced persona and person; he claimed that Lamb's partly fictional character unleashed a literary "richness and colour" not present in Lamb's earlier writing.[6] F. V. Morley held that Lamb created Elia to escape the tragedies of his actual life.[7] Gerald Monsman and Thomas McFarland agree: Elia elides the unutterable horror of murder and madness.[8] Simon P. Hull connects Elia to the *London Magazine*. Elia immerses himself in London's currents while at the same time playfully transcending them.[9] In another recent trend readers have traded biography for poetics, arguing that Elia makes apparent what is implicit in all literary essays: the "I," no matter how ostensibly continuous with the historical self, is a fiction supporting a particular aesthetic.[10]

Each of these views captures one aspect of Lamb's relationship to his persona. But Lamb himself offers support for the last view: his making of Elia exemplifies in extremis what we all do the instant we utter "I." In his review of Hazlitt's *Table Talk*, unpublished during his lifetime, Lamb venerates the essayist, such as Hazlitt, whose persona "attracts, or repels, by strong realities of individual observation, humour, and feeling."[11] If a "series of Miscellaneous Essays" lacks "some pervading character to give a unity to it," it is "ordinarily as tormenting to get through as a set off aphorisms, or a jest-book." The greatest essayists, like Plutarch and Montaigne, "imparted their own personal peculiarities to their themes. By this balm are they preserved."[12] Even Samuel Johnson's Rambler, despite his "ponderous levities and unwieldy efforts at being sprightly," exudes this charm. Johnson's obtrusion of "his particular views of life for universal truths" "binds us to his writings," not any "steady conviction we have of the solidity of his thinking."[13]

Lamb contrasts Steele's Spectator to the radically idiosyncratic persona. The Spectator is so general he can hold any opinion and express himself in any style. He lacks the dramatic flair and unprecedented complexity of a successful literary character.

Lamb, in the guise of a friend of the "Late Elia," describes the primary traits of his famous persona. This "Phil-Elia" writes an obituary of his friend in a January 1823 number of the *London Magazine*. The friend notes that many accused Elia of egotism, because he attributes to himself the experiences of others, like the time he appropriated the experience of a "forlorn" rural youth—Coleridge—in his essay on Christ's Hospital. But if such flowing out of self into another is egotism, then all novelists are such, as well as all playwrights. Regardless of egotism, Elia was "a singular character." Those who didn't fancy him hated him, and many who "once liked him, afterwards became his bitterest haters." He cared little what he said, and who heard him. He was indifferent to the clock and his surroundings. To the "severe religionist he would pass as a free-thinker; while the other faction set down for a bigot." He was largely misunderstood, and probably didn't really comprehend himself. Irony might be to blame. He remained ambiguous, breaking into solemn conversations with a joke. His abrupt and doubt-inducing speech, along with haphazard verbal organization and a stutter, ensured he would never be an orator, even though he "seemed determined that, no one else should play that part when he was present." In appearance, he was small and "ordinary." In times he found himself in "what is called good company," but was unacquainted with the group, he sat silently, to the point he was thought "odd." Then he would "stutter out some senseless pun . . . which stamped his character for the evening." Often the pun fell flat, alienating the company. He attempted wit to "give his poor thoughts articulation." He favored eccentrics, and this choice didn't always endear him to polite society. He didn't care. Though he was "temperate in his meals and diversions," he "always kept a little on this side of abstemiousness." "Only in the use of the Indian weed he might be thought a little excessive." Tobacco was his "solvent of speech." "As the friendly vapour ascended how his prattle would curl up sometimes with it! the ligaments, which tongue-tied him, were loosened, and the stammerer proceed a statist!" Elia didn't like to be treated as a "grave or respectable character," and so was especially wary of old age. He was too childish. Manhood annoyed him (*W,* 2:153).

Charles Lamb, the creator of Elia, kills Elia and creates another character to eulogize, with critical eye, Elia. The result is that Lamb eulogizes himself, alive and dead at once. This move emphasizes the distance between Lamb and character. But Phil-Elia's description of Elia is a description of Lamb, albeit an exaggerated one.

Why blend fact and fiction? Why not fashion a fictional character like Johnson's Rambler or Sterne's Yorick? Or why not hold the "I" close to the historical person, as Montaigne and Hazlitt did? Because of Lamb's love of irony, of the "is" and "is not" perpetually generating new ideas, new things. Elia is a fabrication and a fact. As a fictional character, he speaks as a figure in a novel would, and what he says is therefore not real like Lamb's love for Mary is real. But as a mouthpiece for the Lamb of the Temple, he speaks as a man of flesh, his words rising from the city.

This self-erasure invites questions about language's capacity to convey durable meaning. If the utterances of Elia are truth and lie, then perhaps all words de-signify as they sign, and thus are not to be trusted. This doubt unsettles, since we require semantics to manage our everyday lives. But this skepticism liberates words from their conventions, throws them into fresh associations, infinite possibilities.

Blurred Elia, Hamlet-wise, asks: who are you? Without hesitation you recall those occurrences from your past that have made you, you: your mom and dad, your best friend, town at night, school desks, sex, bats, Yeats, that dream of the boar, and you say, I am the person these things happened to. But you have lived billions of moments. Why focus on these? They support how you want to see yourself during this instant. Ten years earlier, you would have grasped other events; seven years later, you will apprehend others. We are novelists perpetually creating and revising the character we call ourselves.

CHAPTER 40

# *Magazines Increase and Multiply*

Until very recently, readers have tended to envision Elia solely as the quirky presence unifying two *books* of essays, *Elia: Essays Which Have Appeared under That Signature in the "London Magazine"* (1823) and *The Last Essays of Elia: Being a Sequel to the Essays Published under That Name* (1833). But the biblio-Elia, permanent and stable and canonized, is not the same as Elia in his original form, penning ephemeral sentences about London's comings and goings. The essays' magazine shapes aren't always the same as their book forms. The periodical versions are more attuned to the present London scene, snapshots of a peculiar metropolis.

Hazlitt recognized the dynamism of the magazine writer, as opposed to the composer of books. "Literary immortality," he writes, is short-lived in this age of information, speed, and commodity. Best to accept that we can't extricate ourselves from the crowded world and the overabundant gawking of the masses. "We must look to the public for support. Instead of solemn testimonies of the learned, we require smiles of the fair and the polite. If princes scowl upon us, the broad shining face of the people my turn to us with a favourable aspect. Is not this life (too) sweet? Would we change it for the former if we could? . . . The great point is, that we cannot! Therefore, let Reviews flourish—let Magazines increase and multiply—let the Daily and Weekly Newspapers live for ever!"[1]

Hazlitt isn't necessarily happy about earning the smiles of the "fair and the polite," but since there is nothing he can do about it, he decides to embrace the new magazine model of authorship: the writer quickly writes about the quicker "now."

Of course the example of Wordsworth shows that the older model of authorship still pertained: the solitary genius spinning out his most personal visions, regardless of audience. For Wordsworth, the poet doesn't conform to taste; he creates it. But Wordsworth wasn't an urban writer, and so never got the London rush Hazlitt and Lamb did—especially Lamb. Unlike the Lake Poet, Lamb never saw the city as foreign, perverse. Far from an immense global monstrosity, London to Lamb resembled an intimate little town, where everyone seemed to know everyone else, for better or worse.

Lamb's first *London Magazine* essay, in the August 1820 number, assumes a reader who shares Elia's city and his experiences: "Reader, in thy passage from the Bank—where thou hast been receiving thy half-yearly dividends (supposing thou art a lean annuitant like myself)—to the Flower Pot, to secure a place for Dalston, or Shacklewell, or some other thy suburban re- treat northerly,—didst thou never observe a melancholy looking handsome, brick and stone edifice, to the left—where Threadneedle-street abuts upon Bishopsgate?" (*W,* 2:1). So begins "Recollections of the South Sea-House" (the title was shortened to "The South Sea-House" in *Elia,* the collection of the essays). Writer and reader walk the same out-of-the-way streets and, most likely, relish the same sights.

This kind of intimacy, grounded on a shared locale, pervades the *Lon- don Magazine* essays, as does a sense that readers know the same people as the author. In footnotes Lamb cut when the essays were gathered into *Elia,* he frequently references these people, though usually in a facetious fashion. For instance, he footnotes a mention of John Tipp's rooms on Threadneedle Street thus: "I have since been informed, that the present tenant of them is a Mr. Lamb, a gentleman who is happy in the possession of some choice pic- tures, and among them a rare portrait of Milton, which I mean to do myself the pleasure of going to see, and at the same time to refresh my memory with the sight of old scenes. Mr. Lamb has the character of a right courteous and communicative collector" (*W,* 2:307). The Mr. Lamb here is Charles's brother John, who did indeed own a fine old picture of Milton, which he purchased in 1815. Upon his death it went to Charles, who gave it as a dowry to Emma Isola when she married Edward Moxon.

Lamb probably cut this and other footnotes because he was attempting, in making a book, to de-localize the essays, to raise them to a more general audience beyond London.

In October, Lamb followed "Recollections of the South Sea-House" with "Oxford in the Vacation." If the former essay joins the reader in an intimate journey into odd London, the latter, following a typical Lamb rhythm, takes the reader to a pastoral realm opposed to the city's bustle: in this case, Oxford University. Again, though, Elia assumes the reader is a fellow Londoner, and so that he regularly peruses periodicals as such materials are designed to be read, "with cursory eye (which, while it reads, seems as though it reads not)" (*W*, 2:7). Scanning this article—not studying it, as one might a book—the reader has no doubt glanced to the bottom, noted the author, and is asking, who is this Elia? Surely, Elia answers, based on "Recollections of the South Sea-House," you assume I am a clerk. You are correct, and in this life, I spend my days laboring over indigos and silks, while at night I attempt, though spent, to cultivate my true passion, composing sonnets and epigrams. No wonder Elia cherishes holidays, which free him from his urban grind.

The Londoners reading this essay, Elia assumes, understand; they all need an escape from the tumult from time to time, and now is their chance to join him on his vacation to Oxford. And when he happens upon a fellow Londoner there, one G.D., certainly readers will know him as George Dyer, who lives in Clifford's Inn, between Fetter Lane and Chancery Street. Might readers also know Elia's very local allusion in describing this naïve man? You would as soon "strike an abstract idea" as assault this innocent (*W*, 2:10). Those in the serious know would recognize this as a portion of Hazlitt's retort to John Lamb after the elder Lamb socked him during an argument over coloring in Hans Holbein the Younger and Van Dyck. Hazlitt, recall, exclaimed that an actual blow would not harm him, only an abstract idea.

Such seemingly arcane allusions were common among the *London Magazine* writers, especially Lamb and Hazlitt, who were constantly talking to one another in the magazine's pages. A month earlier, in "On the Conversation of Authors," Hazlitt had referred to a visit Lamb made to Oxford some years back; fittingly, he emphasized Lamb's urban sensibility: "The country people thought him an oddity, and did not understand his jokes. It would be strange if they had; for he did not make any while he stayed. But when we crossed the country to Oxford, then he spoke a little. He and the old colleges were hail fellow well met; and in the quadrangles, he 'walked gowned.'"[2] In this last phrase, Hazlitt alludes to Lamb's poem of August 1819, published in the *Examiner*, "Written at Cambridge," in which Lamb feels as if he walks "gowned," even though he never studied at this university.

Lamb connects Elia even more closely to his London circle in providing a lengthy footnote on Dyer's notorious naïveté, known only to those familiar with him. The footnote, which we learn is "not by Elia," chastises "Lamb" for playing jokes on poor Dyer. The anonymous glosser—certainly Lamb himself—knocks Lamb for "gravely" assuring D. that Lord Castlereagh "had acknowledged himself to be the author of Waverly." D. went around repeating this falsehood—Scott, of course, was the author, though he published anonymously—with just as much gravity, making a fool of himself (*W,* 2:313).

Lamb cut this footnote in *Elia*, again probably assuming it was too local for the wider audience he wished to attract. He also excised a lengthy passage in the body of the essay, a humorous account of Dyer's first employment as "usher to a knavish fanatic schoolmaster" (*W,* 2:314). A letter from one W.K. (probably William King) to the *London Magazine* probably convinced Lamb to make this latter revision. The letter complained of mistakes Elia had made in Dyer's biography.[3] Elia replied that any inaccuracies were committed purely as "an error of judgment" (*W,* 2:315).

Lamb in *Elia* retained the local details in his next two *London Magazine* essays, "Christ's Hospital Five and Thirty Years Ago," from November 1820, and "The Two Races of Men," from December. In his piece on his old school, Lamb in the guise of Coleridge describes the day-to-day life of this ancient London institution; he also sketches the student lives of current friends his readers would recognize, such as Valentine Le Grice. In "Two Races of Men," his portraits of John Fenwick as Ralph Bigod and Coleridge as Comberbatch would have been humorously familiar to those in London literary circles.

Lamb's *London Magazine* essay of January 1821, "New Year's Eve," converses with Hazlitt's piece in the same volume, "On Past and Future."[4] Both essays find the future uninteresting (Lamb because he lacks children and forward-looking thoughts, Hazlitt because it is "a dead wall or a thick mist hiding all objects from our view") and the past exhilarating (Lamb since he was lovely and good as a youth, Hazlitt for the reason that "the past is alive and stirring with objects, bright or solemn, and of unfading interest.")

In February, in "Mrs. Battle's Opinions on Whist," Lamb grants a glimpse of his and Mary's weekly gatherings, in which serious card playing was softened by whimsical conversation. The March essay, "A Chapter on Ears," depicts musical evenings at the home of the Novellos. To the essay, Lamb attached a postscript, later removed in *Elia*. He alludes to Hunt's insinuation in the January 31 *Indicator*: Elia doesn't write the *London Magazine* essays; one "Mr. L——b" does." Elia, in the *London*, is furious. How is it that a "plain man must not be allowed *to be?*" "They call this an age of personality: but surely this spirit of anti-personality (if I may so express it) is something worse. . . . When a gentleman is robbed of his identity, where is he?" (*W*, 2:337).

Elia continued to entertain the fiction himself, albeit comically. In November 1821, in the "Lion's Head," the editorial section of the *London Magazine*, Elia clears up a matter concerning his birthplace. A "Correspondent" has noted a discrepancy: Elia has claimed his origin to be both the Temple (in "The Old Benchers of the Inner Temple") and Calne (in "Christ's Hospital Five and Thirty Years Ago"). Elia asks for interpretive latitude: "So by the word 'native,' I may be supposed to mean a town where I might have been born; or where it might be desirable that I should have been born, as being situate in wholesome air, upon a dry chalky soil, in which I delight; or a town, with the inhabitants of which I passed some weeks, a summer or two ago, so agreeably, that they and it became in a manner native to me" (*W*, 2:340).

In April 1821, Lamb once more conversed with Hazlitt in the pages of the *London Magazine*. Whereas Hazlitt's "On People of Sense" attacks philosophical dogmatists and celebrates empiricism, Elia's "All Fools' Day" praises ridiculous ideas, such as those of the dunces in Jesus's parables. Hazlitt is the only living person invited to the April Fools' feast, perhaps because he and Lamb had recently fallen out, and Lamb saw fit to call his difficult friend a dunce.[5]

Up until April 1821, Lamb's Elia essays were topical, alluding to London locales, activities, authors. During this month, however, Lamb broke the pattern to cogitate on the Quaker religion and the poetics of silence. This trend continued in the ensuing months. Lamb needed more room for his mind to move. In May he published "Old and New Schoolmaster," which gently mocks the schoolmaster's obsession with turning experience to information, while indirectly extolling Elia's alternative practice: learning by fits and starts. (Though not concerned with London, the essay nonetheless coincides in the *London Magazine* with Hazlitt's "On Antiquity," which emphasizes the value of learning the past as it relates to the present.)[6] Elia's essay of August 1821, "Jews, Quakers, Scotchmen, and other Imperfect Sympathies," further explores ways of knowing. As we will see in more detail in a later chapter, Elia abhors the strict logic of the Scotsman, partially because his own thought is unsystematic, unfinished, casual.

If "Old and New Schoolmaster" and "Jews, Quakers, Scotchmen, and Other Imperfect Sympathies" examine learning, Elia's November essay, "Grace Before Meat," studies language. In mocking gluttons who pray before devouring their dinners, Elia advocates words appropriate to the context: say grace only before a modest meal. Elia's essay of March 1822, "Distant Correspondents," also scrutinizes language, in this case, the sentences that arouse regardless of distance and time. In "A Dissertation upon Roast Pig," from September 1822, Lamb continues his analysis of language, in this case the speech of imperialism. (Lamb also printed an earlier essay in this number, "A Bachelor's Complaint of the Behaviour of Married People," first published in the *Reflector* back in 1811 or 1812; the month before, August, he reprinted "Confessions of a Drunkard.") In November 1822, Lamb speculated on gender relations in "Modern Gallantry." The piece is political, calling for society to treat women more justly.

Veering out from London into unsystematic philosophy, Lamb during his first two years at the *London Magazine* also delved into his personal experience. In "My Relations," from June 1821, Elia sketches his odd brother and aunt; the next month, in "Mackery End, in Hertfordshire," he introduces us to Mary. These essays are followed in September and October, respectively, by "The Old Benchers of the Inner Temple" and "Witches, and Other Night-Fears," descriptions of Lamb's childhood. ("Witches," a mapping of dark dreams, ran in the same *London Magazine* number as the second part of De Quincey's own nightmare, *Confessions of an English Opium Eater*.)[7] "My First Play," from December 1821, extends Elia's song of innocence. The next essay, "Dream-Children: A Reverie," from January 1822, breaks from Lamb's actual past to the history he wishes he possessed, but does not.

In May and June 1822, Lamb returned to present-day London, with his eye less on the personal and more on the social. "The Praise of Chimney-Sweepers: A May-Day Effusion" calls for gentler treatment of the unfortunate sweepers, and "A Complaint of the Decay of Beggars" does the same for London's vagabonds.

Lamb removed the ending of the London version of the beggar essay when he printed the piece in *Elia*. In the magazine draft, Elia concludes with an anecdote about his friend "L——," Lamb, who heard a female beggar lament that she had seen better days. "'So have I, my good woman,' retorted he, looking up at the welkin which was just then threatening a storm—and the jest (he will have it) was as good to the beggar as a tester.'" The joke was at least better than "consigning her to the stocks, or the parish beadle" (*W*, 2:387).

In addition to these *London Magazine* essays, Lamb completed three pieces on contemporary theater, all titled "The Old Actors." They appeared in February, April, and October 1822. For *Elia*, Lamb reworked them into "On Some of the Old Actors," "On the Artificial Comedy of the Last Century," and "On the Acting of Munden." Each piece elevates acting styles to models for everyday living. If identities are constructs, and not essential, we might as well create captivating characters for ourselves, and value compelling theatrics in others, like London's beggars.

As Lamb created Elia in the *London Magazine* month after month, local-color essays sprouted half-facetious contemplations on life itself, intimate portrayals of Charles's past, casual social commentaries, and vivid appreciations of the art of acting. Just when Lamb decided to publish his Elia essays in a book is unknown. He probably did when he noticed the motifs rising from his *London Magazine* drafts and imagined an aesthetically potent arrangement of the essays. But he also no doubt had sales in mind. The Elia essays were gaining notoriety in the London literary scene. Not surprisingly, the *London Magazine* consistently boosted Lamb in its pages. In addition to the aforementioned notices of Elia by Hazlitt, Clare, Procter, Barton, and Wainewright, an anonymous reviewer of a novel by Louisa Stewart Costello placed Elia in the august company of Sterne and Goldsmith. This was in December 1820. In March 1821, Horace Smith in "Death—Posthumous Memorials—Children," praised the "quaint lugubrious pleasantry" of Elia's essays, as well as their "social yet deep philosophy."[8] In August 1821, Charles Abraham Elton, under the name of Olen, published "Epistle to Elia," which gently chides Elia for lacking commitment to the afterlife.

Beyond the *London Magazine*, the *Edinburgh Review* of May 1823 hailed the "quaint and grave subtleties of Elia" as the *London Magazine*'s best writing.[9] But whereas the liberal *Edinburgh* said yes, the conservative *Blackwood*'s hollered no. In November 1820, a Dr. Olinthus Petre (*a* nom de plume of William Maginn) condemned the "impertinencies of a Cockney scribbler, who signs himself Elia, full of all kinds of personal, and often offensive allusions to every individual who had the misfortune of being educated at the same school as himself."[10] Six months later, Maginn describes how baffled he was to learn that Elia is Lamb, since he has heretofore been a lover of Lamb's writing, especially *Rosamund Gray*. He laments that Lamb has traded Wordsworth, Coleridge, and Southey, now all good Tories, for Cockneys like Hazlitt.

*Charles Lamb*, after a portrait by Daniel Maclise, 1835, for *Fraser's Magazine*.
The caption, provided by Lamb, reads "Yours, ratherish unwell Ch$^s$. Lamb."
(Classic Image / Alamy Stock Photo.)

In October 1822, *London Magazine* announced that the "Essays of Elia" were now being prepared for publication in one volume. In December, Taylor and Hessey, the editors of *London Magazine*, released the book under an 1823 copyright. Contained in octavo-sized boards—which were covered in green morocco and gilt around the edges—were twenty-seven of the twenty-eight essays Lamb published as Elia. The essay not making the cut was "Confessions of a Drunkard," too serious for Elia and too controversial for Lamb. Taking its place was "Valentine's Day," earlier published in the *Examiner* and the *Indicator*.

Lamb made two other substantial changes. He removed, as we know, several footnotes and passages connecting the essays to the London scene. He also rearranged the essays, lifting them from the rush of London's week-to-week randomness into a literary work's structure, the dance, seemingly inevitable, of unity and diversity. Here are the sequences of the *London Magazine* versus *Elia*. (Essays in the magazine list connected by a slash were published in the same month.)

*London Magazine*

"Recollections of the South-Sea House"
"Oxford in the Vacation"
"Christ's Hospital Five and Thirty Years Ago"
"The Two Races of Men"
"New Year's Eve"
"Mrs. Battle's Opinions on Whist"
"A Chapter on Ears"
"All Fools' Day" / "A Quaker's Meeting"
"The Old and New Schoolmaster"
"My Relations"
"Mackery End, in Hertfordshire"
"Jews, Quakers, Scotsmen and Other Imperfect Sympathies"
"The Old Benchers of the Inner Temple".
"Witches, and Other Night-Fears"
"Grace Before Meat"
"My First Play"
"Dream-Children: A Reverie"
"The Old Actors"
"Distant Correspondents"
"The Old Actors"

"The Praise of Chimney-Sweepers"
"A Complaint of the Decay of Beggars in the Metropolis"
"Confessions of a Drunkard"
"A Dissertation upon Roast Pig" / "A Bachelor's Complaint of the Behaviour of
    Married People"
"The Old Actors"
"Modern Gallantry"

*Elia*

"The South-Sea House"
"Oxford in the Vacation"
"Christ's Hospital Five and Thirty Years Ago"
"The Two Races of Men"
"New Year's Eve"
"Mrs. Battle's Opinions on Whist"
"A Chapter on Ears"
"All Fools' Day"
"A Quaker's Meeting"
"The Old and New Schoolmaster"
"Valentine's Day"
"Imperfect Sympathies"
"Witches, and Other Night-Fears"
"My Relations"
"Mackery End, in Hertfordshire"
"Modern Gallantry"
"The Old Benchers of the Inner Temple".
"Grace Before Meat"
"My First Play"
"Dream-Children: A Reverie"
"Distant Correspondents"
"The Praise of Chimney-Sweepers"
"A Complaint of the Decay of Beggars in the Metropolis"
"A Dissertation upon Roast Pig"
"A Bachelor's Complaint of the Behaviour of Married People"
"On Some of the Old Actors"
"On the Artificial Comedy of the Last Century"
"On the Acting of Munden"

Lamb's reshuffling suggests an overall design. The first cluster of essays, from "The South-Sea House" to "Valentine's Day," explores his obsession: the possibility of finding portals (old buildings, vacations, childhood, borrowing, card playing, and such) through which one can pass into a realm—physical or emotional—outside instrumental time. Sadly, these realms exist in the past or in fancy, so they are fleeting and tenuous, if accessible at all.

The next grouping, beginning with "Imperfect Sympathies" and ending with "Grace Before Meat," is about failure to connect. Elia is biased, childhood is nightmare, relatives are unknowable, men are unfair to woman, history forgets local eccentrics, rituals disconnect us from experience.

The next assemblage, running from "My First Play" to "Distant Correspondents," grieves over lost sundials, the passing of first plays, lives desired but unlived, and friends now worlds away.

Social problems unify the next grouping. In his essays on chimney sweeps and beggars, Elia mocks abstract visions of reform that ignore the particularities of the needy. The essay on roast pig also satirizes hypocritical social conventions, as does "A Bachelor's Complaint of the Behaviour of Married People," where the institution of marriage compromises male friendships.

The first twenty-five essays fall on the darker side of a continuum running between melancholy alienation and joyful connection. But none of these pieces is depressing. The slightly naïve Elia finds comedy in the gap between aspiration and reality. Our high hopes, doomed to remain unfulfilled, are laughable. We are like blind men who behave as if they are sighted. We bang into things, run into walls, stumble, fall, barely miss getting run over, all the while believing we are noble animals progressing toward higher states of being. It would be easy to be bitter over this disproportion between fantasy and fact, like Swift is. It would also be easy to view the rift with deadpan indifference, as Camus does. But Elia is too generous, or too innocent, for either move. His attitude is: the world is so painful and stupid and random, why not relieve the agony for a little by laughing at how silly we are?

Fittingly, the model for *Elia* is not philosophy but distracting chit-chat. Just before publication, Lamb asked Taylor include a preface to the collection. It would ask readers to take the essays in the spirit in which they were intended—as "fair construction[s] of after-dinner conversation[s]." Such conversations allow for "the rashness and necessary incompleteness of first thoughts" and forgive "words spoken peradventure after the fourth glass." But then Lamb decided against a preface, since the essays "are *all Preface*." "A

Preface," after all, "is nothing but a talk with the reader; and they do nothing else" (*L*, 2:350).

The essays perform the casual theatrics with which we charm away boredom or sadness or—as Lamb knew all too well—trauma. Lamb fittingly ends *Elia* with three essays celebrating comedic acting. The sequencing of these essays is significant. The first praises Bensley and Dodd for their psychological realism. They invested their characters with such emotional subtlety, it seemed as if they really were those characters. This early form of method acting knits self and performance so closely together we can't tell the difference. The mask becomes real, perhaps even more real than the actor, if reality is intensity, complexity, luminous ambiguity. Become more real, more alive, by acting more brilliantly. If you are in low spirits, change the play.

Lamb's penultimate essay cheers the artificial comedies of the eighteenth century. Elia admires these farces because they play for the sake of playing. Good and evil are secondary to pleasure. Laughter, gusto, joie de vivre trump the causality we expect from everyday reality. Amoral verve is highly moral, since it valorizes generosity toward the charming irrelevancies that make life livable.

Munden gets the final essay. If Bensley and Dodd illustrate how to live into constructed identities, and if Congreve implies that comic identity is the most vital, Munden demonstrates how the skilled comic actor imbues his ordinary environment with extraordinary energy. He so intensely inhabits his space that everything he attends to shines. This is the power of embracing things as unprecedented and unrepeatable particulars and loving them precisely for their idiosyncratic concreteness. The eye becomes a movie camera, in whose lens the most trifling objects turn into portals to the rich and strange.

In Lamb's concluding essays on comedy, his irony is as uncanny and melancholy and big-hearted as ever—and also redemptive. Just as you can transform teacups into raptures, you can torque terror into wit. Life is terrible. Sisters kill mothers. It is also funny, slapstick funny. Gravity knocks you about, but since you know how to go down, nothing hurts as much as it should. Lamb stumbles, Elia breaks the fall.

To call this irony redemptive seems excessive, until we recall the irony of Lamb's Christianity: from the perspective of time, this world is tragic, so we should treat people as mercifully as we can; from the view of eternity, the world has already come and gone, and means nothing, and watching little specks take this earth so seriously is hilarious.

The period during which Lamb composed his first series of Elia essays, from August 1820 to November 1822, is one of the most remarkable in literary history, similar in intensity and richness to Wordsworth's period from 1798 to 1805, when he wrote "Tintern Abbey," the Lucy poems, "Intimations of Immortality," "Resolutions and Independence," and *The Prelude*. The hot core of Lamb's explosion—January 1821 to September 1822, which created "New Year's Eve," "A Chapter on Ears," "A Quaker's Meeting," "Imperfect Sympathies," "Witches, and Other Night-Fears," "Mackery End, in Hertfordshire," "The Old Benchers of Inner Temple," "My First Play," "Dream-Children," "The Praise of Chimney-Sweepers," "A Complaint of the Decay of Beggars in the Metropolis," and "A Dissertation upon Roast Pig"—equals the most fecund one-year period in British literature, Keats's annus mirabilis, 1819, during which the poet produced "The Eve of St. Agnes," "La Belle Dame Sans Merci," and the four majestic odes.

To compare Lamb to Wordsworth is particularly apt. Elia obsessively echoes the Lake Poet, out of both respect and irritation. Lamb's emphasis on the glories of childhood, for instance, is deeply informed by Wordsworth. But where Wordsworth idealizes—the child is a "Philosopher blest" who properly guides our adult lives—Lamb scrutinizes the hard facts. We are lost to childhood joy and terror; they only remind us of what we are bereft of. But this lack doesn't turn Lamb sullen. He discovers a humor in our ridiculous pitiful longings that elevates us above the hurt.

As much as Wordsworth, though, Sterne haunts the Elia essays. The eccentric accountants and benchers and relatives; the hobbyhorses of Elia; the tender feelings; the wacky style: all remind of *Tristram Shandy*. But again, Lamb transgresses his influence. Sterne's novel takes place in a country house, while Elia's essays spread over the variegated city. Lamb's comedy is thus more expansive and socially engaged. Moreover, where Sterne in his masterpiece makes sentiment mostly mockable, Lamb's expressions of ardent feeling, especially in "Dream-Children," flourish between torment and detachment. Hurt for what ought to be; joke at what is.

Sterne gleaned his outrageous style from Burton and Browne, as did Lamb. Elia's baroque puns, conceits, and hyperboles he borrows right from these favorite Renaissance writers, and he feels their melancholy, too. Similar to Burton and Browne, Elia's melancholy is generative, a gentle cynicism that creates compelling questions and open-ended answers. But Lamb diverges from these early modern masters in confessing his own sorrows in harrowing detail. Even though his irony holds him slightly aloof, he delves into the unseemly facets of his life, not to be sensational but to express what fascinated him: his inmost unrest.

The Elia essays were strikingly novel for their time. In contrast to his great Romantic contemporaries Wordsworth and Coleridge, Lamb took the city's grit as his primary passion. Also in opposition to the Lake Poets, he assumed that identity is a construct, and that a self is a theatrical role, and so authenticity is self-consciously playing a character of your own making. For Lamb, averse to grand arguments about Nature and Imagination, the play's the thing, the only thing. Style *is* substance. It's not *what* you say but *how* you say it. And Lamb said it like no one before, celebrating extreme eccentricity as the highest form of expression, in literature as well as life.

Reviews of *Elia* were mixed. On the negative side, the *Monthly Magazine* faulted the book, though it was original and pleasant, for its "disagreeable quaintness and affection" as well as its "revolting indelicacy" and "ridiculous puerility."[11] More positively, the *Monthly Review* lauded Elia for his "flow of original thought," "depth of feeling," "wise and playful humanity," and "vein of mixed humour and melancholy running through every line." Still, some of Lamb's whimsies, peculiarities, and conceits are silly, and might keep his audience limited to the like-minded.[12]

The reviewer for the *British Critic* was also positive, and his assessment was sophisticated. He observed that Elia isn't the same as Lamb and compared Lamb to Sterne. When he finished the collection, he felt as if he were parting "from an agreeable and original friend, whose humour has tickled our fancy even in those instances where we did not coincide with his judgement."[13]

That Lamb's status had risen in the literary world was demonstrated by the argument over who first discovered that Elia was Lamb. Oddly, *Blackwood's* proudly claimed credit, while still mocking Lamb. But Hazlitt probably knew Elia's identity first. He reveals it in his 1822 *Table Talk*, where he relished Lamb's pleasurable imitations of the "old English style," as well as his "marrowy vein" that saves the work from "quaintness." Still, he suspects Lamb's ideas, if expressed in contemporary language, wouldn't amount to much.[14]

# CHAPTER 41

## Emma

During their trip to Cambridge in July 1820, just before Lamb published his first Elia essay in August, the Lambs dined at the house of Mrs. Paris on Trumptington Street. She was the sister of their friend William Ayrton. In attendance was a charming eleven-year-old, Emma Isola. Her grandfather was Agostino Isola, who had taught Spanish and Italian at Cambridge University and actually served as Wordsworth's tutor some thirty years earlier. Emma's father was Charles Isola, former esquire bedell of Cambridge. He was deceased, as was her mother. Emma lived with her Aunt Humphreys, also of Trumptington Street.

The Lambs took to Emma and invited her to London over the Christmas holidays. This visit didn't happen, since Mary fell ill again. She recovered in January, however, and joined Charles on Russell Street, where he had just completed "New Year's Eve." Emma arrived the same month. London invigorated the Cambridge girl: "I arrived quite safe and Miss Lamb was at the Inn waiting for me. The first night I came we went out to spend the evening. The second night Mr. Lamb took me to see the wild beasts at Exeter Change. Saturday night being twelfth night I went to a party and did not return till four in the morning. Yesterday Miss Lamb took me to the theatre at Covent Garden. I cannot tell you how much I liked it. I was so delighted" (*L*, 2:290).

Charles's jokey part of this same letter suggests that Emma animated him and Mary as well. "Emma is a very naughty girl, and has broken three cups, one plate and a slop-basin with mere giddiness. She is looking over me, which is impertinent. But if you can spare her longer than her holidays, we shall be happy to keep her, in hopes of her amendment. She came home at 5 o'clock in the morning with a strange gentleman on Twelfth Night. Will you, dear Miss Humph, permit Emma to stay a week or so beyond her holidays. She is studying algebra & the languages. I teach her *dancing*" (*L,* 2:290).

By the time Emma returned to Cambridge at the end of the month, the Lambs were smitten. As Charles wrote to Miss Humphreys, again in his comic mode, Emma's "bloom [is] somewhat impaired by late hours and dissipation, but her gait, gesture, and general manners (I flatter myself) [are] considerably improved by—*somebody that shall be nameless.* My sister . . . begs me to assure you that Emma has been a very good girl, which, with certain limitations, I must myself subscribe to. I wish I could cure her of making dog's ears in books, and pinching them on poor Pompey [the Lambs' dog], who, for one, I dare say, will heartily rejoyce at her departure" (*L,* 2:292).

Emma began regularly to spend her holidays with the Lambs. They funded her schooling in Dulwich and instructed her themselves. By 1823, when Emma was fourteen (and Lamb had just completed his greatest literary run), the relationship had become so intimate that the young woman lived with the Lambs year-round. Though they never legally adopted her—Miss Humphreys remained her guardian—she became, when Charles was forty-eight and Mary fifty-nine, their de facto daughter.

Now the Lamb who complained in "New Year's Eve" that he had no children to inspire forward-looking thoughts had no excuse to neglect the future. Emma was not to the Lambs as Eppie was to Silas Marner, but she did energize the aging siblings. They found themselves behaving like a thirty-something married couple.

The high spirits Emma displayed on her first visit continued to charm. In a poem celebrating her twenty-first birthday, "To a Young Friend," Lamb called her his "Fond Runagate" and relished her gamboling about the house. In another verse to her, he celebrates her jests, "mad discourse," and "bursts of song" (*L,* 5:53). But Emma's exuberance cramped her learning. In 1827, Charles, somewhat tongue-in-cheek, wrote to Mary Shelley, "I am teaching Emma Latin to qualify her for a superior governess-ship: which we see no prospect of her getting. 'Tis like feeding a child with chopped hay from a spoon. Sisyphus—his labours were as nothing to it." "Actives and passives jostle in her nonsense till a deponent enters, like Chaos, more to embroil the fray. Her prepositions are suppositions; her conjunctions copulative have no connection in them; her concords disagree; her interjections are purely English 'Ah!' and 'Oh!' with a yawn and a gape in the same tongue; and she herself is a lazy, block-heFadly supine" (*L,* 3:110). Lamb tried to remedy Emma's short attention span by facing her away from the window, but she had eyes in the back of her head. When friends passed by, she leapt up and announced them.

Observing Charles's good-natured pedagogical irritations, and probably wearying of them, Mary, who taught Emma French, wrote a supportive sonnet, "To Emma, Learning Latin, and Desponding." She alludes to Coleridge's daughter Sara, gifted in languages.

> A right good scholar shalt thou one day be,
> And that no distant one; when even she,
> Who now to thee a star far off appears,
> That most rare Latinist, the Northern Maid—
> The language-loving Sarah of the Lake—
> Shall hail thee Sister Linguist. (*W,* 5:83)

But Mary had to admit Emma was no great scholar. Charles needed constantly to refresh her Latin, and she remained "sadly deficient" in arithmetic (*L,* 3:181).

Still, Mary most certainly appreciated her and Charles's pedagogical labors. She and her brother were giving Emma the kind of education Mary herself had wanted but never got.

Mary made up for her lack of formal education through strenuous autodidacticism. She taught herself French and Latin—with a little help from Charles—and became proficient enough that she could offer to teach these languages to Fanny Kelly.

Ironically enough, the underschooled Mary ended up educating the woman to whom Charles complained (gently) of Emma's lax scholarship: the maker of *Frankenstein* herself. Charles and Mary met Mary Shelley in 1800, when they entered Godwin's circle.[1] Shelley was thirteen. A few years later, she was reading Mary's and Charles's *Tales from Shakespear* and Charles's *Specimens of English Dramatic Poets.*

That's not all. Mary Shelley was versed in Charles's poetry as well, and included his lines, along with those of Coleridge and her husband Percy Bysshe, in her masterwork. When Victor leaves his family for the university, he laments leaving behind the "old familiar faces." Shelley admired the Elia essays, too. In her 1823 article "Giovanni Villani," she wrote, "I cannot help here alluding to the papers of 'Elia,' which have lately appeared in a periodical publication.[2] When collected together, they must rank among the most beautiful and highly valued specimens of the kind of writing spoken of in the text." She valued *Rosamund Gray*, too. In an 1830 review of *Cloudesley*, a novel of her father, she called Lamb's "beautiful" tale the "most perfect specimen of the species of writing to which we allude."[3]

After Shelley returned to England from Italy in 1823, she socialized with the Lambs often, enjoying those traits that made Mary and Charles popular among London's literary elite. In 1823, she reported to Leigh Hunt's wife that she saw the siblings frequently; she found Mary "ever amiable" and Charles "witty and delightful." She recounted the comical tale, learned from Lamb, of Dyer walking into New River, and she looked forward to sharing with Leigh Hunt one of Charles's witticisms: "'Now some men who are very veracious are called matter-of-fact men, but such a one I should call a matter-of-lie-man.'"[4] In 1827, Shelley expressed her affection to Mary outright: "Believe (if such familiar expression be not unmeet from me) that I love you with all my heart—gratefully and sincerely" (quoted in *L*, 3:111).

The Lambs reciprocated Shelley's love. In addition to writing her warm letters, inviting her to his and Mary's parties, and admiring her famous novel (Lamb found it the "most extraordinary realisation of the idea of being out of nature which had ever been effected"), Charles recommended Shelley to Taylor and Hessey as a writer for the *London Magazine*.[5] Lamb even wrote three comic "songs" to Mary Shelley after he witnessed her crying—perhaps at the Novellos'—over a sad song: "Pity's Tear," "Beauty's Tear," and "A Mother's Tear."[6]

Charles and Emma developed an intimate relationship independent of Mary. From 1825 until Emma married, she and Charles took long walks together. Mary wasn't as strong as she used to be—back when she could conquer Helvylln after a cold draft of water—and Charles could still cover twenty miles a day easily. Moreover, from the spring of 1827 to the spring of 1828, when Emma lived with the Lambs full-time (she was between school and a job), she and Charles found themselves much alone, since Mary had suffered another of "her sad long illnesses." In this case, though the illness deprived Charles of her "society," Mary continued living at home. For "eight or nine weeks together," he could "see her but it [did] her no good" (*L*, 3:127). Without Mary to talk to, and now home all day himself—he had retired from East

EMMA

India House in 1825—Charles conversed with Emma intimately and at length. In the summer of 1829, Charles and Emma were together once again without Mary, who was confined when Emma visited from Bury St. Edmunds, where she was employed as a governess.

Did Mary see Emma as a threat? Charles loved Emma very much, as a letter to Emma's friend Miss Fryer shows. Soon after Emma married the publisher Edward Moxon in 1833, he wrote, "I know in my reason this is a good match but I cannot but remember a companionship of eight years in my almost solitude."[7] The syntax is odd, and the sentiment ambiguous: does he mean he might be a better match for Emma? When he wrote this, he was fifty-eight and she was twenty-five.

Then this strange incident occurred. At the end of April 1833, right around the time Emma became engaged to Edward Moxon, Mary fell ill, and she was unable to help plan the wedding. On the actual wedding day, July 30, 1833, Mary continued insensible. Her caretaker, a Mrs. Walden, remarked, more to herself than anyone, that Emma must be married by now. She lifted a glass of wine, asking Mary's permission to drink to the Moxons' health. Mary felt a "total change of countenance" in her nurse. "It restored me," she wrote, "from that moment: as if by an electrical stroke: to the entire possession of my senses—I never felt so calm and quiet after a similar illness as I do now. I feel as if all tears were wiped away from my eyes, and all care from my heart" (*L,* 3:380).

The simplest way of understanding this is that Mary felt a jolt of clarity when hearing of her adopted daughter's happy moment. But questions linger. Was Mary's recovery caused by her relief of knowing that Emma was now out of the range of her brother's romantic affections? Had she been unconsciously jealous of the younger woman, and now exalted at having a rival out of the way? Was Mary justified in feeling so? Was Charles in love with Emma Isola, his "girl of gold"? (*L,* 3:200).

In his album filled with material about and by Lamb, William Ayrton handwrote the following:

Edward White, Esq. (Ned White, in Lamb-language) was Lamb's fellow-clerk at the India House. He is still living (1848). He thought that Lamb had a more than friendly liking for Emma Isola (afterwards Mrs. Moxon). One day both were together at Torrance's (the pastry-cook, Spring Gardens) where White met them. "We want" said Lamb "to sleep in town in the course of the week." "I can offer you a bed," said White significantly, thinking that his friend contemplated marriage. Lamb and Emma evidently understood the hint, and looked expressive silence.

When Emma's intended union with Moxon was announced, White said to Lamb, "I am much shocked to hear of it: I thought you were to be the happy man." Lamb hung his head, sighed, and said not a word. . . .

(All the foregoing from White, at Puttick's Auction Room, Piccadilly, July 25, 1848.)[8]

Can White be trusted? Neil Bell, in a biographical novel about the Lambs, depicted Charles and Emma as lovers. This was in 1940. Five years later, Katherine Anthony, in her joint biography of the siblings, argued the same, while also hinting that Charles and Mary's relationship might be incestuous. Anthony believes Mary recovered her senses on the wedding day because she had feared she might, in madness, kill Emma, and Emma's marriage to Edward removed that possibility.[9]

Whatever their nature, Charles's feelings for Emma seem to have distressed him greatly. In 1825, that first year of retirement that put Charles much in the company of a sexually mature, spirited, and physically attractive Emma, Charles suffered two bouts of what he termed "nervous fever." In July, he wrote to Coleridge, "This damn'd nervous Fever . . . indisposes me for seeing any friends" (L, 3:7). In September, he complained again, this time to Allsop: "I am very feeble, can scarce move a pen; got home from Enfield on the Friday, and on Monday follow'g was laid up with a most violent nervous fever second this summer, have had Leeches to my Temples, have not had, nor can not get, a night's sleep" (L, 3:25).

For decades Charles had been complaining of low spirits, but not of "nervous fevers." Was he on the verge of a mental collapse, the likes of which he had not seen since 1796? If so, was it his distress over Emma pushing him to sanity's brink?

We can't answer these questions. The evidence, if we can even call it that, is too circumstantial. Furthermore, as Ernest Carson Ross demonstrates in his arduous challenge to White, Bell, and Anthony, Lamb's own contemporaries did not believe Charles loved Emma.[10] Robinson denied the notion outright, as did Talfourd, Mrs. Charles Cowden Clarke, and B. W. Procter, other intimates of the Lambs.

Lamb's own words argue against any romantic longings on his part. In a poem to Emma, he emphasizes her plain appearance and simple heart—not virtues traditionally conducive to erotic desire. He has known much "fairer damsels" and most wants Emma to cultivate interior beauty (*W,* 5:54). In an 1829 letter to Procter, Lamb calls Emma "a silent brown girl" (*L,* 3:202). Lamb also wrote a generous-hearted poem hailing Emma's marriage to Edward Moxon, and he gave them his beloved Milton portrait, formerly owned by his brother, for a dowry. Would a jealous lover do such things?

The nature of Charles's relationship to Emma must remain a mystery.

# CHAPTER 42

# Imperfect Sympathies

During the months leading up to his first meeting with Emma in June 1820 and the publication of his first Elia essay in August of the same year, Charles expressed his "thorough aversion" to Byron's character (*L,* 2:279). (In 1824, Lamb penned a droll quatrain on the recently deceased poet. Manners don't change from climate to climate; "who goes a drunkard will return a sot. / So lordly Juan, damn'd to lasting fame, / Went out a pickle, and came back the same" [*W,* 5:107].) In the autumn, he gently chastised Coleridge for his book-borrowing habits (and so seeded a famous essay), and began socializing with a new friend, Bryan Waller Procter, whom he met through the *London Magazine.* Procter was a contemporary of Byron's at Harrow, a solicitor, and author of *Dramatic Scenes and Other Poems* (1819). Lamb adored this collection. If he had found it printed anonymously in the Garrick Collection—an archive of early modern drama housed in the British Museum—he would have included it in his *Dramatic Specimens.*

Just before Emma visited him and Mary in January 1821, Lamb commented on a very large woman in Cambridge, one Mrs. Smith, who broke "down two benches in Trinity Gardens, one on the confines of St. John's, which occasioned a litigation between the societies as to repairing it. In warm weather she retires into an ice-cellar (literally!) and dates the returns of the years from a hot Thursday some 20 years back. She sits in a room with opposite doors and windows, to let in a thorough draught, which gives her slenderer friends toothaches" (*L*, 2:289).

In the spring, just before traveling to Margate, the Lambs met the Mathewses. The husband, Charles, was a famous comedic actor who had turned his home, Ivy Cottage, near Highgate, into a gallery of portraits of famous actors. Through Mrs. Mathews we see Lamb at forty-six: "Mr. Lamb's first appearance was not prepossessing. His figure was small and mean, and no man was certainly ever less beholden to his tailor. His 'bran' new suit of black cloth . . . was drolly contrasted with his very rusty silk stockings, shown from his knees, and his much too large, *thick* shoes, without polish. . . . His hair was black and sleek, but not formal, and his face the gravest I ever saw, but indicating great intellect, and resembling very much the portraits of Charles I."[1]

Amid these happenings, a tragedy occurred. In addition to Elia rising to literary stardom, a major event of early 1821 concerned his *London Magazine* editor, John Scott. Scott and his Cockney writers had been repeatedly attacked by *Blackwood's*, and Scott had finally had enough. In the November and December issues of 1820 and the January one of 1821, he unleashed a rhetorical barrage on John Gibson Lockhart, one of *Blackwood's* most caustic writers. He charged Lockhart with misrepresenting Hazlitt (by calling the essayist pimpled); revealed that Lockhart was in fact editing *Blackwood's*; and accused Lockhart's father-in-law, Sir Walter Scott, of having ties to the magazine. Even though these allegations were accurate, Lockhart was embarrassed, especially since his famous father-in-law, who liked to remain unsullied, was now implicated in *Blackwood's* dirty work. It was the novelist who turned the situation violent. He told his son-in-law that according to chivalric code, he must challenge Scott to a duel.[2]

Lockhart wanted nothing to do with fighting, nor did John Scott. Lockhart traveled down to London from Edinburgh to find a way out. He and Scott negotiated a way to avoid a duel while retaining honor. Lockhart returned to Scotland glad to be alive. But Sir Walter stepped in again. He traveled to London and convinced Lockhart's friend John Christie to declare against John Scott. This time there was no escape. The editor of *London Magazine* must answer or be viewed as a coward. He answered. The duel was set for February 16 at 9 p.m., near Chalk Farm Tavern.

A week earlier, Lamb had sent Scott "A Chapter on Ears," to which he attached a note "heartily acquiesc[ing]" to Scott's "whole conduct," and wondering if perhaps it would not be Lockhart who would come for the duel—take "pot luck—or shot luck"—but James Hogg, who wrote for *Blackwood's* under the pseudonym "Ettrick Shepherd" (*L,* 2:292).

Scott and his second, P. G. Patmore, arrived fifteen minutes early. The weather was foggy, chilly. Patmore carried the dueling pistols, likely those of his family, and wore a white greatcoat, so he wouldn't be fired upon by mistake. They ordered wine at the tavern and drank two-thirds of the bottle. When they left at 9, they asked the bartender to leave the glasses out. They expected to return.

Christie had meanwhile rounded up his second, James Traill. He informed Traill he did not intend to kill Scott unless he was sure Scott wanted to kill him. He planned to aim wide of his opponent on the first shot. Christie and Traill met Scott and Patmore, and the four walked to the field. Patmore and Traill set the distance, and each duelist was given a pistol. The foes took their places. The signal sounded and the men fired. Scott apparently tried to hit Christie, while Christie deliberately aimed wide of Scott. Neither man was hit. A surgeon, Pettigrew, and his assistant, Morris, appeared. Several minutes passed as the men reloaded.

During this time, if Traill had told Patmore that Christie had deliberately missed, and did not desire to harm Scott, the duel would have ended, since both men had fulfilled the requirements of honor. But Traill failed to communicate this to Patmore. Silence settled on the field once again. The signal was given, and the men fired. Scott missed, but Christie hit Scott on the right side, between rib cage and hipbone. Patmore became furious when he learned that Christie had missed on purpose the first time, and Christie, shocked and remorseful, admitted to Scott that he'd much rather be in his place. Scott died ten days later.

Unlike Christie, Sir Walter Scott exhibited zero remorse. As he told his son-in-law Lockhart, "It would be great hypocrisy in me to say I am sorry for John Scott. He got exactly what he was long fishing for." Nonetheless the famous novelist needed to make nice to his London literary acquaintances. He traveled down to the city to breakfast with Lamb and Haydon. Lamb, who "seems to have felt acutely poor Scott's death," bristled at the Scotsman's feigned regrets; instead of exhibiting his customary good will, he bitterly denounced Scott's uncivilized tribal codes. He preferred "houses to rocks," he said to Sir Walter, and "citizens to wild rustics and highland men."[3]

Six months later, Lamb vented his rage toward the Scottish novelist and his violently archaic ilk in his most biting and perplexing Elia essay, ""Jews, Quakers, Scotchmen, and Other Imperfect Sympathies."[4] This essay seems admirable for its blunt honesty—Elia confesses that he feels "the differences of mankind, national or individual, to an unhealthy excess"—but repulsive for its prejudices (*W*, 2:58). Elia loathes Scotsmen (like Sir Walter), for instance. If the intellect of the Scotsman is rigorous, systematic, and comprehensive, Elia's is among those "essentially anti-Caledonian." Such thinkers "have minds rather suggestive than comprehensive. They have no pretences to much clearness or precision in their ideas, or in their manner of expressing them. . . . They are content with fragments and scattered pieces of Truth. She presents no full front to them—a feature or side-face at the most. Hints and glimpses, germs and crude essays at a system, is the utmost they pretend to. . . . The light that lights them is not steady and polar, but mutable and shifting: waxing, and again waning" (*W*, 2:59).

In contrast, "surmises, guesses, misgivings, half-intuitions, semi-consciousnesses, partial illuminations, dim instincts, embryo conceptions, have no place in [the Scotchman's] brain, or vocabulary. The twilight of dubiety never falls upon him. . . . . Between the affirmative and the negative there is no border-land with him. You cannot hover with him upon the confines of truth, or wander in the maze of a probable argument. He always keeps the path. . . . His taste never fluctuates. His morality never abates. He cannot compromise, or understand middle actions" (*W*, 2:60).

We might fault Elia for generalizing in such passages, taking behaviors he might have noticed in one Scotsman and applying them to all. Otherwise, we laud his openness to ambiguity, flux, complexity, and doubt, since life for most of us is messily uncertain.

But when Elia admits his anti-Semitism, we feel different. Though in the "abstract" he has "no disrespect for Jews," he does not care to be "in habits of familiar intercourse with any of that nation." He does not have "the nerves to enter their synagogues." His "old prejudices cling." The enmity between the Christianity of his ancestors and the Judaism he has been taught to distrust—even if he is liberal now, open-minded—cannot simply vanish (*W*, 2:61).

Moreover, Elia is a racist: though "in the Negro countenance you will often meet with strong traits of benignity . . . I should not like to associate with them, to share my meals and my good-nights with them—because they are black" (*W*, 2:62). He also doesn't like Quakers. They are too pure.

Some readers believe Elia is a mouthpiece for Lamb's own bigotry. But Lamb from his early twenties sided, as we know, with radicals. He sympathized with the famous abolitionist Thomas Clarkson and with the Quaker Lloyds. It is unlikely that a man of such enthusiastic liberal views would be a racist.

Why make the character Elia racist then? But is Elia really a racist in the essay, or is he satirizing racism? That he prides himself on his sensitivity to ambiguity, as opposed to absolutism, certainly contradicts his racist remarks. A man committed to the "both/and" is unlikely to be racist.

Being racist with no reason to be racist, Elia mocks the irrationality of racism. Why does he dislike Negroes? Because they are black. Why does he dislike Quakers? They don't like gossip. Why does he dislike Scotsmen? For being as absolutist as he is when he says he doesn't like Scotsmen.

Elia thus enacts the arbitrariness of racism. Doing so, he exemplifies the suggestiveness, as opposed to directness, he promulgates. Instead of proclaiming that racism is wrong, he demonstrates its evil and foolishness. We are all imperfect in our sympathies. There is no one who is not prejudiced. Own your inescapable biases, and then work toward justice.

After Scott's death, Baldwin needed an editor. Initially, he thought of Talfourd, but was dissuaded by Lamb and Robinson. They believed editing was not compatible with his vocation as a lawyer. But Lamb and Robinson likely had another editor in mind: Hazlitt. Probably on the strength of their recommendation, Baldwin named Hazlitt the editor on March 5, 1821.[5]

Hazlitt was not excited about this job; he did it for the money. He was also distracted by the publication, in April, of his *Table Talk*, for which he had high hopes. They were not met. The majority of reviews, especially in the *British Critic* and the *Quarterly*, went on the attack.

But Hazlitt nonetheless executed his duties as the *London*'s editor admirably. The two numbers he managed, April and May 1821, featured four of his own essays, including "People of Sense"; Lamb's essays on April Fools, Quakers, and schoolmasters; and pieces by Hunt, Procter, and Wainewright. Hazlitt might have even solicited Lamb's "Imperfect Sympathies," likely composed at this time, though not published until August.

After Hazlitt stepped down, Baldwin sold the *London Magazine* to the publishers John Taylor and James Hessey. Unlike Baldwin, the men didn't employ an editor to guide the magazine, only a subeditor, Thomas Hood, who basically helped Taylor run things. The periodical declined quickly.

Regardless, Lamb continued to publish voluminously in its pages. Aside from the Elia essays, he published "The Confessions of H.F.V.H. Delamore, Esq," based on his own time in the stocks at Barnet; "The Gentle Giantess," inspired by the outsized Mrs. Smith of Cambridge; a letter by Elia parodying De Quincey's *London* piece "To a Young Man Whose Education Has Been Neglected"; "Ritson versus John Scott the Quaker," a hoax staged by Elia in which he fabricates the marginalia of two actual literary men; "Guy Faux," an extension of his *Reflector* essay of 1811, "On the Probable Effects of Gunpowder Treason"; and a speculation on the passage in *The Tempest* where Prospero says of Sycorax, "For one thing that she did / They would not take her life." But by August 1825, Lamb was fed up with the *London*'s poor management. He stopped publishing in its pages. By 1829 the magazine had closed.

But Taylor and Hessey did at least one good thing; they inaugurated a monthly dinner among their writers, and through these dinners Lamb met several men who would become good friends, including Hood (the poet and novelist who gave the Lambs their dog Dash and who described Lamb's face as a piece of delicate, odd, old china); Bernard Barton; Henry Francis Cary (translator of Dante, keeper of the printed books in the British Museum, composer of the epigraph on Lamb's tombstone); and Thomas Griffiths Wainewright.[6]

At one of these *London Magazine* parties Lamb met John Clare, the peasant-poet from Helpston, Northamptonshire. Though he attended school until the age of twelve, and then studied in night school, Clare spent most of his childhood and early adulthood working as a field laborer, potboy, gardener, soldier, and lime burner. This work wasn't enough to support him and his family, so in 1818, at the age of twenty-five, Clare applied for parish relief. He studied James Thomson's *The Seasons*. He fell in love with the verse, and he made his own. To keep from being evicted, he tried to sell his verse to Edward Drury, a local bookseller. Fortunately for Clare, Drury was cousin to John Taylor, to whom he sent Clare's poems. Taylor and Hessey published *Poems Descriptive of Rural Life and Scenery* in 1820. The book caught the last wave of the "ploughboy poet" craze, and it was a success. The follow-up, *Village Minstrel and Other Poems*, did not do as well.

Look at "Noon," from *Rural Life and Scenery*.

> All how silent and how still
> Nothing heard but yonder mill;
> While the dazzled eye surveys

> All around a liquid blaze;
> And amid the scorching gleams,
> If we earnest look, it seems
> As if crooked bits of glass
> Seem'd repeatedly to pass.[7]

So stunningly odd was this verse, Taylor struggled to describe it through another medium: "Clare . . . does not regard language in the same way that a
logician does. He considers it collectively rather than in detail, and paints
up to his mind's original by mingling words, as a painter mixes his colours."[8]

Clare, who had spent time in Gypsies' camps as a youth, fascinated Lamb.
Here they are at a *London* dinner.

> On the right hand then of the editor sits Elia, of the pleasant smile,
> and the quick eyes . . . and a wit as quick as his eyes, and sure, as
> Hazlitt described, to stammer out the best pun and the best remark
> in the course of the evening. Next to him, shining verdantly out from
> the grave-coloured suits of the literati, like a patch of turnips amidst
> stubble and fallow, behold our Jack i' the Green—John Clare! In his
> bright, grass-coloured coat, and yellow waistcoat (there are green-
> ish stalks too, under the table), he looks a very cowslip. . . . Elia—
> much more of house Lamb than of grass Lamb—avowedly caring
> little or nothing for pastoral; cottons, nevertheless, very kindly to the
> Northamptonshire poet, and still more to his ale, pledging him again
> and again as "Clarissimus," and "Princely Clare," and sometimes so
> lustily as to make the latter cast an anxious glance into his tankard.
> . . . . But besides the tankard, the two "drouthie neebors" discuss
> poetry in general, and Montegomery's "Common Lot" in particu-
> lar, Lamb insisting on the beauty of the tangential sharp turn of "O!
> she was fair!" thinking, mayhap, of his own Alice W———, and Clare
> swearing "Dal!" (a clarified d———n) "Dal! if it isn't like a dead man
> preaching out of his coffin."[9]

Clare visited Lamb at his home.

> Then there is Charles Lamb . . . he is very fond of snuff which
> seems to sharpen his wit every time he dips his plentiful finger into
> his large bronze colord box and then he sharpens up his head thro[w]s
> himself backward in his chair and stammers at a joke or a pun with
> an inward sort of utterance ere he can give it speech till his tongue

becomes a sort of Packmans strop turning it over and over till at last it comes out wetted as keen as a razor and expectation when she knows him wakens into a sort of danger as bad as cutting your throat but he is a good sort of fellow and if he offends it is innosently done who is not acquainted with Elia and who woud believe him otherwise as soon as the cloath is drawn the wine and he's become comfortable his talk now doubles and threbles into a combination of repetitions urging the same thing over and over again until at last he—leans off with scarcly "good night" in his mouth and dissapears leaving his memory like a pleasant ghost hanging about his vacant chair and there is his sister Bridget a good sort of woman tho her kind cautions and tender admonitions are nearly lost upon Charles who like an undermined river bank leans carlessly over his jollity and recieves the gentle lappings of the waves of womans tongue unheedingly till it ebbs and then in the same carless posture sits and recieves it again tho all is lost on Charles.[10]

When together, the two men were sometimes known as "Tom and Jerry," a reference drawn from Pierce Egan's *Life in London*, a novel that features urban Corinthian Tom and his cousin from the country, Jerry Hawthorne.[11]

In 1822, Clare wrote that Elia's "reveries and vision'd themes / To Care's lorn heart a luscious pleasure prove; / Wild as the mystery of delightful dreams, / Soft as the anguish of remember'd love."[12]

Throughout 1821, Lamb moved back and forth between London and Dalston, wrote Elia essays, received praise and money for them, socialized. And he drank heavily. He confessed to Taylor in late July he had no idea who had brought him home the night before (*L,* 2:307).

De Quincey had dinner with the Lambs around this time. Like De Quincey himself, Lamb had a habit of taking a "great deal" of wine "*during* dinner—none *after* it." So much wine did Lamb take that he passed out at the table—or, as De Quincey delicately put it, fell into "a brief eclipse of sleep." The slumber "descended upon him as softly as a shadow. In a gross person, laden with superfluous flesh, and sleeping heavily, this would have been disagreeable; but in Lamb, thin even to meagreness, spare and wiry as an Arab of the desert, or as Thomas Aquinas, wasted by scholastic vigils, the affection of sleep seemed rather a network of aerial gossamer than of earthly cobweb—more like a golden haze falling upon him gently from the heavens than a cloud exhaling upwards from the flesh." When Lamb awoke from this wine stupor, he "sat for some time in profound silence, and then, with the most startling rapidity, sang out—'Diddle, diddle, dumpkins'; not looking at me, but as if soliloquizing. For five minutes he relapsed into the same deep silence; from which again he started up into the same abrupt utterance of—'Diddle, diddle, dumpkins.'"[13]

Lamb did stay awake long enough to take one trip, in June, to Margate, his second to this resort village on England's southeast coast. Mary joined him. This trip and the earlier one, in 1790, inspired the Elia essay "Old Margate Hoy," a charming sketch of sea life that digresses into a discussion of the gap between expectation and reality: "Will it be thought a digression (it may spare some unwelcome comparisons), if I endeavour to account for the *dissatisfaction* which I have heard so many persons confess to have felt (as I did myself feel in part on this occasion), *at the sight of the sea for the first time?*" (*W*, 2:180).

On this particular trip, the Lambs marveled at a whale foundered on the shore. As Mary Cowden Clarke, who met them there, recalled, Charles talked eagerly about "an extraordinarily large whale that had been captured there, of its having created lively interest in the place, of its having been conveyed away in a strong cart, on which it lay a huge mass of colossal height; when he added with one of his sudden droll penetrating glances:—The *eye* has just gone past our window."[14]

On October 26, John Lamb died. Charles had not seen much of him over the past several years, but the death hit him hard. Though he bore the demise pretty well at first, he writes, as Elia, "afterwards it haunted and haunted me; and though I did not cry or take it to heart as some do, and as I think he would have done if I had died, yet I missed him all day long, and knew not till then how much I had loved him. I missed his kindness, and I missed his crossness, and wished him to be alive again, to be quarrelling with him . . . rather than not have him again" (*W*, 2:103).

Regardless of his differences with—and from—his brother, Charles felt a deep, dark bond. In a poem first printed in 1818, "To John Lamb, Esq, of the South-Sea House" he faintly mocks John's maintenance of the "old authoritative strain" that keeps him, the "elder brother," "up in state." But though convention might hold John above Charles, the brothers see, through a "dim glass," the "old buried forms" and "faces long ago" that bind them—and another (Mary)—to a grim past (*W*, 5:41). John's death must have revived the family's tragedy in Charles's heart. Grieving for John, he mourned his mother again.

Dorothy Wordsworth intuited this suffering. As she wrote to Robinson, she had "great concern" for the Lambs. She feared the "loss [would] be deeply felt."[15] What she didn't know was that Mary had fallen ill again and didn't register the death at all. As Charles wrote to Ayrton, "I think it well that the death of poor John should have happened at a time that my sister can be but half sensible to it. . . . I ventured on my own advice to acquaint her. . . . It does not seem much to have altered her state of mind, and now she will gradually come to herself with nothing new to tell." Lamb admits that "I am in a state of trial, but I do not lose myself" (*L*, 2:314).

Not even a month later, the Lambs lost Admiral Burney, their longtime whist companion. Lamb confessed to Rickman that this loss didn't shock him greatly, since he now felt used to death after his brother's recent passing and, the previous year, the death of Jem White (*L*, 2:315).

Nevertheless, loss was consuming Lamb, as he acknowledged in a contemplative letter to Wordsworth in March 1822. Because of the recent deaths, he feels "a certain deadness to every thing," and wants only to "bury" himself at Dalston. For each person who has died over the past two years, so many parts of him "have been numbed." "One sees a picture, reads an anecdote, starts a casual fancy, and thinks to tell of it to this person in preference to every other—the person is gone whom it would have peculiarly suited. It won't do for *another*. Every departure destroys a class of sympathies. . . . One never hears any thing, but the image of the particular person occurs with whom alone almost you would care to share the intelligence. Thus one distributes oneself about—and now for so many parts of me I have lost the market." How can he play whist without Burney? Lamb chooses his friends carefully, based on his own idiosyncrasies. When the man matches his whimsy, he latches on, hard, and melds the friend inseparably to the activities they mutually love. The joy of this habit is obvious: a life charged with shared strangeness. But when the friend dies, those forms of life he vivified die. Where the friend was in his heart is now a hole. There are no replacements parts. "Common natures do not suffice me. Good people, as they are called, won't serve. I want individuals. I am made up of queer points and I want so many answering needles. The going away of friends does not make the remainder more precious. It takes so much from them as there was a common link. A. B. and C. make a party. A. dies. B. not only loses A. but all A.'s part in C. C. loses A.'s part in B., and so the alphabet sickens by subtraction of interchangeables" (*L*, 2:318–19).

# CHAPTER 43

❧

# *Paris*

Boldly, given Mary's sensitivity to travel and Charles's deep malaise, the Lambs planned a trip to Paris, a city Lamb had wanted to visit since 1802, when Manning was there. This was in June 1822, and it would be their first time abroad. Robinson saw them the night before they left. Charles was in a good mood, but Mary was agitated. "Her courage in going is great."[1]

The siblings sailed from Brighton to Dieppe. A Frenchman accompanied them, as did Sarah James, Mary's nurse. Their old friend James Kenney, the dramatist, was now living in Versailles, along with his wife. Mrs. Kenney, the widow of Holcroft, was French. Charles and Mary would stay with this family and benefit from their knowledge of the language and culture.

On the coach from Dieppe to Paris, Mary fell ill. In Amiens Lamb was "in despair," but somehow found some people he knew, and they helped him get Mary into "proper hands."[2] Did he find a private asylum in Amiens? This seems likely. It appears that Lamb then traveled on to Versailles by himself. If so, he probably had assumed that Mary, deep into her seizure, wouldn't know if he was there or not.

As for Mary, we can't know how she felt during her time in Amiens. However, a fictional fragment she likely composed soon after returning from France in September gives us hints. The story, part of which Charles wrote, is set in France between 1787 and 1788. A Mrs. McKenna has just married a second time. She has moved from England to France with her second husband, a merchant. At one point, she falls into "a very low nervous state" that the least noise worsens. Bizarrely, a French officer in the room above is purposely loud. Mrs. McKenna in general is a neurotic soul, and she worries that her moods will frustrate her husband: "I had made my husband very uncomfortable for a time—teasing him with my dread of hearing bad news." At one point, she stays in a room with a bare tile floor. She worries about hurting herself on the hard surface, and she asks the landlady to spread blankets.[3]

Do these details recall Mary's breakdown in Amiens? Did she hallucinate during her low nervous state about a man above trying to make her worse? Did she feel guilty for irritating Charles, her "husband?" Were blankets spread for her while she remained in "good hands" in Amiens, so she wouldn't hurt herself?

At the Kenneys' home in Versailles, Lamb connected with the Kenneys' little girl, Sophy, whom he referred to as his "dear wife." But Lamb drank too much French wine, perhaps to escape his guilty feelings over leaving Mary. Kenney perceived that Lamb was "more reserved and shut up than usual—avoiding his old friends and not so cordial or amiable as was his wont."[4]

Lamb traveled to Paris. He was accompanied by Kenney's friend John Howard Payne, an American actor who had debuted as Young Norval in *Douglas*, the character Lamb believed he was while in Hoxton, twenty-seven years back. Payne was likely in Paris to escape debts incurred from his failed efforts to produce his own plays in Sadler's Wells. Rumor has it he and his friend Washington Irving were both in love with Mary Shelley. Payne apparently helped Lamb in his arrangements with his sister. Upon returning to England, Lamb submitted some of Payne's plays to Covent Garden. Payne became famous for writing the song "Home, Sweet Home."

In Paris Lamb stayed at the Hôtel de l'Europe on the rue de Valois, close to the Palais Royal. Here he established a rhythm. He "led his own independent life—disappearing sometimes all day, having lived mostly on the river quays on the Odeon side of the Seine, rummaging the bookstalls and print-shops for old books and old prints, returning late at night to the hotel, and skating up the waxed stairs to bed, thoroughly satisfied with the day's work."[5]

Lamb dined with François-Joseph Talma, the famous French actor. He had seen Talma in William Havard's *Regulus* and, when the actor asked his opinion, he did not reply. Talma understood. Lamb wasn't impressed. See me in Juoy's *Scylla*, Talma urged, implying he was much better in that play. Lamb said, "Incidit in Scyllam, qui vult vitare Charybdim" (He runs into Scylla, who wants to avoid Charybdis.) Talma replied, "Ah! you are a rogue; you are a great rogue!" He shook Lamb's hand "cordially" when the evening ended.[6]

Lamb had little to say about his trip to Paris. He did write to John Clare that he had "eaten frogs. The nicest little rabbity things you ever tasted" (*L*, 2:328). And around the same time, to Barron Field he praised the beauty and unifying power of the Seine: "Paris is a glorious picturesque old City. London looks mean and New to it, as the town of Washington would, seen after *it*. But they have no St. Paul's or Westminster Abbey. The Seine, so much despised by Cockneys, is exactly the size to run thro' a magnificent street; palaces a mile long on one side, lofty Edinbro' stone . . . houses on the other. The Thames disunites London and Southwark" (*L*, 2:333).

By the time Lamb was ready to return to London, in mid-August 1822, Mary had landed at the Kenneys'. Characteristically, a sane Mary was impressive. Kenney was "loud in her praise, saying that he thought her a faultless creature—possessing every virtue under heaven."[7] Though Charles needed to go home, Mary had not yet seen Paris, and so she decided not to return with him. Robinson was in France, and he offered to show Mary the city.

Like her brother, she stayed at the Hôtel de l'Europe. Robinson escorted her and Mrs. Kenney through the Palais Royal and the Louvre and along the borough side of the Seine, from which Mary could see the Tuileries. Along this route were print shops and bookstalls. Charles had written his friend a letter recommending that he take exactly that stroll with Mary, but Robinson didn't receive the missive until after the walk. He was pleased to confirm his theory: he could always sympathize with Lamb's likings ("but not generally his dislikings").[8] For her part, Mary loved the "long dreary Boulevards" (*L*, 2:348).

Mary returned to London in September. Perhaps fearing she would suffer another attack, Robinson lent her his overcoat for the journey. It could serve as a straitjacket. The trip home was trouble-free, but the coat didn't make it through UK customs—officials didn't believe a man's coat with the name "Robinson" in it belonged to a woman named "Lamb."

# CHAPTER 44

## Colebrook

Lamb spent the remainder of 1822 writing to friends that he had eaten frogs; refusing to mourn the recently drowned "Percy Bishe," whose voice he found the "most obnoxious squeak I was ever tormented with" (*L*, 2:327); trying to raise money for a fallen-on-hard-times Godwin (he asked Haydon and Sir Walter Scott); critiquing London theater to Payne; summing up his sense of Defoe for Walter Wilson ("His style is . . . beautiful, but plain *& homely*" [*L*, 2:352]); and lamenting a Christmas ruined by too much company.

The year 1823 opened with the publication of *Elia* and Phil-Elia announcing the death of the author, whose humor was anyway "pretty well exhausted" (*W*, 1:151). Lamb obviously meant his obituary at the beginning of 1823 as a jest—Elia lived in many more essays—but the joke turned unintentionally earnest: from this moment on, Lamb's literary career and his life steadily lost the fantastic energy of Elia, and he began to die.

Along with "The Character of Elia," Lamb published another New Year's piece in the January number of the *London Magazine*, "Rejoicings upon the New Year's Coming of Age." Elia personifies the new year as a "young spark" who throws a party for all the days of the year. His jester, April Fool, plays havoc with the seating arrangements, placing Summer Solstice beside Winter and Ash Wednesday between Christmas and Lord Mayor's Day. Dramas and songs and toasts and flirtations and quibbles and conundrums ensue, until the feast concludes with "Valentine and pretty May" taking "their departure together in one of the prettiest silvery twilights a Lover's Day could wish to set in" (*W*, 2:235).

Compared to the marvelous essays of 1822, Elia's annus mirabilis, this is light fare. Unlike the earlier "New Year's Eve," there is no playful "I," no ironic tension, no outlandish humor or style, no drama among temporalities. Several of the *London Magazine* essays of 1823 feel similarly like thinner versions of earlier masterpieces. "The Child Angel: A Dream," from June, recalls "Dream-Children: A Reverie" but lacks its heart-rending drama. The later essay sentimentally tells of how a child angel, though touched with slight mortality, becomes "the Tutelar Genius of Childhood upon Earth" (*W*, 2:145). Elia's July essay, "The Old Margate Hoy," is, like "Oxford in the Vacation," a description of a holiday. While the piece features vigorously stark images ("I love town, or country; but this detestable Cinque Port is neither. I hate these scrubbed shoots, thrusting out their starved foliage from between the horrid fissures of dusty in-nutritious rocks" [*W*, 2:181]), it, too, lacks the ironic play of the earlier works.

But Lamb after 1823 could still rally, as he did in March of that year, with "Old China." In May and December, respectively, he published "Poor Relations" and "Amicus Redivivus." "Blakesmoor, in H——shire" appeared in September 1824, and "The Superannuated Man" and "The Convalescent" came out in May and July 1825, respectively.

Lamb was becoming a literary celebrity, but he wasn't happy about it, since the admirers sucked away his precious time. He wrote to Payne that he was soon to be introduced to "a literary lady . . . whose portentous name is *Plura*, in English 'many things.' Now, of all God's creatures, I detest letters-affecting, authors-hunting ladies. But . . . So Miss Many Things and I are to have a conference" (*L*, 2:358). He complains to Wordsworth of the "d——d people" coming. "By d——d, I only mean deuced. 'Tis these suitors of Penelope that make it necessary to authorize a little for gin and mutton and such trifles" (*L*, 3:5).

But Lamb still enjoyed the company of other writers, especially on April 4, 1823, the evening of the famous Monkhouse gathering, which included Wordsworth, Coleridge, Thomas Moore, and Samuel Rogers. Mary was there, too, and Mary Wordsworth, as was Robinson, who left an account: "During this afternoon, Coleridge alone displayed any of his peculiar talent. He talked much and well. I have not for years seen him in such excellent health and with such fine a flow of spirits. His discourse was addressed chiefly to Wordsworth, on points of metaphysical criticism—Rogers occasionally interposing a remark. The only one of the poets who seemed not to enjoy himself was Moore. He was very attentive to Coleridge, but seemed to relish Lamb, next to whom he was placed."[1]

Moore was attuned to Lamb's new literary celebrity, calling him the hero of the *London Magazine*. He admired Lamb's cleverness but wearied of "the villainous & abortive puns which he miscarries of every minute." Mary didn't fare too well in Moore's eyes. She was to him only "the poor woman who went mad with him in the diligence on the way to Paris."[2] (No wonder Lamb told the prickly Moore that he had always felt an antipathy for him, even though he liked him—drunkenly—now.)

For his part, Lamb praised his oldest friend: "Coleridge was in his finest vein of talk, had all the talk, and let 'em talk as evilly as they do of the envy of Poets, I am sure not one there but was content to be nothing but a listener. The Muses were dumb, while Apollo lectured, on his and their fine art" (*L*, 2:377).

Lamb's biggest publishing event of 1823 was an attack on Robert Southey. In the January number of the *Quarterly Review*, the now-conservative Southey published "The Progress of Infidelity," a review of Henri Gregoire on Deism. As an aside, he referred to Lamb's *Elia* as a book that would be "delightful" if it only had a "sounder religious feeling" (*W*, 1:479n). This angered Lamb, who for all his flippancy never abandoned his Unitarian-like Christianity. He countered in the October number of the *London Magazine*.

Lamb wrote as Elia, claiming that he can't detect any impiety in his sentences. Yes, he is occasionally "betrayed into some levities," but this habit he learned from Southey, who has all his "life been making a jest of the Devil." Southey's joking is fine with Elia, but not when he censures his friends for cracking wise. Elia defends these friends, most notably Hazlitt and Hunt, and reminds Southey that he is a "Dissenter," not a member of Southey's Church of England (*W*, 1:168).

For someone who can write as wittily as Lamb, the "Letter to Southey" is a tedious, lengthy affair. Why would Lamb go to the trouble? He probably had sales in mind. A swipe like Southey's could hurt his bottom line. But his rebuttal reminds us that the nonsensical Lamb retained a serious religious side he was ready to defend. He was also swift to stand up for his two radical friends. He also probably still held a grudge toward the *Quarterly*, which had exposed Mary's madness, asserted "Confessions of a Drunkard" was about

Lamb himself (which it was), and butchered his review of Wordsworth. Finally, Lamb hated hypocrisy, and exposed it in Southey.

Southey wrote remorsefully to Lamb. "Nothing could be further from my mind than any intention or apprehension of any way offending or injuring a man concerning whom I have never spoken, thought, or felt otherwise than with affection, esteem, and admiration." If he had known his piece had offended Lamb, he would gladly have inserted a "note" in the next number of the *Quarterly* to "qualify and explain" what hurt Lamb. Southey was sorry he hadn't done so, and he had no intention of stretching out the controversy. He asked Lamb to please forgive "an unintended offence." He offered to come to Lamb's house to shake hands.[3]

Lamb was quick to forgive. "The kindness of your note has melted away the mist which was upon me" (*L*, 2:407). Lamb was mainly irked at the *Quarterly*, not so much Southey. Come any day next week except Wednesday, he assured his old friend, and we can shake.

Lamb gave his new address to Southey: Colebrook Cottage, Colebrook Row, Islington. "A detached whitish house, close to the New River, end of Colebrook Terrace, left hand from Sadler's wells" (*L*, 2:407–8).

After returning from a summer holiday trip to Tunbridge Wells and Hastings, the Lambs found both their residences—Covent Garden and Dalston—unbearable. The landlord's family in Dalston was constantly fighting—physically, bruising each other—and the landlady on Russell Street argued with her maid. The Lambs wanted quiet, and so they moved to Islington, then a small village just north of London, about a two-and-a-half-mile walk from the Russell Street address. For centuries Islington had been a rural retreat for city dwellers, especially famous for its archery culture. By Lamb's time, urban sprawl had encroached on the ancient fields. Colebrook Row, Lamb's address, was constructed in 1768. ("Colebrook" is now spelled "Colebrooke.") Initially it abutted six acres of nursery, but a brickfield soon replaced the trees. Mary Shelley thought the address pretty humdrum, but it pleased the Lambs. Lamb described it as "a white house, with 6 good rooms; the New River (rather elderly by this time) runs (if a moderate walking pace can be so termed) close to the foot of the house; and behind is a spacious garden, with vines (I assure you), pears, strawberries, parsnips, leeks, carrots, cabbages, to delight the heart of old Alcinous. You enter without passage into a cheerful dining room, all studded over and rough with old Books, and above is a lightsome Drawing

Charles Lamb's house in Islington. (Courtesy of British Museum Images.)

room, 3 windows, full of choice prints. I feel like a great Lord, never having had a house before" (*L*, 2:394).

Lamb reveled in the "exquisite raciness" of his jargonels. He sat under his vine and contemplated "the growth of vegetable nature." He felt like "FATHER ADAM," lapsed, since he drunkenly lopped off some "choice boughs . . . which hung over from a neighbor's garden" and shaded his window. He couldn't calm the neighbor's wife, whose fury made her "not handsome." "There was no buttering her parsnips. She talk'd of the Law. What a lapse to commit on the first day of my happy 'garden-state'" (*L*, 2:395).

The birdlife tickled Lamb, too. George Daniel, a stockbroker's clerk and man of letters, remembers Lamb whistling for the birds to come down from his windowsills and peck his "plum" cake. When Daniel offered him a bull-finch in a cage, Lamb said no. "Every song that it sung from its wiry prison I could never flatter myself was meant for my heart; but rather a wistful note to the passing travelers of air that it were with them, too! This would make me self-reproachful and sad."[4]

Mary had fallen ill around the time of the move. Until Charles got settled, she remained in Dalston with Sarah James. She joined him in September, still weak. During this month, Lamb made his will.

In November, Dyer walked out of Lamb's door and fell into the New River. Lamb's letter to Sarah Hazlitt describing the event, including the "one-eyed" doctor, "dirty and drunk," served as an early draft for "Amicus Redivivus" (*L*, 2:405). Mary Shelley came to tea soon after. Lamb admonished: "Mind how you come" (*L*, 2:407).

Lamb closed 1823 by riffing to Barton on the importance of knowing as little about the "inner construction of the Animal Man" as possible. That keeps you from worrying about the effects of drink on your liver (*L*, 2:409).

Lamb opened 1824 by writing to Barton, now a regular correspondent, again. He now wasn't able to muster as much humor about his dark interiors.

> Do you know what it is to succumb under an insurmountable day-mare,—a whoreson lethargy, Falstaff calls it,—an indisposition to do anything, or to be anything,—a total deadness and distaste—a sus-pension of vitality—an indifference to locality—a numb, soporifical, goodfornothingness—an ossification all over—an oyster-like insensi-bility to the passing events,—a mind-stupor,—a brawny defiance to the needles of a thrusting-in conscience—did you ever have a very bad cold, with a total irresolution to submit to water-gruel processes?—this has been for many weeks my lot, and my excuse—my fingers drag heavily over this paper, and to my thinking it is three and twenty furlongs from here to the end of this demi-sheet—I have not a thing to say—nothing is of more importance than another—I am flatter

than a denial or a pancake . . . duller than a country stage when the
actors are off it—a cipher, an O—I acknowledge life at all, only by an
occasional convulsional cough, and a permanent phlegmatic pain in
the chest—I am weary of the world—Life is weary of me . . . nothing
interests me. . . .if you told me the world will be at an end to-morrow,
I should just say, "will it?"—I have not volition enough left to dot my
*i*'s, much less to comb my EYEBROWS . . . my hand writes, not I, from
habit, as chickens run about a little, when their heads are off—O for
a vigorous fit of gout, cholic, toothache—an earwig in my auditory, a
fly in my visual organs—pain is life—the sharper, the more evidence
of life—but this apathy, this death. (*L,* 2:413–14)

This sounds more like the Coleridge of "Limbo" ("Tis a strange place, this
Limbo . . . where Time & weary Space / Fettered from flight, with night-mair
sense of fleeing, / Strive for their last crepuscular half-being") than Lamb—at
least the Lamb in print.[5] Lamb had been feeling like the similarly depressed
Coleridge for years, and now he found the language to expound upon what
he had been calling his "low spirits." The imagery is sadly ironic. He now
finds himself in the kind of causeless state he longed for in his "The South-
Sea House" and "Oxford in the Vacation." But this condition where nothing
consequential occurs isn't innocence. It is hell. Each moment is as flat and
meaningless as the last. The past doesn't inspire nostalgia but vague regret.
The future doesn't evoke hope but slight dread. This is the dull fever of time
as an infinite succession of indifferent ticks. The malaise brings only more
malaise, apathy over apathy over apathy. Lamb is Coleridge's "Life-in-Death,"
motion without significance, talk just for talk.

But in writing about the despair, Lamb overcomes, at least momentarily,
the despair. As is true of Coleridge's "Limbo," as well as his "Dejection: An
Ode," Lamb's descriptions of his lack of vigor are emphatically alive. Such
is the logic of the Romantic crisis text (Shelley's "Ode to the West Wind"
and Keats's "Ode to Melancholy" are other examples): writing about failure
becomes success. Lamb's letter here should join the great melancholic confessions of the poets.

Barton was concerned. Lamb downplayed. "That peevish letter of mine,
which was meant to convey an apology for my incapacity to write, seems to
have been taken by you in too serious a light. It was only my way of telling
you I had a severe cold." But Lamb returns to his mood, which has nothing
to do with a cold: "The fact is I have been insuperably dull and lethargic for

many weeks, and cannot rise to the vigour of a Letter, much less an Essay"
(*L*, 2:415). The *London Magazine* will have to do without him for now. (He
contributed nothing from December 1823 to September 1824.) He will feel
better in the spring. A month later, though, Lamb still complains to Barton
of his "heavy" head.

In March Charles and Mary hosted a gathering that included Robinson and Manning. The talk turned to religion, and Robinson perceived that
"Lamb's impressions against religion are unaccountably strong, and yet he is
by nature pious. It is the dogmatism of theology which has disgusted Lamb,
and it is that alone which he opposes; he has the organ of theosophy, and is
by nature pious."[6]

Also in the spring of 1824, Lamb met P. G. Patmore, Scott's second in the
duel with Christie. He presents the twilight Lamb: "During the last ten years
of his life, he was never seen in any thing but a suit of uniform black, with
knee-breeches, and (sometimes, not always) gaiters of the same to meet them.
Probably he was induced to admit this innovation by a sort of compromise
with his affection for the colour of other years; for though his dress was 'black'
in name and nature, he always contrived that it should exist only in a state of
rusty brown."[7]

In May Lamb wrote Barton about something other than melancholia:
William Blake. Barton had recently read Blake's "The Chimney Sweeper"
from *Songs of Innocence*. He was curious about the author. Lamb filled him in.

Blake is a real name, I assure you, and a most extraordinary man he is,
if he still be living. [He was, at sixty-six, at 3 Fountain Court, Strand.]
He is the Robert [William] Blake, whose wild designs accompany a
splendid edition of the "Night Thoughts," which you may have seen,
in one of which he pictures the parting of soul and body by a solid
mass of human form floating off, God knows how, from a lumpish
mass . . . left behind on the dying bed. He paints in water-colours
marvellous strange pictures, visions of his brain, which he asserts he
has seen. They have great merit. He has *seen* the old Welsh bards on
Snowdon—he has seen the Beautifullest, the strongest, and the Ugli-
est Man, left alone from the Massacre of the Britons by the Romans,
and has painted them from memory (I have seen his paintings), and
asserts them to be as good as the figures of Raphael and Angelo, but
not better, as they had precisely the same retro-visions and prophetic

visions with [himself]. The painters in oil (which he will have it that neither of them practised) he affirms to have been the ruin of art, and affirms that all the while he was engaged in his Water paintings, Titian was disturbing him, Titian the Ill Genius of Oil Painting. His Pictures—one in particular, the Canterbury Pilgrims (far above Stothard's)—have great merit, but hard, dry, yet with grace. He has written a Catalogue of them with a most spirited criticism on Chaucer, but mystical and full of Vision. His poems have been sold hitherto only in Manuscript. I never read them; but a friend at my desire procured the "Sweep Song." There is one to a tiger, which I have heard recited, beginning:

> Tiger, Tiger, burning bright,
> Thro' the desarts of the night,

which is glorious, but, alas! I have not the book; for the man is flown, whither I know not—to Hades or a Mad House. But I must look on him as one of the most extraordinary persons of the age. (*L*, 2:424–25)

Lamb was one of the few who attended Blake's art exhibition in May 1809. He accompanied Robinson. On the first floor of his brother's sock shop in Golden Square, Soho, Blake presented sixteen paintings, six of which have gone missing, including the massive portrait of the ancient Britons, ten feet by fourteen. Lamb seems to have admired all the paintings at the exhibit (as well as Blake's illustrations of Blair's *The Grave*). Lamb had also read Blake's *Descriptive Catalogue*, the poet's account of the exhibit, "mystical and full of vision." Describing his picture of the ancient Britons, Blake imagines ancient man as a fourfold wonder of himself, strength, beauty, and ugliness. Blake's account of his painting of *The Canterbury Tales*—which Lamb admired for its hard, dry grace—discovers in the pilgrims "visions of . . . eternal principles" (*L*, 2:425).

It is a pity Lamb didn't review the exhibition. The only notice the show (which sold nothing) received was by Robert Hunt, who complained, "The poor man fancies himself a great master, having painted a few wretched pictures, blotted and blurred and very badly drawn." Hunt found the *Catalogue* lacking, too: "a farrago of nonsense . . . the wild effusions of a distempered brain."[8]

Lamb knew lunacy and sensed that Blake could have easily ended up in a madhouse. But he saw in Blake the kind of madness he most valued: not the insanity that blots out individuality but the dazzling eccentricity of a man obsessively following his own genius. Lamb, who complemented Blake by calling him a "mad Wordsworth," saw what Hunt couldn't: an artist for which there did not yet exist categories of interpretation.[9] The same was true of Lamb.

"I must Create a System, or be enslav'd by another Mans." So Blake's Los says in *Jerusalem*, that "perfectly mad poem" Southey had seen on a visit to Blake's, after which he came to the Lambs'. Southey had also said that he admired Blake's "designs & poetic talents," but thought him "a decided madman."[10] Robinson, who conversed with Blake many times, called him "a remarkable man—Shall I call him Artist or Genius—or Mystic or Madman? Probably he is all."[11] Coleridge knew Blake, too, and believed he was a "man of Genius," compared to whose output his own visions were in "the very mire of common-place common-sense."[12]

Lamb also despised systems, and though he wasn't as passionate about construction as Blake (he was more a drifter), he knew that art, verbal or pictorial, could live only as weirdness endlessly upsetting hypnotic abstractions.

At the end of his lovely letter on Blake, Lamb glanced at Byron, who died on April 19, 1824. Byron was "at best a Satyrist,—in any other way he was mean enough." All he could move was "the Spleen." Lamb fears he is behaving unjustly to this poseur but, he admits, "I cannot love him, nor squeeze a tear to his memory" (*L,* 2:426).

CHAPTER 45

Retirement

For the remainder of 1824, Lamb struggled with his own spleen. He complained to Barton: "To have to do anything, to order me a new coat, for instance, tho' my old buttons are shelled like beans, is an effort" (*L*, 2:437). Exacerbating this depression was an eye infection that caused "severe inflammation" (*L*, 2:429). So low-spirited was Lamb he didn't even arrange the yearly excursion. But there was a payoff: Mary got through the year without an attack. Perhaps she could avoid her illness in the future by just staying home.

Charles's job continued to drain him. As he wrote Procter, who had just married, "I am married . . . to a severe step-wife, who keeps me, not at bed and board, but at desk and board, and is jealous of my morning aberrations . . . the damn'd Day-hag BUSINESS" (*L*, 2:443). Charles's other source of income, the *London Magazine,* was in precipitous decline, but he did manage to write two essays for the periodical as 1824 winded down. In September, he returned to his old Elian form with "Blakesmoor, in H——shire," which he followed in November with "Captain Jackson," about imagination combating poverty.

In early 1825, hope came in the form of hyperbole. Lamb wrote to Manning that he had just seen Dr. Tuthill, and the physician had deemed him "*non*-capacitated . . . for business. O joyous imbecility!" (*L*, 2:455). Lamb hoped a letter from Tuthill exaggerating his poor health would liberate him from East India House with a good pension. In early February Lamb submitted this document to the office, along with another medical report from Dr. Gillman. East India acknowledged the papers in its minutes: "A letter from Mr. Charles Lamb, dated the 7th [of February] stating that he has served as Clerk in the Accounting Office for a period of nearly 33 years; enclosing medical certificates of the declining state of his health; and requesting permission to retire from the service under the Act of the 53 Geo. 3, cap. 155, being read: Ordered That the said Letter be referred to the Committee of Accounts to examine and report."[1]

On February 10, Lamb turned fifty. By March 23, he was still waiting to hear the company's response. "I have a glimpse of Freedom," he wrote Barton, "of becoming a Gentleman at large, but I am put off from day to day (L, 2:463).

Six days later the directors accepted Lamb's resignation—"on account of certified ill health"—and offered him a handsome pension. His current income of £730 translated to £450 per year. Lamb left Leadenhall on this day, March 29, 1825, a man of leisure, a state he had coveted for decades. On the way back to Colebrook, he stopped at Robinson's. "I have left the d——d India House for Ever! Give me great joy" (L, 2:465).

To Wordsworth, a week later, he described his feelings.

> I came home forever on Tuesday in last week. The incomprehensible-
> ness of my condition overwhelm'd me. It was like passing from life
> into Eternity. Every year to be as long as three, i.e. to have three times
> as much real time, time that is my own, in it! I wandered about think-
> ing I was happy, but feeling I was not. But that tumultuousness is
> passing off, and I begin to understand the nature of the gift. Holydays,
> even the annual month, were always uneasy joys: their conscious fugi-
> tiveness—the craving after making the most of them. Now, when all is
> holyday, there are no holydays. I can sit at home, in rain or shine with-
> out a restless impulse for walkings. I am daily steadying, and shall soon
> find it as natural to me to be my own master, as it has been irksome to
> have had a master. Mary wakes every morning with an obscure feeling
> that some good has happened to us. (L, 2:466–67)

The giddy Lamb admits that the "certificates" of ill health given to him by Tuthill and Gillman were "friendly lie[s]." But when Mary read the reports, she "shook her head, and said it was all true." Lamb must concur: "Indeed, this last winter I was jaded out, winters were always worse than other parts of the year, because the spirits are worse, and I had no daylight." But now he would be better. Freedom from the India House would bring him the happiness he'd been missing (*L*, 2:467).

Not so. Three months later, he fell into a "damn'd nervous Fever," and into another in September, both of which, as we have seen, debilitated him. What Lamb never would have guessed was happening: far from energizing him, his retirement removed the structure, no matter how stressful, that had distracted him from his brooding. Now he had all the time in the world to do everything, so why not take a day or two, or three, or a week or a month, to do nothing? But in this void time, Lamb had only himself to face: his fears and anxieties, his desires never to be satisfied, his bitterness over his unfair lot. These vexations *became* his existence. He lost the means for separating himself from himself, which is what a daily job, even a joyless one, can do. He regretted retiring.

Charles explored this gap between expectation and reality in his Elian essay of May 1825, "The Superannuated Man." Elia describes the jolt of being released from prison. The inmate is overwhelmed by freedom and knows not what to do: "It seemed to me that I had more time on my hands than I could ever manage. From a poor man, poor in Time, I was suddenly lifted up into a vast revenue; I could see no end of my possessions; I wanted some steward, or judicious bailiff, to manage my estates in Time for me." Without restrictions, the joy of release has vanished: "Having all holidays, I am as though I had none. If Time hung heavy upon me, I could walk it away; but I do *not* walk all day long, as I used to do in those old transient holidays, thirty miles a day, to make the most of them" (*W*, 2:196).

Now, being retired for a while, he is used to his freedom, but time remains frictionless: "I have lost all distinction of season. I do not know the day of the week, or of the month. Each day used to be individually felt by me in its reference to the foreign post days; in its distance from, or propinquity to, the next Sunday. . . . All days are the same" (*W*, 2:198).

Lamb retired did not become Wordsworth, free-ranging poet-sage; he became ill.

In July of the year he retired, just after his first nervous fever of the year, he wrote "The Convalescent." It turns out that the sickroom and the retired state are the same. What else is sickness but "total oblivion of all the works which are going on under [the sun]?" an insensibility to "all the operations of life, except the beatings of one feeble pulse?" "To the world's business he is dead" (*W,* 2:185).

In this fevered chamber, the convalescent cultivates the true state of sickness: "supreme selfishness." He thinks only of how this particular self can get better. He "keeps his sympathy, like some curious vintage, under trusty lock and key, for his own use only." He is "for ever plotting how to do some good to himself; studying little stratagems and artificial alleviations" (*W,* 2:184).

His body is not a microcosm of the cosmos, but the cosmos itself: "He makes the most of himself; dividing himself, by an allowable fiction, into as many distinct individuals, as he hath sore and sorrowing members. Sometimes he meditates—as of a thing apart from him—upon his poor aching head, and that dull pain which, dozing or waking, lay in it all the past night like a log, or palpable substance of pain, not to be removed without opening the very scull, as it seemed, to take it thence" (*W,* 2:185).

Perversely, health he abhors, since ruddiness requires him again to attend to the rhythms of time, its swells and diminishments. But return to responsibility he must, and after a while he appreciates the "wholesome weaning from that preposterous dream of self-absorption—the puffy state of sickness." He can become again, as Elia does at the essay's end, a man of "natural pretension," a "lean and meagre figure," an "insignificant Essayist" (*W,* 2:187).

Lamb had some creative force remaining, but not much. In 1825, he published four more Elia essays in the *London Magazine,* only the first of which, January's bizarre "A Vision of Horns," did not get reprinted in *The Last Essays of Elia.* In this essay, Elia describes a dream of a town where all men sport horns as signs as their wives' infidelity. In April, Lamb released "Barbara S.——," an account of Fanny Kelly's impoverished, honest youth. June saw the publication of "The Wedding," where Elia details the ceremony of Sarah Burney, the daughter of the admiral and Sarah, to John Payne, her cousin. And in August, Lamb published "Imperfect Dramatic Illusion" (later called "Stage Illusion"), his final *London* essay, an analysis of an essential element in comic acting: a fine balance between presenting the character realistically and reminding the audience that the character isn't real.

His persona set aside, in 1825 Lamb published other pieces in the *London Magazine* under his own name. In January he printed "Biographical Memoir of Mr. Liston," a fabricated biography of the actor John Liston. In February appeared "Unitarian Protests," Lamb's attack on the government's requirement that marriages take place within the Church of England. Also in February he released "Autobiography of Mr. Munden," a phony biography like the Liston piece. March saw "Reflections in the Pillory," in which one R——d recounts his experience in the pillory for tax fraud. (No doubt Lamb was drawing once more on his experience in the stocks.) "The Last Peach" came out in April.

Lamb's work appeared in other periodicals in 1825. In the *New Times*, as "Lepus" (the hare), he published six pieces. The first, "Many Friends," describes the frustrations of having too many visitors, which Lamb, especially post-Elia, knew well. "Readers against the Grain" laments the speed with which moderns read, and the shallowness. "Mortifications of an Author" considers this: "No creature is so craving after applause, and so starved and famished for it, as an author: none so pitiful, and so little pitied" (*W*, 1:276). "Tom Pry" sketches a man who pries into the affairs of others; "Tom Pry's Wife" portrays Tom's even more meddlesome wife. Finally, "Egomet" paints a man "whose sin is a total absorption of mind in things relating to himself" (*W*, 1:279).

Lepus lacks the irony, playfulness, largesse, and self-effacement of Elia. He is a sullen, unsocial polemicist. Unappreciative readers and acquaintances have wounded him. He abhors busybodies and narcissists. Lamb dropped this persona after these brief essays, even if the mask suited his increasingly embittered person.

In 1825 Lamb also published, in the *New Monthly Magazine*, "The Illustrious Defunct," a humorous eulogy on the death of the lottery. In the same year, he released in the *New Times* a pun-laden ode to the actor Joseph Grimaldi. He followed these pieces in 1826 with two items for the *New Monthly*: a humorous riff on how actors are now expected to express their religious beliefs; and a portrait of Juke Judkins (signed by Elia), whose inability to purchase good oranges at the theater costs him his lady friend.

Though throughout the first half of the 1820s Lamb grew into a prose star, he never forsook poetry. Aptly, he began the decade by being one of the first to acknowledge publicly Keats's genius. In a July 1820 review (in the *New Times*) of *"Lamia," "Isabella," "The Eve of St. Agnes" and Other Poems*, he elevated the poet to the pantheon (even if he curiously neglected the great odes). In "The Eve of St. Agnes" Lamb discovered a "delicacy worthy of [Coleridge's] Christabel," and he appreciated in "Isabella" stanzas as "nakedly grand and moving in sentiment" as those of Dante, Chaucer, and Spenser

(*W,* 1:201). Among such affirmative assessments, Lamb might have written what he told Robinson: he believed Keats was the greatest poet of the age after Wordsworth. Sadly, by the time this review came out, Keats was so ill from tuberculosis (in mid-September he would sail to Rome to die) that he could hardly relish Lamb's praise.

Lamb's own verse—if not as glorious—often appeared in the same *London Magazine* numbers that featured his major prose. In September 1820, for instance, he published "To R.[J.]S. Knowles, Esq: On His Tragedy of Virginius," celebrating the new play of his friend James Sheridan Knowles, the Irish playwright and actor. The play reaches Lamb's highest standard; so emotionally vivid is its action, it barely requires words. In the same *London* number, Lamb included a sonnet, "Commendatory Verses to the Author of Poems, Published under the Name of Barry Cornwall," in which he tells his friend Procter he need not hide behind a nom de plume; his verse is exquisite, and he should joy openly in its power.

Lamb was also publishing in the *Champion*, John Scott's old magazine, now owned by the still radical John Thelwall. Lamb's lines were appropriately political. In May 1820, Lamb published "Sonnet to Matthew Wood, Esq, Alderman and M.P." "Heroic Wood," the lord mayor of London from 1815 to 1817 and now the city's representative in Parliament, challenged the verdict of the so-called Cato Conspiracy, a plot, hatched in early 1820, to murder the British cabinet and the prime minister. The plan failed, and thirteen were arrested, five of whom were executed. Like many radicals, Wood believed that the plot was instigated by the government to justify the Six Acts, laws recently passed in the wake of the Peterloo Massacre to hinder meetings in the name of reform. In Parliament, Wood argued that one of the supposed plotters, George Edwards, a police spy, was in fact the primary instigator of the plan. One of Wood's most vociferous critics was George Canning, the same who had attacked Lamb and his circle back in 1798 in the *Anti-Jacobin*. In his poem, Lamb encourages Wood to hold his course against the "player's son" (Canning's mother was an actress), the "Zany of Debate— / Who nothing generous ever understood" (*W,* 5:105).

Two months later, Lamb again got political in the *Champion*, in this case addressing Queen Caroline's exclusion from George IV's coronation.[2] Though George married the Princess of Brunswick in 1795, he despised her. The two lived apart. George was free to philander as he pleased, and rumors circulated about Caroline's own romantic exploits. When George III died in January 1820, Caroline returned from an Italian exile to claim her part of the throne. The new king tried to scrounge up enough dirt on her to merit a divorce. He was unsuccessful. Nonetheless, when Caroline tried to force her way into his coronation ceremony, which took place in July 1821, George's bodyguards repulsed her.

Like many who loathed the king's person and policies, Lamb, along with Matthew Wood, supported Caroline. His comical verse of July 1820, "Song for the C[oronatio]n," reflects his position.

> Roi's wife of Brunswick Oels!
> Roi's wife of Brunswick Oels!
> Wot you how she came to him,
> While he supinely dreamt of no ills?
> Vow! but she is a canty Queen,
> And well can she scare each royal orgie.
> To us she ever must be dear,
> Though she's for ever cut by Georgie. (*W,* 1:106)

As was the case in his earlier attack on George, "The Triumph of the Whale," Lamb attacks the monarch's voluptuousness, but he also hints at the royal's lack of sexual vigor. George lies down, while the queen is brisk and lively.

In the same number of the *Champion,* Lamb once more mocked the king, this time in "On a Protected Journey," where he claims that the English will be glad to see George travel to Hanover, since they wish him gone. In May 1820, Lamb indicted the spy system that Wood attacked. "Three Graves," reprinted in the *London Magazine* in 1825, imagines Satan as the sexton of a horrific graveyard where counter-revolutionary spies will rot. In his poem of September 1820, "The Unbeloved," Lamb went after Canning again, unloved by "woman, child, or man in / All this isle" (*W,* 5:106).

The year 1820 saw Lamb turn out other occasional verses. In the July *Morning Chronicle,* he published "To Miss Burney, on Her Character of Blanch in 'Country Neighbors,'" a tribute to the novelist Sarah Burney, half sister to the more famous Fanny. In September, he printed in Leigh Hunt's *Indicator* a sonnet celebrating Hunt himself, "Wit, poet, prose-man, party-man, translator" (*W,* 5:83). In October he included in the *London* a poem to Louisa Martin, whom he had affectionately called, when she was a child, "Monkey." Titled "The Ape," the verse laments how time has aged Louisa.

Occasional verse—addressed to particular people or political events—increasingly became Lamb's poetic medium. Culminating in his 1830 *Album Verses, with a Few Others,* this kind of poetry is eminently less ambitious than his earlier verse. While poems like "The Old Familiar Faces" aspired to universality and permanence, lines such as those to Hunt or Wood highlight their specificity and evanescence: this poem is for the here and now; it has an expiration date.

But such transience galvanized Lamb's prose at the time, too. His *London Magazine* versions of the Elia essays, recall, were alert to the quick shifts in his city scene, and even if Lamb later hoisted the prose onto the more stable platform of a book, the crazed parataxis still flashes the voltage of the street.

Lamb's late verse confirms his commitment to the desultory. The world is a parade of phantoms—every "is" already a "was"—but also of possibility: each instant is spirit.[3]

Lamb's conversation attuned to the circumstantial, too. In the *Monthly Repository*, "S.Y."—author Sarah Flowers Adams, whose father Benjamin was the publisher of the *Cambridge Intelligencer*—describes an evening at Colebrook with the Lambs near the close of 1825. Coleridge was in attendance, and Adams saw the nimble Lamb shine in contrast to the ponderous Comberbatch. Whereas Coleridge propounded visions "based in the study of his own individual nature more than the nature of others," Lamb "seemed not for a moment to rest on self, but to throw his whole soul into the nature of circumstances and things around him." His discourse on the scene—unlike Coleridge's studied monologues—was aptly alert to the uneven rhythm of a dinner party: his sentences were "periodic" bursts, "short, telling, full of wit, philosophy, at times slightly caustic, though that is too strong a word for satire which was of the most good-natured kind." Lamb's attention to the "now" lent his talk a "racy freshness" lacking in Coleridge.[4]

CHAPTER 46

∽⊙∿

*Enfield*

"Without contraries there is no progression," writes Blake in *The Marriage of Heaven and Hell*. This aphorism reaches the heart of Lamb. If Ireland hurt Yeats into poetry, then the office scathed Lamb into Elia, a character desperate to escape ciphering's exhaustion. Where are the portals to the places beyond vocation? Can you find holes in your hell? Yes, but these little Edens appear only if you require them for survival. If they don't materialize, then the polarities required for essay writing never clash, and the gritty Cockney muse softens.

Not only did Lamb leave East India House; he abandoned his beloved London, and so sacrificed his final years to a second erroneous belief (the first being that retirement would please him): he would be happier in a pastoral setting. After visiting the Allsops in Enfield, Middlesex, during the summers of 1825 and 1827, Charles and Mary moved to the small rural village ten miles from the city. They wanted relief from the constant flow of visitors, upsetting to the mental health of Charles and Mary both. In September 1827, they settled into a recently built house in Chase Side, Enfield. Though the house was in excellent condition, Hood found it a "bald-looking yellowish house, with a bit of a garden, and a wasp's nest convenient," which treated Hood's pony and Lamb's thumb to excruciating stings.[1] Predictably, Lamb complained of moving. "You may find some of our flesh sticking to the door

419

posts" of Colebrook, Lamb wrote to Hood. But he hoped the change would bring a "rejuvenescence" (*L,* 3:131).

It didn't. As Lamb wrote to Mary Shelley, "If you ever run away, which is problematical, don't run to a country village, which has been a market town, but is such no longer. Enfield, where we are, is seated most indifferently upon the borders of Middlesex, Essex, and Hertfordshire, partaking of the quiet dulness of the first, & the total want of interest pervading the two latter Counties." There is no cathedral, only one printshop (where Valentines are made), and the bookseller deals only in prose versions of melodrama, "with plates of Ghosts and Murders, and other Subterranean passages." The bakery sells stale macaroons. There are no jewelers. If you "cast your dreary eyes about, up Baker Street . . . it gets worse. There was something like a tape and thread shop at that end, but here—is two apples stuck between a farthing's worth of ginger bread, & the children too poor to break stock." The library has no books, and the only word of London comes in newspapers several days old. "Clowns stand about . . . and spit minutely to relieve ennui" (*L,* 3:239–40).

Still, there was the walking. Charles and Mary did miles of it, almost daily, even if Charles didn't value rural trekking as much as his London strolls. But a beast irritated, comically, this most universal of pleasures. When Patmore visited the Lambs in Enfield, he admired the "large and very handsome dog" Lamb was caring for. This was Dash, and he joined Lamb on "his long rambling daily walks." These rambles were "interminable," and Lamb "made himself a perfect slave to [Dash], whose habits were of the most extravagantly errant nature, for, generally speaking, the creature was half-a-mile off from his companion, either before or behind, scouring the fields or roads in all directions . . . and keeping Lamb in a perfect fever of irritation and annoyance."[2]

His troubles with Dash aside, Lamb actually enjoyed dogs. Before Dash, Charles and Mary owned Prynne and Pompey. The best dog in the world would not have leavened Lamb's Enfield days, however. Maybe drinking, Lamb's darling habit, would. He measured his walks not by miles but by "Ale and Beer." That he walked many "pints" in Enfield is attested by two porterhouses of that village almost shutting down when the Lambs vacated the area for a month or two.[3]

But drink could not reconcile Charles to Enfield either. He tried to walk himself numb, so at least he wouldn't feel the ennui as acutely. But no matter how much he peregrinated in the summer, the "deadly long" day still weighed on him. There was too much time to kill (*L,* 3:225). As Charles exclaimed in an uncharacteristically angry outburst to Patmore, "The most squalid garret in the most confined and noisome purlieu of London would be a paradise to him, compared with the fairest dwelling placed in the loveliest scenery of 'the country.' 'I hate the country!'"[4]

In early 1830, Lamb expressed his ire to Wordsworth. In "dull Enfield" "we have nothing to do with our victuals but to eat them, with the garden but to see it grow, with the tax-gatherer but to hear him knock, with the maid but to hear her scolded. . . . Yet in the self condemned obliviousness, in the stagnation, some molesting yearnings of life not quite kill'd rise, prompting me that there was a London, and that I was of that old Jerusalem." But Lamb can return to the metropolis only in dreams, from which he wakes, to "cry" himself to sleep again. "Oh, let no native Londoner imagine that health, and rest, and innocent occupation, interchange of converse sweet and recreative study, can make the country anything better than altogether odious and detestable." Rural Eden was no paradise; it was fortunate that man, with "promethean felicity and boldness . . . sinned himself out of it" (L, 3:241–42).

# CHAPTER 47

*Three Portraits*

Occasionally visitors from the city alleviated the Enfield boredom. Emma came, of course, as did the Hoods, the Cowden Clarkes, Crabb Robinson, and Edward Moxon. Lamb also had Mary's company, at least when she was sane, and her companionship continued to lift him when everything felt to him, as it did in Enfield, "very gloomy" (*L*, 3:143–44).

A friend of the Cowden Clarkes provides a vivid portrait of Mary and Charles during the late 1820s. "Miss Lamb . . . presented the pleasant appearance of a mild, rather stout, and comely maiden of middle age. Dressed with a quaker-like simplicity in dove-coloured silk, with a transparent kerchief of snow-white muslin folded across her bosom, she at once prepossessed the beholder in her favour, by an aspect of serenity and peace. Her manners were very quiet and gentle, and her voice low. She smiled frequently, but seldom laughed." She related to Charles as an "admiring disciple," with her eyes seldom leaving his face. Even when "apparently engrossed in conversation with others, she would, by supplying some word for which he was at a loss, even when talking in a distant part of the room, show how closely her mind waited upon his."[1]

Unfortunately, we must rely on this colorful language alone to envision Mary at this time. We don't get to see her face until Cary's 1834 painting of her at seventy. She stands in her bonnet, while Charles sits at her left side. The only image we have of her before this is Thomas Hood's caricature of her

Thomas Hood's drawing of Mary Lamb climbing over a stile, for William Hone's
*Table-Book* (1827–28). (The Reading Room / Alamy Stock Photo.)

climbing over a stile. In her oversized bonnet, which covers her face completely, she resembles a child.

Three paintings of Charles, however, were completed around this time.
The first, from 1825, is by Thomas Wageman, who strikingly represented Leigh
Hunt and was famous for his portraits of actors. His Lamb stares straight at
you, indifferent. This is cold melancholia, not the ardent longing Hazlitt captured. We wouldn't be surprised to find this image in a catalogue of inmates
at Bedlam.

The next likeness, completed in May 1826, is by the renowned Henry
Meyer, portraitist of Lord Nelson, Lady Hamilton, and Lord Byron. That
such an esteemed artist would paint Lamb demonstrates Elia's high stature
in London society. Meyer sees the opposite of Wageman: a literary lion. His
Lamb sits on a gold velvet throne. He turns his head slightly to the left, deep

*Portrait of Charles Lamb*, after Thomas Charles Wageman.
(Courtesy of British Museum Images.)

in thought. A sheaf of blank paper rests on a low table to his right. In his right hand, a quill. Behind the paper are two burgundy volumes. In the far background to Lamb's right is his beloved British Museum. To his left is a red velvet curtain. Near Lamb's left hand are rolled-up pages: Elia's work, ready for the press.

Meyer's painting, which Hunt thought "the least unsatisfactory portrait" of his friend, is not Charles but an allegory of "Lamb."[2] The painting shows, in Robinson's words, a "thinking man more like the framer of a system of philosophy than of the genial and gay effusions of Elia."[3]

The other image, which Lamb sent to Coleridge in June 1826, returns Elia to the humor that made him. Completed by Lamb's East India colleague

*Charles Lamb*, after Henry Meyer, oil on canvas, based on a work of 1826.
(© National Portrait Gallery, London.)

Brook Pulham, the etching shows Charles standing in profile. His spindly legs, outsized nose, and knee breeches are prominently displayed. This is about as far from Wageman's sorrow and Meyer's dignity as you can get.

Because of Pulham's mockery of ceremony, Lamb liked his companion's image best. As he wrote to Coleridge in a letter accompanying the picture, the

*Charles Lamb*, by Brook Pulham, 1825. (© National Portrait Gallery, London.)

image "was stolen from my person at one of my unguarded moments by some too partial artist." Even if some friends, notably Procter, believe Pulham does not "flatter" him, Lamb admires how the artist displays his "native character" much more honestly than "can be possible in the restraints of an enforced sitting attitude." The implication is that Wageman and Meyer missed Lamb's authentic posture, which Lamb jokingly equates with the "thinking man," as opposed to a "man in the act of thought." Pulham's portrait models how Lamb would like to communicate with Coleridge: he wants his "thoughts to flow in a sort of undress rather than in the more studied graces of diction" (*L*, 3:46–47).

To say that these three images of Lamb capture all sides of him—the melancholy, the serious, the silly—would be reductive, but certainly the pictures do reveal three personae he was trying to negotiate. After his "fevers" of 1825, his melancholia, and the drinking he did to ease it, Lamb became increasingly worse. Mary's more frequent episodes—one coming just after the Enfield move—contributed to his malaise, as did two losses that come with age: friends (to death) and gusto. The fame Meyer celebrated affected Lamb, too. For the first time in his life, he was a public figure. The status pleased him—his "Elia" mask inspired his greatest prose—but annoyed him as well. He wearied of visits from his admirers. How to combat the pomposity attendant upon fame? Mock the celebrity. This is just what the self-effacing Lamb did, and he appreciated when others jibed at his expense.

Over the last years of his life, from 1826 until the end, as the Wageman character took over, Lamb continued to write. In 1826, he published in the *New Monthly* a series of "Popular Fallacies," in which he wittily overturned conventional maxims, such as "A Bully Is Always a Coward" and an "Ill-Gotten Gain Never Prospers." In the same magazine he also published "The Sanity of True Genius"—as much a wish as a statement—and "Genteel Style in Writing," an appreciation of the writings of Lord Shaftesbury and Sir William Temple.

Lamb also contributed in the last decade of his life to *The Every-day Book* and *The Table-Book* of William Hone. Hone was a flamboyantly contrarian publisher, author, and bookseller. He was tried for blasphemy and acquitted, but he spent three years in prison for debt. In addition to his rebellious political satires, he wrote a biography of William Cobbet and edited and annotated the English medieval miracle plays. His *Every-day Book* and *Table-Book* reflected his passion for the literature of the past. They were collections, spanning multiple volumes, of lore from old England as well as ancient legends and curiosities. The volumes also contained contemporary articles and poems.

Lamb met Hone around 1819 and became friends with him in 1823, when Hone gave Lamb his *Ancient Mysteries* and Lamb returned the favor by gifting him *Elia*. Lamb lent his Colebrook house to Hone while he and Mary were at Enfield, and Hone dedicated his *Every-day Book* to Lamb, who contributed regularly through 1825 and 1826. Lamb also submitted two essays to *The Table-Book*, which appeared in 1827–28.

The pieces for Hone are short, whimsical. A "Remarkable Correspondent," for instance, is written by "February 29," sad to be absent from the round of days except every four years. "The Defeat of Time" imagines Time pitted against fairies, with whom he quarrels and then decides to kill, until a young Shakespeare intercedes. Many of the pieces are in fact about time: the months, the seasons, the day of August 12.

Lamb also wrote for Hone his account of his first school on Fetter Lane and moreover contributed humorous essays on a donkey ("Here was Anti-music with a vengeance; a whole Pan-Dis-Harmonicon in a single lungs of leather!" [*W,* 1:305]) and on squirrels ("We remember at school getting our fingers into the orangery of one of these little gentry [not having a due caution of the traps set there], and the result proved sourer than lemons" [*W,* 1:306].) Lamb additionally reminisced over the ludicrously comical Sir Jeffrey Dunstan, mayor of Garrat and seller of secondhand wigs; and he produced a small piece on the stiles in Enfield and Edmonton, inspired by Hood's sketch of Mary.

In 1828, Lamb wrote for the *Spectator* a piece on theaters that try to improve Shakespeare by altering his endings. For the same magazine in 1830, he completed an article on the ballad, "The Sweet Lass of Richmond Hill." He also penned, for Wilson's *Memoirs of the Life and Times of Daniel De Foe*, a critical piece on the novelist's "secondary" work. For the *Gem*, he composed an essay on Saturday night, where he mentioned the cruel tender mercies of grandmothers like his own: when "a fly had got into a corner of my eye, and I was complaining of it to her, the old Lady deliberately pounded two ounces or more of the finest loaf sugar that could be got, and making me hold open the eye as wide as I could—all innocent of her purpose—she blew from delicate white paper, with a full breath, the whole saccharine contents into the part afflicted, saying, 'There, now the fly is out.' 'Twas most true—a legion of blue-bottles, with the prince of flies at their head, must have dislodged with the torrent and deluge of tears which followed" (*W,* 1:325).

CHAPTER 48

⟨⟨᠗⟩⟩

# Album Verses

Without East India hours, *London Magazine* deadlines, or an insistent muse, Lamb faced an abyss of time. How to fill it? Fanny Kelly might call, as she did in April 1828. Or Lamb might travel into town for a party at the Talfourds, with Wordsworth in attendance. But the dinner parties meant drinking, and now the unemployed Lamb had the luxury of easing his hangovers with the hair of the dog. As Lamb writes in a June 1828 letter, when he attends London parties, "there is a necessity for my drinking too much . . . at and after dinner; then I require spirits at night to allay the crudity of the weaker Bacchus; and in the morning I cool my parched stomach with a fiery libation. Then I am aground in town, and call upon my London friends, and get new wets of ale, porter, & etc.; then ride home, drinking where the coach stops, as duly as Edward set up his Waltham Crosses" (*L*, 3:167).

Though melancholy and drinking heavily, Lamb remained attractive to his friends. In July 1828 the Cowden Clarkes honeymooned in Enfield and frequently called on the Lambs. They enjoyed Lamb's "playful bluntness," which gave the impression of "his liking you well enough to be rough and unceremonious with you; it showed you he felt at home with you."[1] Talfourd perceived this trait in Lamb as well: "Where [Lamb] loved and doted most, he would vent the overflowing of his feelings in words that looked like rudeness."[2]

Lamb cultivated another pastime in the late 1820s: composing verses for the albums of others. Collecting items for personal albums was an increasingly popular pastime of young women. She might include drawings, portraits of friends or public figures, pressed flowers, favorite quotes and poems. Special prizes were poems by others, usually family and friends, written in their own hands. But the most cherished entry of all was a handwritten poem from a famous author, such as Procter or Lamb, preferably addressed to the album's owner.[3]

Many male writers chafed at this "feminine" practice, believing it a degradation of serious literature, which should properly address universal subjects in the form of print, not particular people in personal scrawls. More prominent writers, such as Southey the poet laureate, grew irritated at frequent requests for their autographs. Perhaps worse, the purchase of such albums threatened the sales of poetry books.

Lamb appears to have shared Southey's low estimation of album poetry. That didn't stop him, however, from publishing a collection of this type of verse in 1830.

Ostensibly he published *Album Verses, with a Few Others* to help along his young friend Edward Moxon. Before Moxon married Emma in 1833 and became in effect his son-in-law, Lamb knew him as a promising young publisher and man of letters. When Lamb met him in 1826, Moxon was completing *"The Prospect," and Other Poems* and working as a publisher for Longman. By 1830, the ambitious Moxon had started his own firm on New Bond Street, helped by a £500 loan from the poet-banker Samuel Rogers, also a good friend of Lamb. (Rogers had attended with Lamb the famous Monkhouse party of 1823, and Lamb wrote a sonnet to Rogers when Rogers's brother Daniel died.) Moxon made the most of his loan. After early success, in 1833 he moved to 44 Dover Street. Two years later, Wordsworth chose Moxon as his publisher. In 1839, Moxon printed the first complete volume of Shelley's works, edited by Mary Shelley herself. Because of Shelley's atheistic *Queen Mab*, he was sued for blasphemous libel. Talfourd defended him. Though Moxon was judged guilty, the prosecution recommended no punishment. After Mary Lamb died in 1847, Charles's books went to Moxon. He sold sixty of the best volumes to dealers in America and allegedly destroyed the rest. Moxon eventually published Browning and Tennyson.

Lamb's *Album Verses* was Moxon's first publication. The young man needed a famous name to launch his house, and Lamb generously, if reluctantly, agreed to lend his. (Hunt wrote, "Mr. Moxon has begun his career as a bookseller in singularly high taste. He has no connection but with the select of the earth.")[4] If we take Lamb's dedication of the volume seriously, he didn't much value the work. He calls the poems "Trifles" and claims that Moxon is publishing them not for their merit but so he can demonstrate his skills as a publisher. The verses not only lack quality, Lamb continues; they are also missing cohesiveness. Some are indeed poems Lamb wrote for the albums of different women, while others were "floating about in Periodicals," such as the *London Magazine*. Regardless of their origin, Lamb has "little interest in their publication." They "are simply—Advertisement Verses" (*W,* 5:304).

Are we to take the ever-ironical Lamb literally here? Certainly the poems in this volume—only nine of which are album verses; the rest fall under the sections "Miscellaneous," "Sonnets," "Commendatory Verses," "Acrostics," "Translations from the Latin of Vincent Bourne," "Pindaric Ode to the Tread Mill," "Epicedium," and *The Wife's Trial; or, The Intruding Widow* (a play)— are not Lamb's best. Literary quality aside, however, the book, like Lamb's occasional verses from the early 1820s (some of which appear in the volume), is a meditation on the nature and function of poetry itself.

In the book's first poem, "In the Album of a Clergyman's Lady" (likely Mrs. Williams, for whom Emma worked as governess), Lamb claims that an "Album is a Garden, not for show / Planted, but use." Unlike a traditional poetry book, which aspires to rise above the cycle of growth and decay, the album ripens and rots. It is moreover practical, as opposed to the conventional volume's more fanciful atmosphere. Entries in the album are indeed precious, like family porcelain or religious icons, objects whose value depends on their usefulness, be it emotional or spiritual. Ultimately, the album is "a list of living friends" who will continue to bloom, because they are rooted in the album, when "cold laws" destroy their bodies. Such should a "tender" album be, and Lamb wishes such a book for this lady (*W,* 5:43).

This seemingly simple verse is contradictory. The album is both ephemeral, like a garden, and stable, like porcelain. It is useful in the present moment, since it reminds one of close friends; but it is also oriented toward the future, because it holds memories that will bloom after the friends die.

This interplay between transience and stability isn't always happy, as Lamb's final album verse in the collection shows. In "In My Own Album," first printed as "Verses for an Album" in the *Gem* in 1828, Lamb pictures his own album, when new, as unsullied and bright. Once others have marked its pages, however, "thought, and care, / And friend and foe" stain and burden it. Over time, the significance of the dates is forgotten, and the good wishes inscribed mark only the failure to realize them. Far from an archive of luminous moments, Lamb's album houses "disjointed numbers; sense unknit; / Huge reams of folly, shreds of wit" (*W,* 5:47). Best to close and lock it.

Lamb's sensitivity to the complex temporality of the album verse makes his volume far from a trifle. His twilight poetics suggest that attention to the "now," the more particular the better, gives poems their power. Ironically, the more intensely the lines speak to the present, the more likely their permanence. The poem properly is an ongoing garden whose fresh produce recalls past growths, or a china cabinet preserving plates whose current use memorializes those who once cherished them.

Lamb's acknowledgment of the potency of the autograph reveals, once more, his admirable lack of gender prejudice. For him, the "feminine" habit of fashioning albums, far from degrading Poetry, proves a vibrant model for poetics of the ordinary.[5]

In his other seven album verses in the collection, Lamb addresses women, some known to him, some not, attempting in each case to praise a trait specific to the recipient. Many of the other poems share this specificity. In the "Miscellaneous" section, Lamb includes, in addition to religious poems such as "Angel Help" and "The Christening," two poems to Emma and one to Barton. The "Sonnets" section features verses to Emma (again), Fanny Kelly, and Samuel Rogers. (Lamb's accomplished sonnets "Written at Cambridge," "Work," and "Leisure" also appear, as does one of his strangest, most haunting poems, "The Gipsy's Malison," from 1829, in which Lamb imagines an infant at his mother's breast maturing into a corpse swinging from the gallows. The *Gem* found it too disturbing to publish, but *Blackwood's,* Lamb's old nemesis, took it.) The next sections, "Commendatory Verses" and "Acrostics," are composed of poems all addressed to acquaintances of Lamb. And even if the pieces in the following section, translations of the eighteenth-century Latin poetry of Vincent Bourne, are not Lamb's, the verses nonetheless are occasional. Bourne writes a poem to a dog, another to a friend, David Cook, and still another to a "deaf and dumb artist."

The remaining verses in the book—an ode about Daniel Defoe and a blank-verse play, *The Wife's Trial*—lack the ephemeral intimacy of most of poems mentioned. They feel like addenda, extra pages to give the volume more material heft.

Of all the poems in *Album Verses,* "On an Infant Dying as Soon as Born," from the "Miscellaneous" section, shines as one of Lamb's best, equal to "The Old Familiar Faces" and *Blank Verse.* The occasion for this 1827 poem—first published in the *Gem*—was the actual death of Thomas Hood's firstborn child, a girl. Why should someone die so young, living not long enough even to be named, or to hold her eyes open for more than an instant? "The economy of Heaven is dark" on these questions, and dark, too, on why others live so long. What to do? At least bury with this infant, killed by "doom perverse," her "silver bells" and "baby clothes." This "harmless vanity" ritualizes the death, marks it as an event that will lodge in the memory (*W,* 5:51).

William Jerdan savaged *Album Verses* in the *Literary Gazette*. He called the book "rubbish." Southey, perhaps guilty over attacking Lamb's religion some years back, came quickly to his friend's defense in the *Athenaeum.*[6] Hunt defended Lamb as well; he praised the book's playful quality, not unaware that Jerdan's takedown was probably politically motivated.[7]

Lamb's own anonymous review of his own work, published in Moxon's *Englishmen's Magazine* in August 1831, confirms the poetics his volume implies: "This may be said even of [the poems], that they are not vague verses—to the Moon, or to the Nightingale—that will fit any place—but strictly appropriate to the person that they were intended to gratify; or to the species of chronicle which they were destined to be recorded in. The Verses to a 'Clergyman's Lady'—to the 'Wife of a learned Serjeant'—to a 'Young Quaker'—could have appeared only in an Album, and only in that particular person's Album they were composed for" (*W,* 1:340).

Here once again is the generous ventriloquism, the Keatsian empathy, Lamb displayed in his letters and Procter observed in his talk. This open-hearted attention to objects is precisely what Lamb admired in Bourne's Latin poems: "They fix upon *something*; they ally themselves to common life and objects; their good nature is a Catholicon, sanative of coxcombry, of heartlessness, and of fastidiousness" (*W,* 1:341).

CHAPTER 49

*"Am" to "Have"*

In 1830, the lease on the Enfield residence expired, and the Lambs moved back to London in the summer, to Southampton Row. By the fall, though, they were in Enfield again, renting a property right across the street from their old one. Why didn't the two just stay in the city? Lamb's letter to Barton in July 1829 gives a hint. "Town, with all my native hankering after it, is not what it was. The streets, the shops are left, but all old friends are gone. And in London I was frightfully convinced of this as I past houses and places—empty caskets now. I have ceased to care almost about any body. The bodies I cared for are in graves, or dispersed. My old Clubs, that lived so long and flourished so steadily, are crumbled away" (*L,* 3:224).

There was another reason London didn't work. As Lamb admitted to Moxon on November 12, 1830, London didn't suit Mary's mental state. "I have brought my sister to Enfield, being sure that she had no hope of recovery in London. Her state of mind is deplorable beyond example. I almost fear whether she has strength at her time of life ever to get out of it. Here she must be nursed, and neither see nor hear of anything in the world out of her sick chamber" (*L,* 3:293).

Enfield for now would be Lamb's home, his "hole."

Not happy in London, melancholy in Enfield: where could Lamb be content? Nowhere. But this dissatisfaction wasn't new to Lamb. It was in his fibers. Patmore remarked that Lamb suffered from a "*constitutional* sadness about [his] mind." "Unlike his friends, Coleridge and Wordsworth, Lamb was not a man whose mind was sufficient to itself, and could dwell for ever, if need were, in the world of its own thoughts, or that which the thoughts of others had created for it. He delighted to *visit* those worlds, and fancied there, it may be, his purest and loftiest pleasures. But the *home* of his spirit was the face of the common earth, and in the absence of human faces and sympathies, it longed and yearned for them with a hunger that nothing else could satisfy."[1]

Patmore's misreading of Coleridge notwithstanding (Coleridge flailed in the same limbos as Lamb), the younger man illuminates Lamb's depression: no matter what he is doing, he craves something else. If he roams the realms of his intellect, he wants to grip the earth, with its cities and characters. But among the people and the streets, he craves solitude. Nothing is good enough; everything could be better. In Lamb this isn't peevishness but a constitutional alienation. He wishes Mary were dead; he can't live without her. He falls in love with women he knows will not love him back.

Hence Lamb's equal emphasis, in his best writing, on the comforts of home and the ecstasy of escape. As Elia, he can push deeply into one sphere or the other, without Charles's agonized, and perverse, hunger to turn back the minute he gets there. Elia can slip through the interstices of time into atemporal realms and play, or acknowledge these places aren't real and long for them gently, wittily. Or he can settle into whist or teacups and enjoy the common sounds and tastes; if these comforts don't suffice, he can mock them genially, and imagine exotics that raise the heart. Or Elia can vacillate quickly between unfamiliar and familiar, not overly tied to either pole, keen on relishing what each has to offer.

Lamb complains, I *am* melancholy. I *have* melancholy, Elia jokes.

But without the writing, how to rise from "am" to "have?" Though Lamb continued to compose now and then after 1830, the work wasn't potent enough to pull him from his sorrow. April 1831, however, offered great promise. The ambitious Moxon launched the *Englishman's Magazine*, and he had big plans for Lamb. He wanted to bring back Elia. In the August number, he proclaimed that Elia would soon return for a series of essays under the category of "Peter's Net." That number indeed contained Elia's "Reminiscences of Elliston," a profile of Robert William Elliston, a famous actor and theater manager.

But Lamb was reluctant to revive Elia. As he wrote to Moxon at the end of August, "Leave out the sickening 'Elia' at the end [of my essays] . . . a signature forces [everything] to be all characteristic of one man, Elia . . . which cramped me formerly." Peter's Net, in Lamb's mind, would allow for material beyond what Elia's character would write, perhaps pieces that weren't simply comical. "All is fish" (*L*, 3:318–19).

Still, in September, in the guise of Elia, he published "Recollections of a Late Royal Academician," a profile of portrait painter George Dawe. He followed in October with another Elia essay, "Newspapers Thirty-Five Years Ago," about writing for London papers at the turn of the century.

But by the end of October, the *Englishman's Magazine* failed. Lamb didn't let Elia go, however. An essay he had prepared for a later number of Moxon's magazine—"On the Total Defects of the Quality of Imagination, Observable in the Works of Modern British Artists"—he published, as Elia, in the *Athenaeum*. This was in the winter of 1833. The essay questions the overly literal styles of modern painters, while praising the "wise falsification" of the old masters, who "got at their true conclusions; by not showing the actual appearances, that is, all that was to be seen at any given moment by an indifferent eye, but only what the eye might be supposed to see in the doing or suffering of some portentous action" (*W*, 2:230).

After 1830, Lamb published little else beyond this. In the *Athenaeum* of February 1831, he—as Lamb, not Elia—eulogized the comedian Munden. Munden "was imaginative; he could impress upon an audience an idea—the low one, perhaps, of a leg of mutton and turnips; but such was the grandeur and singleness of his expressions, that that single expression would convey to all his auditory a notion of all the pleasures they had all received from all the legs of mutton and turnips they had ever eaten in their lives. Now, this is not acting, nor do I set down Munden amongst my old actors. He was only a wonderful man, exerting his vivid impressions through the agency of the stage" (*W*, 1:342).

In November 1833, he returned to Elia again, releasing in the *Athenaeum* a piece on presents of game (the kind you eat). In 1834, over four issues, Elia appeared in the *Athenaeum* again, for some "Table Talk." His surreal pithiness remained. "The greatest pleasure I know, is to do a good action by stealth, and to have it found out by accident" (*W*, 1:344). "We are ashamed at the sight of a monkey—somehow as we are shy of poor relations" (*W*, 1:349). "Absurd images are sometimes irresistible. I will mention two. An elephant in a coach-office gravely coming to have his trunk booked;—a mermaid over a fish-kettle cooking her own tail" (*W,* 1:349).

Poetry still trickled as well, mainly occasional lines similar to those in *Album Verses.* In 1831, he published poems to Charles Aders, art collector and friend of Blake; to Louisa Martin, subject of his earlier poem "The Ape"; and to a family whose sons and daughters had drowned. He followed these in 1833 with verses to Edith Southey, wife of the poet; Edward Moxon, on his wedding to Emma; and Thomas Stothard, illustrator of Patlock's tale of glums and gawries, which Lamb devoured at Christ's. In 1834, he celebrated Clara Novello, daughter of the organist Vincent Novello and an accomplished soprano.

Otherwise, Lamb published a ballad, *Satan in Search of a Wife,* in 1831. Lamb's name wasn't on the title page, likely because he was embarrassed. As he wrote to Moxon, who published the work, "I wish you would omit 'by the Author of Elia' *now,* in advertising that damn'd 'Devil's Wedding'" (*L,* 3:354). In *Blackwood's* Lamb printed a farce he wrote back in 1825, *The Pawnbroker's Daughter,* based loosely on *The Merchant of Venice,* though in this case the daughter, Marian, steals her father's jewels by accident, unlike Jessica, who deliberately purloins from Shylock. Marian's father Flint is more compassionate than Shylock, in the end reconciling with his daughter.

Remaining verses from Lamb's final years are oddities: a summary of a tale by Suidas, concerning Hercules; a translation of Palingenius's Latin *Zodiacus Vita*; and another translation from the Latin, Palineniius's "Existence, Considered in Itself, No Blessing," a harrowing poem about overcoming suicide, even if the world be nothing but a "black negation" (*W,* 5:90).

In October 1834, Lamb, as far as we know, wrote his last poem, which was printed in the *Athenaeum* in March 1835. It is called "To Margaret W——," and it likens Margaret to a daisy, which is apt, since *marguerite* is French for the flower. This Margaret exudes "grace" wherever planted, whether "home-seated" in a "lonely bower," or "wedded—a transplanted flower" (*W,* 5:91).

The final big literary event of Lamb's life was Moxon's publication of *The Last Essays of Elia* early in 1833. The book didn't generate the excitement of *Elia,* receiving only two notable reviews, one in the *Literary Gazette* (uneven), another in the *Monthly Repository* (positive). As noted earlier, some of Lamb's most powerful writing appears in the volume, including "Old China," "Poor Relations," "Amicus Redivivus," "Blakesmoor, in H——shire," "The

Superannuated Man," and "The Convalescent." In these essays, the tantaliz-
ing Elian "I" gambols—and gambles. Other essays that brim with the strange
Elia charm are "The Old Margate Hoy," "Detached Thoughts on Books and
Reading," "Captain Jackson," "Barbara S——,"and "Newspapers Thirty-
Five Years Ago." The other pieces Lamb chose from his periodical writing
are "Stage Illusion," "To the Shade of Elliston" and "Ellistoniana" (the earlier
"Reminiscences of Elliston" broken into two essays), "Sanity of True Genius,"
"The Genteel Style of Writing," "The Tombs in the Abbey" (the final part of
"The Letter to Southey," concerning Westminster Abbey charging admission
for entrance), "Some Sonnets of Sir Philip Sidney," "Barrenness of the Imaginative Faculty in the Productions of Modern Art" (earlier published as "On
the Total Defects of the Quality of Imagination, Observable in the Works of
Modern British Artists"), "The Wedding" (published in 1825 to celebrate the
wedding of the Burneys' daughter Sarah, but now, in 1833, a covert lament
over losing Emma to a husband), "Rejoicings upon the New Year's Coming
of Age" (a lesser version of the magnificent "New Year's Eve"), "The Child
Angel: A Dream" (as sentimental as Lamb ever got), and "Popular Fallacies."

CHAPTER 50

## His Great and Dear Spirit Haunts Me

Mary's periods of illness were becoming more frequent and lasting longer. She was ill in 1827, 1829, 1830, 1832, and 1833. The '29 attack lasted twelve weeks, and the '30 fit was the most intense yet. Increasingly, Lamb feared that she would descend into madness and never climb out again. Without his sister's sane presence, he would not be Charles. She was a mother, a wife, a fellow writer and reader, a best friend, a moral guide. So close had they become as they neared the end that even the habits that irritated each other were signs of deepest affection. When Thomas Hood's wife Jane asked Charles if his constant ribbing ever upset Mary, he replied that yes, once he thought he had actually hurt her feelings, and he decided not to tease her for a while. But Mary "did nothing but keep bursting into tears every time she looked at me, and when I asked her what she was crying for, when I was doing all I could to please her, she blubbered out: 'You're changed, Charles, you're changed; what have I done, that you should treat me in this cruel manner?'" He explained his motive for being gentle. "Joke again, Charles," Mary begged, "—I don't know you in this manner. I am sure I should die, if you behaved as you have done for the last few days." I joke for her own good, Charles concluded. "It saved her life then, anyhow."[1]

When lunacy possessed Mary in the summer of 1832, Charles placed her in a private madhouse in Edmonton, run by the Waldens, a husband and wife. When Mary faltered again in April 1833, he once more installed her

439

*Mary Lamb; Charles Lamb*, by Francis Stephen Cary, oil on canvas, 1834.
(© National Portrait Gallery, London.)

there. Since he was frustrated with his Enfield landlords, and he knew Mary might be gone a long time, he moved to Edmonton and lived with Mary in the Waldens' house. As he wrote to Wordsworth from Edmonton, "I am with attentive people, and younger—I am 3 or 4 miles nearer the Great City, Coaches half-price less, and going always, of which I will avail myself. I have few friends left there, one or two tho' most beloved. But London Streets and faces cheer me inexpressibly, tho' of the latter not one known were remaining" (*L*, 3:371).

In the same letter, he reports to Wordsworth that he will soon "lose my old and only walk-companion, whose mirthful spirits were the 'youth of our house,' Emma Isola. I have her now for a little while, but she is too nervous properly to be under such a roof, so she will make short visits, be no more an inmate. With my perfect approval, and more than concurrence, she is to be wedded to Moxon at the end of Augst. So 'perish the roses and the flowers'— how is it?" (*L*, 3:371). (The "roses" quote comes from Wordsworth's *Excursion*.)

One of the few bright spots in Lamb's final years was meeting Walter Savage Landor. When he met Lamb in September 1832, Landor was visiting his home country from Fiesole, the village near Florence where he had been living since 1821. There he wrote his *Imaginary Conversations*, fictional dialogues, scores of them, between significant historical figures. He imagines talks between Diogenes and Plato, Milton and Marvel, Henry VIII and Anne Boleyn, Dante and Beatrice, Achilles and Helen of Troy. Hazlitt, who met Landor in Florence in 1825, thought the book displayed "considerable originality, learning, acuteness, terseness of style, and force of invective," even if the volume "is spoiled and rendered abortive throughout by an utter want to temper, of self-knowledge and decorum."[2] Landor, like Lamb, was just strange enough to accommodate Hazlitt's own oddness, and the two became friends, regardless of Hazlitt's criticism.

Landor had endured far worse attacks than literary ones. After a rambunctious tenure at Oxford, from which he was suspended in 1794 for firing a shotgun at the window of a too-loud Tory student, he eventually found himself, like Byron, fighting for freedom in earnest. In 1808 he rounded up a private army to aid the Spanish in fighting the French. But unlike Hazlitt, who alienated friends at an alarming rate, the eccentrically irascible Landor was highly regarded. He counted among his companions Southey, the Hunts, Crabb Robinson, Browning, and Dickens, who named one of his children Walter Landor.[3]

It was Robinson who introduced Landor to Lamb. Robinson had written to Landor earlier, reporting that he saw Landor's poems lying open before Charles who, "tipsy and sober . . . is ever muttering 'Rose Aylmer.'" (This lyric, Landor's most famous, is devoted to a woman he loved who was shipped away to India, where she perished of cholera. The poem dolefully concludes, "Rose Aylmer, whom these wakeful eyes / May weep, but never see, / A night of memories and of sighs / I consecrate to thee.") In the same letter, Robinson adds that Lamb is haunted by another poem of Landor, *Gebir*, a tale, once more, of doomed love, in which the prince of Spain falls in love with the queen of his enemy country, Egypt.[4]

The visit, which took place at the Lambs' home in Enfield, lasted only an hour. Robinson, Landor, and one Worsley, a friend of Robinson's, appeared mid-morning. Landor was delighted with Mary, and pleased with Lamb's conversation, though Charles, according to Robinson, was not "at his ease," and "nothing in the conversation [was] recollectable." Just before the men departed, Emma appeared; she pleased Landor mightily, and he later wrote poetry about her.[5]

Landor didn't share Robinson's assessment of the visit. So memorable did he find the hour that he wrote these lines:

> Once, and once only, have I seen thy face,
> Elia! once only has thy tripping tongue
> Run o'er my heart, yet never has been left
> Impression on it stronger or more sweet.
> Cordial old man! what youth was in thy years,
> What wisdom in thy levity, what soul
> In every utterance of thy purest breast!
> Of all that ever wore man's form,'tis thee
> I first would spring to at the gate of Heaven.[6]

Commenting on an earlier version of the poem, which he included in an 1834 letter to Lady Blessington, Landor explains that he wrote "*tripping tongue*" because Lamb "stammered and spoke hurriedly." When Lamb met me, Landor continues, he didn't "put on a fine new coat," as Coleridge did, but "met me as if I had been a friend of twenty years' standing; indeed, he told me I had been so, and shewed me some things I had written much longer ago and had utterly forgotten." The admiration was mutual: "The world will never see again two such delightful volumes as 'The Essays of Elia'; no man living is capable of writing the worst twenty pages of them."[7]

As a show of his affection to Lamb and his family, Landor contributed a poem to Emma's album, in which he likens her to "the fairest form, the purest mind" that ever "sprang" from Ausonia, the Italian village of her family.[8]

In thanking Landor for the album, Lamb introduced his new friend to some of his choice nonsense. Lamb knew the Beetham family, about which Landor had apparently complained: "I knew a quarter of a mile of them.

17 brothers and 16 sisters, as they appear to me in memory. There was one of them that used to fix his long legs on my fender, and tell a story of a shark, every night, endless, immortal. How have I grudged the salt-sea ravener not having had his gorge of him! . . . The shortest of the daughters measured 5 foot eleven without her shoes. Well, some day we may confer about them. But they were tall. Surely I have discover'd the longitude" (*L,* 3:361).

Had Lamb lived another ten years or so—Landor lived another *forty-two*—he would have written to him letters as peculiarly comical as his best to Manning.

Lamb's meeting with another literary personage about a year earlier could not have been more different. A thirty-six-year-old Thomas Carlyle called on Lamb in November 1831 and came away sour. (Carlyle had met Lamb earlier, in 1824.) Immediately he stained his diary page with invective, claiming, as we have seen, that Lamb was a "shameless drunkard" "in some considerable degree insane."

Lamb probably did feel to some degree insane at this time, and he was surely drinking hard. His losses pummeled him. Not only Emma's, whose bright presence would dim to him now, but the losses of friends and heroes, too, in rapid succession. As Lamb wrote to Wordsworth in 1830, "There are not now the years that there used to be. The tale of the dwindled age of men, reported of successional mankind, is true of the same man only" (*L,* 3:241).

Already in 1827, Randal Norris, the Temple librarian and sub-treasurer from Lamb's youth, had died. The seventy-six-year-old Norris had been a friend of the Lambs' parents as well as Charles and Mary. After Norris died, Lamb wrote to Robinson, "To the last he called me Charley. I have none to call me Charley now." In this same letter—which Lamb later published, with small revisions, as "A Death-Bed"—he continued, "In him I have a loss the world cannot make up. He was my friend, and my father's friend, for all the life that I can remember. I seem to have made foolish friendships since. Those are the friendships, which outlast a second generation. Old as I am getting, in his eyes I was still the child he knew me" (*W,* 2:246). After Randal died, Lamb arranged for the Temple to assist his widow financially.

In the death of Norris, Lamb lost his last living connection to the Temple, to his childhood. The same year Norris died, Blake succumbed to a liver disease, singing, as he passed from the physical world, hymns of his own making. Lamb didn't know Blake personally, but he admired in Blake what he saw in himself: delicate eccentricity. With Blake's passing, Lamb surely felt the world was profoundly less. In 1829, Lamb's recently met friend John Bates Dibdin, only thirty, died of consumption. Dibdin was a clerk at a London shipping office, and he often found himself at the East India House, where he met Lamb. Dibdin soon guessed Lamb was Elia, and the two become friends. Lamb wrote Dibdin a series of entertaining letters in 1826, when the younger man was in Hastings recruiting for his company. He had taken along a parcel of Lamb's books, in connection to which Lamb sent this advice: "Mary bids me warn you not to read the Anatomy of Melancholy in your present *low way*. You'll fancy yourself a pipkin, or a headless bear, as Burton speaks of. You'll be lost in a maze of remedies for a labyrinth of diseasements, a plethora of cures" (*L*, 3:50–51).

Hazlitt died on September 18, 1830. Impoverished and largely forgotten, he succumbed to stomach cancer in a shabby room in Soho, on Frith Street, in what is now known as Hazlitt Hotel. Lamb described Hazlitt's last days in a letter to Basil Montagu. He was "lying in bed as bad as man can be, that is alive. His complaint is spasms, he has been violently vomiting blood, and nothing stays upon his stomach. I consider him in danger, & am afraid he cannot afford a nurse. Some male friends have been sitting up with him, since the servant of the house was nearly exhausted."[9] One of those friends was Procter, who saw the moribund man as a grim apocalypse of death itself: "[Hazlitt] lay ghastly, shrunk, and helpless, on the bed from which he never afterwards rose. His mind seemed to have weathered all the dangers of extreme sickness, and to be safe and strong as ever. He could not lift his hand from the coverlet; and his voice was changed and diminished to a hoarse whisper, resembling the faint scream that I have heard from birds. I never was so sensible of the power of death before."[10]

Hazlitt appeared to rally the day before his death. He had letters sent announcing his recovery. The next morning, his good spirits continued. He even said to his son, "Well, I've had a happy life." These were his last words. The symptoms returned. William Jr. called Hessey, Hazlitt's publisher; Edward White, a friend and Lamb's colleague at East India House; and Lamb himself. At about 4:30, Hazlitt, age fifty-two, died.[11] The landlady was so eager to show the room to potential lodgers she hid the body under the bed.

Lamb arranged the funeral, which took place five days later in the churchyard of St. Anne in Soho. Only a few others attended. The tombstone—the only one in the cemetery still visible today—bears a lovely memorial, whose essence arrives in these lines: "He lived and died the unconquered champion of truth, liberty and humanity." The composer of the praise—"one whose heart is with him, in the grave"—remains a mystery. One Hazlitt biographer thinks it could be attorney Charles Wells, a fervid admirer of the writer, or Hazlitt's first wife Sarah Stoddart, who retained her affection for her difficult ex-husband.[12] But was it Lamb?

Hazlitt's death stunned Lamb belatedly, as Talfourd observed: Hazlitt's "death did not so much shock Lamb at the time, as it weighed down his spirits afterwards, when he felt the want of those essays which he had used periodically to look for with eagerness in the magazines and reviews which they alone made tolerable to him; and when he realised the dismal certainty that he should never again enjoy that rich discourse of old poets and painters with which so many a long winter's night had been gladdened, or taste life with an additional relish in the keen sense of enjoyment which endeared it to his companion."[13]

Soon after Hazlitt's death, Lamb made a second will. He left everything in trust for his sister, with the residue going to Emma.

On February 6, 1832, Munden died. Closer to our time, this would be akin to Chaplin dying, or Robin Williams: a presence whose "grandeur and singleness of expression" could convey "all the pleasures" the everyday world grants but we forget (*W,* 1:342).

Lamb fell into a savage mood. Robinson wrote in his diary, "Met Kenney at the Athenaeum. He gave me a very melancholy account of Ch. Lamb, which looks like the approach of that catastrophe everyone must fear. His anti-social feeling is quite a disease. I am afraid of going down to him."[14]

On July 25, 1834, Lamb lost the person he loved most, next to Mary— Coleridge, to heart failure. On his deathbed in the Gilmans' house in Highgate, Coleridge requested a volume of his *Poetical Works.* In pencil, near "This Lime-tree Bower My Prison," he wrote "Ch. and Mary Lamb—dear to my heart, yea, as it were, my heart. STC AET. 63, 1834, 1797–1834—37 years!" The dying poet also arranged for a "small plain mourning ring" to be given to Charles Lamb, along with a lock of hair. Five others were granted the same parting gift. Wordsworth was not among them. As Coleridge's prodigious consciousness faded, he said, "I could even be witty.[15]

The editor of the *Athenaeum* asked Lamb to write on Coleridge's death, but Lamb was too stunned to comply. Only in November, four months later, could he muster some words. He set them down, humbly and obscurely, in an album book of Mr. Keymer the bookseller:

When I heard of the death of Coleridge, it was without grief. It seemed to me that he long had been on the confines of the next world,—that he had a hunger for eternity. I grieved then that I could not grieve. But since, I feel how great a part he was of me. His great and dear spirit haunts me. I cannot think a thought, I cannot make a criticism on men or books, without an ineffectual turning and reference to him. He was the proof and touchstone of all my cogitations. . . . He was fifty years my old friend without a dissention. Never saw I his likeness, nor probably the world can see again. (*W,* 1:351).

Lamb didn't attend the funeral, but later visited Highgate, Coleridge's final residence. He wished to speak to the nurse who cared for his friend. So moved was he by her affection he gave her 5 guineas.

For the rest of his days—and there were not many—Lamb out of nowhere would exclaim, in the middle of a conversation about this or that, "Coleridge is dead!"[16]

Coleridge might have done the same in relation to Lamb's death, had the younger Grecian gone first. Coleridge had said of Lamb,

Charles Lamb has more totality and individuality of character than any other man I know, or have ever known in all my life. . . . The wild words that come from him sometimes on religious subjects would shock you from the mouth of any other man, but from him they seem mere flashes of firework. If an argument seems to his reason not fully true, he bursts out in that odd desecrating way: yet his will, the inward man, is, I well know, profoundly religious. Watch him when alone, and you will find him with either a Bible or an old divine, or an old English poet; in such is his pleasure.[17]

A friend of Lamb correctly said, "Lamb never fairly recovered from the death of Coleridge" (*W,* 1:406n).

# CHAPTER 51

## *A Swallow Flying*

Lamb died as he had lived: walking. On Monday, December 22, 1834, about a year after Elia's last essays and five months after Coleridge died, Lamb was strolling from his Edmonton residence on Church Street to Fore Street, where Bell Tavern, a favorite drinking spot, stood. On Edmonton High Street, he stumbled on a stone, fell, sliced open his face. He had probably been drinking. He contracted erysipelas, a skin disease also known as St. Anthony's Fire.

Erysipelas, derived from the Greek "red skin," occurs when streptococcus enters the skin. Wounds, in particular face wounds, are a common conduit for the bacteria. Within forty-eight hours, a hot, painful rash appears at the point of infection, and it swells and spreads. Its texture resembles an orange peel, frequently dotted with blisters and vesicles. Fever, chills, headaches, and vomiting ensue. Sometimes the lymph nodes swell. Those with compromised immune systems are most susceptible to the condition, such as older people and alcoholics. In our time, the infection is easily treated with antibiotics. Lacking these, as Lamb the fifty-nine-year-old drunkard did, erysipelas can intensify into necrotizing fasciitis, a "flesh-eating" infection causing hideous coloring, corrosion, and death. Charles Lamb likely died disfigured and in agony.

Four days after Lamb was cut, Talfourd heard from Mr. Ryle of India House (a co-executor, with Talfourd, of Lamb's will), that his friend was "in danger." Talfourd hurried to Edmonton the next morning, where he found Lamb "weak, and nearly insensible to things passing around him. Now and then a few words were audible, from which it seemed that his mind, in its feebleness, was intent on kind and hospitable thoughts." The last person to whom Lamb wrote a letter, a Mr. Childs, had sent a present of a turkey, and it seemed that the dying man was trying to arrange for some friends to partake of the bird in his absence. But the hardly coherent Lamb couldn't be sure what was going on. He didn't recognize Talfourd, who, after failing to "engage" his old friend's attention, left. "I quitted him," Talfourd continues, "not believing his death so near at hand. In less than an hour afterwards, his voice gradually grew fainter, as he still murmured the names of Moxon, Procter, and some other old friends, and he sank into death as placidly into sleep."[1]

Many thought Mary would collapse. In the immediate wake of the death, and at the funeral, though, she appeared composed. But when Robinson visited her a few days later, he observed, "A stranger would have seen little remarkable about her. She was neither violent nor unhappy; nor was she entirely without sense. She was, however, out of her mind, as the expression is."[2]

Robinson himself elected not to attend the funeral, but Talfourd was there, as were Moxton, Procter, Allsop, Cary, and friends from East India House. Lamb was buried in All Saints Churchyard on Church Street, Edmonton. After consulting Lamb's friends, Moxon asked Wordsworth for some lines to be engraved on the tombstone. Moxon also asked the poet if Talfourd, who was planning his biography, could print some of Lamb's letters to him and Dorothy.

Wordsworth replied that he would send some of Lamb's letters, but that others must be held back, in particular those relating to his own poetry, because "opinions or judgments of friends given in this way are of little value."[3] In the same letter, Wordsworth included his epitaph, which was far too long for a stone, but possibly suitable for a monument in a church. In the end, only three lines were adopted for Lamb's memorial in Edmonton Church, near the memorials of Keats (who spent a significant part of his youth in Edmonton) and Cowper (whose comic ballad of John Gilpin centers on the Bell Inn in Edmonton). The lines, rather too decorous, read: "At the centre of his being lodged / A soul by resignation sanctified . . . / O, he was good, if e'er a good Man lived." Fortunately Wordsworth offered a more personal tribute elsewhere. In "An Extempore Effusion upon the Death of James Hogg," he mourned the vanishing of "the frolic and the gentle" Lamb.[4]

The epitaph ended up being composed by Lamb's friend Cary, the translator of Dante. The poem is not much loved by Elians, especially when com-

Charles Lamb's and Mary Lamb's grave at All Saints Church, Edmonton.
(Courtesy of Northmetpit, Wikimedia Commons.)

pared to Wordsworth's lines. Still, the verse expresses a homely sentiment that Wordsworth's elegiac grandeur lacks.[5]

> Farewell, dear friend; that smile, that harmless mirth,
> No more shall gladden our domestic hearth;
> That rising tear, with pain forbid to flow,
> Better than words no more assuage our woe;
> That hued outstretched from small but well-earned store,
> Yields succour to the destitute no more.
> Yet art thou not all lost; through many an age,
> With sterling sense and humour, shall thy page
> Win many an English bosom, pleased to see
> That old and happier vein revived in thee.
> This for our earth; and if with friends we share
> Our joys in heaven, we hope to meet thee there.

Cary values Lamb's humor, love of domesticity, stalwart Englishness, anti-quarian quirks, and friendship. If the poetry approaches doggerel, the tribute suits the man.

Mary lived the next six years at the Waldens' in Edmonton. Then she was moved to Mrs. Parsons's house in Alpha Road, St. John's Wood. Charles had left enough to provide for her. She died in 1847, and she is buried beside her brother.

In his 1845 note to his long elegy for Charles, Wordsworth wrote, "Mary Lamb was ten years older than her brother, and has survived him as long a time. Were I to give way to my own feelings, I should dwell not only on her genius and intellectual powers, but upon the delicacy and refinement of manner which she maintained inviolable under most trying circumstances. She was loved and honoured by all her brother's friends; and others, some of them strange characters, whom his philanthropic peculiarities induced him to countenance."[6]

Landor also felt moved to write about Mary. In a letter to Robinson not long after Charles's death, he confessed that his recent friend's loss "has grieved me bitterly. Never did I see a human being with whom I was more inclined to sympathise. There is something in the recollection that you took me with you to see him which affects me greatly more than writing or speaking of him could do with any other. When I first heard of the loss that all his friends, and many that were never his friends, sustained in him, no thought took posses-sion of my mind except the anguish of his sister."[7] Landor enclosed a poem, "To the Sister of Elia," which concludes:

> Though the warm day is over, yet [the good and wise] seek
> Upon the lofty peak
>
> Of his pure mind the roseate light that glows
> O'er death's perennial snows.
> Behold him! From the region of the blest
> He speaks: he bids thee rest.[8]

In the years just after Lamb's death, his friends—namely Talfourd, Procter, and Hood—followed Landor and Wordsworth's examples. They sainted Lamb. No one wrote about his gritty politics, his vexed relationship to the empire, his addiction to drink, his debilitating melancholy, his nervous fevers, the almost nauseating vertigo of his irony.

Charles would have mocked their willful blindness.

We have his own obituary, which he wrote in 1827, where he admits he has done little worth noting, save he "once caught a swallow flying." He "confesses a partiality for the production of the juniper berry, was a fierce smoker of Tobacco," and he "is also the true Elia whose Essays are extant in a little volume published a year or two since; and rather better known from that name without a meaning, than from anything he has done or can hope to do in his own" (*W*, 1:320).

If Lamb had been able to write his obituary posthumously, he might have replaced sparrow-flight with another kind of soaring: his passage through the portal he had searched for his whole life, to a place beyond the western sun, where no madness is, or fear. One imagines him tiring quickly, though, of the *nectarous* tranquility. He hankers to press back through the gate, to the turmoil and the whim-whams. He would suffer life's stings all over again for those evenings of whist and gin, or the long London walks with Mary.

# Notes

*PREFACE*

1. Pater, "Appreciations," 177.
2. Woolf, "A Room of One's Own" and "Three Guineas," 8
3. Philip Lopate, in his foreword to *The Essays of Elia,* xv, finds in Lamb and Wallace both "a template for . . . giddy, runaway, self-referential verbal production[s]."
4. Lucas's impeccable *The Life of Charles Lamb* remains pertinent, but it is dated by now. Much new information has emerged, especially letters, and Lucas's hagiographical method is out of favor. Hagiography was de rigueur for the man whom Thackeray called "St. Charles." Thomas Noon Talfourd, Lamb's friend and first book-length biographer, praised Lamb's generosity, wit, sweetness, or character on almost every page, overlooking entirely Lamb's darker parts. This was in his 1837 *Letters of Charles Lamb, with a Sketch of His Life,* which he followed in 1848 with *Final Memorials of Charles Lamb.* Throughout the remainder of the nineteenth century, several biographies were published, most providing important new information on Lamb, all spinning Elia more or less positively. One was by another friend of Lamb: Bryan Waller Procter (Barry Cornwall), *Charles Lamb.* Others were Percy Fitzgerald's *Charles Lamb;* Thomas Craddock's *Charles Lamb;* Alfred Ainger's *Charles Lamb;* Benjamin Ellis Martin's *In the Footprints of Charles Lamb;* and William Carew Hazlitt's *The Lambs.* In addition to Lucas's great biography, other early twentieth-century lives of Lamb include Walter Jerrold's *Lamb* and S. L. Bensusan's *Charles Lamb.*
5. Thompson, "Our Debt to Lamb," 207.
6. Riehl in *That Dangerous Figure* provides an excellent discussion of how Thompson's efforts almost single-handedly ruined Lamb's reputation (98–100).

7. The best biography between Lucas's and more modern lives is Edmund Blunden's *Charles Lamb and His Poetic Contemporaries.* Blunden, a poet who served in the trenches in World War I and edited Winifred Owen's and John Clare's works, set out to establish Lamb as a writer of the same stature as Wordsworth and Coleridge. Katharine Anthony's 1945 *The Lambs* opposes the appreciationists. In her unsentimental biography, largely dismissed as speculative, she argues that Charles and Mary shared incestuous feelings for each another and that Charles was in love with their adopted daughter Emma Isola. (Ernest C. Ross in *Charles Lamb and Emma Isola,* published in 1950, vigorously rebutted Anthony.) In 1964, George L. Barnett published *The Evolution of Elia,* an excellent work of biographical literary criticism in which Barnett shows how salient details of Lamb's life inform his work. Barnett followed this in 1977 with a brief biography of Lamb. In 1982, Winifred Courtney published her fantastic account of the first half of Lamb's life, *Young Charles Lamb.* David Cecil's *A Portrait of Charles Lamb* is, like Barnett's biography, a brief account of Lamb. Jane Aaron in 1991 released *A Double Singleness;* the book considers the lives and letters of the siblings in light of class and gender. Sarah Burton in 2003 published *A Double Life;* though Charles is not the primary focus of the book—his relationship with Mary is—Burton brilliantly reveals the darker sides of Lamb. In her biography of Mary Lamb, Susan Hitchcock also reveals the more sordid details of Lamb (*Mad Mary Lamb*). In *The Devil Kissed Her,* Kathy Watson's detailed descriptions of Mary's insanity and its various "cures" shed light on Charles's own confinement in a Hoxton madhouse in 1795–96.

8. For Lamb and the British Empire, see Fang, "Empire, Coleridge, and Charles Lamb's Consumer Imagination." Other pertinent work on Lamb and the imperialistic East India Company are Baladouni, "Charles Lamb"; and Ledwith, "The East India Company." See also James, "Thomas Manning, Charles Lamb, and Oriental Encounters." James has also done engaging work on Lamb's participation in a network of political radicals of the 1790s who valued Unitarianism, Joseph Priestley, and sympathetic friendship. See her *Charles Lamb, Coleridge and Wordsworth.* David Fairer in *Organising Poetry* also considers this network, as does Alison Hickey in "Double Bonds." In *Charles Lamb,* James also connects Lamb to the tradition of the flâneur, the urban walker who transforms as he moves streets and blocks and buildings into reflections of his shifting moods. Simon Hull's work emphasizes Lamb as an urban writer as well, in particular a member of the Cockney literary school and writer for the *London Magazine.* See his *Charles Lamb, Elia and the "London Magazine."* See also Makdisi, "William Blake, Charles Lamb, and Urban Antimodernity"; Oliver, "Walking and Imagining the City"; and Stewart, "Lamb's London, Magazines and Nostalgia in the Present Tense." For more on Lamb and the Cockney School, see Gregory Dart's *Metropolitan Art and Literature.* For recent work on Lamb and children's literature, see Newbon, "'Squeamish Times'"; Lim, "Appropriate(d) Nursery Reading"; and Roy, "Celebrating 'Wild Tales.'" Aaron's *A Double Singleness* explores Lamb's gender fluidity. An excellent article on Lamb's late album verses is Samantha Matthews's "From Autograph to Print." David Stewart has illuminated Lamb's late occasional verse in "Fleeting, Shadowy Reflections."

9. Recent work has explored darker parts of Lamb's personality that the appreciationists overlooked, ignored, or repressed. Anya Taylor's *Bacchus in Romantic England* delves into Lamb's drinking problem. Burton in *Double Life* and Hitchcock in *Mad Mary Lamb* expose Lamb's own mental health issues—drinking and depression—while Thomas McFarland in "Charles Lamb and the Politics of Survival" and Gerald Monsman in *Confessions of a Poetic Dreamer* show how Lamb's Elia essays are his efforts to work through the trauma of his mother being killed. Jennifer Harris has explored Lamb's own time in a mental institution. See her "Managing Madness." Lamb's erotic life has received little attention—mainly because there is little to go on—but Anthony's study of Lamb's sexuality, though far-fetched, at least treats Lamb the bachelor as a sexual being, as I do in this biography. Duncan Wu in his biography of Hazlitt is the first to argue that Lamb actually visited prostitutes, as did Hazlitt, Wordsworth, and Keats. See *Hazlitt*, 60, 108–9.

## INTRODUCTION

1. Thornbury, *Old and New London*, 1:35–69, 220–33; Borer, *An Illustrated Guide to London 1800*, 29, 38, 46.
2. George Christof Lichtenberg of Göttingen, friend of Lamb's hero Priestley and a connoisseur, like Lamb, of Hogarth, described a typical London thoroughfare in the latter half of the eighteenth century.

In the middle of the street roll chaises, carriages and drays in an unending stream. Above this din and the hum and clatter of ten thousand of tongues and feet, one hears the chimes from church towers, the bells of the postmen, the organs, fiddles and hurdy-gurdies and tambourines of English mountebanks, and the cries of those who sell hot and cold viands in the open at the street corners. Then you will see a bonfire of shavings flaring up as high as the upper floors of the houses, in a circle of merrily shouting beggar-boys, sailors and rogues. Suddenly a man, whose handkerchief has been stolen, will cry "Stop thief" and everyone will begin running and pushing and shoving, many of them not with any idea of catching the thief, but of prigging for themselves perhaps a purse or watch. Before you know where you are a pretty, nicely dressed miss will take you by the hand "Come my lord, come along, let us drink a glass together" or "I'll go with you, if you please." Then there is an accident forty paces from you. "God bless me!" cries one. "Poor creature!" another. Then one stops and must put one's hand in one's pocket for all appear to sympathize with the misfortunes of the poor creature; but all of a sudden they are laughing again because someone has laid down by mistake in the gutter. "Look there, damn me" says a third and the procession passes on.

Quoted in Bayne-Powell, *Travellers in the Eighteenth-Century*, 38.
3. Boswell, *The Journals of James Boswell, 1762–1795*, 12.
4. Dickens, *A Tale of Two Cities*, 159.
5. *The Works of Charles and Mary Lamb*, ed. Lucas, 2:83; hereafter cited parenthetically as *W*, followed by volume and page.

6. *The Letters of Charles and Mary Anne Lamb*, ed. Marrs Jr., 1:72; hereafter cited parenthetically as *M*, followed by volume and page.

7. The phrase is actually Coleridge's, but Lamb loved it.

8. Charles le Grice is the schoolfellow, quoted in Talfourd, *Letters*, 4; Hunt, *Autobiography*, 1:175.

9. Monsman, *Confessions of a Poetic Dreamer*, 155; Hood, *Hood's Own*, 551; Forster, "Charles Lamb," 205; Talfourd, *Letters*, 3; Hall, *A Book of Memories of Great Men and Women of the Age*, 57; Patmore, *My Friends and Acquaintance*, 14.

10. Charles le Grice, quoted in Talfourd, *Letters*, 4.

11. Hood, *Hood's Own*, 551; Patmore, *My Friends and Acquaintance*, 14.

## *1. THE TEMPLE*

1. Thornbury, *Old and New London*, 1:149–81.

2. Wordsworth, *Thirteen Book "Prelude,"* 2:119–20.

3. Lucas, *Life*, 1:3.

4. Aaron in *Double Singleness* insightfully discusses how Mary and Charles struggled with their class status (20–50).

5. Lucas, *Life*, 2461.

6. Procter, *Charles Lamb*, 42.

7. Razzell and Spence, "The History of Infant, Child and Adult Mortality in London, 1550–1850," 271–92.

8. Hazlitt, *Selected Writings*, 8:33.

9. Haydon, *Life, Letters, and Table Talk*, 281. See also Wu's account in *Hazlitt*, 176–78.

10. Quoted in Lucas, *Life*, 2:107; Procter, *Charles Lamb*, 49.

11. For Wordsworth's presence in this essay, see Seturman, "A Note on Lamb's 'Benchers.'"

12. This anecdote was reported by John Chambers, who worked with Lamb at East India Company. It is recounted by Algernon Black in "Charles Lamb," 431.

13. Lucas, *Life*, 2:201–2.

14. Marrs's three-volume edition of Lamb's letters ends in October 1817. All citations of letters after this year come from Lucas's edition, *The Letters of Charles Lamb, to Which Are Added Those of His Sister Mary Lamb*. The letters will be cited parenthetically in the text as *L*, followed by volume and page. This letter on Mary's "rambling" is found at 3:401.

15. De Quincey, *Works*, 10:251.

16. Wordsworth, "Essays upon Epitaphs," in *Prose Works*, 2:45–96.

17. Cowden Clarke and Cowden Clarke, *Recollections of Writers*, 177.

18. Talfourd, *Final Memorials*, 2:226–27.

19. Cowden Clarke and Cowden Clarke, *Recollections of Writers*, 177.

20. Quoted in Lucas, *Life*, 2:241.

21. Talfourd, *Final Memorials*, 2:227.

22. Cowden Clarke and Cowden Clarke, *Recollections of Writers*, 185.

23. Talfourd, *Letters*, 91.

24. For work on Lamb's essay on witches and childhood experience, see Newbon, "'Terrors in Children.'"
25. Wordsworth, *Thirteen-Book "Prelude,"* 2:25.


## 2. CHRIST'S HOSPITAL

1. Hood, *Hood's Own,* 564.
2. Misson, *Memoirs and Observations,* 19.
3. *Gentleman's Magazine.*
4. Thornbury, *Old and New London,* 3:364–79.
5. Coleridge, *Essays on His Times,* 2:26.
6. Hunt, *Autobiography,* 1:96.
7. Hunt, *Autobiography,* 1:113.
8. "As if it were a lily" comes from Hunt, "Deaths of Little Children," 204.
9. Hunt, "Deaths of Little Children," 204.
10. For an excellent discussion of the alternative canon at Christ's in Lamb's time, see Watters, "The Tribe of Sam."
11. Hunt, *Autobiography,* 1:102.
12. Coleridge, *Table Talk,* 1:326.
13. Allan, *Christ's Hospital,* 44.
14. Hunt, *Autobiography,* 1:107.
15. Quoted in Talfourd, *Letters,* 5–6.
16. Talfourd, *Letters,* 5.
17. Hunt, *Autobiography,* 1:143.
18. Coleridge, *Table Talk,* 2:97.
19. Hunt, *Autobiography,* 1:128.
20. For a good discussion of the interplay between the two Christ's essays, see Treadwell, "Impersonation and Autobiography in Lamb's Christ's Hospital Essays."
21. Coleridge, *Biographia Literaria,* 1:10.
22. Katie S. Homar has demonstrated how the classical curriculum at Christ's shaped Lamb's style. See her "'Rehearsing Continually the Part of the Past.'"
23. Coleridge, *Biographia Literaria,* 1:10.
24. Hunt, *Lord Byron,* 2:181.
25. De Quincey, *Works,* 16:387.
26. Procter, *Charles Lamb,* 157.
27. De Quincey, *Works,* 16:387.
28. Cowden Clarke and Cowden Clarke, *Recollections of Writers,* 177.


## 3. EAST INDIA

1. Quoted in Lucas, *Life,* 1:71.
2. Manning, "Memorials of Joseph Paice," 387.
3. De Quincey, *Works,* 10:276.

4. A helpful article on Lamb's biography and the South Sea House is David Chandler's "Charles Lamb and the South Sea House." For the essay's relationship to Lamb's persona, see Monsman, "Charles Lamb's 'Enfranchised Quill.'"

5. Lopate, introduction to *The Art of the Personal Essay*, xxv.

6. Courtney's research on Ann Simmons is thorough and indispensable. *Young Charles Lamb*, 69–83.

7. Quoted in Courtney, *Young Charles Lamb*, 76.

8. Robert Southey, letter to Edward Moxon, February 2, 1836, in *Collected Letters*.

9. "Review of *The Works of Charles Lamb*."

10. Lucas, *Life*, 1:81. Sarah Burton (*A Double Life*) disagrees with Lucas. First of all, there is no clear history of insanity in the Lamb family (even though Talfourd, who knew Lamb well, says there was). And would a man so intensely in love as Lamb have even allowed such a history to impede him, if it existed? (Not inconceivable for the hyper-gallant Lamb.)

11. For Lamb's storytelling technique in this essay, see O'Neill, "'Only What Might Have Been.'"

12. De Quincey, *Works of Thomas De Quincey*, 10:237. The standard biography of De Quincey is Grevel, *The Opium-Eater*. A recent compelling biography is Frances Wilson's *Guilty Thing*.

13. De Quincey, *Works*, 10:238.

14. De Quincey, *Works*, 10:239.

15. De Quincey, *Works*, 10:240.

16. Scott, *History of Torture*, 148–49.

17. Aaron, *A Single Doubleness*, 80.

18. Charles Lamb Papers.

19. Black, "Charles Lamb," 432. Gerald Monsman provides an excellent account of Lamb's juggling literature and labor. See his "Charles Lamb's Elia as Clerk."

20. Black, "Charles Lamb," 432.

21. Lucas, *Life*, 2:143–45.

22. Twitchell, "Concerning Charles Lamb."

23. Robinson, *Diary*, 1:214.

24. David Booth Papers.

25. Charles Lamb Papers.


### 4. SALUTATION AND CAT

1. Lucas, *Life*, 1:75.

2. Southey, letter to Edward Moxon, February 2, 1836, in *Collected Letters*.

3. Talfourd, *Letters*, 100–102.

4. Hunt, *Autobiography*, 1:175.

5. Hunt, *Lord Byron*, 2:40.

6. "Review of *The Works of Charles Lamb*," 306.

7. Watson, *The Devil Kissed Her*, 70–72.

8. Woodring, introduction to *Table Talk*.

9. Dix, *Lions*, 2:376.

10. Coleridge, *Collected Letters*, 1:316–17.
11. Boswell, *The Life of Samuel Johnson*, 505.
12. Southey, letter to Edward Moxon, February 2, 1836, in *Collected Letters*.
13. Quoted in Courtney, *Young Charles Lamb*, 109.
14. In *Coleridge: Early Visions*, 63–120, Richard Holmes recounts Coleridge's development of the Pantisocracy in characteristically riveting detail.
15. James, *Charles Lamb*, 13–54.
16. Wordsworth, *Lyrical Ballads*, 118.
17. Coleridge, *Poetical Works*, 1:181.
18. Coleridge, *Poetical Works*, 1:163.
19. James, *Charles Lamb*, 24.
20. Coleridge, preface to *Poems on Various Subjects*, vii.
21. Coleridge, preface to *Poems on Various Subjects*, vii.
22. Around the time Lamb published these poems, he wrote another poem to Anna, only published about ten years ago. The manuscript resides in the Robert H. Taylor Collection, Manuscripts Division, Department of Rare Books and Special Collections, Princeton University Library. Felicity James printed it in the *Charles Lamb Bulletin* 127 (July 2004).

> Sweet is thy sunny hair,
> O Nymph, divinely fair,
> With whose loose locks, as they stray
> On the pinions of the wind,
> I were well content to play
> All the live-long Summer's day
> Under some tall wood's shade
> In mild oblivion laid,
> Nor heed the busier scenes I left behind.
> Yet not thy sunny hair,
> O Nymph, divinely fair,
> Nor cheek of delicate hue,
> Nor eye of loveliest blue,
> Nor voice of melody,
> O'er my fond heart could so prevail
> As did the soul of sympathy,
> That beam'd a meek and modest grace
> Of pensive softness o'er thy face,
> When thy heart bled to hear the tale
> Of Julia, and the silent secret moan
> The love-lorn maiden pour'd for Savillon.
> Ah! too, like him, far, far I go
> From all my heart holds dear,
> With sorrowing steps and slow,
> And many a starting tear.

Yet could I hope, that thou wouldst not forget,
The love-sick youth, that sighs his soul away
[All journeying on] his weary way
[Then might I leave] with less regret
Each [open lawn], or shadowy grove,
Each [sunny field], or green-wood shade,
Where with my Anna I have stray'd,
Far, far to wander from the maid I love.

### 5. DAY OF HORRORS

1. Susan Hitchcock agrees that we should be careful not to diagnose Mary by today's categories, but she also believes that if Mary were diagnosed today, she would probably be labeled "bipolar." Kathy Watson also holds that Mary was manic-depressive. Russell R. Monroe diverges from this commonly held perception of Mary's mental illness. In *Creative Brainstorms.* he argues that Mary suffered from limbic lobe seizures, as did Edvard Munch. Lisa Appignanesi in *Mad, Bad, and Sad* does a fine job of historically contextualizing Mary's illness (13–52).
2. Talfourd, *Final Memorials*, 2:227.
3. Coleridge, *Collected Letters*, 2:498.
4. Coleridge, *Collected Letters*, 3:941.
5. Talfourd, *Final Memorials*, 227.
6. Burton's description of Charles's behavior in the aftermath of the killing is excellent. *A Double Life*, 91–129.
7. Quoted in Andrews and Scull, *Undertaker of the Mind*, 21. This book provides helpful historical context for understanding madness in the age of Lamb. See also Porter, *Madness*, 62–88; and Shorter, *A History of Psychiatry*, 1–68.
8. Burton, *A Double Life;* Watson, *The Devil Kissed Her;* Hitchcock, *Mad Mary Lamb;* and Appignanesi, *Mad, Bad, and Sad* offer vivid accounts of the sorts of therapies Mary might have endured.
9. Burton provides useful information on how King George's madness affected the laws for the criminally insane, and so, indirectly, Mary (*A Double Life*, 91–95).
10. For an account of Nicholson and the aftermath of her attempt, see Joanne Holland's "Narrating Margaret Nicholson," 1–39.
11. For Hadfield's case, see Eigen, *Witnessing Insanity,* 48–54.
12. Quoted in Appignanesi, *Mad, Bad, and Sad,* 42.
13. Burton, *A Double Life,* 295–302.
14. Burton, *A Double Life,* 295–302.

### 6. UNITARIAN

1. Coleridge, *Poetical Works,* 1:181.
2. Coleridge, *Collected Letters,* 1:137.

3. For Coleridge's quote, see Coleridge, *Collected Letters*, 1:258.
4. Coleridge, *Poetical Works,* 1:179.
5. Priestley, *The Doctrine of Necessity,* 108.
6. Lindsey, preface to *An Answer to Mr. Paine's Age of Reason.*
7. Felicity James's work on Lamb, Coleridge, and Priestley has been very helpful; see her *Charles Lamb*, 20–34.

### 7. MENTION NOTHING OF POETRY

1. Coleridge, *Poetical Works*, 1:158.
2. Wu, *Hazlitt*, 48.
3. Holmes, *Coleridge: Early Visions*, 159–65. Holmes's biography of Coleridge captures his mercurial, volatile character best. For more scholarly versions of Coleridge's life, see Ashton, *The Life of Samuel Taylor Coleridge*; and Lefebure, *Samuel Taylor Coleridge.*
4. Roe, *Fiery Heart,* 175–236.
5. Alexander, *A History of English Literature*, 243.
6. Gardner, *Poetry and Popular Protest*, 120–29.
7. James, *Charles Lamb*, 22–23.
8. Coleridge, *Poetical Works*, 1:275.
9. Coleridge, *Poetical Works*, 1:234–35.
10. Coleridge, *Poetical Works* 1:351–54.

### 8. DIVINE CHIT-CHAT

1. Both James (*Charles Lamb*, 97–101) and Fairer (*Organising Poetry,* 7–10) provide helpful discussions of Lloyd's involvement in the circle of Coleridge and Lamb.
2. Lloyd, "Lines Written on a Friday."
3. Coleridge, *Collected Letters*, 1:256.
4. Quoted in Lucas, *Charles Lamb and the Lloyds*, 14.
5. Coleridge, *Collected Letters*, 1:257.
6. Coleridge, *Collected Letters*, 1:315.
7. I base this assessment on De Quincey's analysis of Lloyd's character in *Works,* 11:199.
8. Cowper, *Memoirs,* 10.
9. For Cowper's biography, see King, *William Cowper.*
10. Cowper, *Poems,* 239.

### 9. NETHER STOWEY

1. Coleridge, *Collected Letters*, 1:308. For a discussion of Coleridge's pastoral yearnings at this time, see Holmes, *Coleridge: Early Visions*, 136–38.
2. Holmes, *Coleridge: Early Visions*, 136–40.
3. Wordsworth, *Thirteen-Book "Prelude,"* 2:229–30.

4. On November 7, 1845, Mary Wordsworth, William's wife, wrote this to Sara, Coleridge's daughter. She said it was her husband's memory. For Coleridge's first meeting with the Wordsworths, see Holmes, *Coleridge: Early Visions*, 149–50.

5. Wordsworth and Wordsworth, *Letters*, 1:188–89.

6. Hazlitt, *Selected Writings*, 9:105.

7. Coleridge, *Collected Letters*, 1:331.

8. Holmes, *Coleridge: Early Visions*, 182–98. For Wordsworth's part in his early friendship with Coleridge and the making of *Lyrical Ballads*, see Gill, *William Wordsworth*, 120–41.

9. Wordsworth, *Lyrical Ballads*, 49. For an excellent recent account of Wordsworth's attitude toward nature at this time, see Nicholson, *The Making of Poetry*.

### *10.* BLANK VERSE

1. James, *Charles Lamb*, 113–14.

2. Coleridge, *Collected Letters*, 1:357–58.

3. Quoted in James, *Charles Lamb*, 115.

4. Coleridge, *Collected Letters*, 1:320.

5. Coleridge, *Collected Letters* 1:320.

6. Southey, letter to Thomas Southey, January 24, 1798, in *Collected Letters*.

7. Coleridge, *Collected Letters*, 2:714.

8. Coleridge, *Collected Letters*, 1:334.

9. Southey, letter to Thomas Southey, January 24, 1798, in *Collected Letters*.

10. Coleridge, *Collected Letters*, 1:390.

11. Lloyd, *Edmund Oliver*, 245. For an excellent discussion of the ins and outs of the Edmund Oliver scandal, see Allan, "Charles Lloyd, Coleridge, and *Edmund Oliver*."

12. Coleridge, *Collected Letters*, 1:407.

13. Coleridge, *Collected Letters*, 1:405.

### *11. PENTONVILLE*

1. Thornbury, *Old and New London,* 2:279–89.

2. Southey, letter to Edward Moxon, February 2, 1836, in *Collected Letters*.

3. Where possible, I rely on Lamb's epistolary drafts of the poems that eventually made their way into *Blank Verse,* in order to view the lines in their most immediate, emotionally raw contexts. In almost all cases, earlier and later drafts are the same, and the differences—usually a spelling out of an ampersand or a removal of bold type—are not significant.

4. *Blank Verse,* 77–79.

5. *Blank Verse,* 85.

6. James, *Charles Lamb*, 131–34.

7. *Blank Verse,* 93.

## 12. FROG AND TOAD

1. *Blank Verse,* 7–13.
2. *Blank Verse,* 11.
3. Godwin, *Enquiry concerning Political Justice,* 365.
4. Southey, letter to C. W. W. Lynn, August 15, 1798, in *Collected Letters.*
5. James, *Charles Lamb,* 1–38.
6. The standard biography of Southey is Speck, *Robert Southey.*
7. Robinson, *Diary,* 1:369.
8. Byron, *Byron's Letters and Journals,* 3:122.
9. Wu, "Ode to a Forgotten Laureate."
10. Holmes, *Coleridge: Early Visions,* 64.
11. Coleridge, *Collected Letters,* 1:293–94.
12. For excellent background on Lamb's novel, see Anderson, "*Rosamund Gray* Reconsidered."
13. Shelley, *Letters of Percy Bysshe Shelley,* 1:111–12.

## 13. QUAKERS

1. Shelley, *Letters of Percy Bysshe Shelley,* 1:111–12.
2. Lucas, *Charles Lamb and the Lloyds,* 175–84.
3. Scully, "The Secular Ethics of Liberal Quakerism," 223.
4. Quoted in Courtney, *Young Charles Lamb,* 181.
5. Courtney, *Young Charles Lamb,* 129–31.
6. For an excellent article on Lamb's ideas on Quakers and silence, see Vigus, "Do 'Friends' Allow Puns?"

## 14. GEORGE DYER

1. Recent work has shown that Dyer was far from a merely comic figure; he was an important player in London radical circles. See Roe, "Radical George"; and Whelan, "George Dyer and Dissenting Culture."
2. Bowring, *Autobiographical Recollections,* 62.
3. Lucas, "G.D., Friend of Lamb."
4. Procter, *Charles Lamb,* 70.
5. Talfourd, *Final Memorials,* 2:137.
6. Talfourd, *Final Memorials,* 2:138.
7. For a discussion of the relationship between this essay and Lamb's life, see Wedd, "Elia the Academic."

## 15. MANNING

1. Ainger, "Notes," 394.
2. For recent work on Lamb's friendship with Manning and Manning's importance as a travel writer, see Weech, "'All Beauties of the Road'"; James, "Thomas Manning,

Charles Lamb, and Oriental Encounters"; and Ades, "Lamb's Correspondence with Thomas Manning."

3. Markham, *Narratives of the Mission of George Bogle*, clv.
4. Markham, *Narratives of the Mission of George Bogle*, 280.
5. Markham, *Narratives of the Mission of George Bogle*, 265.
6. Markham, *Narratives of the Mission of George Bogle*, 278.
7. Manning, letter to William Manning, July 1799.
8. Manning, letter to William Manning, July 1799.
9. Manning, letter to William Manning, July 1799.
10. Manning, letter to William Wilkins, April 24, 1807.
11. Markham, *Narratives of the Mission of George Bogle*, clx.
12. Lucas, *Life*, 2:122.
13. Manning, *Letters to Charles Lamb*, 22.
14. Anderson and Ehrenpreis, "The Familiar Letter in the Eighteenth Century," 269–82.

### 16. GODWIN

1. Southey, letter to Edith Southey, May 15, 1799, in *Collected Letters*.
2. Coleridge, *Collected Letters*, 1:563.
3. The standard introduction to Godwin is Don Locke's *A Fantasy of Reason*.
4. Godwin, *Memoirs of the Author of the "Vindication of the Rights of Woman,"* 133.
5. Robinson, *Diary*, 1:191.
6. Courtney, *Young Charles Lamb*, 262–64.
7. Southey, letter to Edward Moxon, February 2, 1836, in *Collected Letters*.

### 17. ANATOMY OF MELANCHOLY

1. White, *Falstaff's Letters*, xix.
2. White, *Falstaff's Letters*, 10.
3. White, *Falstaff's Letters*, 5.
4. Coleridge, *Collected Letters*, 1:588.
5. Lamb, Commonplace Book.
6. Burton, *Anatomy of Melancholy*, 1:17, 1:14.
7. Burton, *Anatomy of Melancholy*, 1:30.
8. Burton, *Anatomy of Melancholy*, 1:16.

### 18. 27 SOUTHAMPTON BUILDINGS

1. Wu, *Hazlitt*, 113.
2. Lucas, *Life*, 2:262–63.
3. Carlyle, *Notebooks*, 23.
4. Lucas, *Life*, 2:203.
5. Taylor, *Bacchus in Romantic England*, 61–92.
6. Lucas, *Life*, 1:331.

7. Coleridge, *Collected Letters*, 3:340.

8. This is Taylor's valid argument in *Bacchus in Romantic England*.

9. Quoted in Courtney, *Young Charles Lamb*, 218.

10. Quoted in Courtney, *Young Charles Lamb*, 219.

11. Wordsworth and Wordsworth, *The Grasmere Journals*, 24.

12. Hazlitt, *Selected Writings*, 5:324.

13. James, *Charles Lamb*, 175.

14. Southey, letter to Charles Danvers, December 21, 1801, in *Collected Letters*.

15. Pamela Clemit covers Lamb's relationship to *Antonio* in "Lamb and Godwin's Antonio."

16. For Lamb and food, see Lamont, "Charles Lamb, Food, and Feasting"; Watson, "Lamb and Food"; Plotz, *Romanticism and the Vocation of Childhood*, 118–28; and Randal, "Eating and Drinking in Lamb's Essays."

17. For the various ways Lamb's essay on roast pig works as a satire, see Monsman, "Satiric Model for Lamb's 'Dissertation upon Roast-Pig'"; Hull, "Snipe, Roast Pig and Boiled Babies"; and Reiman, "Social and Political Satire in a 'Dissertation upon Roast-Pig.'"

18. Landon, "Chas Farrar Browne," 22.

19. Wu, *Hazlitt*, 59–60.

20. Wu, *Hazlitt*, 87.

### 19. FLÂNEUR

1. Hazlitt, *Selected Writings*, 8:38.

2. For Lamb as flâneur, see James, *Charles Lamb*, 212–13; and Dart, *Metropolitan Art and Literature*, 137–62.

3. Baudelaire, "The Painter of Modern Life."

### 20. JOURNALISM

1. Taylor, *Works of Jeremy Taylor*, 369.

2. These passages as well as the ones from "What Is Jacobinism?" do not appear in Lucas's edition of Lamb's writing, most certainly because they are not signed by Lamb. Courtney, however, convincingly argues that these *Albion* pieces are Lamb's. In this and the next paragraph, I am quoting from her *Young Charles Lamb*, 314–15.

3. Courtney, *Young Charles Lamb*, 315–16.

4. Quoted in Williams, *Lamb's Friend the Census-Taker*, 70–71.

5. Quoted in *W*, 2:430–31.

6. Southey, letter to Joseph Cottle, June 18, 1797, in *Collected Letters*.

7. Quoted in Williams, *Lamb's Friend the Census-Taker*, 24.

8. Quoted in Crosse, "Thomas Poole," 613.

9. Holmes, *Coleridge: Early Visions*, 336.

10. Coleridge, *Collected Letters*, 1:1074.

11. Southey, letter to John Rickman, February 17, 1802, in *Collected Letters*.

12. Procter, *Charles Lamb*, 173.

### 21. BARTHOLOMEW FAIR

1. Wordsworth, *Poems in Two Volumes,* 147.
2. Wordsworth, *Prose Works,* 1:129.
3. For an account of the Wordsworths' complex relationship to London at this time, see Newlyn, "Lamb, Lloyd, London."
4. Wordsworth, *Thirteen-Book "Prelude,"* 2:131–33.

### 22. MARY'S LETTERS

1. Balle, "Mary Lamb and Sarah Stoddart." See also Grayling, *The Quarrel of the Age,* 97.

### 23. LONG AND RUEFUL FACES

1. Coleridge, *Collected Letters,* 2:941.
2. For accounts of Charles and Mary's relationship, see Watson, *The Devil Kissed Her,* 107–10; Burton, *A Double Life,* 209–42; and Hitchcock, *Mad Mary Lamb,* 93–95.
3. Procter, *Charles Lamb,* 37.

### 24. PUNS

1. For Lamb and punning, see Ledbetter, "The Comic Imagination in Lamb and Coleridge."
2. Keats, *Letters,* 70–71.
3. Quoted in Talfourd, *Letters,* 319.
4. Talfourd, *Letters,* 314.
5. Talfourd, *Letters,* 318–19.
6. Procter, *Charles Lamb,* 235.
7. *World's Wit,* 33.
8. *World's Wit,* 32.
9. *World's Wit.*
10. *World's Wit.*
11. Beckinschtein, "Why Clowns Taste Funny," 9669–70.
12. Beck, "Why Do Puns Make People Groan?"
13. Jack Pollack, *The Pun Also Rises,* quoted in Beck, "Why Do Puns Make People Groan?"
14. Lucas, *Life,* 2:407.
15. For more on Hazlitt and Lamb, see Natarajan, "Hazlitt, Lamb, and the Philosophy of Familiarity"; and Hamilton, "The Irritable Genius."
16. Hazlitt, *Selected Writings,* 9:69.
17. Hazlitt, *Selected Writings,* 8:118.
18. Hazlitt, *Selected Writings,* 2:208.
19. Hazlitt, *Selected Writings,* 2:79.
20. Hazlitt, *Selected Writings,* 8:121.
21. Hazlitt, *Selected Writings,* 9:204.

22. Hazlitt, *Selected Writings*, 8:31.
23. Coleridge, *Collected Letters*, 2:990.
24. Hazlitt, *Selected Writings*, 7:165.
25. For more on the Hazlitt scandal in the Lake District, see Wu, *Hazlitt*, 98–99.
26. Quoted in Johnston, *The Hidden Wordsworth*, 570.
27. Wu, *Hazlitt*, 151–54, 272–73.
28. Haverty, *The Far Side of a Kiss*.
29. Wu, *Hazlitt*, 258–59.
30. Hazlitt, *Selected Writings*, 7:231.
31. Hazlitt, *Selected Writings*, 8:32.
32. Garratt, "The Early Friendship of Captain James Burney and Charles Lamb."
33. Samuel Johnson, letter to Hester Thrale, November 14, 1781, *Letters*.
34. "Review of *The Works of Charles Lamb*," 292.
35. Talfourd, *The Works of Charles Lamb*, 294.
36. Hazlitt, *Selected Writings*, 8:32.
37. Hazlitt, *Selected Writings*, 8:33.
38. Hazlitt, *Selected Writings*, 8:33.
39. Hunt, *Examiner*, April 4, 1824, quoted in Lucas, *Life*, 2:116.
40. Hunt, *Examiner*, April 4, 1824, quoted in Lucas, *Life*, 2:116.
41. Hazlitt, *Selected Writings*, 8:33.
42. Talfourd, *Letters*, 347.

### 25. SWEEPS AND BEGGARS

1. Cullingford, *British Chimney Sweeps*, 34–103.
2. For Lamb's relationship to laws concerning beggars and to contemporary representations of beggars, see Harriman-Smith, "Representing the Poor."
3. Harriman-Smith, "Representing the Poor," 52.

### 26. SHIPWRECK

1. Coleridge, *Collected Letters*, 2:1174.
2. Coleridge, *Collected Letters*, 2:1177.
3. Wordsworth and Wordsworth, *Letters*, 2:86.
4. For John Wordsworth, see Reeves, "John Wordsworth."
5. Wordsworth and Wordsworth, *Letters*, 1:545.
6. Matlak, "Captain John Wordsworth's Death at Sea "
7. Wordsworth and Wordsworth, *Letters*, 1:544–45.

### 27. HOGSFLESH

1. For more on *Mr. H.*, see Craik, "Hogsflesh Revisited."
2. Hazlitt, *Selected Writings*, 6:208.
3. Robinson, *Diary*, 1:148.

4. Robinson, *Diary,* 1:148.

5. *Monthly Literary Recreations,* December 1806.

## 28. TALES FROM SHAKESPEAR

1. For the contexts of Godwin's and Lamb's children's literature, see Newbon, "Squeamish Times" and Roy, "Celebrating 'Wild Tales.'" Judith Plotz's reading of Lamb (*Romanticism and the Vocation of Childhood,* 87–128) suggests he is most unsuitable to write strong children's literature. She finds Lamb's vision of childhood selfish and escapist—not without justification.

2. Coleridge, *Collected Letters,* 1:553.

3. Coleridge, *Collected Letters,* 1:354.

4. Hitchcock discusses Mary's struggles between convention and invention: *Mad Mary Lamb,* 160–68. See also Marsden, "Shakespeare for Girls."

5. *Critical Review; or, Annals of Literature.*

## 29. SPECIMENS OF ENGLISH DRAMATIC POETS

1. Quoted in Fox, *A Brief History of the Wesleyan Missions,* 58. For information on Clarkson, I have drawn from 56–67.

2. Robinson, *Diary,* 1:19.

3. Robinson, *Diary,* 1:19.

4. Haydon, *Diary,* 5:53.

5. Hazlitt, *Letters,* 95–101.

6. Patmore, *My Friends and Acquaintance,* 21.

7. Jones, *Hazlitt,* 24.

8. Fitzgerald, *Life, Letters and Writings of Charles Lamb,* 6:128n.

9. Patmore, *My Friends and Acquaintance,* 89.

10. Quoted in Courtney, *Young Charles Lamb,* 348.

11. Browne, *Religio Medici,* 83.

12. Hazlitt, *Letters,* 104.

13. Hazlitt and Hazlitt, *Journals of Sarah and William Hazlitt,* 247.

14. For Lamb and Chapman, see Newman, "'A Trifle Like the Current Undertaking.'"

15. Coleridge, *Collected Letters,* 3:68.

16. Cowden Clarke and Cowden Clarke, *Recollections of Writers,* 130–31. For Keats's interest in Chapman, see Motion, *Keats,* 108–13; and Roe, *John Keats,* 106–14.

17. Review of *The Adventures of Ulysses,* 81.

18. Procter, *An Autobiographical Fragment,* 173. For Hazlitt's use of Lamb for his poetry lectures, see Lockwood, "'He Spoke to Lamb.'"

19. Quoted in Riehl, *That Dangerous Figure,* 9.

20. Melville, "Hawthorne and His Mosses," 137.

21. Quoted in Shokoff, "Charles Lamb and the Elizabethan Dramatists," 10.

### 30. MRS. LEICESTER'S SCHOOL

1. For more on *Mrs. Leicester's School*, see Dobson, "(Re)considering Mary Lamb."
2. "*Mrs. Leicester's School*," 444.
3. Jerrold, *Bon-mots*, 47.
4. Jerrold, *Bon-mots*, 58.
5. Lucas, "A Friend to Charles Lamb."

### 31. NO. 4 INNER TEMPLE LANE

1. Holmes, *Coleridge: Early Visions*, 334.
2. Lucas, *Charles Lamb and the Lloyds*, 159.
3. Hazlitt, *Selected Writings*, 6:292. See also Grayling, *The Quarrel of the Age*, 128–30; and Wu, *Hazlitt*, 128–29.
4. For more historical context for the Lamb's children's poetry, see Ruwe, "Benevolent Brothers and Supervising Mothers."
5. Hitchcock's discussion of *Poetry for Children*, especially "Nurse Green," is especially insightful, *Mad Mary Lamb*, 204–10.
6. Hazlitt, *Selected Writings*, 8:133–14. See also Wu, "William Hazlitt: The Lion of Winterslow."
7. Hazlitt, "Farewell to Essay Writing," quoted in Wu, *Hazlitt*, 406.
8. Hunt, "Among my Books."
9. Procter, *Charles Lamb*, 301.
10. For Lamb's negotiation with imperialism in "Old China," see Fang, "Empire, Coleridge, and Charles Lamb's Consumer Imagination."
11. Wordsworth and Wordsworth, *Letters*, 2:439.
12. Wordsworth and Wordsworth, *Letters*, 2:357.
13. De Quincey, *De Quincey to Wordsworth*, 265.
14. Robinson, *Diary*, 1:204.
15. Wordsworth and Wordsworth, *Letters*, 2:443.

### 32. *THE* REFLECTOR

1. Hull, *The Familiar Essay*, 68–69.
2. Hunt, *A Day by the Fire*, 16, 22, 28.
3. Hunt and Hunt, "The Prince on St. Patrick's Day," 179.
4. Hunt, *Autobiography*, 1:148.
5. Hull, *The Familiar Essay*, 144.
6. For Lamb as a Cockney, see Fulford, "Talking, Walking, and Working"; and Dart, *Metropolitan Art and Literature*, 137–62.
7. Hay, *Young Romantics*, 248–51.
8. Recent interest in Lamb's *Reflector* essays has been high. The *Charles Lamb Bulletin* of 2012 (vol. 156) devoted an entire issue to these early Lamb essays. Among these contributions, see Felicity James's "Lamb's Essays"; Strachan, "Leigh Hunt in March 1812"; and Hull, "Snipe, Roast Pig and Boiled Babies."

9. Russo connects the *Reflector* essays and the Napoleonic Wars in "Charles Lamb's Beloved Liberalism," 451–52. In his discussion, Russo draws from Mary Favret's *War at a Distance.*

### 33. MANIA

1. Robinson, *Diary*, 1:204.
2. Quoted in Lucas, *Life*, 1:307.
3. Quoted in Lucas, *Life*, 1:307.
4. Quoted in Lucas, *Life,* 1:307.
5. Quoted in Lucas, *Life*, 1:307.
6. Robinson, Diaries Typescript, 1:63.
7. Quoted in Lucas, *Life*, 1:308.
8. Wordsworth and Wordsworth, *Letters*, 8:69.
9. Coleridge, *Notebooks*, 119.
10. Coleridge, *Notebooks*, 123.
11. Coleridge, *Collected Letters*, 3:400.
12. Quoted in Lucas, *Life*, 1:424.
13. Robinson, *Diary,* 1:214.
14. Robinson, *Diary,* 1:216.
15. Robinson, *Diary,* 1:218.
16. Robinson, *Diary,* 1:218.
17. Robinson, *Diary,* 1:236.
18. Haydon, *Life,* 1:228.
19. Lucas, *Charles Lamb and the Lloyds,* 169.
20. Robinson, *Diary,* 1:223.
21. Robinson, *Diary,* 1:224.
22. Robinson, *Diary,* 1:238.
23. Gifford, "Review of *The Dramatic Works of John Ford.*"
24. Croker, "Review of Keats's *Endymion*," 205.
25. Robinson, *Diary,* 1:246.
26. Robinson, *Diary,* 1:241.
27. Hunt, *Lord Byron,* 1:427.
28. Wu, *Hazlitt*, 144; Grayling, *The Quarrel of the Age,* 152–53.
29. Quoted in Lucas, *Life*, 1:407.
30. Robinson, *Blake, Coleridge, Lamb*, 44.
31. Lucas, *Life*, 1:336.

### 34. THE MELANCHOLY OF TAILORS

1. Robinson, *Diary,* 1:278.
2. *Champion*, January 14, 1816.
3. Scott, "Living Authors."

4. Thackeray, *The Newcomes*, 215; Wordsworth and Wordsworth, *Letters*, 3:280.
5. Robinson, *Diary*, 1:314.
6. Haydon, *Neglected Genius*, 129.
7. Robinson, *Diary*, 1:298.
8. Robinson, *Diary*, 1:299.


35. *WHICH IS THE GENTLEMAN WE ARE GOING TO LOSE?*

1. Talfourd, *The Works of Charles Lamb*, 94.
2. Talfourd, *The Works of Charles Lamb*, 94.
3. Quoted in Lucas, *Life*, 1:354.
4. Quoted in Lucas, *Life*, 1:386.
5. Cowden Clarke, *The Life and Labors of Vincent Novello*, 14–15.
6. Haydon, *Life*, 1:342. There are two excellent book-length accounts of this so-called Immortal Dinner: Plumly, *The Immortal Evening*; and Hughes-Hallett, *The Immortal Dinner*.
7. Hazlitt, *Selected Writings*, 9:105.
8. Haydon, *Life*, 1:203.
9. Quoted in Lucas, *Life*, 1:436.
10. For the full account of the evening, see Haydon, *Life*, 1:392–95. Unless otherwise noted, all subsequent quotations describing the "Immortal Dinner" are from this source.
11. Haydon, *Diary*, 2:174.
12. Plumly, *The Immortal Evening*, 149.
13. Haydon, *Correspondence and Table-Talk*, 2:413.


36. WORKS

1. Hunt, *Correspondence*, 2:117.
2. Robinson, *Diary*, 1:383.
3. Hunt, "The Works of Charles Lamb," 187.
4. Quoted in Riehl, *That Dangerous Figure*, 12.


37. FANNY

1. Robinson, *Diary*, 2:388
2. For this account of Frances Kelly and George Barnett, I follow Burton's excellent discussion of the affair: *A Double Life*, 306–8.
3. Quoted in Watson, *The Devil Kissed Her*, 181.
4. Lucas, *Life*, 2:382.

## 38. *THE* LONDON MAGAZINE

1. Scott, "Prospectus."
2. For the culture of London magazine writing in Lamb's time, see Dart, *Metropolitan Art and Literature*; Oliver, "Walking and Imagining the City"; Hull, *Charles Lamb*; Parker, *London Magazines*; Stone, "William Hazlitt, Charles Lamb, and the *London Magazine*"; and Stewart, "Lamb's London."
3. Hazlitt, *Selected Writings*, 7:232–33.
4. Parker, *London Magazines*, 44.

## 39. *ELIA*

1. An excellent overview of the origin and pronunciation of Lamb's "Elia" is Stewart, "Elia, Epistles, and Elegy."
2. Lucas, *Life*, 2:59.
3. Barnett, *Charles Lamb*, 89–113.
4. Talfourd, *Letters*, 65–66.
5. Chandler, "'Elia the Real.'"
6. Lucas, *Life*, 2:242.
7. Morley, *Lamb Before Elia*, 77–80.
8. Monsman, *Confessions*; McFarland, "Charles Lamb and the Politics of Survival."
9. Hull, *Charles Lamb*.
10. For Lamb, philosophy, and identity, see Milnes, "Charles Lamb"; Lazar, "Playing Ourselves"; and Klaus, "Elia."
11. This essay is published in *Lamb as Critic*, edited by Roy Park.
12. Lamb and Lamb, "Review of Hazlitt's *Table Talk*," 300.
13. Lamb and Lamb, "Review of Hazlitt's *Table Talk*," 301.

## 40. MAGAZINES INCREASE AND MULTIPLY

1. Hazlitt, "The Periodical Press," in *The Complete Works of William Hazlitt*, 16:220. See also Parker, *London Magazines*, 6.
2. Hazlitt, *Selected Writings*, 8:38.
3. Payne, "Baptist Connections of George Dyer."
4. Stone, "William Hazlitt, Charles Lamb, and the *London Magazine*," 42.
5. Stone, "William Hazlitt, Charles Lamb, and the *London Magazine*," 41.
6. Schoenfield, "Voices Together."
7. Higgins, "Imagining the Exotic."
8. Smith, "Death—Posthumous Memorials—Children," 250.
9. "The Periodical Press," 370.
10. "Letter from Dr. Olinthus Petre," 207.
11. Quoted in Riehl, *That Dangerous Figure*, 15.
12. Quoted in Riehl, *That Dangerous Figure*, 16.
13. Quoted in Riehl, *That Dangerous Figure*, 17.
14. Hazlitt, *Selected Writings*, 6:219–20.

## 41. EMMA

1. Betty T. Bennett helpfully describes Lamb's friendship with Mary Shelley in "Three Unpublished Songs."
2. Mary Shelley, "Giovanni Villani," 285.
3. Mary Shelley, "Cloudesley," 712.
4. Mary Shelley, *Letters of Mary Wollstonecraft Shelley*, 1:403.
5. Talfourd, *The Letters of Charles Lamb*, 332.
6. Bennett, "Three Unpublished Songs," 122.
7. This letter, dated July 30, 1833, does not appear in Lucas's edition of the letters, nor in Marrs's. Housed in the Princeton University Library, it was published in 1945 by Jeremiah Stanton Finch in an article titled "Charles Lamb's Companionship."
8. This album is contained in William S. Ayrton's re-bound copy of Lamb's *Works* (1818), housed in the Huntington Library.
9. Bell, *So Perish the Roses*; Anthony, *The Lambs*.
10. Ross, *Charles Lamb and Emma Isola*.

## 42. IMPERFECT SYMPATHIES

1. Mathews, *Charles Mathews*, 193–94.
2. Wu, *Hazlitt*, 293. For an account of the duel between Scott and Christie, see Parker, *London Magazines*, 20–28; and Wu, *Hazlitt*, 293–95.
3. Quoted in Wu, *Hazlitt*, 295.
4. Wu, *Hazlitt*, 295.
5. Wu, *Hazlitt*, 295–96; Grayling, *The Quarrel of the Age*, 266.
6. An excellent discussion of these dinners appears in Tim Chilcott's *The Publisher and His Circle*, 143–60.
7. Clare, *Major Works*, 24–26.
8. Quoted in Clare, *John Clare: The Critical Heritage*, 48.
9. Hood, *Hood's Own*, 556.
10. Clare, *John Clare by Himself*, 142–43.
11. Bate, *John Clare*, 242.
12. Clare, "To Elia."
13. De Quincey, *Works*, 16:391.
14. Cowden Clarke and Cowden Clarke, *Recollections of Writers*, 27.
15. Wordsworth and Wordsworth, *Letters*, 4:93.

## 43. PARIS

1. Robinson, *Diary*, 1:476.
2. Shelley, *Letters of Mary Wollstonecraft Shelley*, 1:373.
3. Lamb and Lamb, "Narrative of the Travels of a Lady in France." For more information, see James, "The Lambs' Story of Revolutionary France."
4. Shelley, *Letters of Mary Wollstonecraft Shelley*, 1:373.
5. Quoted in Lucas, *Life*, 2:488.

6. Quoted in *Lucas*, Life, 2:488.

7. Shelley, *Letters of Mary Wollstonecraft Shelley*, 1:373.

8. Robinson, *Diary*, 1:478.

### 44. COLEBROOK

1. Robinson, *Diary*, 1:485.

2. Moore, *Diary*, 50.

3. Southey, letter to Charles Lamb, November 19, 1823, in *Collected Letters*.

4. Lucas, *Life*, 2:118.

5. Coleridge, *Poetical Works*, 2:1098.

6. Robinson, *Diary*, 2:4.

7. Lucas, *Life*, 2:174.

8. Hunt, "Mr. Blake's Exhibition."

9. Robinson, *Letters*, 31.

10. Robinson, *Diary*, 1:217.

11. Robinson, *Diary*, 2:24–25.

12. Coleridge, *Collected Letters*, 4:1114.

### 45. RETIREMENT

1. Lucas, *Life*, 2:196.

2. For Lamb's interest in Queen Caroline, see Gardner, "Caroline, Lamb, and Swellfoot."

3. Stewart, "Fleeting, Shadowy Reflections," 142.

4. Lucas, *Life*, 2:156.

### 46. ENFIELD

1. Lucas, *Life*, 2:252.

2. Patmore, *My Friends and Acquaintance*, 30.

3. Lucas, *Life*, 2:252.

4. Patmore, *My Friends and Acquaintance*, 49.

### 47. THREE PORTRAITS

1. Lucas, *Life*, 2:252.

2. Hunt, "Recollections of Lamb," 236.

3. Robinson, *Diary*, 2:42.

### 48. ALBUM VERSES

1. Cowden Clarke and Cowden Clarke, *Recollections of Writers*, 54.

2. Talfourd, *The Works of Charles Lamb*, 316.

3. Matthews, "From Autograph to Print."

4. *Tatler,* June 4, 1831.

5. Matthews, "From Autograph to Print."

6. Southey, "To Charles Lamb," 491.

7. Hunt, "*Album Verses,*" 246–48.


### 49. "AM" TO "HAVE"

1. Patmore, *My Friends and Acquaintance,* 28.


### 50. HIS GREAT AND DEAR SPIRIT HAUNTS ME

1. "Lamb and Hood," 420.

2. Hazlitt, "Landor's Imaginary Conversations," in *The Complete Works of William Hazlitt,* 16:240.

3. Wu, *Hazlitt,* 356–59.

4. Forster, *Walter Savage Landor,* 337.

5. Robinson, *Diary,* 2:175.

6. Landor, *Poetical Works,* 2:283–84.

7. Marguerite, Countess of Blessington, *Literary Life and Correspondence,* 112–13.

8. Landor, *Poetical Works,* 3:236.

9. Charles Lamb to Basil Montague, "Monday," Charles Lamb Collection, Gen MSS 254, box 1, folder 5, Beinecke Library, Yale University, quoted in Wu, *Hazlitt,* 429.

10. Procter, "My Recollections of the Late William Hazlitt."

11. Wu, *Hazlitt,* 428–31.

12. Grayling, *The Quarrel of the Age,* 343–44.

13. Talfourd, *Letters,* 281.

14. Lucas, *Life,* 2:341.

15. Holmes, *Coleridge: Darker Reflections,* 559–60.

16. Talfourd, *Letters,* 305.

17. Coleridge, *Table Talk,* 2:226–27n.


### 51. A SWALLOW FLYING

1. Talfourd, *Letters,* 314

2. Robinson, *Diary,* 2:205.

3. Wordsworth and Wordsworth, *Letters,* 6:113.

4. Wordsworth, *Last Poems,* 306.

5. For the context of Lamb's epitaph, see Matthews, "Epitaphs, Effusions, and *Final Memorials.*"

6. Wordsworth, *Wordsworth's Poetical Works,* 4:457–58.

7. Quoted in Lucas, *Life,* 2:283.

8. Landor, *Poetical Works,* 2:283.

# Bibliography

Aaron, Jane. *A Single Doubleness: Gender and the Writings of Charles and Mary Lamb*. Oxford: Clarendon, 1991.

Ades, John I. "Lamb's Correspondence with Thomas Manning: Reflections on Epistolary Friendship." *Wordsworth Circle* 18, no. 1 (Winter 1987): 45–49.

Ainger, Alfred. *Charles Lamb*. London: Macmillan, 1882.

———. "Notes." In *The Letters of Charles Lamb, Newly Arranged, with Additions*, edited by Alfred Ainger, vol. 1. London: Macmillan, 1904.

Alexander, Michael. *A History of English Literature*. New York: Macmillan Foundation Series / Red Globe, 2013.

Allan, G. A. T. *Christ's Hospital*. London: Town & Country, 1984.

Allan, Richard C. "Charles Lloyd, Coleridge, and *Edmund Oliver*." *Studies in Romanticism* 35, no. 2 (Summer 1996): 245–94.

Anderson, Howard, and Irvin Ehrenpreis. "The Familiar Letter in the Eighteenth Century: Some Generalizations." In *The Familiar Letter in the Eighteenth Century*, edited by Howard Anderson et al. Lawrence: University of Kansas Press, 1966.

Anderson, Phillip B. "*Rosamund Gray* Reconsidered: Charles Lamb's Fiction and Its Contexts." *Philological Review* 33, no. 1 (Spring 2007), 1–14.

Andrews, Jonathon, and Andrew Scull. *Undertaker of the Mind: John Munro and Mad-Doctoring in Eighteenth-Century England*. Berkeley: University of California Press, 2001.

Anthony, Katharine. *The Lambs*. New York: Knopf, 1945.

Appignanesi, Lisa. *Mad, Bad, and Sad: A History of Women and the Mind Doctors*. New York: Norton, 2009.

Ashton, Rosemary. *The Life of Samuel Taylor Coleridge: A Critical Biography*. Oxford: Blackwell, 1996.

Ayrton, William S. Re-bound copy of Lamb's *Works* (1818), Acc. 110244. Huntington Library, San Marino, CA.

Baladouni, Vahé. "Charles Lamb: A Man of Letters and a Clerk in the Accountant's Department of the East India Company." *Accounting Historians Journal* 17, no. 2 (December 1990): 21–36.

Balle, Mary Blanchard. "Mary Lamb and Sarah Stoddart: An Unlikely Friendship." *Charles Lamb Bulletin* 106 (April 1999): 54–65.

Barnett, George Leonard. *Charles Lamb*. New York: Twayne Authors Series, 1977.

———. *The Evolution of Elia*. Indianapolis: Indiana University Press, 1964.

Bate, Jonathan. *John Clare: A Biography*. New York: Farrar, Straus, & Giroux, 2003.

Baudelaire, Charles. "The Painter of Modern Life." In *Baudelaire: Selected Writings on Art and Literature,* edited and translated by P. E. Charvet. New York: Penguin, 1993.

Bayne-Powell, Rosamond. *Travellers in the Eighteenth-Century*. London: J. Murray, 1951.

Beck, Julie. "Why Do Puns Make People Groan?" *Atlantic,* July 10, 2015.

Beckinschtein, Tristan E., et al. "Why Clowns Taste Funny: The Relationship between Humor and Semantic Ambiguity." *Journal of Neuroscience*, June 29, 2011, 9665–71.

Bell, Neil. *So Perish the Roses*. London: Macmillan, 1940.

Bennett, Betty T. "Three Unpublished Songs by Charles Lamb for Mary Shelley." *Wordsworth Circle* 33, no. 3 (Summer 2002): 122–23.

Bensusan, S. L . *Charles Lamb: His Home and Haunts*. Pilgrim Book Series. London: T. C. & E. C. Jack, 1910.

Black, Algernon. "Charles Lamb." *Macmillan Magazine,* November 1878–April1879, 431–32.

Blunden, Edmund. *Charles Lamb and His Poetic Contemporaries*. Cambridge: Cambridge University Press, 1937.

Borer, Mary Cathcart. *An Illustrated Guide to London 1800*. New York: St. Martin's, 1988.

Boswell, James. *The Journals of James Boswell, 1762–1795*. Edited by John Wain. New Haven: Yale University Press, 1994.

———. *The Life of Samuel Johnson*. Edited by David Womersly. New York: Penguin, 2008.

Bowring, Sir John. *Autobiographical Recollections of Sir John Bowring*. Vol. 1. London: Henry S. King, 1877.

Browne, Sir Thomas. *Religio Medici and Other Writings.* Edited by C. H. Herford. London: J. M. Dent, 1920.

Burton, Robert. *The Anatomy of Melancholy.* 2 vols. Edited by A. R. Shilleto. London: G. Bell & Sons, 1912.

Burton, Sarah. *A Double Life: A Biography of Charles and Mary Lamb.* New York: Viking, 2003.

Byron, George Gordon. *Byron's Letters and Journals.* 12 vols. Edited by Leslie A. Marchand. Cambridge, MA: Harvard University Press, 1973–82.

Carlyle, Thomas. *Notebooks,* November 2, 1831. In *A Carlyle Reader: Selections from the Writings of Thomas Carlyle,* edited by G. B. Tennyson. Cambridge: Cambridge University Press, 1984.

Cecil, David. *A Portrait of Charles Lamb.* London: Constable, 1983.

Chandler, David. "Charles Lamb and the South Sea House." *Notes and Queries* 51 (June 2004): 139–43.

———. "'Elia the Real': The Original of Lamb's Nom de Plume." *Review of English Studies* 58 (November 2007): 669–83.

Chilcott, Tom. *The Publisher and His Circle: The Life and Work of John Taylor, Keats's Publisher.* New York: Routledge, 2014.

Clare, John. *John Clare by Himself.* Edited by Eric Robinson and David Powell. New York: Routledge, 2002.

———. *John Clare: The Critical Heritage.* Edited by Mark Storey. New York: Routledge, 1973.

———. *Major Works.* Edited by Eric Robinson and David Powell. Oxford: Oxford University Press, 2008.

———. "To Elia." *London Magazine,* August 1822, 151.

Clemit, Pamela. "Lamb and Godwin's Antonio." *Charles Lamb Bulletin* 85 (January 1994): 13–18.

Coleridge, Samuel Taylor. *Biographia Literaria; or, Biographical Sketches of My Literary Life and Opinions.* 2 vols. Edited by James Engell and W. Jackson Bate. Princeton: Princeton University Press, 1983.

———. *The Collected Letters of Samuel Taylor Coleridge.* 6 vols. Edited by Earl Leslie Griggs. Oxford: Oxford University Press, 1956–71.

———. *Essays on His Times in the "Morning Post" and the "Courier."* 3 vols. Edited by David V. Erdman. Princeton: Princeton University Press, 1978.

———. *Notebooks: A Selection.* Edited by Seamus Perry. Oxford: Oxford University Press, 2002.

———. *Poems on Various Subjects.* London: G. G. & J. Robinson, 1796.

———. *Poetical Works.* 3 vols. Edited by J. C. C. Mays. Princeton: Princeton University Press, 2001.

———. *Table Talk.* 2 vols. Edited by Kathleen Coburn and B. Winer. Princeton: Princeton University Press, 1972.

———. "My Recollections of the Late William Hazlitt." *New Monthly Magazine and Literary Journal*, part 2 (1830): 469–82.

Courtney, Winifred. *Young Charles Lamb, 1775–1802*. New York: New York University Press, 1982.

Cowden Clarke, Charles, and Mary Cowden Clarke. *Recollections of Writers*. 2nd ed. London: Sampson Lowe, Marston, Searle, & Rivington, 1878.

Cowden Clarke, Mary. *The Life and Labors of Vincent Novello, by His Daughter*. London: Novello, 1864.

Cowper, William. *Memoirs of the Most Remarkable and Interesting Parts of the Life of William Cowper, Esq*. London: E. Cox & Son, 1816.

———. *The Poems of William Cowper, Esq*. London: Ernest Fleischer, 1828.

Craddock, Thomas. *Charles Lamb*. London: Simkin, Marshall, 1867.

Craik, T. W. "Hogsflesh Revisited." *Charles Lamb Bulletin* 112 (October 2000): 157–68.

*Critical Review; or, Annals of Literature* 3, no. 11 (1807): 98–99.

Croker, John Wilson. "Review of Keats's *Endymion*." *Quarterly Review*, April 1818, 204–8.

Crosse, Cornelia A. H. "Thomas Poole." *Littell's the Living Age*, 5th ser., 67 (1889): 605–14.

Cullingford, Benita. *British Chimney Sweeps: Five Centuries of Chimney Sweeping*. New York: New Amsterdam Books, 2001.

Dart, Gregory. *Metropolitan Art and Literature, 1810–1840: Cockney Adventures*. Cambridge: Cambridge University Press, 2012.

De Quincey, Thomas. *De Quincey to Wordsworth: A Biography of a Relationship, with the Letters of Thomas De Quincey to the Wordsworth Family*. Edited by John E. Jordan. Berkeley: University of California Press, 1962.

———. *The Works of Thomas De Quincey*. 21 vols. Edited by Greville Lindop. London: Pickering & Chatto, 2000–2003.

Dickens, Charles. *A Tale of Two Cities*. Edited by Richard Maxwell. New York: Penguin, 2003.

Dix, John Ross. *Lions: Living and Dead; or, Personal Recollections of the "Great and Gifted."* 2 vols. London: W. Tweedy, 1854.

Dobson, Meaghan Hanrahan. "(Re)considering Mary Lamb: Imagination and Memory in Mrs. Leicester's School." *Charles Lamb Bulletin* 93 (January 1996): 12–21.

Eigen, Joel Peter. *Witnessing Insanity: Madness and Mad-Doctors in the English Court*. New Haven: Yale University Press, 1995.

Elmes, James. *Notes and Queries* (1859).

Fairer, David. *Organising Poetry: The Coleridge Circle, 1790–1798*. Oxford: Oxford University Press, 2009.

Fang, Karen. "Empire, Coleridge, and Charles Lamb's Consumer Imagination." *SEL: Studies in English Literature, 1500–1900* 43, no. 4 (2003): 815–43.

Favret, Mary. *War at a Distance: Romanticism and the Making of Modern Wartime.* Princeton: Princeton University Press, 2010.

Finch, Jeremiah Stanton. "Charles Lamb's Companionship . . . in Almost Solitude." *Princeton University Library Chronicle* 6, no. 4 (June 1945): 191–92.

Fitzgerald, Percy. *Charles Lamb: His Friends, His Haunts, and His Books.* London: Richard Bentley, 1866.

———, ed. *Life, Letters and Writings of Charles Lamb.* 6 vols. London: Edward Moxon, 1876.

Forster, John. "Charles Lamb." *New Monthly Magazine* 43 (1835).

———. *Walter Savage Landor: A Biography, in Eight Books.* London: Chapman & Hall, 1874.

Fox, William. *A Brief History of the Wesleyan Missions on the Western Coast of Africa.* London: Aylott & Jones, 1851.

Fulford, Tim. "Talking, Walking, and Working: The Cockney Clerk, the Suburban Ramble, and the Invention of Leisure." *Essays in Romanticism* 18 (2011): 75–95.

Gardner, John. "Caroline, Lamb, and Swellfoot." *Charles Lamb Bulletin* 113 (January 2001): 2–22.

———. *Poetry and Popular Protest: Peterloo, Cato Street and the Queen Caroline Controversy.* London: Palgrave, 2011.

Garratt, Edmund. "The Early Friendship of Captain James Burney and Charles Lamb." *Charles Lamb Bulletin* 122 (April 2003): 64–70.

*Gentleman's Magazine* 32 (February 1763): 97.

Gifford, William. "Review of *The Dramatic Works of John Ford.*" *Quarterly Review,* December 1811, 485.

Gill, Stephen. *William Wordsworth: A Life.* Oxford: Clarendon, 1989.

Godwin, William. *Enquiry concerning Political Justice and Its Influence on Morals and Happiness.* 2nd. ed. vol. 1. London: G. G. & J. Robinson, 1796.

———. *Memoirs of the Author of the "Vindication of the Rights of Woman."* 2nd ed. London: J. Johnson, 1798.

Grayling, A. C. *The Quarrel of the Age: The Life and Times of William Hazlitt.* London: Orion, 2001.

Grevel, Lindop. *The Opium-Eater: A Life of Thomas De Quincey.* London: Dent, 1981.

Hall, Samuel Chester. *A Book of Memories of Great Men and Women of the Age: From Personal Acquaintance.* London: Virtue, 1877.

Hamilton, Paul. "The Irritable Genius." *Charles Lamb Bulletin* 27 (1979): 41–51.

Harriman-Smith, James. "Representing the Poor: Charles Lamb and the Vagabondiana." *Studies in Romanticism* 54, no. 4 (Winter 2015): 551–68.

Harris, Jennifer. "Managing Madness: Charles and Mary Lamb, Thomas Noon Talfourd, and Normand House." *Charles Lamb Bulletin* 152 (2010): 94–104.

Haverty, Anne. *The Far Side of a Kiss.* New York: Vintage, 2001.

Hay, Daisy. *Young Romantics: The Shelleys, Byron, and Other Tangled Lives.* New York: Farrar, Straus, & Giroux, 2011.

Haydon, Robert Benjamin. *Correspondence and Table-Talk, with a Memoir by His Son, Frederic Wordsworth Haydon.* 2 vols. Boston: Estes & Lauriat, 1877.

____. *The Diary of Benjamin Robert Haydon.* 5 vols. Edited by Willard Bissell Pope. Cambridge, MA: Harvard University Press, 1960–63.

———. *The Life, Letters, and Table Talk of Benjamin Haydon.* Edited by Richard Henry Stoddard. New York: Scribner's, 1876.

———. *The Life of Benjamin Robert Haydon, Historical Painter, from his Autobiography and Journals.* 2 vols. Edited by Tom Taylor. New York: Harper & Brothers, 1853.

———. *Neglected Genius: The Diaries of Benjamin Robert Haydon, 1808–1846.* Edited by John Joliffe. London: Faber & Faber, 1990.

Hazlitt, Sarah, and William Hazlitt. *The Journals of Sarah and William Hazlitt, 1822–1831.* Edited by Willard Hallam Bonner. Special issue, *University of Buffalo Studies* 24, no. 3 (1959).

Hazlitt, William. *The Complete Works of William Hazlitt.* 21 vols. Edited by P. P. Howe. London: Dent, 1930–34.

———. *The Letters of William Hazlitt.* Edited by Herschel Moreland Sikes, Willard Hallam Bonner, and Gerald Lahey. New York: New York University Press, 1978.

———. *The Selected Writings of William Hazlitt.* 9 vols. Edited by Duncan Wu. London: Pickering & Chatto, 1998.

Hazlitt, William Carew. *The Lambs: Their Lives, Their Friends, and Their Correspondence; New Particulars and New Material.* London: E. Mathews, 1897.

Hickey, Alison. "Double Bonds: Charles Lamb's Romantic Collaborations." *ELH* 63, no. 3 (Fall, 1996): 735–71.

Higgins, David. "Imagining the Exotic: De Quincey and Lamb in the *London Magazine.*" *Romanticism: The Journal of Culture and Criticism* 17, no. 3 (October 2011): 288–98.

Hitchcock, Susan Tyler. *Mad Mary Lamb: Lunacy and Murder in Literary England.* New York: Norton, 2005.

Holland, Joanne. "Narrating Margaret Nicholson: A Character Study in Fact and Fiction." MA thesis, McGill University, 2008.

Holmes, Richard. *Coleridge: Darker Reflections, 1804–1834.* New York: Pantheon, 2001.

———. *Coleridge: Early Visions, 1772–1804.* New York: Pantheon, 1999.

Homar, Katie S. "'Rehearsing Continually the Part of the Past': Lamb's Elia Essays and the Classical Curriculum at Christ's Hospital." *Studies in Romanticism* 53, no. 1 (Spring 2014): 79–101.

Hood, Thomas. *Hood's Own; or, Laughter from Year to Year.* London: Edward Moxon, 1855.

Hughes-Hallett, Penelope. *The Immortal Dinner: A Famous Evening of Genius and Laughter in Literary London, 1817.* New York: New Amsterdam Books, 2002.

Hull, Simon. *Charles Lamb, Elia and the "London Magazine": Metropolitan Muse.* London: Pickering & Chatto, 2010.

———. *The Familiar Essay, Romantic Affect and Metropolitan Culture: The Sweet Security of Streets.* Newcastle upon Tyne: Cambridge Scholars, 2018.

———. "Snipe, Roast Pig and Boiled Babies: Lamb's Consuming Passion." *Charles Lamb Bulletin* 156 (Autumn 2012), 138–48.

Hunt, Leigh. "*Album Verses, with a Few Others.* By Charles Lamb." *Chat of the Week,* August 14, 1830, 246–48.

———. "Among My Books." *Literary Examiner,* July 5–12, 1823, 1–22.

———. *The Autobiography of Leigh Hunt, with Reminisces of Friends and Contemporaries.* 3 vols. London: Smith, Elder, & Sons, 1850.

———. *The Correspondence of Leigh Hunt.* 2 vols. London: Smither, Elder, 1862.

———. *A Day by the Fire and Other Papers Hitherto Uncollected.* London: Sampson Low, Son, & Marston, 1870.

———. "Deaths of Little Children." In *The Indicator, Volumes 1–2.* London: Joseph Appleyard, 1822.

———. *Lord Byron and Some of His Contemporaries, with Recollections of the Author's Life, and of His Visit to Italy.* 2 vols. 2nd ed. London: Henry Colbourn, 1828.

———. "Recollections of Lamb." *Leigh Hunt's London Journal* 2 (January–December 1835): 236–37.

———. "The Works of Charles Lamb." *Examiner,* March 21, 1819, 187.

Hunt, Leigh, and John Hunt. "The Prince on St. Patrick's Day." *Examiner,* March 22, 1812, 177–80.

Hunt, Robert. "Mr. Blake's Exhibition." In *William Blake: The Critical Heritage,* edited by G. E. Bentley Jr. New York: Routledge, 1975.

James, Felicity. *Charles Lamb, Coleridge and Wordsworth: Reading Friendship in the 1790s.* New York: Palgrave Macmillan, 2008.

———. "Lamb's Essays in *The Reflector:* A Bicentenary Celebration." *Charles Lamb Bulletin* 156 (2012), 117–58.

———. "'Sweet Is Thy Sunny Hair': An Unpublished Charles Lamb Poem." *Charles Lamb Bulletin* 127 (July 2004): 54–56.

———. "Thomas Manning, Charles Lamb, and Oriental Encounters." *Poetica: An International Journal of Linguistic-Literary Studies* 76 (2011): 21–35.

James, Louis. "The Lambs' Story of Revolutionary France: A Newly Discovered Fragment." *Charles Lamb Bulletin* 2 (April 1973): 29–32.

Jerrold, Walter, ed. *Bon-mots of Charles Lamb and Walter Jerrold*. London: Dent, 1893.

———. *Lamb*. London: George Bell, 1905.

Johnson, Samuel. *The Letters of Samuel Johnson*. 4 vols. Edited by Bruce Redford. Oxford: Clarendon, 1991.

Johnston, Kenneth R. *The Hidden Wordsworth*. New York: Norton, 2000.

Jones, Stanley. *Hazlitt: A Life*. Oxford: Oxford University Press, 1989.

Keats, John. *The Letters of John Keats*. 4th ed. Edited by Maurice Buxton Forman. Oxford: Oxford University Press, 1952.

King, James. *William Cowper: A Biography*. Durham: Duke University Press, 1986.

Klaus, Carl H. "Elia: Pseudonymous Self Extraordinaire." In *The Made-Up Self: Impersonation in the Personal Essay*. Iowa City: University of Iowa Press, 2010.

"Lamb and Hood." *Christian Examiner,* 5th ser., 7 (July, September, November 1860): 415–34.

Lamb, Charles. Charles Lamb Papers. India Office Records and Private Papers, MSS Eur 008, British Library, London.

———. Charles Lamb Papers. India Office Records and Private Papers, MSS Eur Photo 017, British Library, London.

———. Commonplace Book: "Handwritten Manuscript with Poems, Excerpts, Acrostics, etc." Charles Lamb Collection, container 5, Harry Ransom Center, Austin, TX.

———. David Booth Papers. India Office Records and Private Papers, MSS Eur C 128, British Library, London. [This source contains Lamb's mock reviews.]

Lamb, Charles, and Mary Lamb. *The Letters of Charles and Mary Anne Lamb*. 3 vols. Edited by Edwin W. Marrs Jr. Ithaca: Cornell University Press, 1975–78.

———. *The Letters of Charles Lamb, to Which Are Added Those of His Sister Mary Lamb*. 3 vols. Edited by E. V. Lucas. London: J. M. Dent & Sons / Meuthen, 1935.

———. "Narrative of the Travels of a Lady in France; Aft September 22, 1822–Bef March, 1833." Add MS 57846, British Library, London.

____. "Review of Hazlitt's *Table Talk*." In *Lamb as Critic,* edited by Roy Parks. Omaha: University of Nebraska Press, 1980.

———. *The Works of Charles and Mary Lamb*. 7 vols. Edited by E. V. Lucas. New York: G. P. Putnam's Sons, 1903 / London: Methuen, 1903.

Lamb, Charles, and Charles Lloyd. *Blank Verse*. London: John & Arthur Arch (T. Bensley), 1798.

Lamont, Claire, "Charles Lamb, Food, and Feasting." *Charles Lamb Bulletin* 161 (Spring 2015): 4–14.

Landon, Melvin D. "Chas Farrar Browne, 'Artemus Ward: A Biographical Sketch.'" In *Artemus Ward: His Works, Complete* (New York: G. W. Carleton, 1877), 11–24.

Landor, Walter Savage. *The Poetical Works of Walter Savage Landor.* 3 vols. Edited by Stephen Wheeler. Oxford: Clarendon, 1937.

Lazar, David. "Playing Ourselves: Pseudo-Documentary and Persona." *Antioch Review* 71, no. 2 (Spring 2013): 233–40.

Ledbetter, Gregory. "The Comic Imagination in Lamb and Coleridge." *Charles Lamb Bulletin* 159 (Spring 2014), 11–19.

Ledwith, Frank. "The East India Company." *Charles Lamb Bulletin* 31 (1980): 129–35.

Lefebure, Molly. *Samuel Taylor Coleridge: A Bondage of Opium.* New York: Stein & Day, 1974.

"Letter from Dr. Olinthus Petre, Christopher North Esq." *Blackwood's Edinburgh Magazine,* November 1820, 207–9.

Lim, Jessica W. H. "Appropriate(d) Nursery Reading; or, (Implied) Child Readers: Charles Lamb and the Godwins' Juvenile Library." *Charles Lamb Bulletin* 163 (2016): 55–65.

Lindsey, Theophilus. Preface to *An Answer to Mr. Paine's Age of Reason, by Joseph Priestley.* London, 1794.

Lloyd, Charles. *Edmund Oliver.* New York: Woodstock Books, 1990.

———. "Lines Written on a Friday, the Day in Each Week Formerly Devoted by the Author and His Brothers and Sisters to the Society of Their Grandmother." In *Poems on the Death of Priscilla Farmer.* Bristol: N. Biggs, 1796.

Locke, Don. *A Fantasy of Reason: The Life and Thought of William Godwin.* London: Routledge Kegan & Paul, 1980.

Lockwood, Tim. "'He Spoke to Lamb': Reading and Performance in Hazlitt's Lectures on the Age of Elizabeth." *Charles Lamb Bulletin* (2014): 31–46.

Lopate, Philip. Foreword to *Essays of Elia.* Iowa City: University of Iowa Press, 2003.

———. Introduction to *The Art of the Personal Essay: An Anthology from the Classical Era to the Present.* New York: Anchor, 1995.

Lucas, E. V., ed. *Charles Lamb and the Lloyds.* London: Smith, Elder, 1898.

———. "A Friend to Charles Lamb." *Athenaeum Journal,* June 7, 1902, 723.

———. "G.D., Friend of Lamb." *Cornhill Magazine* 8 (January–June 1905): 120.

———. *The Life of Charles Lamb.* 2 vols. London: G. P. Putnam's Sons, 1905.

Makdisi, Saree. "William Blake, Charles Lamb, and Urban Antimodernity." *SEL: Studies in English Literature, 1500–1900* 56 (2016): 737–56.

Manning, Anne. "Memorials of Joseph Paice." *Athenaeum: Journal of Literature, Science, and the Fine Arts* (1841): 387.

Manning, Thomas. *The Letters of Thomas Manning to Charles Lamb*. Edited by
　　G. A. Anderson. New York: Harper & Brothers, 1926.

———. Letter to William Manning, July 1799, TM/1/1/04, Royal Asiatic Society,
　　London.

———. Letter to William Wilkins, April 24, 1807, TM 5/4, Royal Asiatic Society,
　　London.

Marguerite, Countess of Blessington. *The Literary Life and Correspondence of the
　　Countess of Blessington*. Vol. 3. Edited by Richard Robert Madden. Cambridge:
　　Cambridge University Press, 2012.

Markham, Clements R., ed. *Narratives of the Mission of George Bogle to Tibet and the
　　Journey of Thomas Manning to Lhasa*. New ed. London: Trübner, 1879.

Marsden, Jean I. "Shakespeare for Girls: Mary Lamb and *Tales from Shakespeare*."
　　*Children's Literature: Annual of the Modern Language Association Division on
　　Children's Literature and the Children's Literature Association* 17 (1989): 47–63.

Martin, Benjamin Ellis. *In the Footprints of Charles Lamb*. New York: Scribner's,
　　1894.

Mathews, Mrs. *Charles Mathews, Comedian*. Vol. 3. London: Richard Bentley,
　　1839.

Matlak, Richard. "Captain John Wordsworth's Death at Sea." *Wordsworth Circle* 31,
　　no. 3 (Summer 2000): 127–33.

Matthews, Samantha. "Epitaphs, Effusions, and *Final Memorials*: Wordsworth and
　　the Grave of Charles Lamb." *Charles Lamb Bulletin* 118 (April 2002): 49–63.

———. "From Autograph to Print: Charles Lamb's *Album Verses, with a Few Others*
　　(1830)." *Charles Lamb Bulletin* 154 (October 2011): 143–54.

McFarland, Thomas. "Charles Lamb and the Politics of Survival." In *Romantic
　　Cruxes: The English Essayists and the Spirit of the Age*. Oxford: Clarendon, 1987.

Melville, Herman. "Hawthorne and His Mosses." *Literary World: A Journal of Sci-
　　ence, Literature and Art* 7 (July–December 1850): 135–40.

Milnes, Tim. "Charles Lamb: Professor of Indifference." *Philosophy and Literature*
　　28, no. 2 (October 2004): 324–41.

Misson, Henri. *Memoirs and Observations*. In *Cambridge Companion to English
　　Restoration Theater*, edited by Deborah Payne Fisk. Cambridge: Cambridge
　　University Press, 2000.

Monroe, Russell R. *Creative Brainstorms: The Relationship between Madness and
　　Genius*. New York: Irvington, 1992.

Monsman, Gerald. "Charles Lamb's Elia as Clerk: The Commercial Employment of
　　a Literary Writer." *Wordsworth Circle* 21, no. 3 (Summer 1990): 96–100.

———. "Charles Lamb's 'Enfranchised Quill': The First Two Essays of Elia." *Criti-
　　cism: A Quarterly for Literature and the Arts* 23, no. 3 (Summer 1981): 232–45.

———. *Confessions of a Poetic Dreamer: Charles Lamb's Art of Autobiography*. Dur-
　　ham: Duke University Press, 1984.

————. "Satiric Model for Lamb's 'Dissertation upon Roast-Pig,'" *Nineteenth-Century Prose* 33, no. 1 (Spring 2006): 1–27.

Moore, Thomas. *A Selection from Tom Moore's Diary.* Edited by John Boynton Priestley. Cambridge: Cambridge University Press, 1933.

Morley, F. V. *Lamb Before Elia.* London: J. Cape, 1932.

Motion, Andrew. *Keats.* London: Faber & Faber, 1997.

*"Mrs. Leicester's School; or, History of Several Young Ladies, Related by Themselves,* Godwin, Juvenile Library, Skinner Street, 1809." *Critical Review,* December 1808, 444.

Natarajan, Uttara. "Hazlitt, Lamb, and the Philosophy of Familiarity." *Charles Lamb Bulletin* 24 (October 2003): 110–18.

Newbon, Peter J. "'Squeamish Times': Lamb, Godwin, Wordsworth, and the Controversies of Children's Tales." *Charles Lamb Bulletin* 167 (2018): 18–31.

————. "'Terrors in Children': Charles Lamb, Robert Southey, and the Witch of Endor." *Charles Lamb Bulletin* 151 (July 2010): 72–87.

Newlyn, Lucy. "Lamb, Lloyd, London: A Perspective on Book Seven of *The Prelude.*" *Charles Lamb Bulletin* 47/48 (July–October 1984): 169–85.

Newman, Hilary. "'A Trifle Like the Current Undertaking': Charles Lamb's Adaptation of George Chapman's *The Odyssey.*" *Charles Lamb Bulletin* 148 (October 2009): 141–48.

Nicholson, Adam. *The Making of Poetry.* New York: William Collins, 2019.

Oliver, Susan. "Walking and Imagining the City: The Transatlanticity of Charles Lamb's Essays for the *London Magazine.*" *Charles Lamb Bulletin* 154 (Autumn 2011): 115–30.

O'Neill, Michael. "'Only What Might Have Been': Lamb and Illusion." *Charles Lamb Bulletin* 128 (October 2004): 96–107.

Park, Roy, ed. *Lamb as Critic.* Lincoln: University of Nebraska Press, 1980.

Parker, Mark. *London Magazines and British Romanticism.* Cambridge: Cambridge University Press, 2004.

Pater, Walter. "Appreciations." In *The Selected Writings of Walter Pater,* edited by Harold Bloom. New York: Columbia University Press, 1974.

Patmore, P. G. *My Friends and Acquaintance: Being Memorials, Mind-Portraits, and Personal Recollections of Deceased Celebrities of the Nineteenth Century.* Vol. 1. London: Saunders & Otley, 1854.

Payne, Ernest A. "The Baptist Connections of George Dyer." *Baptist Quarterly* 11, nos. 8/9 (1944): 237–38.

"The Periodical Press." *Edinburgh Review,* May 1823, 349–78.

Plotz, Judith. *Romanticism and the Vocation of Childhood.* New York: Palgrave, 2001.

Plumly, Stanley. *The Immortal Evening: A Legendary Dinner with Keats, Wordsworth, and Lamb.* New York: Norton, 2016.

Porter, Roy. *Madness: A Brief History.* Oxford: Oxford University Press, 2003.

Priestley, Joseph. *The Doctrine of Necessity*. London: J. Johnson, 1777.

Procter, Bryan Waller (Barry Cornwall). *An Autobiographical Fragment and Biographical Notes*. London: Bell & Sons, 1877.

———. *Charles Lamb: A Memoir*. London: Edward Moxon, 1866.

———. "My Recollections of the Late William Hazlitt." *New Monthly Magazine and Literary Journal*, part 2 (1830): 478.

Randal, Fred V. "Eating and Drinking in Lamb's Essays." *ELH* 37, no. 1 (March 1970): 57–76.

Razzell, Peter, and Christine Spence. "The History of Infant, Child and Adult Mortality in London, 1550–1850." *London Journal: A Review of Metropolitan Society Past and Present* 32, no. 3 (2007): 271–92.

Reeves, Florence. "John Wordsworth." *Charles Lamb Bulletin* 46 (April 1984): 125–33.

Reiman, Donald H. "Social and Political Satire in a 'Dissertation upon Roast-Pig.'" *Charles Lamb Bulletin* 151 (1976): 38–41.

Review of *The Adventures of Ulysses*, by Charles Lamb. *Anti-Jacobin Review*, January 1809, 80–81.

Review of *The Works of Charles Lamb, Including His Life and Letters, Collected into One Volume*. Moxon." *British Quarterly Review*, February and May 1848, 292-311.

Riehl, Joseph E. *That Dangerous Figure: Charles Lamb and the Critics*. Columbia, SC: Camden House, 1998.

Robinson, Henry Crabb. *Blake, Coleridge, Lamb, etc: Being Selections from the Remains of Henry Crabb Robinson*. Edited by Edith J. Morley. London: Longman's / Manchester: Manchester University Press, 1922.

———. Diaries Typescript. 23 vols. Dr. Williams's Library, London.

———. *Diary, Reminiscences and Correspondence of Henry Crabb Robinson*. 2 vols. Edited by Thomas Sadler. Boston: Fields, Osgood, 1869.

———. *The Letters of Henry Crabb Robinson*. Edited by Timothy Whelan. Grasmere: Wordsworth Library, 2013.

Roe, Nicholas. *Fiery Heart: The First Life of Leigh Hunt*. New York: Random House, 2005.

———. *John Keats: A New Life*. New Haven: Yale University Press, 2013.

———. "Radical George: Dyer in the 1790s." *Charles Lamb Bulletin* 49 (January 1985): 17–26.

Ross, Ernest C., *Charles Lamb and Emma Isola*. London: Charles Lamb Society, 1950.

Roy, Malini. "Celebrating 'Wild Tales': Lamb and Godwin's Groundwork for Children's Literature." *Charles Lamb Bulletin* 147 (2009): 122–30.

Russo, Brent L. "Charles Lamb's Beloved Liberalism: Eccentricity in the Familiar Essays." *Studies in Romanticism* 52, no. 3 (Fall 2013): 437–57.

Ruwe, Donelle R. "Benevolent Brothers and Supervising Mothers: Ideology in the Children's Verses of Mary and Charles Lamb and Charlotte Smith." *Children's Literature: Annual of the Modern Language Association Division on Children's Literature and the Children's Literature Association* 25 (1997): 87–115.

Schoenfield, Mark. "Voices Together: Lamb, Hazlitt, and the *London*." *Studies in Romanticism* 29, no. 2 (Summer 1990): 257–72.

Scott, George Ryley. *The History of Torture throughout the Ages*. London: Routledge, 2002.

Scott, John. "Living Authors: Lord Byron." *London Magazine,* January 1821, 50–61.

———. "Prospectus." *London Magazine,* January–June 1820, vii–viii.

Scully, Jackie Leech. "The Secular Ethics of Liberal Quakerism." In *Good and Evil: Quaker Perspectives,* edited by Jackie Leech Scully and Pink Dandelion. London: Routledge, 2007.

Seturman, V. S. "A Note on Lamb's 'Benchers': Lamb's 'Intimations.'" *Charles Lamb Bulletin* 37 (January 1982): 92–94.

Shelley, Mary Wollestonecraft. "*Cloudesley: A Tale.* By the Author of Caleb Williams."

*Blackwood's Edinburgh Magazine,* May 1830, 711–17.

———. "Giovanni Villani." *The Liberal* 4 (1823): 281–97.

———. *The Letters of Mary Wollstonecraft Shelley.* 3 vols. Edited by Betty T. Bennett. Baltimore: Johns Hopkins University Press, 1980–88.

Shelley, Percy Bysshe. *The Letters of Percy Bysshe Shelley.* 2 vols. Edited by Frederick Jones. Oxford: Oxford University Press, 1964.

Shokoff, James. "Charles Lamb and the Elizabethan Dramatists." *Wordsworth Circle* 4, no. 1 (Winter 1973): 3–11.

Shorter, Edward. *A History of Psychiatry: From the Era of the Asylum to the Age of Prozac.* New York: Wiley, 1998.

Smith, Horace. "Death—Posthumous Memorials—Children." *London Magazine,* March 1821, 250–54.

Southey, Robert. *The Collected Letters of Robert Southey.* Edited by Lynda Pratt, Tim Fulford, and Ian Packer. Romantic Circles Electronic Editions. https://www.rc.umd.edu/editions/southey_letters.

———. "To Charles Lamb, on the Review of His *Album Verses* in the *Literary Gazette.*" *Athenaeum,* August 7, 1830, 491.

Speck, W. A. *Robert Southey: Entire Man of Letters.* New Haven: Yale University Press, 2005.

Stewart, David G. "Elia, Epistles, and Elegy: Lamb and His Readers." *Charles Lamb Bulletin* 146 (April 2009): 54–67.

———. "Fleeting, Shadowy Reflections: Lamb's Occasional Verse, 1820–1834." *Charles Lamb Bulletin* 154 (October 2011): 131–42.

————. "Lamb's London, Magazines and Nostalgia in the Present Tense." *Charles Lamb Bulletin* 144 (October 2008): 102–13.

Stone, Heather B. "William Hazlitt, Charles Lamb, and the *London Magazine*." *Wordsworth Circle* 44, no. 1 (Winter 2013): 41–44.

Strachan, John. "Leigh Hunt in March 1812: The *Examiner*, the *Reflector*, and 'A Day by the Fire.'" *Charles Lamb Bulletin* 156 (2012): 149–58.

Talfourd, Thomas Noon. *Final Memorials of Charles Lamb; Consistent Chiefly of His Letters Not Before Published, with Sketches of Some of His Companions.* 2 vols. London: Edward Moxon, 1848.

————. *Letters of Charles Lamb, with a Sketch of His Life.* London: Edward Moxon, 1837.

————, ed. *The Works of Charles Lamb, Including His Most Interesting Letters.* London: Bell & Daldy, 1867.

Taylor, Anya. *Bacchus in Romantic England: Writers and Drink, 1780–1830.* London: Palgrave, 1999.

Taylor, Jeremy. *The Works of Jeremy Taylor, D.D., with Some Account of His Life, by the Reverend T.S. Hughes, B.D.* Vol. 5. London: A. J. Valpy, 1831.

Thackeray, William Makepeace. *The Newcomes: Memoirs of a Most Respectable Family.* Edited by Arthur Pendennis. London: Smith, Elder, 1898.

Thompson, Denys. "Our Debt to Lamb." In *Determinations: Critical Essays,* edited by F. R. Leavis. Folcroft, PA: Folcroft Library Editions, 1934.

Thornbury, Walter. *Old and New London: A Narrative of Its History, Its People, Its Places.* 3 vols. Rev. ed. London, Paris, and Melbourne: Cassell, 1878.

Treadwell, James. "Impersonation and Autobiography in Lamb's Christ's Hospital Essays." *Studies in Romanticism* 37, no. 4 (January 1998): 499–521.

Twitchell, Joseph H. "Concerning Charles Lamb." *Scribner's Monthly,* November 1875–April 1875, 726.

Vigus, James. "Do 'Friends' Allow Puns? Lamb on Quakers, Language, and Silence." *Charles Lamb Bulletin* 157 (Spring 2013): 2–17.

Watson, J. R. "Lamb and Food." *Charles Lamb Bulletin* 54 (April 1986): 160–75.

Watson, Kathy. *The Devil Kissed Her: The Story of Mary Lamb.* London: Bloomsbury, 2004.

Watters, Reggie. "The Tribe of Sam: Formative Images and Role-Models from Coleridge's Christ's Hospital." *Coleridge Bulletin,* new ser., 1 (Winter 1992/93): 15–21.

Wedd, Mary. "Elia the Academic." *Charles Lamb Bulletin* 135 (July 2006): 71–81.

Weech, Edward. "'All Beauties of the Road': Thomas Manning's Romantic Visions, from the Lakes to Tibet, 1799–1812." *Charles Lamb Bulletin* 167 (Spring 2018): 7–17.

Whelan, Timothy. "George Dyer and Dissenting Culture, 1777–96." *Charles Lamb Bulletin* 155 (Spring 2012): 9–30.

White, James. *Falstaff's Letters . . . with Notes of the Author Collected from Charles Lamb, Leigh Hunt and Other Contemporaries.* London: B. Robson, 1877.

Williams, Orlo. *Lamb's Friend the Census-Taker: The Life and Letters of John Rickman.* Boston: Houghton Mifflin, 1912.

Wilson, Frances. *Guilty Thing: A Life of Thomas De Quincey.* New York: Farrar, Straus, & Giroux, 2016.

Woodring, Carl. Introduction to *Table Talk,* by Samuel Taylor Coleridge, edited by Carl Woodring, in *The Collected Works of Samuel Taylor Coleridge,* vol. 14. Princeton: Princeton University Press, 1990.

Woolf, Virginia. *"A Room of One's Own" and "Three Guineas."* Edited by Morag Shiach. Oxford: Oxford University Press, 1992.

Wordsworth, William. *Last Poems, 1821–1850.* Edited by Jared Curtis. Ithaca: Cornell University Press, 1999.

———. *Lyrical Ballads and Other Poems, 1797–1800.* Edited by James A. Butler and Karen Green. Ithaca: Cornell University Press, 1993.

———. *Poems in Two Volumes, and Other Poems.* Edited by Jared Curtis. Ithaca: Cornell University Press, 1983.

———. *The Prose Works of William Wordsworth.* 3 vols. Edited by W. J. B. Owen and Jane Worthington Smyser. Oxford: Clarendon, 1974.

———. *The Thirteen Book "Prelude."* 2 vols. Edited by Mark L. Reed. Ithaca: Cornell University Press, 1992.

———. *Wordsworth's Poetical Works.* 5 vols. Edited by E. de Selincourt and Helen Darbishire. Oxford: Clarendon, 1947.

Wordsworth, William, and Dorothy Wordsworth. *The Grasmere Journals.* Edited by Pamela Woof. Oxford: Clarendon, 1991.

———. *The Letters of William and Dorothy Wordsworth.* 8 vols. Edited by Ernest de Selincourt and Alan G. Hill. Oxford: Oxford University Press, 1967–93.

*The World's Wit and Humour, English.* Vol. 3, *Austen to Thackeray.* New York: Review of Reviews, 1906.

Wu, Duncan. "Ode to a Forgotten Laureate." *Independent,* July 15, 2004.

———. *William Hazlitt: The First Modern Man.* Oxford: Oxford University Press, 2008.

———. "William Hazlitt: The Lion of Winterslow." *Independent,* February 1, 2006.

# *Acknowledgments*

I am first of all thankful for the support of my home institution, Wake Forest University, which provided me a research leave for a semester and two generous grants to travel to research libraries and archives in the United Kingdom and across the United States. Jessica Richard, my chairperson, was especially supportive of my research. She was cheerfully willing to write many letters on my behalf (for grant support, for permission to enter archives), and she always had an encouraging word for me when I brought up my most recent stage of Lamb research.

This book would not exist, of course, without the help of several excellent libraries and archives. Aside from the Z. Smith Reynolds Library at Wake Forest—which efficiently sent interlibrary loan books right to my office door and helped me track down hard-to-find editions and articles—I benefited mightily from the Manuscripts and Archives Department of the British Library; Dr. Williams's Library; the Royal Asiatic Society; the Henry W. and Albert A. Berg Collection and Carl H. Pforzheimer Collections at the New York Public Library; the Manuscript and Archives Division at the New York Public Library; the Beinecke Rare Book and Manuscript Library at Yale University; the Firestone Library at Princeton University; the Huntington Library and the Harry Ransom Center at the University of Texas; and the Charles Lamb Archive at the Guildhall Library.

One of the joys of undertaking manuscript and archival research is meeting librarians passionately committed to their rare collections. Dr. David Wykes at the Dr. Williams's Library alerted me to Henry Crabb Robinson materials that helped my understanding of Lamb considerably. At the Royal Asiatic Society, Edward Weech navigated me through the letters of Thomas Manning and showed me new ways that Manning is important to Lamb studies, the history of travel writing, and Romanticism. Charles Carter of the Carl H. Pforzheimer Collection of Shelley and his circle taught me much about children's literature during the Romantic era.

Researching a biography of course requires more than libraries and archives. You need to get information on the ground. Dr. Andrew Wines, assistant head of Christ's Hospital, generously walked me around the school (now located in Horsham), illuminated Lamb's connections to Christ's, and invited me to have lunch with him and the students. He also very helpfully arranged for me to meet with the school's museum director, Elizabeth Bridges, who showed me Lamb's original presentation papers, books inscribed by Lamb, Lamb correspondence, and items donated by the Charles Lamb Society. Jacqueline Fenton gave me a very informative tour of Lamb's Inner Temple, and the Reverend Stuart Owen described to me how Lamb's presence lives on at All Saints Church, Edmonton, where Charles and Mary are buried.

Though there has been no definitive biography of Lamb since 1905—that of the great E. V. Lucas—more specialized life studies have been indispensable: the volumes of Winifred Courtney, Susan Tyler Hitchcock, Sarah Burton, Jane Aaron, and Kathy Watson. Partially because of these scholars, there is, I am happy to say, a Lamb renaissance going on in the academy.

I would like to thank my agent, Matt McGowan, for his insight and support, especially at the beginning of this project. I appreciate Sarah Miller, my first editor at Yale, for taking the project on, and I am thankful to Heather Gold, who stepped in to edit when Sarah moved to another job. At a pivotal moment, Heather was brilliant and supportive. Eva Skewes and Ash Lago, editorial assistants at Yale, were patient and efficient at every part of the process. I have never worked with a copyeditor better than Robin DuBlanc, whose sharp eye for detail is matched by her impeccable sense of style. Tessa Hawkins did a fantastic job proofreading the book in its final stages of production.

I would like to thank the anonymous readers Yale commissioned to review the MS. Their candor, rigor, and acumen improved the book significantly.

Conversations about Lamb with colleagues and friends have been indispensable. Among these valued Wake Forest interlocutors are Jessica Richard,

Joanna Ruocco, Matt Garite, Sarah Hogan, Susan Harlan, Omaar Hena, Amy Catanzano, and Jeff Holdridge. On my many runs with Andy LesterNiles and my many art nights with Kevin Calhoun, I have gone deep into Lamb. My conversations with John McNally and Angus McLachlan are always as humorous as they are scintillating. Joel Tauber's wit, conversation, and empathy have been essential. Phil Arnold, wise man of the wood, has been my Wordsworthian sage all these many years, and he is also disturbingly funny. Likewise, philosophical talks with Terry Price, whom I've known since the first grade, were illuminating, heartening, and hilarious.

I am overjoyed to include my daughter Una among my most important intellectual companions. I started this book when she was twelve. Now she is eighteen. My understanding of Lamb has grown with her understanding of the world. I look forward to many more talks with her: about everything from how slippery nature is to out-and-out Elian nonsense.

When I was right in the middle of this book, I met someone who has now become my partner for life. Our first trip abroad was a giddy mix of Lamb research and new romance. Without her love and support, I would not have finished this book. Thank you, Fielding, for helping me again find my Lambian irony and ecstasy.

# Index

Page numbers in italics indicate illustrations. References to "Lamb" mean Charles Lamb; all other members of the Lamb family are indicated with their personal names like "Mary" or "John" and are alphabetized in subheadings following the "Lamb" entries for Charles.

Gregoire, Henri, 403

Greta Hall (Keswick). *See* Coleridge, Samuel Taylor

Greville, Fulke, 145

Grimaldi, Joseph, 415

Gutch, John Matthew, 170, 177–79; *Narrative of a Singular Imposture Carried out at Bristol by One Mary Baker . . .*, 177

Hadfield, James, 86–87

Hancock, Robert, portraits by: *Charles Lamb, 138, 139,* 345; *Robert Southey, 133; William Wordsworth, 112*

Harris, Jennifer, 455n9

Hart, Hannah, 281, 315

Hartley, David, 74, 76, 90, 104; *Observations on Man,* 72, 90

Hastings, Warren, 54, 57–58

Haverty, Anne: *The Far Side of a Kiss,* 232

Hawkes, Thomas, 102

Hawkins, Thomas: *Origins of English Drama,* 275

Haydon, Benjamin Robert, 61, 232, 268, 302, 314, 328–29, 338–41, 390, 401; *Christ's Triumphant Entry into Jerusalem,* 339–41; "Immortal Dinner" in his *Autobiography,* 339–41; *Leigh Hunt, 301;* life masks for Keats and Wordsworth by, 339

Hayley, William, 42

Hays, Mary, 165–66

Hazlitt, Sarah. *See* Stoddart, Sarah

Hazlitt, William: art criticism by, 230; Coleridge and, 231, 315; death of, 444–45; death of his and Sarah Stoddart's infant son, 284–85; description of Lamb by, 234; divorce from Sarah Stoddart, 232, 271; on Elia's identity, 373, 380; Elizabethan drama and, 276–77; engagement to Sarah Stoddart, 267–68; English grammar book by, 293; epitaph of, 444–45; falling

out with Lamb, 326–27; Gifford and, 316; Holcroft biography by, 293; Hunt and, 301; impressment into military service and, 95; influence on Keats, 228, 230; John Lamb, Jr. in fight with, 12–13, 238, 369; Mary Lamb and, 17; Lamb's friendship and correspondence with, 221–22, 228–38, 254, 255, 271, 281, 297, 311, 345; on Lamb's *John Woodvil,* 184; on Lamb's magazine writing, 361; Lamb's manner with, 210, 233; Lamb's mock obituary for, 267–68; Lamb's praise and defense of, 233, 319, 403; Landor and, 441; Lockhart and, 389; in London, 314–16; in *London Magazine,* 360–61, 370, 373; as *London Magazine* editor, 392; on magazine writer's role, 367–72, 472n2 (Ch. 38); marriage to Sarah Stoddart (first marriage), 270–71, 281; Napoleon admired by, 233; portrait of, *231;* portrait of Charles Lamb by, 228, *229,* 345, 423; productivity of, 347; Robinson and, 267; scandalous conduct of, in Lake District, 232, 467n25; second marriage to Isabella Bridgwater, 233; sexual life of, 191, 465n9; Shakespeare criticism by, 230, 308; Sarah Walker as romantic interest of, 232, 271; in Winterslow, 281, 288; Wordsworth and, 111, 232

Hazlitt, William, works by: "The Fight," 228–30; "The Indian Dancers," 228; *Liber Amoris,* 232; "My First Acquaintance with the Poets," 228; "On Antiquity," 371; "On the Conversation of Authors," 369–70; "On Going on a Journey," 228; *On Human Action,* 228; "On Past and Future," 370; "On People of Sense," 371, 392; "On the Pleasures of Hating," 228, 230–31; *Spirit of the Age,* 361; *Table Talk,* 364, 380, 392

Hazlitt, William (infant son, d. 1809), 284–85